Lecture Notes in Computer Science 4960

Sophia Drossopoulou (Ed.)

Programming Languages and Systems

17th European Symposium on Programming, ESOP 2008
Held as Part of the Joint European Conferences
on Theory and Practice of Software, ETAPS 2008
Budapest, Hungary, March 29-April 6, 2008
Proceedings

Springer

Volume Editor

Sophia Drossopoulou
Imperial College London
Department of Computing
SW7 2BZ London, UK
E-mail: S.Drossopoulou@imperial.ac.uk

Library of Congress Control Number: 2008923060

CR Subject Classification (1998): D.3, D.1, D.2, F.3, F.4, E.1

LNCS Sublibrary: SL 1 – Theoretical Computer Science and General Issues

ISSN 0302-9743
ISBN-10 3-540-78738-0 Springer Berlin Heidelberg New York
ISBN-13 978-3-540-78738-9 Springer Berlin Heidelberg New York

Springer is a part of Springer Science+Business Media

springer.com

Printed in Germany

Typesetting: Camera-ready by author, data conversion by Scientific Publishing Services, Chennai, India
Printed on acid-free paper SPIN: 12244515 06/3180 5 4 3 2 1 0

Foreword

ETAPS 2008 was the 11th instance of the European Joint Conferences on Theory and Practice of Software. ETAPS is an annual federated conference that was established in 1998 by combining a number of existing and new conferences. This year it comprised five conferences (CC, ESOP, FASE, FOSSACS, TACAS), 22 satellite workshops (ACCAT, AVIS, Bytecode, CMCS, COCV, DCC, FESCA, FIT, FORMED, GaLoP, GT-VMT, LDTA, MBT, MOMPES, PDMC, QAPL, RV, SafeCert, SC, SLA++P, WGT, and WRLA), nine tutorials, and seven invited lectures (excluding those that were specific to the satellite events). The five main conferences received 571 submissions, 147 of which were accepted, giving an overall acceptance rate of less than 26%, with each conference below 27%. Congratulations therefore to all the authors who made it to the final programme! I hope that most of the other authors will still have found a way of participating in this exciting event, and that you will all continue submitting to ETAPS and contributing to make of it the best conference in the area.

The events that comprise ETAPS address various aspects of the system development process, including specification, design, implementation, analysis and improvement. The languages, methodologies and tools which support these activities are all well within its scope. Different blends of theory and practice are represented, with an inclination towards theory with a practical motivation on the one hand and soundly based practice on the other. Many of the issues involved in software design apply to systems in general, including hardware systems, and the emphasis on software is not intended to be exclusive.

ETAPS is a confederation in which each event retains its own identity, with a separate Programme Committee and proceedings. Its format is open-ended, allowing it to grow and evolve as time goes by. Contributed talks and system demonstrations are in synchronized parallel sessions, with invited lectures in plenary sessions. Two of the invited lectures are reserved for 'unifying' talks on topics of interest to the whole range of ETAPS attendees. The aim of cramming all this activity into a single one-week meeting is to create a strong magnet for academic and industrial researchers working on topics within its scope, giving them the opportunity to learn about research in related areas, and thereby to foster new and existing links between work in areas that were formerly addressed in separate meetings.

ETAPS 2008 was organized by the John von Neumann Computer Society jointly with the Budapest University of Technology and the Eötvös University, in cooperation with:

- ▷ European Association for Theoretical Computer Science (EATCS)
- ▷ European Association for Programming Languages and Systems (EAPLS)
- ▷ European Association of Software Science and Technology (EASST)

and with support from Microsoft Research and Danubius Hotels.

The organizing team comprised:

Chair	Dániel Varró
Director of Organization	István Alföldi
Main Organizers	Andrea Tósoky, Gabriella Aranyos
Publicity	Joost-Pieter Katoen
Advisors	András Pataricza, Joaõ Saraiva
Satellite Events	Zoltán Horváth, Tihamér Levendovszky, Viktória Zsók
Tutorials	László Lengyel
Web Site	Ákos Horváth
Registration System	Victor Francisco Fonte, Zsolt Berényi, Róbert Kereskényi, Zoltán Fodor
Computer Support	Áron Sisak
Local Arrangements	László Gönczy, Gábor Huszerl, Melinda Magyar, several student volunteers.

Overall planning for ETAPS conferences is the responsibility of its Steering Committee, whose current membership is:

Vladimiro Sassone (Southampton, Chair), Luca de Alfaro (Santa Cruz), Roberto Amadio (Paris), Giuseppe Castagna (Paris), Marsha Chechik (Toronto), Sophia Drossopoulou (London), Matt Dwyer (Nebraska), Hartmut Ehrig (Berlin), Chris Hankin (London), Laurie Hendren (McGill), Mike Hinchey (NASA Goddard), Paola Inverardi (L'Aquila), Joost-Pieter Katoen (Aachen), Paul Klint (Amsterdam), Kim Larsen (Aalborg), Gerald Luettgen (York) Tiziana Margaria (Göttingen), Ugo Montanari (Pisa), Martin Odersky (Lausanne), Catuscia Palamidessi (Paris), Anna Philippou (Cyprus), CR Ramakrishnan (Stony Brook), Don Sannella (Edinburgh), João Saraiva (Minho), Michael Schwartzbach (Aarhus), Helmut Seidl (Munich), Perdita Stevens (Edinburgh), and Dániel Varró (Budapest).

I would like to express my sincere gratitude to all of these people and organizations, the Programme Committee Chairs and members of the ETAPS conferences, the organizers of the satellite events, the speakers themselves, the many reviewers, and Springer for agreeing to publish the ETAPS proceedings. Finally, I would like to thank the Organizing Chair of ETAPS 2008, Dániel Varró, for arranging for us to have ETAPS in the most beautiful city of Budapest

January 2008 Vladimiro Sassone

Preface

It is an honour to be writing the preface of this volume, containing the papers presented at the 17th European Symposium on Programming (ESOP 2008), which took place in Budapest, March 31–April 2, 2008. ESOP is an annual conference devoted to fundamental issues in the specification, analysis, and implementation of programming languages and systems.

This year, ESOP received 104 full submissions out of 136 preliminary submissions. For each submission, at least 3, and on average 3.6, reviews were written. After an intensive electronic meeting (minimizing our carbon footprint) over 4 weeks, the programme committee decided to accept 27 papers, 2 of which are tool presentations.

This volume also contains a summary of the ETAPS invited talk, *Verification of Higher-Order Computation: A Game-Semantic Approach*, given by Luke Ong, and an abstract of the ESOP invited talk, *Constructive Mathematics and Functional Programming*, given by Thierry Coquand.

The papers are listed in the chronological order of their presentation followed by the index of authors.

Thanks go to the authors of all the submitted papers, and to the external referees, who helped us with their excellent reviews. Very many thanks go to the program committee members, for their hard work during the reviewing and the dedicated debates during the selection process.

I am grateful to the EasyChair team for their tool, which provided robust support to all administrative sides of my task.

January 2008 Sophia Drossopoulou

Conference Organization

Programme Committee

Davide Ancona	University of Genova, Italy
Manuel Chakravarty	University of New South Wales, Australia
Dave Clarke	CWI, Netherlands
Adriana Compagnoni	Stevens Institute of Technology, USA
Sophia Drossopoulou	Imperial College London, UK
Manuel Fahndrich	Microsoft Research Redmond, USA
Sabine Glesner	Technical University of Berlin, Germany
Robert Harper	Carnegie Mellon University, USA
Shriram Krishnamurthi	Brown University, USA
Doug Lea	State University of New York at Oswego, USA
Alan Mycroft	University of Cambridge, UK
Peter Müller	ETH Zurich, Switzerland and Microsoft Research, USA
David Naumann	Stevens Institute of Technology, USA
Catuscia Palamidessi	INRIA and Ecole Polytechnique, France
Matthew Parkinson	University of Cambridge, UK
German Puebla	Technical University of Madrid, Spain
Andrei Sabelfeld	Chalmers University of Technology, Sweden
Konstantinos Sagonas	National Technical University of Athens, Greece
Vijay Saraswat	Penn State University and IBM T.J. Watson Research Lab, USA
Eijiro Sumii	Tohoku University, Japan
Walid Taha	Rice University, USA
Frank Tip	IBM T.J. Watson Research Center, USA
Philip Wadler	University of Edinburgh, UK
Joe Wells	Heriot-Watt University, UK

External Reviewers

Umut Acar	Ashish Agarwal	Elvira Albert
Jonathan Aldrich	Tristan Oliver Richard Allwood	Puri Arenas
Aslan Askarov	Robert Atkey	Anindya Banerjee
Amir Ben-Amram	Josh Berdine	Lorenzo Bettini
Michael Beyer	Philippe Bidinger	Roderick Bloem
Eduardo Bonelli	John Boyland	Aleks Bromfield
Steve Brookes	Maria Grazia Buscemi	Diletta Romana Cacciagrano
Marco Carbone	Manuel Carro	Greg Cooper

Ricardo Corin
Andrea Corradini
Veronique Cortier
Karl Crary
Anupam Datta
Giorgio Delzanno
Mariangiola Dezani
Cinzia Di Giusto
Werner Dietl
Gabriel Ditu
Katy Dobson
Derek Dreyer
Rob Ennals
Azadeh Farzan
Boris Feigin
Maribel Fernandez
Pietro Ferrara
Robby Findler
Matthew Flatt
Florent Garnier
Samir Genaim
Prodromos Gerakios
Lars Gesellensetter
Giorgio Ghelli
Miguel Gomez-Zamalloa
Andy Gordon
Giovanna Guerrini
Thomas Göthel
Sebastian Hack
Barry Hayes
Jonathan Hayman
Paula Herber
David Herman
Kohei Honda
Haruo Hosoya
Christine Hundt
Chung-Kil Hur
Joe Hurd
Ralf Huuck
Atsushi Igarashi
Paul Jackson
Bart Jacobs
Jean-Marie Jacquet
Jan Jakubuv
Johan Jeuring
Bengt Jonsson
Gabriele Keller
Paul Kelly
Jens Knoop
Naoki Kobayashi
Giovanni Lagorio
Ivan Lanese
Alan Lawrence
Daniel Lee
Daan Leijen
Xavier Leroy
Roman Leshchinskiy
Dan Licata
Sam Lindley
Francesco Logozzo
Hans-Wolfgang Loidl
Matteo Maffei
Sergio Maffeis
Mila Majster-Cederbaum
Jonathan Mak
Keye Martin
Jacob Matthews
Conor McBride
Stephen McCamant
Jay McCarthy
Jacqueline McQuillan
Ricardo Medel
Peter Mosses
Dimitris Mostrous
Magnus O. Myreen
Gopalan Nadathur
Juan Carlos Nieves
Carlos Olarte
Paulo Oliva
Karol Ostrovsky
Scott Owens
Nikolaos Papaspyrou
Dirk Pattinson
Andrew Pitts
Arnd Poetzsch-Heffter
Didier Remy
Tamara Rezk
Tom Ridge
Stan Rosenberg
Mads Rosendahl
Alejandro Russo
Elke Salecker
Clara Segura
Peter Sewell
Robert Simmons
Christian Skalka
Gregor Snelting
Lex Spoon
Daniel Spoonhower
Sriram Srinivasan
Sam Staton
Gareth Stoyle
Tom Stuart
Henry Sudhof
Dirk Tetzlaff
Peter Thiemann
Ashish Tiwari
Viktor Vafeiadis
Frank Valencia
Pradeep Varma
Mandana Vaziri
Sven Verdoolaege
Mirko Viroli
Eelco Visser
Peng WU
Alisdair Wren
Hongwei Xi
Damiano Zanardini
Gianluigi Zavattaro
Elena Zucca

Table of Contents

Semantics, Parametricity, and Types

Semantics

Functional and Logic Programming

ESOP Invited Talk

Static Analysis

Security I

Concurrency

ETAPS Invited Talk

Program Verification

Security II

A Sound Semantics for OCaml$_{light}$

Scott Owens

University of Cambridge

Abstract. Few programming languages have a mathematically rigorous definition or metatheory—in part because they are perceived as too large and complex to work with. This paper demonstrates the feasibility of such undertakings: we formalize a substantial portion of the semantics of Objective Caml's core language (which had not previously been given a formal semantics), and we develop a mechanized type soundness proof in HOL. We also develop an executable version of the operational semantics, verify that it coincides with our semantic definition, and use it to test conformance between the semantics and the OCaml implementation. We intend our semantics to be a suitable substrate for the verification of OCaml programs.

1 Mechanizing Metatheory

Researchers in programming languages and program verification routinely develop their ideas in the context of core calculi and idealized models. The advantage of the core calculus approach comes from the efficacy of pencil-and-paper mathematics, both for specification and proof; however, these techniques do not scale well. Usable programming languages contain numerous constructs that are designed for practical utility rather than mathematical elegance, and their presence makes the proofs too long and tedious to check reliably by hand. Furthermore, the specifications themselves are subject to errors [1,2]. Formal verification offers a better path: using a proof assistant to formalize an unambiguous semantics and to mechanize high-assurance proofs.

In this paper, we present a formal verification methodology that successfully scales to a programming language that includes a large complement of pragmatic constructs. Although our formal proofs are more detailed than informal pencil-and-paper proofs, they follow the same structure, use the same mathematical techniques, and the proof assistant ensures that they are correct. We did not have to invent new specification or reasoning techniques to succeed, but we did exercise care in the details of our formalization.

We demonstrate the methodology on a substantial fragment of Objective Caml [3, Chapter 1] that we call OCaml$_{light}$ (since its feature set is roughly comparable to that of Caml Light). As a guiding design principle, we try to ensure that OCaml$_{light}$ could form a substrate for applying program verification techniques to a significant subset of real OCaml programs.

We design and formalize the OCaml$_{light}$ type system and operational semantics using Ott [4], a tool for expressing such specifications, and we use the HOL-4 proof assistant [5] to prove a type soundness theorem.[1] We also formalize a deterministic,

[1] We verify all of our proofs in HOL-4, but our techniques apply in most systems based on higher-order logic (HOL), including Isabelle/HOL and Coq.

S. Drossopoulou (Ed.): ESOP 2008, LNCS 4960, pp. 1–15, 2008.

executable version of the operational semantics, and prove that the two correspond. OCaml is not defined formally, so our semantics is a post-hoc attempt to detail the behavior of the language—both as described in the manual and as observed on the implementation. To build confidence that the semantics corresponds to the implemented language, we run test programs on both. Testing is a crucial component in the acceptance of post hoc semantics—we are not associated with the OCaml developers, and the test suite provides tangible evidence that our semantics is accurate.

Our development has taken under six man-months from start to finish, and based on our experience, we believe there is no reason why many well-established programming languages cannot be formally specified and given mechanized metatheories. To summarize our contribution, we demonstrate the feasibility of mathematical specification and mechanized reasoning for a useful fragment of a real-world programming language by:

- creating and formally specifying an operational semantics and type system for OCaml$_{light}$ (Sect. 2). The semantics themselves are a novel contribution; no prior attempt to give OCaml a formal semantics appears in the literature;
- using HOL to mechanize a type soundness proof for OCaml$_{light}$ (Sect. 3), the first of this scale in HOL; and
- demonstrating the reliability of our operational semantics with testing, enabled by the creation and verification of an executable version of the semantics (Sect. 4).

The remainder of this section explains our methodology and related work, and Sect. 5 presents observations and statistics on the mechanization. All of the formalizations, proofs, and tests are available at `http://www.cl.cam.ac.uk/~so294/ocaml`. The specification is written in Ott source, and is accompanied by HOL-4 and LaTeX versions that are generated automatically by Ott. Ott can also generate Isabelle and Coq versions.[2]

Methodology. Our formalization and proofs use standard techniques, all of which are supported by HOL. The abstract syntax of OCaml$_{light}$ is represented by mutually recursive algebraic datatypes, and the type system (which is purely syntactic and non-algorithmic) is expressed with inductively defined relations. The operational semantics is small-step, and is expressed as an inductively defined labeled transition relation over source programs (the labels carry store actions that allow us to avoid explicitly threading the store through the rules). Value and type identifiers are not treated up to α-equivalence, because our semantics never reduces under a value variable binder, and well-typed programs have no free variables. The semantics can reduce under a type variable binding (i.e., the bound expression of a **let**), requiring α-renaming in our proofs; we choose to represent type variables using de Bruijn indices. In the proof we make extensive use of rule induction and structural induction principles. We also rely upon the ability to create functions using well-founded recursion [6], and upon an automated first-order prover [7].

Our OCaml$_{light}$ formalization follows the formal syntactic specification (BNF) in the OCaml manual [3, Chapter 6] as closely as is feasible. This close connection with the source language helps make the semantic rules directly accessible to semanticists

[2] Thanks to Tom Ridge and Gilles Peskine for developing the respective translations.

who are familiar with OCaml, and we believe that direct accessibility is particularly advantageous in the context of program verification, especially by symbolic execution techniques [8,9,10]. A consequence of this choice is that our soundness proof has to deal directly with complex source-level constructs (e.g., n-tuples, n-way recursive lets, and full OCaml-style datatypes and pattern matching) that do not usually appear in lambda calculi. This complexity adds up to a relatively large language definition, roughly comparable, in terms of the number of constructs and semantic rules, to full-scale languages. Our methodology is relatively unsophisticated, but it handles this scaling. Our language does not involve the most semantically intricate features that appear in some programming languages, such as Standard ML's module system, so our methodology remains untested for these situations.

Related Work. There has been extensive work on formalizing language semantics (e.g., POPLmark [11] solutions), and Java, C, and Standard ML (SML) have all been subject to large-scale developments in proof assistants, with varying degrees of success [12,13,14,15,16,17,18,19]. Type soundness has been proved for large subsets of Java [12,15,18], with a similar methodology to ours; however, the formalized versions of Java are significantly simpler than OCaml$_{light}$: for example, they lack parametric polymorphism and pattern matching. Norrish's formalization of C [16] contains some metatheoretic results, but none of them approaches the scale of the OCaml$_{light}$ type soundness proof.

The only prior mechanized type soundness proof for a realistic ML-like language (for SML) [13] follows a methodology that differs significantly from ours. Instead of formalizing SML directly, it uses an internal language (IL) into which SML, including its module system, can be elaborated ([13] proved type soundness only for IL, leaving a formalized elaboration to future work; this work has now been completed [20]). IL is essentially a heavily streamlined version of SML designed to yield an elegant and tractable mechanized soundness proof. In particular, IL does not directly support pattern matching, implicit polymorphism, or n-ary constructs; they are all compiled away by the elaboration. Unlike the IL soundness proof, we do not formalize a generative module system, but our system directly handles some features, such as datatypes and polymorphism, which are handled only by the module system in IL. However, OCaml's semantics differs from SML's in many details, some of which make our job easier (e.g., OCaml does not support local type or exception definitions, equality types, or overloading). Extending OCaml$_{light}$ to add a full SML-like module system would likely require direct proof assistant support for reasoning about binding, or some amount of elaboration, or both.

Another important difference between the SML proof and ours is the setting of the mechanization; the SML proof was carried out in the Twelf proof assistant [21] which differs significantly from HOL:

- HOL is a classical, impredicative logic (with a model in ZFC set theory) whereas Twelf is constructive and predicative.
- Twelf supports higher-order abstract syntax (binding for the programming language being modeled is represented using the binding of the Twelf logic itself) which alleviates the burden of binding-related reasoning in proofs. HOL's logic is not suited for higher-order abstract syntax representations of programming languages.

- Twelf's proof system only supports $\forall\exists$-theorems (i.e., no universal quantification is allowed under an existential quantifier). Syntactic soundness theorems fit into this restriction, but other theorems or program verifications might not (proofs by logical relations are a standard example). HOL faces no such restriction.
- HOL uses a powerful tactic-based proof system that allows common proof steps to be automated using SML programs (such as the first-order logic proof search mentioned above). However, learning to effectively use the system is a non-trivial task, and reading existing proofs can be difficult. Twelf uses a more accessible declarative proof style, but lacks this powerful automation.

Prior SML proof efforts tried to closely follow the mathematical specification of *The Definition of Standard ML* [22], but failed, in part because of its big-step operational semantics, in part because of its bugs, and in part because the proof assistant technology of the time was lacking [1,2,14,17,19]. The Metis [7] and TFL [6] packages, upon which we rely, did not exist at the time.

2 OCaml$_{light}$

To a crude approximation, our OCaml$_{light}$ semantics is a core ML, excluding only modules and objects. In detail, it covers the following features, which form a complete language for writing programs without undue burden:

- definitions
  - variant data types (e.g., $\mathbf{type}\ t\ =\ I\ \mathbf{of\ int}\ |\ C\ \mathbf{of\ char}$),
  - record types (e.g., $\mathbf{type}\ t\ =\ \{ f\ :\ \mathbf{int}\ ;\ g\ :\ \mathbf{bool} \}$),
  - parametric type constructors (e.g., $\mathbf{type}\ 'a\,t\ =\ C\ \mathbf{of}\ 'a$),
  - recursive and mutually recursive combinations of the above,
  - exceptions,
  - values;
- expressions for type annotations, sequencing, and primitive values (functions, lists, tuples, and records);
- **with** (record update), **if**, **while**, **for**, **assert**, **try**, and **raise** expressions;
- let-based polymorphism (with an SML-style value restriction);
- mutually-recursive function definitions via **let rec**;
- pattern matching with nested patterns, **as** patterns, and "or" (|) patterns;
- mutable references with **ref**, :=, and !;
- polymorphic equality (the OCaml = operator);
- 31-bit word semantics for **ints** (using an existing HOL library);
- IEEE-754 semantics for **floats** (using an existing HOL library).

OCaml$_{light}$ overspecifies evaluation ordering relative to the OCaml manual (which makes no guarantees), generally going right-to-left in agreement with our observations of the OCaml bytecode implementation. On the above features it differs from the OCaml implementation in only the following four minor ways (the first three discrepancies could be repaired with a lightweight source-to-source elaboration):

$$
\begin{array}{l}
\mathit{typeconstr}, \mathit{tc} ::= \mathit{typeconstr\_name} \mid \textbf{int} \mid \textbf{exn} \mid \textbf{list} \mid \textbf{option} \mid \textbf{ref} \mid \cdots \\
\mathit{typexpr} ::= \alpha \mid \_ \mid \mathit{typexpr}_1 \rightarrow \mathit{typexpr}_2 \mid \mathit{typexpr}_1 * .... * \mathit{typexpr}_n \mid \mathit{typeconstr} \\
\qquad \mid \mathit{typexpr}\ \mathit{typeconstr} \mid (\ \mathit{typexpr}_1\ ,\ ...,\ \mathit{typexpr}_n\ )\ \mathit{typeconstr} \mid \cdots \\
\mathit{constr} ::= \mathit{constr\_name} \mid \textbf{Match\_failure} \mid \textbf{None} \mid \textbf{Some} \mid \cdots \\
\mathit{constant} ::= \mathit{int\_literal} \mid \mathit{constr} \mid \textbf{true} \mid \textbf{false} \mid [] \mid () \mid \cdots \\
\mathit{unary\_prim} ::= \textbf{raise} \mid \textbf{ref} \mid \textbf{not} \mid ! \mid \sim- \\
\mathit{binary\_prim} ::= = \mid + \mid - \mid * \mid / \mid := \\
\mathit{pattern} ::= \mathit{value\_name} \mid \mathit{constant} \mid \{ \mathit{field}_1 = \mathit{pattern}_1\ ;\ ...\ ;\ \mathit{field}_n = \mathit{pattern}_n \} \\
\qquad \mid \_ \mid \mathit{pattern}\ \textbf{as}\ \mathit{value\_name} \mid (\mathit{pattern}_1 \mid \mathit{pattern}_2) \mid \cdots \\
\mathit{expr} ::= (\ \%\textbf{prim}\ \mathit{unary\_prim}\ ) \mid \mathit{value\_name} \mid \mathit{constant} \mid (\ \mathit{expr}\ :\ \mathit{typexpr}\ ) \\
\qquad \mid \mathit{expr}_1\ ,\ ....,\ \mathit{expr}_n \mid \mathit{constr}\ (\ \mathit{expr}_1\ ,\ ..,\ \mathit{expr}_n\ ) \mid \mathit{expr}_1 :: \mathit{expr}_2 \\
\qquad \mid \{ \mathit{field}_1 = \mathit{expr}_1\ ;\ ...\ ;\ \mathit{field}_n = \mathit{expr}_n \} \mid \mathit{expr}\ .\ \mathit{field} \mid \mathit{expr}_1\ \mathit{expr}_2 \\
\qquad \mid \{\ \mathit{expr}\ \textbf{with}\ \mathit{field}_1 = \mathit{expr}_1\ ;\ ...\ ;\ \mathit{field}_n = \mathit{expr}_n\ \} \mid \textbf{while}\ \mathit{expr}_1\ \textbf{do}\ \mathit{expr}_2\ \textbf{done} \\
\qquad \mid \textbf{let}\ \mathit{pattern} = \mathit{expr}\ \textbf{in}\ \mathit{expr} \mid \textbf{let rec}\ \mathit{letrec\_bindings}\ \textbf{in}\ \mathit{expr} \\
\qquad \mid \textbf{try}\ \mathit{expr}\ \textbf{with}\ \mathit{pattern\_matching} \mid \mathit{location} \mid \cdots \\
\mathit{pattern\_matching}, \mathit{pat\_mat} ::= \mathit{pattern}_1 \rightarrow \mathit{expr}_1 \mid ... \mid \mathit{pattern}_n \rightarrow \mathit{expr}_n \\
\mathit{letrec\_bindings}, \mathit{lrbs} ::= \mathit{letrec\_binding}_1\ \textbf{and}\ ...\ \textbf{and}\ \mathit{letrec\_binding}_n \\
\mathit{letrec\_binding} ::= \mathit{value\_name} = \textbf{function}\ \mathit{pattern\_matching} \\
\mathit{definition} ::= \textbf{let}\ \mathit{let\_binding} \mid \textbf{let rec}\ \mathit{lrbs} \mid \mathit{type\_definition} \mid \mathit{exception\_definition}
\end{array}
$$

Fig. 1. Grammar (excerpt)

- OCaml's record expression evaluation ordering is right-to-left in the order of the labels from the record's type definition, and in OCaml$_{light}$ the ordering is right-to-left based on the record expression only;
- the behavior of partially applied, curried functions with non-exhaustive pattern matches can differ when the pattern matching fails at run time;
- the OCaml$_{light}$ type system rejects programs with duplicate data constructor or record field name definitions; and
- the OCaml$_{light}$ type system enforces a value restriction on let-based polymorphism, and rejects programs that require OCaml's greater permissiveness.

In the future we would like to add support for type abbreviations, pattern matching guards (**when**), mutable records, arrays, and modules. We expect only the last of these to require significant changes to the formalization, and perhaps a lightweight elaboration, because of the more complex type theory underlying OCaml modules.

Although the grammar is too large to show here in its entirety (it has 251 productions), the (Ott generated) excerpt in Fig. 1 demonstrates its general flavor. In a few cases, we treat a source-level construct as syntactic sugar; for example **fun** is locally translated into **function**. Ott turns "$x_1 ... x_n$" in grammars and rules into corresponding list-based HOL code.

2.1 Operational Semantics

The (small-step) operational semantics of OCaml$_{light}$ is phrased as a relation on definitions, programs, and stores; Fig. 2 gives an overview of the main relations and a few of the 137 rules to illustrate interesting aspects of OCaml$_{light}$ and the formalization (*value* and v indicate the Ott-enforced value grammar for *expr*).

$L ::= \epsilon \mid \textbf{ref}\ value\ =\ location \mid\ !\,location\ =\ value \mid location := value$
$program ::= definitions \mid (\%\textbf{prim raise})\ expr$

$\vdash \langle definitions, program, store\rangle \longrightarrow \langle definitions', program', store'\rangle \qquad \vdash expr \xrightarrow{L} expr'$
$\vdash \langle definitions, program\rangle \xrightarrow{L} \langle definitions', program'\rangle \qquad \vdash store \xrightarrow{L} store'$
$\vdash expr\ \textbf{matches}\ pattern\ \rhd\ \{\!\{\ substs\_x\ \}\!\} \qquad \vdash expr\ \textbf{matches}\ pattern$
$\vdash v\ \textbf{with}\ pattern\_matching \longrightarrow expr$

$$\frac{\vdash e_1 \xrightarrow{L} e_1'}{\vdash e_1\ v_0 \xrightarrow{L} e_1'\ v_0}(1) \qquad \frac{}{\vdash \textbf{ref}\ v \overset{\textbf{ref}\ v\,=\,l}{\longrightarrow} l}(2)$$

$$\frac{\vdash v\ \textbf{matches}\ pat\ \rhd\ \{\!\{\ x_1 \leftarrow v_1\ ,\ ..\ ,\ x_m \leftarrow v_m\ \}\!\}}{\vdash v\ \textbf{with}\ pat\ \rightarrow\ e \mid pat_1\ \rightarrow\ e_1 \mid ... \mid pat_n\ \rightarrow\ e_n\ \longrightarrow\ \{\!\{\ x_1 \leftarrow v_1\ ,\ ..\ ,\ x_m \leftarrow v_m\ \}\!\}\ e}(3)$$

$$\frac{\vdash v_1\ \textbf{matches}\ pat_1\ \rhd\ \{\!\{\ substs\_x_1\ \}\!\}\quad ....\quad \vdash v_n\ \textbf{matches}\ pat_n\ \rhd\ \{\!\{\ substs\_x_n\ \}\!\}}{\vdash (\ v_1\ ,\ ....\ ,\ v_n\ )\ \textbf{matches}\ (\ pat_1\ ,\ ....\ ,\ pat_n\ )\ \rhd\ \{\!\{\ substs\_x_1\ @\ ....\ @\ substs\_x_n\ \}\!\}}(4)$$

$$\frac{\begin{array}{l}\neg(v\ \textbf{matches}\ pat_1)\\ \vdash v\ \textbf{matches}\ pat_2\ \rhd\ \{\!\{\ x_1 \leftarrow v_1\ ,\ ..\ ,\ x_n \leftarrow v_n\ \}\!\}\end{array}}{\vdash v\ \textbf{matches}\ pat_1 \mid pat_2\ \rhd\ \{\!\{\ x_1 \leftarrow v_1\ ,\ ..\ ,\ x_n \leftarrow v_n\ \}\!\}}(5) \qquad \frac{\vdash v\ \textbf{matches}\ pat_2}{\vdash v\ \textbf{matches}\ pat_1 \mid pat_2}(6)$$

$$\frac{lrbs = (x_1\ =\ \textbf{function}\ pat\_mat_1\ \textbf{and}\ ...\ \textbf{and}\ x_n\ =\ \textbf{function}\ pat\_mat_n)}{\begin{array}{l}\textbf{recfun}\ (\ lrbs\ ,\ pat\_mat\ )\ \rhd\\ \{\!\{\ x_1 \leftarrow \textbf{let rec}\ lrbs\ \textbf{in}\ x_1\ ,\ ...\ ,\ x_n \leftarrow \textbf{let rec}\ lrbs\ \textbf{in}\ x_n\ \}\!\}\ (\ \textbf{function}\ pat\_mat\ )\end{array}}(7)$$

$$\frac{\begin{array}{l}lrbs = (x_1\ =\ \textbf{function}\ pat\_mat_1\ \textbf{and}\ ...\ \textbf{and}\ x_n\ =\ \textbf{function}\ pat\_mat_n)\\ \textbf{recfun}\ (\ lrbs\ ,\ pat\_mat_1\ )\ \rhd\ e_1\quad ...\quad \textbf{recfun}\ (\ lrbs\ ,\ pat\_mat_n\ )\ \rhd\ e_n\end{array}}{\vdash \textbf{let rec}\ lrbs\ \textbf{in}\ e\ \longrightarrow\ \{\!\{\ x_1 \leftarrow e_1\ ,\ ...\ ,\ x_n \leftarrow e_n\ \}\!\}\ e}(8)$$

$$\frac{}{\begin{array}{l}\vdash \textbf{try}\ (\ \%\textbf{prim raise}\ )\ v\ \textbf{with}\ pattern\_matching\ \longrightarrow\\ \quad \textbf{match}\ v\ \textbf{with}\ pattern\_matching \mid \_\ \rightarrow\ (\ (\ \%\textbf{prim raise}\ )\ v\ )\end{array}}(9)$$

$$\frac{\begin{array}{l}\vdash store \xrightarrow{L} store'\\ \vdash \langle definitions\_value, program\rangle \xrightarrow{L} \langle definitions, program'\rangle\end{array}}{\vdash \langle definitions\_value, program, store\rangle \longrightarrow \langle definitions, program', store'\rangle}(10)$$

Fig. 2. Operational semantics (excerpt)

Contexts. We specify evaluation-in-context with a collection of congruence rules (e.g., Rule 1). Alternative evaluation-context based approaches (in which the context information is encapsulated into a grammar-with-a-hole and hole filling function) can provide a more compact formalization, but initial experimentation showed them to be less convenient for HOL manipulation. HOL's automation works well with congruence rules directly, whereas the process of interpreting the hole filling on a data object (the evaluation context itself) introduced significantly more overhead.

Rule 1 incorporates right-to-left evaluation ordering for OCaml$_{light}$. Dropping the ordering requirement would require only trivial changes to the reduction rules and soundness proof, but looking ahead to testing, or even program verification via symbolic execution [8,9,10], we believe the benefits of a deterministic semantics outweigh the drawbacks of slightly over-specifying the language.

Store. The reduction rules are annotated with labels (L in Fig 2). Whenever the store must be consulted or updated (e.g., Rule 2), the label records the relevant information, both input from and output to the store. Thus, the store does not need to be threaded through the semantics, a formal version of the informal "state convention" of *The Definition of Standard ML.*[3] Rule 10 correlates the program's reduction with a reduction in the store. We anticipate using the labels to conveniently add other features, including I/O and concurrency.

Value Binding. All variable binding in OCaml$_{light}$ is expressed through pattern matching, and the pattern matching rules implement binding with (parallel) substitutions (Rules 3 and 4).[4]

Rule 5 for matching the right side of an "or" pattern must check that the left pattern does not match. HOL's rule induction package forbids a recursive call to the pattern matching relation under the requisite negation because such constructions are not inductive in general. We use a previously defined relation that simply checks pattern matching without building the substitution. This relation is acceptable to HOL because it does not need to discriminate between the cases where the first or second pattern match (Rule 6).

Recursive bindings use a substitution that replaces the bound variables with the entire recursive binding construct (Rules 7 and 8). This is one place where working directly on OCaml source complicates the specification and metatheory; the rule for a single function recursive **let** would be significantly simpler.

Primitives. We denote primitive operators with a special symbol $\%\mathbf{prim}$ to avoid confusing primitives (e.g., $(\%\mathbf{prim}\,+)$), which the semantics must directly interpret, with variables (e.g., $+$), which can be rebound in the source program. Furthermore, it distinguishes partially applied binary primitives (e.g., $(\%\mathbf{prim}\,+)0$), which are values, from other applications, which are not. Evaluation starts with a substitution that replaces identifiers in the initial environment with the corresponding $\%\mathbf{prim}$ values (e.g., substituting $(\%\mathbf{prim}\,+)$ for $+$).

Exceptions. For each congruence rule, there is a corresponding exception rule that discards the immediate context. When an exception reaches a **try** expression it is matched against the **with** portion (Rule 9). If it reaches the top level of a program, the rest of the program is discarded, and no further evaluation occurs.

Curried functions. The semantics of OCaml$_{light}$ differs slightly from OCaml in its treatment of partial pattern matches in curried functions. We reduce function applications one-at-a-time whereas the OCaml implementation does not reduce a curried function until all of its arguments are available. Thus, the following program raises a pattern matching exception on our semantics, but not in the implementation.

$$\mathbf{let}\,f = \mathbf{function}\,1 \rightarrow \mathbf{function}\,\_ \rightarrow 0\,;;\,\mathbf{let}\,\_ = f\,2\,;;$$

[3] The evaluation context approach can also avoid store threading.

[4] We write cons as , and append as @.

Specifying the implemented behavior would entail using the same elaborative pre-pass for detecting multiple-argument functions as the OCaml compiler. We do not believe this to be worth the effort given that the departure is small, and it is only observable in the presence of non-exhaustively matched patterns (whose existence the compiler can detect) which furthermore fail at run time.

2.2 Type System

Figure 3 gives an overview of our type system for OCaml$_{light}$, along with a few of its 173 rules. The type system is mostly syntax directed, but non-algorithmic, due to declarative handling of polymorphism and recursion.

Environments. The E productions describe the environments used by the type system. A binding, EB, can be one of the following, in order: a de Bruijn type variable binding (**TV**), a value binding; a constant data constructor; a parameterized data constructor; a variant type constructor; a record's field name; a record type constructor; or a store location. If our type system checked pattern matches for exhaustiveness, variant type constructors would have to keep a constructor list similar to a record type constructor's field list. Location bindings are introduced only by the top-level store, and type constructor, field, and value constructor bindings are introduced only by top-level definitions. Type variable and value bindings are introduced by **let** expressions, with unbounded nesting.

In an **ok** environment E, all type constructor and type variable references are bound by a prior EB. Also, E contains no duplicate bindings for a location, type constructor, value constructor, or field name. The type constructor restriction (which is enforced in OCaml) is necessary for type soundness; for example, the following program, which gets stuck, would otherwise typecheck since v has type t which, at the field access site, is specified to have a field g:

$$\mathbf{type}\ t = \{f : \mathbf{int}\} ;; \mathbf{let}\ v = \{f = 1\} ;; \mathbf{type}\ t = \{g : \mathbf{bool}\} ;; \mathbf{let}\ \_ = v\,.\,g$$

The constructor and field restrictions do not preclude programs that get stuck, but they are necessary for type preservation (and hence for our soundness proof). In the following example, once v is substituted, the enclosing binding of C is different, and $C\,1$ can no longer be typed.

$$\mathbf{type}\ t = C\,\mathbf{of}\ \mathbf{int} ;; \mathbf{let}\ v = C\,1 ;; \mathbf{type}\ u = C\,\mathbf{of}\ \mathbf{bool} ;; \mathbf{let}\ \_ = v$$

The *absence* of a similar restriction on value name repetition is also necessary for type preservation, because we do not treat value names up to α-equivalence. The following example does not start with a repeated, nested binding, but immediately after v is substituted, x is duplicated in the environment.

$$\mathbf{let}\ v = \mathbf{function}\ x \to x ;; \mathbf{let}\ x = 1 ;; \mathbf{let}\ w = v\,9$$

Polymorphism. A **let** expression with a non-expansive binding introduces a type variable binding into E. The type of the binding can refer to this variable as a well-formed, but opaque, type. When the binding's type is added to E to check the **let** body, it is

$$
\begin{array}{l}
E ::= \mathbf{empty} \mid E, EB \\
EB ::= \mathbf{TV} \mid value\_name : typescheme \mid constr\_name\,\mathbf{of}\, typeconstr \\
\quad \mid constr\_name\,\mathbf{of}\,\forall\, type\_params,\, typexprs : typeconstr \mid typeconstr\_name : kind \\
\quad \mid field\_name : \forall\, type\_params,\, typeconstr\_name \rightarrow typexpr \\
\quad \mid typeconstr\_name : kind\,\{\, field\_name_1 \,;\, \ldots ;\, field\_name_n \,\} \mid location : typexpr \\
\sigma^T ::= \{\!\{\, \alpha_1 \leftarrow typexpr_1 \,,\, \ldots,\, \alpha_n \leftarrow typexpr_n \,\}\!\}
\end{array}
$$

$$
\begin{array}{ll}
E \vdash \mathbf{ok} & E \vdash typexpr : kind \\
\sigma^T \,\&\, E \vdash pattern : typexpr \,\triangleright\, E' & \sigma^T \,\&\, E \vdash expr : typexpr \\
E \vdash definition : E' & E \vdash program : E' \\
E \vdash store : E' & E \vdash \langle program, store \rangle
\end{array}
$$

$$
\frac{\begin{array}{c}\mathbf{shift}\,0\,1\,\sigma^T \,\&\, E, \mathbf{TV} \vdash pat = nexp \,\triangleright\, x_1 : t_1 \,,\, \ldots,\, x_n : t_n \\ \sigma^T \,\&\, E\,@\,x_1 : \forall\, t_1 \,,\, \ldots,\, x_n : \forall\, t_n \vdash e : t\end{array}}{\sigma^T \,\&\, E \vdash \mathbf{let}\, pat = nexp\,\mathbf{in}\, e : t}\ (11)
$$

$$
\frac{\begin{array}{l}E \vdash value\_name \,\triangleright\, value\_name : ts \\ E \vdash t \leq ts\end{array}}{E \vdash value\_name : t}\ (12)
\qquad
\frac{\begin{array}{l}E \vdash \forall\, t' : \mathbf{Type} \\ E \vdash t_1 : \mathbf{Type} \;\; .. \;\; E \vdash t_n : \mathbf{Type} \\ \{\!\{\, t_1 \,,\, \ldots,\, t_n \,\}\!\}\, t' \,\triangleright\, t''\end{array}}{E \vdash t'' \leq \forall\, t'}\ (13)
$$

$$
\frac{\begin{array}{c}\sigma^T \,\&\, E \vdash e : t \\ E \vdash t \leq \sigma^T\, src\_t\end{array}}{\sigma^T \,\&\, E \vdash (\, e : src\_t\,) : t}\ (14)
\qquad
\frac{\begin{array}{c}\sigma^T \,\&\, E \vdash e : t \\ E \vdash field\_name : t \rightarrow t'\end{array}}{\sigma^T \,\&\, E \vdash e\,.\,field\_name : t'}\ (15)
$$

$$
\frac{\begin{array}{l}E\,@\,E' \vdash store : E' \\ E\,@\,E' \vdash program : E''\end{array}}{E \vdash \langle program, store \rangle}\ (16)
\qquad
\frac{\begin{array}{c}E \vdash store : E' \\ \{\!\{\;\}\!\}\,\&\, E \vdash v : t\end{array}}{E \vdash store\,,\, l \mapsto v : E', (\, l : t\,)}\ (17)
$$

$$
\frac{\begin{array}{l}E \vdash field\_name \,\triangleright\, field\_name : \forall\,(\,\alpha_1 \,,\, \ldots,\, \alpha_m\,)\,,\, typeconstr\_name \rightarrow t \\ E \vdash (\, t_1' \,,\, \ldots,\, t_m'\,)\, typeconstr\_name \rightarrow t'' \leq \\ \quad \forall\,(\,\alpha_1 \,,\, \ldots,\, \alpha_m\,)\,,\, (\,\alpha_1 \,,\, \ldots,\, \alpha_m\,)\, typeconstr\_name \rightarrow t\end{array}}{E \vdash field\_name : (\, t_1' \,,\, \ldots,\, t_m'\,)\, typeconstr\_name \rightarrow t''}\ (18)
$$

$$
\frac{\sigma^T \,\&\, E, \mathbf{TV} \vdash pat = nexp \,\triangleright\, (\, x_1 : t_1'\,) \,,\, \ldots,\, (\, x_k : t_k'\,)}{E \vdash \mathbf{let}\, pat = nexp : (\, x_1 : \forall\, t_1'\,) \,,\, \ldots,\, (\, x_k : \forall\, t_k'\,)}\ (19)
$$

Fig. 3. Type system (excerpt)

first generalized into a type scheme (Rule 11). Where the body refers to the binding, the type scheme is instantiated to a type that is valid at the use point (Rules 12 and 13).[5]

One of the more subtle aspects of OCaml$_{light}$ is the treatment of type variables that appear in explicit annotations. These are scoped by top level definitions, and stand in for arbitrary types. Thus, the top-level **let** definition rule (19) creates a substitution σ^T that supplies the types for these variables to Rule 14. Substituting **bool** for $'a$, f in the following program has type **bool** $\rightarrow$ **bool**, which agrees with OCaml.[6]

[5] Each **TV** actually introduces an infinite collection of type variables, indexed by numbers, because a **let** expression can introduce any number of type variables.

[6] The corresponding program in SML is not well typed.

$$\textbf{let}\, f\,(x\;:\;'a)\;:\;'a\;=\;x\,\&\&\,\textbf{true}$$

Stores. Since the store can contain cyclic structures, it is type checked in a context that includes E', the types of the locations in the store (Rule 16). Values in the store cannot have type variables in their enclosed type annotations (hence the empty substitution appears in the Rule 17), because such variables would have escaped their scope at a top-level definition. Thus, before placing a value into the store, the operational semantics replaces all of its type variables with the wildcard type variable _.

Records and Variants. Rules 15 and 18 show how expressions and patterns consult the environment for the types of the fields and constructors.

3 Type Soundness

The type soundness theorem (Theorem 1) ensures that a well-typed program does not get stuck. Our mechanized proof follows the standard methodology of preservation and progress lemmas. These lemmas are proved at three levels: for expressions, for definitions and for top level definition/program/store tuples. They rely on a typical collection of other main lemmas: substitution, weakening, strengthening, type substitution, and validity. The number and size of these lemmas prevents a full presentation here, so we instead highlight several aspects.

Theorem 1. If both $\vdash \langle \epsilon, \mathit{program}, \mathit{store}\rangle \longrightarrow^* \langle \mathit{definitions}', \mathit{program}', \mathit{store}'\rangle$ and $\epsilon \vdash \langle \mathit{program}, \mathit{store}\rangle$ then either
$(\mathit{program}' = \epsilon)$, or $(\exists \mathit{value}.\ \mathit{program}' = (\%\textbf{prim raise})\ \mathit{value})$, or
$\exists \mathit{definitions}''\ \mathit{program}''\ \mathit{store}''.$
$\vdash \langle \mathit{definitions}', \mathit{program}', \mathit{store}'\rangle \longrightarrow \langle \mathit{definitions}'', \mathit{program}'', \mathit{store}''\rangle.$

Type Variable Binding. We use a de Bruijn index encoding of type variables. Shift operations appear in the rules of the type system 19 times, 16 of which occur to generalize a type into a type scheme from a non-polymorphic binder. Since the type variables that appear in source language type annotations are handled with substitutions (Sect. 2.2), the de Bruijn encoding does not require changing the source language at all: indices and shifts exist only in the type rules and the soundness proof (but not the operational semantics). Thus, the de Bruijn encoding does not substantially complicate OCaml$_{light}$.

Unlike value variables, type variables must not be repeated in the context. Otherwise, a type scheme generalization in one **let** expression might capture a type variable introduced by a different **let** expression. The prohibition on repetition is exactly the reason that α-renaming is required in the soundness proof. In the following example, the first evaluation step substitutes the middle **let** underneath the type variable binding introduced by the rightmost **let**.

$$\textbf{let}\, x\;=\;(\,\textbf{function}\,\_\;\rightarrow\;\textbf{let}\, y\;=\;\textbf{function}\, w\;\rightarrow\;w\,\textbf{in}\, y\,)\,\textbf{in}\,\textbf{let}\, z\;=\;x\,\textbf{in}\, z$$

In the proof, this situation corresponds to the polymorphic **let** case of the weakening lemma. Given a **let** expression and typing derivation in $E_1 @ E_2$, we must show that it has a type in $E_1\,,\,'a @ E_2$. In the given derivation, the **let** extends the environment with a type variable that might be $'a$. If so, a new derivation cannot be formed without renaming one of the type variables.

We investigated two proof approaches that do not use an α-aware representation for type variables. The first approach begins by showing an equivariance property: that the result of consistently renaming the type variables in a typing derivation remains a typing derivation. Equivariance is then used in the weakening proof to rename the type variable added by the **let**. The drawback of this approach is that weakening cannot be proved with a rule induction because the renamed derivation does not match up with the induction hypothesis. Instead the induction must be on derivation heights, which requires a significant amount of additional work to formalize in HOL. The second approach combines the statements of equivariance and weakening into a single lemma, which restores the ability to do rule induction.[7] Ultimately, we concluded that both approaches required significantly more work to mechanize than the de Bruijn representation, where the equivariance result is intrinsic to the representation. Since the de Bruijn representation was easy to work with in the proof, we did not consider other equivariant representations.

Lemma 1 states expression weakening for a single de Bruijn type variable.

Lemma 1. If $(\sigma^T \,\&\, E_2 \,@\, E_1 \vdash \mathit{expr} : \mathit{typexpr})$ then
$\sigma^T \uparrow^1_{\mathrm{num\_tv}(E_1)} \,\&\, E_2, \mathbf{TV} \,@\, E_1 \uparrow^1_0 \vdash \mathit{expr} : \mathit{typexpr} \uparrow^1_{\mathrm{num\_tv}(E_1)}$.

Labels. The preservation and progress lemmas are split into pieces according to the transition labels. Lemma 2 states that a well typed program can take a step with some label, and Lemma 3 allows the label to be altered so that it works for a given store. The $\vdash \mathit{store} \xrightarrow{L} \mathit{store}'$ relation updates a store according to a label.

Lemma 2. Suppose that E has no value bindings. If $\sigma^T \,\&\, E \vdash \mathit{expr} : \mathit{typexpr}$ then either expr is a value, or $(\exists \mathit{value}.\ \mathit{expr} = (\%\mathbf{prim\,raise})\ \mathit{value})$, or $(\exists L\ \mathit{expr}'.\ \vdash \mathit{expr} \xrightarrow{L} \mathit{expr}')$.

Lemma 3. Suppose that all of the locations in expr are bound to values in store. If $\vdash \mathit{expr} \xrightarrow{L} \mathit{expr}'$ then $\exists L'\ \mathit{expr}'\ \mathit{store}'.\ \vdash \mathit{expr} \xrightarrow{L'} \mathit{expr}' \ \wedge\ \vdash \mathit{store} \xrightarrow{L'} \mathit{store}'$.

The statement of preservation (Lemma 4) relies on two relations for checking labels. The first $\sigma^T \,\&\, E \vdash L$ ensures that the parts of L that are input into the expression reduction (e.g., the value of a location dereference) are well formed and well typed. The second $\sigma^T \,\&\, E \vdash L \rhd E'$ ensures that the output parts of L (e.g., the location being dereferenced) are well formed and well typed. It also gives the environment bindings created by the output. Thus, the input relation appears in the preservation statement's assumptions and the output in its conclusions.

Lemma 4. Suppose that E has no value bindings.
If $\vdash \mathit{expr} \xrightarrow{L} \mathit{expr}'$ and $\sigma^T \,\&\, E \vdash \mathit{expr} : \mathit{typexpr}$ and $\sigma^T \,\&\, E \vdash L$ then
$\exists E'.\ \sigma^T \,\&\, E \vdash L \rhd E' \ \wedge\ \sigma^T \,\&\, E \,@\, E' \vdash \mathit{expr}' : \mathit{typexpr}$.

[7] Thanks to Tom Ridge for this observation.

The top level preservation theorem for program/store tuples relies on Lemma 4 (lifted to definition sequences) and two other lemmas. The first states that updating a well typed store with a well typed (by the expression output label typing relation) label gives a well typed store. The second states that if a well typed store is updated with a label then the label is well typed (by the expression input label). These parts of the proof are not particularly difficult: the key insight is to split the label checking between two relations.

Store Typing. Not only can the store contain cyclic references as mentioned in Sect. 2.2, but it can also contain constructed and record values. To ensure preservation, the store must be typed in an environment that has bindings for any type definitions that might be needed. Thus, the operational semantics builds a separate record of type definitions as it encounters them. Intermediate computation steps are type checked by converting the type definitions into an environment, then checking the store in this environment, and finally checking the unevaluated definitions with both the type definitions' and the store's environments.

4 Testing and Determinism

Because creating a large semantics is an error-prone activity [1,2], we run a test suite of programs on the semantics to build confidence in its accuracy. Crucially, we can transfer this confidence to others by showing them the test suite. To our knowledge, the testing of full-language-scale semantics has been previously carried out only for the Scheme semantics in the PLT Redex term rewriting system [23] and in ACL2 for a Java Virtual Machine [9,24] (symbolic execution is part of the standard ACL2 methodology, and it has often been applied to test full-scale hardware formalizations). Although both the type system and operational semantics should be tested, our focus here is on the operational semantics, leaving the type system for future work.

Although a mechanized type soundness proof rules out certain kinds of errors, it falls far short of ensuring that the semantics accurately models the intended language. In fact, we discovered an error while preparing the executable semantics, before testing even began. While proving Lemma 5 we discovered that we had omitted the negated premise of the "or" pattern matching rule (Sect. 2.1). This mistake allowed the semantics to non-deterministically return incorrect results in some cases, while remaining perfectly type sound.

Another class of specification mistakes arises from pattern-matching rules that do not find a match when they should. These mistakes do not cause type soundness violations because a **Match_failure** exception is raised when no patterns match. For example, after finishing the type soundness proof, we realized that the rule for record patterns was incorrectly requiring the field lists to be in the same order for both the pattern and value. However, the pattern matcher can be tested for this sort of bug.

Evaluation Function. The first step toward testing the semantics is to create an executable version of it. Although the relational formulation of the semantics could in principle be executed as a logic program (as Twelf does), we chose to create a functional version for execution. This is in part because HOL-4 does not currently support relational execution, but can evaluate functions (and can generate ML code from functions for greater speed). Additionally, since the semantics is deterministic, we would like to prove that fact. We prove determinacy and support testing with the same technique: we create a functional version of the semantics and prove it equal to the relational version.

We use the ability to do functional programming in HOL's logic to implement the single-step execution function using common patterns of functional abstraction to reduce the amount of redundant code and make the definition tractable for a language the size of OCaml$_{light}$. Because HOL is a logic of total functions only, we must prove that the functions always terminate. The proof is not difficult, but the mutually recursive helper functions used to abstract out common patterns make it complicated enough that HOL-4 does not prove termination automatically.

To maintain the correspondence with the labeled transition relation, the store is not an input to the expression reduction function (`red`); instead, the result type for `red` includes cases for interactions with the store. For example, the result for a store lookup reduction indicates the location of the reference, and it supplies a function that is applied to the value in the location to determine the result. Lemma 5 correlates the relational and functional expression semantics using `interp_result`, which applies the information in a label to a reduction result.

Lemma 5. $\vdash \mathit{expr} \xrightarrow{L} \mathit{expr}'$ iff $\texttt{interp\_result}(\texttt{red}(\mathit{expr}), L) = \texttt{Some}\ \mathit{expr}'$.

Unlike the expression semantics, the top-level semantics is not deterministic: the location allocator can use any unallocated location for the new reference. Thus, the `top_red` function is parameterized over an allocation function that, for a given store, returns the next location to use.

Theorem 2. Say that *alloc* is *good* if *alloc*(*store*) never results in a location already mapped in *store*.
$\vdash \langle \mathit{definitions}, \mathit{program}, \mathit{store}\rangle \longrightarrow \langle \mathit{definitions}', \mathit{program}', \mathit{store}'\rangle$ iff
$\exists \mathit{alloc}.\ \mathit{alloc}$ is good $\wedge$
$\texttt{top\_red}(\mathit{alloc}, (\mathit{definitions}, \mathit{store}, \mathit{program})) = \texttt{Some}(\mathit{definitions}', \mathit{store}', \mathit{program}')$.

Test Suite. Our test suite currently contains 145 test cases, each designed to test one or two language features. A test case comprises a program and its expected result, both in OCaml syntax. We convert both into abstract syntax trees using the parser and (slightly modified) AST printer from the OCaml implementation. We use HOL-4's SML code generation on the reduction functions and test ASTs to execute the test cases. The test suite fully covers the reduction function definition.[8]

5 Discussion

The primary challenge we encountered in our formalization and mechanization was the scale of OCaml$_{light}$. The HOL proof techniques we use are typical, and up to the

[8] We check coverage using Standard ML of New Jersey's coverage checking tool. This ensures that every application point is taken by the test suite.

task: rewriting with equational theorems, backward and forward chaining with implicational theorems (including induction principles), instantiating existentially quantified variables, case-splitting, and doing first-order proof search. However, the scale of the language provided a constant source of friction. For example, proof cases involving arbitrarily sized constructs, such as tuples and records, often require inductive lemmas whereas their fixed size counterparts, such as "and" expressions, only involve a case split.

As to the scale, the grammar has 251 productions in 55 non-terminals. Of these, 142 and 36 (respectively) are parts of the source language, and the rest are used in intermediate results and to support the type system and semantics (e.g., notation for substitution). The type system comprises 173 rules that define 28 relations, and the operational semantics comprises 137 rules that define 15 relations. These relations rely on 12 helper functions in addition to the substitution and free variable functions generated by Ott. In total, the specification comprises about 3700 lines of Ott source. The evaluation function is 540 lines of typical functional programming (although in HOL). The proof contains about 9000 lines of HOL broken into 561 stated lemmas and theorems. The entire development has taken the author approximately 6 months to create.

We want to be able to extend the OCaml$_{light}$ specification easily. We believe that the specification achieves this goal thorough the combination of Ott, labeled transitions, and careful planning ahead. However, the HOL proof scripts are fragile with respect to specification changes, including changing variable names or rule ordering. We have taken some initial steps, in conjunction with Ott, to alleviate some of the ordering problems. However, for proofs over definitions as as large as OCaml$_{light}$, acceptable flexibility will come only from significant advances in proof assistant technology for proof maintenance and extension.

6 Conclusion

We have formally specified a type system and operational semantics for a substantial fragment of OCaml. We validated them by proving their type soundness in HOL, and by testing the semantics on a thorough test suite. Throughout the process we have maintained a close connection between our formalization and OCaml source code. Our effort is the first of its complexity with this goal—a goal motivated by our view that the mechanized specification and proofs are not only a final product, but also a starting point for the verification of OCaml programs.

Acknowledgments. We thank Gilles Peskine for his collaboration on parts of the formalization and for sharing his expertise in the OCaml language, and Peter Sewell and Francesco Zappa Nardelli for their work on the initial formalization. We acknowledge the support of EPSRC grants GR/T11715/01 and EP/C510712/1.

References

1. Kahrs, S.: Mistakes and ambiguities in the definition of Standard ML. Technical Report ECS-LFCS-93-257, University of Edinburgh (April 1993)
2. Rossberg, A.: Defects in the revised definition of Standard ML. Technical report, Saarland University, Saarbrücken, Germany (October 2001), Updated 2007/01/22

3. Leroy, X.: The Objective Caml System. 3.10 edn. (2007) `http://caml.inria.fr/pub/docs/manual-ocaml/index.html`.
4. Sewell, P., Zappa Nardelli, F., Owens, S., Peskine, G., Ridge, T., Sarkar, S., Strniša, R.: Ott: Effective tool support for the working semanticist. In: Proc. ICFP (2007)
5. Norrish, M., Slind, K.: HOL-4, `http://hol.sourceforge.net/`
6. Slind, K.: Reasoning about Terminating Functional Programs. PhD thesis, Institut für Informatik, Technische Universität München (1999)
7. Hurd, J.: First-order proof tactics in higher-order logic theorem provers. In: Proc. Design and Application of Strategies/Tactics in Higher Order Logics (2003)
8. Compton, M.: Stenning's protocol implemented in UDP and verified in Isabelle. In: Proc. Australasian Symposium on Theory of Computing (2005)
9. Liu, H., Moore, J.S.: Java program verification via a JVM deep embedding in ACL2. In: Slind, K., Bunker, A., Gopalakrishnan, G.C. (eds.) TPHOLs 2004. LNCS, vol. 3223, Springer, Heidelberg (2004)
10. Ridge, T.: Operational reasoning for concurrent Caml programs and weak memory models. In: Schneider, K., Brandt, J. (eds.) TPHOLs 2007. LNCS, vol. 4732, Springer, Heidelberg (2007)
11. Aydemir, B.E., Bohannon, A., Fairbairn, M., Foster, J.N., Pierce, B.C., Sewell, P., Vytiniotis, D., Washburn, G., Weirich, S., Zdancewic, S.: Mechanized metatheory for the masses: The POPLmark Challenge. In: Hurd, J., Melham, T. (eds.) TPHOLs 2005. LNCS, vol. 3603, Springer, Heidelberg (2005)
12. Klein, G., Nipkow, T.: A machine-checked model for a Java-like language, virtual machine and compiler. Trans. on Prog. Lang. and Systems 28(4), 619–695 (2006)
13. Lee, D.K., Crary, K., Harper, R.: Towards a mechanized metatheory of Standard ML. In: Proc. Principles of Programming Languages (2007)
14. Maharaj, S., Gunter, E.L.: Studying the ML module system in HOL. In: Melham, T.F., Camilleri, J. (eds.) HUG 1994. LNCS, vol. 859, Springer, Heidelberg (1994)
15. Nipkow, T., van Oheimb, D.: Java_{light} is type-safe — definitely. In: POPL (1998)
16. Norrish, M.: C Formalised in HOL. PhD thesis, University of Cambridge (1998)
17. Syme, D.: Reasoning with the formal definition of Standard ML in HOL. In: Joyce, J.J., Seger, C.-J.H. (eds.) HUG 1993. LNCS, vol. 780, Springer, Heidelberg (1994)
18. Syme, D.: Proving Java type soundness. In: Formal Syntax and Semantics of Java, pp. 83–118. Springer, Heidelberg (1999)
19. VanInwegen, M.: The Machine-Assisted Proof of Programming Language Properties. PhD thesis, University of Pennsylvania (1996)
20. Harper, R.: personal correspondence (2007)
21. Harper, R., Licata, D.: Mechanizing metatheory in a logical framework. Journal of Functional Programming 17(4–5), 613–673 (2007)
22. Milner, R., Tofte, M., Harper, R., MacQueen, D.: The Definition of Standard ML (Revised). MIT Press, Cambridge (1997)
23. Matthews, J., Findler, R.B.: An operational semantics for Scheme. Journal of Functional Programming (to appear)
24. Moore, J.S.: Symbolic simulation: An ACL2 approach. In: Gopalakrishnan, G.C., Windley, P. (eds.) FMCAD 1998. LNCS, vol. 1522, Springer, Heidelberg (1998)

Parametric Polymorphism through Run-Time Sealing or, Theorems for Low, Low Prices!

Jacob Matthews[1] and Amal Ahmed[2]

[1] University of Chicago
jacobm@cs.uchicago.edu
[2] Toyota Technological Institute at Chicago
amal@tti-c.org

Abstract. We show how to extend System F's parametricity guarantee to a Matthews-Findler-style multi-language system that combines System F with an untyped language by use of dynamic sealing. While the use of sealing for this purpose has been suggested before, it has never been proven to preserve parametricity. In this paper we prove that it does using step-indexed logical relations. Using this result we show a scheme for implementing parametric higher-order contracts in an untyped setting which corresponds to a translation given by Sumii and Pierce. These contracts satisfy rich enough guarantees that we can extract analogues to Wadler's free theorems that rely on run-time enforcement of dynamic seals.

1 Introduction

There have been two major strategies for hiding the implementation details of one part of a program from its other parts: the static approach and the dynamic approach.

The static approach can be summarized by the slogan "information hiding = parametric polymorphism." In it, the language's type system is equipped with a facility such as existential types so that it can reject programs in which one module makes unwarranted assumptions about the internal details of another, even if those assumptions happen to be true. This approach rests on Reynolds' notion of abstraction [1], later redubbed the "parametricity" theorem by Wadler [2].

The dynamic approach, which goes back to Morris [3], can be summarized by the alternate slogan "information hiding = local scope + generativity." Rather than statically rejecting programs that make unwarranted assumptions, the dynamic approach simply takes away programs' ability to see if those assumptions are correct. It allows a programmer to *dynamically seal* values by creating unique keys ($\mathit{create\text{-}seal} : \rightarrow \mathit{key}$) and using those keys with locking and unlocking operations ($\mathit{seal} : v \times \mathit{key} \rightarrow \mathit{opaque}$ and $\mathit{unseal} : \mathit{opaque} \times \mathit{key} \rightarrow v$ respectively). A value locked with a particular key is opaque to third parties: nothing can be done but unlock it with the same key. Here is a simple implementation written in Scheme, where **gensym** is a function that generates a new, completely unique symbol every time it is called:

(**define** (*create-seal*) (**gensym**))
(**define** (*seal v s1*) (λ (*s2*) (**if** (**eq?** *s1 s2*) *v* (**error**))))
(**define** (*unseal sealed-v s*) (*sealed-v s*))

S. Drossopoulou (Ed.): ESOP 2008, LNCS 4960, pp. 16–31, 2008.

Using this facility a module can hand out a particular value while hiding its representation by creating a fresh seal in its private lexical scope, sealing the value and hand the result to clients, and then unsealing it again whenever it returns. This is the primary information-hiding mechanism in many untyped languages. For instance PLT Scheme [4] uses generative `structs`, essentially a (much) more sophisticated version of seals, to build abstractions for a great variety of programming constructs such as an object system. Furthermore, the idea has seen some use recently even in languages whose primary information-hiding mechanism is static, as recounted by Sumii and Pierce [5].

Both of these strategies seem to match an intuitive understanding of what information-hiding ought to entail. So it is surprising that a fundamental question — what is the relationship between the guarantee provided by the static approach and the dynamic approach? — has not been answered in the literature.

In this paper we take a new perspective on the problem, posing it as a question of parametricity in a multi-language system [6]. After reviewing our previous work on multi-language systems and giving a multi-language system that combines System F (henceforth "ML") and an untyped call-by-value lambda calculus (henceforth "Scheme") (section 2), we use this vantage point to show two results. First, in section 3 we show that dynamic sealing preserves ML's parametricity guarantee even when interoperating with Scheme. For the proof, we define two step-indexed logical relations [7], one for ML (indexed by both types as well as, intuitively, the number of steps available for future evaluation) and one for Scheme (indexed only by steps since Scheme is untyped). The stratification provided by step-indexing is essential for modeling unbounded computation, available in Scheme due to the presence of what amounts to a recursive type, and available in ML via interaction with Scheme. Then we show the fundamental theorems of each relation. The novelty of this proof is its use of what we call the "bridge lemma," which states that if two terms are related in one language, then wrapping those terms in boundaries results in terms that are related in the other. The proof is otherwise essentially standard. Second, in section 4 we restrict our attention to Scheme programs that use boundaries with ML only to implement a contract system [8]. Appealing to the first parametricity result, we give a more useful, contract-indexed relation for dealing with these terms and prove that it relates contracted terms to themselves. In section 4.1 we show that our notion of contracts corresponds to Findler and Felleisen's, and to a translation given by Sumii and Pierce [5, section 8].

We have elided most proofs here. They can be found in this paper's companion technical report [9].

2 A Brief Introduction to Multi-language Systems

To make the present work self-contained, in this section we summarize some relevant material from earlier work [6].

The natural embedding. The natural embedding multi-language system, presented in figure 1 is a method of modeling the semantics of a minimal "ML" (simply-typed, call-by-value lambda calculus) with a minimal "Scheme" (untyped, call-by-value lambda calculus) such that both languages have natural access to foreign values. They receive

$$
\begin{array}{lcl}
\mathbf{e} & = & \mathbf{x} \mid \mathbf{v} \mid (\mathbf{e}\;\mathbf{e}) \mid (op\;\mathbf{e}\;\mathbf{e}) \mid (\mathbf{if0}\;\mathbf{e}\;\mathbf{e}\;\mathbf{e}) \\
 & & \mid (\mathbf{cons}\;\mathbf{e}\;\mathbf{e}) \mid ({}^{\tau}\!M\!S\;\mathsf{e}) \\
\mathbf{v} & = & \lambda\mathbf{x}:\tau.\mathbf{e} \mid \overline{n} \mid \mathbf{nil} \mid (\mathbf{cons}\;\mathbf{v}_1\;\mathbf{v}_2) \mid \mathbf{fst} \mid \mathbf{rst} \\
op & = & + \mid - \\
\tau & = & \mathbf{Nat} \mid \tau \to \tau \mid \tau^* \\
\mathbf{x} & = & \text{ML variables} \\
\mathbf{E} & = & [\,]_M \mid (\mathbf{E}\;\mathbf{e}) \mid (\mathbf{v}\;\mathbf{E}) \mid (op\;\mathbf{E}\;\mathbf{e}) \mid (op\;\mathbf{v}\;\mathbf{E}) \\
 & & \mid (\mathbf{if0}\;\mathbf{E}\;\mathbf{e}\;\mathbf{e}) \mid (\mathbf{cons}\;\mathbf{E}\;\mathbf{e}) \mid (\mathbf{cons}\;\mathbf{v}\;\mathbf{E}) \mid ({}^{\tau}\!M\!S\;\mathsf{E})
\end{array}
$$

$$
\frac{}{\Gamma,\mathbf{x}:\tau \vdash_M \mathbf{x}:\tau}
\qquad
\frac{\Gamma,\mathbf{x}:\tau_1 \vdash_M \mathbf{e}:\tau_2}{\Gamma \vdash_M \lambda\mathbf{x}:\tau_1.\,\mathbf{e}:\tau_1\to\tau_2}
$$

$$
\frac{\Gamma \vdash_M \mathbf{e}_1:\tau_1\to\tau_2 \qquad \Gamma \vdash_M \mathbf{e}_2:\tau_1}{\Gamma \vdash_M (\mathbf{e}_1\;\mathbf{e}_2):\tau_2}
$$

$$
\frac{}{\Gamma \vdash_M \mathbf{nil}:\tau^*}
\qquad
\frac{\Gamma \vdash_M \mathbf{e}_1:\tau \quad \Gamma \vdash_M \mathbf{e}_2:\tau^*}{\Gamma \vdash_M (\mathbf{cons}\;\mathbf{e}_1\;\mathbf{e}_2):\tau^*}
$$

$$
\frac{}{\Gamma \vdash_M \mathbf{rst}:\tau^*\to\tau^*}
\qquad
\frac{}{\Gamma \vdash_M \mathbf{fst}:\tau^*\to\tau}
$$

$$
\frac{}{\Gamma \vdash_M \overline{n}:\mathbf{Nat}}
\qquad
\frac{\Gamma \vdash_M \mathbf{e}_1:\mathbf{Nat} \qquad \Gamma \vdash_M \mathbf{e}_2:\mathbf{Nat}}{\Gamma \vdash_M (op\;\mathbf{e}_1\;\mathbf{e}_2):\mathbf{Nat}}
$$

$$
\frac{\Gamma \vdash_M \mathbf{e}_1:\mathbf{Nat} \qquad \Gamma \vdash_M \mathbf{e}_2:\tau \qquad \Gamma \vdash_M \mathbf{e}_3:\tau}{\Gamma \vdash_M (\mathbf{if0}\;\mathbf{e}_1\;\mathbf{e}_2\;\mathbf{e}_3):\tau}
$$

$$
\frac{\Gamma \vdash_S \mathsf{e}:\mathbf{TST}}{\Gamma \vdash_M ({}^{\tau}\!M\!S\;\mathsf{e}):\tau}
$$

$$
\begin{array}{lll}
\mathscr{E}[((\lambda\mathbf{x}:\tau.\,\mathbf{e})\;\mathbf{v})]_M & \mapsto & \mathscr{E}[\mathbf{e}[\mathbf{v}/\mathbf{x}]] \\
\mathscr{E}[(+\;\overline{n_1}\;\overline{n_2})]_M & \mapsto & \mathscr{E}[\overline{n_1+n_2}] \\
\mathscr{E}[(-\;\overline{n_1}\;\overline{n_2})]_M & \mapsto & \mathscr{E}[\overline{max(n_1-n_2,0)}] \\
\mathscr{E}[(\mathbf{if0}\;\overline{0}\;\mathbf{e}_1\;\mathbf{e}_2)]_M & \mapsto & \mathscr{E}[\mathbf{e}_1] \\
\mathscr{E}[(\mathbf{if0}\;\overline{n}\;\mathbf{e}_1\;\mathbf{e}_2)]_M & \mapsto & \mathscr{E}[\mathbf{e}_2] \quad \text{where } n \neq 0 \\
\mathscr{E}[(\mathbf{fst}\;(\mathbf{cons}\;\mathbf{v}_1\;\mathbf{v}_2))]_M & \mapsto & \mathscr{E}[\mathbf{v}_1] \\
\mathscr{E}[(\mathbf{fst}\;\mathbf{nil})]_M & \mapsto & \mathbf{Error}\text{: nil} \\
\mathscr{E}[(\mathbf{rst}\;(\mathbf{cons}\;\mathbf{v}_1\;\mathbf{v}_2))]_M & \mapsto & \mathscr{E}[\mathbf{v}_2] \\
\mathscr{E}[(\mathbf{rst}\;\mathbf{nil})]_M & \mapsto & \mathbf{Error}\text{: nil}
\end{array}
$$

$$
\begin{array}{lll}
\mathscr{E}[({}^{\mathbf{Nat}}\!M\!S\;\overline{n})]_M & \mapsto & \mathscr{E}[\overline{n}] \\
\mathscr{E}[({}^{\mathbf{Nat}}\!M\!S\;\mathsf{v})]_M & \mapsto & \mathbf{Error}\text{: Non-num} \\
 & & \text{where } \mathsf{v} \neq \overline{n} \text{ for any } n \\
\mathscr{E}[({}^{\tau_1\mapsto\tau_2}\!M\!S(\lambda\mathsf{x}.\mathsf{e}))]_M & \mapsto & \\
\multicolumn{3}{r}{\mathscr{E}[(\lambda\mathbf{x}:\tau_1.({}^{\tau_2}\!M\!S\;((\lambda\mathsf{x}.\mathsf{e})\;(S\!M^{\tau_1}\;\mathbf{x}))))]} \\
\mathscr{E}[({}^{\tau_1\mapsto\tau_2}\!M\!S\;\mathsf{v})]_M & \mapsto & \mathbf{Error}\text{: non-proc} \\
 & & \text{where } \mathsf{v} \neq \lambda\mathsf{x}.\mathsf{e} \text{ for any } \mathsf{x},\mathsf{e} \\
\mathscr{E}[({}^{\tau^*}\!M\!S\;\mathbf{nil})]_M & \mapsto & \mathscr{E}[\mathbf{nil}] \\
\mathscr{E}[({}^{\tau^*}\!M\!S\;(\mathbf{cons}\;\mathsf{v}_1\;\mathsf{v}_2))]_M & \mapsto & \\
\multicolumn{3}{r}{\mathscr{E}[(\mathbf{cons}\;({}^{\tau}\!M\!S\;\mathsf{v}_1)\;({}^{\tau^*}\!M\!S\;\mathsf{v}_2))]} \\
\mathscr{E}[({}^{\tau^*}\!M\!S\;\mathsf{v})]_M & \mapsto & \mathbf{Error}\text{: Non-list} \\
 & & \text{where } \mathsf{v} \text{ is not a pair or } \mathbf{nil}
\end{array}
$$

$$
\begin{array}{lcl}
\mathsf{e} & = & \mathsf{v} \mid (\mathsf{e}\;\mathsf{e}) \mid \mathsf{x} \mid (op\;\mathsf{e}\;\mathsf{e}) \mid (\mathbf{if0}\;\mathsf{e}\;\mathsf{e}\;\mathsf{e}) \\
 & & \mid (pd\;\mathsf{e}) \mid (\mathbf{cons}\;\mathsf{e}\;\mathsf{e}) \mid (S\!M^{\tau}\;\mathbf{e}) \\
\mathsf{v} & = & (\lambda\mathsf{x}.\mathsf{e}) \mid \overline{n} \mid \mathbf{nil} \mid (\mathbf{cons}\;\mathsf{v}_1\;\mathsf{v}_2) \mid \mathbf{fst} \mid \mathbf{rst} \\
op & = & + \mid - \\
pd & = & \mathsf{proc?} \mid \mathsf{nat?} \mid \mathsf{nil?} \mid \mathsf{pair?} \\
\mathsf{x} & = & \text{Scheme variables} \\
\mathsf{E} & = & [\,]_S \mid (\mathsf{E}\;\mathsf{e}) \mid (\mathsf{v}\;\mathsf{E}) \mid (op\;\mathsf{E}\;\mathsf{e}) \mid (op\;\mathsf{v}\;\mathsf{E}) \\
 & & \mid (\mathbf{if0}\;\mathsf{E}\;\mathsf{e}\;\mathsf{e}) \mid (pred\;\mathsf{E}) \mid (\mathbf{cons}\;\mathsf{E}\;\mathsf{e}) \\
 & & \mid (\mathbf{cons}\;\mathsf{v}\;\mathsf{E}) \mid (S\!M^{\tau}\;\mathbf{E})
\end{array}
$$

$$
\frac{\Gamma,\mathsf{x}:\mathbf{TST} \vdash_S \mathsf{e}:\mathbf{TST}}{\Gamma \vdash_S \lambda\mathsf{x}.\,\mathsf{e}:\mathbf{TST}}
$$

$$
\frac{\Gamma \vdash_M \mathbf{e}:\tau}{\Gamma \vdash_S (S\!M^{\tau}\;\mathbf{e}):\mathbf{TST}} \qquad \ldots
$$

$$
\begin{array}{lll}
\mathscr{E}[((\lambda\mathsf{x}.\,\mathsf{e})\;\mathsf{v})]_S & \mapsto & \mathscr{E}[\mathsf{e}[\mathsf{v}/\mathsf{x}]] \\
\mathscr{E}[(\mathsf{v}_1\;\mathsf{v}_2)]_S & \mapsto & \mathbf{Error}\text{: non-proc} \\
 & & \mathsf{v}_1 \neq \lambda\mathsf{x}.\mathsf{e} \\
\mathscr{E}[(+\;\overline{n_1}\;\overline{n_2})]_S & \mapsto & \mathscr{E}[\overline{n_1+n_2}] \\
\mathscr{E}[(-\;\overline{n_1}\;\overline{n_2})]_S & \mapsto & \mathscr{E}[\overline{max(n_1-n_2,0)}] \\
\mathscr{E}[(op\;\mathsf{v}_1\;\mathsf{v}_2)]_S & \mapsto & \mathbf{Error}\text{: non-num} \\
 & & \mathsf{v}_1 \neq \overline{n} \text{ or } \mathsf{v}_2 \neq \overline{n} \\
\mathscr{E}[(\mathbf{if0}\;\overline{0}\;\mathsf{e}_1\;\mathsf{e}_2)]_S & \mapsto & \mathscr{E}[\mathsf{e}_1] \\
\mathscr{E}[(\mathbf{if0}\;\mathsf{v}\;\mathsf{e}_1\mathsf{e}_2)]_S & \mapsto & \mathscr{E}[\mathsf{e}_2] \quad \mathsf{v} \neq \overline{0} \\
\mathscr{E}[(\mathsf{proc?}\;(\lambda\mathsf{x}.\,\mathsf{e}))]_S & \mapsto & \mathscr{E}[\overline{0}] \\
\mathscr{E}[(\mathsf{proc?}\;\mathsf{v})]_S & \mapsto & \mathscr{E}[\overline{1}] \\
 & & \mathsf{v} \neq (\lambda\mathsf{x}.\mathsf{e}) \text{ for any } \mathsf{x},\mathsf{e} \\
\mathscr{E}[(\mathsf{nat?}\;\overline{n})]_S & \mapsto & \mathscr{E}[\overline{0}] \\
\mathscr{E}[(\mathsf{nat?}\;\mathsf{v})]_S & \mapsto & \mathscr{E}[\overline{1}] \\
 & & \mathsf{v} \neq \overline{n} \text{ for any } n \\
\mathscr{E}[(\mathsf{nil?}\;\mathbf{nil})]_S & \mapsto & \mathscr{E}[\overline{0}] \\
\mathscr{E}[(\mathsf{nil?}\;\mathsf{v})]_S & \mapsto & \mathscr{E}[\overline{1}] \quad \mathsf{v} \neq \mathbf{nil} \\
\mathscr{E}[(\mathsf{pair?}\;(\mathbf{cons}\;\mathsf{v}_1\;\mathsf{v}_2))]_S & \mapsto & \mathscr{E}[\overline{0}] \\
\mathscr{E}[(\mathsf{pair?}\;\mathsf{v})]_S & \mapsto & \mathscr{E}[\overline{1}] \\
 & & \mathsf{v} \neq (\mathbf{cons}\;\mathsf{v}_1\;\mathsf{v}_2) \text{ for any } \mathsf{v}_1,\mathsf{v}_2 \\
\mathscr{E}[(\mathbf{fst}\;(\mathbf{cons}\;\mathsf{v}_1\;\mathsf{v}_2))]_S & \mapsto & \mathscr{E}[\mathsf{v}_1] \\
\mathscr{E}[(\mathbf{fst}\;\mathsf{v})]_S & \mapsto & \mathbf{Error}\text{: non-pair} \\
 & & \mathsf{v} \neq (\mathbf{cons}\;\mathsf{v}_1\;\mathsf{v}_2) \text{ for any } \mathsf{v}_1,\mathsf{v}_2 \\
\mathscr{E}[(\mathbf{rst}\;(\mathbf{cons}\;\mathsf{v}_1\;\mathsf{v}_2))]_S & \mapsto & \mathscr{E}[\mathsf{v}_2] \\
\mathscr{E}[(\mathbf{rst}\;\mathsf{v})]_S & \mapsto & \mathbf{Error}\text{: non-pair} \\
 & & \mathsf{v} \neq (\mathbf{cons}\;\mathsf{v}_1\;\mathsf{v}_2) \text{ for any } \mathsf{v}_1,\mathsf{v}_2 \\
\mathscr{E}[(S\!M^{\mathbf{Nat}}\;\overline{n})]_S & \mapsto & \mathscr{E}[\overline{n}] \\
\mathscr{E}[(S\!M^{\tau_1\mapsto\tau_2}\;\mathbf{v})]_S & \mapsto & \\
\multicolumn{3}{r}{\mathscr{E}[(\lambda\mathsf{x}.\,(S\!M^{\tau_2}(\mathbf{v}\;({}^{\tau_1}\!M\!S\,\mathsf{x}))))]} \\
\mathscr{E}[(S\!M^{\tau^*}\;\mathbf{nil})]_S & \mapsto & \mathscr{E}[\mathbf{nil}] \\
\mathscr{E}[(S\!M^{\tau^*}\;(\mathbf{cons}\;\mathbf{v}_1\;\mathbf{v}_2))]_S & \mapsto & \\
\multicolumn{3}{r}{\mathscr{E}[(\mathbf{cons}\;(S\!M^{\tau}\mathbf{v}_1)\;(S\!M^{\tau^*}\;\mathbf{v}_2))]}
\end{array}
$$

Fig. 1. Natural embedding of ML (left) and Scheme (right)

foreign numbers as native numbers, and they can call foreign functions as native functions. Note that throughout this paper we have typeset the nonterminals of our ML language using a **bold font with serifs**, and those of our Scheme language with a light sans-serif font. These font differences are semantically meaningful.

To the core languages we add new syntax, evaluation contexts, and reduction rules that define syntactic boundaries, written ${}^{\tau}\!MS$ and SM^{τ}, to allow cross-language communication. (For this paper we have chosen arbitrarily to make top-level programs be ML programs that optionally call into Scheme, and so we choose $\mathcal{E} = \mathbf{E}$; to make it the other way around we would let $\mathcal{E} = \mathsf{E}$ instead.) We assume we can translate numbers from one language to the other, and give reduction rules for boundary-crossing numbers based on that assumption:

$$\mathcal{E}[(SM^{\mathbf{Nat}}\ \overline{n})]_S \mapsto \mathcal{E}[\overline{n}] \qquad\qquad \mathcal{E}[({}^{\mathbf{Nat}}\!MS\ \overline{n})]_M \mapsto \mathcal{E}[\overline{n}]$$

To convert procedures across languages, we use native proxy procedures. We represent a Scheme procedure in ML at type $\tau_1 \to \tau_2$ by a new procedure that takes an argument of type τ_1, converts it to a Scheme equivalent, runs the original Scheme procedure on that value, and then converts the result back to ML at type τ_2. For example, $({}^{\tau_1\to\tau_2}\!MS\,\lambda\mathsf{x}.\mathsf{e})$ becomes $(\lambda\mathbf{x} : \tau_1.{}^{\tau_2}\!MS\,((\lambda\mathsf{x}.\mathsf{e})\,(SM^{\tau_1}\,\mathbf{x})))$ and vice versa for Scheme to ML. Note that the boundary that converts the argument is an SM^{τ_1} boundary, not an ${}^{\tau_1}\!MS$ boundary—i.e., the direction of conversion reverses for function arguments. Whenever a Scheme value is converted to ML, we also check that value's first order properties: we check to see if a Scheme value is a number before converting it to an ML value of type **Nat** and that it is a procedure value before converting it to an ML value of arrow type (and signal an error if either check fails).

Theorem 1 (Natural embedding type safety [6]). *If* $\vdash_M \mathbf{e} : \tau$, *then either* $\mathbf{e} \mapsto^* \mathbf{v}$, $\mathbf{e} \mapsto^*$ **Error**: *str, or* $\mathbf{e}$ *diverges.*

We showed in prior work that the dynamic checks in this system naturally give rise to higher-order contracts [8,10]; in section 4 of this work we show another way of arriving at the same conclusion, this time equating a contract enforcing that an untyped term e behave as a (closed) type specification τ (which we write e^{τ}) by converting it to and from ML at that type: to a first approximation, $\mathsf{e}^{\tau} = (SM^{\tau}\ ({}^{\tau}\!MS\ \mathsf{e}))$.

2.1 Polymorphism, Attempt One

An omission from the "ML" side of the natural embedding to this point is that it contains no polymorphism. We now extend it to support polymorphism by replacing the simply-typed lambda calculus with System F. When we do so, we immediately hit the question of how to properly handle boundaries. In this subsection, we make what we consider the most straightforward decision of how to handle boundaries and show that it results in a system that does not preserve System F's parametricity property; in the next subsection we refine our strategy using dynamic sealing techniques.

Figure 2 shows the extensions we need to make to figure 1 to support non-parametric polymorphism. To ML's syntax we add type abstractions ($\Lambda\alpha.\ \mathbf{e}$) and type application ($\mathbf{e}\langle\tau\rangle$); to its types we add $\forall\alpha.\ \tau$ and α. Our embedding converts Scheme functions that work polymorphically into polymorphic ML values, and converts ML type abstractions directly into plain Scheme functions that behave polymorphically. For example, ML

$$\mathbf{e} = \cdots \mid \Lambda\alpha.\mathbf{e} \mid \mathbf{e}\langle\tau\rangle$$
$$\mathbf{v} = \cdots \mid \Lambda\alpha.\mathbf{e} \mid ({}^{\mathbf{L}}\mathit{MS}\ \mathsf{v})$$
$$\tau = \cdots \mid \forall\alpha.\tau \mid \alpha \mid \mathbf{L}$$
$$\Delta = \bullet \mid \Delta,\tau$$
$$\mathbf{E} = \cdots \mid \mathbf{E}\langle\tau\rangle$$

$$\frac{\Delta,\alpha;\Gamma \vdash_M \mathbf{e} : \tau}{\Delta;\Gamma \vdash_M (\Lambda\alpha.\mathbf{e}) : \forall\alpha.\tau} \qquad \frac{\Delta;\Gamma \vdash_M \mathbf{e} : \forall\alpha.\tau' \quad \Delta \vdash \tau}{\Delta;\Gamma \vdash_M \mathbf{e}\langle\tau\rangle : \tau'[\tau/\alpha]}$$

$$\mathscr{E}[(\Lambda\alpha.\mathbf{e})\langle\tau\rangle]_M \mapsto \mathscr{E}[\mathbf{e}[\tau/\alpha]]$$
$$\mathscr{E}[({}^{\forall\alpha.\tau}\mathit{MS}\ \mathsf{v})]_M \mapsto \mathscr{E}[(\Lambda\alpha.({}^{\tau}\mathit{MS}\ \mathsf{v}))]$$
$$\mathscr{E}[(\mathit{SM}^{\forall\alpha.\tau}\ \mathbf{v})]_S \mapsto \mathscr{E}[(\mathit{SM}^{\tau[\mathbf{L}/\alpha]}\ \mathbf{v}\langle\mathbf{L}\rangle)]$$
$$\mathscr{E}[(\mathit{SM}^{\mathbf{L}}\ ({}^{\mathbf{L}}\mathit{MS}\ \mathsf{v}))]_S \mapsto \mathscr{E}[\mathsf{v}]$$

Fig. 2. Extensions to figure 1 for non-parametric polymorphism

might receive the Scheme function $(\lambda\mathsf{x}.\mathsf{x})$ from a boundary with type $\forall\alpha.\alpha \to \alpha$ and use it successfully as an identity function, and Scheme might receive the ML type abstraction $(\Lambda\alpha.\lambda\mathbf{x} : \alpha.\mathbf{x})$ as a regular function that behaves as the identity function for any value Scheme gives it.

To support this behavior, the model must create a type abstraction from a regular Scheme value when converting from Scheme to ML, and must drop a type abstraction when converting from ML to Scheme. The former is straightforward: we reduce a redex of the form $({}^{\forall\alpha.\tau}\mathit{MS}\ \mathsf{v})$ by dropping the $\forall$ quantifier on the type in the boundary and binding the now-free type variable in τ by wrapping the entire expression in a Λ form, yielding $(\Lambda\alpha.\ ({}^{\tau}\mathit{MS}\ \mathsf{v}))$.

This works for ML, but making a dual of it in Scheme would be somewhat silly, since every Scheme value inhabits the same type so type abstraction and application forms would be useless. Instead, we would like to allow Scheme to use an ML value of type, say, $\forall\alpha.\alpha \to \alpha$ directly as a function. To make boundaries with universally-quantified types behave that way, when we convert a polymorphic ML value to a Scheme value we need to remove its initial type-abstraction by applying it to some type and then convert the resulting value according to the resulting type. As for which type to apply it to, we need a type to which we can reliably convert any Scheme value, though it must not expose any of those values' properties. In prior work, we used the "lump" type to represent arbitrary, opaque Scheme values in ML; we reuse it here as the argument to the ML type abstraction. More specifically, we add **L** as a new base type in ML and we add the cancellation rule for lumps to the set of reductions: these changes, along with all the other additions required to support polymorphism, are summarized in figure 2.

2.2 Polymorphism, Attempt Two

Although this embedding is type safe, the polymorphism is not parametric in the sense of Reynolds [1]. We can see this with an example: it is well-known that in System F, for which parametricity holds, the only value with type $\forall\alpha.\alpha \to \alpha$ is the polymorphic identity function. In the system we have built so far, though, the term

$$({}^{\forall\alpha.\alpha\to\alpha}\mathit{MS}(\lambda\mathsf{x}.(\mathtt{if0}\ (\mathtt{nat?}\ \mathsf{x})\ (+\ \mathsf{x}\ \bar{1})\ \mathsf{x})))$$

has type $\forall\alpha.\alpha \to \alpha$ but when applied to the type **Nat** evaluates to

$$(\lambda\mathbf{y}.({}^{\mathbf{Nat}}\mathit{MS}((\lambda\mathsf{x}.(\mathtt{if0}\ (\mathtt{nat?}\ \mathsf{x})\ (+\ \mathsf{x}\ \bar{1})\ \mathsf{x})(\mathit{SM}^{\mathbf{Nat}}\mathbf{y})))))$$

Since the argument to this function is always a number, this is equivalent to

$$(\lambda\mathbf{y}.({}^{\mathbf{Nat}}\mathit{MS}((\lambda\mathsf{x}.(+\ \mathsf{x}\ \bar{1}))(\mathit{SM}^{\mathbf{Nat}}\mathbf{y}))))$$

which is well-typed but is not the identity function.

The problem with the misbehaving $\forall\alpha.\alpha \to \alpha$ function above is that while the type system rules out ML fragments that try to treat values of type α non-generically, it still

$$
\begin{aligned}
\mathbf{e} &= \cdots \mid \Lambda\alpha.\mathbf{e} \mid \mathbf{e}\langle\tau\rangle \mid ({}^{\kappa}\mathit{MS}\ \mathsf{e})\\
\mathsf{e} &= \cdots \mid (\mathit{SM}^{\kappa}\ \mathbf{e})\\
\mathbf{v} &= \cdots \mid \Lambda\alpha.\mathbf{e} \mid ({}^{\mathbf{L}}\mathit{MS}\ \mathsf{v})\\
\mathsf{v} &= \cdots \mid (\mathit{SM}^{\langle\beta;\tau\rangle}\ \mathbf{v})\\
\tau &= \cdots \mid \forall\alpha.\tau \mid \alpha \mid \mathbf{L}\\
\kappa &= \mathbf{Nat} \mid \kappa_1 \rightarrow \kappa_2 \mid \kappa^* \mid \forall\alpha.\kappa \mid \alpha \mid \mathbf{L} \mid \langle\alpha;\tau\rangle
\end{aligned}
$$

$$
\frac{\Delta,\alpha;\Gamma \vdash_M \mathbf{e}:\tau}{\Delta;\Gamma \vdash_M (\Lambda\alpha.\mathbf{e}):\forall\alpha.\tau}
\qquad
\frac{\Delta;\Gamma \vdash_M \mathbf{e}:\forall\alpha.\tau' \quad \Delta \vdash \tau}{\Delta;\Gamma \vdash_M \mathbf{e}\langle\tau\rangle : \tau'[\tau/\alpha]}
$$

$$
\frac{\Delta;\Gamma \vdash_S \mathsf{e}:\mathbf{TST} \quad \Delta \vdash \lfloor\kappa\rfloor}{\Delta;\Gamma \vdash_M ({}^{\kappa}\mathit{MS}\ \mathsf{e}) : \lfloor\kappa\rfloor}
\qquad
\frac{\Delta;\Gamma \vdash_M \mathbf{e}:\lfloor\kappa\rfloor \quad \Delta \vdash \lfloor\kappa\rfloor}{\Delta;\Gamma \vdash_S (\mathit{SM}^{\kappa}\ \mathbf{e}):\mathbf{TST}}
$$

$$
\begin{aligned}
\mathcal{E}[(\mathit{SM}^{\forall\alpha.\tau}\ \mathbf{v})]_S &\mapsto \mathcal{E}[(\mathit{SM}^{\tau[\mathbf{L}/\alpha]}\ \mathbf{v}\langle\mathbf{L}\rangle)]\\
\mathcal{E}[(\mathit{SM}^{\mathbf{L}}\ ({}^{\mathbf{L}}\mathit{MS}\ \mathsf{v}))]_S &\mapsto \mathcal{E}[\mathsf{v}]\\[1em]
\mathcal{E}[(\Lambda\alpha.\mathbf{e})\langle\tau\rangle]_M &\mapsto \mathcal{E}[\mathbf{e}[\tau/\alpha]]\\
\mathcal{E}[({}^{\forall\alpha.\kappa}\mathit{MS}\ \mathsf{v})]_M &\mapsto \mathcal{E}[(\Lambda\alpha.({}^{\kappa}\mathit{MS}\ \mathsf{v}))]\\
\mathcal{E}[({}^{\langle\alpha;\tau\rangle}\mathit{MS}\ (\mathit{SM}^{\langle\alpha;\tau\rangle}\ \mathbf{v}))]_M &\mapsto \mathcal{E}[\mathbf{v}]\\
\mathcal{E}[({}^{\langle\alpha;\tau\rangle}\mathit{MS}\ \mathsf{v})]_M &\mapsto \mathbf{Error}\text{: bad value}\\
&\quad (\mathsf{v} \neq \mathit{SM}^{\langle\alpha;\tau\rangle}\ \mathbf{v} \text{ for any } \mathbf{v})
\end{aligned}
\qquad
\begin{aligned}
\lfloor\ \rfloor :\ & \kappa \rightarrow \tau\\
\lfloor\mathbf{Nat}\rfloor &= \mathbf{Nat}\\
\lfloor\kappa_1 \rightarrow \kappa_2\rfloor &= \lfloor\kappa_1\rfloor \rightarrow \lfloor\kappa_2\rfloor\\
\lfloor\kappa^*\rfloor &= \lfloor\kappa\rfloor^*\\
\lfloor\forall\alpha.\kappa\rfloor &= \forall\alpha.\lfloor\kappa\rfloor\\
\lfloor\alpha\rfloor &= \alpha\\
\lfloor\mathbf{L}\rfloor &= \mathbf{L}\\
\lfloor\langle\alpha;\tau\rangle\rfloor &= \tau
\end{aligned}
$$

Fig. 3. Extensions to figure 1 to support parametric polymorphism

allows Scheme programs to observe the concrete choice made for α and act accordingly. To restore parametricity, we use dynamic seals to protect ML values whose implementation should not be observed. When ML provides Scheme with a value whose original type was α, Scheme gets a sealed value; when Scheme returns a value to ML at a type that was originally α, ML unseals it or signals an error if it is not a sealed value with the appropriate key.

This means that we can no longer directly substitute types for free type variables on boundary annotations. Instead we introduce *seals* as type-like annotations of the form $\langle\alpha;\tau\rangle$ that indicate on a boundary's type annotation that a particular type is the instantiation of what was originally a type variable, and *conversion schemes* (indicated with metavariable κ) as types that may also contain seals; conversion schemes only appear as the annotations on boundaries. From a technical standpoint, seals are introduced into a reduction sequence by the type substitution in the type application rule. For a precise definition, a *type substitution* η is a partial function from type variables to closed types. We extend type substitutions to apply to types, conversion schemes, and terms as follows (we show the interesting cases, the rest are merely structural recursion):

$$
\eta(\alpha) \stackrel{\text{def}}{=} \begin{cases} \tau \text{ if } \exists\eta'.\ \eta = \eta',\alpha:\tau \\ \alpha \text{ otherwise} \end{cases}
\qquad
\begin{aligned}
\eta({}^{\kappa}\mathit{MS}\ \mathsf{e}) &\stackrel{\text{def}}{=} {}^{\mathbf{sl}(\eta,\kappa)}\mathit{MS}\ \eta(\mathsf{e})\\
\eta(\mathit{SM}^{\kappa}\ \mathbf{e}) &\stackrel{\text{def}}{=} \mathit{SM}^{\mathbf{sl}(\eta,\kappa)}\ \eta(\mathbf{e})
\end{aligned}
$$

The boundary cases (which use the seal metafunction $\mathbf{sl}(\cdot,\cdot)$ defined below) are different from the regular type cases. When we close a type with respect to a type substitution η, we simply replace all occurrences of free variables with their mappings in η, but when we close a conversion scheme with respect to a type substitution we replace free variables with "sealed" instances of the types in η. The effect of this is that even when we have performed a type substitution, we can distinguish between a type that was concrete in the original program and a type that was abstract in the original program but has been substituted with a concrete type. The $\mathbf{sl}(\cdot,\cdot)$ metafunction maps a type τ (or more generally a conversion scheme κ) to an isomorphic conversion scheme κ where each instance of each type variable that occurs free in τ is replaced by an appropriate sealing declaration, if the type variable is in the domain of η.

Definition 1 (sealing). *The metafunction* $\mathbf{sl}(\eta,\kappa)$ *is defined as follows:*

$$\mathbf{sl}(\cdot,\cdot) \quad : \eta \times \kappa \rightarrow \kappa$$

$$\mathbf{sl}(\eta,\alpha) \stackrel{\text{def}}{=} \begin{cases} \langle \alpha; \eta(\alpha)\rangle & \text{if } \eta(\alpha) \text{ is defined} \\ \alpha & \text{otherwise} \end{cases}$$

$$\mathbf{sl}(\eta,\langle\alpha;\tau\rangle) \stackrel{\text{def}}{=} \langle\alpha;\tau\rangle$$

$$\mathbf{sl}(\eta,L) \stackrel{\text{def}}{=} L$$

$$\mathbf{sl}(\eta,\mathbf{Nat}) \stackrel{\text{def}}{=} \mathbf{Nat}$$

$$\mathbf{sl}(\eta,\kappa_1 \rightarrow \kappa_2) \stackrel{\text{def}}{=} \mathbf{sl}(\eta,\kappa_1) \rightarrow \mathbf{sl}(\eta,\kappa_2)$$

$$\mathbf{sl}(\eta,\forall\alpha.\kappa_1) \stackrel{\text{def}}{=} \forall\alpha.\mathbf{sl}(\eta,\kappa_1)$$

$$\mathbf{sl}(\eta,\kappa^*) \stackrel{\text{def}}{=} \mathbf{sl}(\eta,\kappa)^*$$

We use the *seal erasure* metafunction $\lfloor\ \rfloor$ to project conversion schemes to types. Figure 3 defines these changes precisely. One final subtlety not written in figure 3 is that we treat a seal $\langle\alpha;\tau\rangle$ as a free occurrence of α for the purposes of capture-avoiding substitution, and we treat boundaries that include $\forall\alpha.\tau$ types as though they were binding instances of α. In fact, the production of fresh names by capture-avoiding substitution corresponds exactly to the production of fresh seals for information hiding, and the system would be neither parametric nor even type-sound were we to omit this detail.

3 Parametricity

In this section we establish that the language of figure 3 is parametric, in the sense that all terms in the language map related environments to related results, using a syntactic logical relation. Our parametricity property does not establish the exact same equivalences that would hold for terms in plain System F, but only because the embedding we are considering gives terms the power to diverge and to signal errors. So, for example, we cannot show that any ML value of type $\forall\alpha.\alpha \rightarrow \alpha$ must be the identity function, but we *can* show that it must be either the identity function, the function that always diverges, or the function that always signals an error.

Our proof amounts to defining two logical relations, one for ML and one for Scheme (see figure 4) and proving that the ML (Scheme) relation relates each ML (Scheme) term to itself regardless of the interpretation of free type variables. Though logical relations in the literature are usually defined by induction on types, we cannot use a type-indexed relation for Scheme since Scheme has only one type. This means in particular that the arguments to function values have types that are as large as the type of the function values themselves; thus any relation that defines two functions to be related if the results are related for any pair of related arguments would not be well-founded. Instead we use a minor adaptation of the step-indexed logical relation for recursive types given by Ahmed [7]: our Scheme logical relation is indexed by the number of steps k available for computation. Intuitively, any two values are related for k steps if they cannot be distinguished by any computation running for no more than k steps.

Since we are interested in proving properties of ML terms that may contain Scheme subterms, the ML relation must also be step-indexed — if the Scheme subterms are only related for (say) 50 steps, then the ML terms cannot always be related for arbitrarily many steps. Thus, the ML relation is indexed by both types and steps (as in Ahmed [7]).

The definitions are largely independent (though we do make a few concessions on this front, in particular at the definition of the ML relation at type **L**), but the

$$\mathbf{Rel}_{\tau_1,\tau_2} = \{\mathbf{R} \mid \forall (k,\mathbf{v}_1,\mathbf{v}_2)\in\mathbf{R}.\ \forall j\le k.\ (j,\mathbf{v}_1,\mathbf{v}_2)\in\mathbf{R} \text{ and } ;\vdash \mathbf{v}_1:\tau_1 \text{ and } ;\vdash \mathbf{v}_2:\tau_2\}$$

$$\Delta\vdash\delta \stackrel{\text{def}}{=} \Delta\subseteq \mathsf{dom}(\delta) \text{ and } \forall\alpha\in\Delta.\ \delta_R(\alpha)\in\mathbf{Rel}_{\delta_1(\alpha),\delta_2(\alpha)}$$

$$\delta\vdash\gamma_M\le^k\gamma'_M:\Gamma_M \stackrel{\text{def}}{=} \forall(\mathbf{x}:\tau)\in\Gamma_M.\ \gamma_M(\mathbf{x})=\mathbf{v}_1,\ \gamma'_M(\mathbf{x})=\mathbf{v}_2 \text{ and } \delta\vdash\mathbf{v}_1\lessapprox^k_M\mathbf{v}_2:\tau$$

$$\delta\vdash\gamma_S\le^k\gamma'_S:\Gamma_S \stackrel{\text{def}}{=} \forall(\mathsf{x}:\mathbf{TST})\in\Gamma_S.\ \gamma_S(\mathsf{x})=\mathsf{v}_1,\ \gamma'_S(\mathsf{x})=\mathsf{v}_2 \text{ and } \delta\vdash\mathsf{v}_1\lessapprox^k_S\mathsf{v}_2:\mathbf{TST}$$

$$\delta\vdash\gamma\le^k\gamma':\Gamma \stackrel{\text{def}}{=} \Gamma=\Gamma_M\cup\Gamma_S,\ \gamma=\gamma_M\cup\gamma_S,\ \gamma'=\gamma'_M\cup\gamma'_S \text{ and } \delta\vdash\gamma_M\le^k\gamma'_M:\Gamma_M \text{ and } \delta\vdash\gamma_S\le^k\gamma'_S:\Gamma_S$$

$$\Delta;\Gamma\vdash\mathbf{e}_1\lesssim_M\mathbf{e}_2:\tau \stackrel{\text{def}}{=} \forall k\ge 0.\ \forall\delta,\gamma_1,\gamma_2.\ \Delta\vdash\delta \text{ and } \delta\vdash\gamma_1\le^k\gamma_2:\Gamma \Rightarrow \delta\vdash\delta_1(\gamma_1(\mathbf{e}_1))\lesssim^k_M\delta_2(\gamma_2(\mathbf{e}_2)):\tau$$

$$\delta\vdash\mathbf{e}_1\lesssim^k_M\mathbf{e}_2:\tau \stackrel{\text{def}}{=} \forall j<k.\ (\mathbf{e}_1\hookrightarrow^j \mathbf{Error}\text{: s} \Rightarrow \mathbf{e}_2\hookrightarrow^* \mathbf{Error}\text{: s}) \text{ and } (\forall\mathbf{v}_1.\ \mathbf{e}_1\hookrightarrow^j\mathbf{v}_1 \Rightarrow \exists\mathbf{v}_2.\ \mathbf{e}_2\hookrightarrow^*\mathbf{v}_2 \text{ and } \delta\vdash\mathbf{v}_1\lessapprox^{k-j}_M\mathbf{v}_2:\tau)$$

$$\delta\vdash\mathbf{v}_1\lessapprox^k_M\mathbf{v}_2:\alpha \stackrel{\text{def}}{=} (k,\mathbf{v}_1,\mathbf{v}_2)\in\delta_R(\alpha)$$

$$\delta\vdash{}^{\mathbf{L}}\!MS\ \mathsf{v}_1\lessapprox^k_M{}^{\mathbf{L}}\!MS\ \mathsf{v}_2:\mathbf{L} \stackrel{\text{def}}{=} \forall j<k.\ \delta\vdash\mathsf{v}_1\lessapprox^j_S\mathsf{v}_2:\mathbf{TST}$$

$$\delta\vdash\overline{n}\lessapprox^k_M\overline{n}:\mathbf{Nat} \quad \textit{(unconditionally)}$$

$$\delta\vdash\lambda\mathbf{x}:\tau_1.\mathbf{e}_1\lessapprox^k_M\lambda\mathbf{x}:\tau_1.\mathbf{e}_2:\tau_1\to\tau_2 \stackrel{\text{def}}{=} \forall j<k.\ \forall\mathbf{v}_1,\mathbf{v}_2.\ \delta\vdash\mathbf{v}_1\lessapprox^j_M\mathbf{v}_2:\tau_1 \Rightarrow \delta\vdash\mathbf{e}_1[\mathbf{v}_1/\mathbf{x}]\lesssim^j_M\mathbf{e}_2[\mathbf{v}_2/\mathbf{x}]:\tau_2$$

$$\delta\vdash\Lambda\alpha.\mathbf{e}_1\lessapprox^k_M\Lambda\alpha.\mathbf{e}_2:\forall\alpha.\tau \stackrel{\text{def}}{=} \forall j<k.\ \forall \text{ closed } \tau_1,\tau_2.\ \forall\mathbf{R}\in\mathbf{Rel}_{\tau_1,\tau_2}.\ \delta,\alpha:(\tau_1,\tau_2,\mathbf{R})\vdash\mathbf{e}_1[\tau_1/\alpha]\lesssim^j_M\mathbf{e}_2[\tau_2/\alpha]:\tau$$

$$\delta\vdash[\mathbf{v}_1,\cdots,\mathbf{v}_n]\lessapprox^k_M[\mathbf{v}'_1,\cdots,\mathbf{v}'_n]:\tau^* \stackrel{\text{def}}{=} \forall j<k.\ \forall i\in 1\ldots n.\ \delta\vdash\mathbf{v}_i\lessapprox^j_M\mathbf{v}'_i:\tau$$

$$\Delta;\Gamma\vdash\mathsf{e}_1\lesssim_S\mathsf{e}_2:\mathbf{TST} \stackrel{\text{def}}{=} \forall k\ge 0.\ \forall\delta,\gamma_1,\gamma_2.\ \Delta\vdash\delta \text{ and } \delta\vdash\gamma_1\le^k\gamma_2:\Gamma \Rightarrow \delta\vdash\delta_1(\gamma_1(\mathsf{e}_1))\lesssim^k_S\delta_2(\gamma_2(\mathsf{e}_2)):\mathbf{TST}$$

$$\delta\vdash\mathsf{e}_1\lesssim^k_S\mathsf{e}_2:\mathbf{TST} \stackrel{\text{def}}{=} \forall j<k.\ (\mathsf{e}_1\hookrightarrow^j \mathbf{Error}\text{: s} \Rightarrow \mathsf{e}_2\hookrightarrow^* \mathbf{Error}\text{: s}) \text{ and } (\forall\mathsf{v}_1.\ \mathsf{e}_1\hookrightarrow^j\mathsf{v}_1 \Rightarrow \exists\mathsf{v}_2.\ \mathsf{e}_2\hookrightarrow^*\mathsf{v}_2 \text{ and } \delta\vdash\mathsf{v}_1\lessapprox^{k-j}_S\mathsf{v}_2:\mathbf{TST})$$

$$\delta\vdash\overline{n}\lessapprox^k_S\overline{n}:\mathbf{TST} \quad \textit{(unconditionally)}$$

$$\delta\vdash(SM^{\langle\alpha;\tau_1\rangle}\ \mathbf{v}_1)\lessapprox^k_S(SM^{\langle\alpha;\tau_2\rangle}\ \mathbf{v}_2):\mathbf{TST} \stackrel{\text{def}}{=} (k,\mathbf{v}_1,\mathbf{v}_2)\in\delta_R(\alpha) \text{ and } \delta_1(\alpha)=\tau_1 \text{ and } \delta_2(\alpha)=\tau_2$$

$$\delta\vdash\lambda\mathsf{x}.\mathsf{e}_1\lessapprox^k_S\lambda\mathsf{x}.\mathsf{e}_2:\mathbf{TST} \stackrel{\text{def}}{=} \forall j<k. \forall\mathsf{v}_1,\mathsf{v}_2.\ \delta\vdash\mathsf{v}_1\lessapprox^j_S\mathsf{v}_2:\mathbf{TST} \Rightarrow \delta\vdash\mathsf{e}_1[\mathsf{v}_1/\mathsf{x}]\lesssim^j_S\mathsf{e}_2[\mathsf{v}_2/\mathsf{x}]:\mathbf{TST}$$

$$\delta\vdash\mathbf{nil}\lessapprox^k_S\mathbf{nil}:\mathbf{TST} \quad \textit{(unconditionally)}$$

$$\delta\vdash(\mathbf{cons}\ \mathsf{v}_1\ \mathsf{v}_2)\lessapprox^k_S(\mathbf{cons}\ \mathsf{v}'_1\ \mathsf{v}'_2):\mathbf{TST} \stackrel{\text{def}}{=} \forall j<k.\ \delta\vdash\mathsf{v}_1\lessapprox^j_S\mathsf{v}'_1:\mathbf{TST} \text{ and } \delta\vdash\mathsf{v}_2\lessapprox^j_S\mathsf{v}'_2:\mathbf{TST}$$

Fig. 4. Logical approximation for ML terms (middle) and Scheme terms (bottom)

proofs cannot be, since an ML term can have an embedded Scheme subexpression and vice versa. Instead, we prove the two claims by simultaneous induction and rely on a critical "bridge lemma" (lemma 1, see below) that lets us carry relatedness between languages.

Preliminaries. A *type relation* δ is a partial function from type variables to triples $(\tau_1, \tau_2, \mathbf{R})$, where τ_1 and τ_2 are closed types and R is a set of triples of the form $(k, \mathbf{v}_1, \mathbf{v}_2)$ (which intuitively means that $\mathbf{v}_1$ and $\mathbf{v}_2$ are related for k steps). We use the following notations: If $\delta(\alpha) = (\tau_1, \tau_2, \mathbf{R})$ then $\delta_1(\alpha) = \tau_1$, $\delta_2(\alpha) = \tau_2$, and $\delta_R(\alpha) = \mathbf{R}$. We also treat δ_1 and δ_2 as type substitutions. In the definition of the logical relation we only allow *downward closed* relations as choices for $\mathbf{R}$; *i.e.* relations that relate two values for k steps must also relate them for all $j < k$ steps. We make this restriction because downward closure is a critical property that would not otherwise hold.

A Scheme (ML) substitution γ_S (γ_M) is a partial map from Scheme (ML) variables to closed Scheme (ML) values, and a substitution $\gamma = \gamma_S \cup \gamma_M$ for some γ_S, γ_M. We say that $e \hookrightarrow v$ (or **Error**: s) if in all evaluation contexts $\mathscr{E}[e] \mapsto \mathscr{E}[v]$ (or **Error**: s).

Lemma 1 (bridge lemma). *For all $k \geq 0$, type environments Δ, type relations δ such that $\Delta \vdash \delta$, types τ such that $\Delta \vdash \tau$, both of the following hold:*

1. *For all e_1 and e_2, if $\delta \vdash \mathsf{e}_1 \lesssim_S^k \mathsf{e}_2 : \textbf{TST}$ then $\delta \vdash ({}^{\mathbf{sl}(\delta_1,\tau)}MS\ \mathsf{e}_1) \lesssim_M^k ({}^{\mathbf{sl}(\delta_2,\tau)}MS\ \mathsf{e}_2) : \tau$.*
2. *For all $\mathbf{e}_1$ and $\mathbf{e}_2$, if $\delta \vdash \mathbf{e}_1 \lesssim_M^k \mathbf{e}_2 : \tau$, then $\delta \vdash (SM^{\mathbf{sl}(\delta_1,\tau)}\ \mathbf{e}_1) \lesssim_S^k (SM^{\mathbf{sl}(\delta_2,\tau)}\ \mathbf{e}_2) : \textbf{TST}$.*

Proof. By induction on τ. All cases are straightforward given the induction hypotheses.

With the bridge lemma established, the fundamental theorem (and hence the fact that logical approximation implies contextual approximation) is essentially standard. We restrict the parametricity theorem to seal-free terms; otherwise we would have to show that any sealed value is related to itself at type α which is false. (A conversion strategy is seal-free if it contains no instances of $\langle\alpha;\tau\rangle$ for any α. A term is seal-free if it contains no conversion strategies with seals.) This restriction is purely technical, since the claim applies to open terms where seals may be introduced by closing environments.

Theorem 2 (parametricity / fundamental theorem). *For all seal-free terms $\mathbf{e}$ and e:*

1. *If $\Delta;\Gamma \vdash_M \mathbf{e} : \tau$, then $\Delta;\Gamma \vdash \mathbf{e} \lesssim_M \mathbf{e} : \tau$.*
2. *If $\Delta;\Gamma \vdash_S \mathsf{e} : \textbf{TST}$, then $\Delta;\Gamma \vdash \mathsf{e} \lesssim_S \mathsf{e} : \textbf{TST}$.*

Proof. By simultaneous induction on the derivations $\Delta;\Gamma \vdash_M \mathbf{e} : \tau$ and $\Delta;\Gamma \vdash_S \mathsf{e} : \textbf{TST}$. The boundary cases both follow from lemma 1.

4 From Multi-language to Single-Language Sealing

Suppose that instead of reasoning about multi-language programs, we want to reason about Scheme terms but also to use a closed ML type τ as a behavioral specification for a Scheme term — **Nat** means the term must evaluate to a number, **Nat** $\rightarrow$ **Nat** means the term must evaluate to a function that returns a number under the promise that the context

$$\mathsf{Rel} = \{\mathsf{R} \mid \forall (k, \mathsf{v}_1, \mathsf{v}_2) \in \mathsf{R}.\ \forall j \le k.\ (j, \mathsf{v}_1, \mathsf{v}_2) \in \mathsf{R}\}$$

$$\begin{array}{ll}
\sigma \vdash \mathsf{e}_1 \leq^k \mathsf{e}_2 : \tau & \stackrel{\text{def}}{=} \forall j < k.\ (\mathsf{e}_1 \hookrightarrow^j \textbf{Error}\text{: s} \Rightarrow \mathsf{e}_2 \hookrightarrow^* \textbf{Error}\text{: s})\ \text{and} \\
& \quad (\forall \mathsf{v}_1.\ \mathsf{e}_1 \hookrightarrow^j \mathsf{v}_1 \Rightarrow \\
& \qquad \exists \mathsf{v}_2.\ \mathsf{e}_2 \hookrightarrow^* \mathsf{v}_2\ \text{and}\ \sigma \vdash \mathsf{v}_1 \leqq^{k-j} \mathsf{v}_2 : \tau) \\
\sigma \vdash \mathsf{v}_1 \leqq^k \mathsf{v}_2 : \alpha & \stackrel{\text{def}}{=} (k, \mathsf{v}_1, \mathsf{v}_2) \in \sigma(\alpha) \\
\sigma \vdash \overline{n} \leqq^k \overline{n} : \textbf{Nat} & \textit{(unconditionally)} \\
\sigma \vdash \lambda \mathsf{x}.\mathsf{e}_1 \leqq^k \lambda \mathsf{x}.\mathsf{e}_2 : \tau_1 \to \tau_2 & \stackrel{\text{def}}{=} \forall j < k.\ \forall \mathsf{v}_1, \mathsf{v}_2.\ \sigma \vdash \mathsf{v}_1 \leqq^j \mathsf{v}_2 : \tau_1 \Rightarrow \\
& \qquad \sigma \vdash \mathsf{e}_1[\mathsf{v}_1/\mathsf{x}] \leq^j \mathsf{e}_2[\mathsf{v}_2/\mathsf{x}] : \tau_2 \\
\sigma \vdash [\mathsf{v}_1, \cdots, \mathsf{v}_n] \leqq^k [\mathsf{v}'_1, \cdots, \mathsf{v}'_n] : \tau^* & \stackrel{\text{def}}{=} \forall j < k.\ \forall i \in 1 \ldots n.\ \sigma \vdash \mathsf{v}_i \leqq^j \mathsf{v}'_i : \tau \\
\sigma \vdash \mathsf{v}_1 \leqq^k \mathsf{v}_2 : \forall \alpha.\tau & \stackrel{\text{def}}{=} \forall j < k.\ \forall \mathsf{R} \in \mathsf{Rel}.\ \sigma, \alpha : \mathsf{R} \vdash \mathsf{v}_1 \leqq^j \mathsf{v}_2 : \tau
\end{array}$$

Fig. 5. Behavioral specification for polymorphic contracts

will always provide it a number, and so on. We can implement this using boundaries with the program fragment $\mathsf{e}^\tau = \mathit{SM}^\tau\ ({}^\tau\!\mathit{MS}\ \mathsf{e})$.

It is easy to check that such terms are always well-typed as long as e itself is well-typed. Therefore, since we have defined a contract as just a particular usage pattern for boundaries, we have by virtue of theorem 2 that every contracted term corresponds to itself, so intuitively every contracted term of polymorphic type should behave parametrically. However, the logical relation we defined in the previous section is not particularly convenient for proving facts about contracted Scheme terms, so instead we give another relation in figure 5 that we think of as the "contracted-Scheme-terms" relation, which gives criteria for two Scheme terms being related at an ML type (which we now interpret as a behavioral contract). Here σ is an *untyped* mapping from type variables α to downward-closed relations R on Scheme values: that is, $\sigma = (\alpha_1 \mapsto \mathsf{R}_1, \cdots, \alpha_n \mapsto \mathsf{R}_n)$ where each $\mathsf{R}_i \in \mathsf{Rel}$ (see figure 5).

Our goal is to prove that closed, contracted terms are related to themselves under this relation. Proving this directly is intractable, but we can prove it by showing that boundaries "reflect their relations"; *i.e.* that if $\delta \vdash \mathbf{e}_1 \lesssim^k_M \mathbf{e}_2 : \tau$ then for some appropriate σ we have that $\sigma \vdash (\mathit{SM}^\tau\ \mathbf{e}_1) \leq^k (\mathit{SM}^\tau\ \mathbf{e}_2) : \tau$ and vice versa; this is the claim we show in lemma 2 (bridge lemma 2) below, and the result we want is an easy corollary when combined with theorem 2. Before we can precisely state the claim, though, we need some machinery for specifying what relationship between δ and σ we want to hold.

Definition 2 (hybrid environments). *An hybrid environment ϕ is a partial map from type variables to tuples of the form (S, R) or $(M, \tau_1, \tau_2, \boldsymbol{R})$.*

The intuition is that a hybrid environment is a tagged union of a Scheme environment σ (each element of which is tagged with S) and an ML environment δ (each element of which is tagged with M). Given such a hybrid environment, one can mechanically derive both a Scheme and an ML representation of it by keeping native elements as-is and wrapping foreign elements in the appropriate boundary:

Definition 3 (Scheme and ML projections of hybrid environments). *For a hybrid environment ϕ, if $\phi(\alpha) = (S, \mathsf{R})$, then:*

$$\sigma_\phi(\alpha) \stackrel{\text{def}}{=} \mathsf{R}$$
$$\delta_\phi(\alpha) \stackrel{\text{def}}{=} (\boldsymbol{L}, \boldsymbol{L}, \{(k, ({}^{\boldsymbol{L}}\mathit{MS}\ \mathsf{v}_1), ({}^{\boldsymbol{L}}\mathit{MS}\ \mathsf{v}_2)) \mid (k, \mathsf{v}_1, \mathsf{v}_2) \in \mathsf{R}\})$$

If $\phi(\alpha) = (M, \tau_1, \tau_2, \boldsymbol{R})$*, then:*

$$\sigma_\phi(\alpha) \stackrel{\text{def}}{=} \{(k, (\mathit{SM}^{\langle\alpha;\tau_1\rangle}\ \boldsymbol{v}_1), (\mathit{SM}^{\langle\alpha;\tau_2\rangle}\ \boldsymbol{v}_2)) \mid (k, \boldsymbol{v}_1, \boldsymbol{v}_2) \in \boldsymbol{R}\}$$
$$\delta_\phi(\alpha) \stackrel{\text{def}}{=} (\tau_1, \tau_2, \boldsymbol{R})$$

We say that $\Delta \vdash \phi$ if for all $\alpha \in \Delta$, $\phi(\alpha)$ is defined, and if $\phi(\alpha) = (\mathrm{S}, \mathsf{R})$ then $\mathsf{R} \in \mathsf{Rel}$, and if $\phi(\alpha) = (\mathrm{M}, \tau_1, \tau_2, \mathbf{R})$ then $\mathbf{R} \in \mathbf{Rel}_{\tau_1,\tau_2}$. We also define operations $c_1(\cdot,\cdot)$ and $c_2(\cdot,\cdot)$ (analogous to $\mathbf{sl}(\cdot,\cdot)$ defined earlier) from hybrid environments ϕ and types τ to conversion schemes κ:

Definition 4 (closing with respect to a hybrid environment). *For* $i \in \{1,2\}$*:*

$$c_i(\phi,\alpha) \stackrel{\text{def}}{=} \begin{cases} \boldsymbol{L} & \text{if } \phi(\alpha) = (S, \mathsf{R}) \\ \langle\alpha;\tau_i\rangle & \text{if } \phi(\alpha) = (M, \tau_1, \tau_2, \boldsymbol{R}) \\ \alpha & \text{otherwise} \end{cases}$$

$$c_i(\phi, \mathbf{Nat}) \stackrel{\text{def}}{=} \mathbf{Nat}$$
$$c_i(\phi, \boldsymbol{L}) \stackrel{\text{def}}{=} \boldsymbol{L}$$
$$c_i(\phi, \tau_1 \to \tau_2) \stackrel{\text{def}}{=} c_i(\phi, \tau_1) \to c_i(\phi, \tau_2)$$
$$c_i(\phi, \forall\alpha.\tau') \stackrel{\text{def}}{=} \forall\alpha.c_i(\phi, \tau')$$
$$c_i(\phi, \tau^*) \stackrel{\text{def}}{=} c_i(\phi, \tau)^*$$

The interesting part of the definition is its action on type variables. Variables that ϕ maps to Scheme relations are converted to type **L**, since when Scheme uses a polymorphic value in ML its free type variables are instantiated as **L**. Similarly, variables that ϕ maps to ML relations are instantiated as seals because when ML uses a Scheme value as though it were polymorphic it uses dynamic seals to protect parametricity.

Now we can show that contracts respect the relation in figure 5 via a bridge lemma.

Lemma 2 (bridge lemma 2). *For all* $k \geq 0$*, type environments* Δ*, hybrid environments* ϕ *such that* $\Delta \vdash \phi$*,* τ *such that* $\Delta \vdash \tau$*, and for all terms* e_1*,* e_2*,* $\boldsymbol{e}_1$*,* $\boldsymbol{e}_2$*:*

1. *If* $\delta_\phi \vdash \boldsymbol{e}_1 \lesssim^k_M \boldsymbol{e}_2 : \tau$ *then* $\sigma_\phi \vdash (\mathit{SM}^{c_1(\phi,\tau)}\ \boldsymbol{e}_1) \leq^k (\mathit{SM}^{c_2(\phi,\tau)}\ \boldsymbol{e}_2) : \tau$.
2. *If* $\sigma_\phi \vdash \mathsf{e}_1 \leq^k \mathsf{e}_2 : \tau$ *then* $\delta_\phi \vdash {}^{c_1(\phi,\tau)}\mathit{MS}\ \mathsf{e}_1 \lesssim^k_M ({}^{c_2(\phi,\tau)}\mathit{MS}\ \mathsf{e}_2) : \tau$.

Proof. Induction on τ. All cases are easy applications of the induction hypotheses.

Theorem 3. *For any seal-free term* e *such that* $\vdash_S \mathsf{e} : \boldsymbol{TST}$ *and for any closed type* τ*, we have that for all* $k \geq 0$*,* $\vdash \mathsf{e}^\tau \leq^k \mathsf{e}^\tau : \tau$.

Proof. By theorem 2, for all $k \geq 0$, $\vdash ({}^\tau\mathit{MS}\ \mathsf{e}) \lesssim^k_M ({}^\tau\mathit{MS}\ \mathsf{e}) : \tau$. Thus, by lemma 2, we have that for all $k \geq 0$, $\vdash (\mathit{SM}^\tau\ ({}^\tau\mathit{MS}\ \mathsf{e})) \leq^k (\mathit{SM}^\tau\ ({}^\tau\mathit{MS}\ \mathsf{e})) : \tau$.

Definition 5 (relational equality). *We write* $\sigma \vdash \mathsf{e}_1 = \mathsf{e}_2 : \tau$ *if for all* $k \geq 0$*,* $\sigma \vdash \mathsf{e}_1 \leq^k \mathsf{e}_2 : \tau$ *and* $\sigma \vdash \mathsf{e}_2 \leq^k \mathsf{e}_1 : \tau$.

Corollary 1. *For any seal-free term* e *such that* $\vdash_S \mathsf{e} : \boldsymbol{TST}$ *and for any closed type* τ, *we have that* $\vdash \mathsf{e}^\tau = \mathsf{e}^\tau : \tau$.

4.1 Dynamic Sealing Replaces Boundaries

The contract system of the previous section is a multi-language system, but just barely, since the only part of ML we make any use of is its boundary form to get back into Scheme. In this section we restrict our attention to Scheme plus boundaries used only for the purpose of implementing contracts, and we show an alternate implementation of contracts that uses dynamic sealing. Rather than the concrete implementation of dynamic seals we gave in the introduction, we opt to use (a slight restriction of) the more abstract constructs taken from Sumii and Pierce's $\lambda_{\texttt{seal}}$ language [5]. Specifically, we use the following extension to our Scheme model:

$$
\begin{array}{lcl}
\mathsf{e} & = & \cdots \mid \nu\mathsf{sx}.\,\mathsf{e} \mid \{\mathsf{e}\}_{\mathsf{se}} \mid (\textbf{let}\ \{\mathsf{x}\}_{\mathsf{se}} = \mathsf{e}\ \textbf{in}\ \mathsf{e}) \\
\mathsf{v} & = & \cdots \mid \{\mathsf{v}\}_{\mathsf{sv}} \\
\mathsf{se} & = & \mathsf{sx} \mid \mathsf{sv} \\
\mathsf{sx} & = & [\text{variables distinct from } \mathsf{x}] \\
\mathsf{sv} & = & [\text{unspecified, unique brands}] \\
\mathsf{E} & = & \cdots \mid \{\mathsf{E}\}_{\mathsf{sv}} \mid (\textbf{let}\ \{\mathsf{x}\}_{\mathsf{sv}} = \mathsf{E}\ \textbf{in}\ \mathsf{e})
\end{array}
$$

$$
\begin{array}{rcl}
\mathscr{E}[\nu\mathsf{sx}.\,\mathsf{e}]_S & \mapsto & \mathscr{E}[\mathsf{e}[\mathsf{sv}/\mathsf{sx}]] \\
 & & \text{where } \mathsf{sv} \text{ fresh} \\
\mathscr{E}[(\textbf{let}\ \{\mathsf{x}\}_{\mathsf{sv}_1} = \{\mathsf{v}\}_{\mathsf{sv}_1}\ \textbf{in}\ \mathsf{e})]_S & \mapsto & \mathscr{E}[\mathsf{e}_1[\mathsf{v}/\mathsf{x}]] \\
\mathscr{E}[(\textbf{let}\ \{\mathsf{x}\}_{\mathsf{sv}_1} = \mathsf{v}\ \textbf{in}\ \mathsf{e})]_S & \mapsto & \textbf{Error}\text{: bad value} \\
 & & \text{where } \mathsf{v} \neq \{\mathsf{v}'\}_{\mathsf{sv}_1} \text{ for any } \mathsf{v}'
\end{array}
$$

We introduce a new set of seal variables sx that stand for seals (elements of sv) that will be computed at runtime. They are bound by $\nu\mathsf{sx}.\,\mathsf{e}$, which evaluates its body (e) with sx bound to a freshly-generated sv. Two operations make use of these seals. The first, $\{\mathsf{e}\}_{\mathsf{se}}$, evaluates e to a value and then itself becomes an opaque value sealed with the key to which se evaluates. The second, $(\textbf{let}\ \{\mathsf{x}\}_{\mathsf{se}} = \mathsf{e}_1\ \textbf{in}\ \mathsf{e}_2)$, evaluates e_1 to a value; if that value is an opaque value sealed with the seal to which se evaluates, then the entire unsealing expression evaluates to e_2 with x bound to the value that was sealed, otherwise the expression signals an error.[1]

Using these additional constructs we can demonstrate that a translation essentially the same as the one given by Sumii and Pierce [5, figure 4] does in fact generate parametrically polymorphic type abstractions. Their translation essentially attaches a higher-order contract [8] τ to an expression of type τ (though they do not point this out). It extends Findler and Felleisen's notion of contracts, which does not include polymorphic types, by adding an environment ρ that maps a type variable to a tuple consisting of a seal and a symbol indicating the party (either $+$ or $-$ in Sumii and Pierce) that has the power to instantiate that type variable, and translating uses of type variable α in a contract to an appropriate seal or unseal based on the value of $\rho(\alpha)$. We define it as follows: when p and q are each parties ($+$ or $-$) and $p \neq q$,

---

[1] This presentation is a simplification of $\lambda_{\texttt{seal}}$ in two ways. First, in $\lambda_{\texttt{seal}}$ the key position for a sealed value or for an unseal statement may be an arbitrary expression, whereas here we syntactically restrict expressions that appear in those positions to be either seal variables or seal values. Second, in $\lambda_{\texttt{seal}}$ an unseal expression has an "else" clause that allows the program to continue even if an unsealing operation fails; we do not allow those clauses.

$$
\begin{array}{lcl}
E^{p,q}_{\mathbf{Nat}}(\rho,\mathsf{e}) & = & (+\ \mathsf{e}\ 0) \\
E^{p,q}_{\tau^*}(\rho,\mathsf{e}) & = & (\mathbf{let}\ ((v\ e))\ (\mathbf{if0}\ (\mathsf{nil?}\ v) \\
& & \qquad \mathsf{nil} \\
& & \qquad (\mathbf{if0}\ (\mathsf{pair?}\ v) \\
& & \qquad\quad (\mathsf{cons}\ E^{p,q}_{\tau}(\rho,(\mathsf{fst}\ \mathsf{v}))\ E^{p,q}_{\tau^*}(\rho,(\mathsf{rst}\ \mathsf{v}))) \\
& & \qquad\quad (\mathsf{wrong}\ \texttt{"Non-list"})))) \\
E^{p,q}_{\tau_1\to\tau_2}(\rho,\mathsf{e}) & = & (\mathbf{let}\ ((v\ e))\ (\mathbf{if0}\ (\mathsf{proc?}\ v) \\
& & \qquad (\lambda\, x.\ E^{p,q}_{\tau_2}(\rho,(\mathsf{v}\ E^{q,p}_{\tau_1}(\rho,\mathsf{x})))) \\
& & \qquad (\mathsf{wrong}\ \texttt{"Non-proc"}))) \\
E^{p,q}_{\forall\alpha.\tau'}(\rho,\mathsf{e}) & = & \nu\mathsf{sx}.\ E^{p,q}_{\mathsf{e}}(\rho,\alpha\mapsto(\mathsf{sx},q),\mathsf{e}) \\
E^{p,q}_{\alpha}(\rho,\alpha\mapsto(\mathsf{sx},p),\mathsf{e}) & = & \{\mathsf{e}\}_{\mathsf{sx}} \\
E^{p,q}_{\alpha}(\rho,\alpha\mapsto(\mathsf{sx},q),\mathsf{e}) & = & (\mathbf{let}\ \{\mathsf{x}\}_{\mathsf{sx}} = \mathsf{e}\ \mathbf{in}\ \mathsf{x})
\end{array}
$$

The differences between our translation and Sumii and Pierce's are as follows. First, we have mapped everything into our notation and adapted to our types (we omit booleans, tuples, and existential types and add numbers and lists). Second, our translations apply to arbitrary expressions rather than just variables. Third, because we are concerned with the expression violating parametricity as well as the context, we have to seal values provided by the context as well as by the expression, and our decision of whether to seal or unseal at a type variable is based on whether the party that instantiated the type variable is providing a value with that contract or expecting one. Fourth, we modify the result of $\forall\alpha.\tau$ so that it does not require application to a dummy value. (The reason we do this bears explanation. There are two components to a type abstraction in System F — abstracting over an interpretation of a variable and suspending a computation. Sumii and Pierce's system achieves the former by generating a fresh seal, and the latter by wrapping the computation in a lambda abstraction. In our variant, $\forall\alpha.\tau$ contracts still abstract over a free contract variable's interpretation, but they do not suspend computation; for that reason we retain fresh seal generation but eliminate the wrapper function.)

Definition 6 (boundary replacement). *$\mathscr{R}[\mathsf{e}]$ is defined as follows:*

$$\mathscr{R}[\mathsf{e}^{\tau}] = E^{+,-}_{\tau}(\bullet,\mathscr{R}[\mathsf{e}]) \qquad \mathscr{R}[(\mathsf{e}_1\ \mathsf{e}_2)] = (\mathscr{R}[\mathsf{e}_1]\ \mathscr{R}[\mathsf{e}_2]) \qquad \ldots$$

Theorem 4 (boundary replacement preserves termination). *If* $;\vdash_S \mathsf{e} : \mathit{TST}$, *then* $\mathsf{e} \mapsto^* \mathsf{v}_1 \Leftrightarrow \mathscr{R}[\mathsf{e}] \mapsto^* \mathsf{v}_2$, *where* $\mathsf{v}_1 = \overline{n} \Leftrightarrow \mathsf{v}_2 = \overline{n}$.

This claim is a special case of a more general theorem that requires us to consider open contracts. The term $\mathsf{v}^{\forall\alpha.\alpha\to\alpha}$ where v is a procedure value reduces as follows:

$$
\begin{array}{rcl}
\mathsf{v}^{\forall\alpha.\alpha\to\alpha} & = & (\mathit{SM}^{\forall\alpha.\alpha\to\alpha}({}^{\forall\alpha.\alpha\to\alpha}\mathit{MS}\ \mathsf{v})) \\
& \mapsto^3 & (\mathit{SM}^{\mathbf{L}\to\mathbf{L}}({}^{\langle\alpha;\mathbf{L}\rangle\to\langle\alpha;\mathbf{L}\rangle}\mathit{MS}\ \mathsf{v})) \\
& \mapsto^2 & \lambda\mathsf{x}.(\mathit{SM}^{\mathbf{L}}\ ((\lambda\mathbf{y}:\mathbf{L}.\ ({}^{\langle\alpha;\mathbf{L}\rangle}\mathit{MS}\ (\mathsf{v}\ (\mathit{SM}^{\langle\alpha;\mathbf{L}\rangle}\ \mathbf{y}))))\ ({}^{\mathbf{L}}\mathit{MS}\ \mathsf{x}))) \\
& = & \lambda\mathsf{x}.(\mathit{SM}^{\mathbf{L}}\ ({}^{\langle\alpha;\mathbf{L}\rangle}\mathit{MS}\ (\mathsf{v}\ (\mathit{SM}^{\langle\alpha;\mathbf{L}\rangle}\ ({}^{\mathbf{L}}\mathit{MS}\ \mathsf{x})))))
\end{array}
$$

Notice that the two closed occurrences of α in the original contracts become two different configurations of boundaries when they appear open in the final procedure. These correspond to the fact that negative and positive occurrences of a type variable with respect to its binder behave differently. Negative occurrences, of the form $(\mathit{SM}^{\langle\alpha;\mathbf{L}\rangle}\ ({}^{\mathbf{L}}\mathit{MS}\ldots))$, act as dynamic seals on their bodies. Positive occurrences, of the form $(\mathit{SM}^{\mathbf{L}}\ ({}^{\langle\alpha;\mathbf{L}\rangle}\mathit{MS}\ldots))$, dynamically unseal the values their bodies produce. So, we write open contract variables as $\alpha-$ (for negative occurrences) and $\alpha+$ (for positive occurrences).

Now we are prepared to define another logical relation, this time between contracted Scheme terms and $\lambda_{\mathtt{seal}}$ terms. We define it as follows, where p owns the given expressions, q is the other party, and ρ maps type variables to seals and owners:

$$\begin{array}{lcl} p;q;\rho \vdash \mathsf{e}_1 =^k_{seal} \mathsf{e}_2 & \stackrel{\text{def}}{=} & \forall j<k.\ (\mathsf{e}_1 \mapsto^j \textbf{Error}: \mathrm{s} \Rightarrow \mathsf{e}_2 \mapsto^* \textbf{Error}: \mathrm{s})\ \text{and} \\ & & \quad (\forall \mathsf{v}_1.\ \mathsf{e}_1 \mapsto^j \mathsf{v}_1 \Rightarrow \exists \mathsf{v}_2.\ \mathsf{e}_2 \mapsto^* \mathsf{v}_2\ \text{and}\ p;q;\rho \vdash \mathsf{v}_1 =^{k-j}_{seal} \mathsf{v}_2) \\ & & \forall j<k.\ (\mathsf{e}_2 \mapsto^j \textbf{Error}: \mathrm{s} \Rightarrow \mathsf{e}_1 \mapsto^* \textbf{Error}: \mathrm{s})\ \text{and} \\ & & \quad (\forall \mathsf{v}_1.\ \mathsf{e}_2 \mapsto^j \mathsf{v}_2 \Rightarrow \exists \mathsf{v}_2.\ \mathsf{e}_1 \mapsto^* \mathsf{v}_1\ \text{and}\ p;q;\rho \vdash \mathsf{v}_1 =^{k-j}_{seal} \mathsf{v}_2) \\ p;q;\rho \vdash \mathsf{v}_1{}^{\alpha-} =^k_{seal} \{\mathsf{v}_2\}_{\mathsf{sv}} & \stackrel{\text{def}}{=} & \rho(\alpha) = (\mathsf{sx}, q)\ \text{and}\ \forall j<k.\ p;q;\rho \vdash \mathsf{v}_1 =^j_{seal} \mathsf{v}_2 \\ & \vdots & \\ p;q;\rho \vdash (\lambda \mathsf{x}.\mathsf{e}_1) =^k_{seal} (\lambda \mathsf{x}.\mathsf{e}_2) & \stackrel{\text{def}}{=} & \forall j<k, \mathsf{v}_1, \mathsf{v}_2.\ \ q;p;\rho \vdash \mathsf{v}_1 =^j_{seal} \mathsf{v}_2 \Rightarrow \\ & & \qquad p;q;\rho \vdash \mathsf{e}_1[\mathsf{v}_1/\mathsf{x}] =^j_{seal} \mathsf{e}_2[\mathsf{v}_2/\mathsf{x}] \end{array}$$

The rest of the cases are defined as in the Scheme relation of figure 4. An important subtlety above is that two sealed terms are related only if they are locked with a seal owned by the *other* party, and that the arguments to functions are owned by the party that does *not* own the function. The former point allows us to establish this lemma, after which we can build a new bridge lemma and then prove the theorem of interest:

Lemma 3. *If* $p;q;\rho,\alpha : (\mathsf{sx}, p) \vdash \mathsf{e}_1 =^k_{seal} \mathsf{e}_2$ *(and* α *not free in* e_1*), then* $p;q;\rho \vdash \mathsf{e}_1 =^k_{seal} \mathsf{e}_2$*. Similarly if* $p;q;\rho \vdash \mathsf{e}_1 =^k_{seal} \mathsf{e}_2$*, then* $p;q;\rho,\alpha : (\mathsf{sx}, p) \vdash \mathsf{e}_1 =^k_{seal} \mathsf{e}_2$*.*

Proof. We prove both claims simultaneously by induction on k.

Lemma 4. *For any two terms* e_1 *and* e_2 *such that* e_1*'s open type variables (and their ownership information) occur in* ρ*, and so do the open type variables in* τ*, then if* $(\forall k.p;q;\rho \vdash \mathsf{e}_1 =^k_{seal} \mathsf{e}_2)$ *then* $(\forall k.p;q;\rho \vdash \mathsf{e}_1{}^{\tau} =^k_{seal} E^{p,q}_{\tau}(\rho, \mathsf{e}_2)$*.*

Proof. By induction on τ. The $\forall\alpha.\tau$ case requires the preceding lemma.

Theorem 5. *If* $\rho \vdash \gamma_1 =_{seal} \gamma_2 : \Gamma$*,* e*'s open type variables occur in* ρ*,* $\Delta;\Gamma \vdash_S \mathsf{e} : \textbf{TST}$*, and* e *only uses boundaries as contracts, then* $\forall k.p;q;\rho \vdash \gamma_1(\mathsf{e}) =^k_{seal} \gamma_2(\mathscr{R}[\mathsf{e}])$*.*

Proof. Induction on the derivation $\Delta;\Gamma \vdash_S \mathsf{e} : \textbf{TST}$. Contract cases appeal to lemma 4.

This theorem has two consequences: first, contracts as we have defined them in this paper can be implemented by a variant on Sumii and Pierce's translation, and thus due to our earlier development their translation preserves parametricity; and second, since Sumii and Pierce's translation is itself a variant on Findler-and-Felleisen-style contracts, our boundary-based contracts are actually contracts in that sense.

Finally, notice that if we choose $\mathscr{E} = \mathsf{E}$ then there is no trace of ML left in the language we are considering; it is pure Scheme with contracts. But, strangely, the contract system's parametricity theorem relies on the fact that parametricity holds in ML.

5 Related Work and Conclusions

We have mentioned Sumii and Pierce's investigation of dynamic sealing [11, 5] many times in this paper. Sumii and Pierce also investigate logical relations for encryption

[12], which is probably the most technically similar paper in their line of research to the present work. In that work, they develop a logical relation that tracks secret keys as a proof technique for establishing the equivalence of programs that use encryption to hide information. One can think of our development as a refinement of their relation that allows Turing-complete "attackers" (which in particular may not terminate) and that clarifies the fundamental connection between parametricity and dynamic sealing.

Zdancewic, Grossman, and Morrisett's notion of *principals* [13, 14] and their associated proof technique are also related. Compared to their work, the present proof technique establishes a much stronger property, but it is comparatively more difficult to scale to more sophisticated programming language features such as state or advanced control features. Rossberg [15,16] discusses the idea of preserving abstraction safety by the use of dynamically-generated types that are very similar to our $\langle\alpha;\tau\rangle$ sealed conversion schemes. The property we have proven here is much stronger than the abstraction properties established by Rossberg; however, his analysis considers a more complicated type system than we do. It is certainly worth investigating how well the multi-language technique presented here maps into Rossberg's setting, but we have not done so yet.

The thrust of this paper has been to demonstrate that the parametricity property of System F is preserved under a multi-language embedding with Scheme, provided we protect all values that arise from terms that had quantified types in the original program using dynamic seals. We think this fact is in itself interesting, and has the interesting consequence that polymorphic contracts are also parametric in a meaningful sense, in fact strong enough that we can derive "free theorems" about contracted Scheme terms (see the technical report [9] for examples). But it also suggests something broader. Rather than just knowing that parametricity continues to hold in System F after the extension, we would like the stronger property that the extension does not weaken System F's contextual equivalence relation at all; in other words to design an embedding such that $e_1 \simeq_{ctxt} e_2$ when considering only contexts without boundaries implies that $e_1 \simeq_{ctxt} e_2$ in contexts with boundaries. This may be a useful way to approach the full-abstraction question raised by Sumii and Pierce.

References

1. Reynolds, J.C.: Types, abstraction and parametric polymorphism. In: IFIP Congress, pp. 513–523 (1983)
2. Wadler, P.: Theorems for free! In: Functional Programming Languages and Computer Architecture (FPCA), pp. 347–359 (1989)
3. Morris Jr., J.H.: Types are not sets. In: POPL (1973)
4. Flatt, M.: PLT MzScheme: Language manual. Technical Report TR97-280, Rice University (1997), `http://www.plt-scheme.org/software/mzscheme/`
5. Sumii, E., Pierce, B.: A bisimulation for dynamic sealing. In: POPL (2004)
6. Matthews, J., Findler, R.B.: Operational semantics for multi-language programs. In: POPL (2007), Extended version: University of Chicago Technical Report TR-2007-8, under review
7. Ahmed, A.: Step-indexed syntactic logical relations for recursive and quantified types. In: ESOP. pp. 69–83 (2006), Extended version: Harvard University Technical Report TR-01-06, `http://ttic.uchicago.edu/~amal/papers/lr-recquant-techrpt.pdf`
8. Findler, R.B., Felleisen, M.: Contracts for higher-order functions. In: ICFP (2002)

9. Matthews, J., Ahmed, A.: Parametric polymorphism through run-time sealing, or, theorems for low, low prices! (extended version). Technical Report TR-2008-01, University of Chicago (2008)
10. Findler, R.B., Blume, M.: Contracts as pairs of projections. In: FLOPS (2006)
11. Pierce, B., Sumii, E.: Relating cryptography and polymorphism. Unpublished manuscript (2000)
12. Sumii, E., Pierce, B.: Logical relations for encryption. Journal of Computer Security (JSC) 11(4), 521–554 (2003)
13. Zdancewic, S., Grossman, D., Morrisett, G.: Principals in programming languages. In: ICFP (1999)
14. Grossman, D., Morrisett, G., Zdancewic, S.: Syntactic type abstraction. ACM Transactions on Programming Languages and Systems 22, 1037–1080 (2000)
15. Rossberg, A.: Generativity and dynamic opacity for abstract types. In: Miller, D. (ed.) PADL, Uppsala, Sweden, ACM Press, New York (2003), Extended version: `http://www.ps.uni-sb.de/Papers/generativity-extended.html`
16. Rossberg, A.: Typed Open Programming – A higher-order, typed approach to dynamic modularity and distribution. Phd thesis, Universität des Saarlandes, Saarbrücken, Germany. Preliminary version (2007)

Regular Expression Subtyping for XML Query and Update Languages

James Cheney

University of Edinburgh

Abstract. XML database query languages such as XQuery employ regular expression types with structural subtyping. Subtyping systems typically have two presentations, which should be equivalent: a declarative version in which the subsumption rule may be used anywhere, and an algorithmic version in which the use of subsumption is limited in order to make typechecking syntax-directed and decidable. However, the XQuery standard type system circumvents this issue by using imprecise typing rules for iteration constructs and defining only algorithmic typechecking, and another extant proposal provides more precise types for iteration constructs but ignores subtyping. In this paper, we consider a core XQuery-like language with a subsumption rule and prove the completeness of algorithmic typechecking; this is straightforward for XQuery proper but requires some care in the presence of more precise iteration typing disciplines. We extend this result to an XML update language we have introduced in earlier work.

1 Introduction

The Extensible Markup Language (XML) is a World Wide Web Consortium (W3C) standard for tree-structured data. Regular expression types for XML [14] have been studied extensively in XML processing languages such as XDuce [13] and CDuce [1], as well as projects to extend general-purpose programming languages with XML features such as Xtatic [10] and OCamlDuce [9]. Moreover, subtyping (based on regular tree language inclusion) plays an important role in all of these systems.

XQuery is a W3C standard XML database query language [6]. Static typechecking is important in XML database applications because type information is useful for optimizing queries and avoiding expensive run-time checks and revalidation. XQuery provides for static typing using regular expression types and subtyping. However, XQuery's type system is imprecise in some situations involving iteration (`for`-loops). In particular, if the variable $\$x$ has type[1] $a[b[]^*, c[]^?]$, then the query

```
for $y in $x/* return $y
```

is assigned type $(b[]|c[])^*$ in XQuery, but in fact the result will always match the regular expression type $b[]^*, c[]^?$. The reason for this inaccuracy is that XQuery's type system

[1] We use the compact notation for regular expression types introduced by Hosoya, Vouillon and Pierce [14] in preference to the more verbose XQuery or XML Schema syntaxes.

S. Drossopoulou (Ed.): ESOP 2008, LNCS 4960, pp. 32–47, 2008.

typechecks a `for` loop by converting the type of the body of the expression (here, $\$x/a$ with type $b[]^*, c[]^?$) to the "factored" form $(\alpha_1|\ldots|\alpha_n)^q$, where q is a quantifier such as ?, +, or $*$ and each α_i is an atomic type (i.e. a data type such as `string` or single element type $a[\tau]$).

More precise type systems have been contemplated for XQuery-like languages, including a precursor to XQuery designed by Fernandez, Siméon, and Wadler [8]. Most recently, Colazzo et al. [5] have introduced a core XQuery language called μXQ, with a regular expression-based type system that performs "path correctness" analysis and provides more precise types for iterations using techniques similar to those in [8], but does not support subtyping. In μXQ, the above expression is assigned the more accurate type $b[]^*, c[]^?$; however, the example cannot be assigned the less precise type $(b[]|c[])^*$ since subtyping was not incorporated into the original formulation of μXQ.

Combining subtyping with accurate typing for iteration constructs is especially important for XML updates. We are developing a statically-typed update language called FLUX [2] in which ideas from μXQ are essential for typechecking updates involving iteration. Using XQuery-style factoring for iteration in FLUX would make it impossible to typecheck updates that modify data without modifying the overall schema of the database—a very common case. For example, using XQuery-style factoring for iteration in FLUX, we would not be able to verify statically that given a database of type $a[b[\texttt{string}]^*, c[]^?]$, the result of an update that modifies some b elements and deletes some c elements still has type $a[b[\texttt{string}]^*, c[]^?]$, rather than $a[(b[\texttt{string}]|c[])^*]$.

One question left unresolved in previous work on both μXQ and FLUX is the relationship between declarative and algorithmic presentations of the type system (in the terminology of [16, Ch. 15–16]). Declarative derivations permit arbitrary uses of the *subsumption rule*:

$$\frac{\Gamma \vdash e : \tau \quad \tau <: \tau'}{\Gamma \vdash e : \tau'}$$

whereas algorithmic derivations limit the use of this rule in order to ensure that typechecking is syntax-directed and decidable. The declarative and algorithmic presentations of a system should agree. If they agree, then declarative typechecking is decidable algorithmically; if they disagree, then the algorithmic system is *incomplete*, that is, it rejects programs that should typecheck according to the declarative rules.

The XQuery standard avoided this issue by defining typechecking algorithmically, that is, building subsumption into several rules and omitting a general subsumption rule. Subtyping was omitted from μXQ, because it interferes with μXQ's "path correctness" component [5, Sec. 4.4] . Subtyping was considered in our initial work on FLUX [3], but we were initially unable to establish that typechecking was decidable.

In this paper we develop the foundations of subtyping for XML query and update languages. Our main contributions relative to previous work [5,3] are definitions and proofs of completeness of algorithmic typechecking (and hence decidability of declarative typechecking) for μXQ and FLUX, extended with subtyping and type, query, and update recursion. We follow the standard technique of proving that declarative derivations can always be normalized to algorithmic derivations [16, Ch. 16]. However, for μXQ's more precise iteration type discipline, completeness of algorithmic typechecking

[2] "FunctionaL Updates for XML"; earlier called LUX ("Lightweight Updates for XML") in [3].

does not follow directly by the obvious structural induction. Instead, we must establish a stronger property based on the semantics of regular expression types.

The structure of the rest of the paper is as follows. Section 2 reviews regular expression types and subtyping. Section 3 introduces the core language μXQ, discusses examples highlighting the difficulties involving subtyping in μXQ, and proves decidability of declarative typechecking. We also review the FLUX core update language in Section 4, discuss examples, and extend the proof of decidability of declarative typechecking to FLUX. Sections 5–6 sketch related and future work and conclude. Space limitations preclude a satisfying self-contained exposition of the μXQ and FLUX languages; the reader is encouraged to consult the earlier papers for further details [5,3].

2 Regular Expression Types and Subtyping

For the purposes of this paper, *XML values* are trees built up out of booleans $b \in Bool = \{\mathtt{true}, \mathtt{false}\}$, strings $w \in \Sigma^*$ over some alphabet Σ, and labels $l, m, n \in Lab$, according to the following syntax:

$$\bar{v} ::= b \mid w \mid n[v] \qquad v ::= \bar{v}, v \mid (\,)$$

Values include *tree values* $\bar{v} \in Tree$ and *forest values* $v \in Val$. We write v, v' for the result of appending two forest values. This operation is associative with unit $(\,)$.

We consider a regular expression type system with structural subtyping, similar to those considered in several transformation and query languages for XML [14,5,8]. The syntax of types and type environments is as follows.

$$\begin{array}{ll}
\text{Atomic types} & \alpha ::= \mathtt{bool} \mid \mathtt{string} \mid n[\tau] \\
\text{Sequence types} & \tau ::= \alpha \mid (\,) \mid \tau|\tau' \mid \tau,\tau' \mid \tau^* \mid X \\
\text{Type definitions} & \tau_0 ::= \alpha \mid (\,) \mid \tau_0|\tau_0' \mid \tau_0,\tau_0' \mid \tau_0^* \\
\text{Type signatures} & E ::= \cdot \mid E, \mathtt{type}\ X = \tau_0
\end{array}$$

We call types of the form $\alpha \in Atom$ *atomic* types (or sometimes tree or singular types), and types $\tau \in Type$ of all other forms *sequence types* (or sometimes forest or plural types). It should be obvious that a value of singular type must always be a sequence of length one (that is, a tree); plural types may have values of any length. There exist plural types with only values of length one, but which are not syntactically singular (for example $\mathtt{int}|\mathtt{bool}$). As usual, the $+$ and $?$ quantifiers can be defined as follows: $\tau^+ = \tau, \tau^*$ and $\tau^? = \tau|(\,)$. We abbreviate $n[(\,)]$ as $n[]$.

Our type language differs slightly from the standard approaches to regular expression types [14,5]. In [14], it was shown that Kleene star can be translated away by introducing type variables and definitions, modulo a syntactic restriction on top-level occurrences of type variables in type definitions. We include Kleene star as a primitive, and permit (mutually) recursive type declarations, but forbid any top-level occurrences type variables in definitions τ_0. Therefore Kleene star is *not* definable in terms of the other operations here; this is why we include it as a primitive. For example, $\mathtt{type}\ X = nil[]|cons[a, X]$ and $\mathtt{type}\ Y = leaf[]|node[Y, Y]$ are allowed but $\mathtt{type}\ X' = (\,)|a[], X'$ and $\mathtt{type}\ Y' = b[]|Y', Y'$ are not. The equation for X' defines the regular tree language $a[]^*$, and would be permitted in XDuce, while that for Y' defines a context-free tree language that is not regular and is forbidden in XDuce.

An environment E is well-formed if all type variables appearing in definitions are themselves declared in E. Given a well-formed environment E, we write $E(X)$ for the definition of X. A type τ denotes the set of values $[\![\tau]\!]_E$, defined as follows.

$$[\![\texttt{string}]\!]_E = \Sigma^* \qquad [\![\texttt{bool}]\!]_E = \mathit{Bool} \qquad [\![\,()\,]\!]_E = \{\,()\,\}$$
$$[\![n[\tau]]\!]_E = \{n[v] \mid v \in [\![\tau]\!]_E\} \qquad [\![X]\!]_E = [\![E(X)]\!] \quad [\![\tau|\tau']\!]_E = [\![\tau]\!]_E \cup [\![\tau']\!]_E$$
$$[\![\tau, \tau']\!]_E = \{v, v' \mid v \in [\![\tau]\!]_E, v' \in [\![\tau']\!]_E\}$$
$$[\![\tau^*]\!]_E = \{\,()\,\} \cup \{v_1, \ldots, v_n \mid v_1 \in [\![\tau]\!]_E, \ldots, v_n \in [\![\tau]\!]_E\}$$

Formally, $[\![\tau]\!]_E$ is defined by a least fixed point construction which we gloss over. Henceforth, we treat E as fixed and define $[\![\tau]\!] \triangleq [\![\tau]\!]_E$. This semantics validates standard identities such as associativity of ',' ($[\![(\tau_1, \tau_2), \tau_3]\!] = [\![\tau_1, (\tau_2, \tau_3)]\!]$), unit laws ($[\![\tau, \,()\,]\!] = [\![\tau]\!] = [\![\,()\,, \tau]\!]$), and idempotence of '*' ($[\![(\tau^*)^*]\!] = [\![\tau^*]\!]$).

In addition, we define a binary *subtyping* relation on types. A type τ_1 is a subtype of τ_2 ($\tau_1 <: \tau_2$), by definition, if $[\![\tau_1]\!] \subseteq [\![\tau_2]\!]$. Our types can be translated to XDuce types, so subtyping reduces to XDuce subtyping; although this problem is EXPTIME-complete in general, the algorithm of [14] is well-behaved in practice. Therefore, we shall not give explicit inference rules for checking or deciding subtyping, but treat it as a "black box".

3 Query Language

We review an XQuery-like core language based on μXQ [5]. In μXQ, we distinguish between *tree variables* $\bar{x} \in \mathit{TVar}$, introduced by `for`, and *forest variables*, $x \in \mathit{Var}$, introduced by `let`. We write $\hat{x} \in \mathit{Var} \cup \mathit{TVar}$ for an arbitrary variable. The other syntactic classes of our variant of μXQ include booleans, strings, and labels introduced above, function names $F \in \mathit{FSym}$, expressions $e \in \mathit{Expr}$, and programs $p \in \mathit{Prog}$; the abstract syntax of expressions and programs is defined as follows:

$$\begin{aligned} e ::= {} & () \mid e, e' \mid n[e] \mid w \mid x \mid \texttt{let}\; x = e \;\texttt{in}\; e' \mid F(e_1, \ldots, e_n) \\ \mid {} & b \mid \texttt{if}\; c \;\texttt{then}\; e \;\texttt{else}\; e' \mid \bar{x} \mid \bar{x}/\texttt{child} \mid e :: n \mid \texttt{for}\; \bar{x} \in e \;\texttt{return}\; e' \\ p ::= {} & \texttt{query}\; e : \tau \mid \texttt{declare function}\; F(x_1{:}\tau_1, \ldots, x_n{:}\tau_n) : \tau\; \{e\}\texttt{;}\; p \end{aligned}$$

The distinguished variables x in `let` $x = e$ `in` $e'(x)$ and $\bar{x}$ in `for` $\bar{x} \in e$ `return` $e'(\bar{x})$ are bound in $e'(x)$ and $e'(\bar{x})$ respectively. Here and elsewhere, we employ common conventions such as identifying expressions modulo α-renaming.

To simplify the presentation, we split μXQ's projection operation $\bar{x}/\texttt{child} :: l$ into two expressions: child projection ($\bar{x}/\texttt{child}$) which returns the children of $\bar{x}$, and node name filtering ($e :: n$) which evaluates e to an arbitrary sequence and selects the nodes labeled n. Thus, the ordinary child axis expression $\bar{x}/\texttt{child} :: n$ is syntactic sugar for $(\bar{x}/\texttt{child}) :: n$ and the "wildcard" child axis is definable as $\bar{x}/\texttt{child} :: * = \bar{x}/\texttt{child}$. Built-in operations such as string equality may be provided as additional functions F.

$$\boxed{\Gamma \vdash e : \tau}$$

$$\frac{\bar{x}{:}\alpha \in \Gamma}{\Gamma \vdash \bar{x} : \alpha} \quad \frac{x{:}\tau \in \Gamma}{\Gamma \vdash x : \tau} \quad \frac{w \in \Sigma^*}{\Gamma \vdash w : \mathtt{string}} \quad \frac{b \in \mathit{Bool}}{\Gamma \vdash b : \mathtt{bool}}$$

$$\frac{}{\Gamma \vdash () : ()} \quad \frac{\Gamma \vdash e : \tau}{\Gamma \vdash n[e] : n[\tau]} \quad \frac{\Gamma \vdash e : \tau \quad \Gamma \vdash e' : \tau'}{\Gamma \vdash e, e' : \tau, \tau'} \quad \frac{\Gamma \vdash e_1 : \tau_1 \quad \Gamma, x{:}\tau_1 \vdash e_2 : \tau_2}{\Gamma \vdash \mathtt{let}\ x = e_1\ \mathtt{in}\ e_2 : \tau_2}$$

$$\frac{\Gamma \vdash c : \mathtt{bool} \quad \Gamma \vdash e_1 : \tau_1 \quad \Gamma \vdash e_2 : \tau_2}{\Gamma \vdash \mathtt{if}\ c\ \mathtt{then}\ e_1\ \mathtt{else}\ e_2 : \tau_1 | \tau_2} \quad \frac{\bar{x}{:}n[\tau] \in \Gamma}{\Gamma \vdash \bar{x}/\mathtt{child} : \tau} \quad \frac{\Gamma \vdash e : \tau \quad \tau :: n \Rightarrow \tau'}{\Gamma \vdash e :: n : \tau'}$$

$$\frac{\Gamma \vdash e_1 : \tau_1 \quad \Gamma \vdash \bar{x}\ \mathtt{in}\ \tau_1 \rightarrow e_2 : \tau_2}{\Gamma \vdash \mathtt{for}\ \bar{x} \in e_1\ \mathtt{return}\ e_2 : \tau_2} \quad \frac{F(\overline{\tau}) : \tau_0 \in \Delta \quad \Gamma \vdash e_i : \tau_i}{\Gamma \vdash F(\overline{e}) : \tau_0} \quad \frac{\Gamma \vdash e : \tau \quad \tau <: \tau'}{\Gamma \vdash e : \tau'}$$

$$\boxed{\Gamma \vdash p\ \mathtt{prog}}$$

$$\frac{\Gamma \vdash e : \tau}{\Gamma \vdash \mathtt{query}\ e : \tau\ \mathtt{prog}} \quad \frac{F \text{ not declared in } p \quad F(\overline{\tau}) : \tau_0 \in \Delta \quad \Gamma, \overline{x} : \overline{\tau} \vdash e : \tau_0 \quad \Gamma \vdash p\ \mathtt{prog}}{\Gamma \vdash \mathtt{declare\ function}\ F(\overline{\tau}) : \tau_0\ \{e\};\ p\ \mathtt{prog}}$$

Fig. 1. Query and program well-formedness rules

$$\boxed{\tau :: n \Rightarrow \tau'}$$

$$\frac{}{n[\tau] :: n \Rightarrow n[\tau]}$$

$$\frac{E(X) :: n \Rightarrow \tau}{X :: n \Rightarrow \tau} \quad \frac{\alpha \neq n[\tau]}{\alpha :: n \Rightarrow ()}$$

$$\frac{}{() :: n \Rightarrow ()} \quad \frac{\tau_1 :: n \Rightarrow \tau_2}{\tau_1^* :: n \Rightarrow \tau_2^*}$$

$$\frac{\tau_1 :: n \Rightarrow \tau_1' \quad \tau_2 :: n \Rightarrow \tau_2'}{\tau_1, \tau_2 :: n \Rightarrow \tau_1', \tau_2'}$$

$$\frac{\tau_1 :: n \Rightarrow \tau_1' \quad \tau_2 :: n \Rightarrow \tau_2'}{\tau_1 | \tau_2 :: n \Rightarrow \tau_1' | \tau_2'}$$

$$\boxed{\Gamma \vdash \bar{x}\ \mathtt{in}\ \tau \rightarrow e : \tau'}$$

$$\frac{}{\Gamma \vdash \bar{x}\ \mathtt{in}\ () \rightarrow e : ()} \quad \frac{\Gamma \vdash \bar{x}\ \mathtt{in}\ E(X) \rightarrow e : \tau}{\Gamma \vdash \bar{x}\ \mathtt{in}\ X \rightarrow e : \tau}$$

$$\frac{\Gamma, \bar{x}{:}\alpha \vdash e : \tau}{\Gamma \vdash \bar{x}\ \mathtt{in}\ \alpha \rightarrow e : \tau} \quad \frac{\Gamma \vdash \bar{x}\ \mathtt{in}\ \tau_1 \rightarrow e : \tau_2}{\Gamma \vdash \bar{x}\ \mathtt{in}\ \tau_1^* \rightarrow e : \tau_2^*}$$

$$\frac{\Gamma \vdash \bar{x}\ \mathtt{in}\ \tau_1 \rightarrow e : \tau_1' \quad \Gamma \vdash \bar{x}\ \mathtt{in}\ \tau_2 \rightarrow e : \tau_2'}{\Gamma \vdash \bar{x}\ \mathtt{in}\ \tau_1, \tau_2 \rightarrow e : \tau_1', \tau_2'}$$

$$\frac{\Gamma \vdash \bar{x}\ \mathtt{in}\ \tau_1 \rightarrow e : \tau_1' \quad \Gamma \vdash \bar{x}\ \mathtt{in}\ \tau_2 \rightarrow e : \tau_2'}{\Gamma \vdash \bar{x}\ \mathtt{in}\ \tau_1 | \tau_2 \rightarrow e : \tau_1' | \tau_2'}$$

Fig. 2. Auxiliary judgments

Colazzo et al. [5] provided a denotational semantics of μXQ queries with the descendant axis but without recursive functions. This semantics is sound with respect to the typing rules in the next section and can be extended to handle recursive functions using operational techniques (as in the XQuery standard). However, we omit the semantics since it is not needed in the rest of the paper.

3.1 Type System

Our type system for queries is essentially that introduced for μXQ by [5], excluding the path correctness component. We consider typing environments Γ and global declaration environments Δ, defined as follows:

$$\Gamma ::= \cdot \mid \Gamma, x{:}\tau \mid \Gamma, \bar{x}{:}\alpha \qquad \Delta ::= \cdot \mid \Delta, F(\overline{\tau}) : \tau_0$$

Note that in Γ, tree variables may only be bound to atomic types. As usual, we assume that variables in type environments are distinct; this convention implicitly constrains all inference rules. We also write $\Gamma <: \Gamma'$ to indicate that $\mathrm{dom}(\Gamma) = \mathrm{dom}(\Gamma')$ and $\Gamma'(\hat{x}) <: \Gamma(\hat{x})$ for all $\hat{x} \in \mathrm{dom}(\Gamma)$.

The main typing judgment for queries is $\Gamma \vdash e : \tau$; we also define a program well-formedness judgment $\Gamma \vdash p\;\texttt{prog}$ which typechecks the bodies of functions. Following [5], there are two auxiliary judgments, $\Gamma \vdash \bar{x}\;\texttt{in}\;\tau \to s : \tau'$, used for typechecking for-expressions, and $\tau :: n \Rightarrow \tau'$, used for typechecking label matching expressions $e :: n$. The rules for these judgments are shown in Figures 1 and 2.

We consider the typing rules to be implicitly parameterized by a fixed global declaration environment Δ. Functions in XQuery have global scope so we assume that the declarations for all the functions declared in the program have already been added to Δ by a preprocessing pass. Additional declarations for built-in functions might be included in Δ as well.

The rules involving type variables in Figure 2 look up the variable's definition in E. These judgments only inspect the top-level of a type; they do not inspect the contents of element types $n[\tau]$. Since type definitions τ_0 have no top-level type variables, both judgments are terminating. (This was argued in detail by Colazzo et al. [5, Lem. 4.6].)

3.2 Examples

We first revisit the example in the introduction in order to illustrate the operation of the rules. Recall that $\bar{x}/*$ is translated to $\bar{x}/\texttt{child}$ in our core language.

$$\dfrac{\dfrac{}{\Gamma \vdash \bar{x}/\texttt{child} : b[]^*, c[]^?} \quad \dfrac{\mathcal{D}}{\Gamma \vdash \bar{y}\;\texttt{in}\;b[]^*, c[]^? \to \bar{y} : b[]^*, c[]^?}}{\Gamma \vdash \texttt{for}\;\bar{y} \in \bar{x}/\texttt{child}\;\texttt{return}\;\bar{y} : b[]^*, c[]^?}$$

where we define $\Gamma = \bar{x}{:}a[b[]^*, c[]^?]$ and subderivation $\mathcal{D}$ is

$$\mathcal{D} = \dfrac{\dfrac{\dfrac{\dfrac{}{\Gamma, \bar{y}{:}b[] \vdash \bar{y} : b[]}}{\Gamma \vdash \bar{y}\;\texttt{in}\;b[] \to \bar{y} : b[]}}{\Gamma \vdash \bar{y}\;\texttt{in}\;b[]^* \to \bar{y} : b[]^*} \quad \dfrac{\dfrac{\dfrac{}{\bar{x}{:}a[b[]^*, c[]], \bar{y}{:}c[] \vdash \bar{y} : c[]}}{\Gamma \vdash \bar{y}\;\texttt{in}\;c[] \to \bar{y} : c[]}}{\Gamma \vdash \bar{y}\;\texttt{in}\;c[]^? \to \bar{y} : c[]^?}}{\Gamma \vdash \bar{y}\;\texttt{in}\;b[]^*, c[]^? \to \bar{y} : b[]^*, c[]^?}$$

Note that this derivation does not use subsumption anywhere. Suppose we wished to show that the expression has type $b[]^*, (c[]^? | d[]^*)$, a supertype of the above type. There are several ways to do this. We could simply use subsumption at the end of the derivation. Alternatively, we could have used subsumption in one of the subderivations such as $\Gamma, \bar{y}{:}c[]^? \vdash \bar{y} : c[]^?$, to conclude, for example, that $\Gamma, \bar{y}{:}c[]^? \vdash \bar{y} : c[]^? | d[]^*$. This is valid since $c[]^? <: c[]^? | d[]^*$.

Suppose, instead, that we actually wanted to show that the above expression has type $(b[d[]^*] | c[]^?)^*$, also a supertype of the derived type. There are again several ways of doing this. Besides using subsumption at the end of the derivation, we could use it on $\Gamma \vdash \bar{x}/\texttt{child} : b[]^*, c[]^?$ to obtain $\Gamma \vdash \bar{x}/\texttt{child} : (b[d[]^*] | c[]^?)^*$. To complete the derivation, we would then need to replace derivation $\mathcal{D}$ with $\mathcal{D}'$:

$$\mathcal{D}' = \dfrac{\dfrac{\overline{\Gamma, \bar{y}{:}b[d[]^*] \vdash \bar{y} : b[d[]^*]}}{\Gamma \vdash \bar{y}\ \mathtt{in}\ b[d[]^*] \to \bar{y} : b[d[]^*]} \quad \dfrac{\dfrac{\overline{\Gamma, \bar{y}{:}c[] \vdash \bar{y} : c[]}}{\Gamma \vdash \bar{y}\ \mathtt{in}\ c[] \to \bar{y} : c[]}}{\Gamma \vdash \bar{y}\ \mathtt{in}\ c[]^? \to \bar{y} : c[]^?}}{\dfrac{\Gamma \vdash \bar{y}\ \mathtt{in}\ b[d[]^*]|c[]^? \to \bar{y} : b[d[]^*]|c[]^?}{\Gamma \vdash \bar{y}\ \mathtt{in}\ (b[d[]^*]|c[]^?)^* \to \bar{y} : (b[d[]^*]|c[]^?)^*}}$$

Not only does $\mathcal{D}'$ have different structure than $\mathcal{D}$, but it also requires subderivations that were not syntactically present in $\mathcal{D}$.

The above example illustrates why eliminating uses of subsumption is tricky. If subsumption is used to weaken the type of the first argument of a `for`-expression according to $\tau_1' <: \tau_1$, then we need to know that we can transform the corresponding derivation $\mathcal{D}$ of $\Gamma \vdash \bar{x}\ \mathtt{in}\ \tau_1 \to e : \tau_2$ to a derivation of $\mathcal{D}'$ of $\Gamma \vdash \bar{x}\ \mathtt{in}\ \tau_1' \to e : \tau_2'$ for some $\tau_2' <: \tau_2$. But the derivations $\mathcal{D}$ and $\mathcal{D}'$ may bear little resemblance to one another.

Now we consider a typechecking a recursive query. Suppose we have[3] `type` $\mathit{Tree} = \mathit{tree}[\mathit{leaf}[\mathtt{string}]|\mathit{node}[\mathit{Tree}^*]]$ and function definition

$$\begin{array}{l}\mathtt{declare\ function}\ \mathit{leaves}(x : \mathit{Tree}) : \mathit{leaf}[\mathtt{string}]^*\ \{\\ \quad x/\mathit{leaf}, \mathtt{for}\ \bar{z} \in x/\mathit{node}/\mathit{tree}\ \mathtt{return}\ \mathit{leaves}(\bar{z})\\ \};\end{array}$$

This uses a construct e/n that is not in core μXQ, but we can expand e/n to $\mathtt{for}\ \bar{y} \in e\ \mathtt{return}\ \bar{y}/\mathtt{child} :: n$; thus, we can derive a rule

$$\dfrac{\Gamma \vdash e : l[\tau] \quad \tau :: n \Rightarrow \tau'}{\Gamma \vdash e/n : \tau'} \iff \dfrac{\Gamma \vdash e : l[\tau] \quad \dfrac{\dfrac{\overline{\Gamma, \bar{y}{:}l[\tau] \vdash \bar{y}/\mathtt{child} : \tau} \quad \tau :: n \Rightarrow \tau'}{\Gamma, \bar{y}{:}l[\tau] \vdash \bar{y}/\mathtt{child} :: n : \tau'}}{\Gamma \vdash \bar{y}\ \mathtt{in}\ l[\tau] \to \bar{y}/\mathtt{child} :: n : \tau'}}{\Gamma \vdash \mathtt{for}\ \bar{y} \in e\ \mathtt{return}\ \bar{y}/\mathtt{child} :: n : \tau'}$$

Using this derived rule and the fact that $x : \mathit{Tree}$ and the definition of Tree, we can see that $x/\mathit{leaf} : \mathit{leaf}[\mathtt{string}]$ and $x/\mathit{node} : \mathit{node}[\mathit{Tree}^*]$, and so $x/\mathit{node}/\mathit{tree} : \mathit{tree}[\mathit{leaf}[\mathtt{string}]|\mathit{node}[\mathit{Tree}^*]]^*$. So the body of the `for`-loop can be typechecked with $\bar{z} : \mathit{tree}[\mathit{leaf}[\mathtt{string}]|\mathit{node}[\mathit{Tree}^*]]$. To check the function call $\mathit{leaves}(\bar{z})$, we need subsumption to see that $\mathit{tree}[\mathit{leaf}[\mathtt{string}]|\mathit{node}[\mathit{Tree}^*]] <: \mathit{Tree}$. It follows that $\mathit{leaves}(\bar{z}) : \mathit{leaf}[\mathtt{string}]^*$, so the `for`-loop has type $(\mathit{leaf}[\mathtt{string}]^*)^*$. Again using subsumption, we can conclude that

$$x/\mathit{leaf}, \mathit{leaves}(x/\mathit{node}/\mathit{tree}) : \mathit{leaf}[\mathtt{string}], (\mathit{leaf}[\mathtt{string}]^*)^* <: \mathit{leaf}[\mathtt{string}]^*\ .$$

Notice that although we could have used subsumption in several more places, we really *needed* it in only two places: when typechecking a function call, and when checking the result of a function against its declared type.

3.3 Algorithmic Completeness and Decidability

The standard approach (see e.g. Pierce [16, Ch. 16]) to deciding declarative typechecking is to define algorithmic judgments that are syntax-directed and decidable, and then show that the algorithmic system is complete relative to the declarative system.

[3] We use a somewhat artificial definition of *Tree* here to simplify the example.

Definition 1 (Algorithmic derivations). *The algorithmic typechecking judgments* $\Gamma \mapsto e : \tau$ *and* $\Gamma \mapsto \bar{x}$ in $\tau_0 \to e : \tau$ *are defined by taking the rules of Figures 1 and 2, removing the subsumption rule, and replacing the function application rule with*

$$\frac{F(\overline{\tau}) : \tau \in \Gamma \quad \Gamma \mapsto e_i : \tau_i' \quad \tau_i' <: \tau_i}{\Gamma \mapsto F(\overline{e}) : \tau}$$

It is straightforward to show that algorithmic derivability is decidable and sound with respect to the declarative system:

Lemma 1 (Decidability). *For any* $\bar{x}, e, n$, *there exist computable partial functions* f_n, g_e, $h_{\bar{x},y}$ *such that for any* Γ, τ_0, *we have:*

1. $f_n(\tau_0)$ *is the unique* τ *such that* $\tau_0 :: n \Rightarrow \tau$.
2. $g_x(\Gamma)$ *is the unique* τ *such that* $\Gamma \mapsto e : \tau$, *when it exists.*
3. $h_{\bar{x},e}(\Gamma, \tau_0)$ *is the unique* τ *such that* $\Gamma \mapsto \bar{x}\ \mathtt{in}\ \tau_0 \to e : \tau$, *when it exists.*

Theorem 1 (Algorithmic Soundness). *(1) If* $\Gamma \mapsto e : \tau$ *is derivable then* $\Gamma \vdash e : \tau$ *is derivable. (2) If* $\Gamma \mapsto \bar{x}\ \mathtt{in}\ \tau_0 \to e : \tau$ *is derivable then* $\Gamma \vdash \bar{x}\ \mathtt{in}\ \tau_0 \to e : \tau$ *is derivable.*

The main result of this section is the corresponding completeness property (Theorem 2 below). A typical proof of completeness involves showing by induction that occurrences of the subsumption rule can be "permuted" downwards in the proof past other rules, except for function applications where subtyping checks are performed. Completeness for μXQ requires strengthening this induction hypothesis. To see why, consider the rules:

$$\frac{\overset{*}{\Gamma \vdash e_1 : \tau_1} \quad \Gamma, x{:}\tau_1 \vdash e_2 : \tau_2}{\Gamma \vdash \mathtt{let}\ x = e_1\ \mathtt{in}\ e_2 : \tau_2} \quad \frac{\overset{*}{\Gamma \vdash e_1 : \tau_1} \quad \Gamma \vdash \bar{x}\ \mathtt{in}\ \tau_1 \to e_2 : \tau_2}{\Gamma \vdash \mathtt{for}\ \bar{x} \in e_1\ \mathtt{return}\ e_2 : \tau_2} \quad \frac{\overset{*}{\Gamma \vdash e : \tau} \quad \tau :: n \Rightarrow \tau'}{\Gamma \vdash e :: n : \tau'}$$

If the subderivation labeled $*$ in the above rules follows by subsumption, however, we cannot do anything to get rid of the subsumption rule using the induction hypotheses provided by Theorem 2. Instead we need an additional lemma that ensures that the judgments are all *downward monotonic*. Downward monotonicity means, informally, that if we replace the "input" types (including those in Γ) in a derivable judgment with subtypes, then the judgment remains derivable with a smaller "output" type.

The downward monotonicity property (Lemma 3 below) is *almost* easy to prove by direct structural induction (simultaneously on all judgments). The cases involving expression-directed typechecking rules are all straightforward inductive steps; however, for the cases involving type-directed judgments, the induction steps do not go through. The difficulty is illustrated by the following cases. For derivations of the form

$$\frac{\tau_1 :: n \Rightarrow \tau_2}{\tau_1^* :: n \Rightarrow \tau_2^*} \qquad \frac{\Gamma \vdash \bar{x}\ \mathtt{in}\ \tau_1 \to e : \tau_2}{\Gamma \vdash \bar{x}\ \mathtt{in}\ \tau_1^* \to e : \tau_2^*}$$

we are stuck: knowing that $\tau_1' <: \tau_1^*$ does not necessarily tell us anything about a subtyping relationship between τ_1' and τ_1. For example, if $\tau_1' = aa$ and $\tau_1 = a$, then we have $aa <: a^*$ but not $aa <: a$. Instead, we need to proceed by an analysis of the semantics of regular expression types and subtyping.

We briefly sketch the argument, which involves an excursion into the theory of regular languages over partially ordered alphabets. Here, the "alphabet" is the set of atomic types and the regular sets are the sets of sequences of atomic types that are subtypes of a type τ. The *homomorphic extension* of a (possibly partial) function $h : \mathit{Atom} \rightharpoonup \mathit{Type}$ on atomic types is defined as

$$\hat{h}(()) = () \qquad \hat{h}(\alpha) = h(\alpha) \qquad \hat{h}(\tau^*) = \hat{h}(\tau)^*$$
$$\hat{h}(\tau_1, \tau_2) = \hat{h}(\tau_1), \hat{h}(\tau_2) \quad \hat{h}(\tau_1|\tau_2) = \hat{h}(\tau_1)|\hat{h}(\tau_2) \quad \hat{h}(X) = \hat{h}(E(X))$$

(Note again that this definition is well-founded, since top-level type variables cannot be expanded indefinitely.) If h is partial, then $\hat{h}$ is defined only on types whose atoms are in $\mathrm{dom}(h)$. We can then show the following general property of partial homomorphic extensions. Detailed proofs are in a companion technical report [4].

Lemma 2. *If $h : \mathit{Atom} \rightharpoonup \mathit{Type}$ is downward monotonic, then its homomorphic extension $\hat{h} : \mathit{Type} \rightharpoonup \mathit{Type}$ is downward monotonic.*

Lemma 3 (Downward monotonicity). *(1) If $\tau_1 :: n \Rightarrow \tau_2$ and $\tau_1' <: \tau_1$ then $\tau_1' :: n \Rightarrow \tau_2'$ for some $\tau_2' <: \tau_2$. (2) If $\Gamma \Vdash e : \tau$ and $\Gamma' <: \Gamma$ then $\Gamma' \Vdash e : \tau'$ for some $\tau' <: \tau$. (3) If $\Gamma \Vdash \bar{x} \;\mathtt{in}\; \tau_1 \to e : \tau_2$ and $\Gamma' <: \Gamma$ and $\tau_1' <: \tau_1$ then $\Gamma' \Vdash \bar{x} \;\mathtt{in}\; \tau_1' \to e : \tau_2'$ for some $\tau_2' <: \tau_2$.*

Proof (Sketch). We work in terms of the partial functions f_n, g_e, and $h_{\bar{x},e}$ from Theorem 1. The lemma follows from the downward monotonicity of f_n, g_e, and $h_{\bar{x},e}$ in their type and context arguments. For (1), we show that $f_n = \hat{F}_n$ where $F_n(\alpha) = n[\tau]$ if $\alpha = n[\tau]$, $F_n(\alpha) = ()$ otherwise; observe that F_n is total and monotone. For parts (2) and (3), we strengthen the induction hypothesis by showing that g_e is downward monotonic and that $h_{\bar{x},e}(\Gamma, -) = \hat{g}_e(\Gamma, x{:}(-))$ by simultaneous induction on the structure of algorithmic derivations. The downward monotonicity of $h_{\bar{x},e}(\Gamma, -)$ (which is needed in part (2)) follows again from Lemma 3.

Theorem 2 (Algorithmic Completeness). *(1) If $\Gamma \vdash e : \tau$ then there exists $\tau' <: \tau$ such that $\Gamma \Vdash e : \tau'$. (2) If $\Gamma \vdash \bar{x} \;\mathtt{in}\; \tau_1 \to e : \tau_2$ then there exists $\tau_2' <: \tau_2$ such that $\Gamma \Vdash \bar{x} \;\mathtt{in}\; \tau_1 \to e : \tau_2'$.*

Proof. Induction on the structure of derivations, appealing to Lemma 3 as necessary.

4 Update Language

We now introduce the core FLUX update language, which extends the syntax of queries with statements $s \in \mathit{Stmt}$, procedure names $P \in \mathit{PSym}$, tests $\phi \in \mathit{Test}$, directions $d \in \mathit{Dir}$, and two new cases for programs:

$$\begin{aligned} s &::= \mathtt{skip} \mid s; s' \mid \mathtt{if}\; e \;\mathtt{then}\; s \;\mathtt{else}\; s' \mid \mathtt{let}\; x = e \;\mathtt{in}\; s \mid P(\bar{e}) \\ &\mid \mathtt{insert}\; e \mid \mathtt{delete} \mid \mathtt{rename}\; n \mid \mathtt{snapshot}\; x \;\mathtt{in}\; s \mid \phi?s \mid d[s] \\ \phi &::= n \mid * \mid \mathtt{bool} \mid \mathtt{string} \qquad d ::= \mathtt{left} \mid \mathtt{right} \mid \mathtt{children} \mid \mathtt{iter} \\ p &::= \cdots \mid \mathtt{update}\; s : \tau \Rightarrow \tau' \mid \mathtt{declare\;procedure}\; P(\bar{x} : \bar{\tau}) : \tau \Rightarrow \tau' \;\{s\};\; p \end{aligned}$$

$$\boxed{\sigma; v \vdash s \Rightarrow^{\mathtt{U}} v'}$$

$$\frac{\sigma \vdash e \Rightarrow v}{\sigma;\, ()\, \vdash \mathtt{insert}\ e \Rightarrow^{\mathtt{U}} v} \quad \frac{\sigma[x := v]; v \vdash s \Rightarrow^{\mathtt{U}} v'}{\sigma; v \vdash \mathtt{snapshot}\ x\ \mathtt{in}\ s \Rightarrow^{\mathtt{U}} v'} \quad \frac{\sigma; v \vdash s \Rightarrow^{\mathtt{U}} v'}{\sigma; n[v] \vdash \mathtt{children}[s] \Rightarrow^{\mathtt{U}} n[v']}$$

$$\frac{\sigma;\, ()\, \vdash s \Rightarrow^{\mathtt{U}} v'}{\sigma; v \vdash \mathtt{left}[s] \Rightarrow^{\mathtt{U}} v', v} \quad \frac{\sigma; t_1 \vdash S \Rightarrow^{\mathtt{U}} v_1' \quad \sigma; v_2 \vdash \mathtt{iter}[s] \Rightarrow^{\mathtt{U}} v_2'}{\sigma; t_1, v_2 \vdash \mathtt{iter}[s] \Rightarrow^{\mathtt{U}} v_1', v_2'} \quad \frac{}{\sigma;\, ()\, \vdash \mathtt{iter}[s] \Rightarrow^{\mathtt{U}} ()}$$

Fig. 3. Operational semantics of selected updates

FLUX is based on a novel *functional*, *local* approach to updates which carefully controls side-effects; it is based on ideas from a database update language called CPL+ introduced by Liefke and Davidson [15]. Each update statement operates on a part of the mutable store (or database) that is "in focus". This locality helps ensure that updates are deterministic and relatively easy to typecheck.

Updates include standard constructs such as the no-op `skip`, sequential composition, conditionals, and `let`-binding. *Atomic updates* directly modify the focused part of the tree. The atomic update operations include insertion `insert` e, which inserts a value into an empty input; deletion `delete`, which deletes the focused input; and `rename` n, which renames the focused input provided it is a single tree.

Tests are operations $\phi?s$ that perform s if the type of the input focus matches the type test ϕ, otherwise do nothing. The node label test n matches tree type $n[\tau]$; the wildcard test $*$ matches tree types $m[\tau]$ for any m; and tests `bool` and `string` match the respective base types. The ? operator binds tightly; for example, $\phi?s; s' = (\phi?s); s'$.

The navigation updates $d[s]$ move the focus to another (smaller) part of the tree, and perform s on the new focus. The `left` and `right` directions focus on the empty sequence "before" or "after" the current focus, which may be a sequence. The `children` direction focuses on the child sequence of a tree. The `iter` direction focuses on each singular value in a sequence.

The `snapshot` operation `snapshot` x `in` s binds x to the input focus value and then applies an update s. Note that `snapshot` is the only way to read from the mutable store, and that the value of x is immutable, so no aliasing ensues.

We lack space to formalize the full semantics of updates. Figure 3 shows some illustrative operational semantics rules, defining the judgment $\sigma; v \vdash s \Rightarrow^{\mathtt{U}} v'$ whose informal meaning is "given immutable environment σ, s updates mutable store v to v'". Here, σ is an environment mapping (tree) variables to (tree) values. The remaining rules, along with additional explanation and examples, may be found in [3].

We distinguish between *singular* (unary) updates which apply only when the context is a tree value and *plural* (multi-ary) updates which apply to a sequence. Tests $\phi?s$ are always singular. The `children` operator applies a plural update to all of the children of a single node; the `iter` operator applies a singular update to all of the elements of a sequence. Other updates can be either singular or plural in different situations. Our type system tracks multiplicity as well as input and output types in order to ensure that updates are well-behaved.

$$\boxed{\Gamma \vdash^a \{\tau\}\ s\ \{\tau'\}}$$

$$\frac{}{\Gamma \vdash^a \{\tau\}\ \texttt{skip}\ \{\tau\}} \quad \frac{\Gamma \vdash^a \{\tau\}\ s\ \{\tau'\} \quad \Gamma \vdash^a \{\tau'\}\ s'\ \{\tau''\}}{\Gamma \vdash^a \{\tau\}\ s; s'\ \{\tau''\}} \quad \frac{\Gamma \vdash e : \tau \quad \Gamma, x{:}\tau \vdash^a \{\tau_1\}\ s\ \{\tau_2\}}{\Gamma \vdash^a \{\tau_1\}\ \texttt{let}\ x = e\ \texttt{in}\ s\ \{\tau_2\}}$$

$$\frac{\Gamma \vdash e : \texttt{bool} \quad \Gamma \vdash^a \{\tau\}\ s\ \{\tau_1\} \quad \Gamma \vdash^a \{\tau\}\ s'\ \{\tau_2\}}{\Gamma \vdash^a \{\tau\}\ \texttt{if}\ e\ \texttt{then}\ s\ \texttt{else}\ s'\ \{\tau_1|\tau_2\}} \quad \frac{\Gamma, x{:}\tau \vdash^a \{\tau\}\ s\ \{\tau'\}}{\Gamma \vdash^a \{\tau\}\ \texttt{snapshot}\ x\ \texttt{in}\ s\ \{\tau'\}}$$

$$\frac{\Gamma \vdash e : \tau}{\Gamma \vdash^* \{()\}\ \texttt{insert}\ e\ \{\tau\}} \quad \frac{}{\Gamma \vdash^a \{\tau\}\ \texttt{delete}\ \{()\}} \quad \frac{}{\Gamma \vdash^1 \{n'[\tau]\}\ \texttt{rename}\ n\ \{n[\tau]\}}$$

$$\frac{\alpha <: \phi \quad \Gamma \vdash^1 \{\alpha\}\ s\ \{\tau\}}{\Gamma \vdash^1 \{\alpha\}\ \phi?s\ \{\tau\}} \quad \frac{\alpha \not<: \phi}{\Gamma \vdash^1 \{\alpha\}\ \phi?s\ \{\alpha\}} \quad \frac{\Gamma \vdash^* \{\tau\}\ s\ \{\tau'\}}{\Gamma \vdash^1 \{n[\tau]\}\ \texttt{children}[s]\ \{n[\tau']\}}$$

$$\frac{\Gamma \vdash^* \{()\}\ s\ \{\tau'\}}{\Gamma \vdash^a \{\tau\}\ \texttt{left}[s]\ \{\tau', \tau\}} \quad \frac{\Gamma \vdash^* \{()\}\ s\ \{\tau'\}}{\Gamma \vdash^a \{\tau\}\ \texttt{right}[s]\ \{\tau, \tau'\}} \quad \frac{\Gamma \vdash_{\texttt{iter}} \{\tau\}\ s\ \{\tau'\}}{\Gamma \vdash^* \{\tau\}\ \texttt{iter}[s]\ \{\tau'\}}$$

$$\frac{\Gamma \vdash^a \{\tau_1\}\ s\ \{\tau_2'\} \quad \tau_2' <: \tau_2}{\Gamma \vdash^a \{\tau_1\}\ s\ \{\tau_2\}} \quad \frac{P(\overline{\tau}) : \sigma \Rightarrow \sigma_2 \in \Delta \quad \sigma_1 <: \sigma \quad \Gamma \vdash \overline{e} : \overline{\tau}}{\Gamma \vdash^a \{\sigma_1\}\ P(\overline{e})\ \{\sigma_2\}}$$

$$\boxed{\Gamma \vdash_{\texttt{iter}} \{\tau\}\ s\ \{\tau'\}}$$

$$\frac{}{\Gamma \vdash_{\texttt{iter}} \{()\}\ s\ \{()\}} \quad \frac{\Gamma \vdash^1 \{\alpha\}\ s\ \{\tau\}}{\Gamma \vdash_{\texttt{iter}} \{\alpha\}\ s\ \{\tau\}} \quad \frac{\Gamma \vdash_{\texttt{iter}} \{E(X)\}\ s\ \{\tau\}}{\Gamma \vdash_{\texttt{iter}} \{X\}\ s\ \{\tau\}} \quad \frac{\Gamma \vdash_{\texttt{iter}} \{\tau_1\}\ s\ \{\tau_2\}}{\Gamma \vdash_{\texttt{iter}} \{\tau_1^*\}\ s\ \{\tau_2^*\}}$$

$$\frac{\Gamma \vdash_{\texttt{iter}} \{\tau_1\}\ s\ \{\tau_1'\} \quad \Gamma \vdash_{\texttt{iter}} \{\tau_2\}\ s\ \{\tau_2'\}}{\Gamma \vdash_{\texttt{iter}} \{\tau_1, \tau_2\}\ s\ \{\tau_1', \tau_2'\}} \quad \frac{\Gamma \vdash_{\texttt{iter}} \{\tau_1\}\ s\ \{\tau_1'\} \quad \Gamma \vdash_{\texttt{iter}} \{\tau_2\}\ s\ \{\tau_2'\}}{\Gamma \vdash_{\texttt{iter}} \{\tau_1|\tau_2\}\ s\ \{\tau_1'|\tau_2'\}}$$

$$\boxed{\Gamma \vdash p\ \texttt{prog}}$$

$$\frac{\Gamma \vdash^* \{\tau_1\}\ s\ \{\tau_2\}}{\Gamma \vdash \texttt{update}\ s : \tau_1 \Rightarrow \tau_2\ \texttt{prog}} \quad \frac{P \text{ not declared in } p \qquad P(\overline{\tau}) : \sigma_1 \Rightarrow \sigma_2 \in \Delta \quad \Gamma, \overline{x}{:}\overline{\tau} \vdash^* \{\sigma_1\}\ s\ \{\sigma_2\} \quad \Gamma \vdash p\ \texttt{prog}}{\Gamma \vdash \texttt{declare procedure}\ P(\overline{x} : \overline{\tau}) : \tau_1 \Rightarrow \tau_2\ \{s\}\texttt{;}\ p\ \texttt{prog}}$$

Fig. 4. Update and additional program well-formedness rules

4.1 Type System

In typechecking updates, we extend the global declaration context Δ with procedure declarations:

$$\Delta ::= \cdots \mid \Delta, P(\overline{\tau}) : \tau_1 \Rightarrow \tau_2$$

There are two typing judgments for updates: singular well-formedness $\Gamma \vdash^1 \{\alpha\}\ s\ \{\tau'\}$ (that is, in type environment Γ, update s maps tree type α to type τ'), and plural well-formedness $\Gamma \vdash^* \{\tau\}\ s\ \{\tau'\}$ (that is, in type environment Γ, update s maps type τ to type τ'). Several of the rules are parameterized by a multiplicity $a \in \{1, *\}$. In addition, there is an auxiliary judgment $\Gamma \vdash_{\texttt{iter}} \{\tau\}\ s\ \{\tau'\}$ for typechecking iterations. The rules for update well-formedness are shown in Figure 4. We also need an auxiliary subtyping relation involving atomic types and tests: we say that $\alpha <: \phi$ if $[\![\alpha]\!] \subseteq [\![\phi]\!]$. This is characterized by the rules:

$$\frac{}{\texttt{bool} <: \texttt{bool}} \quad \frac{}{\texttt{string} <: \texttt{string}} \quad \frac{}{n[\tau] <: n} \quad \frac{}{n[\tau] <: *}$$

$$\dfrac{\dfrac{\dfrac{\vdots}{\vdash_{\mathtt{iter}} \{a[b[]^*, c[]]\}\ a?\mathtt{children}[s]\ \{a[(b[], c[])^*, c[]]\}} \quad \vdash_{\mathtt{iter}} \{d[]\}\ a?\mathtt{children}[s]\ \{d[]\}}{\vdash_{\mathtt{iter}} \{a[b[]^*, c[]], d[]\}\ a?\mathtt{children}[s]\ \{a[(b[], c[])^*, c[]], d[]\}}}{\vdash^* \{a[b[]^*, c[]], d[]\}\ \mathtt{iter}\ [a?\mathtt{children}[s]]\ \{a[(b[], c[])^*, c[]], d[]\}}$$

Fig. 5. Example partial update derivation, where $s = \mathtt{iter}\ [b?\mathtt{right\ insert}\ c[]]$

Remark 1. In most other XML update proposals (including XQuery! [12] and the draft XQuery Update Facility [2]), side-effecting update operations are treated as *expressions* that return `()`. Thus, we could perhaps typecheck such updates as expressions of type `()`. This would work fine as long as the values reachable from the free variables in Γ never change; however, the updates available in these languages can and do change the values of variables. Thus, to make this approach sound Γ may need to be updated to take these changes into account, perhaps using a judgment $\Gamma \vdash e : \mathtt{()} \mid \Gamma'$, where Γ' is the updated type environment reflecting the types of the variables after evaluating side-effects in e. This approach quickly becomes difficult to manage, especially if it is possible for different variables to "alias", or refer to overlapping parts of the data accessible from Γ, and adding side-effecting functions further complicates matters.

This is *not* the approach to update typechecking that is taken in FLUX. Updates are syntactically distinct from queries, and a FLUX update typechecking judgment such as $\Gamma \vdash^a \{\tau\}\ s\ \{\tau'\}$ assigns an update much richer type information that describes the type of part of the database before and after running s. The values of variables bound in Γ are immutable in the variable's scope, so their types do not need to be updated. Similarly, procedures must be annotated with expected input and output types. We do not believe that these annotations are burdensome in a database setting since a typical update procedure would be expected to preserve the (usually fixed) type of the database.

4.2 Examples

The interesting typing rules are those involving `iter`, tests, and `children`, `left`/`right`, and `insert`/`rename`/`delete`. The following example should help illustrate how the rules work for these constructs. Consider the high-level update:

```
insert after a/b value c[]
```

which can be translated to the following core FLUX statement:

$$\mathtt{iter}\ [a?\mathtt{children}\ [\mathtt{iter}\ [b?\ \mathtt{right\ insert}\ c[]]]]$$

Intuitively, this update inserts a c after every b under a top-level a. Now consider the input type $a[b[]^*, c[]], d[]$. Clearly, the output type *should* be $a[(b[], c[])^*, c[]], d[]$. To see how FLUX can assign this type to the update, consider the derivation shown in Figure 5.

As a second example, consider the procedure declaration

$$\begin{array}{l}\mathtt{declare\ procedure}\ \mathit{leafupd}(x{:}\mathtt{string}) : \mathit{Tree} \Rightarrow \mathit{Tree}\ \{\\ \quad \mathtt{iter}[\mathtt{children}[\mathtt{iter}[\mathit{leaf}?\mathtt{children}[\mathtt{delete};\ \mathtt{insert}\ x];\\ \qquad\qquad\qquad \mathit{node}?\mathtt{children}[\mathtt{iter}[\mathit{leafupd}(x)]]]]]\\ \};\end{array}$$

$$\cfrac{\cfrac{\cfrac{\cfrac{\cfrac{\cfrac{\cfrac{\mathit{leafupd}(\mathtt{string}) : \mathit{Tree} \Rightarrow \mathit{Tree} \in \Delta \quad \mathit{tree}[...] <: \mathit{Tree} \quad x{:}\mathtt{string} \vdash x : \mathtt{string}}{x{:}\mathtt{string} \vdash^1 \{\mathit{tree}[\mathit{leaf}[\mathtt{string}]|\mathit{node}[\mathit{Tree}^*]]\}\ \mathit{leafupd}(x)\ \{\mathit{Tree}\}}}{x{:}\mathtt{string} \vdash_{\mathtt{iter}} \{\mathit{tree}[\mathit{leaf}[\mathtt{string}]|\mathit{node}[\mathit{Tree}^*]]\}\ \mathit{leafupd}(x)\ \{\mathit{Tree}\}}}{x{:}\mathtt{string} \vdash_{\mathtt{iter}} \{\mathit{Tree}\}\ \mathit{leafupd}(x)\ \{\mathit{Tree}\}}}{x{:}\mathtt{string} \vdash_{\mathtt{iter}} \{\mathit{Tree}^*\}\ \mathit{leafupd}(x)\ \{\mathit{Tree}^*\}}}{x{:}\mathtt{string} \vdash^* \{\mathit{Tree}^*\}\ \mathtt{iter}[\mathit{leafupd}(x)]\ \{\mathit{Tree}^*\}}}{x{:}\mathtt{string} \vdash^1 \{\mathit{node}[\mathit{Tree}^*]\}\ \mathtt{children}[\mathtt{iter}[\mathit{leafupd}(x)]]\ \{\mathit{node}[\mathit{Tree}^*]\}}}{x{:}\mathtt{string} \vdash^1 \{\mathit{node}[\mathit{Tree}^*]\}\ \mathit{node}?\mathtt{children}[\mathtt{iter}[\mathit{leafupd}(x)]]\ \{\mathit{node}[\mathit{Tree}^*]\}}$$

Fig. 6. Partial derivation for body of *leafupd*

This procedure updates all leaves of a tree to x. As with the recursive query discussed in Section 3.2, this procedure requires subtyping to typecheck the recursive call. We also need subtyping to check that the return type of the expression matches the declaration. A partial typing derivation for part of the body of the procedure involving a recursive call is shown in Figure 6.

4.3 Algorithmic Completeness and Decidability

To prove update typechecking decidable, we must again carefully control the use of subsumption. The appropriate algorithmic typechecking judgment is defined as follows:

Definition 2 (Algorithmic derivations for updates). *The algorithmic typechecking judgments $\Gamma \blacktriangleright^a \{\tau\}\ s\ \{\tau'\}$ and $\Gamma \blacktriangleright_{\mathtt{iter}} \{\tau\}\ s\ \{\tau'\}$ are obtained by taking the rules in Figure 4, removing the subsumption rule, and replacing the procedure call rule with*

$$\frac{P(\overline{\sigma}) : \sigma \Rightarrow \sigma' \in \Delta \quad \tau <: \sigma \quad \Gamma \blacktriangleright \overline{e} : \overline{\tau} \quad \overline{\tau} <: \overline{\sigma}}{\Gamma \blacktriangleright^a \{\tau\}\ P(\overline{e})\ \{\sigma'\}}$$

Moreover, all subderivations of expression judgments in an algorithmic derivation of an update judgment must be algorithmic.

The proof of completeness of algorithmic update typechecking has the same structure as that for queries. Again, proof details are in the technical report [4].

Lemma 4 (Decidability for updates). *Let a, s be given. Then there exist computable functions $j_{a,s}$ and k_s such that:*

1. *$j_{a,s}(\Gamma, \tau_1)$ is the unique τ_2 such that $\Gamma \blacktriangleright^a \{\tau_1\}\ s\ \{\tau_2\}$, if it exists.*
2. *$k_s(\Gamma, \tau_1)$ is the unique τ_2 such that $\Gamma \blacktriangleright_{\mathtt{iter}} \{\tau_1\}\ s\ \{\tau_2\}$, if it exists.*

Theorem 3 (Algorithmic soundness for updates). *(1) If $\Gamma \blacktriangleright^* \{\tau\}\ s\ \{\tau'\}$ is derivable then $\Gamma \vdash^* \{\tau\}\ s\ \{\tau'\}$ is derivable. (2) If $\Gamma \blacktriangleright_{\mathtt{iter}} \{\tau\}\ e\ \{\tau'\}$ is derivable then $\Gamma \vdash_{\mathtt{iter}} \{\tau\}\ e\ \{\tau'\}$ is derivable.*

Lemma 5 (Downward monotonicity for updates). *(1) If $\Gamma \blacktriangleright^a \{\tau_1\}\ s\ \{\tau_2\}$ and $\Gamma' <: \Gamma$ and $\tau_1' <: \tau_1$ then $\Gamma' \blacktriangleright^a \{\tau_1'\}\ s\ \{\tau_2'\}$ for some $\tau_2' <: \tau_2$. (2) If $\Gamma \blacktriangleright_{\mathtt{iter}} \{\tau_1\}\ s\ \{\tau_2\}$ and $\Gamma' <: \Gamma$ and $\tau_1' <: \tau_1$ then $\Gamma' \blacktriangleright_{\mathtt{iter}} \{\tau_1'\}\ s\ \{\tau_2'\}$ for some $\tau_2' <: \tau_2$.*

Theorem 4 (Algorithmic completeness for updates). *(1) If* $\Gamma \vdash^{a} \{\tau_1\}\ s\ \{\tau_2\}$ *then there exists* $\tau_2' <: \tau_2$ *such that* $\Gamma \vdash\!\!\blacktriangleright^{a} \{\tau_1\}\ s\ \{\tau_2'\}$. *(2) If* $\Gamma \vdash_{\mathtt{iter}} \{\tau_1\}\ s\ \{\tau_2\}$ *then there exists* $\tau_2' <: \tau_2$ *such that* $\Gamma \vdash\!\!\blacktriangleright_{\mathtt{iter}} \{\tau_1\}\ s\ \{\tau_2'\}$.

5 Related and Future Work

This work is directly motivated by our interest in using regular expression types for XML updates, using richer typing rules for iteration as found in μXQ [5]. Fernandez, Siméon and Wadler [8] earlier considered an XML query language with more precise typechecking for iteration, but this proposal required additional type annotations; we only require annotations on function or procedure declarations.

For brevity, the core languages in this paper omitted many features of full XQuery, such as the descendant, attribute, parent and sibling axes. The attribute axis is straightforward since attributes always have text content. In μXQ, the descendant axis was supported by assigning $\bar{x}$/`descendant-or-self` the type formed by taking the union of all (finitely many) tree types that are reachable from the type of $\bar{x}$. XQuery handles other axes by discarding type information. Our algorithmic completeness proof still appears to work if these axes are added with XQuery- or μXQ-style typing rules.

FLUX's functional, local approach to updates draws on ideas first explored in the CPL+ database update language by Liefke and Davidson [15] (unfortunately this work is not well-known even in the database community). This approach is fundamentally different from the other XML update language proposals of which we are aware (such as XQuery! [11] and the draft W3C XQuery Update Facility [2]). Most such proposals contemplate adding unrestricted side-effecting update operations as additional XQuery expressions, which would undermine many of XQuery's advantages as a purely functional language, such as clear semantics and equational optimization laws. Moreover, to the best of our knowledge, static typechecking and subtyping have not even been considered for these languages and seem likely to encounter difficulties for reasons we outlined in Section 4.1 and discussed in more depth in [3].

On the other hand, XQuery! and related proposals are clearly more expressive than FLUX, and have been incorporated into mature XQuery implementations such as Galax [7]. Although we currently have a prototype that implements the core typechecking algorithm described here as well as the operational semantics described in [3], further work is needed to develop a robust implementation inside an XML database system and evaluate scalability, optimization, and high-level update language design issues.

6 Conclusions

Static typechecking is important in a database setting because type (or "schema") information is useful for optimizing queries and avoiding expensive run-time checks or re-validation. The XQuery standard, like other XML programming languages, employs regular expression types and subtyping. However, its approach to typechecking iteration constructs is imprecise, due to the use of "factoring" which discards information about the order of elements in the result of an iteration operation such as a `for`-loop. While this imprecision may not be harmful for typical queries, it is disastrous for typechecking updates that are supposed to preserve the type of the database.

In this paper we have considered more precise typing disciplines for XQuery-style iterative queries and updates in the core languages μXQ and FLUX respectively. In order to ensure that these type systems are well-behaved and that typechecking is decidable, it is important to prove the completeness of an algorithmic presentation of typechecking in which the use of subtyping rules is limited so that typechecking remains syntax-directed. We have shown how to do so for the core μXQ and FLUX languages, and believe the proof technique will extend to handle other features not included in the paper. These results provide a solid foundation for subtyping in XML queries and updates.

Acknowledgments. Thanks to Peter Buneman and Stijn Vansummeren for many discussions on update languages. The author was supported by EPSRC grant R37476.

References

1. Benzaken, V., Castagna, G., Frisch, A.: CDuce: An XML-centric general-purpose language. In: ICFP 2003: Proceedings of the eighth ACM SIGPLAN international conference on Functional programming, pp. 51–63. ACM Press, New York, NY, USA (2003)
2. Chamberlin, D., Florescu, D., Robie, J.: XQuery update facility. W3C Working Draft (July 2006), `http://www.w3c.org/TR/xqupdate/`
3. Cheney, J.: LUX: A lightweight, statically typed XML update language. In: ACM SIGPLAN Workshop on Programming Language Technology and XML (PLAN-X 2007), pp. 25–36 (2007)
4. Cheney, J.: Regular expression subtyping for XML query and update languages. Technical report, arXiv.org (2008), arXiv:0801.0714v1
5. Colazzo, D., Ghelli, G., Manghi, P., Sartiani, C.: Static analysis for path correctness of XML queries. J. Funct. Program. 16(4-5), 621–661 (2006)
6. Draper, D., Fankhauser, P., Fernández, M., Malhotra, A., Rose, K., Rys, M., Siméon, J., Wadler, P.: XQuery 1.0 and XPath 2.0 formal semantics. W3C Recommendation (January 2007), `http://www.w3.org/TR/xquery-semantics/`
7. Fernández, M.F., Siméon, J., Choi, B., Marian, A., Sur, G.: Implementing XQuery 1.0: The Galax experience. In: VLDB 2003, pp. 1077–1080 (2003)
8. Fernández, M.F., Siméon, J., Wadler, P.: A semi-monad for semi-structured data. In: Van den Bussche, J., Vianu, V. (eds.) ICDT 2001. LNCS, vol. 1973, pp. 263–300. Springer, Heidelberg (2001)
9. Frisch, A.: OCaml + XDuce. In: ICFP 2006: Proceedings of the eleventh ACM SIGPLAN international conference on Functional programming, pp. 192–200. ACM Press, New York, NY, USA (2006)
10. Gapeyev, V., Garillot, F., Pierce, B.C.: Statically typed document transformation: An Xtatic experience. In: Castagna, G., Raghavachari, M. (eds.) PLAN-X, BRICS, pp. 2–13 (2006)
11. Ghelli, G., Rose, K., Siméon, J.: Commutativity analysis in XML update languages. In: Schwentick, T., Suciu, D. (eds.) ICDT 2007. LNCS, vol. 4353, pp. 374–388. Springer, Heidelberg (2006)
12. Ghelli, G., Re, C., Siméon, J.: XQuery!: An XML query language with side effects. In: Grust, T., Höpfner, H., Illarramendi, A., Jablonski, S., Mesiti, M., Müller, S., Patranjan, P.-L., Sattler, K.-U., Spiliopoulou, M., Wijsen, J. (eds.) EDBT 2006. LNCS, vol. 4254, pp. 178–191. Springer, Heidelberg (2006)
13. Hosoya, H., Pierce, B.C.: XDuce: A statically typed XML processing language. ACM Trans. Internet Technology 3(2), 117–148 (2003)

14. Hosoya, H., Vouillon, J., Pierce, B.C.: Regular expression types for XML. ACM Trans. Program. Lang. Syst. 27(1), 46–90 (2005)
15. Liefke, H., Davidson, S.B.: Specifying updates in biomedical databases. In: SSDBM 1999, pp. 44–53 (1999)
16. Pierce, B.C.: Types and Programming Languages. MIT Press, Cambridge (2002)

A Theory of Hygienic Macros

David Herman and Mitchell Wand

College of Computer and Information Science
Northeastern University
Boston, MA 02115
{dherman,wand}@ccs.neu.edu

Abstract. Hygienic macro systems, such as Scheme's, automatically rename variables to prevent unintentional variable capture—in short, they "just work." Yet hygiene has never been formally presented as a *specification* rather than an algorithm. According to folklore, the definition of hygienic macro expansion hinges on the preservation of alpha-equivalence. But the only known notion of alpha-equivalence for programs with macros depends on the results of macro expansion! We break this circularity by introducing explicit binding specifications into the syntax of macro definitions, permitting a definition of alpha-equivalence independent of expansion. We define a semantics for a first-order subset of Scheme-like macros and prove hygiene as a consequence of confluence.

The subject of macro hygiene is not at all decided, and more research is needed to precisely state what hygiene formally means and [precisely which] assurances it provides.

—Oleg Kiselyov [1]

1 What Are Hygienic Macros?

Programming languages with hygienic macros automatically rename variables to prevent subtle but common bugs arising from unintentional variable capture—the experience of the practical programmer is that hygienic macros "just work." Numerous macro expansion algorithms for Scheme have been developed over many years [2,3,4,5,6], and the Scheme standard has included hygienic macros since R^4RS [7].

Yet to date, a formal specification for hygiene has been an elusive goal. Intuitively, macro researchers have always understood hygiene to mean *preserving* α*-equivalence*. In particular, performing an α-conversion of a bound variable should not result in a macro expansion that accidentally captures the renamed variable. But this idea has never been made precise.

Why should such a simple idea be so hard to formalize? The problem is this: since the only known binding forms in Scheme are the core forms, the binding structure of a Scheme expression does not become apparent until after it has been fully expanded to core Scheme. Thus α-equivalence is only well-defined for Scheme programs that have been fully expanded, with no remaining instances of

S. Drossopoulou (Ed.): ESOP 2008, LNCS 4960, pp. 48–62, 2008.

macros. So if the conventional wisdom is correct, the definition of hygienic macro expansion relies on α-equivalence, but the definition of α-equivalence relies on the results of macro expansion! This circularity is clearly paradoxical, and the definition of hygiene has consequently remained a mystery.

But in practice, well-behaved macros follow regular binding disciplines consistently, independent of their particular expansion. For example, Scheme's `let` construct can be macro-defined using `lambda`, yet programmers rely on knowing the binding structure of `let` without actually thinking about its expansion. If the semantics of macros only had access to this binding structure in such a way that we could reason formally about the scope of Scheme programs without resorting to operational reasoning about their expansion, we could cut the Gordian knot and specify both α-equivalence and hygiene in an intuitive and precise way.

To put it more succinctly, we argue that *the binding structure of a macro is a part of its interface.* In this paper, we make that interface explicit as a type annotation. Our type system is novel but incorporates ideas both from the shape types of Culpepper and Felleisen [8] and nominal datatypes of Gabbay and Pitts [9]. With the aid of these type annotations, we define a notion of α-equivalence for Scheme programs with *first-order* macros, i.e., macros that do not expand into subsequent macro definitions, and prove hygiene as a consequence of confluence. We discuss higher-order macros as future work in Section 9.

The organization of this paper is as follows. The next section introduces λ_m, a Scheme-like language with typed macros. Section 3 defines the α-equivalence relation for λ_m, and Section 4 introduces the macro type system. Section 5 defines the macro expansion semantics. The next two sections present the key correctness theorems: type soundness in Section 6 and hygiene in Section 7. In Section 8 we present a front end for parsing S-expressions as λ_m expressions. Section 9 concludes with a discussion of related and future work.

2 λ_m: An Intermediate Language for Modeling Macros

In Scheme, macro expansion transforms S-expressions into a small, fixed set of core forms which the underlying compiler or interpreter is designed to recognize. Expansion eliminates uses of macros by translating them according to their definitions, repeating this process recursively until there are no derived forms left to translate. Thus macro expansion consumes programs in surface syntax:

```
(let ((x (sqrt 2)))
  (let ((y (exp x)))
    (lambda (f)
      (f y))))
```

and produces programs with only the internal forms recognized by the compiler:

$$((\lambda x.\, ((\lambda y.\, \lambda f.\, f\ y)\ (exp\ x)))\ (sqrt\ 2))$$

We use a distinct syntax for core forms to highlight the fact that they indicate the completion of macro expansion. We use S-expressions not simply to describe

Scheme, but as a simple and general model of tree-structured syntax. Because macro expansion operates on partially expanded programs, which may contain both core forms and S-expressions yet to be expanded, a model for macros must incorporate both syntactic elements.

To that end, we define an intermediate language for modeling macro expansion, called λ_m. The core forms are based on the λ-calculus, but with additional forms for local binding of macro definitions and macro application.[1]

$$
\begin{aligned}
e &::= v \mid \lambda v.\, e \mid e\ e \mid \texttt{let syntax}\ x\ \texttt{=}\ m\ \texttt{in}\ e\ \texttt{end} \mid op[\![s]\!]^{\sigma} \\
v &::= x \mid ?a \\
op &::= v \mid m \\
m &::= \texttt{macro}\ p : \sigma \Rightarrow e \\
p &::= ?a \mid \texttt{(}\overline{p}\texttt{)} \\
s &::= e \mid op \mid \texttt{(}\overline{s}\texttt{)}
\end{aligned}
$$

Unlike the surface syntax of Scheme, the syntax of λ_m consists not just of S-expressions but also expressions e, whose syntactic structure is fixed and manifest. Of course, macros admit arbitrary syntactic extension in the form of S-expressions, so S-expressions s appear in the grammar as the arguments to macro applications. Here too, though, the syntactic structure is made apparent via a *shape type annotation* σ. We return in detail to shape types in Section 2.2. Variables v come in two sorts: *program variables* x, which are standard, and *pattern variables* $?a$, which are bound in macro argument patterns and used in their definitions. Thus, for example, $\lambda x.\, x$ is a traditional λ-abstraction, but $\lambda ?a.\, ?a$ might appear in the body of a macro as a λ-abstraction whose bound variable will be provided from one of the macro's inputs. Macro operators op are either variable references or macro expressions. Macros m contain a pattern p, a type annotation σ, and a template expression e. A pattern p is a tree of pattern variables (assumed not to contain duplicates). Finally, an S-expression s is a tree of expressions or macro operators. The latter form is used to pass macros as arguments to other macros.

The syntax of λ_m may seem unfamiliar compared to the simple S-expressions of Scheme. After all, Scheme applications $\texttt{(}\overline{s}\texttt{)}$ look different from λ_m applications $op[\![s]\!]^{\sigma}$ and in Scheme, pattern variables are indistinguishable from program variables. However, given shape-annotated macro definitions, we can easily parse surface S-expression syntax into λ_m. We describe this process in Section 8.

2.1 Tree Locations

In order to address context-sensitive properties of terms, we use the mechanism of *tree locations* [10] to identify subterms by their position. Tree structures in our language take the general form $t ::= L \mid \texttt{(}\overline{t}\texttt{)}$ for some non-terminal of leaves L. For any such tree structure, we can select a subtree as a path from the root of the tree to the node containing the subtree. A *tree location* ℓ is an element of $\mathbb{N}^*$. Given a tree t, the subtree $t.\ell$ is defined by $t.\epsilon = t$ and $\texttt{(}\overline{t}\texttt{)}.i\,\ell = t_i.\ell$.

[1] Throughout this paper we use an overbar notation ($\overline{x}$) to represent sequences.

2.2 Binding Specifications

Macro definitions and applications in λ_m are explicitly annotated with shape types. The purpose of these annotations is to fix the structure of macros, including their scoping structure. For example, the following macro m matches four pattern variables, $?a, ?b, ?e_1$, and $?e_2$:

$$\texttt{macro}\ \texttt{(}?a\ ?b\ ?e_1\ ?e_2\texttt{)} : \texttt{(}\langle 0\rangle\ \langle 1\rangle\ \textsf{expr}^0\ \textsf{expr}^{0,1}\texttt{)}$$
$$\Rightarrow \lambda ?a.\,((\lambda ?b.\,?e_2)\ ?e_1)$$

The shape type $\sigma = \texttt{(}\langle 0\rangle\ \langle 1\rangle\ \textsf{expr}^0\ \textsf{expr}^{0,1}\texttt{)}$ tells us that pattern variables $?a$ and $?b$ are placed in binding positions in the macro template, pattern variable $?e_1$ is used in the scope of $?a$ alone, and $?e_1$ appears inside the scope of both $?a$ and $?b$. Maintaining the bindings in order—$?a$ is bound outside, $?b$ inside—makes it possible to resolve references unambiguously even if both $?a$ and $?b$ are instantiated with the same variable. For example, this tells us that $m[\![\texttt{(}x\ x\ x\ x\texttt{)}]\!]^\sigma =_\alpha m[\![\texttt{(}x\ y\ x\ y\texttt{)}]\!]^\sigma \neq_\alpha m[\![\texttt{(}x\ y\ y\ x\texttt{)}]\!]^\sigma$.

Shape types are defined by the following grammar:

$$\tau ::= \textsf{expr} \mid \sigma \rightarrow \textsf{expr}$$
$$\beta ::= \langle \ell\rangle \mid \textsf{expr}^{\ell,\overline{\ell}}$$
$$\sigma ::= \tau \mid \beta \mid \texttt{(}\overline{\sigma}\texttt{)}$$

The base types τ include the type of expressions and the types of macros, which receive S-expressions as arguments and produce expressions. Binding types β express the scope of S-expressions. A binder type $\langle \ell\rangle$ corresponds to a variable in binding position. The location ℓ represents the position in the macro S-expression where the binder occurs. A body type $\textsf{expr}^{\ell,\overline{\ell}}$ corresponds to an expression inside the scope of one or more binders; the locations $\overline{\ell}$ indicate the positions in the macro S-expression of each of the binders that are in scope, in the order in which they are bound, outermost first.

2.3 From S-Expressions to the Lambda Calculus

Once a λ_m program has been fully expanded, it consists only of core forms, which in our simple model corresponds to the untyped λ-calculus. We say a program is in *expansion-normal form* (ENF) if it obeys the familiar grammar:

$$e ::= x \mid \lambda x.\,e \mid e\ e$$

If ENF is the internal language of the compiler or evaluator, then S-expressions are the surface language used by the programmer. The syntax of the surface language is a restricted subset of λ_m S-expressions:

$$s ::= x \mid \texttt{(}\overline{s}\texttt{)}$$

Thus we can envision an idealized pipeline for the evaluation of programs with macros as shown in Figure 1.

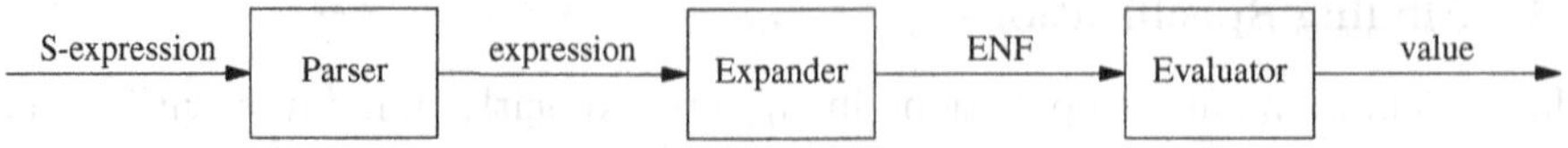

Fig. 1. Pipeline for an idealized evaluator with macro expansion

In real Scheme implementations, parsing is interleaved with macro expansion as the syntactic roles of expressions gradually become apparent. This is different from our idealized pipeline, which completely separates parsing from expansion. This is due to the fact that complete type information makes it possible to parse an S-expression before macro expansion. We return to the front end in Section 8.

3 Alpha-Equivalence

We follow Gabbay and Pitts [9] in using variable swapping to define α-equivalence. Swapping is defined by:

$$\begin{array}{lll} (v_1\ v_2) \cdot v_1 &= v_2 & \\ (v_1\ v_2) \cdot v_2 &= v_1 & \\ (v_1\ v_2) \cdot v &= v & \text{if } v \notin \{v_1, v_2\} \\ (v_1\ v_2) \cdot \lambda v.\, e &= \lambda((v_1\ v_2) \cdot v).\, ((v_1\ v_2) \cdot e) & \\ (v_1\ v_2) \cdot \textbf{(}\overline{s}\textbf{)} &= \textbf{(}\overline{(v_1\ v_2) \cdot s}\textbf{)} & \\ \textit{etc.} & & \end{array}$$

The *support* of a term is the set of variables it contains:

$$\begin{array}{ll} \mathit{supp}(v) &= \{v\} \\ \mathit{supp}(\lambda v.\, e) &= \{v\} \cup \mathit{supp}(e) \\ \mathit{supp}(\textbf{(}\overline{s}\textbf{)}) &= \bigcup_i \mathit{supp}(s_i) \\ \textit{etc.} & \end{array}$$

A variable v is fresh with respect to a finite set of terms S, written $v \# S$, if for all terms $s \in S$, $v \notin \mathit{supp}(s)$. We write $v \# s_1, \ldots, s_n$ where $n \geq 1$ to mean $v \# \{s_1, \ldots, s_n\}$.

We also define the notion of simultaneously introducing multiple, distinct fresh variables by overloading the freshness relation for variable mappings. If S is a set of terms and Z is a mapping $\{\overline{\ell \mapsto z}\}$ then we write $Z \# S$ to mean

$$\forall \ell \in \mathit{dom}(Z) \,.\, Z(\ell) \# S \text{ and } \forall \ell, \ell' \in \mathit{dom}(Z) \,.\, Z(\ell) = Z(\ell') \Rightarrow \ell = \ell'$$

We identify the binders of a form by collecting the set of binding positions identified in the form's shape type. The function $\mathit{bp}(\sigma)$ produces the set of binding positions of a shape type, and the function $\mathit{pp}(p)$ identifies the positions of pattern variables in a macro pattern.

$$\begin{array}{ll} \mathit{bp}(\textbf{(}\overline{\sigma}\textbf{)}) &= \bigcup_i \{i\,\ell \mid \ell \in \mathit{bp}(\sigma_i)\} \\ \mathit{bp}(\langle \ell \rangle) &= \{\epsilon\} \\ \mathit{bp}(\textbf{expr}^{\overline{\ell}}) &= \mathit{bp}(\tau) = \emptyset \end{array} \qquad \begin{array}{ll} \mathit{pp}(\textbf{(}\overline{p}\textbf{)}) &= \bigcup_i \{i\,\ell \mid \ell \in \mathit{pp}(p_i)\} \\ \mathit{pp}(?a) &= \{\epsilon\} \end{array}$$

We can use bp to compute the set of binders of a macro application $binders(\sigma, s)$ as a mapping from binding positions ℓ to their actual binders $s.\ell$:

$$binders(\sigma, s) = \{\ell \mapsto s.\ell \mid \ell \in bp(\sigma)\}$$

3.1 Shape-Directed Conversion

Consider the following Scheme expression, with all occurrences of the variable `x` labelled for the sake of explanation.

$$\texttt{(let ((x}^1\ \texttt{x}^2\texttt{))}$$
$$\quad \texttt{(x}^3\ \texttt{(lambda (x}^4\texttt{) x}^5\texttt{)))}$$

In order to α-convert $\texttt{x}^1$ to a fresh name `z`, we must be careful to rename only the occurrences of `x` bound by $\texttt{x}^1$, which in this example includes only $\texttt{x}^3$. Because macros may have arbitrary shape, a structural induction on the S-expression would be insufficient to recognize which instances of `x` were which. Instead, we define a notion of *shape-directed conversion* $(Z\ X)^\sigma \cdot s$, which follows the structure of a form's binding specification rather than its syntax.

$$\begin{array}{llll}
(Z\ X)^{\tau} & \cdot\ s & = s & \\
(Z\ X)^{\langle \ell \rangle} & \cdot\ x & = z & \text{if } z = Z(\ell) \\
(Z\ X)^{\langle \ell \rangle} & \cdot\ v & = v & \text{if } \ell \notin dom(Z) \\
(Z\ X)^{\mathsf{expr}^{\ell,\overline{\ell'}}} & \cdot\ e & = (z\ x) \cdot (Z\ X)^{\mathsf{expr}^{\overline{\ell'}}} \cdot e & \text{if } z = Z(\ell) \text{ and } x = X(\ell) \\
(Z\ X)^{\mathsf{expr}^{\ell,\overline{\ell'}}} & \cdot\ e & = (Z\ X)^{\mathsf{expr}^{\overline{\ell'}}} \cdot e & \text{if } \ell \notin dom(Z) \\
(Z\ X)^{\mathbf{(}\overline{\sigma}\mathbf{)}} & \cdot\ \mathbf{(}\overline{s}\mathbf{)} & = \mathbf{(}\overline{(Z\ X)^{\sigma_i} \cdot s_i}\mathbf{)} & \\
(Z\ X)^{\mathbf{(}\overline{\sigma}\mathbf{)}} & \cdot\ ?a & = ?a &
\end{array}$$

The key to the definition of shape-directed conversion is the fourth rule, which swaps a bound variable with its corresponding fresh name in an expression within its scope. Because body types order their bound variables from the outside in, occurrences of the variable x are renamed to z only after performing all inner renamings, in case x is shadowed by an inner binding.

3.2 Alpha-Equivalence

The definition of α-equivalence appears in Figure 2. The first four rules parallel the rules of α-equivalence for the λ-calculus, but note that we do not convert pattern variables $?a$ used in binding positions. The rule for macro bindings converts the macro name and proceeds inductively. The next rule is key: to compare two macro applications, their operators must be equivalent, and their arguments must be equivalent once we α-convert their bound variables. Checking these involves several conditions. First, the two expressions must bind exactly the same pattern variables, if any; we ensure this by requiring that at any binding position ℓ, $s.\ell$ binds an ordinary program variable x if and only if $s'.\ell$ binds an ordinary program variable x'. We collect the binder mappings X and X' for the

$$\frac{}{v =_\alpha v} \qquad \frac{e =_\alpha e'}{\lambda ?a.\, e =_\alpha \lambda ?a.\, e'} \qquad \frac{z \# e, e' \quad (z\ x) \cdot e =_\alpha (z\ x') \cdot e'}{\lambda x.\, e =_\alpha \lambda x'.\, e'} \qquad \frac{e_1 =_\alpha e_1' \quad e_2 =_\alpha e_2'}{e_1\ e_2 =_\alpha e_1'\ e_2'}$$

$$\frac{m =_\alpha m' \qquad z \# e, m, e', m' \quad (z\ x) \cdot e =_\alpha (z\ x') \cdot e'}{\texttt{let syntax } x \texttt{ = } m \texttt{ in } e \texttt{ end} =_\alpha \texttt{let syntax } x' \texttt{ = } m' \texttt{ in } e' \texttt{ end}}$$

$$\frac{\begin{array}{c} op =_\alpha op' \\ \forall \ell \in bp(\sigma) \,.\, \exists x = s.\ell \Leftrightarrow \exists x' = s'.\ell \\ X = binders(\sigma, s) \qquad X' = binders(\sigma, s') \\ Z = \{\ell \mapsto z \mid \ell \in bp(\sigma), \exists x = s.\ell\} \qquad Z \# s, s' \\ (Z\ X)^\sigma \cdot s =_\alpha (Z\ X')^\sigma \cdot s' \end{array}}{op[\![s]\!]^\sigma =_\alpha op'[\![s']\!]^\sigma}$$

$$\frac{\begin{array}{c} \forall \ell \in pp(p) \,.\, p.\ell = ?a_\ell \text{ and } p'.\ell = ?a'_\ell \text{ and } ?z_\ell \# e, e' \\ \forall \ell, \ell' \in pp(p) \,.\, ?z_\ell = ?z_{\ell'} \Rightarrow \ell = \ell' \\ (\overline{?z_\ell\ ?a_\ell}) \cdot p = (\overline{?z_\ell\ ?a'_\ell}) \cdot p' \\ (\overline{?z_\ell\ ?a_\ell}) \cdot e =_\alpha (\overline{?z_\ell\ ?a'_\ell}) \cdot e' \end{array}}{(\texttt{macro } p : \sigma \Rightarrow e) =_\alpha (\texttt{macro } p' : \sigma \Rightarrow e')} \qquad \frac{\forall i \,.\, s_i =_\alpha s'_i}{(\overline{s}) =_\alpha (\overline{s'})}$$

Fig. 2. Alpha-equivalence of λ_m programs

two respective forms, and we choose a mapping of fresh binders Z, being careful not to α-convert at locations that bind pattern variables. Finally, we compare the α-converted arguments s and s'. The rule for comparing macros is somewhat simpler. We choose fresh pattern variables $?z_\ell$ to replace the pattern variables in either macro, and compare both their patterns and templates. Finally, compound S-expressions are compared inductively.

3.3 Instantiation

Identifying binders in a shape type positionally is convenient for the theory, since it results in one canonical representation for each distinct type. However, for some operations it is necessary to identify binders by name. We present an alternate form of shape types $\hat{\sigma}$ which use variables rather than locations to represent their binding structure:

$$\hat{\beta} ::= \langle v \rangle \mid \textsf{expr}^{v,\overline{v}}$$
$$\hat{\sigma} ::= \tau \mid \hat{\beta} \mid (\overline{\hat{\sigma}})$$

We write $\hat{\sigma} = \sigma[X]$ to denote the instantiation of a nameless shape type σ with the concrete variable names of a variable mapping X.

The free and bound variables of an expression are computed via shape-directed generalizations of the standard operations $FV(s, \hat{\sigma})$ and $BV(s, \hat{\sigma})$ (omitted for space). The following theorem ensures that we can always replace an S-expression with an α-equivalent S-expression with fresh binders.

Theorem 1 (Freshness). *Let s be an S-expression and S be a finite set of S-expressions. Then there exists an S-expression $s' =_\alpha s$ such that $BV(s', \hat{\sigma}) \# S$.*

Proof. Induction on the structure of s. For each binding in s, choose fresh binders that are not in $supp(S)$.

It easy to show that if e and e' are in ENF, then $e =_\alpha e'$ if and only if the two expressions are α-equivalent as λ-terms.

4 Type Checking

The job of the type checker is to confirm that each macro definition conforms to its specification and that each use of a macro conforms to its interface. Excerpts of the type checking algorithm are presented in Figure 3. The type system uses two environments to track the two dimensions of binding in λ_m. The *program environment* $\Gamma ::= \bullet \mid \Gamma[v := \tau]$ tracks the scope of variables from binding forms such as λ and `let syntax`. The *pattern environment* $\Phi \in \{\bullet\} \cup PVar \to Shape$ tracks the binding of pattern variables for the current macro (if any). This environment is constructed by pairing the structure of a macro pattern p with an instantiation of the macro's type annotation:

$$penv(\mathbf{(}\overline{p}\mathbf{)}, \mathbf{(}\overline{\hat{\sigma}}\mathbf{)}) = \bigcup_i penv(p_i, \hat{\sigma}_i)$$
$$penv(?a, \hat{\sigma}) = \{?a \mapsto \hat{\sigma}\}$$

The type rule [T-MacDef] permits only non-nested macro definitions by requiring an empty pattern environment. Rule [T-MacApp] checks macro arguments with their annotated type instantiated with the actual binders. Rule [T-PBody] checks a pattern variable reference with a body type, ensuring that all the necessary pattern variables have been bound in the proper order. Rule [T-PAbs] checks abstractions with pattern variable binders. We discuss [T-PRef] in the next section. Rule [T-Body] binds a variable from a body type in the program environment. Rule [T-Macro] forms a pattern environment Φ and checks the template against its annotated type (subject to well-formedness constraints), filtering out any pattern variables from the program environment; the first-order macros of λ_m cannot refer to pattern variables outside their own scope.

4.1 The Aliasing Problem

The design of our type system led us to discover a peculiarity of Scheme macros. Consider the following macro:

```
(define-syntax K
  (syntax-rules ()
    ((K a b)
     (lambda (a)
       (lambda (b) a)))))
```

$$\boxed{(\Gamma, \Phi) \vdash e : \textsf{expr}}$$

$$[\text{T-MacDef}]\quad \frac{(\Gamma, \bullet) \vdash m : \sigma \rightarrow \textsf{expr} \qquad (\Gamma[m := \sigma \rightarrow \textsf{expr}], \bullet) \vdash e : \textsf{expr}}{(\Gamma, \bullet) \vdash \texttt{let syntax}\ x\ \texttt{=}\ m\ \texttt{in}\ e\ \texttt{end} : \textsf{expr}}$$

$$[\text{T-MacApp}]\quad \frac{(\Gamma, \Phi) \vdash op : \sigma \rightarrow \textsf{expr} \qquad (\Gamma, \Phi) \vdash s : \sigma[binders(\sigma, s)]}{(\Gamma, \Phi) \vdash op[\![s]\!]^{\sigma} : \textsf{expr}}$$

$$[\text{T-PBody}]\quad \frac{\Phi(?a) = \textsf{expr}^{\overline{?b}} \qquad \Gamma|_{pvar} = \overline{[?b := \textsf{expr}]}}{(\Gamma, \Phi) \vdash ?a : \textsf{expr}}$$

$$[\text{T-PAbs}]\quad \frac{\Phi(?a) = \langle ?a \rangle \qquad (\Gamma[?a := \textsf{expr}], \Phi) \vdash e : \textsf{expr}}{(\Gamma, \Phi) \vdash \lambda ?a.\, e : \textsf{expr}}$$

$$[\text{T-PRef}]\quad \frac{\Phi(?a) = \langle ?a \rangle \qquad \Gamma|_{pvar} = \Gamma'[?a := \textsf{expr}]}{(\Gamma, \Phi) \vdash ?a : \textsf{expr}}$$

$$\boxed{(\Gamma, \Phi) \vdash e : \hat{\beta}}$$

$$[\text{T-Body}]\quad \frac{(\Gamma[v := \textsf{expr}], \Phi) \vdash e : \textsf{expr}^{\overline{v'}}}{(\Gamma, \Phi) \vdash e : \textsf{expr}^{v, \overline{v'}}}$$

$$\boxed{(\Gamma, \Phi) \vdash op : \sigma \rightarrow \textsf{expr}}$$

$$[\text{T-Macro}]\quad \frac{wf(\sigma) \qquad (\Gamma|_{var}, penv(p, \sigma[pvars(p)])) \vdash e : \textsf{expr}}{(\Gamma, \Phi) \vdash (\texttt{macro}\ p : \sigma \Rightarrow e) : \sigma \rightarrow \textsf{expr}}$$

Fig. 3. Excerpts from the λ_m type system

One might expect that any application of `K` would produce an expression equivalent to $\lambda x.\, \lambda y.\, x$. But consider the application `(K x x)`: even in a hygienic macro system, this would expand into $\lambda x.\, \lambda x.\, x$! The binding structure of `K` is thus dependent on its actual arguments. We call this dependency the *aliasing problem.*

To resolve this ambiguity, we propose a simple rule we call the *shadow restriction*, enforced by the type rule [T-PRef]. A pattern binder $?a$ (i.e., of type $\langle ?a \rangle$) may only occur in an expression position if no other intervening pattern binders are in scope. For example, $\lambda ?a.\, (\lambda ?b.\, ?b)$ is legal but $\lambda ?a.\, (\lambda ?b.\, ?a)$ is ill-typed. In particular, this prohibits the definition of the `K` macro above. This restriction might seem draconian, but in fact `K` can easily be rewritten:

```
(define-syntax K′
  (syntax-rules ()
    ((K′ a b)
     (lambda (a)
       (let ((tmp a))
         (lambda (b) tmp))))))
```

Note that even with standard, untyped Scheme macros, this new definition always exhibits the intended behavior, in that even `(K′ x x)` expands into an expression equivalent to $\lambda x.\, \lambda y.\, x$.

4.2 Alpha-Equivalence Preserves Type

Theorem 2 gives us the freedom to use α-equivalent S-expressions without affecting the types.

Lemma 1. $(\Gamma, \Phi) \vdash s : \sigma[X] \Leftrightarrow (\Gamma, \Phi) \vdash (Z\ X)^{\sigma} \cdot s : \sigma[Z]$

Theorem 2 (Alpha-equivalence preserves type). *If* $(\Gamma, \Phi) \vdash s : \hat{\sigma}$ *and* $s =_{\alpha} s'$ *then* $(\Gamma, \Phi) \vdash s' : \hat{\sigma}$.

5 Macro Expansion

In this section, we specify our macro expansion semantics. We begin with a notion of compatibility, defined via expansion contexts.

5.1 Expansion Contexts

An expansion context C^{σ} is an S-expression with a hole $[\,]$, which produces an S-expression of shape σ when filled with an expression e. When the shape of a context is clear or irrelevant, we omit it for brevity.

$$
\begin{array}{lll}
C^{\mathsf{expr}^{\overline{\ell}}} & ::= [\,] \mid \lambda v.\, C^{\mathsf{expr}} \mid C^{\mathsf{expr}}\ e \mid e\ C^{\mathsf{expr}} & \\
& \mid\ \mathtt{let\ syntax}\ x\ \mathtt{=}\ C^{\sigma \to \mathsf{expr}}\ \mathtt{in}\ e\ \mathtt{end} & \\
& \mid\ \mathtt{let\ syntax}\ x\ \mathtt{=}\ m\ \mathtt{in}\ C^{\mathsf{expr}}\ \mathtt{end} & \\
& \mid\ C^{\sigma \to \mathsf{expr}}(s) \mid op[\![C^{\sigma}]\!]^{\sigma} & \\
C^{(\overline{\sigma})} & ::= (\overline{s}^{1..i-1}\ C^{\sigma_i}\ \overline{s}^{i+1..|\overline{\sigma}|}) & i \in 1..|\overline{\sigma}| \\
C^{\sigma \to \mathsf{expr}} & ::= \mathtt{macro}\ p : \sigma \Rightarrow C^{\mathsf{expr}} &
\end{array}
$$

5.2 Variable Conventions

The heart of hygienic macro expansion is the management of bindings to prevent accidental capture. Different expansion algorithms achieve this in different ways. For the *specification* of hygienic macro expansion, we simply specify the necessary conditions on variables under which expansion can proceed.

Analogous to the Barendregt variable convention [11], the *transparent* predicate allows a macro definition to be substituted into an application only if no intervening bindings can capture free variable references in the macro template. This condition is sometimes referred to as *referential transparency.*

$$\mathit{transparent}(s, \hat{\sigma}, s', \hat{\sigma}') \Leftrightarrow BV(s, \hat{\sigma}) \cap FV(s', \hat{\sigma}') = \emptyset$$

This condition alone is not enough to prevent unintended capture. The predicate *hygienic* requires a macro template's bindings to be fresh before performing an application. This prevents the bindings in the template from capturing references in the macro's arguments.

$$\mathit{hygienic}(s, \hat{\sigma}, s') \Leftrightarrow BV(s, \hat{\sigma}) \# s'$$

5.3 Expansion Semantics

The semantics of macro expansion involves two rules. The first rule connects macro applications to their definitions via the substitution operation $s[x := m]^{\hat{\sigma}}$, which uses the shape type $\hat{\sigma}$ to traverse the structure of s.

$$
\begin{array}{lll}
v[x := m]^{\mathsf{expr}} & = v & (v \neq x) \\
(\lambda x.\, e)[x := m]^{\mathsf{expr}} & = \lambda x.\, e & \\
(\lambda v.\, e)[x := m]^{\mathsf{expr}} & = \lambda v.\, (e[x := m]^{\mathsf{expr}}) & (v \neq x) \\
x[x := m]^{\sigma \to \mathsf{expr}} & = m & \\
v[x := m]^{\sigma \to \mathsf{expr}} & = v & (v \neq x) \\
e[x := m]^{\mathsf{expr}^{x,\overline{v}}} & = e & \\
e[x := m]^{\mathsf{expr}^{v,\overline{v'}}} & = e[x := m]^{\mathsf{expr}^{\overline{v'}}} & (v \neq x) \\
etc. & &
\end{array}
$$

A macro substitution step is defined by the rule:

$$
\begin{array}{l}
\texttt{let syntax}\ x\ \texttt{=}\ m\ \texttt{in}\ e\ \texttt{end} \longmapsto_{\mathsf{subst}} e[x := m]^{\mathsf{expr}} \\
\quad \text{if } \mathit{transparent}(e, \mathbf{expr}, m, \mathit{type}(m))
\end{array}
$$

Note that the variable convention must be fulfilled to prevent the context of the macro application from capturing free variable references in the macro template.

The second rule of macro expansion performs a macro transcription step, expanding an individual macro application. This rule is carried out in two parts. The first part, *pattern matching*, matches the macro pattern against the actual sub-expressions, producing a substitution ρ:

$$
\begin{array}{ll}
\mathit{match}(\mathbf{(}\overline{p}\mathbf{)}, \mathbf{(}\overline{s}\mathbf{)}) & = \bigcup_i \mathit{match}(p_i, s_i) \\
\mathit{match}(?a, s) & = \{?a \mapsto s\}
\end{array}
$$

Next, *transcription* instantiates all pattern variables in the template with the substitution function ρ:

$$
\begin{array}{ll}
\mathit{transcribe}(x, \rho) & = x \\
\mathit{transcribe}(?a, \rho) & = \rho(?a) \\
\mathit{transcribe}(\lambda v.\, e, \rho) & = \lambda(\mathit{transcribe}(v, \rho)).\, (\mathit{transcribe}(e, \rho)) \\
\mathit{transcribe}(e_1\ e_2, \rho) & = (\mathit{transcribe}(e_1, \rho))\ (\mathit{transcribe}(e_2, \rho)) \\
\mathit{transcribe}(op[\![s]\!]^{\sigma}, \rho) & = (\mathit{transcribe}(op, \rho))[\![\mathit{transcribe}(s, \rho)]\!]^{\sigma} \\
\mathit{transcribe}(m, \rho) & = m \\
\mathit{transcribe}(\mathbf{(}\overline{s}\mathbf{)}, \rho) & = \mathbf{(}\overline{(\mathit{transcribe}(s, \rho))}\mathbf{)}
\end{array}
$$

The macro transcription step is defined as the rule:

$$
\begin{array}{l}
(\texttt{macro}\ p : \sigma \Rightarrow e)[\![s]\!]^{\sigma} \longmapsto_{\mathsf{trans}} \mathit{transcribe}(e, \mathit{match}(p, s)) \\
\quad \text{if } \mathit{transparent}(s, \hat{\sigma}, e, \mathbf{expr}) \text{ and } \mathit{hygienic}(e, \mathbf{expr}, s) \\
\quad \text{where } \hat{\sigma} = \sigma[\mathit{binders}(\sigma, s)]
\end{array}
$$

The first variable convention also applies to this rule, since binders introduced in the actual arguments of the macro application should not capture free references from the template. The second convention prevents binders introduced from the body of the template from capturing references in the actual arguments.

We define the binary relation $\longmapsto_\varepsilon$ to be the compatible closure of the combined rules $\longmapsto_{\mathsf{subst}} \cup \longmapsto_{\mathsf{trans}}$ on S-expressions up to α-equivalence, i.e., the least relation such that $s_1 \longmapsto_\varepsilon s_2$ if there exist S-expressions s'_1, s'_2, a context C, and expressions e_1, e_2 such that $s_1 =_\alpha s'_1$, $s_2 =_\alpha s'_2$, $s'_1 = C[e_1]$, $s'_2 = C[e_2]$, and either $e_1 \longmapsto_{\mathsf{subst}} e_2$ or $e_1 \longmapsto_{\mathsf{trans}} e_2$.

The binary relation $\mapsto\!\!\!\twoheadrightarrow_\varepsilon$ is the reflexive, transitive closure of $\longmapsto_\varepsilon$.

6 Type Soundness

The type soundness proof is in the style of Wright and Felleisen [12]. The Preservation Lemma is proved for any S-expression s; it is reused in this more general form for the proof of confluence.

Lemma 2 (Preservation). *If $(\Gamma, \Phi) \vdash s : \hat{\sigma}$ and $s \longmapsto_\varepsilon s'$ then $(\Gamma, \Phi) \vdash s' : \hat{\sigma}$.*

Proof. The proof depends on three lemmas that guarantee that macro substitution, pattern matching, and transcription respectively preserve type, as well as a decomposition lemma. Theorem 2 ensures that choosing α-equivalent terms to satisfy the variable conventions is also type-preserving.

Lemma 3 (Progress). *If $\vdash e : \mathsf{expr}$ then either e is in ENF or there exists an e' such that $e \longmapsto_\varepsilon e'$.*

Proof. Macro substitution is defined for all well-typed S-expressions, as is *match*. Theorem 1 allows us to choose α-equivalent terms that satisfy the variable conventions for the expansion rules.

Theorem 3 (Type soundness). *If $\vdash e : \mathsf{expr}$ and $e \mapsto\!\!\!\twoheadrightarrow_\varepsilon e'$ and $e' \not\longmapsto_\varepsilon$, then e' is in ENF and $\vdash e' : \mathsf{expr}$.*

7 Hygiene

Theorem 4 (Confluence). *Let s be an S-expression such that $(\Gamma, \Phi) \vdash s : \hat{\sigma}$.*

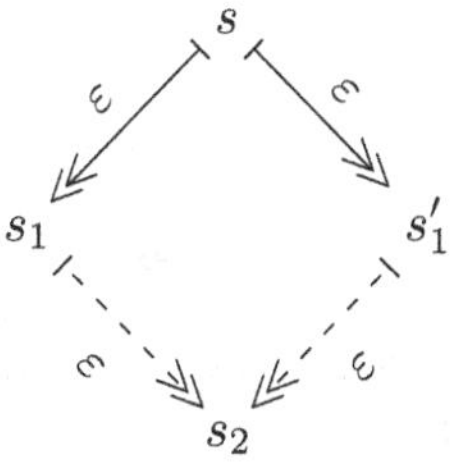

Proof. In the style of Barendregt [11], Chapter 11, §1. The proof involves marking a redex and tracking the marked redex and any copies or expansions of that marked term through multiple expansion steps. The central lemma shows that both macro substitution and transcription commute with expansion of marked redexes.

At last, the final Hygiene Theorem follows immediately from confluence.

Theorem 5 (Hygiene). *Let* e_0 *be an expression such that* $\vdash e_0 : \textsf{expr}$. *If* $e_0 =_\alpha e_0'$, $e_0 \longmapsto\!\!\!\!\rightarrow_\varepsilon e$, *and* $e_0' \longmapsto\!\!\!\!\rightarrow_\varepsilon e'$ *such that* e *and* e' *are in ENF, then* $e =_\alpha e'$.

This theorem provides the crucial guarantee of hygienic macros, namely that α-conversion of λ_m programs is semantics-preserving.

8 Front End

The parsing algorithm uses the same environments as the type system in order to distinguish the sorts of variables as well as annotate macro applications with types. Excerpts of this parsing algorithm are presented in Figure 4. Because function application in Scheme is denoted by parenthesization rather than invoking a special application macro, the rule for parsing function applications inserts an explicit reference to a built-in macro `@`. This is similar to the technique used in PLT Scheme [13], in which implicit function applications are rewritten to explicit applications of `#%app`.

Scheme implementations generally provide a standard library of macros. The primitive forms `lambda` and `@` can be implemented as built-in macros in the initial context of a Scheme program:

$$
\begin{array}{l}
C_0 = \texttt{let syntax} \\
\qquad\quad \texttt{lambda} = (\texttt{macro}\ \texttt{((}?a\texttt{)}\ ?e\texttt{)} : \texttt{((}\langle 00\rangle\texttt{)}\ \textsf{expr}^{00}\texttt{)} \Rightarrow \lambda ?a.\, ?e) \\
\qquad\quad \texttt{@} = (\texttt{macro}\ \texttt{(}?e_1\ ?e_2\texttt{)} : \texttt{(}\textsf{expr}\ \textsf{expr}\texttt{)} \Rightarrow ?e_1\ ?e_2) \\
\quad\ \texttt{in}\ [\,]\ \texttt{end}
\end{array}
$$

The parser must account for these macros in its initial environment:

$$
\begin{array}{ll}
\Gamma_0(\texttt{lambda}) & = \texttt{((}\langle 00\rangle\texttt{)}\ \textsf{expr}^{00}\texttt{)} \rightarrow \textsf{expr} \\
\Gamma_0(\texttt{@}) & = \texttt{(}\textsf{expr}\ \textsf{expr}\texttt{)} \rightarrow \textsf{expr}
\end{array}
$$

$$
\begin{array}{ll}
\mathit{parse}(\Gamma, \Phi, x, \textsf{expr}) & = \begin{cases} ?x \text{ if } x \in \mathit{dom}(\Phi) \\ x \ \ \text{if } x \notin \mathit{dom}(\Phi) \end{cases} \\
\mathit{parse}(\Gamma, \Phi, \texttt{(let-syntax ((}x\ s_1\texttt{))}\ s_2\texttt{)}, \textsf{expr}) & = \texttt{let syntax}\ x\ \texttt{=}\ m\ \texttt{in}\ e\ \texttt{end} \\
\quad \text{where } \mathit{parseMacro}(s_1) = m & \\
\qquad \text{and } \mathit{parse}(\Gamma[x := \mathit{type}(m)], \Phi, s_2, \textsf{expr}) = e & \\
\mathit{parse}(\Gamma, \Phi, \texttt{(}x\ \overline{s}\texttt{)}, \textsf{expr}) & = \mathit{op}[\![s']\!]^\sigma \\
\quad \text{where } \mathit{parseOperator}(\Gamma, \Phi, x) = (\mathit{op}, \sigma \rightarrow \textsf{expr}) & \\
\qquad \text{and } \mathit{binders}(\Phi, \sigma, \texttt{(}\overline{s}\texttt{)}) = X & \\
\qquad \text{and } \mathit{parse}(\Gamma, \Phi, \texttt{(}\overline{s}\texttt{)}, \sigma[X]) = s' & \\
\mathit{parse}(\Gamma, \Phi, \texttt{(}s_1\ s_2\texttt{)}, \textsf{expr}) & = \mathit{parse}(\Gamma, \Phi, \texttt{(@}\ s_1\ s_2\texttt{)}, \textsf{expr}) \\
\quad \text{if } s_1 \notin \mathit{dom}(\Gamma) \text{ and } ?s_1 \notin \mathit{dom}(\Phi) &
\end{array}
$$

Fig. 4. Excerpts of the type-directed parsing algorithm

9 Related and Future Work

Hygienic macros are over twenty years old, and many macro systems have been designed to facilitate or guarantee hygiene [2,5,3,6]. Several have been defined in a rigorous and formal way, but none provides a specification for hygiene, nor any satisfying account for the guarantees it provides. Our work shares a common observation with the *syntactic closures* macro system [4], namely that macro programmers know the binding structure of macros *a priori*; their work provides an API rather than a theory. Our primitive `lambda` and `@` macros resemble the *micros* of Krishnamurthi [14].

Several syntactic extension mechanisms have been designed for languages other than Scheme [15,16]. MacroML [17] is particularly relevant since it automatically prevents unintended variable capture. Their system is restrictive: binding forms can only extend ML's `let` form, and macros cannot inspect or destructure their syntactic arguments. Our work allows destructuring of S-expressions while still preserving the integrity of expressions. Our work also provides a theory of α-equivalence. Previous work on *staged notational definitions* [18] provides a meta-language SND for reasoning about MacroML programs; we believe our system more closely matches the informal reasoning used by macro programmers.

The shape types of Culpepper and Felleisen [8] are similar in expressive power to ours, allowing destructuring of S-expressions and synthesis of arbitrary binding forms. Our work extends theirs by accounting for binding structures. Crucially, this provides us with our account of α-equivalence and hygiene. Our use of types for expressing bindings was inspired by the nominal datatypes of Gabbay and Pitts [9].

Gasbichler [19] provides a detailed formal account of a rich macro system in order to study the interaction of hygienic macros and module systems. Our work is concerned instead with the guarantees provided by hygiene. Griffin [20] and Bove and Arbilla [21] also provide formal accounts of notational definitions and macros, respectively. The former is based on a higher-order representation of binding forms, the latter on de Bruijn indices. We have taken an explicitly-named approach in order to explore the connection between hygiene and α-equivalence. Both works prove key correctness properties, but in the context of a language with only top-level macro definitions, i.e., without lexically scoped macros.

Finally, we note that the design of our shape types bears some resemblance to the *locally nameless* approach to binding structures [22,23,24]. In particular, our macro types use tree locations ℓ in order to avoid using an α-equivalence relation on shape types, but when destructuring a type, we instantiate these locations with concrete names. We intend to investigate this relationship further.

There is much more to discover of the theory of hygienic macros. Our elementary type system is not yet expressive enough to permit important idioms in common use, including recursive macros, variable-length lists and list-patterns [25], and case dispatch. Another important next step will be to understand the type structure of *higher-order* macros, which expand into subsequent macro definitions. We intend to investigate the connection to staged types for this question.

Other areas for future exploration include procedural macros, inference for shape types, and support for intentional capture.

References

1. Kiselyov, O.: How to write seemingly unhygienic and referentially opaque macros with syntax-rules. In: Scheme Workshop (2002)
2. Kohlbecker, E., Friedman, D.P., Felleisen, M., Duba, B.: Hygienic macro expansion. In: LISP and Functional Programming (1986)
3. Clinger, W., Rees, J.: Macros that work. In: POPL (1991)
4. Bawden, A., Rees, J.: Syntactic closures. In: LISP and Functional Programming, pp. 86–95 (1988)
5. Kent Dybvig, R., Bruggeman, R.H.,, C.: Syntactic abstraction in Scheme. Lisp and Symbolic Computation 5(4), 295–326 (1993)
6. van Tonder, A.: SRFI 72: Hygienic macros. Online (September 2005)
7. Clinger, W., Rees, J.: Revised^4 report on the algorithmic language Scheme. Technical report (1991)
8. Culpepper, R., Felleisen, M.: Taming macros. In: Karsai, G., Visser, E. (eds.) GPCE 2004. LNCS, vol. 3286, Springer, Heidelberg (2004)
9. Gabbay, M.J., Pitts, A.M.: A new approach to abstract syntax with variable binding. Formal Aspects of Computing 13(3–5), 341–363 (2001)
10. Gorn, S.: Explicit definitions and linguistic dominoes. In: Systems and Computer Science, Proceedings of the Conference held at Univ. of Western Ontario (1967)
11. Barendregt, H.P.: The Lambda Calculus: Its Syntax and Semantics. revised edn. North-Holland, Amsterdam (1984)
12. Wright, A.K., Felleisen, M.: A syntactic approach to type soundness. Information and Computation 115(1), 38–94 (1994)
13. Flatt, M.: PLT MzScheme: Language manual. Technical Report PLT-TR2007-1-v371, PLT Scheme Inc. (2007), `http://www.plt-scheme.org/techreports/`
14. Krishnamurthi, S.: Linguistic Reuse. PhD thesis, Rice University (May 2001)
15. de Rauglaudre, D.: Camlp4 reference manual. Online (September 2003)
16. Sheard, T., Peyton Jones, S.: Template metaprogramming for Haskell. In: Chakravarty, M.M.T. (ed.) Haskell Workshop, pp. 1–16 (2002)
17. Ganz, S.E., Sabry, A., Taha, W.: Macros as multi-stage computations: Type-safe, generative, binding macros in MacroML. In: ICFP 2001, pp. 74–85 (2001)
18. Taha, W., Johann, P.: Staged notational definitions. In: Pfenning, F., Smaragdakis, Y. (eds.) GPCE 2003. LNCS, vol. 2830, pp. 97–116. Springer, Heidelberg (2003)
19. Gasbichler, M.: Fully-parameterized, first-class modules with hygienic macros. PhD thesis, University of Tübingen (August 2006)
20. Griffin, T.: Notational definition—a formal account. In: LICS 1988, pp. 372–383 (1988)
21. Bove, A., Arbilla, L.: A confluent calculus of macro expansion and evaluation. In: LISP and Functional Programming, pp. 278–287. ACM Press, New York (1992)
22. McKinna, J., Pollack, R.: Some lambda calculus and type theory formalized. Journal of Automated Reasoning 23, 373–409 (1999)
23. Gordon, A.D.: A mechanisation of name-carrying syntax up to alpha-conversion. In: Workshop on HOL Theorem Proving and its Applications, pp. 413–425 (1994)
24. McBride, C., McKinna, J.: Functional pearl: I am not a number—I am a free variable. In: Haskell Workshop, pp. 1–9 (2004)
25. Kohlbecker, E.E., Wand, M.: Macro-by-example: Deriving syntactic transformations from their specifications. In: Principles of Programming Languages (1987)

A Hybrid Denotational Semantics for Hybrid Systems

Olivier Bouissou[1] and Matthieu Martel[2]

[1] CEA LIST - Laboratoire MeASI
F-91191 Gif-sur-Yvette Cedex, France
Olivier.Bouissou@cea.fr
[2] ELIAUS-DALI Laboratory - Université de Perpignan Via Domitia
F-66860 Perpignan Cedex, France
Matthieu.Martel@univ-perp.fr

Abstract. In this article, we present a model and a denotational semantics for hybrid systems. Our model is designed to be used for the verification of large, existing embedded applications. The discrete part is modeled by a program written in an extension of an imperative language and the continuous part is modeled by differential equations. We give a denotational semantics to the continuous system inspired by what is usually done for the semantics of computer programs and then we show how it merges into the semantics of the whole system. The semantics of the continuous system is computed as the fix-point of a modified Picard operator which increases the information content at each step.

1 Introduction

The importance of static analysis techniques [6] for software validation is no longer to be outlined. Their application to highly critical programs has become a major challenge for many industries. Such programs are often automatically generated, imperative programs which are embedded into a heterogeneous system. They mostly behave as follows: they capture information from the physical environment via sensors, treat it using numerical computations and then modify the environment via actuators. The analysis of such programs requires either to over-approximate the physical environment, which often leads to an imprecise analysis, or to analyze the hybrid system made of the continuous environment and the discrete program [5,14]. We use this approach. The analysis of hybrid systems requires as a starting point a formal description of their behavior. We need to give a coherent interpretation of both the discrete and the continuous subsystems. The formalization of a continuous system using the same notions as for a computer program is already a challenge of its own. The continuous variables move along a continuous function of the real time while the discrete system is defined, in a denotational semantics approach, as a function between discrete environments [24]. In this article, we propose a formalism for modeling hybrid systems together with a description of their behavior as a *hybrid denotational semantics*: the evolution of the hybrid system is a function between hybrid

S. Drossopoulou (Ed.): ESOP 2008, LNCS 4960, pp. 63–77, 2008.

environments (containing a discrete *and* a continuous part) which is computed as the least fix-point of a sequence of approximations.

Our model for hybrid systems is designed for an implementation level and ensures a clear separation of the discrete and the continuous subsystems. They are modeled in two different formalisms (see Sects. 2.1 and 2.2) which allows the analysis of one program within various environments for example. Despite this heterogeneity, we give a unique description of the behavior of the hybrid system. First, we suppose that the discrete part is completely determined and we give a semantics $[\![\kappa]\!]$ for the continuous part (Sect. 3). It is computed as the fix-point of an operator Γ which acts on partially defined functions and we show that this fix-point is actually the limit of Tarski's iterates [22]. The semantics $[\![\Delta]\!]$ of the purely discrete part of the system is computed using the standard semantics of imperative languages (as in [24]). We add denotations for some hybrid actions that represent sensors and actuators, and show how these are combined to $[\![\kappa]\!]$ to form the hybrid semantics $[\![\Omega]\!]^{\mathcal{H}}$ (Sect. 4). For conciceness reasons, we ommit in this paper most of the proofs of the presented results. An extended version containing them with more details on the theory of ODEs can be found in [3].

Running Example. We will illustrate this article with a simplified version of the well-known two tanks problem [18]. It consists of *one* water tank (Fig. 1.1(a)) filled by a constant flow i with two evacuation tubes: one at the bottom, which has a valve v than can be open or closed, and one at height h. The continuous system is the height x of the water in the tank, whose evolution is governed by the ordinary differential equation of Fig. 1(b). The discrete part is a controller whose goal is to maintain x between safe bounds by closing/opening the valve.

Related Work. The modeling of hybrid systems with hybrid automata was initiated by Henzinger [16]. They are finite state automata to which we add at each node a *flow equation* describing the continuous dynamics at this point. Their operational semantics was introduced in the early papers and their analysis using model checking techniques has been well studied [12,17]. A denotational semantics for these models was recently proposed by Edalat [11] and proved to be equivalent to the operational semantics. Since the first results, many models for hybrid systems and verification methods were proposed. These include hybrid process algebra like HyPa [8] or Hybrid Chi [23]. Meanwhile, Hybrid-CC [15] introduced hybrid components to the concurrent constraints theory. All these

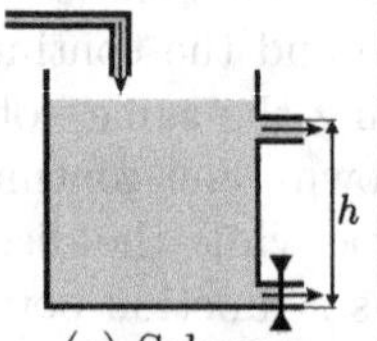

(a) Scheme.

$$\dot{x} = \begin{cases} i - k_1\sqrt{x} - k_2\sqrt{x-h} & \text{if } x \geq h \text{ and } v \text{ open} \\ i - k_2\sqrt{x-h} & \text{if } x \geq h \text{ and } v \text{ closed} \\ i - k_1\sqrt{x} & \text{if } x \leq h \text{ and } v \text{ open} \\ i & \text{otherwise} \end{cases}$$

(b) Continuous System.

Fig. 1.1. One Tank Example

models are generally used as high level abstract formalisms to reason about the principles of hybrid systems. However, when the verification of industrial size, critical systems is at stake, they are not fully sufficient. First, for safety reasons, the analysis of the embedded source code is always necessary. Secondly, for industrial size problems, it is necessary to have a clear distinction between discrete and continuous states to allow the modeling process of the both parts to be executed by different engineers. Most of the models we cited are not well-suited for these requirements, although some advances have been made for the separation issue [1]. The main difficulty in the formalization of hybrid systems is to give a coherent meaning to the continuous and the discrete parts. Edalat et al. proposed a formalization of differential calculus and of the solutions of differential equations in the theory of Scott domains, both for the mono-variate [9] and multi-variate [10] cases. We used their theory as a starting point for our work to define the denotational semantics of the continuous subsystem.

Notations and Mathematical Background. In this article, $\mathbb{R}$ denotes the set of real numbers, $\mathbb{R}_+$ the set of non-negative real numbers and $\mathbb{N}$ denotes the natural integers. The set of compact intervals over $\mathbb{R}$ is $\mathbb{I}(\mathbb{R})$. For $i \in \mathbb{I}(\mathbb{R})$, we write $\underline{i}$ (resp. $\overline{i}$) its lower (resp. upper) bound. We define its width $w(i) = \overline{i} - \underline{i}$ and its midpoint $mid(i) = \frac{\overline{i}+\underline{i}}{2}$. In Sect. 3, we use some advanced techniques of the theory of *ordinary differential equations* (ODEs). We assume that the reader is familiar with the basics of this theory, and give here just the main results that we will use. The main theorem that we will use concerns the iterates of the Picard operator $P_I(F, y_0)$. Given $I \in \mathbb{I}(\mathbb{R})$, a continuous function F and $y_0 \in \mathbb{R}$, $P_I(F, y_0)$ is a map between continuous functions defined by $P_I(F, y_0)(f) = \lambda x.y_0 + \int_{\underline{I}}^{x} F(f(s), s)ds$. It gives a characterisation of the solution of an initial value problem (IVP) as a fixpoint and it provides a way to compute it via successive approximation, as shown by Theorem 1.

Theorem 1 (Properties of the Picard operator). *Let $\dot{y} = F(y)$, $y(0) = y_0$ be an IVP. A continuous, differentiable function f on (a, b), with $0 \in (a, b)$, is a solution to the IVP if and only if it satisfies:*

$$\forall t \in (a, b),\ f(t) = P_{(a,b)}(F, y_0)(y)(t) \ . \tag{1}$$

If F is globally Lipschitz on $\mathbb{R}$, the Picard iterates *defined by $f_0 \in C^0([a, b])$, $f_{n+1} = P_{[a,b]}(F, y_0)(f_n)$ converge uniformly on (a, b). So, whatever the choice of f_0, if we iteratively compute $f_{n+1} = P_{[a,b]}(F, y_0)(f_n)$, the sequence converges toward the solution of the IVP on (a, b).*

2 Our Model for Hybrid Systems

Our goals for this model of hybrid systems are the following. First, the discrete part should remain close to existing embedded software. Secondly, the action of sensors and actuators must be clearly identified. Finally, we want the continuous and discrete systems to be modeled separately for two reasons. First, to analyze the behavior of a controller in different physical environments without rewriting the entire system, the distinction between the plant (i.e. the discrete part) and the environment must be clear. Secondly, for existing industrial applications, the discrete part (i.e. the program) is already written, so we want a model of the hybrid systems that can use this program "as it is". An obvious solution would consist of building a cartesian product between the continuous states and the states of the program. For combinatorial reasons, our approach consists of first describing a model for continuous subsystems (Sect. 2.1) and then a model for discrete subsystems (Sect. 2.2).

2.1 Model for the Continuous Subsystem

The continuous part contains variables evolving continuously with time such as the water height in the tank or the temperature of the air. They are usually modelled by an *ordinary differential equation*; for example, the temperature y of a room with a heater is given by an ODE like $\dot{y} = 5 - 0.1y$. Let κ be the continuous model, its expressiveness depends on the set of functions F that we allow to define the IVP $\dot{y} = F(y),\ y(0) = y_0$. We need to capture two phenomena: a change in the dynamics due to the environment itself and a change due to the discrete program. The first arises for example when the water passes above the tube (see (2)) while the second appears when the valve is closed.

To capture the changes due to the actuators, we let F have *boolean parameters*: $F = F(y, t, \boldsymbol{k})$, where $\boldsymbol{k}$ vector of boolean valued. We write $F_k(y, t) = F(y, t, k)$ for every possible value of k. To capture the changes induced by the environment itself, we let each F_k be a continuous, piecewise Lipschitz function. Thus, F_k behaves differently in different regions of the space, which is precisely the kind of changes we wanted to model. We recall that a function g is piecewise Lipschitz if there exist finitely many real numbers $x_0 < x_1 < \cdots < x_n$ such that the restriction of g to $[x_i, x_{i+1}]$ is Lipschitz. The theory of differential equations remain unchanged with such functions, except that the solutions are now continuous but only piecewise differentiable functions. Especially, the Picard iterates still converge uniformly on every interval.

The continuous model κ is a triple $\kappa = (F, (F_k)_{k \in \boldsymbol{k}}, y_0)$ where $(F_k)_{k \in \boldsymbol{k}}$ is the set of possible modes. We write $F_{\boldsymbol{k}}$ for $(F_k)_{k \in \boldsymbol{k}}$. F is the function defining the IVP and is such that there exists $t_0 < t_1 < \cdots < t_n < \ldots$ such that the restriction of F to $[t_i, t_{i+1}]$ is equal to one of the F_k. The model representing the evolution of the liquid height in the one-tank system is $(F, \{F_0, F_1\}, y_0)$ where (F_0, F_1) are given by (2).

$$F_k(x) = \begin{cases} i - k * k_1\sqrt{x} - k_2\sqrt{x - h} & \text{if } x \geq h \\ i - k * k_1\sqrt{x} & \text{otherwise} \end{cases} \tag{2}$$

2.2 Model for the Discrete Subsystem

We want the discrete model Δ to remain close to existing embedded software. We thus start with a set of standard statements which are common to any imperative language (*stmt* in Fig. 2.1): assignemnts, **if** statements, **while** loops, arithmetic

stmt := v = *exp* | **while**(*bool*) *stmt* | **if**(*bool*) **then** *stmt* **else** *stmt*
| *stmt*;*stmt* | *hyb_stmt*
exp := c | *exp*+*exp* | *exp*-*exp* | *exp***exp* ...
bool := v<exp | v>exp | *bool*∨*bool* | ...
hyb_stmt := **sens**.y?x | **act**.k!c | **wait** c

Fig. 2.1. Statements for the discrete system

and boolean expressions. This core language can be extended to more complex statements without perturbing the semantics of the hybrid system as they represent purely discrete actions. In addition, we have three hybrid actions. First, a **sens** action for the sensors: the action of **sens.y?x** is to bind the variable **x** to the value of the continuous variable **y** at the time the action is executed. Then, a **act** action for the actuators: the action of **act.k!c** is to change the continuous dynamics by choosing the function F_c among all the possible dynamics $F_{\boldsymbol{k}}$. Finally, a **wait** action for the passing of time: we suppose that all discrete and hybrid actions are instantaneous and we model the fact that they were not by explicitly adding these **wait** statements. The effect of **wait c** is to move time forward by **c** seconds. This formalism is very close to existing imperative languages and, in most cases, the programs already contain, as comments, the hybrid statements. For example, the loops of industrial programs are usually precisely cadenced and we often see in the codes comments indicating their frequency such as "this loop runs at 8kHz". Thus, adding a **wait** command at the end of the loop to model its cadence is easy. Using this syntax, we can write a controller for the one tank system that measures the height x of the water with a sensor and open the valve if x is too high (see Listing 1). We suppose that closing the valve takes two seconds, so the controller must predict the height of the water two seconds later (via the function `anticipate`) and start the opening if this predicted value is too high.

```
int main() {
  sensor x;              // sensors declaration
  actuator k;            // actuators declaration
  while (true) {
    sens.x?h;
    if (h>h_max)
      act.k!1; throw( alarm );
    h_in_2_secs = anticipate(h);
    if (h_in_2_secs > h_max)
      act.k!1;
    wait (0.01);      // delay action
  }
}
```

Listing 1. Controller for a one-tank system.

This model for hybrid systems conforms to our three requirements, and we designed it such that it prohibits physically impossible phenomena like continuous state jumps or Zeno effects. Actually, time is driven by the discrete subsystem through the **wait** statements, thus there must exist a minimum time between two mode switchings (because the discrete program is finite), which prohibits Zeno phenomena. We now give a formal, denotational semantics for this model of hybrid systems.

3 Continuous Semantics

In this section, we give a formal, denotational semantics of the continuous model. Let us recall that the continuous part of an hybrid system is represented as $\kappa = (F, F_{\boldsymbol{k}}, y_0)$ where $F_{\boldsymbol{k}}$ is a family of piecewise Lipschitz continuous functions and $y_0 \in \mathbb{R}$ is the initial condition (we suppose $t_0 = 0$). Each F_k is supposed to be globally α-Lipschitz on $\mathbb{R}$, so that there exists a unique maximal solution on $\mathbb{R}$ to each ODE $\dot{y} = F_k(y,t)$. We first give the intuition for the continuous semantics and then we describe the lattice structure that we manipulate (Sect. 3.1) and the computation of the semantics as a fix-point (Sect. 3.2).

In an analogy with standard denotational semantics, we want to express the semantics of κ as a function mapping an initial environment to a final value. If we know the behavior of the discrete part of the system, we know the times at which the parameters $k \in \boldsymbol{k}$ switch. Thus, we know completely the function F and the semantics of κ maps an initial value to the semantics of the IVP:

$$\dot{y} = F(y,t), \;\; y(0) = y_0 \;\; . \tag{3}$$

Basically, the semantics of the IVP is its maximal solution, i.e. a piecewise differentiable, continuous function $y : \mathbb{R}_+ \to \mathbb{R}$ which satisfies (3). Thus, the semantics of κ is a function $[\![\kappa]\!]$ mapping an initial *environment* (i.e. the initially available information y) to the solution of the IVP. The computation of $[\![\kappa]\!](y)$ requires the computation of a fix-point, in the sense of Banach's fix-point theory, as shown by Theorem 1. We translate this fix-point computation into Tarski's fix-point theory: $[\![\kappa]\!](y)$ is computed as the fix-point of an operator Γ and we prove this is the supremum of the iterates $\Gamma^n(\bot)$. Γ is defined on elements with partial information and it updates them by increasing their information content. Our notion of partial information is the following: a function has only partial information if it is defined on a finite interval $[0, X]$ for some $X \in \mathbb{R}_+$ and its value at each point is bounded, i.e. is an interval. Thus, the maximal elements are the real-valued functions defined on $\mathbb{R}_+$ and our semantics will construct one of these (the solution of (3)) as the limit of an approximations sequence, each approximation being a partially defined, interval-valued function.

3.1 The Lattice of Interval-Valued Functions

We now define the set of partially defined, interval-valued functions. We also define an order and shows that this order provides a lattice structure.

Definition 1 (*Partial, interval-valued functions*). *Let $X \in \mathbb{R}_+$. $\mathcal{IF}_X$ is the set of interval-valued functions defined on $[0, X]$: $\mathcal{IF}_X = \{f : [0, X] \to \mathbb{I}(\mathbb{R})\}$ For such a function, we define its* upper $\overline{f}$ *and* lower $\underline{f}$ *functions as the two real-valued functions such that $\forall x \in [0, X],\ f(x) = [\underline{f}(x), \overline{f}(x)]$.*

When $\underline{f}$ (respectively $\overline{f}$) is right-continuous (respectively left-continuous), f is (Scott) continuous and write $\mathcal{IF}^0_X$ the set of all *continuous*, partial, interval-valued functions. We recall that a function f is right-continuous if when t tends toward x from above, $f(t)$ tends toward $f(x)$; the left-continuity is the opposite. We provide the set $\mathcal{IF}^0_X$ with a *complete partial order* structure with the pointwise reverse order: $f \sqsubseteq_X g \Leftrightarrow \forall x \in [0, X],\ g(x) \subseteq f(x)$. This order means that at every point in $[0, X]$, g is more informative than f. Clearly, $(\mathcal{IF}^0_X, \sqsubseteq_X)$ is a CPO (actually, it is a continuous Scott domain [9]). The left-(resp. right) continuity of $\overline{f}$ (resp. $\underline{f}$) is a necessary condition for f to be Scott-continuous [9] *and* for $\mathcal{IF}^0_X$ to be a CPO; consider for example the piecewise linear functions $f_n \in \mathcal{IF}^0_1$ defined by $f_n(x) = [0, 1]$ if $x \in [0, \frac{1}{2}]$, $f_n(x) = [0, 1 - \frac{n}{2}(x - \frac{1}{2})]$ if $x \in [\frac{1}{2}, \frac{1}{2} + \frac{1}{n}]$ and $f_n(x) = [0, \frac{1}{2}]$ otherwise. Clearly, $f = \bigsqcup_n f_n$ is not continuous in $\frac{1}{2}$, while each f_n is. The right-continuity condition imposes that $\overline{f}(x) = 1$ for $x \in [0, \frac{1}{2}[$ and $\overline{f}(x) = \frac{1}{2}$ for $x \in [\frac{1}{2}, 1]$.
$\mathcal{IF}^0_\infty$ is the natural extension of $\mathcal{IF}^0_X$ to functions defined on $\mathbb{R}_+$. We now build the set of interval functions defined over arbitrary intervals of $\mathbb{R}$.

Definition 2 (*Arbitrary long, interval-valued functions*). *The set of all continuous, partial, interval-valued functions is* $\mathcal{D}^0 = \left(\bigcup_{X \in \mathbb{R}_+} \mathcal{IF}^0_X\right) \cup \mathcal{IF}^0_\infty$. *For* $f \in \mathcal{D}^0$, *we note* X_f *the upper bound of its domain:* $X_f = sup(dom(f))$. *The value* X_f *is the maximum time until which* f *is defined; if* f *is defined on* $\mathbb{R}_+$, *then* $X_f = \infty$.

Note that for all $X \geq 0$, the set of continuous, real-valued functions $\mathcal{C}^0([0, X])$ is embedded into $\mathcal{D}^0$ by the function $\gamma : f \mapsto \lambda x.[f(x), f(x)]$. Thus, we will identify a map $f \in \mathcal{C}^0([0, X])$ with the map $\lambda x.[f(x), f(x)]$ and write $f \in \mathcal{D}^0$. We extend the order $\sqsubseteq_X$ to $\mathcal{D}^0$ by requiring that g is greater than f if it is more precise on a longer interval than f:

$$f \sqsubseteq g \Leftrightarrow X_f \leq X_g \text{ and } f \sqsubseteq_{X_f} g_{|[0, X_f]} \text{ and } \forall x \in [X_f, X_g],\ g(x) \subseteq f(X_f) \tag{4}$$

where $g_{|[0, X_f]}$ denotes the restriction of g to $[0, X_f]$. Figure 3.1 gives an example of comparable functions (left, the dark one being bigger than the light one) and an example of incomparable functions (right). The third hypothesis in (4) states that g remains bounded by the last value of f on $[X_f, X_g]$. It is necessary for $\mathcal{D}^0$ to be a CPO: in any increasing chain f_n, the functions $\overline{f_n}$ and $\underline{f_n}$ are bounded, thus $(\underline{f_n})$ is a bounded increasing sequence (with respect to the pointwise order for real-valued functions), so it has a limit $\underline{f}$. Equivalently, $(\overline{f_n})$ has a limit $\overline{f}$,

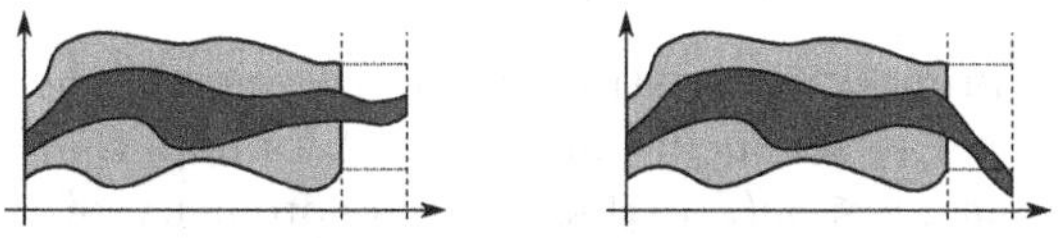

(a) Comparable functions. (b) Incomparable functions.

Fig. 3.1. Order on partially defined functions

which proves the existence of $\bigsqcup_n f_n = [\underline{f}, \overline{f}]$. We extend $(\mathcal{D}^0, \sqsubseteq)$ with a bottom $\bot$ and a top $\top$ element such that $\forall f \in \mathcal{D}^0,\ \bot \sqsubseteq f \sqsubseteq \top$. We also define the join and meet operators $\sqcup$ and $\sqcap$ as follows. Let $f, g \in \mathcal{D}^0$, with $X_f \leq X_g$. Then, $f \sqcup g \in \mathcal{IF}^0_{X_g}$ and $f \sqcap g \in \mathcal{IF}^0_{X_f}$ are defined by:

$$f \sqcup g(x) = \begin{cases} f(x) \cap g(x) & \text{if } x \in [0, X_f] \\ f(X_f) \cap g(x) & \text{otherwise} \end{cases} \qquad f \sqcap g(x) = f(x) \cup g(x)$$

This definition of $f \sqcup g$ supposes that $\forall x \in [0, X_f],\ f(x) \cap g(x) \neq \emptyset$. If this is not true, $f \sqcup g = \top$.

Proposition 1. *$(\mathcal{D}^0, \sqsubseteq, \top, \bot, \sqcup, \sqcap)$ is a continuous lattice.*

Let us remark that $\mathcal{D}^0$ is a lattice and a CPO, so every increasing chain does have a supremum. It is however *not* a complete lattice as there exist infinite sequences without supremum. For example, let us consider the sequence of functions $\varphi_n \in \mathcal{IF}^0_{1-\frac{1}{n}}$ defined by $\varphi_n(x) = [-\frac{1}{1-x}, \frac{1}{1-x}]$. Clearly, this sequence does not have a supremum in $\mathcal{D}^0$ except $\top$, while there are infinitely many $f \in \mathcal{D}^0$ greater than f_n for all n (for example, the constant function with value 0).We next define some basic operations on $\mathcal{D}^0$ that adapt the classical operations on real-valued functions. The arithmetic operators $+, -, *, /$ are defined as an extension of the interval arithmetic. For $\odot \in \{+, -, *, /\}$ and $f, g \in \mathcal{IF}^0_X$, we define $f \odot g \in \mathcal{IF}^0_X$ as $\forall x \in [0, X],\ f \odot g(x) = \{y \odot z \mid y \in f(x) \text{ and } z \in g(x)\}$. We next define the composition, primitive and width of functions in $\mathcal{D}^0$.

Definition 3 (*Function composition, Primitive and Width*).
The composition *of a continuous, real-valued function $F : \mathbb{R} \to \mathbb{R}$ and a partial, interval-valued function $f \in \mathcal{IF}^0_X$ is the function $F \circ_X f \in \mathcal{IF}^0_X$ defined by: $\forall x \in [0, X], (F \circ_X f)(x) = \{F(y) \ :\ y \in f(x)\}$. $F \circ_X f$ is well defined because F is continuous and $f(x)$ is an interval, so $F \circ f(x)$ is an interval for all x. We naturally extend the notion of function composition to $\mathcal{D}^0$ and define the composition operator $\circ$ as: $\forall F : \mathbb{R} \to \mathbb{R}$ and $f \in \mathcal{D}^0$, $F \circ f = F \circ_{X_f} f$.*
The primitive *of a function $f \in \mathcal{IF}^0_X$ is $I_X(f) \in \mathcal{IF}^0_X$ defined by: $\forall x \in [0, X],\ I_X(f)(x) = \left[\int_0^x \underline{f}(s)ds, \int_0^x \overline{f}(s)ds\right]$. This primitive operator is extended to $\mathcal{D}^0$ straightforwardly: for $f \in \mathcal{D}^0$, we set $I(f) = I_{X_f}(f)$.*
The width *of a function $f \in \mathcal{D}^0$ is computed as the maximum width of all intervals $f(x)$: $w(f) = \max_{x \in [0, X_f]} w(f(x))$.*

Proposition 2. *The operator $\circ$ is monotone and continuous. The width w is a monotone, continuous function from $(\mathcal{D}^0, \sqsubseteq)$ to $([0, \infty[, \preceq)$ where $x \preceq y \Leftrightarrow y \leq x$.*

The proof of this proposition is straightforward: we use the monotonicity of functions with respect to set inclusion for $\circ$ and we note that for two intervals i_1, i_2, $i_2 \subseteq i_1 \Rightarrow w(i_2) \leq w(i_1)$, thus the monotonicity of w. The primitive operator is not monotone, as it does not preserve the third condition for the order $\sqsubseteq$ (Equation (4)). However, the second condition is preserved thanks to the monotonicity of the primitive for real-valued functions.

Among all the functions of $\mathcal{D}^0$, one is of special interest for us: y_∞, the maximal solution of (3). We compute it by successive approximations and thus need to measure the quality of our approximation. Following Keye Martin's measure theory [19], a measurement is a continuous function μ from a CPO $\mathcal{D}$ into the set of nonnegative real numbers with reverse ordering: $[0,\infty[^*$ that reveals the distance of $f \in \mathcal{D}$ to the maximal elements of $\mathcal{D}$, which have measure 0. The measurement must be coherent with the informational order on $\mathcal{D}$: the more informative f, the smaller its measure. It must also be the case that if we *measure* that the sequence f_n converges towards 0 ($\lim_{n\to\infty} \mu(f_n) = 0$), then the sequence f_n *does* converge towards a maximal element ($\bigsqcup_n f_n = f$, $\mu(f) = 0$). For a formal definition of a measurement, please refer to [19], Chapter 2. In our case, the maximal elements of $\mathcal{D}^0$ are the real-valued functions defined on $\mathbb{R}_+$. These functions have a null width and an infinitely long domain of definition. Thus, a measurement must takes both aspects into account.

Definition 4 (*The measurement* μ). *Let $f \in \mathcal{D}^0$. We let $\mu(f) = w(f) + \frac{1}{X_f}$.*

Clearly, $\mu(f)$ is null if and only if f is maximal, so in particular $\mu(y_\infty) = 0$.

Proposition 3. *μ is a measurement, i.e.:*

(i) *it is a Scott continuous map from $(\mathcal{D}^0, \sqsubseteq)$ into $[0,\infty[^*$.*
(ii) *for all $f \in \mathcal{D}^0$ such that $\mu(f) = 0$ and all sequences $f_n \ll f$, we have $\lim_{n\to\infty} \mu(f_n) = 0 \Rightarrow \sqcup_n f_n = f$*

We recall that the far away *relation $f \ll g$ means that for every increasing chain φ_n with a supremum greater than g, the elements φ_n must become greater than f at some $N \in \mathbb{N}$.*

We thus have built a lattice $\mathcal{D}^0$ and defined three operators on it: I, $\circ$ and w. We also have a measurement μ on $\mathcal{D}^0$ which characterizes its maximal elements, i.e. the real-valued functions defined on $\mathbb{R}_+$. We use μ in the next section.

3.2 The Semantics

$[\![\kappa]\!](y)$ is computed as the least fix-point of the operator $\Gamma_{F,y_0} : \mathcal{D}^0 \to \mathcal{D}^0$ that acts as follows: a function $f \in \mathcal{IF}^0_X$, it first updates the available information by bringing each $f(x)$ closer to $y_\infty(x)$ and then it extends the function to the right by assigning a value to $f(x)$ for $x \in [X, X+1]$. The first step uses an iteration of the Picard operator (Sect. 1) while the second step extends the function in such a way that if f encloses the solution at X, then the extension encloses y_∞ on $[X, X+1]$. This is possible because F is α-Lipschitz, so y_∞ cannot grow faster than $e^{\alpha x}$. We recall that the Picard operator is defined as $P_{[0,X_f]}(F, y_0)(f) = \lambda x.y_0 + \int_0^x F(f(s))ds = y_0 + I(F \circ f)$.

Definition 5 (*Updating operator*). *Let $f \in \mathcal{D}^0$, we suppose $X_f < \infty$. Let F be a continuous, globally α-Lipschitz function and $y_0 \in \mathbb{R}$. Then, $\Gamma_{F,y_0}(f) \in \mathcal{IF}^0_{X_f+1}$ is defined by:*

$$\Gamma_{F,y_0}(f)(x) = \begin{cases} P_{[0,X_f]}(F,y_0)(f)(x) & \textit{if } x \le X_f \\ J + F(J) * [-e^\alpha, e^\alpha] * (x - X), & \\ \quad \textit{with } J = P_{[0,X_f]}(F,y_0)(f)(X) \textit{ otherwise} & \end{cases}$$

If $f \in \mathcal{IF}^0_\infty$, $\Gamma_{F,y_0}(f) = P_{[0,\infty[}(F,y_0)(f)$. $\Gamma_{F,y_0}(\bot)$ *is the function defined on* $[0,0]$ *with value* y_0.

An example of the effect of Γ_{F,y_0} on a partial function is shown on Fig. 3.2. The black line represents y_∞; Figure 3.2(a) shows the updating mechanism, while Fig. 3.2(b) is the extension. The operator Γ_{F,y_0} is not monotone on $\mathcal{D}^0$, but we know that it has a fix-point: y_∞. We will show in the following that this fix-point can be computed as the supremum of the Γ_{F,y_0} iterates, i.e. $y_\infty = \bigsqcup_n \Gamma^n_{F,y_0}(\bot)$.

Proposition 4. *Let* $f \in \mathcal{IF}^0_X$. Γ_{F,y_0} *verifies the invariant:*

$$\forall x \in [0,X], y_\infty(x) \in f(x) \Rightarrow \forall x \in [0, X+1], y_\infty(x) \in \Gamma_{F,y_0}(f)(x) \ .$$

The iterates $f_{n+1} = \Gamma_{F,y_0}(f_n)$, starting from $f_0 = \bot$, form a sequence of approximation of y_∞: they enclose it and their width converge toward 0. On Table 1 the figures show how the iterates of Γ_{F,y_0} converge to a real valued function. The semantics of the continuous subsystem $\kappa = (F, F_{\boldsymbol{k}}, y_0)$ maps $f \in \mathcal{D}^0$ with the least fix-point of Γ_{F,y_0} starting from f: $[\![\kappa]\!](f) = \bigsqcup_n \Gamma^n_{F,y_0}(f)$. We now give the main result of this section.

Theorem 2. *The solution* y_∞ *of* (3) *is a fix-point of* Γ_{F,y_0} *and*

$$[\![\kappa]\!](\bot) = Fix(\Gamma_{F,y_0}) = \bigsqcup_n \Gamma^n_{F,y_0}(\bot) = y_\infty \ .$$

4 Hybrid Semantics

Let us now give the semantics of the complete hybrid system. The hybrid model is a pair $\Omega = (\Delta, \kappa)$ consisting of a model Δ for the discrete system and a model κ for the continuous environment that define two dynamical systems that run in parallel and, from time to time, communicate. On the one hand,data are passed from κ to Δ via the sensors. This communication requires that both dynamical systems reached the same time before the data is exchanged. The **sens** actions must thus be blocking. On the other hand, orders are passed from

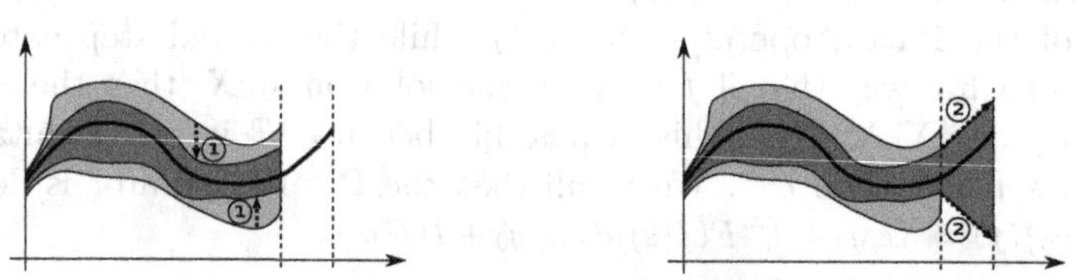

(a) Update the information

(b) Extends the information

Fig. 3.2. The updating operator (two steps)

Δ to κ via the actuators. Indeed, the discrete system only indicates to the continuous system what its semantics will be, i.e. it chooses one of the possible functions F_k. This communication needs not to be blocking as it does not affect the value of the continuous variables but only their future behavior. The hybrid denotations for **sens** and **act** respect these facts. The semantics $[\![\Omega]\!]^{\mathcal{H}}$ of Ω is a function between hybrid environments. The discrete environment is altered by the discrete subsystem while the continuous one is computed only when needed, i.e. when a **sens** is found.

4.1 Hybrid Environments

A hybrid environment consists of a pair made of a discrete and a continuous environment. The discrete environment σ_δ binds every discrete variable $v \in Var$ to a value and the time *time* to a positive real value. It also contains the function F that defines the semantics of the continuous variables. This function F is piecewisely defined by the discrete program through the **act** statements and thus storing F is equivalent to storing the sequence of all executed **act** actions. The discrete environment thus stores both the value of the variables, the execution time, as well as the sequence of modifications brought to the continuous system. We write Σ_Δ the set of all discrete environments, $\Sigma_\Delta = \{(Var \to Val) * (\{time\} \to \mathbb{R}_+) * (F : \mathbb{R}_+ \times \mathbb{R} \to \mathbb{R})\}$. The continuous environment σ_κ contains an approximation of the physical variables $y \in \mathcal{D}^0$ and the set of functions F_k defining the continuous dynamics, i.e. the set of possible continuous modes that are available for the discrete program to chose. We write Σ_κ the set of all continuous environments, $\Sigma_\kappa = \{(y \in \mathcal{D}^0) * (F_k \mid F_k : \mathbb{R}_+ \times \mathbb{R} \to \mathbb{R})\}$. As usual, we write $\sigma_\delta.X$ (resp. $\sigma_\kappa.Y$) the the value of a variable $X \in Var \cup \{time, F\}$ (resp. $Y \in \{y\} \cup F_{\boldsymbol{k}}$) in the discrete (resp. continuous) environment. We write $\Sigma^{\mathcal{H}}$ the set of all hybrid environments:

$$\Sigma^{\mathcal{H}} = \left\{ (\sigma_\delta, \sigma_\kappa) \;\middle|\; \begin{array}{c} \sigma_\delta \in \Sigma_\Delta \text{ and } \sigma_\kappa \in \Sigma_\kappa \text{ and} \\ \exists (t_n), (c_n) \text{ s.t. } \forall i \in \mathbb{N},\ \forall t \in [t_i, t_{i+1}[, \\ \sigma_\delta.F(t) = \sigma_\kappa.F_{c_i}(t) \end{array} \right\} . \tag{5}$$

We write $\Pi_\delta : (\sigma_\delta, \sigma_\kappa) \mapsto \sigma_\delta$ and $\Pi_\kappa : (\sigma_\delta, \sigma_\kappa) \mapsto \sigma_\kappa$ the two projections of an hybrid environment into a discrete (resp. continuous) one.

4.2 Hybrid Denotations

The denotation of the purely discrete parts of the language are defined as usual for imperative languages (see [24] for example). We have denotations for numerical (resp. boolean) expressions $[\![exp]\!]$ (resp. $[\![bool]\!]$) which are functions between a discrete environment and a numerical (resp. boolean) value. Every discrete statement *stmt* also has a denotation which is a function between discrete environmnents. We extend them to hybrid environments: $[\![exp]\!]^{\mathcal{H}}(\sigma_\delta, \sigma_\kappa) = [\![exp]\!](\sigma_\delta)$, $[\![bool]\!]^{\mathcal{H}}(\sigma_\delta, \sigma_\kappa) = [\![bool]\!](\sigma_\delta)$, and $[\![stms]\!]^{\mathcal{H}}(\sigma_\delta, \sigma_\kappa) = [\![stms]\!](\sigma_\delta)$. The denotation of a **wait** is a function from $\Sigma^{\mathcal{H}}$ to $\Sigma^{\mathcal{H}}$ that modifies the value of time: $[\![\mathbf{wait}(c)]\!]^{\mathcal{H}}(\sigma_\delta, \sigma_\kappa) = (\sigma_\delta[time \mapsto \sigma_\delta.time + c, \sigma_\kappa)$. The denotation of an action **sens.y?x** (Equation (6) with $n = \lfloor \sigma_\delta.time + 1 \rfloor$) is a function from $\Sigma^{\mathcal{H}}$ to $\Sigma^{\mathcal{H}}$ that modifies a pair $(\sigma_\delta, \sigma_\kappa)$ as follows: it first updates σ_κ to ensure that $\sigma_\kappa.y$ has a value at time $\sigma_\delta.time$ and then it binds x with this value in σ_δ. The first step is done by applying $\lfloor \sigma_\delta.time + 1 \rfloor$ times the operator Γ_{F,y_0} (see Sect. 3.2) to $\sigma_\kappa.y$ with $F = \sigma_\delta.F$ and $y_0 = \sigma_\kappa.y(0)$.

$$[\![\mathbf{sens}.\mathrm{y?x}]\!]^{\mathcal{H}}(\sigma_\delta, \sigma_\kappa) = \begin{pmatrix} \sigma'_\kappa = \sigma_\kappa[y \mapsto \Gamma^n_{\sigma_\delta.F,y(0)}(y)], \\ \sigma'_\delta = \sigma_\delta[x \mapsto mid(\sigma'_\kappa.y(\sigma_\delta.time))] \end{pmatrix} . \tag{6}$$

The denotation of an action **act.k!c** (Equation (7)) is a function from $\Sigma^{\mathcal{H}}$ to $\Sigma^{\mathcal{H}}$ that modifies$(\sigma_\delta, \sigma_\kappa)$ as follows: σ_κ is left unchanged and in σ_δ, the function F is modified so that it takes the value of $\sigma_\kappa.F_c$ for times greater than $\sigma_\delta.time$.

$$[\![\mathbf{act}.\mathrm{k!c}]\!]^{\mathcal{H}}(\sigma_\delta, \sigma_\kappa) = \left(\sigma_\delta \left[F \mapsto \lambda t, y. \begin{cases} \sigma_\delta.F(y,t) & \text{if } t \le \sigma_\delta.time \\ \sigma_\kappa.F_c(y,t) & \text{otherwise} \end{cases} \right], \sigma_\kappa \right) . \tag{7}$$

We can compute the hybrid semantics $[\![\Delta]\!]^{\mathcal{H}}$ of the discrete program by combining these denotations. This does not however compute the semantics of the continuous environment, this is the role of the semantics of the hybrid system.

4.3 Hybrid Semantics

The semantics of the hybrid model $\Omega = (\Delta, \kappa)$ is a function between hybrid environments: $[\![\Omega]\!]^{\mathcal{H}} : \Sigma^{\mathcal{H}} \to \Sigma^{\mathcal{H}}$. $[\![\Omega]\!]^{\mathcal{H}}$ alters a pair $(\sigma_\delta, \sigma_\kappa)$ as follows. It computes $(\sigma'_\delta, \sigma'_\kappa) = [\![\Delta]\!]^{\mathcal{H}}(\sigma_\delta, \sigma_\kappa)$ and two cases occur. If $\sigma'_\kappa = \sigma_\kappa$, the discrete program has no effect on the environment, i.e. either there are no **sens** statements in it, or they have no effect on σ_κ. This is the case only if $\sigma_\kappa.y$ is a fix-point of Γ_{F,y_0}, i.e. $\sigma_\delta.y = [\![\kappa]\!](\sigma_\delta.y)$. In this case, we have computed both the continuous semantics and the discrete one, so we set $[\![\Omega]\!]^{\mathcal{H}}(\sigma_\delta, \sigma_\kappa) = (\sigma'_\delta, \sigma'_\kappa)$. On the other hand, if $\sigma'_\kappa \neq \sigma_\kappa$, the program has modified the environment and thus brought $\sigma_\delta.y$ closer to $[\![\kappa]\!](\sigma_\delta.y)$. σ'_δ (resp. σ'_κ) is only an approximation of the result of the discrete (resp. continuous) system and we must iterate the process to obtain a better approximation. We thus propagate σ'_κ into the discrete subsystem, i.e. we apply $[\![\Delta]\!]^{\mathcal{H}}$ to $(\sigma_\delta, \sigma'_\kappa)$ and repeat the operation. The semantics $[\![\Omega]\!]^{\mathcal{H}}$ is computed as a fix-point of a function that applies $[\![\Delta]\!]$ consecutively until the semantics of the continuous environment has been computed. The formal definition of $[\![\Omega]\!]^{\mathcal{H}}$ is given in (8). Let us note that $[\![\Omega]\!]^{\mathcal{H}}$ is actually the only fix-point of the function $\Gamma^{\mathcal{H}}$ just like $[\![\kappa]\!]$ was the only fix-point of Γ_{F,y_0} in Sect. 3. $[\![\Omega]\!]^{\mathcal{H}}$ is compatible with the continuous semantics $[\![\kappa]\!]$ presented in Sect. 3: the continuous environment is finally computed as the fix-point of the operator Γ_{F,y_0} as in Sect. 3.2. It is also compatible with the standard denotational semantics of imperative languages: if Δ does not have any hybrid actions, then $[\![\Omega]\!]^{\mathcal{H}}$ is precisely the semantics of the discrete program as defined in [24] for example.

$$\begin{aligned} [\![\Omega]\!]^{\mathcal{H}} &= Fix(\Gamma^{\mathcal{H}}) \text{ where} \\ \Gamma^{\mathcal{H}}(\varphi)(\sigma_\delta, \sigma_\kappa) &= (\sigma'_\delta, \sigma'_\kappa) \text{ with } \begin{cases} \sigma'_\delta = \Pi_\delta([\![\Delta]\!]^{\mathcal{H}}(\sigma_\delta, \sigma'_\kappa)) \\ \sigma'_\kappa = \Pi_\kappa\left(\varphi(\sigma_\delta, \Pi_\kappa([\![\Delta]\!]^{\mathcal{H}}(\sigma_\kappa, \sigma_\delta)))\right) \end{cases} \end{aligned} . \tag{8}$$

4.4 Example

To illustrate that our semantics really computes the behavior of the hybrid system, let us consider a simplified version of the one-tank controller (see the

Table 1. First three iterations of the semantics computation

Statement	Iteration 1			Iteration 2			Iteration 3		
	t	h	x	t	h	x	t	h	x
Initial environment	0	$\bot$	$\bot$	0	$\bot$	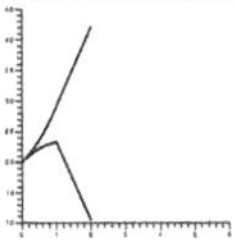	0	$\bot$	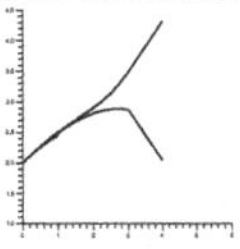
`wait(1);`	1			1			1		
`sens.x?h;`		2.0	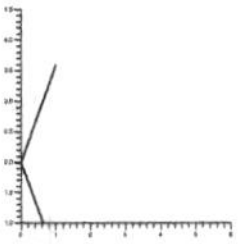		2.45	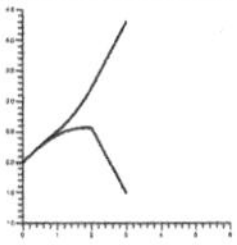		2.48	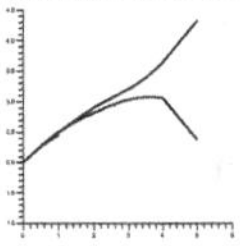
`if (h>h_max) act.k!1;`	$F \mapsto F_0$			$F \mapsto F_0$			$F \mapsto F_0$		
`wait(1);`	2			2			2		
`sens.x?h;`		2.8	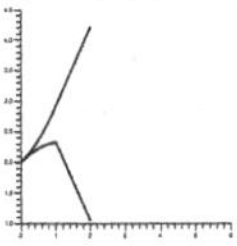		2.85	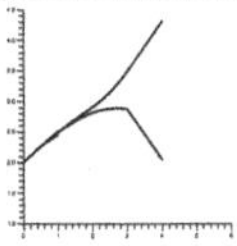		2.95	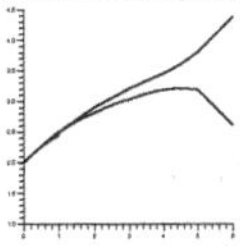
`if(h>h_max) act.k!1;`	$F \mapsto F_0$			$F \mapsto F_0$			$F \mapsto \lambda t.(t < 2)?F_0; F_1$		

first column of Tab. 1). We only consider two iterations of the **while** loop (which has a period of one second) and forget about the anticipation mechanism. The continuous system is still given by (2), with $i = 2$, $k_1 = k_2 = 1$, $h = 3$, $h\_max = 2.9$, and the initial value for the height of water x is $x_0 = 2$. We have two possible continuous dynamics : F_0 (the valve is closed) and F_1 (the valve is open). Initially, the valve is closed, i.e. we start with the dynamic F_0. Table 1 shows the first three iterations of the computation of the semantics of the system. For each line of the program, we indicate how the variables are changed (t is the time, h the discrete variable and x the continuous one). For the **act** statement, we indicate how it changes the function F of the hybrid environment. The notation $\lambda t.(t < 2)?F_0; F_1$ means that $F(t) = F_0(t)$ if $t < 2$, and $F(t) = F_1(t)$ otherwise.

5 Conclusion

In this article, we presented a new approach to hybrid systems that can be used for the modeling and analysis of large critical embedded programs. Our model is based on a clear separation of the discrete and the continuous systems: ordinary differential equations with boolean parameters are used to model the continuous system, an imperative language with hybrid statements is used for the discrete part. The emphasis has been placed on making this model as unintrusive as possible for existing software, so we believe that we can use it for industrial size problems. We defined the semantics of our model in two steps: first, we extended results by Edalat and Lieutier [9] to consider the maximal solutions of IVP on $\mathbb{R}_+$ and we presented the semantics of the continuous model as a function mapping the initial condition to the maximal solution. The semantics of the hybrid system is then an extension of the standard denotational semantics of imperative languages in which actions of sensors and actuators are defined.

To the best of our knowledge, this is the first attempt to integrate into the semantics of imperative languages the continuous environment that models the programs inputs. We are not aware of any equivalent, operationally defined models. We believe that our model is expressive enough to encode most of Henzinger's hybrid automata, but both models are based on very different asumptions (for example, we consider that time is driven by the discrete system) so that it is difficult to formally compare them.

This work is a first step toward the validation of embedded software with their environment. The analysis of such systems using, for example, abstract interpretation techniques [6] requires two stages. First, the continuous system must be abstracted in a non-naive way. The theory of guaranteed integration of ODE [21] brings us the adequate tools for the safe abstraction of the continuous system. Validated ODE solvers [4] compute interval bounds that are proved to contain the solution. This can be seen as a valid abstraction in the theory of abstract interpretation. For the analysis of the discrete part, the use of an implementation level model allows us to use existing methods [7,13]. These methods must however be completed so that they consider time: the main difficulty in the analysis of the discrete system is to carefully analyze the time at which every statement is executed (this is necessary for the sensor actions to be precise enough) This modification of standard static analysis techniques to our framework will be our main concern for future work. Another interesting application of our approach for hybrid systems is to modify standard strictness [20] or termination analysis [2] so that they fit to our model. This could be used to solve, in an approximate way, the reachability problem of a discrete state in a hybrid system, which is known to be undecidable [16]. Several methods have been proposed for its simplification [17]; we believe that our approach may be efficiently used for its approximate solution as it benefits from all the static analysis based methods for programming languages.

References

1. Alur, R., Grosu, R., Hur, Y., Kumar, V., Lee, I.: Modular specification of hybrid systems in charon. In: Lynch, N.A., Krogh, B.H. (eds.) HSCC 2000. LNCS, vol. 1790, Springer, Heidelberg (2000)
2. Berdine, J., Chawdhary, A., Cook, B., Distefano, D., O'Hearn, P.: Variance analyses from invariance analyses. In: POPL, pp. 211–224 (2007)
3. Bouissou, O., Martel, M.: A hybrid denotational semantics of hybrid systems - extended version, `http://hal.archives-ouvertes.fr/hal-00177031/`
4. Bouissou, O., Martel, M.: GRKLib: a guaranteed runge-kutta library. In: International Symposium on Scientific Computing, Computer Arithmetic and Validated Numerics, IEEE, Los Alamitos (2006)

5. Cousot, P.: Integrating physical systems in the static analysis of embedded control software. In: Yi, K. (ed.) APLAS 2005. LNCS, vol. 3780, pp. 135–138. Springer, Heidelberg (2005)
6. Cousot, P., Cousot, R.: Abstract interpretation: a unified lattice model for static analysis of programs by construction or approximation of fixpoints. In: POPL, pp. 238–252. ACM Press, New York (1977)
7. Cousot, P., Cousot, R., Feret, J., Mauborgne, L., Monniaux, A.M.D., Rival, X.: The ASTREÉ analyzer. In: Sagiv, M. (ed.) ESOP 2005. LNCS, vol. 3444, Springer, Heidelberg (2005)
8. Cuijpers, P., Reniers, M.: Hybrid process algebra. Journal of Logic and Algebraic Programming 62(2), 191–245 (2005)
9. Edalat, A., Lieutier, A.: Domain theory and differential calculus. Mathematical Structures in Computer Science 14(6), 771–802 (2002)
10. Edalat, A., Lieutier, A., Pattinson, D.: A computational model for multi-variable differential calculus. In: Sassone, V. (ed.) FOSSACS 2005. LNCS, vol. 3441, Springer, Heidelberg (2005)
11. Edalat, A., Pattinson, D.: Denotational Semantics of Hybrid Automata. In: Aceto, L., Ingólfsdóttir, A. (eds.) FOSSACS 2006 and ETAPS 2006. LNCS, vol. 3921, pp. 231–245. Springer, Heidelberg (2006)
12. Alur, R., et al.: The algorithmic analysis of hybrid systems. Theoretical Computer Science 138(1), 3–34 (1995)
13. Goubault, E., Martel, M., Putot, S.: Asserting the precision of floating-point computations: A simple abstract interpreter. In: Le Métayer, D. (ed.) ESOP 2002. LNCS, vol. 2305, pp. 209–212. Springer, Heidelberg (2002)
14. Goubault, E., Martel, M., Putot, S.: Some future challenges in the validation of control systems. In: ERTS (2006)
15. Gupta, V., Jagadeesan, R., Saraswat, V.: Computing with continuous change. Science of Computer Programming 30(1–2), 3–49 (1998)
16. Henzinger, T.A.: The theory of hybrid automata. In: Symposium on Logic in Computer Science, pp. 278–292. IEEE Computer Society Press, Los Alamitos (1996)
17. Henzinger, T.A., Ho, P.H., Wong-Toi, H.: Algorithmic analysis of nonlinear hybrid systems. IEEE Transactions on Automatic Control 43, 540–554 (1998)
18. Kowalewski, S., Stursberg, O., Fritz, M., Graf, H., Preuß, I.H.J.: A case study in tool-aided analysis of discretely controlled continuous systems: the two tanks problem. In: Antsaklis, P.J., Kohn, W., Lemmon, M.D., Nerode, A., Sastry, S.S. (eds.) HS 1997. LNCS, vol. 1567, Springer, Heidelberg (1999)
19. Martin, K.: A Foundation for Computation. PhD thesis, Department of Mathematics, Tulane University (2000)
20. Mycroft, A.: Abstract interpretation and Optimizing Transformations for Applicative Programs. PhD thesis, University of Edinburgh (1981)
21. Nedialkov, N.S., Jackson, K.R., Corliss, G.F.: Validated solutions of initial value problems for ordinary differential equations. Applied Mathematics and Computation 105(1), 21–68 (1999)
22. Tarski, A.: A lattice-theoretical fixpoint theorem and its applications. Pacific Journal of Mathematics 5, 285–309 (1955)
23. van Beek, D., Man, K., Reniers, M., Rooda, J., Schiffelers, R.: Syntax and consistent equation semantics of hybrid chi. Journal of Logic and Algebraic Programming 68(1-2), 129–210 (2006)
24. Winskel, G.: The formal semantics of programming languages: An introduction. MIT Press, Cambridge (1993)

Full Abstraction for Linda

Cinzia Di Giusto and Maurizio Gabbrielli

Dip. Scienze dell'Informazione, Università di Bologna
Bologna, Italy
{digiusto,gabbri}@cs.unibo.it

Abstract. This paper investigates full abstraction of a trace semantics for two Linda-like languages. The first language provides primitives for adding and removing messages from a shared memory, local choice, parallel composition and recursion. The second one adds the possibility of checking for the absence of a message in the store. After having defined a denotational semantics based on traces, we obtain fully abstract semantics for both languages by using suitable abstractions in order to identify different traces which do not correspond to different operational behaviours.

1 Introduction

One of the fundamental purposes of a semantics is to provide a rigorous mean for proving the correctness of programs w.r.t. some behavioural specification. Several different tools (operational, denotational, algebraic and logic) can be used to this aim and ideally one would like to have a compositional and fully abstract semantics.

Compositionality is of course an important feature since it is the foundation for managing large systems complexity when considering program verification, analysis and (modular) design. Most of the above mentioned tools indeed allow to obtain rather easily a compositional semantics.

Full abstraction is also a desirable feature since it allows to simplify and "economize" as much as possible a semantics while preserving its correctness. However, in general this is a rather difficult target to achieve. To be more precise and to set the ground for the content of this paper, following [4,9,12] we can summarize the terms of the problem as follows. Given a language L, define a semantics that associates to each process (or program) P in L a set of observable properties $\mathcal{O}(P)$. This is usually done in operational terms by using a transition system and a suitable definition of $\mathcal{O}(P)$ which identifies computational aspects relevant for a specific class of applications. In case such semantics is compositional, i.e. if we can reconstruct $\mathcal{O}(P\ op\ Q)$ from $\mathcal{O}(P)$ and $\mathcal{O}(Q)$ for any operator *op* of the language L, we have a satisfactory semantics, since the observational equivalence on processes induced by $\mathcal{O}(P)$ is preserved by contexts. More precisely, we have that $\mathcal{O}(P) = \mathcal{O}(Q)$ iff, for any context $C[\bullet]$, $\mathcal{O}(C[P]) = \mathcal{O}(C[Q])$.

However often this is not the case and in order to obtain a compositional semantics some richer semantic structures than those used in $\mathcal{O}(P)$ need to be considered. For example, as we will see in Section 4, typically pairs representing the input/output behaviour of a process are not sufficient to obtain compositionality and one has to use

S. Drossopoulou (Ed.): ESOP 2008, LNCS 4960, pp. 78–92, 2008.

traces. It can happen that these richer semantic structures "add too much" in the sense that the semantics $[\![\cdot]\!]$ based on them allows to distinguish processes which have the same behaviour w.r.t. $\mathcal{O}(P)$, under any possible context. In this case suitable abstractions must be used in $[\![\cdot]\!]$ in order to obtain a fully abstract result which, in general, can be stated as follows: $[\![P]\!] = [\![Q]\!]$ iff, for any context $C[\bullet]$, $\mathcal{O}(C[P]) = \mathcal{O}(C[Q])$ holds.

In this paper we investigate the full abstraction problem, as described above, for two variants of Linda. Linda is a programming paradigm [11] which allows interprocess communication through a shared data space, also called tuple space, where processes can post and retrieve messages (also called tuples). The shared memory paradigm offers some advantages since it decouples communication between processes: communication is in fact asynchronous and processes do not need to be aware of each other identity or location. Indeed, the Linda paradigm has received also a commercial interest, mainly due to the applications which use the Java Spaces from Sun Microsystems [10] and TSpaces from IBM [13] models, both based on Linda (a more detailed comparison of Linda implementations can be found in [19]). Distributed Linda-like languages have also been investigated. Notably, Klaim [17] is an implemented language based on the Linda paradigm where the central store is replaced by several distributed local stores and processes mobility among different locations is supported.

Fully abstract semantics based on traces for input/output observables have been studied many years ago for several concurrent languages, as we shall discuss in Section 6. However, to the best of our knowledge no one has yet addressed this problem for a Linda-like language.

Many different formalizations and variants of Linda have been defined. Here we use essentially the process-algebraic formalization of Linda introduced in [6,7] and we consider the very basic Linda dialects. The first one, which we call Linda-core, apart from the usual operators in process algebra (choice, parallel composition, recursion) contains the two Linda primitives in and out which allow to remove and add messages to the store, respectively. For Linda-core we define a compositional, fixpoint trace semantics which is correct but not fully abstract when considering the input/output pairs. Hence we introduce a suitable abstraction on traces and show that this allows us to obtain a fully abstract semantics. The second dialect (Linda-inp) enriches the syntax of Linda-core by allowing also a construct (inp) which allows to check the absence of information in the store. We prove that in this case a much simpler abstraction on traces is sufficient to obtain a full abstraction result. This accounts for the augmented expressive power of the language with inp, which can be formally proven by using the techniques in [6,20]. Unfortunately, due to the saturation operator, the fully abstract semantics are not compositional. This is unavoidable in our trace model, since the properties that we need to abstract depend on sets of traces (rather than on single ones). Of course this does not mean that in general a compositional fully abstract semantics based on traces does not exist. However, in case it existed, it would use traces substantially more complicated than ours.

The remainder of the paper is organized as follows. Section 2 introduces the Linda languages under consideration while Section 3 defines their denotational semantics. We then provide the fully abstract semantics for the core language in Section 4. Section 5 contains the main theorem on the full abstraction for the language extended with the *inp* primitive. Finally, Section 6 concludes by discussing some related works.

2 Preliminaries

In this section, following the process algebraic view of Linda proposed in [6] we recall the syntax of the Linda languages that we consider and their operational semantics.

2.1 Linda-Core

As previously mentioned, Linda is a paradigm which provides a simple model to describe communication between processes. The central notion in Linda is the one of *tuple space*. A tuple space is a shared data space (i.e. a common store) where all the *tuples* representing the information to be exchanged are stored. Here we shall abstract from the specific nature of tuples assuming that these are elementary messages. Communication is represented by the concurrent and asynchronous activity of several processes which add or remove messages from the common store. I.e. the sender dispatches a message through a non-blocking operation which adds the tuple in the tuple space. Then the message has an independent existence until a receiver retrieves and removes it from the shared space. Such kind of communication is called *generative* (see [11]).

Processes of the language Linda-core, denoted by $P, Q, \ldots$, are then given by the following grammar:

$$P ::= \mathbf{0} \mid out(a).P \mid in(a).P \mid P \mid P \mid P + P \mid recX.P \tag{1}$$

where we assume that $a \in Msg$ and Msg denotes the set of all possible messages (or tuples), ranged over by $a, b, \ldots$.

Intuitively $\mathbf{0}$ represents the process that does nothing. Then the process $out(a).P$ adds the message a to the store and then behaves as P. The message a which has been added to the store will be visible to other processes only after the completion of the $out(a)$ action, however note that other interpretations are possible for this primitive (see [5]). If a is present in the tuple space, $in(a).P$ removes the message and then behaves as P. Otherwise if a is not present, the process $in(a).P$ is suspended until a becomes available in the store. The parallel construct $P \mid Q$ is interpreted in terms of interleaving. The process $P + Q$ can non-deterministically choose to behave either as P or as Q (hence we have a form of local choice). Finally we have the recursion operator where we assume that guarded recursion is used (i.e. the process $recX.X$ is not allowed).

The operational semantics of Linda-core is described by means of a transition system $T = (Conf, \rightarrow)$. Configurations $Conf$ are pairs of the form $\langle P, \mathcal{M} \rangle$ where P is a process and $\mathcal{M}$ is a multiset containing tuples, also called tuple space or store. The transition relation $\rightarrow \subseteq Conf \times Conf$ is the least relation satisfying the rules in Table 1, which should be self-explaining, provided we introduce the following notation.

Notation 1. *To describe updates in the store we will use* $\oplus$ *and* $\ominus$ *to denote multisets union and difference, respectively. So* $\mathcal{M} \oplus \{a\}$ *means that a message (a tuple) '* a *' has been added to the store while* $\mathcal{M} \ominus \{a\}$ *indicates that a copy of '* a *' has been removed.*

Table 1. An operational semantics An operational semantics for Linda-core

R1	$\langle out(a).P, \mathcal{M}\rangle \rightarrow \langle P, \mathcal{M} \oplus \{a\}\rangle$
R2	$\langle in(a).P, \mathcal{M} \oplus \{a\}\rangle \rightarrow \langle P, \mathcal{M}\rangle$
R3	$\dfrac{\langle P, \mathcal{M}\rangle \rightarrow \langle P', \mathcal{M}'\rangle}{\langle P \mid Q, \mathcal{M}\rangle \rightarrow \langle P' \mid Q, \mathcal{M}'\rangle}$ and $\dfrac{\langle Q, \mathcal{M}\rangle \rightarrow \langle Q', \mathcal{M}'\rangle}{\langle P \mid Q, \mathcal{M}\rangle \rightarrow \langle P \mid Q', \mathcal{M}'\rangle}$
R4	$\langle P + Q, \mathcal{M}\rangle \rightarrow \langle P, \mathcal{M}\rangle$ and $\langle P + Q, \mathcal{M}\rangle \rightarrow \langle Q, \mathcal{M}\rangle$
R5	$\dfrac{\langle P[recX.P/X], \mathcal{M}\rangle \rightarrow \langle P', \mathcal{M}'\rangle}{\langle recX.P, \mathcal{M}\rangle \rightarrow \langle P', \mathcal{M}'\rangle}$

Table 2. The rule for inp

R6	$\langle inp(a)?P : Q, \mathcal{M} \oplus \{a\}\rangle \rightarrow \langle P, \mathcal{M}\rangle$
	$\langle inp(a)?P : Q, \mathcal{M}\rangle \rightarrow \langle Q, \mathcal{M}\rangle$ provided $a \notin \mathcal{M}$

A transition $\langle P, \mathcal{M}\rangle \rightarrow \langle Q, \mathcal{M}'\rangle$ then means that the process P reduces to Q, possibly by producing some changes in the store which evolves from $\mathcal{M}$ to $\mathcal{M}'$. A sequence of configurations is called run or computation. The reflexive transitive closure of $\rightarrow$ is denoted by $\Rightarrow$. By using the transition system described above we can characterize several different notions of observables. The ones we are interested in here consider simply the input/output behaviour of a process in terms of the tuple space. The input is therefore the initial tuple space, while the output is the final store produced by a process which cannot further proceed in the computation (denoted by $\not\rightarrow$) either because it is suspended on an in operation or because it has consumed all the actions. More precisely we define the observables as follows.

Definition 1 (Observables $\mathcal{O}(P)$). *Let P be a Linda process. We define:*
$\mathcal{O}(P) = \{(\mathcal{M}_1, \mathcal{M}_n) \mid \langle P, \mathcal{M}_1\rangle \Rightarrow \langle P_n, \mathcal{M}_n\rangle \not\rightarrow\}$

2.2 Linda-inp

We will now introduce a slightly different variant of Linda, called Linda-inp, obtained by adding a new operator $inp(a)?P : Q$ which allows also to check whether a message is not present in the store. More precisely, the previous construct checks whether the store contains the message a: if the message is present in the store then the process continues with P, otherwise with Q.

Therefore we will add to the grammar in (1) the following primitive:

$$P ::= inp(a)?P : P \tag{2}$$

The operational semantics for Linda-inp is obtained by (a transition system defined by) adding to the rules of Table 1 the rules contained in Table 2. The observables can be defined as before.

3 Denotational Semantics

It is easy to see that the operational semantics which associates to a process P its observables $\mathcal{O}(P)$ is not compositional. For example consider the processes $Q = out(b)$ and $P = out(a).in(a).out(b)$. Then $\mathcal{O}(P) = \mathcal{O}(Q)$ holds, however, considering the process $R = in(a).out(ok)$ we have that $(\emptyset, \{ok\}) \in \mathcal{O}(P \mid R) \setminus \mathcal{O}(Q \mid R)$ which means that the observables of a parallel composition cannot be obtained from the observables of the two processes being composed (in parallel). This problem is in general well known, in fact in order to obtain a compositional model more informative structures than input/output pairs have been used. In particular, models based on traces (or sequences) have been used for many concurrent languages, starting from the early works on dataflow languages [16], imperative ones [4] and concurrent constraint programming [9].

In the following we will define a compositional semantics which correctly models the $\mathcal{O}(P)$ observables and which is based on traces. This semantics is similar to those used for timed Linda in [8] (and therefore to that one of [9]), even though the technical treatment is different. In fact in [8], where maximal parallelism was assumed, the denotational model used traces of pairs of tuple spaces, representing the input and the output at each step of the computation. Here, due to the interleaving semantics and to local choice, this kind of sequences is not sufficient to obtain a correct model. Essentially the problem is that we have to distinguish the processes $out(a) \mid in(a)$ and $out(a).in(a) + in(a).out(a)$ (because when starting with an empty store the second process can produce an empty store as a result) and this cannot be done by using simply input/output pairs. Hence, here we consider a denotational model which associates to a process a set of sequences of the form $\alpha_1, \ldots, \alpha_n$ where each α_i is an element of the set $\mathcal{A} = \{in(a), out(a), \overline{in}(a), \overline{inp}(a) \mid a \in Msg\}$ (where Msg denotes all the possible messages, as previously mentioned). The first two kinds of actions in $\mathcal{A}$ are obvious as they represent the corresponding operations on the store, $\overline{in}(a)$ and $\overline{inp}(a)$ are used to express absence of information. We denote with $\mathcal{S}$ the set of all possible sequences defined in this way.

We introduce now two denotational semantics (one for each language we are considering) based on traces which are compositional by construction. Such semantics are the least functions $[\![\cdot]\!] : Processes \rightarrow 2^{\mathcal{S}}$, which satisfy the equations in Table 3 for Linda-core and the equations in Table 3 plus that in Table 4 for Linda-inp. The order on functions here is the one induced by set inclusion on the co-domain. Well known fixpoint results allow to obtain the semantics as the least fixpoint of the operators defined implicitly by the equations in the Tables.

3.1 Denotational Semantics for Linda-Core

The equations should be self-explanatory apart from a few details. The denotation of the **0** process is the empty sequence, while the equations D2 and D3 show the expected behaviour for the basic primitives. Note that in equation D3 we have two cases: the first one corresponds to the case in which a is present in the store, thus the computation can proceed (with the sequence s) after the in action. On the other hand, the $\overline{in}(a)$ action represents the absence of a in the store, in which case the computation terminates (the

Table 3. A denotational semantics for Linda-core

D1 $[\![\mathbf{0}]\!] = \{\epsilon\}$

D2 $[\![out(a).P]\!] = \{out(a) \cdot s \mid s \in [\![P]\!]\}$

D3 $[\![in(a).P]\!] = \{in(a) \cdot s \mid s \in [\![P]\!]\} \cup \{\overline{in}(a)\}$

D4 $[\![P \mid Q]\!] = [\![P]\!] \,\tilde{|}\, [\![Q]\!]$

where the operator $\tilde{|}$ is inductively defined as follow:

$$(x \cdot s) \,\tilde{|}\, y = y \,\tilde{|}\, (x \cdot s) = \{(x \cdot t) \mid t \in s \,\tilde{|}\, y\} \;\cup\; \{y \cdot x \cdot s\}$$

$$(x \cdot s) \,\tilde{|}\, (y \cdot t) = (y \cdot t) \,\tilde{|}\, (x \cdot s) =$$
$$\{(x \cdot u) \mid u \in s \,\tilde{|}\, (y \cdot t)\} \cup \{(y \cdot u) \mid u \in (x \cdot s) \,\tilde{|}\, t\}$$

with $x, y \in \mathcal{A}$ and $s, t, u \in \mathcal{S}$.

D5 $[\![P + Q]\!] = [\![P]\!] \cup [\![Q]\!]$

D6 $[\![recX.P]\!] = [\![P[recX.P/X]]\!]$

process is suspended). The parallel operator is interpreted in terms of interleaving as usual, while since the choice is local, it can be modeled by a simple set union. Recursion is treated in the usual way.

In order to show that the denotational semantics is correct w.r.t. our notion of observables we define the evaluation of a trace as follows ($\uparrow$ means undefined).

Definition 2. *Given a trace $s \in \mathcal{S}$ and a store $\mathcal{M}$, the function $eval_1(s, \mathcal{M})$ is defined by the following cases:*

$$eval_1(\epsilon, \mathcal{M}) = \mathcal{M}$$
$$eval_1(out(x) \cdot t, \mathcal{M}) = eval_1(t, \mathcal{M} \oplus \{x\})$$
$$eval_1(in(x) \cdot t, \mathcal{M}) = \begin{cases} eval_1(t, \mathcal{M} \ominus \{x\}) & \textit{if } x \in \mathcal{M} \\ \uparrow & \textit{otherwise} \end{cases}$$
$$eval_1(\overline{in}(x) \cdot t, \mathcal{M}) = \begin{cases} \mathcal{M} & \textit{if } x \notin \mathcal{M} \textit{ and } t = \epsilon \\ \uparrow & \textit{otherwise} \end{cases}$$

The correctness is then stated by the following proposition which can be proved by using a fixpoint characterization of the semantics $[\![\cdot]\!]$. This can be obtained by first considering an interpretation as a mapping $I : Processes \to 2^{\mathcal{S}}$ which associates to each process a denotation (i.e. a set of sequences). The set $\mathcal{I}$ of all the interpretations is easily seen to be a cpo with the ordering induced by $\subseteq$. An operator $\mathcal{F} : \mathcal{I} \to \mathcal{I}$ is obtained by substituting $[\![\cdot]\!]$ for $\mathcal{F}(I)$ in equations D1-D5 and in the left hand side of equation D6, and by replacing $[\![\cdot]\!]$ for I in the right hand side of equation D6. The semantics $[\![\cdot]\!]$ is then the least fixpoint of $\mathcal{F}$, which can be obtained as the least upper bound of $\{\mathcal{F}^n(\bot) \mid n \geq 0\}$, where $\bot$ is the least interpretation, $\mathcal{F}^0(\bot) = \bot$ and

Table 4. The equations for Linda-inp

D7	$[\![inp(a)?P : Q]\!] = \{in(a) \cdot s \mid s \in [\![P]\!]\} \cup \{\overline{inp}(a) \cdot s \mid s \in [\![Q]\!]\}$

$\mathcal{F}^n(\bot) = \mathcal{F}(\mathcal{F}^{n-1}(\bot))$. This allows us to prove the proposition by induction on the structure of processes and on induction on the powers $\mathcal{F}^n(\bot)$ of the operator.

Proposition 1 (Correctness). *Given a Linda-core process P,* $\mathcal{O}(P) = \{(\mathcal{M}_0, eval_1(s, \mathcal{M}_0)) \mid s \in [\![P]\!]$ *and* $eval_1(s, \mathcal{M}_0) \neq \uparrow\}$ *holds.*

3.2 Denotational semantics for Linda-inp

When considering the Linda-inp language the denotational semantics can be obtained from Table 3 by adding the equation in Table 4. This difference w.r.t. the case of Linda core is due to the presence of the inp, which is described by Equation D7: since when a is present both the $inp(a)$ and the $in(a)$ construct are modeled in the same way, when a is not present we have to distinguish the two cases (by using $\overline{in}(a)$ and $\overline{inp}(a)$) since it would not be correct to use the evaluation given in Definition 2 for the $in(a)$.

In order to prove the correctness of the model introduced above we need to add to $eval_1$ the new cases obtaining the evaluation function $eval_2$:

Definition 3. *Given a trace $s \in \mathcal{S}$ and a store $\mathcal{M}$, the function $eval_2(s, \mathcal{M})$ is defined by the following cases:*

$$eval_2(\overline{inp}(x) \cdot t, \mathcal{M}) = \begin{cases} eval_2(t, \mathcal{M}) & \text{if } x \notin \mathcal{M} \\ \uparrow & \text{otherwise} \end{cases}$$

$$eval_2(\alpha(x) \cdot t, \mathcal{M}) = eval_1(\alpha(x) \cdot t, \mathcal{M}) \text{ for } \alpha \neq \overline{inp}$$

Using the same technique of Proposition 1 it can be easily proved the following theorem that states the correctness of the denotational model:

Proposition 2 (Correctness). *Given a Linda-inp process P,* $\mathcal{O}(P) = \{(\mathcal{M}_0, eval_2(s, \mathcal{M}_0)) \mid s \in [\![P]\!]\}$ *holds.*

4 Full Abstraction for Linda-Core

The aim of this section is to obtain a fully abstract semantics for the Linda-core language. The semantics introduced in the previous section represents a too fine description of the actions that affect the store, since it records all the possible changes while the observables capture only the initial and the final state. It is therefore immediate to find processes which have a different denotation, while having the same input/output behaviour under any possible context.

In order to obtain full abstraction we saturate the denotational semantics by adding all those traces which, intuitively, represent a computation whose input/output behaviour, in any possible context, can be simulated by a trace which is already in the semantics. The formal definition is as follows.

Definition 4 (Saturation). *Let $T \subseteq S$ be a set of traces. We define the saturation of T as the minimal set $Sat(T)$ which satisfies the following rules:*

i) if $s \in T$ then $s \in Sat(T)$
ii) if $s \cdot out(a) \cdot t \cdot in(a) \cdot v \in Sat(T)$ then $s \cdot t \cdot v \in Sat(T)$
iii) if $s{\cdot}out(a){\cdot}t{\cdot}in(a){\cdot}v \in Sat(T)$ then $s{\cdot}out(a){\cdot}t{\cdot}in(a){\cdot}out(a){\cdot}in(a){\cdot}v \in Sat(T)$
iv) $s \in Sat(T)$ iff $s \cdot in(a) \cdot out(a) \in Sat(T)$
v) if $s \cdot out(a) \cdot t \in Sat(T)$ then $s \cdot t' \in Sat(T)$ where $t' \in \{out(a) \,\tilde{|}\, t\}$
vi) all the traces in T of the form $t \cdot \overline{in}(a) \cdot u$ with $u \neq \epsilon$ are removed;

According to the previous definition in $Sat(T)$ we add all the traces which (i) are derived (inductively) from the traces in T by performing the following operations: (ii) Removing complementary actions $out(a)$ and $in(a)$ which appear, in this order, in different places of the sequence; it is rather clear that this does not change the operational behaviour described by the original sequence. (iii) Adding a "stuttering step" represented by a sequence $out(a) \cdot in(a)$ of two complementary actions is also allowed, provided that both these actions occur before (in this order) in the sequence. Intuitively, if the $out(a)$ action does not appear before in the sequence we cannot add it, since the presence of a could trigger some new computation; moreover, since the multiplicity of a message is relevant, also in case the sequence contains $out(a)$ and not $in(a)$ we cannot add the sequence $out(a) \cdot in(a)$ because after the added $out(a)$ we would have one more a than in the original sequence, which, again, could trigger new computations. (iv) Stuttering steps of the form $in(a) \cdot out(a)$ can be safely added and removed only at the end of a sequence. (v) As stated in [5] an output prefix $out(a).P$ is observably equivalent to $out(a) \mid P$, note that from this rule follows that the core-language cannot observe the order of appearance of messages. (vi) Finally, $\overline{in}(a)$ represents a process suspended because the message a is not present in the store, hence it is not correct to assume that other actions could take place afterwards. Clearly this is not anymore true (apart from rule (vi)) in presence of a construct which allows to check for absence of information, as we will see in the next section.

The fully abstract semantics is obtained by applying the saturation defined above to the semantics $[\![\cdot]\!]$.

In order to prove the full abstraction result we proceed by steps. First we prove that the abstraction introduced by Sat is correct (under any context) w.r.t. $\mathcal{O}(P)$. This result is obtained by first showing that the construction of $Sat([\![P]\!])$ does not add any trace that does not respect the observables of P. This is the content of the following Proposition, whose proof is immediate

Proposition 3. *Given a process P,* $\mathcal{O}(P) = \{(\mathcal{M}_0, eval_1(s, \mathcal{M}_0)) | s \in Sat([\![P]\!])\}$.

Now we are ready to state that the abstract (saturated) semantics is correct under any context w.r.t. the chosen observation criteria. A context $C[\bullet]$ is defined as a process with a hole, that is, a process where a subprocess is left unspecified. $C[P]$ is then the process obtained from $C[\bullet]$ by replacing $\bullet$ for the process P.

Theorem 2 (Correctness for Linda-core). *Given two Linda-core process A and B, if* $Sat([\![A]\!]) = Sat([\![B]\!])$ *then, for every context* $C[\bullet]$, $\mathcal{O}(C[A]) = \mathcal{O}(C[B])$ *holds.*

Proof. We will first prove $\mathcal{O}(C[A]) \subseteq \mathcal{O}(C[B])$. Let $(\mathcal{M}_0, \mathcal{M}_1) \in \mathcal{O}(C[A])$ then following from Proposition 1 there exists $s \in [\![C[A]]\!]$ such that $\mathcal{M}_1 = eval_1(s, \mathcal{M}_0)$. Since the denotational semantics we provide is compositional $s = c\,\tilde{o}\,t$ for some suitable $\tilde{o}$, where $c \in [\![C[\bullet]]\!]$ and $t \in [\![A]\!]$.

Since $[\![A]\!] \subset Sat([\![A]\!]) = Sat([\![B]\!])$ then $t \in Sat([\![B]\!])$ therefore two cases could arise: (1) $t \in [\![B]\!]$ hence $s \in [\![C[B]]\!]$ and $(\mathcal{M}_0, \mathcal{M}_1) \in \mathcal{O}(C[B])$. (2) $t \notin [\![B]\!]$ then there exists $u \in [\![B]\!]$ such that u is derived from t following the rules in definition 4 and $eval_1(t, \mathcal{M}_0) = eval_1(u, \mathcal{M}_0)$. Hence by induction on the structure of c it can be easily proved that $eval_1(c\,\tilde{o}\,u, \mathcal{M}_0) = \mathcal{M}_1$ and therefore $(\mathcal{M}_0, \mathcal{M}_1) \in \mathcal{O}(C[B])$.

The other set inclusion $\mathcal{O}(C[B]) \subseteq \mathcal{O}(C[A])$ is symmetrical. □

To obtain full abstraction we need now to prove the converse of the above theorem. This is the central result of this section and is the content of the following.

Theorem 3. *Given two Linda-core processes A and B, if $Sat([\![A]\!]) \neq Sat([\![B]\!])$ then there exists a context $C[\bullet]$ such that $\mathcal{O}(C[A]) \neq \mathcal{O}(C[B])$.*

Proof. Suppose that there exists $t \in Sat([\![A]\!]) \setminus Sat([\![B]\!])$ and consider a generic $s \in Sat([\![B]\!])$ (thus $t \neq s$). From the definition of Sat it follows that we can choose s and t as the shortest sequences such that: (i) they do not contain sub-sequences of the form $out(x) \cdot u \cdot in(x) \cdot out(x) \cdot in(x)$, (ii) they do not contain suffixes of the form $in(x) \cdot out(x)$, (iii) every output appears as soon as possible and (iv) between two consecutive inputs the outputs are ordered in lexicographic order.

Then assume that t and s have the following form: $t = r \cdot \alpha(x) \cdot t_1$, $s = r \cdot \beta(y) \cdot s_1$ where the common prefix r can also be empty and $\alpha, \beta \in \mathcal{A}$ with $\alpha \neq \beta$.

The proof is by cases, where we analyze the first couple of different actions α and β. In each case we will construct a context $C[\bullet]$ which allows to distinguish A and B (that is, a context such that $\mathcal{O}(C[A]) \neq \mathcal{O}(C[B])$). In the proof we will use the following notation: if $in(a_1), in(a_2), \ldots, in(a_n)$ are all the input actions which appear, in this order, in the sequence r (which can also contain other out actions), then $InComp(r)$ denotes the sequence $out(a_1) \cdot out(a_2) \cdots out(a_n)$: intuitively this sequence is a sort of complement (w.r.t. in actions) of r which allows to proceed in the computation when composed in parallel with r. Furthermore, in order to further simplify the notation, in the following we will use these assumptions:

$$c_1 = InComp(r)$$

c_2 is a sequence consisting of as many $in(x)$ as the $out(x)$ in r

c_3 is a sequence consisting of as many $in(y)$ as the $out(y)$ in r

We have then the following cases:

1. let $\beta(y) \cdot s_1 = \epsilon$, thus $t = r \cdot \alpha(x) \cdot t_1$ and $s = r$. Depending on t we can construct the following distinguishing contexts $C[\bullet]$:
   (a) if $t = r \cdot out(x) \cdot t_1$ then $C[\bullet] = \bullet \mid c_1.c_2.in(x).out(ok)$;
   (b) if $t = r \cdot in(x) \cdot t_1$ noticing that $t_1 \neq out(x)$, the following context can be provided $C[\bullet] = \bullet \mid c_1.out(x).InComp(t_1)$.

   The symmetric case is completely analogous.

2. $\alpha(x) = in(x)$ and $\beta(y) = in(y)$ $(x \neq y)$ then in order to separate the two processes we need to make further distinctions (note that by construction $t_1 \neq out(x)$):
   (a) if $eval_1(t_1, \emptyset) \neq \{x\}$ then $C[\bullet] = \bullet \mid c_1.c_3.out(x)$
   (b) if $eval_1(t_1, \emptyset) = \{x\}$ and the actions $out(y)$, $in(y)$ do not appear in t_1 then $C[\bullet] = \bullet \mid c_1.c_3.out(x).InComp(t_2)$
   (c) otherwise since $out(y)$ appears in t_1, it can be provided the following context $C[\bullet] = \bullet \mid c_1.c_3.out(x).in(y).out(y).out(y)$.
3. $\alpha(x) = out(x)$ and $\beta(y) = in(y)$ or vice versa: then it can be easily shown that the context $C[\bullet] = \bullet \mid c_1.c_2.c_3.in(x).out(ok)$ allows to distinguish A and B.
4. $\alpha(x) = out(x)$ and $\beta(y) = out(y)$ (with $x \neq y$). By hypothesis we can choose $t = r \cdot out(x) \ldots in(v) \ldots$ and $s = r \cdot out(y) \ldots in(w) \ldots$ where $in(v)$ and $in(w)$ are the first input actions after $out(x)$ and $out(y)$ respectively. Moreover $out(x)$ does not appear before $in(w)$ in s. Then two cases could arise if $v \neq x$ then the context $C[\bullet] = \bullet \mid c_1.c_4.c_5$ where c_4 and c_5 are sequences of as many $in(v)$ and $in(w)$ as the $out(v)$ and $out(w)$ that precedes the two input actions respectively. Instead if $v = x$ then we can safely assume $in(w)$ does not appear in s and the context $C[\bullet] = \bullet \mid c_1.c_5.InComp(t_1)$ can distinguish the two processes.
5. There are some remaining cases, where the two sequences are different because of a $\overline{in}$ action. However, due to the construction of our semantics, $r \cdot \overline{in}(x) \in Sat_2(\llbracket A \rrbracket)$ iff $r \cdot in(x) \cdot s \in Sat_2(\llbracket A \rrbracket)$. Therefore we can omit to consider the sequence $r \cdot \overline{in}(x)$ and just consider the case of the sequence $r \cdot in(x) \cdot s$, which is included above.

This completes the proof. □

The previous two theorems can be summarized in the following corollary.

Corollary 1 (Full Abstraction for Linda-core). *Given two Linda-core processes A and B, $Sat(\llbracket A \rrbracket) = Sat(\llbracket B \rrbracket)$ iff, for any context $C[\bullet]$, $\mathcal{O}(C[A]) = \mathcal{O}(C[B])$ holds.*

5 Full Abstraction for Linda-inp

Now we move to consider the language Linda-inp where we can test for the absence of a message in the store by using the primitive inp. As underlined in the introduction, such a possibility augments the expressive power of the language. In semantic terms this means that we can construct more powerful contexts, thus allowing to discriminate processes which were identified by Linda-core contexts. As a simple example, consider the two processes $A = out(a).out(b)$ and $B = out(b).out(a)$. These processes cannot be distinguished (w.r.t. the observables $\mathcal{O}$) by any Linda-core contexts, indeed the corresponding traces $out(a) \cdot out(b)$ and $out(b) \cdot out(a)$ are identified by the saturation operation. However, the context $C[\bullet] = \bullet \mid in(a).(inp(b)?out(nok) : out(ok))$ allows to distinguish them, since it allows to check that a is present and b is absent in the store. Indeed we have that $(\emptyset, ok \in \mathcal{O}(C[A]) \setminus \mathcal{O}(C[B]))$. This example shows that a fully abstract semantics for Linda-inp must induce a finer equivalence on processes than Sat or, in other terms, that a less abstract operation has to be used to saturate sequences. However the Denotational semantics provided in Section 3.2 is not fully abstract. In fact, consider the two processes $A = inp(a)?\mathbf{0} : \mathbf{0}$ and $B = in(a) + A$: these two processes cannot be distinguish by any context, yet they have a different denotational semantics. Thus we need the following definition.

Definition 5 (Saturation for Linda-inp). *Let $T \subseteq S$ be a set of traces. We define the inp-saturation of T as the set $Sat_2(T)$ which is obtained by performing the following steps (in this order) on T:*

1. *all the traces in T of the form $t \cdot \overline{in}(a) \cdot u$ with $u \neq \epsilon$ are removed;*
2. *all the $\overline{in}(x)$ actions in all traces are replaced by $\overline{inp}(x)$ (for any x).*

Condition 1 ensures that we obtain correct traces once we have performed the transformation in 2. In fact, $\overline{in}(a)$ comes from the evaluation of $in(a)$, when a is not present. Since such an evaluation is suspended, it is not correct to assume that some action can be performed later. Thus, before transforming $\overline{in}(a)$ into $\overline{inp}(a)$ (and therefore moving from the $eval_1$ of Definition 2 to $eval_2$ of Definition 3) we have to delete these traces. The correctness of the saturation is stated by the following proposition which can be easily proved.

Proposition 4. *Given a process P, $\mathcal{O}(P) = \{(\mathcal{M}_0, eval_2(s, \mathcal{M}_0)) | s \in Sat_2(\llbracket P \rrbracket)\}$*

Theorem 4. *Given two Linda-inp processes A and B, if $Sat_2(\llbracket A \rrbracket) = Sat_2(\llbracket B \rrbracket)$ then, for every context $C[\bullet]$, $\mathcal{O}(C[A]) = \mathcal{O}(C[B])$ holds.*

Proof. We will first prove $\mathcal{O}(C[A]) \subseteq \mathcal{O}(C[B])$. Let $(\mathcal{M}_0, \mathcal{M}_1) \in \mathcal{O}(C[A])$ then following from Proposition 2 there exists $s \in \llbracket C[A] \rrbracket$ such that $\mathcal{M}_1 = eval_2(s, \mathcal{M}_0)$. Since the denotational semantics we provide is compositional $s = c\ \tilde{\circ}\ t$ for some suitable $\tilde{\circ}$, where $c \in \llbracket C[\bullet] \rrbracket$ and $t \in \llbracket A \rrbracket$.

Applying the rules in definition 5 we can construct a trace t' s.t. $eval_2(t, \mathcal{M}_0) = eval_2(t', \mathcal{M}_0)$. Hence $t' \in Sat_2(\llbracket A \rrbracket)$. Since $Sat_2(\llbracket A \rrbracket) = Sat_2(\llbracket B \rrbracket)$, $t' \in Sat_2(\llbracket B \rrbracket)$ two cases could arise: (1) $t' \in \llbracket B \rrbracket$ hence $s \in \llbracket C[B] \rrbracket$ and $(\mathcal{M}_0, \mathcal{M}_1) \in \mathcal{O}(C[B])$. Or (2) $t' \notin \llbracket B \rrbracket$ therefore there exists $u \in \llbracket B \rrbracket$ where some of the actions $\overline{in}$ have been replaced with $\overline{inp}$ and $eval_2(t, \mathcal{M}_0) = eval_2(u, \mathcal{M}_0)$. Hence by induction on the structure of c it can be easily proved that $eval_2(c\ \tilde{\circ}\ u, \mathcal{M}_0) = \mathcal{M}_1$ and therefore $(\mathcal{M}_0, \mathcal{M}_1) \in \mathcal{O}(C[B])$.

The other set inclusion $\mathcal{O}(C[B]) \subseteq \mathcal{O}(C[A])$ is symmetrical. □

Theorem 5. *Given two Linda-inp processes A and B, if $Sat_2(\llbracket A \rrbracket) \neq Sat_2(\llbracket B \rrbracket)$ then there exists a context $C[\bullet]$ such that $\mathcal{O}(C[A]) \neq \mathcal{O}(C[B])$.*

Proof. Suppose that there exists $t \in Sat_2(\llbracket A \rrbracket) \setminus Sat_2(\llbracket B \rrbracket)$ and consider a generic $s \in Sat_2(\llbracket B \rrbracket)$. Since $s \neq t$ by hypothesis, let $t = r \cdot \alpha_1(x_1) \cdots \alpha_n(x_n)$ and $s = r \cdot \beta_1(y_1) \cdots \beta_m(y_m)$ where the common prefix r can also be empty and $\alpha_1, \ldots, \alpha_n$, $\beta_1, \ldots, \beta_m \in \mathcal{A}$ with $\alpha_1 \neq \beta_1$.

The proof is by cases, where we analyze the first different actions α_1 and β_1 in the sequences t and s. In each case we will construct a context $C[\bullet]$ which allows to distinguish A and B (that is, a context such that $\mathcal{O}(C[A]) \neq \mathcal{O}(C[B])$). As in the proof of Theorem 3, if $in(a_1), in(a_2), \ldots, in(a_n)$ are all the input actions which appear, in this order, in the sequence r then $InComp(r)$ denotes the sequence $out(a_1) \cdot out(a_2) \cdots out(a_n)$. Furthermore, in order to further simplify the notation, in the following we will use these assumptions:

$c_1 = InComp(r)$
c_2 is a sequence consisting of as many $in(a)$ as the $out(a)$ in r
c_3 is a sequence consisting of as many $in(b)$ as the $out(b)$ in r

We have then the following cases:

1. $t = r \cdot out(a) \cdot t_1$ and $s = r$; In this case $C[\bullet] = \bullet \mid c_1.c_2.in(a).out(ok)$ allows to distinguish A and B.
2. $t = r \cdot in(a) \cdot t_1$ and $s = r$; then $C[\bullet] = out(a).\bullet \mid c_1.c_2.inp(a)?out(ok) : out(no)$ is the distinguishing context.
3. $t = r \cdot out(a) \cdot t_1$ and $s = r \cdot out(b) \cdot s_1$. We have the following sub-cases:
   (a) If the number of $out(a)$ in t is different from the number of $out(a)$ in s then it can be easily proved that there is a context that distinguishes the two programs (essentially it is a context that *counts* the occurrences of the $out(a)$). Similarly if we are considering the b's. The following is an example.

   Example 1. If $t = out(a) \cdot in(a) \cdot out(a) \cdot out(b)$ and $s = out(b) \cdot out(a)$ then we can build the distinguishing context

   $$C[\bullet] = \bullet \mid in(a).out(a).inp(a)?out(ok) : out(no)$$

   (b) Now suppose that the number of $out(a)$ (or $out(b)$) is the same in t and s. If in t_1 or in s_1 there is an input action again it is easy to provide a distinguishing context, either by blocking the execution of the rest of the trace after the input or by querying the store for the presence/absence of messages in the store. The following provide an example.

   Example 2. If $t = out(a) \cdot in(b) \cdot out(b)$ and $s = out(b) \cdot in(b) \cdot out(a)$ then we can consider the distinguishing context

   $$C[\bullet] = \bullet \mid in(a).out(b).inp(b)?out(ok) : out(no)$$

   (c) If in t_1 and in s_1 there are only outputs then either there is an output action which is not present in one of the two traces, and in this case it is straightforward to build a distinguishing context, or the output actions of a sequence are a permutation of output actions of the other sequence; also in this case it is easy to construct a context that distinguishes the two processes by checking the presence of a message and the absence of the other one, as shown by the following.

   Example 3. If $t = out(a) \cdot out(b)$ and $s = out(b) \cdot out(a)$ then the distinguishing context $C[\bullet] = \bullet \mid in(a).inp(b)?out(ok) : out(no)$ (as seen in the initial part of this Section).

4. $t = r \cdot out(a) \cdot t_1$, $s = r \cdot in(b) \cdot s_1$ and $s' = r \cdot \overline{inp}(b) \in Sat_2([\![B]\!])$. It suffices to consider $C[\bullet] = \bullet \mid c_1.c_2.c_3.in(a).out(ok)$.
5. $t = r \cdot out(a) \cdot t_1$, $s = r \cdot in(b) \cdot s_1$ and $s' = r \cdot \overline{inp}(b) \cdot s_2 \in Sat_2([\![B]\!])$. The following situations may arise:

(a) if $out(a) \notin s_2$ then $C[\bullet] = \bullet \mid c_1.c_2.c_3.in(a).out(ok)$;
(b) if $in(b) \notin t_1$ then $C[\bullet] = out(b).\bullet \mid c_1.inp(b)?out(ok) : out(no)$;
(c) otherwise the only significant case is when $s' = r \cdot \overline{inp}(b) \cdot out(a) \cdot t_1$ and therefore a suitable context can be constructed observing that the order of the actions is different (i.e. b is consumed in two different positions). This is shown in the following.

Example 4. If $t = out(a)$ and $s = in(b) \cdot out(b) \cdot out(a)$ recalling that $s' = \overline{inp}(b) \cdot out(a)$ we can build the distinguishing context $C[\bullet] = out(b).\bullet \mid in(b).out(b).inp(b)?out(ok) : out(no)$

6. $t = r \cdot in(a) \cdot t_1$, $s = r \cdot in(b) \cdot s_1$ and $s = r \cdot \overline{inp}(b) \in Sat_2(B)$. In this case $C[\bullet] = out(a).\bullet \mid c_1.c_2.c_3.inp(a)?out(ok) : out(no)$.
7. $t = r \cdot in(a) \cdot t_1$, $s = r \cdot in(b) \cdot s_1$ and $s' = r \cdot \overline{inp}(b) \cdot s_2 \in Sat_2([\![B]\!])$. We should here distinguish between the following further cases
   (a) if $out(a) \notin t_1$ and $in(a) \notin s_2$ then $C[\bullet] = out(a).\bullet \mid c_1.c_3$;
   (b) otherwise the worst possible scenario happens when $s_2 = in(a) \cdot t_1$ and t_1 and s_1 are "symmetrical" in a and b. As already shown in some preceding cases, when the order of the actions changes it is always possible to find a distinguishing context. This is shown in the following, last example.

Example 5. Given $A = inp(a)?(out(a).in(b).out(b)) : (in(b).out(b))$, and $B = inp(b)?(out(b).in(a).out(a)) : (in(a).out(a))$ thus $Sat_2([\![A]\!]) = \{in(a) \cdot out(a) \cdot in(b) \cdot out(b), \overline{inp}(a) \cdot in(b) \cdot out(b), \dots\}$ and $Sat_2([\![B]\!]) = \{in(b) \cdot out(b) \cdot in(a) \cdot out(a), \overline{inp}(b) \cdot in(a) \cdot out(a), \dots\}$ and the following context can distinguish between the two programs: $C[\bullet] = \bullet \mid inp(a)?out(ok1) : (inp(b)?out(ok2) : out(no))$.

8. There are some remaining cases, where the two sequences are different because of a $\overline{inp}$ action. However, due to the construction of our semantics, $r \cdot \overline{inp}(x) \in Sat_2([\![A]\!])$ iff $r \cdot in(x) \cdot s \in Sat_2([\![A]\!])$. Therefore we can omit to consider the sequence $r \cdot \overline{inp}(x)$ and just consider the case of the sequence $r \cdot in(x) \cdot s$, which is included above.

This completes the proof. □

The previous two theorems can be summarized in the following corollary.

Corollary 2 (Full Abstraction for Linda-inp). *Given two Linda-inp processes A and B, $Sat_2([\![A]\!]) = Sat_2([\![B]\!])$ iff, for any context $C[\bullet]$, $\mathcal{O}(C[A]) = \mathcal{O}(C[B])$ holds.*

6 Conclusions and Related Work

We have studied the full abstraction problem for two variants of the Linda paradigm. For the first one, the core Linda language, we have provided a trace semantics which is fully abstract w.r.t. the input/output notion of observables. This has been obtained by using a suitable abstraction in order to identify different traces which do not represent meaningful operational differences. The second language, Linda-inp, allows also checking for the absence of information. The augmented expressive power of this language permits us to obtain a full abstraction result by using a much simpler abstraction.

In the specific context of Linda, full abstraction has been previously investigated by [3] which used also techniques inspired by [12]. The results in [3] are completely different from ours, since in such a paper a semantics based on sequences is shown to be fully abstract with respect to a notion of observable which consider traces of computations. We prefer to consider a coarser notion of observables, consisting in the input/output behaviour, which accounts for a "black box" use of processes. Clearly our notion of observables leads to a more difficult full abstraction result, being the denotational model based on traces.

Results similar to ours have been obtained in the context of concurrent constraint programming (CCP) by De Boer and Palamidessi [9], however this language differs from Linda since it does not allow to remove information from the store. This monotonic nature of CCP makes its semantic treatment simpler, hence the results in [9] cannot be applied directly to the languages we consider here. Also Brookes [4] provides a trace model and a full abstraction result for a shared variable parallel language which is substantially different from Linda. The same applies to the results in [12].

More generally, full abstraction results have been provided for many concurrent languages and in quite various settings, which however are different from the case we consider here. In fact, even though our core Linda language can be seen as a fragment of asynchronous CCS (and therefore of asynchronous π-calculus), all the full abstraction results available for these languages consider different observational equivalences from ours. Probably the closer work in this sense is [2], where full abstraction of a trace semantics w.r.t. may testing equivalence has been studied. Note however that may testing is different from the observational equivalence that we consider (which is based on the input-output behaviour). For example, the processes $in(a).in(b)$ and $in(b).in(a)$ are may testing equivalent (see [2]) while they are not equivalent in our case, since they can be distinguished by the context $out(a)$.

Several other papers consider barbed equivalences and their relations with bisimulation, (notably [1] for asynchronous π-calculus and [6] for Linda-like process algebras) which, as previously mentioned, are completely different from the equivalence we consider. It is also worth noticing that the construct inp, which is not available in π-calculus and in CCS, change considerably the semantics of the language, thus for Linda-inp one cannot use existing results for CCS or π-calculus. For example, [6] shows that in presence of inp the coarse congruence contained in barbed equivalence is a new, specific congruence called inp-bisimulation while for the core language it is the usual one.

Recently, full abstraction results for π-calculus with contextual equivalence [18] and for Java-like languages with testing equivalence have been obtained in [15] (by considering weak bisimulation) and in [14] (by using a model based on traces). Also in these cases the considered equivalences are different from ours.

Our results can be extended along several lines. We have described a fully abstract semantics which is not compositional since the abstractions that we need on sequences are inherently non compositional. It would therefore be interesting to determine whether a simple, compositional, fully abstract semantics based on sequences actually exists.

Secondly we could investigate some other of the (many) dialects of Linda which exist in the literature. In particular we are planning to investigate the case of the language Klaim [17], which supports distribution and mobility. Finally it would be interesting to consider full abstraction results for other notions of observational equivalences.

References

1. Amadio, R.M., Castellani, I., Sangiorgi, D.: On bisimulations of the asynchronous π-calculus. Theor. Comput. Sci. 195(2), 291–324 (1998)
2. Boreale, M., Nicola, R.D., Pugliese, R.: Trace and testing equivalence on asynchronous processes. Inf. Comput. 172(2), 139–164 (2002)
3. Brogi, A., Jaquet, J.-M.: Modeling coordination via asynchronous communication. In: Proceedings of the 2nd COORD 1997, London, UK, pp. 238–255. Springer, Heidelberg (1997)
4. Brookes, S.D.: Full abstraction for a shared-variable parallel language. Information and Computation 127(2), 145–163 (1996)
5. Busi, N., Gorrieri, R., Zavattaro, G.: Three semantics of the output operation for generative communication. In: Proceedings of the 2nd COORD 1997, London, UK, pp. 205–219. Springer, Heidelberg (1997)
6. Busi, N., Gorrieri, R., Zavattaro, G.: A process algebraic view of linda coordination primitives. Theor. Comput. Sci. 192(2), 167–199 (1998)
7. Busi, N., Gorrieri, R., Zavattaro, G.: On the turing equivalence of linda coordination primitives. Theor. Comput. Sci. 230(1-2), 260–261 (2000)
8. de Boer, F.S., Gabbrielli, M., Meo, M.C.: A timed linda language and its denotational semantics. Fundamenta Informaticae 63(4) (2004)
9. de Boer, F.S., Palamidessi, C.: A fully abstract model for concurrent constraint programming. In: Proceedings TAPSOFT/CAAP 1991, vol. 1, pp. 296–319. Springer, New York (1991)
10. Freeman, E., Arnold, K., Hupfer, S.: JavaSpaces Principles, Patterns, and Practice. Addison-Wesley Longman Ltd, Essex, UK (1999)
11. Gelernter, D.: Generative communication in linda. ACM Trans. Program. Lang. Syst. 7(1), 80–112 (1985)
12. Horita, E., de Bakker, J.W., Rutten, J.J.M.M.: Fully abstract denotational models for nonuniform concurrent languages. Inf. Comput. 115(1), 125–178 (1994)
13. IBM. Tspaces, `http://www.almaden.ibm.com/cs/TSpaces/index.html`
14. Jeffrey, A., Rathke, J.: Java jr.: Fully abstract trace semantics for a core java language. In: Sagiv, M. (ed.) ESOP 2005. LNCS, vol. 3444, pp. 423–438. Springer, Heidelberg (2005)
15. Jeffrey, A.S.A., Rathke, J.: Full abstraction for polymorphic pi-calculus. Theoretical Computer Science (to appear, 2007)
16. Jonsson, B.: A model and proof system for asynchronous networks. In: Proc. of the 4th ACM symposium on Principles of distributed computing, pp. 49–58. ACM Press, New York (1985)
17. Nicola, R.D., Ferrari, G.L., Pugliese, R.: Klaim: A kernel language for agents interaction and mobility. IEEE Transactions on Software Engineering 24(5), 315–330 (1998)
18. Pierce, B.C., Sangiorgi, D.: Behavioral equivalence in the polymorphic pi-calculus. In: Proceedings of the 24th ACM SIGPLAN-SIGACT, pp. 242–255. ACM Press, New York (1997)
19. Wells, G., Clayton, P., Chalmers, A.G.: A Comparison of Linda Implementations in Java. In: Communicating Process Architectures 2000, september 2000, pp. 63–76 (2000)
20. Zavattaro, G.: Towards a hierarchy of negative test operators for generative communication. Electr. Notes Theor. Comput. Sci. 16(2) (1998)

Practical Programming with Higher-Order Encodings and Dependent Types*

Adam Poswolsky[1] and Carsten Schürmann[2]

[1] Yale University
poswolsky@cs.yale.edu
[2] IT University of Copenhagen
carsten@itu.dk

Abstract. Higher-order abstract syntax (HOAS) refers to the technique of representing variables of an object-language using variables of a meta-language. The standard first-order alternatives force the programmer to deal with superficial concerns such as substitutions, whose implementation is often routine, tedious, and error-prone. In this paper, we describe the underlying calculus of Delphin. Delphin is a fully implemented functional-programming language supporting reasoning over higher-order encodings and dependent types, while maintaining the benefits of HOAS. More specifically, just as representations utilizing HOAS free the programmer from concerns of handling explicit contexts and substitutions, our system permits programming over such encodings without making these constructs explicit, leading to concise and elegant programs. To this end our system distinguishes bindings of variables intended for instantiation from those that will remain uninstantiated, utilizing a variation of Miller and Tiu's ∇-quantifier [1].

1 Introduction

Logical frameworks are meta-languages used to represent information. Any system supporting the declaration of custom datatypes is providing a framework for representing information. Church's simply typed λ-calculus is arguably the first logical framework that supports higher-order encodings, which means that binding constructs of the object language (the information modeled) are expressed in terms of the binding constructs of the λ-calculus. This deceptively simple idea allows for encodings of complex data structures without having to worry about the representation of variables, renamings, or substitutions that are prevalent in logic derivations, typing derivations, operational semantics, and more.

The logical framework LF [2] is essentially an extention of Church's λ-calculus with dependent types and signatures. A signature contains a collection of constants used to construct objects of different types, also known as datatype constructors. Dependent types and type families (type level constants that need to be indexed by objects) can capture invariants about representations that are

* This research has been funded by NSF grants CCR-0325808 and CCR-0133502.

S. Drossopoulou (Ed.): ESOP 2008, LNCS 4960, pp. 93–107, 2008.

impossible with just simple types. A list can be indexed by its length. An expression can be indexed by its type. An evaluation relation can be represented as a type indexed by two expressions, its input and output. The list goes on.

Neither the simply typed λ-calculus nor LF are suitable for programming. Neither framework permits the definition of recursive functions by cases. They are logical frameworks, whose sole purpose is the representation of syntax modulo variable renaming and substitution. Furthermore, we must be careful when adding anything to LF. For example, the addition of case analysis would inevitably lead to *exotic* terms, i.e. typeable terms that do not correspond to any concrete term in the object-language being encoded. The existence of such exotic terms would eliminate the main benefits of higher-order encodings.

Thus, the first challenge of designing a calculus of recursive functions supporting higher-order encodings is to cleanly separate the two function spaces for representation and computation. Our Delphin calculus defines a computation level supporting function definition by case analysis and recursion without extending the representation level LF. Therefore, all of LF's representational features and properties are preserved.

The second challenge of designing our calculus is supporting recursion under representation level (LF) functions. We solve this problem by distinguishing between two methods of variable binding. The *function type constructor* $\forall$ (or $\supset$ when non-dependent) binds variables that are intended for instantiation, which means that computation is delayed until application. Additionally, we provide a *newness type constructor* ∇ to bind variables that will always remain *uninstantiated* and hence computation will not be delayed. The introduction form of ∇ is the ν (pronounced *new*) construct, $\nu x.\ e$, where x can occur free in e. Evaluation of e occurs while the binding x remains uninstantiated. Therefore, for the scope of e, the variable x behaves as a constant in the signature, which we will henceforth call a parameter. One may view ν as a method of dynamically extending the signature.

The Delphin calculus distinguishes between *parameters* (extensions of the signature) and *objects* (built from constants and parameters). The type $A^{\#}$ refers to a parameter of type A. Intuitively, the type $A^{\#}$ is best viewed as a subtype of A. Although all parameters of type A do have type A, the converse does not necessarily hold.

The presence of parameters introduce concerns with respect to case analysis. When performing case analysis over a type, we cannot only consider the constants declared in the signature, but we must also consider parameters. To this end, Delphin permits a versatile definition of cases. Pattern variables of type $A^{\#}$ will be used to capture these additional cases.

Our ∇-type constructor is related to Miller and Tiu's ∇-quantifier [1], where they distinguish between eigenvariables intended for instantiation from those representing scoped constants. In their logic, the formula $(\forall x.\ \forall y.\ \tau(x,\ y)) \supset \forall z.\ \tau(z,\ z)$ is provable, whereas $(\nabla x.\ \nabla y.\ \tau(x,\ y)) \supset \nabla z.\ \tau(z,\ z)$ is not. Similarly, the Delphin type $(\forall x.\ \forall y.\ \tau(x,\ y)) \supset \forall z.\ \tau(z,\ z)$ is inhabited by

Types $A, B ::= a \mid A\ M \mid \Pi x{:}A.\ B$	Signature $\Sigma ::= \cdot \mid \Sigma, a{:}K \mid \Sigma, c{:}A$
Objects $M, N ::= x \mid c \mid M\ N \mid \lambda x{:}A.\ N$	Context $\Gamma ::= \cdot \mid \Gamma, x{:}A$
Kinds $K ::= \mathit{type} \mid \Pi x{:}A.\ K$	

Fig. 1. The logical framework LF

$\lambda f.\ \lambda z.\ f\ z\ z$. However, the type $(\nabla x.\ \nabla y.\ \tau(x,\ y)) \supset \nabla z.\ \tau(z,\ z)$ is in general not inhabited because nothing might be known about $\tau(z,\ z)$.

In this paper we describe our calculus of recursive functions and its implementation in the Delphin programming language. Delphin is available for download at `http://www.cs.yale.edu/~delphin`. We begin this paper with an overview of the logical framework LF in Section 2. We motivate the Delphin language in Section 3, and provide examples in Section 4. We discuss its static semantics in Section 5 followed by the operational semantics in Section 6. Next, we present some meta-theoretical results in Section 7. An advanced example with combinator transformations is given in Section 8. We briefly discuss some implementation details in Section 9. Finally, we describe related work in Section 10 before we conclude and assess results in Section 11.

2 Logical Framework LF

The Edinburgh logical framework [2], or LF, is a meta-language for representing deductive systems defined by judgments and inference rules. Its most prevalent features include dependent types and the support for the higher-order encodings of syntax and hypothetical judgments.

We present the syntactic categories of LF in Figure 1. Function types assign names to their arguments in $\Pi x{:}A.\ B$. We write $A \to B$ as syntactic sugar when x does not occur in B. Types may be indexed by objects and we provide the construct $A\ M$ to represent such types. We write x for variables while a and c are type and object constants (or constructors), respectively. We often refer to a as a type family. These constants are provided in a fixed collection called the signature. The functional programmer may interpret the signature as the collection of datatype declarations.

In the presence of dependencies, not all types are valid. The *kind* system of LF acts as a type system for types. We write $\Gamma \vdash^{\mathsf{lf}} M : A$ for valid objects and $\Gamma \vdash^{\mathsf{lf}} A : K$ for valid types, in a context Γ that assigns types to variables. The typing and kinding rules of LF are standard [2] and are omitted here in the interest of brevity. All LF judgments enjoy the usual weakening and substitution properties on their respective contexts, but exchange is only permitted in limited form due to dependencies. We take $\equiv_{\alpha\beta\eta}$ as the underlying notion of definitional equality between LF-terms. Terms in β-normal η-long form are also called canonical forms.

Theorem 1 (Canonical forms). *Every well-typed object $\Gamma \vdash^{\mathsf{lf}} M : A$ possesses a unique canonical form (modulo α-renaming) $\Gamma \vdash^{\mathsf{lf}} N : A$, such that $M \equiv_{\alpha\beta\eta} N$.*

Encodings consist of a signature and a representation function, which maps elements from our domain of discourse into canonical forms in our logical framework.

We say that an encoding is *adequate* if the representation function ($\ulcorner - \urcorner$) is a compositional bijection (one that commutes with substitution). We next present examples of a few adequate encodings. We write the signature to the right of the representation function.

Example 1 (Natural numbers).

$$\begin{array}{lll} & & \text{nat} : \mathit{type} \\ \ulcorner 0 \urcorner = \text{z} & & \text{z} \;\; : \text{nat} \\ \ulcorner n+1 \urcorner = \text{s} \ulcorner n \urcorner & & \text{s} \;\; : \text{nat} \rightarrow \text{nat} \end{array}$$

Example 2 (Expressions). As another example, we choose the standard language of untyped λ-terms $t ::= x \mid \textbf{lam}\ x.t \mid t_1 @ t_2$. The encoding $\ulcorner t \urcorner$ is as follows:

$$\begin{array}{lll} \ulcorner x \urcorner & = x & \text{exp} : \mathit{type} \\ \ulcorner \textbf{lam}\ x.t \urcorner & = \text{lam}\ (\lambda x{:}\text{exp}.\ \ulcorner t \urcorner) & \text{lam} : (\text{exp} \rightarrow \text{exp}) \rightarrow \text{exp} \\ \ulcorner t_1 @ t_2 \urcorner & = \text{app}\ \ulcorner t_1 \urcorner \ulcorner t_2 \urcorner & \text{app} : \text{exp} \rightarrow \text{exp} \rightarrow \text{exp} \end{array}$$

In this example, we represent object-level variables x by LF variables x of type exp, which is recorded in the type of lam. As a result, we get substitution for free: $\ulcorner [t_1/x]t_2 \urcorner = [\ulcorner t_1 \urcorner / x] \ulcorner t_2 \urcorner$.

Example 3 (Natural deduction calculus). Let $A, B ::= A \Rightarrow B \mid p$ be the language of formulas. We will use $\Rightarrow$ as an infix operator below. We write $\mathcal{E} ::\vdash A$ if $\mathcal{E}$ is a derivation in the natural deduction calculus. Natural deduction derivations $\mathcal{E} ::\vdash A$ are encoded in LF as $\ulcorner \mathcal{E} \urcorner : \text{nd}\ \ulcorner A \urcorner$, whose signature is given below.

$$\dfrac{\begin{array}{c}\overline{\vdash A}\,u \\ \vdots \\ \vdash B\end{array}}{\vdash A \Rightarrow B}\,\mathsf{impi} \qquad \dfrac{\vdash A \qquad \vdash A \Rightarrow B}{\vdash B}\,\mathsf{impe}$$

$$\begin{array}{l} \text{o} : \mathit{type} \\ \Rightarrow : \text{o} \rightarrow \text{o} \rightarrow \text{o} \\ \\ \text{nd} : \text{o} \rightarrow \mathit{type} \\ \text{impi} : (\text{nd}\ A \rightarrow \text{nd}\ B) \rightarrow \text{nd}\ (A \Rightarrow B) \\ \text{impe} : \text{nd}\ (A \Rightarrow B) \rightarrow \text{nd}\ A \rightarrow \text{nd}\ B. \end{array}$$

We omit the leading Πs from the types when they are inferable. This is, for example, common practice in Twelf. The logical framework LF draws its representational strength from the existence of canonical forms, providing an induction principle that allows us to prove adequacy.

3 Delphin Calculus

The Delphin calculus is specifically designed for programming with (higher-order) LF encodings. It distinguishes between two levels: computational and representational. Its most prominent feature is its newness type constructor ∇, which binds uninstantiable parameters introduced by our ν construct. Figure 2 summarizes all syntactic categories of the Delphin calculus.

We use δ to distinguish between *representational types* A, *parameters* $A^{\#}$, and *computational types* τ.[1] Representational types A are the LF types defined

[1] In the corresponding technical report [3] we also allow for computation-level parameters $\tau^{\#}$, which we omit here for the sake of simplicity.

Types	δ	$::= \tau \mid A \mid A^{\#}$
Computational Types	τ, σ	$::= \top \mid \forall \alpha {\in} \delta.\ \tau \mid \exists \alpha {\in} \delta.\ \tau \mid \nabla x {\in} A^{\#}.\ \tau$
Variables	α	$::= x \mid u$
Expressions	e, f	$::= \alpha \mid M \mid \text{unit} \mid e\ f \mid (e,\ f) \mid \nu x {\in} A^{\#}.\ e \mid e \backslash x$
		$\mid \mu u {\in} \tau.\ e \mid \text{fn}\ (c_1 \mid \ldots \mid c_n)$
Cases	c	$::= \epsilon \alpha {\in} \delta.\ c \mid \nu x {\in} A^{\#}.\ c \mid c \backslash x \mid e \mapsto f$

Fig. 2. Syntactic Definitions of Delphin

in Section 2. We write $A^{\#}$ to denote parameters of type A. Through this distinction we strengthen pattern matching as well as permit functions that range over parameters. It is best to view $A^{\#}$ as a subtype of A. We also distinguish representation-level and computation-level variables by x and u, respectively. Computational types are constructed from four type constructors: the unit type constructor $\top$, the function type constructor $\forall$, the product type constructor $\exists$, and the *newness* type constructor ∇.

Computational types τ disallow computing anything of LF type A. This is necessary as LF types may depend on objects of type A, and we chose to disallow dependencies on computation-level expressions. This separation ensures that the only objects of type A are LF terms M. Although computation cannot result in an object of type A, it may result in an object of type $\exists x {\in} A.\ \top$. We abbreviate this type as $\langle A \rangle$ and summarize all abbreviations in Figure 3.

Since $\forall$ and $\exists$ range over δ, they each provide three respective function and pairing constructs– over A, τ, and $A^{\#}$. For example, a function of type $\forall x {\in} \text{o}.\ \langle \text{nd}\ x \rangle$ computes natural deduction derivations for any formula. In contrast, a function of type $\forall x {\in} \text{o}^{\#}.\ \langle \text{nd}\ x \rangle$ only works on parameters.

As already stated, functions may range over any type δ. We write $\delta \supset \tau$ for $\forall \alpha {\in} \delta.\ \tau$ when α does not occur in τ, which will always be the case when δ is a τ. We define values of Delphin functions as a list of cases fn $(c_1 \mid \ldots \mid c_n)$, which means that we do not introduce an explicit computation-level λ-term. This technique allows us to avoid aliasing of bound variables, which significantly simplifies the presentation of our calculus in the presence of dependent types.

We write a single case as $e \mapsto f$ where e is the *pattern* and f is the *body*. Patterns may contain pattern variables, which are explicitly declared. We use ϵ to declare pattern variables of any type representing objects or parameters. For example, fn $\epsilon u {\in} \tau.\ u \mapsto u$ encodes the identity function on type τ. Multiple cases are captured via alternation, $c_1 \mid c_2$, and $\cdot$ stands for an empty list of cases. A Delphin level λ-binder $\lambda \alpha {\in} \delta.\ e$ may thus be expressed as fn $\epsilon \alpha {\in} \delta.\ \alpha \mapsto e$.

Function application is call-by-value and is written as $e\ f$. During computation, e is expected to yield a set of cases c, of which one that matches the argument is selected and executed. During the matching process, ϵ-bound pattern variables are appropriately instantiated.

The Delphin type for dependent pairs is denoted by $\exists \alpha {\in} \delta.\ \tau$, and its values are pairs of the form $(e,\ f)$, where both e and f are values. We write $\delta \star \tau$ when α does not occur in τ, which will always be the case when δ is a τ. Pairs are eliminated via case analysis.

$$\begin{aligned}
\delta \supset \tau &= \forall \alpha{\in}\delta.\ \tau \\
\delta \star \tau &= \exists \alpha{\in}\delta.\ \tau \\
\langle A \rangle &= \exists x{\in}A.\ \top \\
\langle M \rangle &= (M, \text{unit}) \\
\lambda \alpha{\in}\delta.\ e &= \text{fn}\ \epsilon\alpha{\in}\delta.\ \alpha \mapsto e \\
\text{case}\ e\ \text{of}\ cs &= (\text{fn}\ cs)\ e
\end{aligned}
\qquad
\begin{aligned}
&\text{let}\ (\alpha{\in}\delta,\ u{\in}\tau) = e\ \text{in}\ f \\
&\quad = \text{case}\ e\ \text{of}\ \epsilon\alpha{\in}\delta.\ \epsilon u{\in}\tau.\ (\alpha,\ u) \mapsto f \\
&\text{let}\ \langle x \rangle = e\ \text{in}\ f \\
&\quad = \text{case}\ e\ \text{of}\ \epsilon x{\in}A.\ \langle x \rangle \mapsto f \\
&\textbf{let}\ \alpha = e\ \text{in}\ f \\
&\quad = (\lambda \alpha{\in}\delta.\ f)\ e
\end{aligned}$$

Fig. 3. Abbreviations

Delphin's newness type constructor is written as $\nabla x{\in}A^{\#}.\ \tau$ and the corresponding values are $\nu x{\in}A^{\#}.\ e$, where e is a value. In Section 6 we will see that a term $\nu x{\in}A^{\#}.\ e$ will *always* evaluate to a term $\nu x{\in}A^{\#}.\ e'$. In other words, evaluation in an extended signature results in values in the same extended signature. Just as ν dynamically extends the signature, the ∇-type is eliminated via $e \backslash x$, which dynamically shrinks the signature to its form before x was introduced.

One may perform case analysis over a ∇-type. This gives us a way to translate between values of the ∇-type and LF's Π-type. For example, we can utilize case analysis to convert between the value $\langle \lambda x.\ M\ x \rangle$ and $\nu x.\ \langle M\ x \rangle$. A Delphin function that would convert the former into the latter would have type $\langle \Pi x : A.\ B \rangle \supset \nabla x{\in}A^{\#}.\ \langle B \rangle$ and be written as $\text{fn}\ \epsilon y{\in}(\Pi x : A.\ B).\ \langle y \rangle \mapsto \nu x{\in}A^{\#}.\ \langle y\ x \rangle$.

Conversely, a function of type $\nabla x{\in}A^{\#}.\ \langle B \rangle \supset \langle \Pi x : A.\ B \rangle$ can be written as $\text{fn}\ \epsilon y{\in}(\Pi x : A.\ B).\ (\nu x{\in}A^{\#}.\ \langle y\ x \rangle) \mapsto \langle y \rangle$. Notice that the pattern is $\langle y\ x \rangle$, illustrating an example of higher-order matching. Just as we introduced the ∇-type to reason over higher-order encodings, we can employ higher-order matching to get rid of it again.

We also remark that we have $\nu\alpha.\ c$ and $c \backslash \alpha$ over cases, which have a similar meaning to their counterparts over expressions. By allowing these constructs to range over cases, we add further flexibility in what we can express with pattern (ϵ-bound) variables. For example, this is useful in implementing *exchange* properties as well as the properties that will be proved in Lemma 1.

Finally, we turn to the usual recursion operator $\mu u{\in}\tau.\ e$. Note that μ can only recurse on Delphin computational types τ and not on LF types A.

4 Examples

We illustrate Delphin with a few examples building on the encodings of natural numbers and expressions given in Section 2.

Example 4 (Addition). The function plus adds two natural numbers.

$$\begin{aligned}
&\mu\mathsf{plus}{\in}\langle \text{nat} \rangle \supset \langle \text{nat} \rangle \supset \langle \text{nat} \rangle. \\
&\quad \text{fn}\ \langle \text{z} \rangle \mapsto \text{fn}\ \epsilon M{\in}\text{nat}.\langle M \rangle \mapsto \langle M \rangle \\
&\quad \mid \epsilon N{\in}\text{nat}.\langle \text{s}\ N \rangle \mapsto \text{fn}\ \epsilon M{\in}\text{nat}.\langle M \rangle \mapsto \text{let}\ \langle x \rangle = (\mathsf{plus}\ \langle N \rangle\ \langle M \rangle)\ \text{in}\ \langle \text{s}\ x \rangle
\end{aligned}$$

Example 5 (Interpreter).

$$
\begin{array}{l}
\mu\mathsf{eval} \in\langle \text{exp}\rangle \supset \langle \text{exp}\rangle.\\
\quad \text{fn } \epsilon E_1{\in}\text{exp}.\ \epsilon E_2{\in}\text{exp}.\ \langle \text{app } E_1\ E_2\rangle\\
\qquad\qquad \mapsto \text{case } (\mathsf{eval}\ \langle E_1\rangle,\ \mathsf{eval}\ \langle E_2\rangle) \text{ of}\\
\qquad\qquad\quad \epsilon F{\in}\text{exp} \to \text{exp}.\ \epsilon V{\in}\text{exp}.\ (\langle \text{lam } F\rangle,\ \langle V\rangle) \mapsto \mathsf{eval}\ \langle F\ V\rangle\\
\quad \mid\ \epsilon E{\in}\text{exp} \to \text{exp}.\ \langle \text{lam } E\rangle\ \mapsto \langle \text{lam } E\rangle
\end{array}
$$

Example 6 (Beta Reduction). We can reduce redices under λ-binders.

$$
\begin{array}{l}
\mu\mathsf{evalBeta} \in\langle \text{exp}\rangle \supset \langle \text{exp}\rangle.\\
\quad \text{fn } \epsilon E_1{\in}\text{exp}.\ \epsilon E_2{\in}\text{exp}.\ \langle \text{app } E_1\ E_2\rangle\\
\qquad\qquad \mapsto \text{case } (\mathsf{evalBeta}\ \langle E_1\rangle,\ \mathsf{evalBeta}\ \langle E_2\rangle) \text{ of}\\
\qquad\qquad\quad \epsilon F{\in}\text{exp} \to \text{exp}.\ \epsilon V{\in}\text{exp}.\ (\langle \text{lam } F\rangle,\ \langle V\rangle) \mapsto \mathsf{evalBeta}\ \langle F\ V\rangle\\
\qquad\qquad\quad \mid\ \epsilon x{\in}\text{exp}^{\#}.\ \epsilon V{\in}\text{exp}.\ (\langle x\rangle,\ \langle V\rangle) \mapsto \langle \text{app } x\ V\rangle\\
\quad \mid\ \epsilon E{\in}\text{exp} \to \text{exp}.\ \langle \text{lam } E\rangle\\
\qquad\qquad \mapsto \text{case } (\nu x{\in}\text{exp}^{\#}.\ \mathsf{evalBeta}\ \langle E\ x\rangle) \text{ of}\\
\qquad\qquad\quad \epsilon E'{\in}\text{exp} \to \text{exp}.(\nu x{\in}\text{exp}^{\#}.\ \langle E'\ x\rangle) \mapsto \langle \text{lam } E'\rangle\\
\quad \mid\ \epsilon x{\in}\text{exp}^{\#}.\ \langle x\rangle \mapsto \langle x\rangle
\end{array}
$$

The $\langle \text{lam } E\rangle$ case illustrates how we handle higher-order terms. Since E is of functional type, we create a parameter x to continue computation with $(E\ x)$ under ν. The term $\nu x{\in}\text{exp}^{\#}.\ \mathsf{evalBeta}\ \langle \text{E } x\rangle$ has type $\nabla x{\in}\text{exp}^{\#}.\ \langle\text{exp}\rangle$. Although the introduction of parameters is easy, eliminating them is more difficult. We do this by case analysis, by first stipulating the existence of an E' of functional type and then match against $\langle E'\ x\rangle$. This illustrates an example of higher-order matching. The parameter x cannot escape its scope because E' was declared outside of the scope of x. This lack of dependency is reflected by the lexical scoping in the Delphin code above: the pattern variable $\epsilon E'$ is declared to the left of νx.

Finally, the base case is required for completeness. New parameters are introduced in the lam case and we specify here that they reduce to themselves.

Example 7 (Variable Counting). For the final example in this section, we write a function that counts the number of variable occurrences in untyped λ-terms. For example, the number of variables in $\ulcorner \textbf{lam}\ x.\ x@(\textbf{lam}\ y.\ x@y)\urcorner$ is $\ulcorner 3\urcorner$.

$$
\begin{array}{lll}
\multicolumn{3}{l}{\mu\mathsf{cntvar}{\in}\langle \text{exp}\rangle \supset \langle \text{nat}\rangle.}\\
\quad \text{fn } \epsilon E_1{\in}\text{exp}.\epsilon E_2{\in}\text{exp}.\langle \text{app } E_1\ E_2\rangle & \mapsto \mathsf{plus}\ (\mathsf{cntvar}\ \langle E_1\rangle)\ (\mathsf{cntvar}\ \langle E_2\rangle)\\
\quad \mid\ \epsilon E{\in}(\text{exp} \to \text{exp}).\langle \text{lam } E\rangle & \mapsto \text{case } (\nu x{\in}\text{exp}^{\#}.\ \mathsf{cntvar}\ \langle \text{E } x\rangle) \text{ of}\\
 & \quad \epsilon N{\in}\text{nat}.(\nu x{\in}\text{exp}^{\#}.\ \langle N\rangle) \mapsto \langle N\rangle\\
\quad \mid\ \epsilon x{\in}\text{exp}^{\#}.\ \langle x\rangle & \mapsto \langle \text{s z}\rangle
\end{array}
$$

We explain the $\langle \text{lam } E\rangle$ case. Since E is of functional type, we create a parameter $x{:}\text{exp}^{\#}$ and recurse on $\langle E\ x\rangle$. From the very definition of natural numbers in Example 1, we deduce that it is impossible for the result to depend on x and express this by matching against $\langle N\rangle$ instead of $\langle N'\ x\rangle$. Note that if it was possible for x to occur in the result then this case would only match, during runtime, in situations where the x did not occur free in the result. Therefore, if the programmer leaves out essential cases then it is possible to get stuck, corresponding to a *match non-exhaustive* error, just as in ML.

5 Static Semantics

Before presenting the typing rules, the role of context deserves special attention.

$$\text{Contexts } \Omega ::= \cdot \mid \Omega, \alpha{\in}\delta \mid \Omega, x\overset{\triangledown}{\in}A^{\#}$$

A Delphin context, Ω, serves two purposes. Besides assigning types to variables, it also distinguishes between variables intended for instantiation from uninstantiable parameters. We write $\alpha{\in}\delta$ to express variables α that will be instantiated, such as pattern variables. Alternatively, we write $x\overset{\triangledown}{\in}A^{\#}$ to store information about uninstantiable parameters, introduced by ν. The distinction between $x{\in}A^{\#}$ and $x\overset{\triangledown}{\in}A^{\#}$ is highlighted by comparing $\lambda x{\in}A^{\#}.\ e$ and $\nu x{\in}A^{\#}.\ e$. The first binds a parameter that is intended for instantiation while the latter will remain uninstantiated. We do not allow reorderings of Ω because of dependencies. Additionally, we assume all declarations in Ω to be uniquely named, and we achieve this goal by tacitly renaming variables. During the actual execution of Delphin programs, Ω only contains declarations of the latter form, which one may interpret as an extension to the signature. In comparison, computation in ML always occurs with a fixed signature.

Definition 1 (Casting). *In order to employ LF typing, we define $\|\Omega\|$ as casting of a context Ω, which throws out all declarations $u{\in}\tau$ and converts $x{\in}A$, $x{\in}A^{\#}$, and $x\overset{\triangledown}{\in}A^{\#}$ all into $x{:}A$, yielding an LF context Γ.*

5.1 Type System

In the presence of dependencies, not all types are valid. We write $\Omega \vdash \delta$ wff for valid types and Ω ctx for valid contexts, but omit both judgments here due to space considerations. We write $\Omega \vdash e \in \delta$ for the central derivability judgment, which we present in Figure 4. Note that the rules have implicit premises using the validity judgments to ensure that the context and all types are well-formed. We make these explicit in the corresponding Technical Report [3].

The variable rules τvar and var$^{\#}$ allow one to use assumptions in the context of types τ and $A^{\#}$, respectively. The only term of type $A^{\#}$ is a variable x.

The rule isLF is the only rule for type A and stipulates that in order for an expression M to be an LF term, we must be able to type it using the LF typing judgment under $\|\Omega\|$ (Definition 1).

The rest of the rules deal with computational types τ. Function types are introduced via cases c. The introduction rule impI expresses that all branches must have the same type. Note that we allow for an empty list of cases which may be used to write a function over an empty type. Functions are eliminated through application with impE. The elimination refines τ under a substitution $[f/\alpha]$ replacing all occurrences of α by f. Formally, we use simultaneous substitutions but refer the interested reader to the corresponding technical report [3] for details. If δ is a computational-type σ, then α cannot occur free in τ and this substitution will be vacuous.

$$\frac{(u{\in}\tau)\ \text{in}\ \Omega}{\Omega \vdash u \in \tau}\,\tau\textsf{var} \qquad \frac{((x{\in}A^{\#})\ \text{or}\ (x\overset{\triangledown}{\in}A^{\#}))\ \text{in}\ \Omega}{\Omega \vdash x \in A^{\#}}\,\textsf{var}^{\#} \qquad \frac{\|\Omega\| \Vdash^{\text{lf}} M : A}{\Omega \vdash M \in A}\,\textsf{isLF}$$

$$\frac{i \geq 0, \text{For all}\ i, \Omega \vdash c_i \in \tau}{\Omega \vdash \text{fn}\ (c_1 \mid \ldots \mid c_n) \in \tau}\,\textsf{impI} \qquad \frac{\Omega \vdash e \in \forall\alpha{\in}\delta.\,\tau \qquad \Omega \vdash f \in \delta}{\Omega \vdash e\ f \in \tau[f/\alpha]}\,\textsf{impE}$$

$$\frac{\Omega, x\overset{\triangledown}{\in}A^{\#} \vdash e \in \tau}{\Omega \vdash \nu x{\in}A^{\#}.\, e \in \nabla x{\in}A^{\#}.\,\tau}\,\textsf{new} \qquad \frac{\Omega \vdash e \in \nabla x'{\in}A^{\#}.\,\tau}{\Omega, x\overset{\triangledown}{\in}A^{\#}, \Omega_2 \vdash e\backslash x \in \tau[x/x']}\,\textsf{pop}$$

$$\frac{\Omega \vdash e \in \delta \qquad \Omega \vdash f \in \tau[e/\alpha]}{\Omega \vdash (e,\ f) \in \exists\alpha{\in}\delta.\,\tau}\,\textsf{pairI} \qquad \frac{\Omega, u{\in}\tau \vdash e \in \tau}{\Omega \vdash \mu u{\in}\tau.\, e \in \tau}\,\textsf{fix} \qquad \frac{}{\Omega \vdash \text{unit} \in \top}\,\textsf{top}$$

....

$$\frac{\Omega, \alpha{\in}\delta \vdash c \in \tau}{\Omega \vdash \epsilon\alpha{\in}\delta.\, c \in \tau}\,\textsf{cEps} \qquad \frac{\Omega \vdash e \in \delta \qquad \Omega \vdash f \in \tau[e/\alpha]}{\Omega \vdash e \mapsto f \in \forall\alpha{\in}\delta.\,\tau}\,\textsf{cMatch}$$

$$\frac{\Omega, x\overset{\triangledown}{\in}A^{\#} \vdash c \in \tau}{\Omega \vdash \nu x{\in}A^{\#}.\, c \in \nabla x{\in}A^{\#}.\,\tau}\,\textsf{cNew} \qquad \frac{\Omega \vdash c \in \nabla x'{\in}A^{\#}.\,\tau}{\Omega, x\overset{\triangledown}{\in}A^{\#}, \Omega_2 \vdash c\backslash x \in \tau[x/x']}\,\textsf{cPop}$$

Fig. 4. Delphin Typing Rules

Cases contain explicit pattern variables, which are simply added to the context in cEps. The actual function type is introduced in cMatch illustrating that functions are defined via case analysis. In the branch $e \mapsto f$, e is the pattern and f is the body. The type of f is refined by its pattern via a substitution $\tau[e/\alpha]$. This expresses how different bodies may have different types, all depending on their corresponding pattern. As we define functions by cases, we do not need to refine the context Ω. Additionally, our distinction between computation-level and representation-level types ensures that this substitution is always defined. Finally, we also have a ν and $c\backslash x$ construct over cases, via cNew and cPop. These have similar semantics to their counterparts on expressions, discussed next.

The introduction form of ∇ is called new. As discussed in Section 3, the type $\nabla x{\in}A^{\#}.\,\tau$ declares $x\overset{\triangledown}{\in}A^{\#}$ as a new parameter. The expression $\nu x{\in}A^{\#}.\, e$ evaluates e where the parameter x can occur free. Previously, our examples have shown how to utilize higher-order matching via case-analysis to eliminate these types. However, the elimination rule pop eliminates a ∇-type via an application-like construction, $e\backslash x$, which shifts computation of e to occur without the uninstantiable parameter x. If $\Omega \vdash e \in \nabla x'{\in}A^{\#}.\,\tau$, then x' is a fresh uninstantiable parameter with respect to the context Ω. Therefore, in an extended context $\Omega, x\overset{\triangledown}{\in}A^{\#}, \Omega_2$, we can substitute x for x' and yield a term of type $\tau[x/x']$. The following lemma illustrates examples where this is useful.

Lemma 1. *The following types are inhabited.*

1. $\nabla x{\in}A^{\#}.\,(\tau \supset \sigma) \supset (\nabla x{\in}A^{\#}.\,\tau \supset \nabla x{\in}A^{\#}.\,\sigma)$
2. $(\nabla x{\in}A^{\#}.\,\tau \supset \nabla x{\in}A^{\#}.\,\sigma) \supset \nabla x{\in}A^{\#}.\,(\tau \supset \sigma)$
3. $\nabla x{\in}A^{\#}.\,(\tau \star \sigma) \supset (\nabla x{\in}A^{\#}.\,\tau \star \nabla x{\in}A^{\#}.\,\sigma)$
4. $(\nabla x{\in}A^{\#}.\,\tau \star \nabla x{\in}A^{\#}.\,\sigma) \supset \nabla x{\in}A^{\#}.\,(\tau \star \sigma)$

Proof. We only show 1 and 2, the other 2 cases are straightforward.

1. $\lambda u_1{\in}\nabla x{\in}A^{\#}.\,(\tau \supset \sigma).\ \lambda u_2{\in}(\nabla x{\in}A^{\#}.\,\tau).\ \nu x{\in}A^{\#}.\ (u_1\backslash x)\ (u_2\backslash x)$
2. $\lambda u_1{\in}(\nabla x{\in}A^{\#}.\,\tau \supset \nabla x{\in}A^{\#}.\,\sigma).$
   $\text{fn}\ \epsilon E{\in}(\nabla x{\in}A^{\#}.\,\tau).\ \nu x{\in}A^{\#}.\ ((E\backslash x) \mapsto (u_1\ E)\backslash x)$

Finally, pairs are introduced via pairI and eliminated using case analysis. The typing rules for recursion (fix) and unit (top) are standard.

6 Operational Semantics

Definition 2 (Values). *The set of values of are:*

$$\textit{Values: } v ::= \text{unit} \mid \text{fn}\ (c_1 \mid \ldots \mid c_n) \mid \nu x{\in}A^{\#}.\ v \mid (v_1,\ v_2) \mid M$$

As usual for a call-by-value language, functions are considered values. A newness term $\nu x{\in}A^{\#}.\ v$ is a value only if its body is a value, which is achieved via evaluation under the ν-construct. LF terms M are the only values (and expressions) of type A, and pairs are considered values only if their components are values. Therefore, $\langle M\rangle$ is the only value of type $\langle A\rangle$ (Figure 3).

We present the small-step operational semantics, $\Omega \vdash e \rightarrow f$, in Figure 5. The first rule illustrates that the evaluation of $\nu x{\in}A^{\#}.\ e$ simply evaluates e under the context extended with x. The declaration is marked as $x\overset{\triangledown}{\in}A^{\#}$ as this represents an extension to the signature. Evaluation under ν drives our ability to reason under LF λ-binders. Additionally, we evaluate $e'\backslash x$ by first evaluating e' down to $\nu x'{\in}A^{\#}.\ e$ and then substitute x for x'. Therefore, we see that $e'\backslash x$ behaves much like an application.

The small-step operational semantics for cases, $\Omega \vdash c \rightarrow c'$, is also shown in Figure 5. The first rule non-deterministically instantiates the pattern variables. In our implementation we delay this choice and instantiate them by unification during pattern matching, which is discussed briefly in Section 9. The next three rules allow us to work with ν over cases, which is the same for the ν over expressions. We provide a rule to reduce the pattern of a case branch, which can be any arbitrary expression. In Section 4 we discussed how a program could get stuck, which corresponds to a *match non-exhaustive* error. However, we say that a program "coverage checks" if the list of patterns is exhaustive.

Recall that all LF terms possess a unique canonical form. Given any Delphin term, we implicitly reduce all LF terms to canonical form allowing us to express matching via syntactic equality in the rule marked with *.

$$\frac{\Omega, x \stackrel{\triangledown}{\in} A^{\#} \vdash e \rightarrow f}{\Omega \vdash \nu x{\in}A^{\#}.\, e \rightarrow \nu x{\in}A^{\#}.\, f} \qquad \frac{\Omega \vdash e \rightarrow e'}{\Omega \vdash (e,\ f) \rightarrow (e',\ f)} \qquad \frac{\Omega \vdash f \rightarrow f'}{\Omega \vdash (e,\ f) \rightarrow (e,\ f')} \qquad \frac{\Omega \vdash e \rightarrow e'}{\Omega \vdash e\ f \rightarrow e'\ f}$$

$$\frac{\Omega \vdash f \rightarrow f'}{\Omega \vdash e\ f \rightarrow e\ f'} \qquad \frac{\Omega \vdash e \rightarrow f}{\Omega, x \stackrel{\triangledown}{\in} A^{\#}, \Omega_2 \vdash e\backslash x \rightarrow f\backslash x} \qquad \frac{}{\Omega, x \stackrel{\triangledown}{\in} A^{\#}, \Omega_2 \vdash (\nu x'{\in}A^{\#}.\, e)\backslash x \rightarrow e[x/x']}$$

$$\frac{}{\Omega \vdash (\text{fn } (c_1 \mid \ldots \mid c_n))\backslash x \rightarrow \text{fn } ((c_1\backslash x) \mid \ldots \mid (c_n\backslash x))} \qquad \frac{\Omega \vdash c_i \rightarrow c_i'}{\Omega \vdash (\text{fn } (\ldots \mid c_i \mid \ldots))\ v \rightarrow (\text{fn } (\ldots \mid c_i' \mid \ldots))\ v}$$

$$\frac{}{\Omega \vdash (\text{fn } (\ldots \mid v \mapsto e \mid \ldots))\ v \rightarrow e}\,* \qquad \frac{}{\Omega \vdash \mu u{\in}\tau.\, e \rightarrow e[\mu u{\in}\tau.\, e/u]}$$

....

$$\frac{\Omega \vdash v \in \delta}{\Omega \vdash \epsilon\alpha{\in}\delta.\, c \rightarrow c[v/\alpha]} \qquad \frac{\Omega, x \stackrel{\triangledown}{\in} A^{\#} \vdash c \rightarrow c'}{\Omega \vdash \nu x{\in}A^{\#}.\, c \rightarrow \nu x{\in}A^{\#}.\, c'} \qquad \frac{\Omega \vdash c \rightarrow c'}{\Omega, x \stackrel{\triangledown}{\in} A^{\#}, \Omega_2 \vdash c\backslash x \rightarrow c'\backslash x}$$

$$\frac{}{\Omega, x \stackrel{\triangledown}{\in} A^{\#}, \Omega_2 \vdash (\nu x'{\in}A^{\#}.\, c)\backslash x \rightarrow c[x/x']} \qquad \frac{\Omega \vdash e \rightarrow e'}{\Omega \vdash (e \mapsto f) \rightarrow (e' \mapsto f)}$$

Fig. 5. Small-Step Operational Semantics

7 Meta-theoretic Results

We show here that Delphin is type-safe when all cases are exhaustive.

Lemma 2 (Substitution)
If $\Omega \vdash e \in \delta$ and $\Omega, \alpha{\in}\delta \vdash f \in \tau$, then $\Omega \vdash f[e/\alpha] \in \tau[e/\alpha]$.

Proof *We actually prove this for a more general notion of simultaneous substitutions. See Technical Report [3] for details.*

Theorem 2 (Type Preservation)
If $\Omega \vdash e \in \tau$ and $\Omega \vdash e \rightarrow f$ then $\Omega \vdash f \in \tau$.

Proof *By induction on the structure of $\mathcal{E} :: \Omega \vdash e \rightarrow f$ and $\mathcal{F} :: \Omega \vdash c \rightarrow c'$. See Technical Report [3] for details.*

Corollary 1 (Soundness). *Parameters cannot escape their scope. If $\Omega \vdash e \in \tau$ and $\Omega \vdash e \rightarrow e'$ then all parameters in e and e' are declared in Ω.*

Theorem 3 (Progress)
Under the condition that all cases in e are exhaustive, if $\Omega \vdash e \in \tau$ and Ω only contains declarations of the form $x \stackrel{\triangledown}{\in} A^{\#}$, then $\Omega \vdash e \rightarrow f$ or e is a value.

Proof *By induction over $\mathcal{E} :: \Omega \vdash e \in \tau$. In matching (rule *) we assume that cases are exhaustive and defer to an orthogonal "coverage check." The Delphin implementation contains a prototype coverage algorithm extending ideas from [4], but a formal description is left for future work. Although the problem of checking an arbitrary list of cases is undecidable, it is always possible to generate an exhaustive list of cases for any type δ.*

8 Combinator Example

Recall the definition of the natural deduction calculus from Example 3. We will give an algorithmic procedure that converts natural deduction derivations into the Hilbert calculus, i.e. simply typed λ-terms into combinators. We omit the declaration of inferable pattern variables (as is also allowed in the implementation).

$$\frac{}{\vdash A \supset B \supset A}\,\mathsf{K} \qquad \frac{\vdash A \supset B \quad \vdash A}{\vdash B}\,\mathsf{MP} \qquad \frac{}{\vdash (A \supset B \supset C) \supset (A \supset B) \supset (A \supset C)}\,\mathsf{S}$$

$$\begin{array}{ll} \multicolumn{2}{l}{\text{comb} : \text{o} \to \mathit{type},} \\ \text{K} & : \text{comb } (A \Rightarrow B \Rightarrow A) \\ \text{MP} & : \text{comb}(A \Rightarrow B) \to \text{comb } A \\ & \quad \to \text{comb } B \\ \text{S} & : \text{comb } ((A \Rightarrow B \Rightarrow C) \Rightarrow \\ & \qquad (A \Rightarrow B) \Rightarrow A \Rightarrow C) \end{array}$$

Our translation follows a two-step algorithm. The first step is bracket abstraction, or ba, which internalizes abstraction. If M has type (comb $A \to$ comb B) and N has type (comb A) then we can use ba to get a combinator, d, of type (comb $A \Rightarrow B$). Subsequently, we can do (MP d N) to get a term that is equivalent to (M N) in combinator logic. Formally, ba is written as.

$$\begin{array}{l} \mu\mathsf{ba} \in \forall A{\in}\text{o}.\ \forall B{\in}\text{o}.\ \langle \text{comb } A \to \text{comb } B\rangle \supset \langle \text{comb } (A \Rightarrow B)\rangle. \\ \ \text{fn } A \mapsto \\ \quad (\text{fn } A \mapsto \text{fn } F \mapsto \langle \text{MP (MP S K) K}\rangle \\ \quad\ \mid B \mapsto \text{fn } \langle \lambda x.\ \text{MP } (D_1\ x)\ ((D_2{:}\text{comb A} \to \text{comb } C)\ x)\rangle \\ \qquad\qquad\qquad \mapsto \text{ let } \langle D_1'\rangle = (\mathsf{ba}\ A\ (C \Rightarrow B)\ \langle D_1\rangle) \text{ in} \\ \qquad\qquad\qquad\quad\ \text{let } \langle D_2'\rangle = (\mathsf{ba}\ A\ \ C\ \langle D_2\rangle) \text{ in } \langle \text{MP (MP S } D_1')\ D_2'\rangle \\ \qquad\quad \mid \langle \lambda x.\ U\rangle \mapsto \langle \text{MP K } U\rangle) \end{array}$$

Next we write the function convert which traverses a natural deduction derivation and uses ba to convert them into Hilbert style combinators. In this function, we will need to introduce new parameters of (nd A) and (comb A) together. In order to hold onto the relationship between these parameters, we pass around a function of type $\forall A{\in}\text{o}.\ \forall D{\in}(\text{nd } A)^{\#}.\ \langle\text{comb } A\rangle$. We will employ type aliasing and abbreviate this type as convParamFun.

$$\begin{array}{l} \mu\mathsf{convert} \in \mathsf{convParamFun} \supset \forall A{\in}\text{o}.\ \forall D{\in}\langle\text{nd } A\rangle.\ \langle\text{comb } A\rangle. \\ \quad \lambda f{\in}\ \mathsf{convParamFun}. \\ \qquad \text{fn } (B \Rightarrow C) \mapsto \text{fn } \langle \text{impi } D'\rangle \mapsto \\ \qquad\qquad (\text{case } (\nu d{\in}(\text{nd } B)^{\#}.\ \nu d_u{\in}(\text{comb } B)^{\#}. \\ \qquad\qquad\quad \text{let } f' = \text{fn } B \mapsto \text{fn } d \mapsto \langle d_u\rangle \\ \qquad\qquad\qquad\qquad \mid (\epsilon B'.\ \epsilon d'.\ \nu d.\ \nu d_u.\ (B' \mapsto \text{fn } d' \mapsto \\ \qquad\qquad\qquad\qquad\quad (\text{let } R = f\ B'\ d' \text{ in } \nu d.\ \nu d_u.\ R)\backslash d\backslash d_u))\backslash d\backslash d_u \\ \qquad\qquad\quad \text{in } \mathsf{convert}\ f'\ C\ \langle D'\ d\rangle) \\ \qquad\qquad \text{of } \nu d{\in}(\text{nd } B)^{\#}.\ \nu d_u{\in}(\text{comb } B)^{\#}.\ \langle D''\ d_u\rangle \mapsto \mathsf{ba}\ B\ \ C\ \langle D''\rangle) \\ \qquad \mid A \mapsto \text{fn } \langle \text{impe } D_1\ (D_2{:}\text{nd } B)\rangle \mapsto \\ \qquad\qquad\qquad \text{let } \langle U_1\rangle = (\mathsf{convert}\ f\ (B \Rightarrow A)\ \langle D_1\rangle) \text{ in} \\ \qquad\qquad\qquad \text{let } \langle U_2\rangle = (\mathsf{convert}\ f\ B\ \langle D_2\rangle) \text{ in } \langle \text{MP } U_1\ U_2\rangle \\ \qquad \mid A \mapsto \text{fn } \epsilon x{\in}(\text{nd } A)^{\#}.\ \langle x\rangle \mapsto f\ A\ x \end{array}$$

The first argument to convert is a computation-level function f of type convParamFun that handles the parameters.

The first case, $\langle$impi $D\rangle$, requires recursion under a representation-level λ. We create two new parameters (or equivalently extend the signature with) d and d_u in order to continue our computation by recursing on $\langle D'\ d\rangle$. As we are in an extended signature, if f was a total function on input, it is no longer total. We therefore extend the function f into f' mapping d to d_u before recursing. We then use the same techniques from Examples 6 and 7 to abstract the result into an LF function D'' exploiting that d cannot occur free in the result. Finally, we employ ba to yield our desired combinator.

The second case does not create any parameters and hence all recursive calls are called with f. Finally, the last case handles the parameters by simply calling the input function f which has been built up to handle all parameters.

The above definition of f' illustrates how one can build up parameter functions. The second branch of f' utilizes $e\backslash x$ and $c\backslash x$ (Section 5.1) to ensure that the input function f is not executed in scope of d and d_u. The Delphin implementation offers a shorthand to extend a function f by writing "f `with` $d \mapsto d_u$".

Example 8 (Sample Execution)

$\nu A.$ convert (fn $\cdot$) $(A \Rightarrow A)$ $\langle$impi $\lambda x.\ x\rangle$
$\ldots \to \nu A.$ case $(\nu d.\ \nu d_u.$ convert (fn $A \mapsto$ fn $d \mapsto \langle d_u\rangle \mid \ldots)$ A $\langle d\rangle)$
of $\nu d.\ \nu d_u.\ \langle D''\ d_u\rangle \mapsto$ ba A A $\langle D''\rangle$
$\ldots \to \nu A.$ case $(\nu d.\ \nu d_u.$ (fn $A \mapsto$ fn $d \mapsto \langle d_u\rangle \mid \ldots)$ A $d)$
of $\nu d.\ \nu d_u.\ \langle D''\ d_u\rangle \mapsto$ ba A A $\langle D''\rangle$
$\ldots \to \nu A.$ case $(\nu d.\ \nu d_u.\ \langle d_u\rangle)$ of $\nu d.\ \nu d_u.\ \langle D''\ d_u\rangle \mapsto$ ba A A $\langle D''\rangle$
$\ldots \to \nu A.$ ba A A $\langle \lambda x.\ x\rangle$
$\ldots \to \nu A.$ $\langle$MP (MP S K) K$\rangle$

9 Implementation

An implementation is available at `http://www.cs.yale.edu/~delphin`. Delphin is implemented in approximately 12K lines of code in SML/NJ offering a powerful type reconstruction algorithm, typechecker, and evaluator.

The non-deterministic instantiation of pattern variables from Section 6 is implemented by using logic variables to delay the choice until matching. Additionally, when writing a curried function with multiple arguments we look at all the arguments together before committing to a branch. We implement this feature by partially evaluating functions. For example, convert $(A \Rightarrow A)$ will result in a function with three cases rather than committing to the first branch. This is an enhancement to allow the programmer to write more concise code.

We employ a unification/matching algorithm based on the one designed by Dowek et al. [5], but extended to handle parameters. Therefore, we only allow LF patterns that fall into the decidable pattern fragment of higher-order unification. Formally, this means that we only allow LF patterns of the form $E\ x_1\ \ldots\ x_n$ where x_i is a fresh parameter (with respect to E) and all x_i's are distinct. It is important to note that this restriction is only an implementation limitation as it is also possible to use different unification algorithms.

The Delphin code for all examples in this paper and many more can be found on our website. We have implemented a function translating HOL proofs into Nuprl proofs (approximately 400 lines of code) and a Hindley-Milner style type-inference algorithm for Mini-ML (approximately 300 lines of code).

10 Related Work

Twelf: LF is well suited for *representation* but does not directly afford the ability to reason over representations. Twelf utilizes a logic programming methodology to conduct such reasoning by providing meta-level constructs to interpret a type family as a function. Delphin affords the user the ability to write the functions themselves, and we envision this will replace the underlying meta-logic of Twelf.

Higher-order encodings: The predecessor of our work was on the ∇-calculus [6], which provided a stack based system only supporting a simply-typed logical framework. The ∇ also referred to something different than what it does here.

Our work is related to Miller and Tiu's [1]. In their setting, they use ∇ as a logic quantifier designed to reason about scoped constants. However, their reasoning occurs over formulas *with* an explicit local context. In our setting there is only a global context, which renders it more useful for functional programming.

Pientka[7] also proposes a system for programming with HOAS, however only for a simply-typed logical framework. Programming over HOAS resorts to the explicit handling of substitutions and contexts. In contrast, we believe the purpose of HOAS is to provide an implicit notion of substitution. Therefore, we provide a computation-level in the same spirit, keeping these constructs hidden.

Dependent types: DML provides indexed datatypes whose domains were recently generalized to LF objects to form the ATS/LF system. In contrast, the Cayenne language supports full dependent types and even computation with types, rendering it more expressive but at the expense of an undecidable type checker. Agda and Epigram are two more languages inspired by dependent type theories. All but the ATS/LF system lack support for higher-order encodings. Although ATS/LF supports HOAS they resort to encoding the context explicitly, or as they say representing terms as *terms-in-contexts*. By making this information explicit they can reason about parameters in the context, but they must also define substitutions. We suspect that they can also add a ∇-type similar to ours.

Freshness: Also related to our work are programming languages with freshness [8], such as FreshML, which utilizes Fraenkel-Mostowski (FM) set theory to provide a built-in α-equivalence relation for first-order encodings. This allows for limited support of HOAS as substitution lemmas must still be explicit, albeit easier to write. Lately, Pottier has developed a logic for reasoning about values and the names they contain in FreshML [9]. As the creation of names is a *global* effect in FreshML, his work is used to prove that names cannot escape their scope, which is an inherent property of Delphin's type system.

11 Conclusion

In this paper we have presented the underlying calculus and semantics of the Delphin programming language. This is the only functional system tackling programming over a logical framework with both higher-order encodings and dependent types. The novelty of this work is in providing a way to reason under LF λ-binders, such that the notions of context and substitutions remain implicit in computations as well as representations.

Acknowledgments. We would like to thank Jeffrey Sarnat and Lucas Dixon for many helpful discussions on this and many earlier designs of the system.

References

1. Miller, D., Tiu, A.: A proof theory for generic judgments. ACM Trans. on Computational Logic 6(4), 749–783 (2005)
2. Harper, R., Honsell, F., Plotkin, G.: A framework for defining logics. Journal of the Association for Computing Machinery 40(1), 143–184 (1993)
3. Poswolsky, A., Schürmann, C.: Extended report on Delphin: A functional programming language with higher-order encodings and dependent types. Technical Report YALEU/DCS/TR-1375, Yale University (2007)
4. Schürmann, C., Pfenning, F.: A coverage checking algorithm for LF. In: Basin, D., Wolff, B. (eds.) TPHOLs 2003. LNCS, vol. 2758, Springer, Heidelberg (2003)
5. Dowek, G., Hardin, T., Kirchner, C., Pfenning, F.: Unification via explicit substitutions: The case of higher-order patterns. Rapport de Recherche 3591, INRIA (December 1998) Preliminary version appeared at JICSLP 1996 (1996)
6. Schürmann, C., Poswolsky, A., Sarnat, J.: The ∇-calculus. Functional programming with higher-order encodings. In: Typed Lambda Calculus and Applications, TLCA (2005)
7. Pientka, B.: A type-theoretic foundation for programming with higher-order abstract syntax and first-class substitutions. In: Principles of Programming Languages, POPL (2008)
8. Gabbay, M., Pitts, A.M.: A new approach to abstract syntax with variable binding. Formal Aspects Computing 13(3-5), 341–363 (2002)
9. Pottier, F.: Static name control for FreshML. In: Twenty-Second Annual IEEE Symposium on Logic In Computer Science (LICS 2007), Wroclaw, Poland (July 2007)

Programming in JoCaml (Tool Demonstration)

Louis Mandel[1] and Luc Maranget[2]

[1] LRI, UNIV PARIS-SUD 11, CNRS, Orsay F-91405
INRIA FUTURS, Orsay F-91893
[2] INRIA PARIS - ROCQUENCOURT, Le Chesnay F-78153
{Louis.Mandel,Luc.Maranget}@inria.fr

Abstract. JoCaml is a language for concurrent and distributed programming. The language is an extension of Objective Caml with concurrent features inspired by the join-calculus.

We here present the recent release of JoCaml, motivate our fundamental design choices, compare the new release with previous ones, and give a taste of JoCaml by means of a few examples.

1 Introduction

JoCaml is a language for programming concurrent and distributed systems. It is based on ML for the computational part, and on the join-calculus for the concurrent part.

The join-calculus is a name passing calculus. The purpose of such calculi is to describe concurrent and distributed systems. Programming such systems is a different, although related, issue, since a good model offers suitable abstractions that help programmers.

Our language, JoCaml, is an extension of Objective Caml (OCaml), a popular dialect of ML. By choosing to extend an existing language, and not to design one of our own, we first intend to minimize our work. We also intend to benefit from functional programming, from pre-existing code base, and from a population of programmers open to innovation.

Up to three new keywords, JoCaml is a conservative extension of OCaml: OCaml programs retain their type and behavior. But we understand compatibility in a stronger sense: JoCaml provides a concurrent extension of ML that strictly adheres to the spirit of functional programming. Channel definitions and synchronization behaviors are programmed concisely, by the high-level join-definition concept, and declaratively, by the introduction of ML pattern matching of messages in channel definitions. Moreover, channels are typed polymorphically, as functions are in ML, types being inferred. Channels are first class-values that, amongst other things, can be passed as arguments to functions, sent as messages on channels, and occur as members of modules. This, with the polymorphic typing of channels, is our way to code re-use for concurrent components.

JoCaml web site is `http://jocaml.inria.fr/`. The site offers a source release (dating June 2007), links to articles, and a 70 pages tutorial and reference manual. We have programmed a few applications in the language ourselves. Amongst

S. Drossopoulou (Ed.): ESOP 2008, LNCS 4960, pp. 108–111, 2008.

expression	::= *ocaml-expression*	
	| def x_1(p_1) & ... & x_n(p_n) = *process*	
	...	join-definition
	or x_k(p'_k) & ... & x_m(p'_m) = *process*	
	in *expression*	
	| spawn *process*	process execution
process	::= x(*expression*)	message sending
	| reply *expression* to x	reply to synchronous channel
	| *process* & *process*	parallel composition
	| *expression* ; *process*	sequential composition
	| let ... in *process*	local value definition
	| def ... in *process*	local channel definition

Fig. 1. JoCaml syntax

those, a distributed ray tracer is the most mature. The ray tracer is available on the web site and its source code amounts to about 7000 lines.

2 The New JoCaml

The new JoCaml system is a re-implementation from scratch of the previous prototype. It focuses on compatibility with OCaml. Any OCaml source code is a valid JoCaml source code and JoCaml can also call external OCaml libraries that do not need to be re-compiled.

Briefly, we proceed by altering the OCaml compiler from parsing phase to first intermediate code generation, and by enriching the thread library of OCaml with specific support. Compiler alteration is justified by specific typing and pattern matching compilation, which both need to be perform inside the compiler. Compiler alteration is limited in the sense that we change or add a few thousand lines in the compiler original source files, add a few source files, and retain the OCaml formats for binary files.

Our focus over compatibility and limited alteration of OCaml, made us abandon the mobility features of the join-calculus. Nevertheless, there are useful distributed programs that can be written without code mobility.

Moreover, the new JoCaml extends the synchronization mechanism of the join-calculus with pattern matching. It allows to define synchronization not only on the presence of a message on a channel, but also on the value of the message.

3 A Join-Definition

JoCaml adds the new syntactical category of *processes* to OCaml syntax (Fig. 1). In contrast to expressions processes yield no result and execute asynchronously. Additionally, JoCaml slightly extends OCaml expressions. The `spawn` *proc* construct introduces processes in expressions: *proc* is executed asynchronously and spawn returns immediately.

The join-definition is the distinctive feature of the join-calculus: it defines several channels and their reception behavior at the same time. In JoCaml, join-definitions are introduced by def and can occur both in processes and expressions. We illustrate join-definitions by the example of a concurrent buffer based on the two-lists implementation of functional FIFO queues.

```
type 'a buffer = { put: 'a -> unit; get: unit -> 'a }

let create_buffer () =
  def state(xs,ys) & put(x) = state(x::xs,ys) & reply () to put
   or state(xs,y::ys) & get() = state(xs,ys) & reply y to get
   or state(_::_ as xs,[]) & get() =
     state([], List.rev xs) & reply get() to get
  in
  spawn state([],[]) ;
  {put=put; get=get;}
```

Our buffers are records, a pure OCaml concept, the novelty resides in the join-definition (def... in above). Three channels are defined: `state`, `put` and `get`. Channel `state` is *asynchronous*. Message sending on an asynchronous channel is an elementary process, as illustrated by `spawn state([],[])` above, for instance. By contrast, `put` and `get` are synchronous channels. Message sending on a synchronous channel yields a result, and thus is an expression. In fact, to the sender, synchronous channels behave as functions and have functional types.

The behavior of the buffer is expressed by three *reaction rules* that compete (or) for consuming messages. A reaction rule consists in a *join-pattern* and in a *guarded process* (separated by =). The semantics is as follows: when there are messages pending on all the channels in the join-pattern and they match the patterns present as formal arguments, then the guarded process may be fired. The guarded process is executed asynchronously, but may transmit return values to the callers of synchronous channels (reply/to).

The idea of the buffer is to store the FIFO queue (implemented by a pair of lists) as a message on the channel `state`. By the organization of join-patterns, which all include `state`, and the fact that there is at most one message on this channel, exclusive access to the internal state of the buffer is granted to the callers of synchronous `put` and `get`.

The first join-pattern `state(xs,ys) & put(x)` is satisfied whenever there are messages on both `state` and `put`. The behavior of the guarded process is to perform two actions in parallel (`&` in processes): (1) send a new message on `state` where the value `x` is added to the list `xs` and (2) return the value `()` to the caller of `put`.

The second join-pattern `state(xs,y::ys) & get()` is satisfied when there are messages on both `state` and `put` *and* that the message on `state` matches the pattern `(xs,y::ys)`. That is, the message is a pair whose second component is a non-empty list. The process guarded by this join-pattern removes one value from the buffer and returns it to the caller of `get`. The last join-pattern `state(_::_ as xs,[]) & get()` is satisfied when there is a message on `get` and a message on `state` that matches a pair whose first component is a non-empty list and second component is an empty list. The corresponding guarded process transfers elements from one end of the queue to the other and performs `get` again. Notice that there is no join-pattern that satisfies `state([],[]) & get()`. As a consequence, a call to `get` is blocked when the buffer is empty.

To initialize the buffer, a message `([],[])` is sent on `state`. The spawn construct is here necessary, since the message sending appears in expression context (the body of the function `create_buffer`).

4 Distributed Computation

The join-calculus provides a transparent model for distributed computation. Guarded processes always execute on the site where they are defined but can be fired from any site. More precisely given a channel c, the sending of a message on c can be performed on any site (provided c is known), while the reception on c can occur only on the site where c is defined. This is by design, and comes in sharp contrast to the model of the π-calculus, where it is sufficient to know c to perform emission and reception on c.

Obviously, the join semantics is much easier to implement than the π semantics in a distributed setting. Basically, message sending to a remote site decomposes into a transport phase and a synchronization phase (join-pattern matching), the latter being performed locally on the receiving site.

However, performing the transport phase (and the related global naming of sites and channels) does not upgrade concurrent JoCaml into distributed JoCaml as if by magic. Two important issues arise that are not really expressed in the join model: channel publication and failures. We addressed those pragmatically, so as not to delay the release of the new JoCaml.

When they start, sites (JoCaml programs) have nothing in common. But, so as to initiate communication, sites need to share at least a few channel names. To that aim, JoCaml provides a *name service* that basically is a repository of channel names, indexed by plain strings. In contrast to the JoCaml language, there is no type safety at all. As to failures, our treatment is rather unsophisticated as we rely exclusively over direct routing: communicating sites are connected by a bi-directional link (a TCP socket). Then, the failure of the link, is interpreted by one partner as the failure of the other partner. We plan to improve these two points in future releases.

5 Conclusion

JoCaml is one amongst many recent language that offer serious support for concurrency and distribution (Erlang, Cω, Alice, Scala to cite a few). In our view, JoCaml main contribution resides in the programming style it favors: a smooth integration of functional programming for concurrent and distributed applications. Our tool demonstration will focus on this point.

Playing with $\mathcal{TOY}$: Constraints and Domain Cooperation

Sonia Estévez-Martín[1], Antonio J. Fernández[2], and Fernando Sáenz-Pérez[3,*]

[1] Univ. Complutense de Madrid, Dpto. de Sistemas Informáticos y Comp, Spain
[2] Univ. de Málaga. Dpto. de Lenguajes y Ciencias de la Computación, Spain
[3] Univ. Complutense de Madrid, Dpto. de Inteligencia Artificial e Ing. SW, Spain

Abstract. This paper describes $\mathcal{TOY}$, an implementation of a Constraint Functional Logic Programming scheme $CFLP(C)$, where C is a coordination domain involving the cooperation among several constraint domains $D_1, ..., D_n$ via a mediatorial domain M. This implementation follows a cooperative goal solving calculus for $CFLP(C)$ based on lazy narrowing, invocation of solvers for each domain D_i, and projection operations for converting D_i constraints into D_j constraints with the aid of mediatorial constraints supplied by M. Mediatorial constraints allow solving programs that require constraints of different domains, and projection may improve performance, allowing certain solvers to profit from (the projected forms) of constraints originally intended for other solvers. As a relevant concrete instance of our $CFLP(C)$, we implemented the cooperation among Herbrand, real arithmetic and finite domain constraints, and the mediatorial constraints relate numeric variables belonging to the last two domains. These mediatorial constraints are the bridge `#== :: int -> real -> bool` (that evaluates to true if their arguments are equivalent -i.e., the real value is considered to represent the integer one- and false otherwise), and the antibridge `#/== :: int -> real -> bool` (with a countermeaning).

1 Introduction

$\mathcal{TOY}$ [1] is a constraint functional logic language and system, designed to support the main declarative programming styles and their combination. From `http://toy.sourceforge.net` the preferred distribution for $\mathcal{TOY}$ can be downloaded. There are some possibilities: Choose either a binary distribution (a portable application that does not need installation) or a source-code distribution (which requires SICStus Prolog previously installed). Therefore, almost any platform can run $\mathcal{TOY}$ (e.g., the system can be started as a Windows application or in a Linux console). It features a command interpreter for submitting goals and system commands. In addition, it has been connected to ACIDE [2],

* First and third authors were partially supported by the Spanish National Projects MERIT-FORMS (TIN2005-09027-C03-03) and PROMESAS-CAM(S-0505/TIC/0407). Second author was partially supported by Spanish MCyT projects under contracts TIN2005-08818-C04-01 and TIN-2007-67134.

S. Drossopoulou (Ed.): ESOP 2008, LNCS 4960, pp. 112–115, 2008.

a graphical and configurable integrated development environment. Further developments are also guided to port the system to free Prolog interpreters such as B-Prolog.

Programs in $\mathcal{TOY}$ can include definitions of types, operators, lazy functions in Haskell style, as well as definitions of predicates in Prolog style. A predicate is viewed as a particular kind of function whose right-hand side is true. A function definition consists of an optional *type declaration* and one or more *defining rules*, which are possibly conditional rewrite rules. Both functions and predicates must be well-typed with respect to a polymorphic type system [3].

Programs can use constraints within the definitions of both predicates and functions. Constraints supported by the system include symbolic equations and disequations [4], linear and non-linear arithmetic constraints over the real numbers [5] and finite domain constraints [6].

$\mathcal{TOY}$ computations solve goals and display computed answers. $\mathcal{TOY}$ solves goals by means of a demand driven lazy narrowing strategy [7] combined with constraint solving. Answer constraints can represent bindings for logic variables, as in answers computed by a Prolog system. Some features of $\mathcal{TOY}$ are:

1. *Curried style.* This allows that partial applications of curried functions can be used to express functional values as partial patterns.
2. *Non-deterministic functions.* These are defined either by means of defining rules with overlapping left-hand sides or using extra variables in the right-hand side that do not occur in the left-hand side.
3. *Sharing* for values of all variables which occur in the left-hand sides of defining rules and have multiple occurrences in the right-hand side and/or the conditions. Sharing implements so-called *call-time choice* semantics of non-deterministic functions.
4. *Higher-order functions* in the style of Haskell, except that lambda abstractions are not allowed. In $\mathcal{TOY}$, higher-order can be naturally combined with non-determinism.
5. *Dynamic Cut.* Optimization that detects deterministic functions at compile time, and the generated code includes a test for detecting at run-time the computations that can actually be pruned [8].
6. *Finite Failure.* The primitive Boolean function *fails* is a direct counterpart to finite failure in Prolog.

2 Constraint Functional Logic Programming Scheme $CFLP(C)$

$\mathcal{TOY}$ implements a Constraint Functional Logic Programming scheme $CFLP(D)$ over a parametrically given constraint domain D, proposed in [9]. $CFLP(D)$ is a logical and semantic framework for lazy Constraint Functional Logic Programming over D, which provides a clean and rigorous declarative semantics for $CFLP$ languages.

In particular, D is the *coordination domain* C introduced in [10] as the amalgamated sums of the domains to be coordinated, $D_1, \ldots, D_n$, along with a *mediatorial domain M* which supplies special communication constraints, called bridges, used to impose the equivalence between values of different base types.

The Cooperative Constrained Lazy Narrowing Calculus $CCLNC(C)$ presented in [10] provides a fully sound formal framework for functional logic programming with cooperating solvers over various constraint domains. $CCLNC(C)$ has been proved fully sound w.r.t. $CRWL(C)$ semantics [9].

3 Cooperation in $\mathcal{TOY}$: Bridges and Projections

$\mathcal{TOY}$ comes equipped with solvers corresponding to three constraint domains:

1. *Herbrand*, with equality and disequality constraints.
2. *Real Arithmetic*, with arithmetical constraints over real numbers.
3. *Finite domain*, with constraints over integer numbers.

The Herbrand Solver is always available, and the real and finite domain solvers can be optionally loaded. With the aim of extending the system applicability, a mechanism for solver cooperation on these domains has been recently incorporated. This mechanism has two main pillars: *Bridges*, necessary for solver communication, and *Projections*, that improve the efficiency of some programs.

A bridge is a special kind of 'hybrid' constraint which allows the communication among the real and finite ('pure') domains and instantiates a variable occurring at one end of a bridge whenever the other end becomes a numeric value. Note that, a bridge constraint can be used to impose an integral constraint over its right argument. As an example, suppose we want to know if two different lines can meet at one integer point. A line can be described algebraically by the linear equation `y = m * x + b`, and the corresponding $\mathcal{TOY}$ program is:

Program
`meetLines M1 B1 M2 B2=(X,Y)`
`<== X #== RX,`
`    Y #== RY,`
`    RY == M1*RX + B1,`
`    RY == M2*RX + B2`

Goal	Answer
`meetLines 2 4 1 2 == L`	`L -> (-2, 0)`
`meetLines 1 1 1 2 == L`	`no %parallel`
`meetLines 1 1 3 2 == L`	`no %real point`

Projection takes place during goal solving whenever a pure constraint is submitted to its solver. At that moment, projection builds a mate constraint which is submitted to the mate solver (think of finite domain solver as the mate of real solver, and vice versa). Projection rules described in [10,11] relying on the available bridges are used for building mate constraints. For example, suppose we want to calculate the intersection of a triangular region (defined in the continuous plane) with an $(N \times N)$-size square discrete grid (defined in the discrete plane). A $\mathcal{TOY}$ program that solves the problem, for any given even integer number N, is shown below; the triangular region is described by the inequalities whereas the square grid is described by the finite domain constraints (i.e., those labelled with # and the function *labeling/2*).

Program	Mate Constraints
`bothIn L X Y N :- X#==RX, Y#==RY, N#==NX,`	
`RY >= (NX/2) - 0.5,` ⇒	`Y #>= ⌈NX/2 #- 0.5⌉,`
`RY - RX <= 0.5,` ⇒	`Y #- X #<= ⌊0.5⌋,`
`RY + RX <= NX + 0.5,` ⇒	`Y #+ X #<= ⌊NX #+ 0.5⌋,`
`domain [X,Y] 0 N,` ⇒	`0<=RX, RX<=N, 0<=RY, RY<=N`
`labeling L [X,Y]`	

Mate constraints, generated during goal solving, allow the finite domain solver to drastically prune the domains of `X` and `Y`. Therefore, if we have a huge grid and a tiny triangle and the projection is enabled, then the computation time is drastically reduced. Note that not all the constraints are projected, for example the labeling constraint.

We have borrowed the idea of constraint projection from the work of P. Hofstedt [12], adapting it to our $CFLP$ scheme and adding bridge constraints as a novel technique which makes projections more flexible and compatible with type discipline.

References

1. Arenas, P., Fernández, A., Gil, A., López, F., Rodríguez, M., Sáenz, F.: $\mathcal{TOY}$. In: Caballero, R., Sánchez, J. (eds.) A Multiparadigm Declarative Language. Version 2.3.0 (2007), Available at `http://toy.sourceforge.net`
2. Sáenz-Pérez, F.: ACIDE: An Integrated Development Environment Configurable for LaTeX. The PracTeX Journal 2007(3) (2007)
3. Damas, L., Milner, R.: Principal type-schemes for functional programs. In: POPL 1982, pp. 207–212. ACM Press, New York (1982)
4. Arenas, P., Gil, A., López, F.: Combining Lazy Narrowing with Disequality Constraints. In: Penjam, J. (ed.) PLILP 1994. LNCS, vol. 844, pp. 385–399. Springer, Heidelberg (1994)
5. Hortalá, T., López, F., Sánchez, J., Ullán, E.: Declarative Programming with Real Constraints. Research Report SIP 5997, U.C.M (1997)
6. Fernández, A.J., Hortalá, T., Sáenz, F., del Vado, R.: Constraint Functional Logic Programming over Finite Domains. Theory Pract. Log. Program. 7(5), 537–582 (2007)
7. Loogen, R., López-Fraguas, F.J., Rodríguez-Artalejo, M.: A demand driven computation strategy for lazy narrowing. In: Penjam, J., Bruynooghe, M. (eds.) PLILP 1993. LNCS, vol. 714, pp. 184–200. Springer, Heidelberg (1993)
8. Caballero, R., García-Ruiz, Y.: Implementing dynamic cut in toy. Electr. Notes Theor. Comput. Sci. 177, 153–168 (2007)
9. López, F., Rodríguez, M., del Vado, R.: A new generic scheme for functional logic programming with constraints. Higher-Order and Symbolic Computation 20(1/2), 73–122 (2007)
10. Estévez, S., Fernández, A.J., Hortalá, M.T., Rodríguez, M., del Vado, R.: A fully sound goal solving calculus for the cooperation of solvers in the CFLP scheme. ENTCS 177, 235–252 (2007)
11. Estévez, S., Fernández, A., Hortalá, T., Rodríguez, M., Sáenz, F., del Vado, R.: A Proposal for the Cooperation of Solvers in Constraint Functional Logic Programming. ENTCS 188, 37–51 (2007)
12. Hofstedt, P., Pepper, P.: Integration of declarative and constraint programming. Theory Pract. Log. Program. 7(1-2), 93–121 (2007)

Typing Safe Deallocation

Gérard Boudol

INRIA, 06902 Sophia Antipolis, France

Abstract. In this work we address the problem of proving, by static analysis means, that allocating and deallocating regions in the store provides a safe way to achieve memory management. That is, the goal is to provably ensure that a program does not use pointers into a deallocated region. A well-known approach to this problem is the one of Tofte and Talpin. Our first contribution is to provide a simple proof, by means of a subject reduction property, of type safety for their region calculus. Our second, main contribution is that we actually do this for an extension of Tofte-Talpin's calculus, featuring a primitive construct for deallocating regions, similar to C's `free`, that allows one to circumvent the strict stack-of-regions discipline enforced in Tofte-Talpin's calculus. Our static analysis consists in a novel type and effect system, extending the one of Tofte and Talpin, where we record deallocation effects.

1 Introduction

Some years ago, Tofte and Talpin [15,16] proposed a new memory model for higher-order, typed languages, as an alternative to explicit allocation/deallocation of memory (e.g. `malloc/free` in C) and garbage collection. The main idea is to introduce, in an intermediate language for the compilation process, a block-structured (letregion ρ in e) construct, allocating a new region in the memory for the evaluation of e, and deallocating it upon termination.[1] Experience has shown that, as reported in [17], introducing region management in this way allows the compiler to produce code for ML programs that executes quite efficiently, even without the support of a garbage collector. Moreover, memory management with regions is *provably safe*, and this is one of the most remarkable achievements of Tofte and Talpin's approach.

The safety proof is not so easy, however. The original proof in [16] used a quite elaborate coinductive technique. A number of research works have been done since then on this topic [2,4,5,6,8,11,18], in order to better understand why the apparently simple typing of the letregion construct is actually safe, and to get a simpler proof. Indeed, this construct allows for reusing a dead region, even though there are still pointers in that region in the code, thus creating dangling pointers. Moreover, the same pointers can also be subsequently reused, holding

[1] This idea was previously mentioned in [14]: "*Since the locations belonging to a private region cannot be accessed after the expression returns, they can be safely deallocated when the expression returns.*" However, the semantics given in this paper did not involve deallocation, and this statement was not proved.

S. Drossopoulou (Ed.): ESOP 2008, LNCS 4960, pp. 116–130, 2008.

values of a different type. The difficulty is then to prove that the pointers in the code that actually refer to defunct regions are guaranteed by typing to never be used. The syntactic proof of [5], following the standard steps of a type safety proof (see [20]), seems to be adopted as the classical one by now (see [13]). It formalizes deallocation as the substitution of a dead region • for the deallocated region everywhere in the current configuration, including in the values stored in the memory. In [5] it is shown that this semantics is bisimilar to the original one of [16]. However, using an explicit notion (•) of a deallocated region modifies (and overloads) the semantics of the letregion construct, with a rewriting phase that is not present in the original formulation, and therefore a truly direct, syntactic proof of type safety for Tofte-Talpin's region calculus is yet to be done. Our first contribution is to give a fresh look at this problem.

To prove that region deallocation is safe, we have to ensure that when a region is deallocated, it should not be used by the rest of the computation (i.e. the evaluation context). This is done in [16] by means of a sophisticated *consistency predicate*, supporting a coinductive proof technique. We shall do this here by means of a type and effect system. The idea is very simple. First, we decompose the (letregion ρ in e) construct of Tofte and Talpin as follows:

$$(\mathsf{letregion}\ \rho\ \mathsf{in}\ e) = (\mathsf{new}\ \rho\ \mathsf{in}\ (\mathsf{free\_after}\ \rho\ e))$$

where (new ρ in e') allocates a new region, with scope e', and (free_after ρ e) deallocates the region ρ when the computation of e is terminated. Such a decomposition was introduced in [1].[2] Then we introduce a new kind of effects, which we call negative effects, or *deallocation effects*, associated with the latter construct in the type system, and we check that there is no conflict with the ordinary, "positive," or *usage* effects, in order to ensure that regions required in future computations are not deleted in the current computation. Typically, assuming a left-to-right evaluation order, as in [16], the negative effect of e_0 in $(e_0 e_1)$ should not intersect the positive effect of e_1, in order for the application to be typable. With this refined (flow-sensitive) effect system, which directly extends the one of [16], we are able to show the safety of region deallocation, by means of a Subject Reduction argument, as explained below (Section 4).

The idea of using explicit deallocation effects suggests that we could further decompose the (letregion ρ in e) construct of Tofte and Talpin, introducing an explicit, atomic instruction for region deallocation. We write this as (dispose ρ), and we define

$$(\mathsf{free\_after}\ \rho\ e) = (\mathsf{let}\ x = e\ \mathsf{in}\ (\mathsf{dispose}\ \rho)\ ;\ x)$$

(see [19] for a similar decomposition). Quite obviously, the deallocation effects are introduced by the dispose instruction, and our proof of type safety actually deals with the refined region calculus, where the letregion construct is replaced by new and dispose. The latter, which could also be defined in terms of free_after and termination (), was considered, in various concrete syntactic forms, in a

[2] In [1], the allocation operation is also separated from the creation of a new name. We shall comment on this below. The free_after construct is denoted (region ρ in e) in [5]. An analogous expression (*private* ρ e) was used in [14], though with different semantics.

number of papers: it is denoted freerg in [8,18], deleteregion in [9,10] and release in [12] (with different semantics), and free in [19]. One reason for using such an explicit region deallocation construct is that, as noted very early in [1,3], the strict stack discipline enforced in Tofte and Talpin's calculus is too constraining to cope with situations where it would be much more efficient to reclaim a region without waiting for the end of its lexical scope. It is then natural to use such an explicit deallocation construct, for optimization purposes, but the problem of ensuring that this operation is safe comes out again, and it is a difficult one.

A specific difficulty, noted in [1], is that *"for correctness it is important that a region be allocated only once and deallocated only once during its lifetime."* The "allocated-only-once" is a built-in feature of the (new ρ in e) construct, but regarding deallocation, it seems appropriate to use ideas from linear logic, and this is indeed what is done in a number of works, see for instance [7,8,18,19]. However, as we show below, resorting to linear logic techniques is not a necessity. Indeed, introducing deallocation effects makes it very easy to control the "deallocated-only-once" feature in our flow-sensitive effect system: it is enough to ensure that a region occurring in the deallocation effect of a subexpression is not in the (negative) effect of the rest of the computation. Our static analysis for provably ensuring the safety of explicit region deallocation is then much simpler than previously given ones.

The paper is organized as follows: in a first section, we introduce our extended region calculus, and describe its operational semantics. In a next section, we introduce our type and effect system, featuring the notion of a deallocation effect. We then establish a Subject Reduction property up to region renaming, and derive from it our Type Safety result. A brief conclusion is given. For lack of space, most of the proofs are omitted.

2 The Extended Region Calculus

In this section we introduce our region calculus, extending the one of Tofte and Talpin with an explicit primitive construct for deallocating regions, and we describe its operational semantics. We assume given two disjoint denumerable sets $\mathcal{R}eg\mathcal{V}ar$ and $\mathcal{R}eg\mathcal{C}st$ of *region variables* and *region constants*, respectively ranged over by ρ and r. The set $\mathcal{R}eg = \mathcal{R}eg\mathcal{V}ar \cup \mathcal{R}eg\mathcal{C}st$ of *region names*, is ranged over by ϱ. We also assume given a denumerable set $\mathcal{L}oc$ of *memory locations*, or *pointers*, range over by p, $q\ldots$, and a denumerable set $\mathcal{V}ar$ of *variables*, ranged over by x, $y,\ldots f$, $g\ldots$. The syntax is as follows:

$$
\begin{array}{lll}
a := (r,p) & & \textit{addresses}\\
v ::= () \mid a & & \textit{values}\\
w ::= \lambda x e & & \textit{storable values}\\
e ::= x \mid v \mid (w\,@\,\varrho) \mid (e_0 e_1) \mid (\mathsf{let}\ x = e_0\ \mathsf{in}\ e_1) & & \textit{expressions}\\
\quad\ \mid (\mathsf{new}\ \rho\ \mathsf{in}\ e) \mid (\mathsf{dispose}\ \varrho) & &
\end{array}
$$

The expression $(w\,@\,\varrho)$, pronounced "w at ϱ" in [16], is meant to create a new pointer in region ϱ with contents w. As usual, the variable x is bound in λxe, and ρ is bound in (new ρ in e), whereas it is free in $(w\,@\,\rho)$ and (dispose ρ).

We denote by $\mathsf{reg}(e)$ the set of region constants and region variables that occur (free) in e, and by $\mathsf{ref}(e)$ the set of addresses occurring in e. The expression e is said to be *closed* if no variable or region variable occurs free in it. We denote by $\{x \mapsto v\}e$ and $\{\rho \mapsto \varrho\}e$ the capture-avoiding substitutions of values and region names in e. We shall consider expressions up to α-conversion, that is up to the renaming of bound variables and regions. We use the notation $(\lambda x e_1 e_0)$, that is $(w e_0)$ where $w = \lambda x e_1$, as a synonym of $(\mathsf{let}\ x = e_0\ \mathsf{in}\ e_1)$, and we also write this as $e_0 \,;\, e_1$ whenever x is not free in e_1.

In a more realistic language, there would be more (storable) values, like booleans, integers, pairs, and so on, with appropriate constructs to use these values, like conditional branching, etc. We regard the region calculus of Tofte and Talpin [16] as a sub-language, where $(\mathsf{new}\ \rho\ \mathsf{in}\ e)$ and $(\mathsf{dispose}\ \varrho)$ are replaced by $(\mathsf{letregion}\ \rho\ \mathsf{in}\ e)$, with

$$
\begin{aligned}
(\mathsf{letregion}\ \rho\ \mathsf{in}\ e) &=_{\mathrm{def}} (\mathsf{new}\ \rho\ \mathsf{in}\ (\mathsf{free\_after}\ \rho\ e)) \quad \text{where}\\
(\mathsf{free\_after}\ \varrho\ e) &=_{\mathrm{def}} (\mathsf{let}\ x = e\ \mathsf{in}\ (\mathsf{dispose}\ \varrho) \,;\, x)
\end{aligned}
$$

as explained in the Introduction.

In order to show our safety result, we use a small-step semantics for the language. The evaluation of an expression consists, as usual, in reducing a *redex* inside an *evaluation context*, in the context of a *store*. The redexes and evaluation contexts are as follows:

$$
\begin{array}{rll}
u ::= & (w\,@\,r) \mid (av) \mid (\lambda x e v) & \textit{redexes}\\
 & \mid (\mathsf{new}\ \rho\ \mathsf{in}\ e) \mid (\mathsf{dispose}\ r) & \\
\mathbf{E} ::= & [] \mid \mathbf{E}[\mathbf{F}] & \textit{evaluation contexts}\\
\mathbf{F} := & ([]\,e) \mid (a\,[]) \mid (\lambda x e\,[]) & \textit{frames}
\end{array}
$$

Definition (Stuck Expressions) 2.1. *An expression e is* stuck *if and only if $e = \mathbf{E}[e']$ where e' is either a variable, or $(w\,@\,\rho)$, or $(()e')$, or $(\mathsf{dispose}\ \rho)$.*

Notice that a closed stuck expression has the form $\mathbf{E}[(()e)]$. The following is a standard fact:

Lemma 2.2. *For any expression e, either*

(i) *e is a value, or*

(ii) *e is a stuck expression, or*

(iii) *there exist an evaluation context $\mathbf{E}$ and a redex u such that $e = \mathbf{E}[u]$.*

As in [16], a *store* s is a mapping from a finite set $\mathsf{dom}(s)$ of region constants to *regions*, where a region is a mapping from a finite set of locations to storable values. We denote by $\mathsf{Dom}(s)$ the set $\{\,(r,p) \mid r \in \mathsf{dom}(s)\ \&\ p \in \mathsf{dom}(s(r))\,\}$, and we write $s(r,p)$ for $s(r)(p)$ where $(r,p) \in \mathsf{Dom}(s)$. We define, for $R \subseteq \mathcal{R}eg$ and $r \in \mathcal{R}eg\mathcal{C}st$:

$$
\begin{aligned}
\mathsf{dom}(s \upharpoonright R) &= R \cap \mathsf{dom}(s)\\
r \in \mathsf{dom}(s \upharpoonright R) &\Rightarrow (s \upharpoonright R)(r) = s(r)\\
s \backslash r &= s \upharpoonright (\mathsf{dom}(s) - \{r\})
\end{aligned}
$$

We shall in fact use the notations $f \upharpoonright X$ and $f \backslash x$ for any partial function $f : A \rightharpoonup B$, with $x \in A$ and $X \subseteq A$.

$$\begin{array}{rcll}
(s, \mathbf{E}[(w @ r)]) & \rightarrow & (s + \{(r,p) \mapsto w\}, \mathbf{E}[(r,p)]) & r \in \mathsf{dom}(s), \\
&&& p \notin \mathsf{dom}(s(r)) \\
(s, \mathbf{E}[((r,p)v)]) & \rightarrow & (s, \mathbf{E}[(wv)]) & r \in \mathsf{dom}(s), \\
&&& p \in \mathsf{dom}(s(r)), \\
&&& s(r,p) = w \\
(s, \mathbf{E}[(\lambda xev)]) & \rightarrow & (s, \mathbf{E}[\{x \mapsto v\}e]) & \\
(s, \mathbf{E}[(\mathsf{new}\ \rho\ \mathsf{in}\ e)]) & \rightarrow & (s + \{r \mapsto \emptyset\}, \mathbf{E}[\{\rho \mapsto r\}e]) & r \notin \mathsf{dom}(s) \\
(s, \mathbf{E}[(\mathsf{dispose}\ r)]) & \rightarrow & (s \backslash r, \mathbf{E}[()]) &
\end{array}$$

Fig. 1. Reduction

In the operational semantics, we use the notations of [16] for extending or updating the store with new regions, namely $s + \{r \mapsto \emptyset\}$ and $s + \{(r,p) \mapsto w\}$. The reduction relation consists in a transition relation between *configurations*, that are pairs (s, e) of a store and an expression to evaluate. This is defined in Figure 1. The evaluation of an application $(e_0 e_1)$ is standard. We nevertheless examine the various steps in details, since our typing will rely on these: first, one computes the function e_0 until an address a is obtained, possibly by reducing an expression $(w @ r)$. Next, the argument e_1 is computed, producing a value v. Then, to evaluate the resulting expression (av), a read operation occurs, returning the value contained in the store at address a. This value should be a function λxe, and we now have to evaluate $(\mathsf{let}\ x = v\ \mathsf{in}\ e)$, as usual, that is: the value v is bound to x, and finally one proceeds evaluating $\{x \mapsto v\}e$. Regarding the construct $(\mathsf{new}\ \rho\ \mathsf{in}\ e)$, evaluating it consists in allocating a new region constant r in the store, which is bound to ρ in e for the rest of the computation,[3] while evaluating $(\mathsf{dispose}\ r)$ deallocates the region named r from the store and terminates. Then one can check that the $(\mathsf{letregion}\ \rho\ \mathsf{in}\ e)$ construct has the same semantics as in [16]. Notice in particular that in allocating a new region, reducing $(\mathsf{new}\ \rho\ \mathsf{in}\ e)$, we do not require that the new name does not occur in e, nor in the evaluation context $\mathbf{E}$, nor in some value currently recorded in the store. Then one can reuse a region name that still occurs in the configuration, with the only proviso that the name is not in the domain of the current store.

3 The Type and Effect System

3.1 Effects, Types, Judgements and Rules

Our main technical novelty in this work consists, as explained in the Introduction, in refining the notion of an effect, introducing negative, *deallocation effects* that are distinct from the usual "positive" effects of creating, reading or updating a region. In this work, it will be unnecessary to distinguish various kinds of positive effects. Then an *effect* here is a pair $\varphi = (\varphi^+, \varphi^-)$ of a positive effect φ^+ and a negative effect φ^-, which both are finite sets of region names. The standard

[3] For simplicity, we use region substitution $\{\rho \mapsto r\}e$ instead of a region environment.

$$\frac{}{\Sigma;\Gamma,x:\tau\vdash x:\emptyset,\tau}\qquad\frac{}{\Sigma;\Gamma\vdash ():\emptyset,\mathbb{1}}\qquad\frac{}{\Sigma,(r,p):\zeta;\Gamma\vdash (r,p):\emptyset,\zeta_r}$$

$$\frac{\Sigma;\Gamma,x:\tau\vdash e:\varphi,\sigma}{\Sigma;\Gamma\vdash \lambda xe:(\tau\xrightarrow{\varphi}\sigma)}\qquad\frac{\Sigma;\Gamma\vdash w:\zeta}{\Sigma;\Gamma\vdash (w\,@\,\varrho):(\{\varrho\},\emptyset),\zeta_\varrho}$$

$$\frac{\Sigma;\Gamma\vdash e_0:\varphi_0,(\tau\xrightarrow{\varphi_2}\sigma)_\varrho\quad \Sigma;\Gamma\vdash e_1:\varphi_1,\tau}{\Sigma;\Gamma\vdash (e_0e_1):(\varphi_0+\varrho)\cup\varphi_1\cup\varphi_2,\sigma}\ \begin{cases}\varphi_0^-\cap(\{\varrho\}\cup\varphi_1^\pm\cup\varphi_2^\pm)=\emptyset\\ \varphi_1^-\cap(\{\varrho\}\cup\varphi_2^\pm)=\emptyset\end{cases}$$

$$\frac{\Sigma;\Gamma\vdash e_0:\varphi_0,\tau\quad \Sigma;\Gamma,x:\tau\vdash e_1:\varphi_1,\sigma}{\Sigma;\Gamma\vdash (\mathsf{let}\ x=e_0\ \mathsf{in}\ e_1):\varphi_0\cup\varphi_1,\sigma}\ \varphi_0^-\cap\varphi_1^\pm=\emptyset$$

$$\frac{\Sigma;\Gamma\vdash e:\varphi,\tau}{\Sigma;\Gamma\vdash (\mathsf{new}\ \rho\ \mathsf{in}\ e):\varphi\backslash\rho,\tau}\ \rho\notin\Sigma,\Gamma,\tau\qquad\frac{}{\Sigma;\Gamma\vdash (\mathsf{dispose}\ \varrho):(\emptyset,\{\varrho\}),\mathbb{1}}$$

Fig. 2. The type and effect system: expressions

set-theoretic notions, like inclusion, union, etc. are extended componentwise to effects. In the following we write $\varphi^\pm$ for $\varphi^+\cup\varphi^-$, $\varphi+\varrho$ for $\varphi\cup(\{\varrho\},\emptyset)$, and $\varphi\backslash\varrho$ for $\varphi-(\{\varrho\},\{\varrho\})$. The types are standard:

$$\tau,\ \sigma\ldots ::= t\ \mid\ \mathbb{1}\ \mid\ \zeta_\varrho \qquad \textit{types}$$

$$\zeta ::= (\tau\xrightarrow{\varphi}\sigma) \qquad \textit{storable value types}$$

The type $\mathbb{1}$ is also often denoted unit. As in [16], $(\tau\xrightarrow{\varphi}\sigma)_\varrho$ is the type of addresses in region ϱ of the store where one finds a functional value of type $(\tau\xrightarrow{\varphi}\sigma)$. As usual, a functional type records the latent effect φ a function of this type may have when applied to an argument.

There are two kinds of judgments in our type and effect system. A judgment $\Sigma;\Gamma\vdash e:\varphi,\tau$ means that under the assumptions Σ and Γ, the expression e is anticipated to have an effect φ, and has type τ. Similarly, a judgment $\Sigma;\Gamma\vdash w:\zeta$ means that, under the assumptions Σ and Γ, the storable value w has type ζ (and no effect, since this is a value). The component Σ in these judgments is the region typing context, which maps a finite set $\mathsf{dom}(\Sigma)$ of region constants to region typings, where a region typing is a map from a finite set of locations to types of storable values. The set $\{\,(r,p)\mid r{\in}\mathsf{dom}(\Sigma)\ \&\ p{\in}\mathsf{dom}(\Sigma(r))\,\}$ is denoted $\mathsf{Dom}(\Sigma)$, and a region typing context is written $(r_1,p_1):\zeta_1,\ldots,(r_m,p_m):\zeta_m$. The Γ component is, as usual, a typing context, mapping a finite set of variables to types. In the typing rule for $(\mathsf{new}\ \rho\ \mathsf{in}\ e)$, we write $\rho\notin\Sigma,\Gamma,\tau$ to mean that the variable ρ does not occur in Σ, Γ (that is, in the types assigned by these typing contexts) and τ.

The rules of the type and effect system are given in Figure 2, which we now comment. First we point out that the negative effects are, as expected, introduced when typing an expression $(\mathsf{dispose}\ \varrho)$, while a positive effect results from a storing operation $(w\,@\,\varrho)$ and reading a (functional) value from the store, in an application. Our effect system then checks that a subexpression does not deallocate a region in which some future effect is anticipated. In our core language, where we adopt a left-to-right evaluation order, the only subexpressions that have a "future" are e_0 in $(e_0 e_1)$ and $(\mathsf{let}\ x = e_0\ \mathsf{in}\ e_1)$, and e_1 in $(e_0 e_1)$, where in the latter case, the effects that may arise after evaluating e_1 are the effect of reading the function from the store (at address e_0), and the latent effect of that function. Then in typing the application $(e_0 e_1)$, we have the constraint that the region in which the value resulting from evaluating e_0 is stored should not be disposed of before the actual reading operation occurs, that is $\varrho \notin (\varphi_0^- \cup \varphi_1^-)$. Similarly, e_0 should not have the effect of removing regions that may be used in the rest of the computation, that is $\varphi_0^- \cap \varphi_1^\pm = \emptyset = \varphi_0^- \cap \varphi_2^\pm$, and finally, e_1 should not delete regions occurring in the latent effect of the function, that is $\varphi_1^- \cap \varphi_2^\pm = \emptyset$. The constraint in typing a $(\mathsf{let}\ x = e_0\ \mathsf{in}\ e_1)$ is similar. These constraints mean in particular that one cannot deallocate twice the same region. Indeed, in our calculus where allocating (via new) and deallocating (via dispose) a region are not restricted to follow the strict block-structured discipline of [16], it would be generally unsafe (and not very useful) to deallocate several times the same region. For instance, evaluating an expression of the form

$$(\mathsf{new}\ \rho_0 \cdots \mathsf{dispose}\ \rho_0 \cdots (\mathsf{new}\ \rho_1 \cdots \mathsf{dispose}\ \rho_0 \cdots (w\ @\ \rho_1) \cdots))$$

could result in assigning to ρ_1 the same region r that has been assigned to ρ_0, since r has been disposed of, but then the second instruction $(\mathsf{dispose}\ \rho_0)$ has the effect of deleting the region associated with ρ_1, and the evaluation of $(w\ @\ \rho_1)$ then fails in this case. In the rule for $(\mathsf{new}\ \rho\ \mathsf{in}\ e)$, we could require $\rho \in \varphi^-$, in order to ensure that the region assigned to ρ has been disposed of when the evaluation exits its scope, but this would be just an indication, because the effects anticipated by typing are not guaranteed to occur (though it is guaranteed that no other effect can possibly occur).

Regarding the derived constructs that are involved in the Tofte and Talpin's sub-calculus, one can see that a derived typing rule is

$$\frac{\Sigma; \Gamma \vdash e : \varphi, \tau}{\Sigma; \Gamma \vdash (\mathsf{free\_after}\ \varrho\ e) : \varphi \cup (\emptyset, \{\varrho\}), \tau}\ \varrho \notin \varphi^-$$

and consequently

$$\frac{\Sigma; \Gamma \vdash e : \varphi, \tau}{\Sigma; \Gamma \vdash (\mathsf{letregion}\ \rho\ \mathsf{in}\ e) : \varphi \backslash \rho, \tau}\ \rho \notin \Sigma, \Gamma, \tau, \varphi^-$$

One may then observe that in typing expressions of the derived sub-calculus the negative effect is always empty, and conclude that, up to the identification of $(\varphi^+, \emptyset)$ with the single effect φ^+, what we get is exactly the usual typing for Tofte and Talpin's region calculus, without any constraint on the effect.

Now let us see an example of a typable expression, inspired from examples in [1,18]. Let w be a typable storable value, e a typable expression using (via the variable x) this value from region ρ (and possibly having other positive effects in this region), and let e' be a typable expression that has no effect in region ρ. Then the following is typable:

$$\begin{array}{l}\mathsf{new}\ \rho\ \mathsf{in}\ \mathsf{let}\ x = (w\ @\ \rho)\ \mathsf{in} \\ \mathsf{new}\ \rho'\ \mathsf{in}\ \mathsf{let}\ f = (\lambda x (\mathsf{let}\ y = (\mathsf{free\_after}\ \rho\ e)\ \mathsf{in}\ e')\ @\ \rho')\ \mathsf{in} \\ (\mathsf{free\_after}\ \rho'\ (f x))\end{array}$$

This example shows, first, that regions may have arbitrarily overlapping extent [1]: here the evaluation will execute the sequence

$$\mathsf{new}\ \rho \cdots \mathsf{new}\ \rho' \cdots \mathsf{dispose}\ \rho \cdots \mathsf{dispose}\ \rho'$$

Second, in the code for the function f, the region constant assigned to ρ can be disposed of without waiting for the call (fx) to end, since this region is only used in a first part of the computation of (fx). As another example, one can see that with a conditional branching construct, typed as follows:

$$\frac{\Sigma;\Gamma \vdash e : \varphi, \mathsf{bool} \quad \Sigma;\Gamma \vdash e_i : \varphi_i, \tau}{\Sigma;\Gamma \vdash (\mathsf{if}\ e\ \mathsf{then}\ e_0\ \mathsf{else}\ e_1) : \varphi \cup \varphi_0 \cup \varphi_1, \tau}\ \varphi^- \cap (\varphi_0^\pm \cup \varphi_1^\pm) = \emptyset$$

then if a branch does not use region ϱ, one can immediately dispose of it, while in the other branch this action is deferred after the use of values in that region. (As above with the new construct, we could additionally require $\varphi_0^- = \varphi_1^-$ in this rule.)

To show the type safety result, we have to extend the typing to configurations. In order to type the store, one should have enough assumptions in the region typing context: any address in the store should be the subject of a typing assumption. Moreover, the value stored at some address should have type as prescribed by the region typing context. Finally, for a configuration to be typable, we shall require a "well-formedness" property, asserting that any region in which the computation may have an effect should be allocated in the store. Indeed, it is essential for safety to preserve the property that accesses to the memory never fail. Our definition is therefore as follows:

Definition (Typing Configurations) 3.1.

$$\text{(i)}\quad \Sigma;\Gamma \vdash s \quad \Leftrightarrow_{\text{def}} \quad \begin{cases} \mathsf{Dom}(s) \subseteq \mathsf{Dom}(\Sigma) \\ (r,p) \in \mathsf{Dom}(s) \ \Rightarrow\ \Sigma;\Gamma \vdash s(r,p) : \Sigma(r,p) \end{cases}$$

$$\text{(ii)}\quad \Sigma;\Gamma \vdash (s,e) : \varphi, \tau \quad \Leftrightarrow_{\text{def}} \quad \begin{cases} \Sigma;\Gamma \vdash s \ \&\ \Sigma;\Gamma \vdash e : \varphi, \tau \\ \forall r.\ r \in \varphi^\pm \ \Rightarrow\ \begin{cases} r \in \mathsf{dom}(s)\ \& \\ \mathsf{dom}(\Sigma(r)) \subseteq \mathsf{dom}(s(r)) \end{cases} \end{cases}$$

3.2 Some Properties

We notice a few facts that will be used in our proof of type safety. First, the type and effect system reflects the fact that a value has no effect:

Remark 3.2. $\Sigma;\Gamma \vdash v : \varphi, \tau \ \Rightarrow\ \varphi = \emptyset$

Second, some errors are, as usual, statically precluded by typing:

Remark 3.3. *A closed stuck expression is not typable.*

Finally, one can show some standard properties relating typing and substitution:

Lemma (Substitution) 3.4.

(i) $\Sigma;\Gamma \vdash v : \psi, \tau \ \&\ \Sigma;\Gamma, x : \tau \vdash e : \varphi, \sigma \ \Rightarrow\ \Sigma;\Gamma \vdash \{x \mapsto v\}e : \varphi, \sigma$

(ii) *If* $\Sigma;\Gamma \vdash e : \varphi, \tau$ *and* r *does not occur in* $\Sigma;\Gamma \vdash e : \varphi, \tau$ *then* $\{\rho \mapsto r\}(\Sigma;\Gamma \vdash e : \varphi, \tau)$.

$$\frac{}{\Sigma;\Gamma\vdash [\,] : (\tau \xrightarrow{\emptyset} \tau)} \qquad \frac{\Sigma;\Gamma\vdash \mathbf{E} : (\theta \xrightarrow{\varphi_1} \sigma) \quad \Sigma;\Gamma\vdash \mathbf{F} : (\tau \xrightarrow{\varphi_0} \theta)}{\Sigma;\Gamma\vdash \mathbf{E}[\mathbf{F}] : (\tau \xrightarrow{\varphi_0\cup\varphi_1} \sigma)}\ \varphi_0^- \cap \varphi_1^\pm = \emptyset$$

$$\frac{\Sigma;\Gamma\vdash e : \varphi_0,\tau}{\Sigma;\Gamma\vdash ([\,]e) : ((\tau \xrightarrow{\varphi_1} \sigma)_\varrho \xrightarrow{(\varphi_0+\varrho)\cup\varphi_1} \sigma)}\ \varphi_0^- \cap (\{\varrho\}\cup\varphi_1^\pm) = \emptyset$$

$$\frac{}{\Sigma,(r,p) : (\tau \xrightarrow{\varphi} \sigma);\Gamma\vdash ((r,p)\,[\,]) : (\tau \xrightarrow{\varphi+r} \sigma)} \qquad \frac{\Sigma;\Gamma,x:\tau\vdash e : \varphi,\sigma}{\Sigma;\Gamma\vdash (\lambda x e\,[\,]) : (\tau \xrightarrow{\varphi} \sigma)}$$

Fig. 3. The type and effect system: evaluation contexts

For the proof of our main result, it will be convenient to decompose the typing of an expression of the form $\mathbf{E}[e]$ into a typing of e and a typing of the evaluation context. (An alternative is to use a "Replacement Lemma", see [20] for instance.) The type system for evaluation contexts allows one to infer judgments of the form $\Sigma;\Gamma\vdash\mathbf{E} : (\tau \xrightarrow{\varphi} \sigma)$, meaning that if the context is filled with an expression of type τ, then it will return a result of type σ, while producing effects as indicated by φ. There are constraints regarding the effects similar to the ones that hold for expressions. The rules are given in Figure 3. Then we introduce an alternative way to type expressions, by means of judgments of the form $\Sigma;\Gamma \Vdash e : \varphi,\tau$, established as follows:

$$\frac{\Sigma;\Gamma\vdash e : \varphi_0,\tau \quad \Sigma;\Gamma\vdash \mathbf{E} : (\tau \xrightarrow{\varphi_1} \sigma)}{\Sigma;\Gamma \Vdash \mathbf{E}[e] : \varphi_0\cup\varphi_1,\sigma}\ \varphi_0^- \cap \varphi_1^\pm = \emptyset$$

We can prove that this provides us with just an equivalent way of typing:

LEMMA 3.5.

(i) $\Sigma;\Gamma \Vdash e : \varphi,\tau \;\Rightarrow\; \Sigma;\Gamma\vdash e : \varphi,\tau$

(ii) *If* $\Sigma;\Gamma\vdash\mathbf{E}[e] : \varphi,\tau$ *then there exist* φ_0, φ_1 *and* σ *such that* $\Sigma;\Gamma\vdash e : \varphi_0,\sigma$ *and* $\Sigma;\Gamma\vdash\mathbf{E} : (\sigma \xrightarrow{\varphi_1} \tau)$ *with* $\varphi = \varphi_0\cup\varphi_1$ *and* $\varphi_0^- \cap \varphi_1^\pm = \emptyset$.

4 Type Safety

A technical difficulty in showing the soundness of typing deallocation is that there is a discrepancy between the operational semantics and typing as regards the generation of new regions. More specifically, to establish Subject Reduction would require that the fresh name generated when reducing $(\mathsf{new}\ \rho\ \mathsf{in}\ e)$ be as fresh as possible, and in particular, that it does not occur in the expression e, in order for the substitution of the new name to yield a valid typing judgment. On the opposite side, from the operational point of view, it could be beneficial, and therefore allowed (as it is), to reuse a name that has been disposed of, even though it could still occur in the expression e, in a dead pointer to a deallocated region for instance. Our way to reconcile the typing with the operational semantics is to establish a Subject Reduction property *up to simulation* (where a "simulation" is half a bisimulation – but we do not need any coinductive machinery). The idea is actually very simple: it is to show that, to preserve the typing along a given computation, one may have to, not exactly follow, but simulate the actual computation by just making "better" (from the typing point of view) choices of new region names and pointers, while still maintaining a tight correspondence with the given computation, by means of a region and pointer renaming. Safety will then result from the fact that the use of dangling pointers is precluded by typing, *cf.* Definition 3.1(ii).

4.1 The Simulation Relation

We introduce a relation over configurations (s, e), that will be proved to be a simulation. More precisely our simulation relates (s, e) to (s', e') by means of a *translation* $\mathbf{t}$, in such a way that, if (s, e) is typable and (s', e') performs a transition, then one can choose regions and pointers so that (s, e) performs a similar transition, resulting in similar configurations, while preserving typability. The translation, relating region constants to regions constants, and pointers to pointers, may evolve along the transitions, either because a new pointer is created, or because a region constant is created, or reused.

DEFINITION (TRANSLATIONS) 4.1. *A* translation $\mathbf{t}$ *is a pair* $(\mathbf{r}, \mathbf{p})$ *where*

(i) $\mathbf{r}$ *is a mapping from a finite subset* $\mathsf{dom}(\mathbf{r})$ *of* $\mathcal{RegCst}$ *to* $\mathcal{RegCst}$*,*

(ii) $\mathbf{p}$ *is a function with the same domain as* $\mathbf{r}$*, such that, for any* $r \in \mathsf{dom}(\mathbf{r})$*,* $\mathbf{p}(r)$ *is an injective mapping from a finite subset* $\mathsf{dom}(\mathbf{p}(r))$ *of* $\mathcal{Loc}$ *to* $\mathcal{Loc}$*.*

We denote by $\mathcal{T}$ the set of translations. We also write $\mathbf{p}(r)$ as $\mathbf{p}_r$. We extend the inclusion relation to translations, as follows:

$$(\mathbf{r}, \mathbf{p}) \subseteq (\mathbf{r}', \mathbf{p}') \quad \Leftrightarrow_{\text{def}} \quad \begin{cases} \mathbf{r} \subseteq \mathbf{r}' \ \& \\ r \in \mathsf{dom}(\mathbf{r}) \ \Rightarrow \ \mathbf{p}_r \subseteq \mathbf{p}'_r \end{cases}$$

For each translation $\mathbf{t} = (\mathbf{r}, \mathbf{p})$, we define the partial mapping $\langle\mathbf{t}\rangle$ on expressions and storable values, by induction on the structure, as follows – omitting the cases where the translation just goes through the structure of the expression:

$$\begin{aligned} \langle\mathbf{t}\rangle(r, p) &= (\mathbf{r}(r), \mathbf{p}_r(p)) && \text{if } r \in \mathsf{dom}(\mathbf{r}) \ \& \ p \in \mathsf{dom}(\mathbf{p}_r) \\ \langle\mathbf{t}\rangle(w \mathbin{@} r) &= (\langle\mathbf{t}\rangle w \mathbin{@} \mathbf{r}(r)) && \text{if } r \in \mathsf{dom}(\mathbf{r}) \\ \langle\mathbf{t}\rangle(\mathsf{dispose}\ r) &= (\mathsf{dispose}\ \mathbf{r}(r)) && \text{if } r \in \mathsf{dom}(\mathbf{r}) \end{aligned}$$

We write:

$$e \rhd_{\mathbf{t}} e' \quad \Leftrightarrow_{\text{def}} \quad e \in \mathsf{dom}(\langle\mathbf{t}\rangle) \ \& \ e' = \langle\mathbf{t}\rangle(e)$$

The syntactic structure of e' is identical to the one of e whenever $e \rhd_{\mathbf{t}} e'$: the expression e' is obtained from e by renaming region constants and pointers. The following should be obvious:

REMARKS 4.2.

(i) *For any expression* e*, if we let* $\mathbf{t}_e = (\mathbf{r}, \mathbf{p})$ *where* $\mathbf{r} = \{\, (r, r) \mid r \in \mathsf{reg}(e) \,\}$ *and* $\mathbf{p}_r = \{\, (p, p) \mid (r, p) \in \mathsf{ref}(e) \,\}$ *for* $r \in \mathsf{reg}(e)$*, then* $\mathbf{t}_e \in \mathcal{T}$ *and* $e \rhd_{\mathbf{t}_e} e$*.*

(ii) *If* $e \in \mathsf{dom}(\langle \mathbf{t} \rangle)$ *then* $\langle \mathbf{t} \rangle e$ *is a value (resp. a redex, resp. a stuck expression) if and only if* e *is a value (resp. a redex, resp. a stuck expression).*
(iii) *If* $e \rhd_{\mathbf{t}} e'$ *and* $\mathbf{t} \subseteq \mathbf{t}'$ *then* $e \rhd_{\mathbf{t}'} e'$.

The relation $\rhd_{\mathbf{t}}$ is compatible with substitution:

LEMMA 4.3.
(i) $v \rhd_{\mathbf{t}} v' \ \&\ e \rhd_{\mathbf{t}} e' \ \Rightarrow\ \{x \mapsto v\}e \rhd_{\mathbf{t}} \{x \mapsto v'\}e'$
(ii) $r \in \mathsf{dom}(\mathbf{r}) \ \&\ e \rhd_{\mathbf{r},\mathbf{p}} e' \ \Rightarrow\ \{\rho \mapsto r\}e \rhd_{\mathbf{r},\mathbf{p}} \{\rho \mapsto \mathbf{r}(r)\}e'$.

We define what it means for a translation $\mathbf{t}$ to *comply* with an effect, which intuitively means that the translation does not confuse the region constants involved in the effect:

DEFINITION 4.4. *A translation* $\mathbf{t} = (\mathbf{r}, \mathbf{p})$ complies *with the effect* φ, *in notation* $\mathbf{t} \propto \varphi$ *if and only if* $\varphi^{\pm} \cap \mathcal{R}eg\mathcal{C}st \subseteq \mathsf{dom}(\mathbf{r})$ *and* $\mathbf{r} \restriction \varphi^{\pm}$ *is injective.*

Clearly

$$\mathbf{t} \propto \varphi \ \&\ \psi \subseteq \varphi \ \Rightarrow\ \mathbf{t} \propto \psi \tag{1}$$

Our simulation on configurations is indexed by a translation $\mathbf{t}$ and an effect φ. We first define the relation $\rhd_{\mathbf{t}}^{\varphi}$ on stores, as follows:

DEFINITION 4.5. *Let* $\mathbf{t} = (\mathbf{r}, \mathbf{p})$ *be a translation and* φ *an effect such that* $\mathbf{t} \propto \varphi$. *Then* $s \rhd_{\mathbf{t}}^{\varphi} s'$, *read "*$s$ *simulates* s' *up to* φ *modulo* $\mathbf{t}$,*" if and only if*
(i) $\mathbf{r}(\varphi^{\pm}) \subseteq \mathsf{dom}(s')$
(ii) $r \in \varphi^{+} \ \&\ (r,p) \rhd_{\mathbf{t}} (r',p') \ \Rightarrow\ \begin{cases} (r,p) \in \mathsf{Dom}(s) \Leftrightarrow (r',p') \in \mathsf{Dom}(s') \\ (r,p) \in \mathsf{Dom}(s) \ \Rightarrow\ s(r,p) \rhd_{\mathbf{t}} s'(r',p') \end{cases}$

It should be obvious that

$$s \rhd_{\mathbf{t}}^{\varphi} s' \ \&\ \psi \subseteq \varphi \ \Rightarrow\ s \rhd_{\mathbf{t}}^{\psi} s' \tag{2}$$

Then we define

$$(s,e) \rhd_{\mathbf{t}}^{\varphi} (s',e') \ \Leftrightarrow_{\mathrm{def}}\ s \rhd_{\mathbf{t}}^{\varphi} s' \ \&\ e \rhd_{\mathbf{t}} e'$$

4.2 Main Result

Now we show the Subject Reduction property suggested above: if (s_0, e_0) is typable, and simulates (s_1, e_1), and if the latter performs a transition to (s_1', e_1') then there is a choice of regions and a typable configuration (s_0', e_0') which simulates (modulo the updated region translation) (s_1', e_1'), and is the result of the corresponding transition from (s_0, e_0). This property can be drawn:

$$\begin{array}{ccc} (s_1, e_1) & \longrightarrow & (s_1', e_1') \\ \Delta & & \Delta \\ \Sigma; \Gamma \vdash (s_0, e_0) : \varphi, \tau & \dashrightarrow & \Sigma'; \Gamma \vdash (s_0', e_0') : \psi, \tau \end{array}$$

LEMMA (SUBJECT REDUCTION up to SIMULATION) 4.6.
If $\Sigma;\Gamma \vdash (s_0, e_0) : \varphi, \tau$ *and* $(s_1, e_1) \to (s_1', e_1')$ *with* $(s_0, e_0) \rhd_{\mathbf{t}}^{\varphi} (s_1, e_1)$ *then there exist* s_0', e_0', Σ' *and* ψ *such that* $(s_0, e_0) \to (s_0', e_0')$ *and* $\Sigma';\Gamma \vdash (s_0', e_0') : \psi, \tau$ *with* $(s_0', e_0') \rhd_{\mathbf{t}'}^{\psi} (s_1', e_1')$ *for some* $\mathbf{t}' \in \mathcal{T}$.
PROOF: by case on the transition $(s_1, e_1) \to (s_1', e_1')$.

- $(s_1, \mathbf{E}_1[(w' \,@\, r')]) \to (s_1 + \{(r', p') \mapsto w'\}, \mathbf{E}_1[(r', p')])$ with $r' \in \mathsf{dom}(s_1)$ and $p' \notin \mathsf{dom}(s_1(r'))$. We have $e_0 = \mathbf{E}_0[(w \,@\, r)]$ with $r \in \mathsf{dom}(\mathbf{r})$, $r' = \mathbf{r}(r)$ and $w \rhd_{\mathbf{t}} w'$. By Lemma 3.5(ii), there exist φ_0, φ_1 and σ such that $\Sigma;\Gamma \vdash (w \,@\, r) : \varphi_0, \sigma$ and $\Sigma;\Gamma \vdash \mathbf{E}_0 : (\sigma \xrightarrow{\varphi_1} \tau)$ with $\varphi = \varphi_0 \cup \varphi_1$ and $\varphi_0^- \cap \varphi_1^{\pm} = \emptyset$. Then $\sigma = \zeta_r$ with $\Sigma;\Gamma \vdash w : \zeta$, and $\varphi_0 = (\{r\}, \emptyset)$. We have $r \in \varphi^+$, and therefore $r \in \mathsf{dom}(s_0)$ by Definition 3.1(ii). We distinguish two cases.

(a) If there exists p such that $\mathbf{p}_r(p) = p'$, that is $(r, p) \rhd_{\mathbf{t}} (r', p')$ then $p \notin \mathsf{dom}(s_0(r))$ by Definition 4.5(ii), and therefore

$$(s_0, e_0) \to (s_0', e_0') \quad \text{where} \quad \begin{cases} s_0' = s_0 + \{(r,p) \mapsto \lambda x e\} \\ e_0' = \mathbf{E}_0[(r,p)] \end{cases}$$

Since $r \in \varphi^+$ and $(r,p) \notin \mathsf{Dom}(s_0)$ we have, by Definition 3.1(ii), $(r,p) \notin \mathsf{Dom}(\Sigma)$, and $\Sigma, (r,p) : \zeta; \Gamma \vdash (r,p) : \emptyset, \zeta_r$. Then $\Sigma, (r,p) : \zeta; \Gamma \vdash (s_0', e_0') : \varphi_1, \tau$ by Lemma 3.5(i) and $\varphi_1 \subseteq \varphi$. Then obviously $\mathbf{t} \propto \varphi_1$ (see (1) above), and

$$\mathbf{r}(\varphi_1^{\pm}) \subseteq \mathbf{r}(\varphi^{\pm}) \subseteq \mathsf{dom}(s_1) = \mathsf{dom}(s_1')$$

by Definition 4.5(i). If $r'' \in \varphi_1^+$ and $(r'', p'') \rhd_{\mathbf{t}} (r', p')$ then $r'' = r$ since $\mathbf{r} \restriction \varphi^{\pm}$ is injective, and $p'' = p$ since $\mathbf{p}_r$ is injective, hence $(r'', p'') \in \mathsf{Dom}(s_0')$. From this we easily conclude $(s_0', e_0') \rhd_{\mathbf{t}}^{\varphi_1} (s_1', e_1')$.

(b) Otherwise, that is if there is no $p \in \mathsf{dom}(\mathbf{p}_r)$ such that $\mathbf{p}_r(p) = p'$, let p be such that $(r,p) \notin \mathsf{Dom}(\Sigma)$. Then $(r,p) \notin \mathsf{Dom}(s_0)$ by Definition 3.1(i), and therefore

$$(s_0, e_0) \to (s_0', e_0') \quad \text{where} \quad \begin{cases} s_0' = s_0 + \{(r,p) \mapsto \lambda x e\} \\ e_0' = \mathbf{E}_0[(r,p)] \end{cases}$$

Since $\Sigma, (r,p) : \zeta; \Gamma \vdash (r,p) : \emptyset, \zeta_r$ we have $\Sigma, (r,p) : \zeta; \Gamma \vdash (s_0', e_0') : \varphi_1, \tau$ by Lemma 3.5(i). Let $\mathbf{t}' = (\mathbf{r}, \mathbf{p}')$ where $\mathbf{p}' = \mathbf{p} + \{(r,p) \mapsto (r', p')\}$. Then $\mathbf{p}_r'$ is injective, and since $\varphi_1 \subseteq \varphi$ we have $\mathbf{t}' \propto \varphi_1$ (see (1) above) and $\mathbf{r}(\varphi_1^{\pm}) \subseteq \mathbf{r}(\varphi^{\pm}) \subseteq \mathsf{dom}(s_1) = \mathsf{dom}(s_1')$. There is no (r'', p'') such that $r'' \in \varphi_1^+$ and $(r'', p'') \rhd_{\mathbf{t}} (r', p')$, since otherwise we would have $r'' = r$, for $\mathbf{r} \restriction \varphi^{\pm}$ is injective, by Definition 4.4, and this would contradict our assumption (b). From this it is easy to conclude $(s_0', e_0') \rhd_{\mathbf{t}'}^{\varphi_1} (s_1', e_1')$, using Remark 4.2(iii).

- $(s_1, \mathbf{E}_1[((r', p')v')]) \to (s_1, \mathbf{E}_1[(w'v')])$ with $r' \in \mathsf{dom}(s_1)$, $p' \in \mathsf{dom}(s_1(r'))$ and $s_1(r', p') = w'$. We have $e_0 = \mathbf{E}_0[((r,p)e_2)]$ with $(r,p) \rhd_{\mathbf{t}} (r', p')$ and $e_2 \rhd_{\mathbf{t}} v'$, hence e_2 is a value v, by Remark 4.2(ii), and therefore $((r,p)e_2)$ is a redex. By Lemma 3.5(ii) there exist φ_0, φ_1 and σ such that $\Sigma;\Gamma \vdash ((r,p)v) : \varphi_0, \sigma$ and $\Sigma;\Gamma \vdash \mathbf{E}_0 : (\sigma \xrightarrow{\varphi_1} \tau)$ with $\varphi_0^- \cap \varphi_1^{\pm} = \emptyset$ and $\varphi = \varphi_0 \cup \varphi_1$. Then $(r,p) \in \mathsf{Dom}(\Sigma)$ with $\Sigma(r,p) = (\theta \xrightarrow{\psi_0} \sigma)_r$ and $\Sigma;\Gamma \vdash v : \psi_1, \theta$ with $\varphi_0 = (\psi_0 + r) \cup \psi_1$. Since $r \in \varphi^+$, we have $r \in \mathsf{dom}(s_0)$ by Definition 3.1(ii), hence $p \in \mathsf{dom}(s_0(r))$ and $s_0(r,p) \rhd_{\mathbf{t}} s_1(r', p')$ by Definition 4.5(ii), that is $s_0(r,p) = w$ with $w \rhd_{\mathbf{t}} w'$. Then $\Sigma;\Gamma \vdash w : (\theta \xrightarrow{\psi_0} \sigma)$ by Definition 3.1(i), and we have

$$(s_0, e_0) \rightarrow (s_0, e'_0) \quad \text{where} \quad e'_0 = \mathbf{E}_0[(wv)]$$

By Lemma 3.5(i) we have $\Sigma; \Gamma \vdash (s_0, e'_o) : \psi, \tau$ where $\psi = \psi_0 \cup \psi_1 \cup \varphi_1 \subseteq \varphi$, and it is obvious that $\mathbf{t} \propto \psi$ and $(s_0, e'_0) \rhd^{\psi}_{\mathbf{t}} (s_1, e'_1)$ (see the remarks (1) and (2) above).

- $(s_1, \mathbf{E}_1[(\lambda x e'_2 v')]) \rightarrow (s_1, \mathbf{E}_1[\{x \mapsto v'\} e'_2])$. In this case we use the Substitution Lemma 3.4(i). The details are left to the reader.

- $(s_1, \mathbf{E}_1[(\mathsf{new}\ \rho\ \mathsf{in}\ e'_2)]) \rightarrow (s_1 + \{r' \mapsto \emptyset\}, \mathbf{E}_1[\{\rho \mapsto r'\} e'_2])$ with $r' \notin \mathsf{dom}(s_1)$. We have $e_0 = \mathbf{E}_0[(\mathsf{new}\ \rho\ \mathsf{in}\ e_2)]$ with $e_2 \rhd_{\mathbf{t}} e'_2$, and there exist φ_0, φ_1 and σ such that $\Sigma; \Gamma \vdash (\mathsf{new}\ \rho\ \mathsf{in}\ e_2) : \varphi_0, \sigma$ and $\Sigma; \Gamma \vdash \mathbf{E}_0 : (\sigma \xrightarrow{\varphi_1} \tau)$ with $\varphi_0^- \cap \varphi_1^\pm = \emptyset$ and $\varphi = \varphi_0 \cup \varphi_1$ by Lemma 3.5(ii). Let r be a fresh region constant, that does not occur in the statement $\Sigma; \Gamma \vdash (s_0, e_0) : \varphi, \tau$, nor in $\mathsf{dom}(\mathbf{r})$. In particular, $r \notin \mathsf{dom}(s_0)$, and therefore

$$(s_0, e_0) \rightarrow (s'_0, e'_0) \quad \text{where} \quad \begin{cases} s'_0 = s_0 + \{r \mapsto \emptyset\} \\ e'_0 = \mathbf{E}_0[\{\rho \mapsto r\} e_2] \end{cases}$$

We have $\Sigma; \Gamma \vdash e_2 : \varphi'_0, \sigma$ with $\rho \notin \Sigma, \Gamma, \tau$ and $\varphi_0 = \varphi'_0 \backslash \rho$. Then by Lemma 3.4(ii) we have $\Sigma; \Gamma \vdash \{\rho \mapsto r\} e_2 : \{\rho \mapsto r\} \varphi'_0, \sigma$, hence $\Sigma; \Gamma \vdash (s'_0, e'_0) : \psi, \tau$ by Lemma 3.5(i), where $\varphi^\pm \subseteq \psi^\pm \subseteq \varphi^\pm \cup \{r\}$. Let $\mathbf{t}' = (\mathbf{r}', \mathbf{p}')$ where $\mathbf{r}' = \mathbf{r} + \{r \mapsto r'\}$ and $\mathbf{p}' = \mathbf{p} + \{r \mapsto \emptyset\}$. If $r'' \in \mathsf{dom}(\mathbf{r})$ is such that $\mathbf{r}(r'') = r'$ then $r'' \notin \psi^\pm$ by Definition 4.5(i) since $r' \notin \mathsf{dom}(s_1)$, and therefore $\mathbf{r}' \upharpoonright \psi^\pm$ is injective, hence $\mathbf{t}' \propto \psi$. Clearly $\mathbf{r}'(\psi^\pm) \subseteq \mathsf{dom}(s'_1)$, since $\mathbf{r}(\varphi^\pm) \subseteq \mathsf{dom}(s_1)$ by Definition 4.5(i). It is then easy to conclude $(s'_0, e'_0) \rhd^{\psi}_{\mathbf{t}'} (s'_1, e'_1)$, using Lemma 4.3(ii).

- $(s_1, \mathbf{E}_1[(\mathsf{dispose}\ r')]) \rightarrow (s_1 \backslash r', \mathbf{E}_1[()])$. We have $e_0 = \mathbf{E}_0[(\mathsf{dispose}\ r)]$ with $r \in \mathsf{dom}(\mathbf{r})$ and $\mathbf{r}(r) = r'$. Then

$$(s_0, e_0) \rightarrow (s'_0, e'_0) \quad \text{where} \quad \begin{cases} s'_0 = s_0 \backslash r \\ e'_0 = \mathbf{E}_0[()] \end{cases}$$

and by Lemma 3.5(ii) there exist ψ and σ such that $\Sigma; \Gamma \vdash \mathbf{E}_0 : (\mathbb{1} \xrightarrow{\psi} \tau)$ with $r \notin \psi^\pm$ and $\varphi = \psi \cup (\emptyset, \{r\})$. Then we have $\Sigma; \Gamma \vdash (s'_0, e'_0) : \psi, \tau$, thanks to Lemma 3.5(i). We obviously have $\mathbf{t} \propto \psi$ (see the remark (1) above). Assume that $r'' \in \psi^\pm$ is such that $\mathbf{r}(r'') = r'$. Since $\mathbf{r} \upharpoonright \varphi^\pm$ is injective, we should then have $r'' = r$, but this is impossible since $r \notin \psi^\pm$. This shows $\mathbf{r}(\psi^\pm) \subseteq \mathsf{dom}(s'_1)$. Now assume that $r'' \in \psi^+$ is such that $(r'', p'') \rhd_{\mathbf{t}} (r', p')$. Then we should have $r'' = r$ since $\mathbf{r} \upharpoonright \varphi^\pm$ is injective, but this is impossible since $r \notin \psi^\pm$. From this we easily conclude that $s'_0 \rhd^{\psi}_{\mathbf{t}} s'_1$, and therefore $(s'_0, e'_0) \rhd^{\psi}_{\mathbf{t}} (s'_1, e'_1)$. ❑

We can now use this lemma to show that a typable closed expression does not run into an error. We first define the erroneous configurations.

Definition (Faulty Configuration) 4.7. *A configuration (s, e) is faulty if either*

(i) *e is a stuck expression, that is $\mathbf{E}[e']$ where e' is either a variable, or $(\lambda x e' @ \rho)$, or $(()e')$, or $(\mathsf{dispose}\ \rho)$, or*

(ii) *e writes in a deallocated region, that is $e = \mathbf{E}[(w @ r)]$ with $r \notin \mathsf{dom}(s)$, or*

(iii) *e uses a dangling pointer, that is $e = \mathbf{E}[((r, p)v)]$ with $(r, p) \notin \mathsf{Dom}(s)$.*

Then our main result is as follows:

THEOREM (TYPE SAFETY) 4.8. *If (s,e) is a closed, typable configuration, and $(s,e) \xrightarrow{*} (s',e')$, then the configuration (s',e') is not faulty.*

PROOF: first we notice that closedness is preserved by reduction. We have $\Sigma;\Gamma \vdash (s,e) : \varphi,\tau$. Let R be a finite subset of $\mathcal{R}eg\mathcal{C}st$ which contains all the region constants involved in the judgment $\Sigma;\Gamma \vdash (s,e) : \varphi,\tau$ (including the name occurring in values stored in s, etc.). Let us define $\mathbf{t} = (\mathbf{r},\mathbf{p})$ as follows: $\mathbf{r} = \{\,(r,r) \mid r \in R\}$ and, for $r \in R$, $\mathbf{p}_r$ maps any address (r,p) occurring in the judgment $\Sigma;\Gamma \vdash (s,e) : \varphi,\tau$ onto itself. Clearly $\mathbf{t} \in \mathcal{T}$, $e \rhd_{\mathbf{t}} e$ (see Remarks 4.2(i)-(iii)), $\mathbf{t} \propto \varphi$ and $s \rhd_{\mathbf{t}}^{\varphi} s$ since $\varphi^{\pm} \subseteq \mathsf{dom}(s)$ by Definition 3.1(ii), and therefore $(s,e) \rhd_{\mathbf{t}}^{\varphi} (s,e)$. Then by Lemma 4.6 there exist (s'',e''), Σ', ψ and $\mathbf{t}' = (\mathbf{r}',\mathbf{p}')$ such that $(s,e) \xrightarrow{*} (s'',e'')$ with $\Sigma';\Gamma \vdash (s'',e'') : \psi,\tau$ and $(s'',e'') \rhd_{\mathbf{t}'}^{\psi} (s',e')$, and in particular $e \rhd_{\mathbf{t}'} e'$. Then by Remarks 3.3 and 4.2(ii), e' is not a stuck expression. If $e' = \mathbf{E}'[(w' \mathbin{@} r')]$ then $e'' = \mathbf{E}[(w \mathbin{@} r)]$ with $\mathbf{r}'(r) = r'$ and $r \in \psi^{+}$ by Lemma 3.5(ii), and therefore $r \in \mathsf{dom}(s'')$ by Definition 3.1(ii), hence $r' \in \mathsf{dom}(s')$ by Definition 4.5. If $e' = \mathbf{E}'[((r',p')e_1)]$ then $e'' = \mathbf{E}[((r,p)e_0)]$ with $(r,p) \rhd_{\mathbf{t}'} (r',p')$, and $r \in \psi^{+}$ by Lemma 3.5(ii). We conclude as in the previous case. ❑

Given a closed, typable expression e with effect φ, which does not contain any memory address, this result applies in particular to an initial configuration (s,e) where $s = \{\, r \mapsto \emptyset \mid r \in \mathsf{reg}(e) \cup \varphi^{\pm}\,\}$. (We conjecture that for such an expression, there exists a typing such that $\varphi^{\pm} \subseteq \mathsf{reg}(e)$.)

5 Conclusion

In this work we have presented a new static analysis for a language with explicit manipulations of memory regions. Our type and effect system is a direct generalization of the one of Tofte and Talpin. We also have introduced a new method for proving type safety in such a language, establishing a "subject reduction up-to-simulation" property that makes apparent the fact that, if we choose "properly" the names created along the computation, then the typing is preserved. We believe that our idea of introducing explicit deallocation effects, which are in some sense dual to the capabilities of [18], and to the set of "currently allocated regions" of [4], can be adapted to richer settings. In particular, in an extended version of this work, we shall show how to deal with region polymorphism and aliasing. We also think our technique could be extended to deal with explicit allocation, as proposed in [1] for instance, by introducing anticipated and actual allocation effects. We preferred not to consider such an extended language here, mainly for the purpose of keeping the exposition simple.

It would be interesting to see whether our static analysis could justify the safety of some of the optimizations, as decribed in [1] for instance, to Tofte and Talpin's compilation from the call-by-value λ-calculus into the region calculus. More generally, it would be interesting to see whether one can take some advantage in using the typed language we have presented as an intermediate language in the compilation process of functional languages.

References

1. Aiken, A., Fähndrich, M., Levien, R.: Better static memory management: improving region-based analysis of higher-order languages. In: PLDl 1995, pp. 174–185 (1995)
2. Banerjee, A., Heintze, N., Riecke, J.: Region analysis and the polymorphic lambda-calculus. In: LICS 1999, pp. 88–97 (1999)
3. Birkedal, L., Tofte, M., Vejlstrup, M.: From region inference to von Neumann machines via region representation inference. In: POPL 1996, pp. 171–183 (1996)
4. Calcagno, C.: Stratified operational semantics for safety and correctness of the region calculus. In: POPL 2001, pp. 155–165 (2001)
5. Calcagno, C., Helsen, S., Thiemann, P.: Syntactic type soundness results for the region calculus. Information and Computation 173(2), 199–221 (2002)
6. Dal Zilio, S., Gordon, A.: Region analysis and a π-calculus with groups. J. of Functional Programming 12(3), 229–292 (2002)
7. Fähndrich, M., DeLine, R.: Adoption and focus: practical linear types for imperative programming. In: PLDI 2002, pp. 13–24 (2002)
8. Fluet, M., Morrisett, G., Ahmed, A.: Linear regions are all you need. In: Sestoft, P. (ed.) ESOP 2006 and ETAPS 2006. LNCS, vol. 3924, Springer, Heidelberg (2006)
9. Gay, D., Aiken, A.: Memory management with explicit regions. In: PLDI 1998, pp. 313–323 (1998)
10. Gay, D., Aiken, A.: Language support for regions. In: PLDI 2001, pp. 70–80 (2001)
11. Helsen, S., Thiemann, P.: Syntactic type soundness for the region calculus. HOOTS 2000, ENTCS 41(3), 1–19 (2001)
12. Henglein, F., Makholm, H., Niss, F.: A direct approach to control-flow sensitive region-based memory management. In: PPDP 2001, pp. 175–186 (2001)
13. Henglein, F., Makholm, H., Niss, F.: Effect Types and Region-Based Memory Management. In: Pierce, B.C. (ed.) Chap. 3 of Advanced Topics in Types and Programming Languages, pp. 87–135. MIT Press, Cambridge (2005)
14. Lucassen, J.M., Gifford, D.K.: Polymorphic effect systems. In: POPL 1988, pp. 47–57 (1988)
15. Tofte, M., Talpin, J.-P.: Implementation of the typed call-by-value λ-calculus using a stack of regions. In: POPL 1994, pp. 188–201 (1994)
16. Tofte, M., Talpin, J.-P.: Region-based memory management. Information and Computation 132(2), 109–176 (1997)
17. Tofte, M., Birkedal, L., Elsman, M., Hallenberg, N.: A retrospective on region-based memory management. HOSC 17(2), 245–265 (2004)
18. Walker, D., Crary, K., Morrisett, G.: Typed memory management via static capabilities. TOPLAS 22(4), 701–771 (2000)
19. Walker, D., Watkins, K.: On regions and linear types. In: ICFP 2001, pp. 181–192 (2001)
20. Wright, A., Felleisen, M.: A syntactic approach to type soundness. Information and Computation 115(1), 38-94 1994

Iterative Specialisation of Horn Clauses

Christoffer Rosenkilde Nielsen, Flemming Nielson, and Hanne Riis Nielson

Technical University of Denmark
{crn,nielson,riis}@imm.dtu.dk

Abstract. We present a generic algorithm for solving Horn clauses through iterative specialisation. The algorithm is generic in the sense that it can be instantiated with any decidable fragment of Horn clauses, resulting in a solution scheme for general Horn clauses that guarantees soundness and termination, and furthermore, it presents sufficient criteria for completeness. We then demonstrate the use of the framework, by creating an instance of it, based on the decidable class $\mathcal{H}_1$, capable of solving a non-trivial protocol analysis problem based on the Yahalom protocol.

1 Introduction

Horn clauses have proven to be useful in many areas of computer science. They are very expressive (they are, in fact, Turing complete [1]) and yet they maintain a high clarity due to the simple format. This makes them attractive for many theoretical developments, as well as for practical purposes exemplified by the Prolog language.

Their usefulness has, however, also been restricted for the very same reasons that they are interesting: unrestricted Horn clauses are Turing complete. Thus Horn clause-based problems are often undecidable, and, similarly, Horn clause-based algorithms often have termination problems.

In this paper we shall show how to circumvent the first shortcoming, namely that problems formulated in unrestricted Horn clauses may be undecidable, thereby making Horn clauses more attractive for theoretical purposes such as static analysis. Specifically, we shall present a framework for finding, and iteratively improving the precision of, a model for any set of unrestricted Horn clauses. The framework is shown to guarantee soundness (i.e. it always returns a correct model) and termination, and it may in some cases also provide completeness (i.e. the model is the least model). Completeness depends on the chosen instance of the framework, as the framework is generic in the sense that it can be instantiated with any known decidable fragment of Horn clauses.

The general structure of our iterative framework is shown in Fig. 1. It is parameterised on a decidable fragment $\mathcal{H}$ of Horn clauses and given a formula φ the first step is to check whether φ is in $\mathcal{H}$, if so, then we can immediately construct its least model, denoted $\mathcal{N}(\varphi)$ on the figure, and we are done.

If φ is not in $\mathcal{H}$, then we apply an $\mathcal{H}$*-relaxation*, $\mathcal{R}$, and the resulting formula, $\tilde{\varphi} = \mathcal{R}(\varphi)$, will be in $\mathcal{H}$. The relaxation guarantees that the least model of this

S. Drossopoulou (Ed.): ESOP 2008, LNCS 4960, pp. 131–145, 2008.

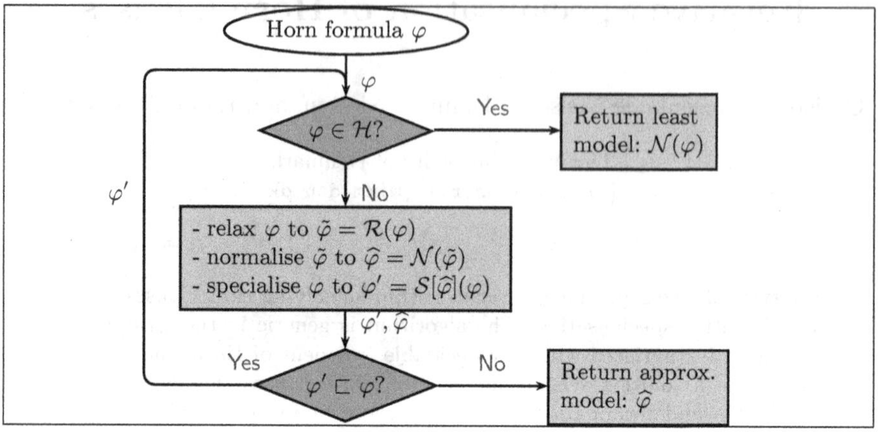

Fig. 1. Iterative scheme

formula (denoted $\widehat{\varphi} = \mathcal{N}(\tilde{\varphi})$ on the figure) is also a model of φ, but it is possibly too large to be useful by itself. It may, however, contain useful information that can be used to *specialise* the original formula φ; this operation is denoted $\varphi' = \mathcal{S}[\widehat{\varphi}](\varphi)$ on Fig. 1. In order to compare the new and the original formula, we introduce a well-founded, *simplification ordering*, $\sqsubseteq$, over formulae; if the new formula is an improvement of the old, according to this ordering, then the above steps can be repeated. Otherwise the iteration stops and $\widehat{\varphi}$ will be the resulting (approximative) model of φ.

The remainder of the paper is organised as follows. In Sect. 2 we give the background in Horn clauses necessary for understanding the development. We then, formally, present the iterative scheme in Sect. 3 and show that it satisfies several attractive properties. To illustrate its usefulness, we present an instance of the scheme in Sect. 4, using the decidable fragment of Horn clauses $\mathcal{H}_1$, and afterwards in Sect. 5 demonstrate how this instance can be used for verifying cryptographic protocols, by applying it to a specific analysis problem based on one of the well-known protocols of the literature; the Yahalom key-distribution protocol. Finally, Sect. 6 reflects and concludes.

2 Horn Clauses

The standard syntax of Horn clauses is presented in Table 1 and should be read as follows. A Horn *formula* $\varphi \in \mathbf{HC}$ is a finite set of implications, usually referred to as *clauses*. Every clause c is on the form $g_0 \Leftarrow g_1, \ldots, g_l$ where the literals g_0 and $g_1, \ldots, g_l$ are the head and the precondition of c, respectively. A *literal* is of the form $\mathsf{p}(t_1, \ldots, t_m)$ where p is an m-ary predicate symbol and t_i is a term built up from variables (indicated by a capitalised first letter) through constructor applications. In the following, we shall sometimes refer to constructors of arity 0 as *constants*, and clauses without preconditions as *facts*, written without the implication arrow.

Table 1. Horn syntax

$\varphi ::= \{c_1, \ldots, c_k\}$	$g ::= \mathsf{p}(t_1, \ldots, t_m)$
$c ::= g_0 \Leftarrow g_1, \ldots, g_l$	$t ::= X \mid f(t_1, \ldots, t_n)$

We let expressions, e, range over formulae, clauses, literals and terms, and define $\mathsf{Var}(e)$, $\mathsf{Con}(e)$, and $\mathsf{Pred}(e)$, to be the set of variable, constructor and predicate symbols, respectively, that occur in e[1]. A term, t, is called *ground* if it consists of no variables, i.e. $\mathsf{Var}(t) = \emptyset$, and for a given formula, φ, the set of all ground terms built from $\mathsf{Con}(\varphi)$ is called its *Herbrand universe*, denoted H_φ.

Horn formulae are interpreted relative to an interpretation $\rho \in \mathbf{R}$ that maps predicate symbols to corresponding term relations; i.e. an m-ary predicate symbol is mapped to an m-ary term relation which is a subset of H_φ^m. Letting θ denote a substitution mapping variables to ground terms, we then define a satisfaction relation $\models$ as presented[2] in Table 2.

Table 2. Satisfaction relation

$\rho \models \varphi$	iff	$\forall c \in \varphi : \rho \models c$
$\rho \models g_0 \Leftarrow g_1, \cdots, g_l$	iff	$\forall \theta : \wedge_{i=1}^{l} (\rho, \theta \models g_i) \Rightarrow (\rho, \theta \models g_0)$
$\rho, \theta \models \mathsf{p}(t_1, \ldots, t_m)$	iff	$\langle t_1\theta, \ldots, t_m\theta \rangle \in \rho(\mathsf{p})$

An interpretation ρ, that satisfies a Horn formula φ is called a model of φ. We then state the following well-known result [2]:

Proposition 1 (Least model). *The set of models of a Horn formula $\varphi \in$ **HC** constitutes a Moore family (i.e. it is closed under intersection), and thus it has a unique least model: $\rho_\varphi = \bigcap\{\rho \mid \rho \models \varphi\}$.*

Given a set of Horn clauses we usually want to answer questions such as *membership* (does $\langle t_1, \ldots, t_m \rangle$ belong to the least model of p) or *non-emptiness* (is p mapped to a non-empty set in the least model). Unfortunately, unrestricted Horn clauses are Turing complete [1], and these questions may be undecidable. Therefore we are particularly interested in subsets of Horn clauses where they are decidable, and we shall refer to these fragments as *decidable classes.*

All our questions concern the least model of the formula, but as this model may include infinite sets, we need a finite representation. This representation can itself be expressed by Horn clauses, but now in a form that allows membership in the least model to be determined in a straightforward manner (i.e. linear time).

[1] Variables occurring in a clause are implicitly universally quantified in that clause; thus, without loss of generality, one may assume that variables in different clauses are α-renamed apart.

[2] We adopt the usual postfix notation for substitutions, i.e. $\theta\theta'$ stands for $\theta' \circ \theta$; for an expression e then $e\theta$ represents the expression resulting from replacing all variables $X \in dom(\theta)$ in e with their corresponding ground terms. When convenient, we shall use the notation $[X \mapsto t]$ for the substitution mapping only the variable X to the ground term t.

Table 3. A normal form for Horn clauses

(N1)	$\mathsf{p}(X_1,\ldots,X_m)$	$\Leftarrow$	$\mathsf{q}_1(X_1),\ldots,\mathsf{q}_m(X_m)$	,	$\forall_{i\neq j}\ X_i \neq X_j \wedge m \geq 2$
(N2)	$\mathsf{p}(f(X_1,\ldots,X_n))$	$\Leftarrow$	$\mathsf{q}_1(X_1),\ldots,\mathsf{q}_n(X_n)$	,	$\forall_{i\neq j}\ X_i \neq X_j$

Such a form is called a *normal form*, and a transformation from a decidable class into a normal form is referred to as a *normalisation*, when it preserves the set of models from the original formula and can be performed through a finite number of operations. We present an example of a normal form in Table 3; notice that we require the heads to be *linear*, i.e. no variable occurs twice. This normal form essentially describes context-free grammars in a succinct manner and provides a linear time lookup for both membership and non-emptiness.

To ease the understanding of the development in the following sections, the reader may think of this particular normal form whenever we refer to an unspecified normal form for Horn clauses, bearing in mind, of course, that the results still apply to any other normal form as well. We shall write $\widehat{\varphi} \in \widehat{\mathbf{HC}}$ to denote a formula on normal form.

3 Iterative Scheme

The general idea in the iterative framework was already explained in Sect. 1. We shall now present the key ingredients that, in addition to the normalisation introduced above, include the relaxation mechanism, the specialisation function and the simplification ordering.

3.1 The Refinement Scheme

Recall first that $\mathbf{HC}$ and $\widehat{\mathbf{HC}}$ denote the (infinite) sets of Horn formulae and normalised Horn formulae, respectively. We then define the premise of our intuition as follows: there exists a function that takes a general Horn formula and returns an over-approximative formula (ie. a formula, for which all models are also models of the original formula, and thus it has a weakly larger least model) which belongs to some decidable class $\mathcal{H}$. We shall call such a function an *$\mathcal{H}$-relaxation* and formally define it as follows:

Definition 1 ($\mathcal{H}$-Relaxation). *Let $\mathcal{H} \subseteq \mathbf{HC}$, then a function $\mathcal{R} : \mathbf{HC} \to \mathcal{H}$ is an $\mathcal{H}$-relaxation if:*

$$\forall \varphi : \forall \rho : \quad \rho \models \mathcal{R}(\varphi) \Rightarrow \rho \models \varphi$$

As $\mathcal{H}$ is decidable, then there exists a function that takes a formula $\varphi \in \mathcal{H}$ and returns a normalised formula that represents its unique least model ρ_φ. Such a function is usually called an *$\mathcal{H}$-normalisation*:

Definition 2 ($\mathcal{H}$-Normalisation). *Let $\mathcal{H} \subseteq \mathbf{HC}$, then a function $\mathcal{N} : \mathcal{H} \to \widehat{\mathbf{HC}}$ is an $\mathcal{H}$-normalisation if:*

$$\forall \varphi \in \mathcal{H} : \forall \mathsf{p} \in \mathsf{Pred}(\varphi) : \quad t \in \rho_\varphi(\mathsf{p}) \Leftrightarrow t \in \rho_{\mathcal{N}(\varphi)}(\mathsf{p})$$

Notice that the definition allows the normalised formula to also include auxiliary predicates.

The combination of the relaxation and the normalisation establishes that we can always find some model of a formula. However, we are usually only interested in the least model or a model close to the least model. Naturally, if $\mathcal{R}$ returns a formula with the same least model as the original, then the result is precise and we are done. But this is usually not the case, and often the approximation will be too coarse to be useful for the intended purpose. In this case, we may inspect this coarse model and look for information that allow us to produce a safe transformation of the formula, that may produce better results. This is called a specialisation.

Definition 3 (Specialisation). *A specialisation is a higher-order function* $\mathcal{S} : \widehat{\mathbf{HC}} \to \mathbf{HC} \to \mathbf{HC}$ *that satisfies:*

$$\forall\widehat{\varphi} : \forall\varphi : \forall\rho \subseteq \rho_{\widehat{\varphi}} : \quad \rho_{\widehat{\varphi}} \models \varphi \Rightarrow (\rho \models \mathcal{S}[\widehat{\varphi}](\varphi) \Leftrightarrow \rho \models \varphi)$$

A specialisation takes an approximative normal formula $\widehat{\varphi}$ and specialises the formula φ, such that the specialisation $\mathcal{S}[\widehat{\varphi}](\varphi)$ maintains the set of models, smaller than or equal to the $\rho_{\widehat{\varphi}}$.

The fourth, and last, ingredient we shall require for the iterative scheme, is an order that ensures termination.

Definition 4 (Simplification ordering). *A relation* $\sqsubseteq : \mathbf{HC} \times \mathbf{HC}$ *is a simplification ordering if it is a well-founded, partial order.*

When convenient, we shall use familiar notation $\sqsupseteq$ for the inverse of $\sqsubseteq$ and likewise $\sqsupset$ and $\sqsubset$ for their respective strict counterparts.

The combination of these operators is then supposed to form the basis of the iterative scheme, for finding solutions for unrestricted Horn problems. However, for this to be achieved, we shall furthermore require them to form an $\mathcal{H}$-refinement scheme:

Definition 5 ($\mathcal{H}$-Refinement Scheme). *A quadruple* $(\mathcal{R}, \mathcal{N}, \mathcal{S}, \sqsubseteq)$*; consisting of an* $\mathcal{H}$*-relaxation, an* $\mathcal{H}$*-normalisation, a specialisation, and a simplification ordering, is an* $\mathcal{H}$*-refinement scheme if:*

$$\forall\varphi : \forall\widehat{\varphi} : \forall \mathsf{p} \in \mathsf{Pred}(\varphi) : \quad \widehat{\varphi} = \mathcal{N}(\mathcal{R}(\varphi)) \Rightarrow (\rho_{\widehat{\varphi}}(\mathsf{p}) \supseteq \rho_{\mathcal{R}(\mathcal{S}[\widehat{\varphi}](\varphi))}(\mathsf{p}))$$

3.2 The Iterative Scheme

The refinement scheme forms the basis of the larger iterative scheme, that was graphically presented in Fig. 1 in Sect. 1. Essentially, for any decidable class $\mathcal{H}$ for which there exists an $\mathcal{H}$-refinement scheme, $(\mathcal{R}, \mathcal{N}, \mathcal{S}, \sqsubseteq)$, the iterative scheme will find a best solution to any unrestricted Horn problem.

The algorithm can terminate in two ways: (1) Either the scheme eventually produces a specialisation within $\mathcal{H}$, which is therefore decidable, and the result is the least model of the input formula; or (2) the scheme eventually fails to improve the formula further, with respect to $\sqsubseteq$, and the result is then the best known model of the input formula.

3.3 Properties of the Scheme

As part of justifying the proposed scheme, we shall show that it satisfies three key properties: we shall prove that the algorithm always terminates, that the normalised output represents a model of the input formula, and that if the algorithm produces a formula within the decidable class, then the corresponding normal form represents the least model of the original input formula.

First we shall give the termination result.

Theorem 1 (Termination). *The algorithm will always terminate.*

Proof. Assuming that the functions $\mathcal{R}$, $\mathcal{N}$, and $\mathcal{S}$ are terminating, then the result follows directly from the fact that $\sqsubseteq$ is well-founded. □

The next result states that the algorithm is sound and justifies the iterative approach.

Theorem 2 (Soundness). *The algorithm will always produce a model of the input formula φ. Each iteration (weakly) improves precision of this model.*

Proof. Notice that, if the algorithm terminates in the ith iteration, then the result is either $\mathcal{N}(\varphi_i)$ or $\mathcal{N}(\mathcal{R}(\varphi_i))$. Thus, the proof amounts to show that these normalised clauses represent models of the input formula for all i and that each iteration retains the set of models smaller than or equal to found model ; i.e. that $\forall \rho \subseteq \rho_{\widehat{\varphi}_i} : (\rho \models \varphi_i \Leftrightarrow \rho \models \varphi)$. This is proven by induction.

For $i = 0$ the result holds trivially. For the iterative step, let $\widehat{\varphi}_i = \mathcal{N}(\mathcal{R}(\varphi_i))$ such that $\rho_{\widehat{\varphi}_i} \models \varphi_i$, and assume that $\forall \rho \subseteq \rho_{\widehat{\varphi}_i} : (\rho \models \varphi_i \Leftrightarrow \rho \models \varphi)$. Next, let $\varphi_{i+1} = \mathcal{S}[\widehat{\varphi}_i](\varphi_i)$ and $\widehat{\varphi}_{i+1} = \mathcal{N}(\mathcal{R}(\varphi_{i+1}))$. Now, according to the definition of a relaxation and normalisation, this means that $\rho_{\widehat{\varphi}_{i+1}} \models \varphi_{i+1}$. Furthermore, by the definition of a refinement scheme, we have $\forall \rho : \forall \mathsf{p} \in \mathsf{Pred}(\varphi_i) : \rho_{\widehat{\varphi}_i}(\mathsf{p}) \supseteq \rho_{\mathcal{R}(\varphi_{i+1})}(\mathsf{p})$, and thus, by definition of the normalisation, $\forall \rho : \forall \mathsf{p} \in \mathsf{Pred}(\varphi_i) : \rho_{\widehat{\varphi}_i}(\mathsf{p}) \supseteq \rho_{\widehat{\varphi}_{i+1}}(\mathsf{p})$. Hence, by definition of a specialisation and the assumption, and as the specialisation does not introduce any new predicates, we have that $\forall \rho \subseteq \rho_{\widehat{\varphi}_{i+1}} : (\rho \models \varphi_{i+1} \Leftrightarrow \rho \models \varphi_i \Leftrightarrow \rho \models \varphi)$. □

And lastly we have the partial completeness result:

Theorem 3 (Partial Completeness). *If the algorithm terminates in* (1), *then it produces the least model of the input formula φ.*

Proof. The result follows directly from the proof for Theorem 2. □

4 Application to $\mathcal{H}_1$

This section presents one instance of the iterative framework, or more precisely, a specific refinement scheme. For this, we have chosen the decidable subclass $\mathcal{H}_1$, originally introduced in [3]. $\mathcal{H}_1$ describes strongly recognisable relations; i.e. finite unions of Cartesian products of recognisable tree languages. In fact, every clause in $\mathcal{H}_1$ is normalisable (to the normal form presented in Sect. 2) and the equivalent normal form can be constructed in deterministic exponential time [3].

Previously, this class has proven very useful for static analysis purposes, both for specifying a Control-Flow Analysis of Spi [3] as well as for verifying real implementations of cryptographic protocols in the C language [4]. Yet, as we shall see in Sect. 5.1, a direct attempt at specifying protocol analysis, results in clauses outside this class. This motivates the use of the iterative scheme of Sect. 3.

We begin by briefly introducing the $\mathcal{H}_1$-class itself, whereafter we will define the operators in the $\mathcal{H}_1$-refinement scheme, $(r, n, s, \leq)$, needed for using the iterative scheme of Fig. 1.

4.1 The Class $\mathcal{H}_1$

We shall say the two variables X and Y are *connected* within a set of literals $\{g_1, \ldots, g_k\}$ if there exists a sequence of literals $g_{p_1} \ldots g_{p_l}$ with $l \geq 1$ and $g_{p_i} \in \{g_1, \ldots, g_k\}$ such that $X \in \mathsf{Var}(g_{p_1})$, $Y \in \mathsf{Var}(g_{p_l})$ and $\mathsf{Var}(g_{p_i}) \cap \mathsf{Var}(g_{p_{i+1}}) \neq \emptyset$ for all $1 \leq i \leq l-1$.

We then say that the clause $g_0 \Leftarrow g_1, \ldots, g_k$ has the property H1 if it satisfies the requirements given in Table 4. Here we call two variables *siblings* in a literal or term, if they occur as arguments of a common parent; i.e. X, Y are siblings in $\mathsf{p}(X, Y)$ and $\mathsf{p}(Z, f(X, Y))$ but not in $\mathsf{p}(X, f(Y))$.

Table 4. Property $H1$ for clauses of the form $g_0 \Leftarrow g_1, \ldots, g_k$

(H1.1)	g_0 is linear.
(H1.2)	If $X, Y \in \mathsf{Var}(g_0)$ are connected in $\{g_1, \ldots, g_k\}$, then they are siblings in g_0.

A formula φ belongs to the class $\mathcal{H}_1$ if all clauses in φ have property H1.

Example 1. Consider, as a small, running example, the following clause, borrowed from the protocol analysis case study in Sect. 5.1:

$$\mathsf{net}(\langle X_{enc}, \{X_{n_b}\}_{X_{k_{ab}}}\rangle) \Leftarrow \mathsf{net}(\langle\{\langle b, X_{k_{ab}}, n_a, X_{n_b}\rangle\}_{k_{as}}, X_{enc}\rangle)$$

Here $\langle t_1, \ldots, t_n\rangle$ is an n-ary constructor and $\{t_1\}_{t_2}$ a binary constructor.

This clause is *not* in $\mathcal{H}_1$ as the variables X_{enc} and X_{n_b} (and similarly X_{enc} and $X_{k_{ab}}$) are connected in the precondition but are not siblings in the head, thus violating the rule (H1.2) in Table 4.

4.2 Relaxation Operator

We now want to define a relaxation function, that always produces clauses within $\mathcal{H}_1$. In [5] it is shown how general Horn clauses can be approximated by $\mathcal{H}_1$ clauses. We shall follow this approach, but slightly improve it, as the relaxation operator we suggest, for clauses violating (H1.2), is more precise as compared to the approximation technique suggested in [5].

Let e be an expression. We then write $e[X \rightsquigarrow t]$ for the expression that is as e, except that the leftmost occurrence of X is replaced by t. We shall also employ the shorthand notation α for a sequence of literals $g_1, \ldots, g_l$ when convenient, and point-wise extend substitutions and $\models$ for this. We then define a function $r(\varphi) = \bigcup\{r(c) \mid c \in \varphi\}$ as follows:

$$r(g \Leftarrow \alpha) = \begin{cases} r(g[X \rightsquigarrow X'] \Leftarrow \alpha[X \mapsto X'], \alpha) & (a) \text{ if } g \Leftarrow \alpha \text{ violates (H1.1)} \\ & \text{and where } X' \text{ is fresh} \\ r(g \Leftarrow \alpha[X \mapsto X'],\ \mathsf{p}(X, Z_1, \ldots, Z_k)) \cup & (b) \text{ if } g \Leftarrow \alpha \text{ violates (H1.2)} \\ \{\mathsf{p}(X, Z_1, \ldots, Z_k) \Leftarrow \alpha\} & \text{and where } X' \text{ and } \mathsf{p} \text{ are fresh} \\ \{g \Leftarrow \alpha\} & (c) \text{ otherwise} \end{cases}$$

In both (a) and (b) X is the leftmost variable that gives rise to the violation, and in (b) the siblings $Z_1, \ldots, Z_k$ of X in g are carried on to the auxiliary predicate, to retain the highest amount of precision.

From the definition it is apparent that the set of clauses generated by r will always be in $\mathcal{H}_1$, and that, if applied to a set of clauses already within $\mathcal{H}_1$, r will be the identity function. Furthermore, as the set of variables in a clause is always finite, it should be fairly obvious that r will always terminate.

Now, prior to showing that r indeed constitutes a relaxation function, we shall give an auxiliary result that benefits the presentation of the proof.

Fact 4. If $\rho \models c$ then $\forall X, X' : \rho \models c[X \mapsto X']$.

Which allows us to establish the following result.

Lemma 1. *The function r is a relaxation operator.*

Proof. The proof proceeds by induction in the derivation sequence establishing $r(\varphi)$:

- (a), remembering that $Y \notin \mathsf{Var}(g \Leftarrow \alpha)$ the result follows from Fact 4 :

$$\begin{aligned} & \rho \models g[X \rightsquigarrow X'] \Leftarrow \alpha[X \mapsto X'], \alpha \\ \Rightarrow\ & \rho \models (g[X \rightsquigarrow X'] \Leftarrow \alpha[X \mapsto X'], \alpha)[X' \mapsto X] \\ \Rightarrow\ & \rho \models g \Leftarrow \alpha, \alpha \\ \Rightarrow\ & \rho \models g \Leftarrow \alpha \end{aligned}$$

- (b) is shown analogously, relying on the fact that the auxiliary predicate p does not occur in the head of any other clause and thus the precondition in the first clause can only be satisfied if the second clause is satisfied.
- (c) holds vacuously. □

Example 2 (Example 1 continued). Recall that the clause from Example 1 was not in $\mathcal{H}_1$, as the variables X_{enc} and X_{n_b} violated rule (H1.2). Thus, the relaxation r applied to this clause will decouple these variables, resulting in the following two clauses, now both in $\mathcal{H}_1$.

$$\begin{aligned} \{\ & \mathsf{net}(\langle X_{enc}, \{X_{n_b}\}_{X_{k_{ab}}}\rangle) \Leftarrow \mathsf{net}(\langle\{\langle b, X_{k_{ab}}, n_a, X_{n_b}\rangle\}_{k_{as}}, X'\rangle), \mathsf{p}(X_{enc}), \\ & \mathsf{p}(X_{enc}) \Leftarrow \mathsf{net}(\langle\{\langle b, X_{k_{ab}}, n_a, X_{n_b}\rangle\}_{k_{as}}, X_{enc}\rangle) \qquad \} \end{aligned}$$

4.3 $\mathcal{H}_1$-Normalisation

Normalising a set of $\mathcal{H}_1$-clauses amounts to bringing the clauses onto the normal form given in Table 3. This is a well-known procedure that was initially described in a direct manner in [3] and later using resolution techniques in [5]. Basically the procedure consists of iteratively extending the set of normal clauses by simplifying non-normal clauses using the current set of normal clauses, this procedure is continued until no further simplification can be performed; then the non-normal clauses are redundant and can be removed.

4.4 Specialisation Operator

The specialisation is supposed to utilise information in a given normal form approximation $\widehat{\varphi}$ of a formula φ, to produce a new formula φ', that maintains the set of models smaller than or equal to $\rho_{\widehat{\varphi}}$, but may yield smaller approximations. One approach to define such an operator, is to define a function that safely eliminates variables from the formula.

First we shall require a formulation of which ground terms a variable may be substituted by in a clause.

Definition 6 (Substitution set). *The substitution set for* $X \in \mathsf{Var}(\varphi)$ *is given by* $\mathcal{T}_\varphi(X) = \{X\theta \mid \bigwedge_{i=0}^{l} \rho_\varphi, \theta \models g_i \ \wedge \ (g_0 \Leftarrow g_1, \ldots, g_l) \in \varphi\}$.

Unfortunately, some of these substitution sets may be infinite and we are therefore particularly interested in the set $\mathcal{F}_\varphi$ of variables $X \in \mathsf{Var}(\varphi)$ for which $\mathcal{T}_\varphi(X)$ is finite. However, it may not always be feasible to determine the complete set $\mathcal{F}_\varphi$, or the corresponding substitution sets, and thus we shall say that a *finiteness substitution mapping* I_φ is permissable if $dom(I_\varphi) \subseteq \mathcal{F}_\varphi$ and $\forall X \in dom(I_\varphi) : I_\varphi(X) \supseteq \mathcal{T}_\varphi(X)$.

As neither the relaxation nor the normalisation renames variables, and as $\rho_{\widehat{\varphi}} \models \varphi$, it follows that for all $X \in \mathsf{Var}(\varphi)$ then $\mathcal{T}_\varphi(X) \subseteq \mathcal{T}_{\widehat{\varphi}}(X)$. Thus a permissable $I_{\widehat{\varphi}}$ is also a permissable I_φ, and the idea is then use the former to perform a *complete expansion* of the formula. This is done by the function, $s : \widehat{\mathbf{HC}} \to \mathbf{HC} \to \mathbf{HC}$, defined as follows:

$$s[\widehat{\varphi}](\varphi) = \bigcup \{\varphi\theta \mid dom(\theta) = dom(I_{\widehat{\varphi}}) \ \wedge \ \forall X \in dom(\theta) : X\theta \in I_{\widehat{\varphi}}(X)\}$$

Note that $s[\widehat{\varphi}]$ is the identity function if there are no variables in φ with finite substitution sets in $I_{\widehat{\varphi}}$.

Lemma 2. *The function s is a specialisation function.*

Proof. Assume $\widehat{\varphi}$, φ and ρ, such that $\rho \subseteq \rho_{\widehat{\varphi}}$. We then have

$$\begin{aligned}
&\rho \models s[\widehat{\varphi}](\varphi)\\
\Leftrightarrow\ &\rho \models \bigcup \{\varphi\theta \mid dom(\theta) = dom(I_{\widehat{\varphi}}) \ \wedge \ \forall X \in dom(\theta) : X\theta \in I_{\widehat{\varphi}}(X)\}\\
\Leftrightarrow\ &\rho \models \bigcup \{\varphi\theta \mid dom(\theta) = dom(I_{\widehat{\varphi}}) \ \wedge \ \forall X \in dom(\theta) : X\theta \in \mathcal{T}_{\widehat{\varphi}}(X)\}\\
\Leftrightarrow\ &\rho \models \bigcup \{\varphi\theta \mid dom(\theta) = dom(I_{\widehat{\varphi}}) \ \wedge \ \forall (g_0 \Leftarrow g_1, \ldots, g_l) \in \varphi : \ \textstyle\bigwedge_{i=0}^{l} \rho_{\widehat{\varphi}} \models g_i\theta\}\\
\Leftrightarrow\ &\rho \models \bigcup \{\varphi\theta \mid dom(\theta) = dom(I_{\widehat{\varphi}}) \ \wedge \ \forall (g_0 \Leftarrow g_1, \ldots, g_l) \in \varphi : \ \textstyle\bigwedge_{i=0}^{l} \rho \models g_i\theta\}\\
\Leftrightarrow\ &\rho \models \bigcup \{\varphi\theta \mid dom(\theta) = dom(I_{\widehat{\varphi}}) \ \wedge \ \rho \models \varphi\theta\}\\
\Leftrightarrow\ &\rho \models \varphi
\end{aligned}$$

In the second and fourth step we use that $\rho \subseteq \rho_{\widehat{\varphi}}$ □

It then only remains to show how $I_{\widehat{\varphi}}$ can be determined for $\mathcal{H}_1$, or more specifically, for the normal form in Table 3. Such a mapping can be obtained by the following inductively defined procedure:

$$\frac{\forall(\mathsf{p}(t) \Leftarrow \alpha) \in \widehat{\varphi} : \ \mathsf{Pred}(\alpha) \subseteq dom(F)}{\begin{array}{c}\mathsf{p} \in dom(F) \ \ \wedge \\ \forall(\mathsf{p}(f(X_1,\ldots,X_n)) \Leftarrow \mathsf{q}_1(X_1),\ldots,\mathsf{q}_n(X_n)) \in \widehat{\varphi} : \\ \forall\langle t_1,\ldots,t_n\rangle \in F(\mathsf{q}_1) \times \cdots \times F(\mathsf{q}_n) : \\ f(t_1,\ldots,t_n) \in F(\mathsf{p})\end{array}}$$

$$\frac{\forall(g \Leftarrow \alpha) \in \widehat{\varphi} : \ \mathsf{p}(X) \in \alpha \Rightarrow \mathsf{p} \in dom(F)}{X \in dom(I_{\widehat{\varphi}}) \quad \wedge \quad \forall(g \Leftarrow \alpha) \in \widehat{\varphi} : \mathsf{p}(X) \in \alpha \Rightarrow F(\mathsf{p}) \subseteq I_{\widehat{\varphi}}(X)}$$

The mapping is built by first finding a mapping F, of the unary predicates with a finite mapping in $\rho_{\widehat{\varphi}}$, and then use this to build $I_{\widehat{\varphi}}$.

Example 3 (Example 1 continued). Assume the finiteness substitution mapping $I_{\widehat{\varphi}} = [X_{n_b} \mapsto \{n_b\}, X_{k_{ab}} \mapsto \{k_{ab}, m_\bullet\}]$, then a complete expansion of the clause from Example 1 is:

$$\begin{array}{l}\{\ \mathsf{net}(\langle X_{enc}, \{n_b\}_{k_{ab}}\rangle) \Leftarrow \mathsf{net}(\langle\{\langle b, k_{ab}, n_a, n_b\rangle\}_{k_{as}}, X_{enc}\rangle), \\ \ \ \ \mathsf{net}(\langle X_{enc}, \{n_b\}_{m_\bullet}\rangle) \Leftarrow \mathsf{net}(\langle\{\langle b, m_\bullet, n_a, n_b\rangle\}_{k_{as}}, X_{enc}\rangle)\ \ \}\end{array}$$

4.5 Simplification Ordering

As the specialisation expands the clauses of the formula, an obvious choice of simplification ordering is an ordering where clauses are greater than their expanded counterpart.

$$\forall\varphi : \forall\varphi' : \quad \varphi \leq \varphi' \Leftrightarrow (\exists\widehat{\varphi} : \varphi = s[\widehat{\varphi}](\varphi'))$$

It follows that equivalence resolves to equality, and thus the check in 4 in the iterative scheme will amount to the test for identity. We then have the result:

Lemma 3. *The operator $\leq$ is a simplification ordering.*

Proof. We have trivially that $\leq$ is a partial order. That it is also well-founded follows from the fact that any formula φ can only hold a finite set of variables. As a complete expansion (modulo identity) will only expand each clause into a finite set of new clauses, and each expanded clause will have a strictly lower number of variables, then any formula can only be completely expanded a finite number of times. □

4.6 $\mathcal{H}_1$-Refinement Scheme

Finally, to show that the different ingredients work together as intended, we must show that they form an $\mathcal{H}_1$-refinement scheme.

Lemma 4. *The quadruple $(r, n, s, \leq)$ forms an $\mathcal{H}_1$-refinement scheme.*

Proof. To prove this, we must show that for all t and for all $\mathsf{p} \in \mathsf{Pred}(\varphi)$, then $t \in \rho_{r(s[\widehat{\varphi}](\varphi))}(\mathsf{p})$ implies $t \in \rho_{\widehat{\varphi}}(\mathsf{p})$, when $\widehat{\varphi} = n(r(\varphi))$. But as the specialisation only eliminates variables, and the relaxation only decouples variables, we have that $t \in \rho_{r(s[\widehat{\varphi}](\varphi))}(\mathsf{p})$ implies $t \in \rho_{s[\widehat{\varphi}](r(\varphi))}(\mathsf{p})$. But then the result follows directly, as $\rho_{r(\varphi)} = \rho_{n(r(\varphi))} = \rho_{\widehat{\varphi}}$, and thus $t \in \rho_{s[\widehat{\varphi}](r(\varphi))}(\mathsf{p})$ implies $t \in \rho_{\widehat{\varphi}}(\mathsf{p})$ by definition of the specialisation, which gives the result we seek. □

5 Worked Example

In this section, we shall give an example of how Horn clauses can be used for formalising some analysis problems in a succinct and clear manner. But, as we shall also see, such specifications easily end up outside any known decidable classes, motivating the use of the iterative scheme.

We have chosen our example from protocol analysis, more specifically the validation of the key-distribution protocol Yahalom [6], which is given in the classical Alice-Bob notation as follows:

1.	$A \rightarrow B$	:	A, N_A
2.	$B \rightarrow S$	:	$B, \{A, N_A, N_B\}_{K_{BS}}$
3.	$S \rightarrow A$	:	$\{B, K_{AB}, N_A, N_B\}_{K_{AS}}, \{A, K_{AB}\}_{K_{BS}}$
4.	$A \rightarrow B$	:	$\{A, K_{AB}\}_{K_{BS}}, \{N_B\}_{K_{AB}}$

Yahalom is considered a secure protocol (cf. [6,7]), but it is an interesting case study, because it proves troublesome for many analyses. In particular, independent attribute analyses, such as [8], will yield false positives for Yahalom, in the presence of several principals.

5.1 Modelling Protocols

Modelling protocol narrations in Horn clauses is relatively straightforward, as Horn clauses provide the means for an almost direct translation from the Alice-Bob notation. One such translation scheme was presented intuitively in [9] and refined in [10], and we shall draw inspiration from these approaches.

We assume that all messages are sent on one global network, and that all principals have access to this network. This is supposed to be a realistic model of the Internet, without adding an extra layer of security to the protocol, and we will describe it through the predicate net. Secondly, we shall model encryptions and tuples through constructors, but to ease readability, we will employ the familiar notation $\{t_1\}_{t_2}$ for the binary encryption constructor, and $\langle t_1, \ldots, t_n \rangle$ for the n-ary tupling constructor.

The result of this method of translation, for one instance of Yahalom, is given in Table 5. Here we have adopted the notation $g, g' \Leftarrow \alpha$ as a shorthand for the clauses $g \Leftarrow \alpha$ and $g' \Leftarrow \alpha$. To stress the intent of the protocol, we add predicates on the form p_key for recording the ground terms that principal p binds and believes to be the distributed key; e.g. k_{ab}.

Each step of the protocol is translated into one clause, where the right-hand side represents the requirements imposed by the sender, and the left-hand side

Table 5. Yahalom in Horn clauses

1.	$\mathsf{net}(\langle a, n_a\rangle)$
2.	$\mathsf{net}(\langle b, \{\langle X_a, X_{n_a}, n_b\rangle\}_{k_{bs}}\rangle) \Leftarrow \mathsf{net}(\langle X_a, X_{n_a}\rangle)$
3.	$\mathsf{net}(\langle\{\langle b, k_{ab}, X_{n_a}, X_{n_b}\rangle\}_{k_{as}}, \{\langle a, k_{ab}\rangle\}_{k_{bs}}\rangle) \Leftarrow \mathsf{net}(\langle b, \{\langle a, X_{n_a}, X_{n_b}\rangle\}_{k_{bs}}\rangle)$
4.	$\mathsf{net}(\langle X_{enc}, \{X_{n_b}\}_{X_{k_{ab}}}\rangle), \mathsf{a\_key}(X_{k_{ab}}) \Leftarrow \mathsf{net}(\langle\{\langle b, X_{k_{ab}}, n_a, X_{n_b}\rangle\}_{k_{as}}, X_{enc}\rangle)$
5.	$\mathsf{b\_key}(X_{k_{ab}}) \Leftarrow \mathsf{net}(\langle\{\langle a, X_{k_{ab}}\rangle\}_{k_{bs}}, \{n_b\}_{X_{k_{ab}}}\rangle)$

the message sent upon the network in that particular step. In addition to the four steps of the protocol, a fifth step is added to reflect the reception of the fourth message. The modelling captures the basic assumption of the protocol, namely that the initiator a and the server s both know the two other principals on advance, but that the responder b does not necessarily need to initially know (or trust) a.

Notice that the specification allows a relational analysis as the relationship between variables in each message is remembered. As mentioned above, this is required for correctly validating Yahalom. In this example, we have, for simplicity, chosen to model only one instance of the protocol, but the methodology could be extended to also model multiple instances between multiple principals, maintaining the relational property, by using standard approximation techniques. This is, however, beyond the scope of this paper.

5.2 Network Attacker and Analysis

After modelling how the legitimate principals of the system interact, we usually want to apply an analysis for ensuring that the protocol cannot be compromised by one or more malicious principals.

One method, that has been employed successfully numerous times before, is modelling the so-called Dolev-Yao attacker [11], also known as the hardest network attacker [12], and investigate whether various security properties are upheld in presence of this attacker. In the Dolev-Yao model, the capabilities of this attacker are defined to be: (1) receive and intercept all messages sent on the global network and send new messages onto the global network; (2) decrypt encrypted messages, if it knows the encryption key, and construct new encryptions from known terms; (3) decompose and compose tuples; and (4) generate new ground terms. The attacker can, in principle, compose and decompose tuples of any arity. However, in [8] it is shown that restricting the attacker to work on a limited set of arities, does not limit its capabilities, as long as the set includes all arities occurring in the protocol and at least one additional arity. This means that a Dolev-Yao attacker, for a specific protocol, is directly translatable into Horn clauses. If we let $\mathcal{K}$ denote the set of occurring arities (for Yahalom this set is $\{2, 3, 4\}$), we can create an extended set $\mathcal{K}_+ = \mathcal{K} \cup \{1\}$, as tuples of arity 1 never occurs, and a generic Dolev-Yao attacker can then be formulated as in Table 6.

The attacker is described through a predicate dy, storing its accumulated knowledge. The first three rules are then straightforward, and the rule (DY4)

Table 6. Dolev-Yao attacker in Horn clauses

(DY1)	$\mathsf{dy}(X) \Leftarrow \mathsf{net}(X)$	
	$\mathsf{net}(X) \Leftarrow \mathsf{dy}(X)$	
(DY2)	$\mathsf{dy}(X) \Leftarrow \mathsf{dy}(\{X\}_{X_{key}}), \mathsf{dy}(X_{key})$	
	$\mathsf{dy}(\{X\}_{X_{key}}) \Leftarrow \mathsf{dy}(X), \mathsf{dy}(X_{key})$	
(DY3)	$\mathsf{dy}(X_1), \ldots, \mathsf{dy}(X_k) \Leftarrow \mathsf{dy}(\langle X_1, \ldots, X_k \rangle)$	if $k \in \mathcal{K}_+$
	$\mathsf{dy}(\langle X_1, \ldots, X_k \rangle) \Leftarrow \mathsf{dy}(X_1), \ldots, \mathsf{dy}(X_k)$	
(DY4)	$\mathsf{dy}(m_\bullet)$	

expresses that the attacker may generate arbitrary ground terms, but, in the modelling, all of these are coalesced into one equivalence class represented by the canonical name $m_\bullet$. Note, that a direct consequence of the rule (DY1) is that the attacker's knowledge and the net are identical.

A conjunction of a protocol description with the attacker in Table 6 constitutes an instance of an analysis problem, and the least model of such a problem allows us to investigate certain properties of the protocol. In its most simple form, such as the formula in Table 5, the protocol descriptions allow direct verification of confidentiality (and integrity through the predicates a_key and b_key) but many other properties can be verified as well using annotation techniques [8].

5.3 Results

Even small analysis problems, such as the one presented in this section, falls, to the best of our knowledge, outside the decidable fragments of Horn Clauses. Hence we must rely on the iterative scheme to determine a best model of our analysis problem.

For this, we have implemented the iterative scheme in OCaml[3]. The result is an extremely succinct implementation; the normalisation itself is constrained to 110 lines of code. As the implementation is intended to be self-explanatory and intuitively correct, several optimisations have been omitted. However, as the normalisation can easily normalise formulae consisting of several thousand $\mathcal{H}_1$-clauses, it suffices for our needs, and the simplicity of the code leaves less room for errors.

Applying the iterative scheme to the Yahalom analysis problem presented above, i.e. the conjunction of Table 5 and Table 6, yields the following specialised clauses, after a single iteration of the algorithm:

1.	$\mathsf{net}(\langle a, n_a \rangle)$
2.	$\mathsf{net}(\langle b, \{\langle X_a, X_{n_a}, n_b \rangle\}_{k_{bs}} \rangle) \Leftarrow \mathsf{net}(\langle X_a, X_{n_a} \rangle)$
3.	$\mathsf{net}(\langle \{\langle b, k_{ab}, X_{n_a}, n_b \rangle\}_{k_{as}}, \{\langle a, k_{ab} \rangle\}_{k_{bs}} \rangle) \Leftarrow \mathsf{net}(\langle b, \{\langle a, X_{n_a}, n_b \rangle\}_{k_{bs}} \rangle)$
4.	$\mathsf{net}(\langle \{\langle a, k_{ab} \rangle\}_{k_{bs}}, \{n_b\}_{k_{ab}} \rangle), \mathsf{a\_key}(k_{ab}) \Leftarrow \mathsf{net}(\langle \{\langle b, k_{ab}, n_a, n_b \rangle\}_{k_{as}}, \{\langle a, k_{ab} \rangle\}_{k_{bs}} \rangle)$
5.	$\mathsf{b\_key}(k_{ab}) \Leftarrow \mathsf{net}(\langle \{\langle a, k_{ab} \rangle\}_{k_{bs}}, \{n_b\}_{k_{ab}} \rangle)$

We omit the clauses for the attacker, as all variables occurring in them have trivially infinite substitution sets, thus these clauses remain unchanged.

[3] available at `http://www.imm.dtu.dk/~{}crn`

Observe first, that the formula is now contained in $\mathcal{H}_1$, and thus the resulting normal form represents its least model. This means that the analysis result is complete, and inspecting it shows that $\mathsf{a\_key}$ and $\mathsf{b\_key}$ can only be bound to k_{ab}. Hence one instance of the protocol serves its purpose and will always successfully establish the intended shared key between the principals. We also find that $k_{as}, k_{bs}, k_{ab} \notin \mathsf{dy}$, which guarantees confidentiality of all the shared keys, including the newly distributed one. Both of these results were expected as Yahalom is, as already mentioned, considered a secure protocol.

6 Conclusion

Horn clauses have many applications. One example, as we have shown, is that it allows for a clear and intuitive specification of protocol analysis problems. However, as is often the case with clean and simple analysis specifications, the resulting instances of analysis problems are outside any of the known decidable fragments of Horn clauses, threatening the analysis itself with being a mere theoretical exercise.

This paper presents an iterative scheme for solving Horn clauses that guarantees termination and soundness, and may in some cases even give completeness. It relies on a chosen known decidable class of Horn clauses and a sound approximation method; the latter being achieved by iteratively specialising the analysis problem and improving the analysis result, until either no further improvements can be made or the analysis result is complete.

We also sketched a methodology for specifying static analyses of cryptographic protocols, in particular we validated the non-trivial key-distribution protocol Yahalom. Our example was concerned with only a single instance of the protocol, but even this simple scenario was sufficient to push the problem beyond the known decidable classes. This demonstrates the complications of containing problems within the decidable domains of Horn logic, but also illustrates the usability of the scheme, as it still successfully determined a complete result for the analysis problem.

We expect the iterative scheme to also prove useful beyond protocol analysis, as deciding the least model or a sufficiently small model of Horn clause-based problems, is attractive to many different branches of theoretical computer science.

References

1. Tärnlund, S.Å.: Horn clause computability. BIT 17(2), 215–226 (1977)
2. van Emden, M.H., Kowalski, R.A.: The semantics of predicate logic as a programming language. J. ACM 23(4), 733–742 (1976)
3. Nielson, F., Nielson, H.R., Seidl, H.: Normalizable horn clauses, strongly recognizable relations, and spi. In: Hermenegildo, M.V., Puebla, G. (eds.) SAS 2002. LNCS, vol. 2477, pp. 20–35. Springer, Heidelberg (2002)
4. Goubault-Larrecq, J., Parrennes, F.: Cryptographic protocol analysis on real c code. In: Cousot, R. (ed.) VMCAI 2005. LNCS, vol. 3385, pp. 363–379. Springer, Heidelberg (2005)

5. Goubault-Larrecq, J.: Deciding h_1 by resolution. Inf. Process. Lett. 95(3), 401–408 (2005)
6. Burrows, M., Abadi, M., Needham, R.M.: A logic of authentication. ACM Trans. Comput. Syst. 8(1), 18–36 (1990)
7. Paulson, L.C.: Relations between secrets: Two formal analyses of the yahalom protocol. Journal of Computer Security 9(3), 197–216 (2001)
8. Bodei, C., Buchholtz, M., Degano, P., Nielson, F., Nielson, H.R.: Static validation of security protocols. Journal of Computer Security 13(3), 347–390 (2005)
9. Blanchet, B.: An efficient cryptographic protocol verifier based on prolog rules. In: CSFW, pp. 82–96. IEEE Computer Society, Los Alamitos (2001)
10. Seidl, H., Verma, K.N.: Cryptographic protocol verification using tractable classes of horn clauses. In: Reps, T., Sagiv, M., Bauer, J. (eds.) Wilhelm Festschrift. LNCS, vol. 4444, pp. 97–119. Springer, Heidelberg (2007)
11. Dolev, D., Yao, A.C.C.: On the security of public key protocols. IEEE Transactions on Information Theory 29(2), 198–207 (1983)
12. Nielson, F., Nielson, H.R., Hansen, R.R.: Validating firewalls using flow logics. Theor. Comput. Sci. 283(2), 381–418 (2002)

Constructive Mathematics and Functional Programming (Abstract)

Thierry Coquand

Department of Computer Science and Engineering,
Göteborg University and Chalmers University of Technology
Sweden
coquand@cs.chalmers.se

Around thirty years ago, P. Martin-Löf [12] suggested that the intuitionistic theory of types, originally designed as a formal system for constructive mathematics, could be viewed as a programming language. The conclusion of this paper stresses the mutual benefit of relating constructive mathematics and computer programming. In one direction one gets a precise system of notations for both statements and proofs, and one obtains the computerization of abstract intuitionistic mathematics that was asked by Bishop [2]. In the other direction, computer programming "gets access to the whole conceptual apparatus of pure mathematics".

In the first part of this talk we shall survey some recent works that illustrate this relation and its fruitfulness. One line of work, close to Bishop, represents real numbers and numerical functions [4,13] in type theory. Another line is concerned with algorithms on finite combinatorial structure (graphs, hypermaps, finite groups). One main example is the complete formalization of a proof of the four color theorem by G. Gonthier and B. Werner. The report on this work [9] points out as well the mutual benefits of this correspondence: "Although this work is purportedly about using computer programming to help doing mathematics, we expect that most of its fallout will be in the reverse direction - using mathematics to help programming computers". A related work, also dealing with hypermaps, aims at obtaining formal specification in geometric modeling [6], and presents algorithms that can be designed in this way [7]. There is also on-going work [8] on the formalization of finite group theory.

The second part will reflect on the design of type theory as a *functional* programming language. The analogy between type theory and functional programming was pointed out already by Martin-Löf [12] (for instance the correspondence between canonical and non-canonical form of expressions and the notion of constructors and selectors, respectively, of Landin [11]). This analogy should go further and type theory should benefit in using more the powerful system of notations provided by functional programming. (In particular, *where expressions* correspond to local abbreviations, definitions and lemmas, functions defined by *pattern-matching* correspond to definitions by case and proofs by case analysis, uses of *recursive definitions* correspond to inductive arguments, *module systems* can be used to structure proofs; the system Agda [1] follows these analogies.)

S. Drossopoulou (Ed.): ESOP 2008, LNCS 4960, pp. 146–147, 2008.

The work of B. Gregoire and X. Leroy [10] illustrates well also this analogy by showing how an evaluation machine for functional programming can be modified in a simple way to provide an efficient algorithm for testing convertibility in type theory. We explain finally how we can precise further the representation of type theory as a functional programming language using some recent results in domain theory [3,5].

References

1. Agda home page, `http://appserv.cs.chalmers.se/users/ulfn/wiki/agda.php`
2. Bishop, E.: Mathematics as a numerical language. In: 1970 Intuitionism and Proof Theory (Proc. Conf., Buffalo, N.Y., 1968), pp. 53–71. North-Holland, Amsterdam (1970)
3. Berger, U.: Continuous Semantics for Strong Normalization. CiE, 23-34 (2005)
4. Bertot, Y.: Affine functions and series with co-inductive real numbers. Mathematical Structures in Computer Science 17(1), 37–63 (2007)
5. Coquand, T., Spiwack, A.: A proof of strong normalisation using domain theory. LMCS 3(4:12) (2007)
6. Dufourd, J.-F.: A hypermap framework for computer-aided proofs in surface subdivisions: genus theorem and Euler's formula. In: SAC 2007, pp. 757–761 (2007)
7. Dufourd, J.-F.: Design and formal proof of a new optimal image segmentation program with hypermaps. Pattern Recognition 40(11), 2974–2993 (2007)
8. Gonthier, G., Mahboubi, A., Rideau, L., Tassi, E., Théry, L.: A Modular Formalisation of Finite Group Theory. In: Schneider, K., Brandt, J. (eds.) TPHOLs 2007. LNCS, vol. 4732, pp. 86–101. Springer, Heidelberg (2007)
9. Gonthier, G.: A computer-checked proof of the Four Colour Theorem. (unpublished)
10. Grégoire, B., Leroy, X.: A compiled implementation of strong reduction. In: ICFP 2002, pp. 235–246 (2002)
11. Landin, P.J.: The mechanical evaluation of expressions. Computer Journal 6(4) (1964)
12. Martin-Löf, P.: Constructive mathematics and computer programming. In: Logic, methodology and philosophy of science, VI (Hannover, 1979), Stud. Logic Found. Math., 104, pp. 153–175. North-Holland, Amsterdam (1982)
13. O'Connor, R.: A monadic, functional implementation of real numbers. Mathematical Structures in Computer Science 17(1), 129–159 (2007)

Ranking Abstractions

Aziem Chawdhary[1], Byron Cook[2], Sumit Gulwani[2], Mooly Sagiv[3], and Hongseok Yang[1]

[1] Queen Mary, University of London
[2] Microsoft Research
[3] Tel Aviv University

Abstract. We propose an abstract interpretation algorithm for proving that a program terminates on all inputs. The algorithm uses a novel abstract domain which uses ranking relations to conservatively represent relations between intermediate program states. One of the attractive aspects of the algorithm is that it abstracts information that is usually not important for proving termination such as program invariants and yet it distinguishes between different reasons for termination which are not usually maintained in existing abstract domains. We have implemented a prototype of the algorithm and shown that in practice it is fast and precise.

1 Introduction

This paper develops sound algorithms for inferring that C programs terminate on all possible inputs. The oldest trick in the book of termination proofs for programs (e.g., [18]) is the ranking function proof. In this method, we find a function p that maps program states into a well-founded ordered set, such that $p(\sigma) > p(\sigma')$ whenever σ' is a state reachable from state σ.

Despite the enormous progress in synthesizing ranking functions (e.g., [3]), modern programming language features such as nested loops lead to non-linear behaviours which make it hard to apply existing techniques to synthesize ranking functions in a sound and precise way directly to the C code.

Recently, [17] introduced the *disjunctive well-foundedness* principle in order to split the termination argument into multiple ranking relations, corresponding to different situations in the program. The main idea is to use a finite set of ranking functions $r_1, r_2, \ldots, r_n$ each of which is well-founded, and to require in addition that the relation between any two intermediate states in the program is included in one of the relations, i.e.,

$$\tau^+ \quad \subseteq \quad \bigcup_{i=1}^{n} r_i \tag{1}$$

where τ is the transition system describing the meaning of the program and τ^+ is the non-reflexive transitive closure of τ. This principle localizes termination proofs by allowing the use of simpler ranking function synthesizers to handle more complicated termination proofs.

However, [17] leaves two open problems: (a) what is the best way to find the set of ranking functions $r_1, r_2, \ldots, r_n$ and (b) how to effectively check the condition in

S. Drossopoulou (Ed.): ESOP 2008, LNCS 4960, pp. 148–162, 2008.

Eq. 1. Notice that this is a safety question which can be attacked by any abstract interpreter [10]. However it may be expensive to check the condition by the abstract interpreter or the interpreter may fail due to imprecision.

In this paper we solve these two problems together in a novel way. The first problem is solved by developing abstract domains which are parameterized by sets of ranking functions. The meaning of each of the relations (ranking functions) overapproximates the relations between intermediate states in the program. We employ standard iterative fixpoint computations to compute a set of ranking functions or determine that the program may diverge. The ranking synthesizer is invoked with larger and larger relations obtained by composing the current approximation with every possible command. Notice that calling the ranking synthesizer allows us to abstract away information that is not necessary for termination, but maintains enough distinctions between different ranking functions. When a fixpoint is reached the condition in Eq. 1 is guaranteed to hold and thus there is no need to perform the inclusion check above. The efficiency provided by our domain is underlined by result which we prove, that, for a particular base abstract domain, fixpoint calculations are guaranteed to converge, at most, in two steps. For more refined domains we lose the guarantee of two, but in our experimental results we find that fixpoints converge in few iterations.

Related Work. Program termination has been studied extensively with many impressive algorithms for automatically inferring termination for functional (e.g.,[13]), logic (e.g., [6,4]) and imperative programs (e.g., [3,7,19,1]). The result in [17] encourages the use of existing safety analyzers in order to prove termination (e.g., SLAM [7] or Octagon [2]). The point of departure of this work is to define a new abstract domain, designed with termination in mind, rather than to re-use existing domains for safety. Termination analysis requires a precise treatment of disjunction, and information about well-foundedness, and we suggest that domains which target these properties will be more appropriate for termination analysis than domains designed for wholly other purposes. Our work follows [7,2] by employing the disjunctive well foundedness principle [17] in order to split the termination argument into multiple ranking relations corresponding to different situations in the program.

By tailoring our abstract domain to termination we obtain a very efficient termination prover for imperative programs. In particular it is faster than TERMINATOR, which relies on SLAM [7], and variance analyses based on Octagon or Polyhedra [2]. The variance analysis we describe in this paper uses rank functions natively, in contrast to the non-native variance analyses proposed in [2] which were constructed from existing domains for invariance. In contrast to [2] we directly abstract ranking relations which allow us to be more precise in the cases where the underlying abstract domain used for invariance analysis is too coarse (e.g., non-disjunctive) and our analysis can be more efficient when the underlying domain records complicated invariants that are not needed for proving termination. In contrast to [7], we iteratively compute ranking functions without the use of counterexample guided refinement.

Our abstract domain is related to the abstraction used in size-change termination [13]. In both cases, program fragments are abstracted in terms of measures decreased or preserved by the fragments. The major difference is that our domain contains only those abstract elements that mean terminating program fragments (unless the elements are $\top$), whilst size-change termination analyses can have an (non-$\top$) abstract element that denotes a diverging program fragment. As a result, size-change termination analyses have to check whether (the concretization of) an abstracted program terminates, whereas our analysis can skip this rather expensive checking.

2 Informal Description of the Analysis

In this section we informally describe the new analysis using an example. Later, in Section 3, we provide a more formal description.

Consider the program:

```
1    while (x>0 ∧ y>0) {
2        if (∗) then { x=x−1; y=∗; } else { y=y−1; }
3    }
```

This program illustrates the limitation of known termination analyses. The Octagon-based and Polyhedra-based termination analyses from [2] can quickly (*i.e.* in 0.02s) infer that the relation ${}^{\backprime}x \geq 0 \wedge {}^{\backprime}x \geq x$ holds between any state at ℓ=2 and any previous state at ℓ=2, where ${}^{\backprime}x$ and x denote previous and current values of x respectively. (Note that ${}^{\backprime}x$ is denoting *some* previous value of x, and not necessarily the *last* value). Unfortunately, this relation is insufficient to prove termination of the loop, as it is not (disjunctively) well-founded—the condition sufficient for proving termination as described in [2].

In contrast TERMINATOR can prove the example terminating, but at a great cost (16s). TERMINATOR finds the following disjunctively well-founded relation at ℓ=2:

$$({}^{\backprime}x \geq 0 \wedge {}^{\backprime}x{-}1 \geq x) \vee ({}^{\backprime}y \geq 0 \wedge {}^{\backprime}y{-}1 \geq y)$$

To find this relation TERMINATOR performs three rounds of refinement on the relation itself and 9 rounds of abstraction/refinement for the checking of the 3 candidate assertions, resulting in the discovery of 21 transition predicates.

The termination analysis in this paper gives us TERMINATOR's accuracy at the speed of the Octagon-based termination analysis. The new analysis finds the relation

$$({}^{\backprime}x \geq 0 \wedge {}^{\backprime}x{-}1 \geq x) \vee ({}^{\backprime}y \geq 0 \wedge {}^{\backprime}y{-}1 \geq y \wedge {}^{\backprime}x{=}x)$$

in 0.02s.

Concretely, the new analysis uses a disjunctive domain of ranking relations conjoined with the information about unchanged variables. That is: disjunctions of relations of the form $T_e \wedge V_X$, where

$$V_X \stackrel{\text{def}}{=} \bigwedge_{x \in X} {}^{\backprime}x{=}x, \qquad T_e \stackrel{\text{def}}{=} {}^{\backprime}e \geq 0 \wedge {}^{\backprime}e{-}1 \geq e,$$

and ${}^{\backprime}e$ is the expression e with all variables x replaced by their corresponding pre-primed versions ${}^{\backprime}x$. Let R represent the transition relation of the loop body of our program in DNF:

$$R \stackrel{\text{def}}{=} C_1 \vee C_2,$$
$$C_1 \stackrel{\text{def}}{=} {}^{\backprime}x > 0 \wedge {}^{\backprime}y > 0 \wedge x{=}{}^{\backprime}x{-}1, \qquad C_2 \stackrel{\text{def}}{=} {}^{\backprime}x > 0 \wedge {}^{\backprime}y > 0 \wedge x{=}{}^{\backprime}x \wedge y{=}{}^{\backprime}y{-}1.$$

Our analysis begins by taking each disjunct in R and performing rank-function synthesis on it. In this case we get

$$\mathsf{RFS}(C_1) = x \quad \text{and} \quad \mathsf{RFS}(C_2) = y.$$

For each disjunct, the analysis also computes a set of variables whose values do not change. In this example, it determines that C_1 can change both x and y, but C_2 does not change variable x. Thus, we begin our analysis with the initial abstract state $A_0 \stackrel{\text{def}}{=} T_x \vee (T_y \wedge V_{\{x\}})$, that is,

$$A_0 \quad = \quad (`x \geq 0 \wedge `x{-}1 \geq x) \vee (`y \geq 0 \wedge `y{-}1 \geq y \wedge `x{=}x).$$

Note that A_0 overapproximates the loop body R.

The meaning of this initial abstract state (*i.e.* $\gamma(A_0)$) is set of all finite sequences of program states $s_i s_{i+1} \ldots s_{i+n}$ such that

$$\big(s_i(x){\geq}0 \wedge s_i(x){-}1{\geq}s_{i+n}(x)\big) \vee \big(s_i(y){\geq}0 \wedge s_i(y){-}1{\geq}s_{i+n}(y) \wedge s_i(x){=}s_{i+n}(x)\big).$$

The analysis then computes the next abstract state A_1 that overapproximates the relational composition of A_0 and R. It takes each disjunction from A_0 and each disjunction from R, composes them, performs rank function synthesis, infers variables that do not change, and constructs the union of the new ranking relations together with A_0. In this case we find:

$$\begin{array}{rr} \mathsf{RFS}(T_x; C_1) = x & \mathsf{RFS}(T_x; C_2) = x \\ \mathsf{RFS}((T_y \wedge V_{\{x\}}); C_1) = x & \mathsf{RFS}((T_y \wedge V_{\{x\}}); C_2) = y \end{array}$$

We also find that the last composition $(T_y \wedge V_{\{x\}}; C_2)$ does not change x. Thus,

$$A_1 \quad = \quad \big(A_0 \vee T_x \vee T_x \vee T_x \vee (T_y \wedge V_{\{x\}})\big) \quad = \quad A_0.$$

Since A_0 is a fixpoint and A_0 overapproximates R, we know that $\forall i > 0.\ R^i \subseteq A_0$, that is, $R^+ \subseteq A_0$. Thus, because A_0 is disjunctively well-founded, [17] tells us that R is well-founded—meaning that the loop of our program guarantees termination.

Note that rank function synthesis is extremely efficient, meaning that our implementation of the analysis can compute the relation A_0 for $\ell = 2$ as fast as the Octagon-based termination analyzer (*i.e.* in 0.02s) [2]. In contrast to the Octagon-based analyzer, however, we compute a relation that is sufficiently strong to establish termination.

To sum up, the essence of our method is that we symbolically execute the body of the loop, and then perform abstraction by calling a rank synthesis engine. This in effect abstracts all information except those that are relevant to termination.

3 Formal Description

In this section we provide a rigorous description of the proposed termination analysis.

3.1 Programming Language

We consider a simple while language in the paper. Let Vars be a finite set of program variables $x, y, z, \ldots$ and let r represent real numbers.

$$
\begin{array}{lcl}
e & ::= & x \mid r \mid e+e \mid r \times e \\
b & ::= & e{=}e \mid e{\neq}e \mid b \wedge b \mid b \vee b \mid \neg b \\
a & ::= & x{:=}e \mid x{:=}* \mid \mathtt{assume}(b) \\
c & ::= & a \mid c;c \mid \mathtt{while}\, b\, c \mid c \,[]\, c
\end{array}
$$

Note that the language has two forms of assignments, normal assignment $x{:=}e$ and nondeterministic random assignment $x{:=}*$. The nondeterministic assignment is used to model some features of a common programming language, for example C, that are not covered by our language above. Also notice that the language does not include the conditional statement. It can be encoded with assume and the nondeterministic choice operator $[]$: $(\mathtt{if}\ b\ c_0\ c_1) \stackrel{\text{def}}{=} ((\mathtt{assume}(b); c_0) \,[]\, (\mathtt{assume}(\neg b); c_1))$.

The semantics of our language is standard. We remind the reader of only the storage model used in the semantics:

$$\mathsf{St} \stackrel{\text{def}}{=} \mathsf{Vars} \rightarrow \mathsf{Real}.$$

This model shows that we assume real variables in this paper. However, changing the type of variables from reals to integers or rationals will not affect the results of the paper, except the ones for the fast termination in Lemma 1 and Theorem 2.

3.2 Abstract Domain

Our analysis is parameterized by a domain for representing relations on states. The domain is specified by the following data:

1. A set D and a monotone function $\gamma_r : D \rightarrow \mathcal{P}(\mathsf{St} \times \mathsf{St})$ (where the target $\mathcal{P}(\mathsf{St} \times \mathsf{St})$ is ordered by the subset relation).
2. An abstract identity element d_{id} in D, that satisfies

$$\Delta_{\mathsf{St}} \subseteq \gamma_r(d_{\mathsf{id}})$$

   where Δ_{St} is the identity relation on St.
3. An operator $\mathsf{RFS}\colon D \rightarrow \mathcal{P}_{\mathsf{fin}}(D) \uplus \{\top\}$, which synthesizes ranking functions. We assume the following two conditions for this operator:
   (a) RFS computes an overapproximation:

$$\mathsf{RFS}(d){\neq}\top \implies \gamma_r(d) \subseteq \bigcup\{\gamma_r(d') \mid d' \in \mathsf{RFS}(d)\}.$$

   (b) $\mathsf{RFS}(d)$ denotes a well-founded relation:

$$\mathsf{RFS}(d){\neq}\top \implies \bigcup\{\gamma_r(d') \mid d' \in \mathsf{RFS}(d)\} \text{ is well-founded.}$$

4. An abstract transfer function $\mathsf{trans}(a)$ for each atomic commands a (i.e., assignments or assume statements). The function $\mathsf{trans}(a)$ has type $D \to \mathcal{P}_{\mathsf{fin}}(D)$, and satisfies

$$\forall d \in D.\ (\gamma_r(d); [\![a]\!]) \subseteq \bigcup\{\gamma_r(d') \mid d' \in \mathsf{trans}(a)(d)\}$$

where the semicolon means the usual composition of relations and $[\![a]\!]$ is the standard relational meaning of the atomic command a.
5. An abstract composition operator $\mathsf{comp}\colon D \times D \to D$ such that

$$\gamma_r(d); \gamma_r(d') \quad \subseteq \quad \gamma_r(\mathsf{comp}(d, d')).$$

Intuitively, the data above means that we have a set D of relations, some of which are well-founded. This set comes with an algorithm RFS, which overapproximates a relation by a ranking relation. It also has operators, trans and comp, that soundly model all the atomic commands and concrete relation composition. One example of D is the set of conjunction of linear constraints. In this case, we can use a linear rank synthesis engine, which we denote LINEARRANKSYN, and define RFS as will be shown in Section 3.4.

The abstract domain $\mathcal{A}$ of our analyzer is:

$$\mathcal{A} \stackrel{\text{def}}{=} (\mathcal{P}_{\mathsf{fin}}(D))^{\top} \quad (\text{i.e., } \mathcal{P}(D) \uplus \{\top\}).$$

It is ordered by the the subset order $\sqsubseteq$ extended with $\top$. That is, $A \sqsubseteq A'$ iff

$$A' = \top, \qquad \text{or} \qquad (A, A' \in \mathcal{P}_{\mathsf{fin}}(D) \text{ and } A \subseteq A').$$

Each abstract element A in $\mathcal{A}$ denotes a set of finite or infinite sequences of states, which we call *traces*. The element $\top$ denotes the set of all traces, including infinite ones, and non-$\top$ elements A denote a set of *finite* nonempty traces whose initial and final states are related by some d in A. Let $\gamma_r(A)$ be $\bigcup\{\gamma_r(d) \mid d \in A\}$, the disjunction of d's in A, and define $\mathcal{T}$ to be the set of all nonempty traces:

$$\mathcal{T} \stackrel{\text{def}}{=} \mathsf{St}^{+} \cup \mathsf{St}^{\infty}.$$

The formal meaning of A is given by a concretization function γ:

$$\gamma \ : \ \mathcal{A} \to \mathcal{P}(\mathcal{T})$$
$$\gamma(A) \stackrel{\text{def}}{=} \textbf{if } (A{=}\top) \textbf{ then } \mathcal{T} \textbf{ else } \{\tau \mid \tau \text{ is nonempty, finite, and } \tau_0[\gamma_r(A)]\tau_{|\tau|-1}\}$$

where $|\tau|$ is the length of the trace τ, and τ_n is the n-th state of the trace τ, and notation $s[r]s'$ means that s, s' are related by r. For instance, when $[x : n, y : m]$ is a state mapping x and y to n and m, a finite trace

$$[x : 1, y : 1][x : 2, y : 2][x : 5, y : 3][x : -2, y : 2]$$

belongs to $\gamma(\{`x{-}1 \geq x,\ `y{-}1 \geq y\})$, because x has a smaller value in the final state than in the initial state.

Our domain $\mathcal{A}$ is a complete semi-lattice. The join of a family $\{A_i\}_{i \in I}$ of elements in $\mathcal{A}$ is given by the union of all A_i's, if none of A_i's is $\top$ and the union is finite. Otherwise, the join is $\top$.

3.3 Generic Analysis

Our generic analyzer is an abstract interpretation, defined in a denotational style.

For functions $f\colon D \to \mathcal{A}$ and $g\colon D \times D \to D$, let $f^\dagger, g^\dagger$ be their liftings on $\mathcal{A}$:

$$f^\dagger : \mathcal{A} \to \mathcal{A} \qquad g^\dagger : \mathcal{A} \times \mathcal{A} \to \mathcal{A}$$
$$f^\dagger(A) \stackrel{\text{def}}{=} \textbf{if } (A{=}\top) \textbf{ then } \top \textbf{ else } \bigsqcup_{d \in A} f(d)$$
$$g^\dagger(A, B) \stackrel{\text{def}}{=} \textbf{if } (A{=}\top \vee B{=}\top) \textbf{ then } \top \textbf{ else } \bigsqcup_{d \in A, d' \in B} \{g(d, d')\}.$$

Using these liftings, we define the generic analyzer as follows: [1]

$$\begin{aligned}
&[\![c]\!]^\# : \mathcal{A} \to \mathcal{A}\\
&[\![a]\!]^\# A \stackrel{\text{def}}{=} (\mathsf{trans}(a))^\dagger A\\
&[\![c_0; c_1]\!]^\# A \stackrel{\text{def}}{=} ([\![c_1]\!]^\# \circ [\![c_0]\!]^\#) A\\
&[\![c_0 \,[\!]\, c_1]\!]^\# A \stackrel{\text{def}}{=} [\![c_0]\!]^\# A \sqcup [\![c_1]\!]^\# A\\
&[\![\mathtt{while}\, b\, c]\!]^\# A \stackrel{\text{def}}{=} \textbf{let } F \stackrel{\text{def}}{=} \lambda A'.[\![\mathtt{assume}(b); c]\!]^\#(\{d_{\mathsf{id}}\} \sqcup A') \textbf{ and } A_s \stackrel{\text{def}}{=} \{d_{\mathsf{id}}\} \sqcup A\\
&\qquad \textbf{in } [\![\mathtt{assume}(\neg b)]\!]^\# (\mathsf{comp}^\dagger(A_s, \mathsf{fix}\,(\mathsf{RFS}^\dagger \circ F)))
\end{aligned}$$

Intuitively, the argument A represents a set of finite or infinite traces that happen before the command c. The analyzer computes an overapproximation of all traces that are obtained by continuing the execution of c from the end of traces in A.

Our definition assumes an operator fix. The fix operator takes a function of the form $\mathsf{RFS}^\dagger \circ F : \mathcal{A} \to \mathcal{A}$, and returns an abstract element A in the image of $\mathsf{RFS}^\dagger$ such that

$$A = \top \;\vee\; (A \neq \top \wedge (\mathsf{RFS}^\dagger \circ F)(A) \neq \top \wedge \gamma_r((\mathsf{RFS}^\dagger \circ F)(A)) \subseteq \gamma_r(A)).$$

One can use the standard fixpoint iteration to define fix,[2] because the above condition holds for all post fixpoints A of $(\mathsf{RFS}^\dagger \circ F)$ (that are in the image of $\mathsf{RFS}^\dagger$). However, this is not mandatory. In fact, a more optimized fix operator is used in the analysis of Section 3.4, which in some cases does not even compute a post fixpoint.

The most interesting case of the analysis is the loop. The best way to understand this case is to assume that fix is the standard fixpoint operator and to see a sequence generated during the iterative fixpoint computation:

$$\begin{aligned}
A_0 &= \{\},\\
A_1 &= A_0 \sqcup (\mathsf{RFS}^\dagger \circ F)\{d_{\mathsf{id}}\}\\
&= (\mathsf{RFS}^\dagger \circ F)\{d_{\mathsf{id}}\}\\
A_2 &= A_1 \sqcup (\mathsf{RFS}^\dagger \circ F)(\{d_{\mathsf{id}}\} \sqcup (\mathsf{RFS}^\dagger \circ F)\{d_{\mathsf{id}}\})\\
&= (\mathsf{RFS}^\dagger \circ F)\{d_{\mathsf{id}}\} \sqcup (\mathsf{RFS}^\dagger \circ F)^2\{d_{\mathsf{id}}\},\\
A_3 &= A_2 \sqcup (\mathsf{RFS}^\dagger \circ F)(\{d_{\mathsf{id}}\} \sqcup (\mathsf{RFS}^\dagger \circ F)\{d_{\mathsf{id}}\} \sqcup (\mathsf{RFS}^\dagger \circ F)^2\{d_{\mathsf{id}}\})\\
&= (\mathsf{RFS}^\dagger \circ F)\{d_{\mathsf{id}}\} \sqcup (\mathsf{RFS}^\dagger \circ F)^2\{d_{\mathsf{id}}\} \sqcup (\mathsf{RFS}^\dagger \circ F)^3\{d_{\mathsf{id}}\},\\
&\ldots
\end{aligned}$$

[1] In the definition, we view RFS, trans(a) as functions of type $D \to (\mathcal{P}_{\mathsf{fin}}(D))^\top$.

[2] In this case, fix $(\mathsf{RFS}^\dagger \circ F)$ is defined by the limit of the sequence $\{A_n\}$ where $A_0 = \{\}$ and $A_{n+1} = A_n \sqcup (\mathsf{RFS}^\dagger \circ F)(A_n)$.

Here we used the fact that $\mathsf{RFS}^\dagger \circ F$ preserves $\sqcup$. Note that in each step, we apply the lifted rank-synthesis algorithm $\mathsf{RFS}^\dagger$ to the analysis result of the loop body $F(A_n)$. This application of RFS throws away all the information from $F(A_n)$, except the one necessary for proving termination. Another thing to note is that the input A is not used in this fixpoint computation at all. As the expansion of A_3 shows, the fixpoint computation effectively starts with $(\mathsf{RFS}^\dagger \circ F)\{d_{\mathsf{id}}\}$, which means the results of running the loop body once on all states. The input A, together with $\{d_{\mathsf{id}}\}$, is pre-composed later to the computed fixpoint. This change of the starting point is crucial for the soundness of our analysis, because it ensures that the analyzer overapproximates the relation between any states (not just initial states) at a loop and the following states at the same loop (so that we can apply a known termination proof rule based on disjunctively well-founded relations [17]).

Given a program c, the analyzer works as follows:

$$
\begin{aligned}
\textsc{Analysis}(c) \overset{\text{def}}{=}\ & \textbf{let } A = [\![c]\!]^{\#}(\{d_{\mathsf{id}}\}) \\
& \textbf{in if } (A \neq \top) \textbf{ then } (\textbf{return } \text{“Terminates”}) \textbf{ else } (\textbf{return } \text{“Unknown”}).
\end{aligned}
$$

Theorem 1. *If* $\textsc{Analysis}(c)$ *returns "Terminates", then c terminates on all states.*

The proof of this theorem is given in the full version of the paper [5]. There we also clarify what we mean by "terminates on all states", by defining a concrete trace semantics of commands based on Cousot's work [9].

3.4 Linear Rank Abstraction

The linear rank abstraction is an instance of our generic analysis, by the domain of linear constraints and a linear ranking synthesis algorithm $\textsc{LinearRankSyn}$.

Let r represent real numbers. Consider constraints C defined by the grammar below:

$$
\begin{aligned}
E &::= x \mid {}^{\backprime}x \mid x' \mid r \mid E + E \mid r \times E \\
P &::= E = E \mid E \neq E \mid E < E \mid E > E \mid E \leq E \mid E \geq E \\
C &::= P \mid \mathsf{true} \mid C \wedge C
\end{aligned}
$$

This grammar ensures that all the constraints are the conjunction of linear constraints. Note that a constraint can have three kinds of variables; a normal variable x denoting the current value of program variable x; a pre-primed variable ${}^{\backprime}x$ storing the initial value of x; post-primed variables y' that usually denotes values which were once stored in program variables during computation. We assume that there are finitely many normal variables (Vars) and finitely many pre-primed variables (‘Vars), and that there is a one-to-one correspondence between these two kinds of variables. For post-primed variables, however, we assume an infinite set.

Each constraint means a relation on St. For each state s, let ${}^{\backprime}s$ be a function from ‘Vars to Real such that for every pre-primed variable ${}^{\backprime}x$, ${}^{\backprime}s({}^{\backprime}x)$ is $s(x)$ for the corresponding normal variable x. The meaning function γ_r of constraints C is defined as follows:

$$
\gamma_r(C) \overset{\text{def}}{=} \{(s_0, s_1) \mid ({}^{\backprime}s_0, s_1 \models \exists X'.C)\}
$$

where X' is the set of post-primed variables in C and $\models$ is the usual satisfaction relation in first-order logic. Note that all post-primed variables in the constraint C are implicitly existentially-quantified.

The linear rank abstraction uses the set of constraints C as the parameter set D of the generic analysis. The identity element d_{id} is the identity relation

$$d_{\mathsf{id}} \stackrel{\text{def}}{=} \bigwedge_{x \in \mathsf{Vars}} `x{=}x.$$

Assume that we are given an enumeration $x_0, \ldots, x_n$ of all program variables in Vars. Call an expression E *normalized,* when (1) E does not contain any pre or post primed variables and (2) it is of the form $a_{i_0} \times x_{i_0} + \ldots a_{i_k} \times x_{i_k} + a$ with $a_{i_0} = 1$ or -1 and $i_0 < i_1 \ldots < i_k$. Note that in a normalized expression E, the coefficient of the first variable in E according to the given enumeration is 1 or -1. Conceptually, LINEARRANKSYN implements a function of the type:[3]

$$D \to (\{(E, r) \mid E \text{ is normalized and } r \text{ is a positive real}\}) \uplus \{\top\}.$$

The output $\top$ indicates that the algorithm fails to discover a ranking function, because (the implementation of) the algorithm is incomplete or the input constraint defines a non-well-founded relation between pre-primed variables and normal variables. The other output (E, r) means that the algorithm succeeds to find a ranking function which overapproximates the given constraint. Concretely, for a normalized expression E and a positive real r, let

$$T_{E,r} \stackrel{\text{def}}{=} (`E \geq 0 \wedge `E{-}r \geq E),$$

where expression $`E$ is $E$ with all normal variables $x$ replaced by corresponding pre-primed variables $`x$. The output (E, r) of LINEARRANKSYN(C) means that

$$(\exists X'.C) \implies T_{E,r}$$

where X' is the set of all post-primed variables in C.

Assume that we have chosen a fixed positive real dec for the analysis, which is very small (in particular smaller than 1). Using LINEARRANKSYN and dec, we define the operator RFS as follows:

$$\mathsf{RFS}(C) \stackrel{\text{def}}{=} \begin{cases} \{\} & \text{if } C \vdash \mathsf{false} \\ \{T_{E,\mathsf{dec}}\} & \text{else if LINEARRANKSYN}(C){=}(E,r) \text{ and } r \geq \mathsf{dec} \\ \top & \text{otherwise} \end{cases}$$

where $\vdash$ is a sound (but not necessarily complete) theorem prover. Note that the result of RFS is always of the form $T_{E,\mathsf{dec}}$, so the second subscript of T is not necessary. From now on, we write T_E for $T_{E,\mathsf{dec}}$.

[3] Usually the implementation of linear rank synthesis returns a tuple (E, r, b) where E is an expression without any pre or post primed variable whose value is decreasing, r is a decrement, and b is a lower bound of E. Our analysis picks the absolute value a of the coefficient of the first variable x_i in E, transforms E/a to a normal form E', and regards $(E' - b/a, r/a)$ as an output from LINEARRANKSYN.

The abstract transfer functions for atomic commands are defined following Floyd's strongest postcondition semantics:

$$\llbracket x{:=}{*} \rrbracket^{\#} C \stackrel{\text{def}}{=} \{C[x'/x]\} \quad (x' \text{ is fresh})$$
$$\llbracket x{:=}e \rrbracket^{\#} C \stackrel{\text{def}}{=} \{C[x'/x] \wedge x{=}(e[x'/x])\} \quad (x' \text{ is fresh})$$
$$\llbracket \texttt{assume}(b) \rrbracket^{\#} C \stackrel{\text{def}}{=} \textbf{if } (C \wedge b \vdash \mathsf{false}) \textbf{ then } \{\}$$
$$\textbf{else } \{C_0, \ldots, C_n \mid C_0 \vee \ldots \vee C_n = \mathsf{norm}(C \wedge b)\}.$$

Here norm is the standard transformation that takes a formula in the propositional logic and transforms the formula to disjunctive normal form.

Next, we define the abstract composition comp. Let fresh be an operator on constraints C that renames all post-primed variables fresh. Let ‘Vars be the set of pre-primed variables. The abstract composition is defined as follows

$$\mathsf{comp}(C_0, C_1) \stackrel{\text{def}}{=} \textbf{let } (C_2 = \mathsf{fresh}(C_1)) \textbf{ in } \Big(C_0[Y'/\mathsf{Vars}] \wedge C_2[Y'/\text{‘}\mathsf{Vars}]\Big).$$

The variable set Y' in the definition denotes a set of fresh post-primed variables, that has as many elements as Vars. The two substitutions there replace a normal variable x and the corresponding pre-primed variable ‘x by the same post-primed variable x'.

Finally, we specify a fix operator. For each function $(\mathsf{RFS}^{\dagger} \circ F)$ on sets of constraints C, let $\{G_n\}_n$ be the standard fixpoint iteration sequence: $G_0 = \{\}$ and $G_{n+1} = G_n \sqcup (\mathsf{RFS}^{\dagger} \circ F)(G_n)$. Given G, our fix operator returns the first G_n such that

$$G_n{=}\top \quad \vee \quad \Big(G_n{\neq}\top \ \wedge \ G_{n+1}{\neq}\top \ \wedge \ \forall C \in G_{n+1}.\, \exists C' \in G_n.\, C \vdash C'\Big).$$

This definition assumes that some G_n satisfies the above property. If such a G_n does not exist, the fix operator is not defined, so the analysis can diverge during the fixpoint computation. In Theorem 2, we will discharge this assumption and prove the termination of the linear rank abstraction.

Example 1. Consider the program c below:

$$\texttt{while } (x > 0 \wedge y > 0) \ (x{:=}x{-}1 \mathbin{[]} y{:=}y{-}1).$$

Given c, the analysis starts the fixpoint computation from the empty set $A_0 = \{\}$. The first iteration of the fixpoint computation is done in two steps. First, it applies the abstract transfer function of the loop body to $\{d_{\mathsf{id}}\} \cup A_0 = \{d_{\mathsf{id}}\}$:

$$\llbracket \texttt{assume}(x{>}0 \wedge y{>}0); (x{:=}x{-}1 \mathbin{[]} y{:=}y{-}1) \rrbracket^{\#}(\{d_{\mathsf{id}}\})$$
$$= \llbracket x{:=}x{-}1 \mathbin{[]} y{:=}y{-}1 \rrbracket^{\#}\{d_{\mathsf{id}} \wedge x{>}0 \wedge y{>}0\}$$
$$= \llbracket x{:=}x{-}1 \rrbracket^{\#}\{d_{\mathsf{id}} \wedge x{>}0 \wedge y{>}0\} \cup \llbracket y{:=}y{-}1 \rrbracket^{\#}\{d_{\mathsf{id}} \wedge x{>}0 \wedge y{>}0\}$$
$$= \llbracket x{:=}x{-}1 \rrbracket^{\#}\{\text{‘}x{=}x \wedge \text{‘}y{=}y \wedge x{>}0 \wedge y{>}0\} \cup \llbracket y{:=}y{-}1 \rrbracket^{\#}\{\text{‘}x{=}x \wedge \text{‘}y{=}y \wedge x{>}0 \wedge y{>}0\}$$
$$= \{\text{‘}x{=}x' \wedge \text{‘}y{=}y \wedge x'{>}0 \wedge y{>}0 \wedge x{=}x'{-}1, \quad \text{‘}x{=}x \wedge \text{‘}y{=}y' \wedge x{>}0 \wedge y'{>}0 \wedge y{=}y'{-}1\}.$$

Next, the analysis calls LINEARRANKSYN twice with each of the two elements in the result set above. These function calls return x and y, from which the analysis constructs two ranking relations below:

$$T_x \stackrel{\text{def}}{=} (\text{‘}x{\geq}0 \ \wedge \ \text{‘}x{-}\mathsf{dec} \geq x) \quad \text{and} \quad T_y \stackrel{\text{def}}{=} (\text{‘}y{\geq}0 \ \wedge \ \text{‘}y{-}\mathsf{dec} \geq y).$$

The result A_1 of the first iteration is $\{T_x, T_y\}$.

The second fixpoint iteration computes:

$$A_1 \sqcup (\mathsf{RFS}^\dagger \circ [\![\texttt{assume}(x{>}0 \wedge y{>}0); (x{:=}x{-}1 \,[\!]\, y{:=}y{-}1)]\!]^\#)A_1.$$

We show that the abstract element on the right hand side of the join, denoted A_2', is again A_1, so that the fixpoint computation converges here. To compute A_2', the analyzer first transforms A_1 according to the abstract meaning of the loop body. This results in a set with four elements:

$$\begin{array}{l}\{\, T_x[x'/x] \wedge x'{>}0 \wedge y{>}0 \wedge x{=}x'{-}1, \quad T_x[y'/y] \wedge x{>}0 \wedge y'{>}0 \wedge y{=}y'{-}1, \\ \;\; T_y[x'/x] \wedge x'{>}0 \wedge y{>}0 \wedge x{=}x'{-}1, \quad T_y[y'/y] \wedge x{>}0 \wedge y'{>}0 \wedge y{=}y'{-}1 \,\}.\end{array}$$

The first two elements come from transforming T_x according to the left and right branches of the loop body. The other two elements are obtained similarly from T_y. Next, the analysis calls LINEARRANKSYN with all the four elements above. These four calls return x, x, y and y, which represent well-founded relations T_x, T_x, T_y, T_y. Thus, A_2' is the same as T_x and T_y, and the fixpoint computation stops here.

After the fixpoint computation, the analysis composes the identity relation $\{d_{\mathsf{id}}\}$ with the result of the fixpoint computation:

$$\begin{aligned}\mathsf{comp}^\dagger(\{d_{\mathsf{id}}\}, \{T_x, T_y\}) &= \{`x{=}x_0' \wedge `y{=}y_0' \wedge T_x[x_0'/`x],\ `x{=}x_0' \wedge `y{=}y_0' \wedge T_y[y_0'/`y]\} \\ &= \{T_x,\ T_y\}.\end{aligned}$$

Finally, we apply $[\![\texttt{assume}(\neg(x > 0 \wedge y > 0))]\!]^\#$ to the set above, which gives a set with four constraints:

$$\{\, T_x \wedge x \leq 0, \quad T_x \wedge y \leq 0, \quad T_y \wedge x \leq 0, \quad T_y \wedge y \leq 0 \,\}.$$

Since the result is not $\top$, the analysis concludes that the given program c terminates. □

In the example above, the fixpoint computation converges after two iterations. In the first iteration, which computes A_1, it finds ranking functions, and in the next iteration, it confirms that the ranking functions are preserved by the loop. In fact, we can prove that the fixpoint computation of the analysis always follows the same pattern, and finishes in two iterations. Suppose that LINEARRANKSYN is well-behaved, such that

1. RFS always computes an optimal ranking function, in the sense that

$$(\mathsf{RFS}(C) = \{T_E\} \wedge \gamma_r(C) \subseteq \gamma_r(T_{E+b})) \implies b \geq 0,$$

2. RFS depends only on the (relational) meaning of its argument.

Lemma 1. *For all commands c and normalized expressions E, if there is a constraint* $C \in [\![c]\!]^\#\{T_E\}$ *such that* $\mathsf{RFS}(C) = \{T_F\}$ *and* $\gamma_r(C) \neq \emptyset$*, then F is of the form* $E - b$ *for some nonnegative b.*

Proof. The proof appears in the full version of this paper [5]. □

Theorem 2 (Fast Convergence). *Suppose that the theorem prover $\vdash$ is complete. Then, for all commands c, the fixpoint iteration of*

$$G = \lambda A.\ (\mathsf{RFS}^\dagger \circ [\![c]\!]^\#)(\{d_{\mathsf{id}}\} \sqcup A)$$

terminates at most in two steps. Specifically, $G^2(\{\})$ is $\top$, or the result of $\mathsf{fix}\,G$ *is $\{\}$ or $G(\{\})$.*

Proof. Suppose that $G^2(\{\})$ is not $\top$. This implies that both $G(\{\})$ and $G^2(\{\})$ are finite sets of T_E's for normalized expressions E, because $G(= \mathsf{RFS}^\dagger \circ [\![c]\!]^\#)$ preserves $\top$. If $G(\{\})$ is empty, $\{\}$ is the fixpoint of G, thus becoming the result of $\mathsf{fix}\,G$, as claimed in the theorem. To prove the other nonempty case, suppose that $G(\{\})$ is a nonempty finite collection $A = \{T_{E_1}, \ldots, T_{E_n}\}$. We need to show that for each T_F in $G(A)$, there exists $T_{E_i} \in A$ such that $T_F \vdash T_{E_i}$, which is equivalent to $\gamma_r(T_F) \subseteq \gamma_r(T_{E_i})$ due to the completeness assumption about the prover. Pick T_F in $G(A)$. Since $G(= \mathsf{RFS}^\dagger \circ [\![c]\!]^\#)$ preserves the join operator, there exists T_{E_i} in A such that $T_F \in G(\{T_{E_i}\})$. This means that $\mathsf{RFS}(C) = \{T_F\}$ for some constraint C in $[\![c]\!]^\#(T_{E_i})$. Note that since RFS filters out all the provably inconsistent constraints and the prover is assumed complete, $\gamma_r(C)$ is not empty. Thus, by Lemma 1, there is a nonnegative b such that $F = E - b$. This gives the required $\gamma_r(T_F) \subseteq \gamma_r(T_E)$. □

Note that the theorem suggests that we could have used a different fix operator that does not call the prover at all and just returns $G^2(\{\})$. We do not take this alternative in the paper, since it is too specific for the RFS operator in this section; if RFS also keeps track of equality information, this two-step convergence result no longer holds.

Refinement with simple equalities. The linear rank abstraction cannot prove the termination of the program in Section 2. When the linear rank abstraction is run for the program, it finds the ranking functions x and y for the true and false branches of the program, but loses the information that the else branch does not change the value of x, which is crucial for the termination proof. As a result, the linear rank abstraction returns $\top$, and reports, incorrectly, the possibility of nontermination.

One way to solve this problem and improve the precision of the linear rank abstraction is to use a more precise RFS operator that additionally keeps simple forms of equalities. Concretely, this refinement keeps all the definitions of the linear rank abstraction, except that it replaces the rank synthesizer RFS of the linear rank abstraction by RFS′ below:

$$\mathsf{RFS}'(C) \stackrel{\text{def}}{=} \textbf{if } (\mathsf{RFS}(C){=}\top) \textbf{ then } \top \textbf{ else } \{T_E \wedge (\wedge_{(C \vdash `x=x)} `x{=}x) \mid T_E \in \mathsf{RFS}(C)\}.$$

When this refined analysis is given the program in Section 2, it follows the informal description in that section and proves the termination of the program.

4 Experimental Evaluation

In order to evaluate the utility of our approach we have implemented the analysis in this paper, and then compared it to several known termination tools. The tools used in the experiments are as follows:

	1	2	3	4	5	6
LR	0.01 ✓	0.01 ✓	0.08 ✓	0.09 ✓	0.02 ✓	0.06 ✓
O	0.11 ✓	0.08 ✓	6.03 ✓	1.02 ✓	0.16 ✓	0.76 ✓
P	1.40 ✓	1.30 ✓	10.90 ✓	2.12 ✓	1.80 ✓	1.89 ✓
T	6.31 ✓	4.93 ✓	T/O -	T/O -	33.24 ✓	3.98 ✓

(a) Results from experiments with termination tools on arithmetic examples from the Octagon Library distribution.

	1	2	3	4	5	6	7	8	9	10
LR	0.23 ✓	0.20 ⊘	0.00 ⊘	0.04 ✓	0.00 ✓	0.03 ✓	0.07 ✓	0.03 ✓	0.01 ⊘	0.03 ✓
O	1.42 ✓	1.67 ⊘	0.47 ⊘	0.18 ✓	0.06 ✓	0.53 ✓	0.50 ✓	0.32 ✓	0.14 ⊘	0.17 ✓
P	4.66 ✓	6.35 ⊘	1.48 ⊘	1.10 ✓	1.30 ✓	1.60 ✓	2.65 ✓	1.89 ✓	2.42 ⊘	1.27 ✓
T	10.22 ✓	31.51 ⊘	20.65 ⊘	4.05 ✓	12.63 ✓	67.11 ✓	298.45 ✓	444.78 ✓	T/O -	55.28 ✓

(b) Results from experiments with termination tools on small arithmetic examples taken from Windows device drivers. Note that the examples are small as they must currently be hand-translated for the three tools.

	1	2	3	4	6	7	8	9	10	11	12
LR	0.19 ✓	0.02 ✓	0.01 †	0.02 †	0.02 †	0.01 †	0.04 †	0.01 †	0.03 †	0.02 †	0.01 †
O	0.30 †	0.05 †	0.11 †	0.50 †	0.10 †	0.17 †	0.16 †	0.12 †	0.35 †	0.86 †	0.12 †
P	1.42 ✓	0.82 ✓	1.06 †	2.29 †	2.61 †	1.28 †	0.24 †	1.36 ✓	1.69 †	1.56 †	1.05 †
T	435.23 ✓	61.15 ✓	T/O -	T/O -	75.33 ✓	T/O -	T/O -	T/O -	T/O -	T/O -	10.31 †

(c) Results from experiments with termination tools on arithmetic examples from the POLYRANK distribution.

Fig. 1. Experiments with 4 termination provers/analyses. **LR** is used to represent LINEARRANKTERM, **O** is used to represent OCTATERM, an Octagon-based variance analysis. **P** is POLYTERM, a Polyhedra-based variance analysis. The **T** represents TERMINATOR [8]. Times are measured in seconds. The timeout threshold was set to 500s. ✓="a proof was found". †="false counterexample returned". T/O = "timeout". ⊘="termination bug found". Note that pointers and aliasing from the device driver examples were removed by a careful hand translation when passed to the tools **O**, **P** and **LR**. Note that a time of 0.00 means that the analysis was too fast to be measured by the timing utilities used.

LR) LINEARRANKTERM is the new variance analysis that implements the linear rank abstraction with simple equalities in Section 3.4. This tool is implemented using CIL [15] allowing the analysis of programs written in C. However, no notion of shape is used in these implementations, restricting the input to only arithmetic programs. The tool uses RANKFINDER [16] as its linear rank synthesis engine and uses the Simplify prover [11] to filter out inconsistent states and check the implication between abstract states.

O) OCTATERM is the variance analysis [2] induced by the octagon analysis OCTANAL [14].

P) POLYTERM is the variance analysis [2] similarly induced from the polyhedra analysis POLY based on the New Polka Polyhedra library [12].

T) TERMINATOR [8].

These tools, except for TERMINATOR, were all run on a 2GHz AMD64 processor using Linux 2.6.16. TERMINATOR was executed on a 3GHz Pentium 4 using Windows XP SP2. Using different machines is unfortunate but somewhat unavoidable due to constraints on software library dependencies, etc. Note, however, that TERMINATOR running on the faster machine was still slower overall, so the qualitative results are meaningful. In any case, the running times are somewhat incomparable since on failed proofs TERMINATOR produces a counterexample path, but LINEARRANKTERM, OCTATERM and POLYTERM give a suspect pair of states.

Fig. 1 contains the results from the experiments performed with these analyses.[4] For example, Fig. 1(a) shows the outcome of the provers on example programs included in the OCTANAL distribution. Example 3 is an abstracted version of heapsort, and Example 4 of bubblesort.

Fig. 1(b) contains the results of experiments on fragments of Windows device drivers. These examples are small because we currently must hand-translate them before applying all of the tools but TERMINATOR.

Fig. 1(c) contains the results from experiments with the 4 tools on examples from the POLYRANK distribution.[5] The examples can be characterized as small but famously difficult (*e.g.* McCarthy's 91 function). Note that LINEARRANKTERM performs poorly on these examples because of the limitations of RANKFINDER. Many of these examples involve phase changes or tricky arithmetic in the algorithm.

From these experiments we can see that LINEARRANKTERM is very fast and precise. The prototype we have developed indicates that a termination analyzer using abstractions based on ranking functions shows a lot of promise.

Acknowledgements. We would like to thank Peter O'Hearn for encouragements and insightful comments on our work, Andrey Rybalchenko for explaining the subtleties of linear ranking functions and RANKFINDER, and Amir Ben-Amram and Neil Jones for helping us to understand the size-change termination. We also acknowledge detailed comments on the paper from Amir and anonymous referees, which help us to improve the presentation of the paper. Chawdhary was supported by a Microsoft PhD studentship, and Yang was supported by EPSRC.

References

1. Balaban, I., Pnueli, A., Zuck, L.: Ranking abstraction as companion to predicate abstraction. In: Wang, F. (ed.) FORTE 2005. LNCS, vol. 3731, Springer, Heidelberg (2005)
2. Berdine, J., Chawdhary, A., Cook, B., Distefano, D., O'Hearn, P.: Variance analyses from invariance analyses. In: POPL 2007 (2007)
3. Bradley, A., Manna, Z., Sipma, H.: Termination of polynomial programs. In: Cousot, R. (ed.) VMCAI 2005. LNCS, vol. 3385, Springer, Heidelberg (2005)

[4] The programs used in our experiments except the ones for drivers are available in http://www.dcs.qmul.ac.uk/~aziem/esop. Unfortunately, we could not put the driver examples in the web page, because that might cause a problem related to intellectual property.

[5] Note also that there is no benchmark number 5 in the original distribution. We have used the same numbering scheme as in the distribution so as to avoid confusion.

4. Bruynooghe, M., Codish, M., Gallagher, J., Genaim, S., Vanhoof, W.: Termination analysis through combination of type based norms. ACM Trans. Progam. Lang. Syst. 29(2) (2007)
5. Chawdhary, A., Cook, B., Gulwani, S., Sagiv, M., Yang, H.: Ranking abstractions. Manuscript (2008), `http://www.dcs.qmul.ac.uk/~aiem/paper/esop08-full.pdf`
6. Codish, M., Taboch, C.: A semantic basis for the termination analysis of logic programs. The Journal of Logic Programming 41(1) (1999)
7. Cook, B., Podelski, A., Rybalchenko, A.: Termination proofs for systems code. In: PLDI 2006 (2006)
8. Cook, B., Podelski, A., Rybalchenko, A.: Terminator: Beyond safety. In: Ball, T., Jones, R.B. (eds.) CAV 2006. LNCS, vol. 4144, Springer, Heidelberg (2006)
9. Cousot, P.: Constructive design of a hierarchy of semantics of a transition system by abstract interpretation. Theoretical Comput. Sci. 277(1–2), 47–103 (2002)
10. Cousot, P., Cousot, R.: Systematic design of program analysis frameworks. In: POPL 1979 (1979)
11. Detlefs, D., Nelson, G., Saxe, J.: Simplify: A theorem prover for program checking (2003)
12. Jeannet, B.: NewPolka polyhedra library, `http://pop-art.inrialpes.fr/people/bjeannet/newpolka/index.html`
13. Lee, C.S., Jones, N.D., Ben-Amram, A.M.: The size-change principle for program termination. In: POPL 2001 (2001)
14. Miné, A.: The Octagon abstract domain. Higher-Order and Symbolic Comput. 19, 31–100 (2006)
15. Necula, G., McPeak, S., Rahul, S., Weimer, W.: CIL: Intermediate Language and Tools for Analysis and Transformation of C Programs. In: Horspool, R.N. (ed.) CC 2002. LNCS, vol. 2304, Springer, Heidelberg (2002)
16. Podelski, A., Rybalchenko, A.: A complete method for the synthesis of linear ranking functions. In: Steffen, B., Levi, G. (eds.) VMCAI 2004. LNCS, vol. 2937, Springer, Heidelberg (2004)
17. Podelski, A., Rybalchenko, A.: Transition invariants. In: LICS 2004 (2004)
18. Turing, A.M.: Checking a large routine. In: Report of a Conference on High Speed Automatic Calculating Machines, pp. 67–69 (1948), Reprinted In: The early British computer conferences. Charles Babbage Institute Reprint Series for the History of Computing, vol. 14, MIT Press, Cambridge (1989)
19. Yahav, E., Reps, T., Sagiv, M., Wilhelm, R.: Verifying temporal heap properties specified via evolution logic. Logic Journal of IGPL (September 2006)

Non-disjunctive Numerical Domain for Array Predicate Abstraction

Xavier Allamigeon[1,2]

[1] EADS Innovation Works, SE/CS – Suresnes, France
[2] CEA, LIST MeASI – Gif-sur-Yvette, France
firstname.lastname@eads.net

Abstract. We present a numerical abstract domain to infer invariants on (a possibly unbounded number of) consecutive array elements using array predicates. It is able to represent and compute affine equality relations over the predicate parameters and the program variables, without using disjunctions or heuristics. It is the cornerstone of a sound static analysis of one- and two-dimensional array manipulation algorithms. The implementation shows very good performance on representative benchmarks. Our approach is sufficiently robust to handle programs traversing arrays and matrices in various ways.

1 Introduction

Program analysis now involves a large variety of methods able to infer complex program invariants, by using specific computer-representable structures, such as intervals [1], octagons [2], linear (more exactly affine) equality constraints [3], or affine inequality constraints [4]. Each abstract domain induces an equivalence relation: two abstract elements are equivalent if and only if they represent the same concrete elements. In this context, an *equivalence class* corresponds to a set of equivalent abstract elements, called *representatives*. Although all representatives are equivalent, they may not be identically treated by abstract operators or transfer functions, which implies that the choice of a "bad" representative may cause a loss of precision. Most numerical domains (for instance, reduced product [5]) are provided with a reduction operator which associates each abstract element to a "good" equivalent element, which will allow gaining precision.

Unfortunately, in some abstract domains, it may not be possible to define a precise reduction operator, because for some equivalence classes, the notion of "good" representatives may depend on further analysis steps, or on parts of the program not yet analyzed. This difficulty appears in abstract domains based on universally quantified predicates ranging over (a possibly unbounded number of) consecutive array elements (first introduced in [6]). The abstract elements of these domains consist of a predicate $\mathbf{p}$ and two parameters u and v: $\mathbf{p}(u, v)$ means that all the elements whose index is between u and v (both included) contain values for which the statement $\mathbf{p}$ holds. These predicates are then combined with classic numerical abstractions to bind their parameters to the values of the program variables.

S. Drossopoulou (Ed.): ESOP 2008, LNCS 4960, pp. 163–177, 2008.

```
1:   int i, n, p; bool t[n];
2:   assert 0 <= p <= n;
3:   i := 0;
4:   while i < n do
5:      t[i] := 0;
6:      i := i+1;
7:   done;
8:   while i > p do
9:      t[i-1] := 1;
10:     i := i-1;
11:  done;
12:
```

```
int i, n; bool t[n];
i := 0;
while i < n do
   t[i] := 0;
   i := i+1;
done;
while ... do
   if ... then
      write_one();
   else
      write_zero();
   end;
done;
```

```
write_one() {
   if i > 0 then
      t[i-1] := 1;
      i := i-1;
   end;
}

write_zero() {
   if i < n then
      t[i] := 0;
      i := i+1;
   end;
}
```

Fig. 1. Incrementing then decrementing array manipulations

Fig. 2. Both incrementing and decrementing array manipulations. The notation ... stands for a non-deterministic condition.

Overview of the Problem. As an example, let us try to analyze the first loop of the program given in Fig. 1, which initializes the array t with the boolean 0. For that purpose, we introduce the predicate **zero** (which means that the associated array elements contain the value 0), combined with the affine inequality domain. Informally, the loop invariant consists in joining the abstract representations Σ_k of the concrete memory states arising after exactly k loop iterations. For example, after one loop iteration ($k = 1$), the instruction t[i] := 0 has assigned a zero to the array element of index 0, so that **zero**(u, v), with $u = v = 0$, $i = 1$ and $n \geq 1$. Similarly, after ten loop iterations, the ten first array elements have been initialized, thus **zero**(u, v), with $u = 0$, $v = 9$, $i = 10$ and $n \geq 10$. It can be shown that joining all the abstract states Σ_k with $k \geq 1$, *ie* which have entered the loop at least once, yields the invariant **zero**(u, v), with $u = 0$, $v = i - 1$, and $1 \leq i \leq n$. We now have to join this invariant with Σ_0 to obtain the whole loop invariant. The abstract state Σ_0 represents the concrete memory states which have not entered the loop. Since the array t is not initialized, Σ_0 is necessarily represented by a *degenerate* predicate, *ie* a predicate **zero**(l, m) such that $l > m$, which ranges over an empty set of array elements. Degenerate predicates naturally form an equivalence class, containing an infinite number of representatives, while non-degenerate predicates form classes containing a unique representative. Now, choosing the degenerate predicate **zero**(u, v) with $u = 0$, $v = -1$, $i = 0$, and $n \geq 0$, to represent Σ_0, yields the expected loop invariant $u = 0$, $v = i$, and $0 \leq i \leq n$. On the contrary, if we choose **zero**(u, v) with $u = 10$, $v = 9$, $i = 0$, and $n \geq 0$, we obtain an invariant **zero**(u, v) with much less precise affine inequality relations, in which, in particular, the value of u is not known exactly anymore (it ranges between 0 and 10). Therefore, the representative **zero**$(0, -1)$ is a judicious choice in the first loop analysis. But choosing the same representative for the second loop analysis will lead to a major loss of precision. The second loop partly initializes the array with the boolean 1 between from the index $n-1$ to the index p. Using a predicate **one** to represent array elements containing the value 1, the analysis yields the expected invariant only if the representative $\mathbf{one}(t, s)$ with $t = n$ and $s = n - 1$ is chosen to represent the class of degenerate predicates **one**.

This example illustrates that the choice of right representatives for the degenerate classes to avoid loss of precision, is not an obvious operation, even for simple one-dimensional array manipulations. In [6,7], some solutions are proposed to overcome the problem: (i) use heuristics to introduce the right degenerate predicates. This solution is clearly well-suited for the analysis of programs involving very few different natures of loops, such as incrementing loops always starting from the index 0 of the arrays, but is not adapted for more complex array manipulations. In particular, we will see in Sect. 4 that even classic matrix manipulation algorithms involve various different configurations for degenerate predicates. (ii) partition degenerate and non-degenerate predicates, instead of merging them in a single (and convex) representation. However such a disjunction may lead to an algorithmic explosion, since at least one disjunction has to be preserved for each predicate, including at control points located after loops: for example, the expected invariant at the control point 12 in Fig. 1 is $\mathbf{zero}(u, v) \wedge \mathbf{one}(s, t)$ with $u = 0$, $v = p - 1$, $s = p$, and $t = n - 1$. Without further information on n and p, this invariant contains non-degenerate and degenerate configurations of both predicates $\mathbf{zero}(u, v)$ and $\mathbf{one}(s, t)$. Partitioning these configurations yields the disjunction $(n = p = 0) \vee (n > p = 0) \vee (p = n > 0) \vee (0 < p < n)$. And, if the program contains instructions after control point 12, the disjunction must be propagated through the rest of the program analysis. Therefore, this approach may not scale up to programs manipulating many arrays.[1] (iii) partition traces [8], for instance unroll loops, in order to distinguish traces in which non-degenerate predicates are inferred, from others. This solution is adapted to simple loops: as an example, for the loop located at control point 4 in Fig. 1, degenerate predicates occur only in the trace which does not enter the loop. But, in general, it may be difficult to automatically discover well-suited trace partitions: for example, in Fig. 2, traces in which the functions `write_one` and `write_zero` are called the same number of times, or equivalently, $i = n$, should be distinguished from others, since they contain a degenerate form of the predicate **one**. Besides, if traces are not ultimately merged, trace partitioning may lead to an algorithmic explosion for the same reasons as state partitions, while merging traces amounts to the problem of merging non-degenerate and degenerate predicates in a non-disjunctive way.

As we aim at building an efficient and automatic static analysis, we do not consider any existing solution as fully satisfactory.

Contributions. We present a numerical abstract domain to be combined with array predicates. It represents sets of equivalence classes of predicates, by inferring

[1] However, some techniques could allow merging disjunctions in certain cases. We will see at the end of Sect. 3 that these techniques coincide with the join operation that we develop in this paper.

affine invariants on some representatives of each class. In particular, the right representatives are automatically discovered, without any heuristics. As it is built as an extension of the affine equality constraint domain [3,9], it does not use any disjunctive representations. Several abstract transfer functions are defined, all are proven to be sound. This domain allows the construction and the implementation of a sound static analysis of array manipulations. It is adapted to array predicates ranging over the elements of one-dimensional or two-dimensional arrays. Our work does not focus on handling a very large and expressive family of predicates relative to the content of the array itself, but rather on the complexity due to the automatic discovery of affine relations among program variables and predicate parameters, hence of right representatives for degenerate predicates. Therefore, the analysis has been experimented on programs traversing arrays and matrices in various ways. In all cases, the most precise invariants are discovered, which proves the robustness of our approach.

Section 2 presents the principles of the representation of equivalence classes of array predicates. Section 3 introduces the domain of *formal affine spaces* to abstract sets of equivalence classes of array predicates by affine invariants on some of their representatives. In Sect. 4, the construction of the array analysis and experiments are discussed. Finally, related work is presented in Sect. 5.

2 Principles of the Representation

As explained in Sect. 1, array predicates are related by an equivalence relation, depending on their nature (degenerate or non-degenerate): for an one-dimensional array predicate $\mathbf{p}$, two representations $\mathbf{p}(u, v)$ and $\mathbf{p}(u', v')$ are equivalent if and only if both are degenerate, *ie* $u > v \wedge u' > v'$, or they are equal ($u = u' \wedge v = v'$). More generally, given predicates with p parameters, we assume that there exists an equivalence relation $\sim$ over $\mathbb{R}^{\mathsf{p}}$, defining the equivalence of two numerical p-tuples of predicate parameters.

Given a program with n scalar variables, a memory state can be represented by an element of $\mathbb{R}^{\mathsf{n}+\mathsf{p}}$, where each scalar variable is associated to one of the n first dimensions, and array predicate parameters are mapped to the p last ones. Then, the equivalence relation $\sim$ can be extended to $\mathbb{R}^{\mathsf{n}+\mathsf{p}}$ to characterize memory states which are provided with equivalent predicates: two memory states M, N in $\mathbb{R}^{\mathsf{n}+\mathsf{p}}$ are equivalent, which is denoted by $M \simeq N$, if and only if M and N coincide on their n first dimensions, and if the p-tuples formed by the p last dimensions are equivalent w.r.t. $\sim$. We adopt the notation $[M]$ to represent the equivalence class of M, *ie* the set of elements equivalent to M.

We have seen in Sect. 1 that the representation of equivalence classes by arbitrarily-chosen representative elements may lead to a very complex invariant, possibly not precisely representable in classic numerical domains. Our solution consists in representing an equivalence class by a *formal representative* instead: it consists in a $(\mathsf{n}+\mathsf{p})$-tuple, whose n first coordinates contain values in $\mathbb{R}$, while the p last ones (related to predicate parameters) contain *formal variables*, taken in a given set $\mathcal{X}$. A formal representative R is provided with a set of valuations over $\mathcal{X}$: each valuation ν maps R to a point $R\nu$ of $\mathbb{R}^{\mathsf{n}+\mathsf{p}}$, by replacing each formal variable x in R by the value $\nu(x) \in \mathbb{R}$. Then, an equivalence class C can be represented by a formal representative R and a set of valuations V such that for any $\nu \in V$, the element $R\nu$ is in the class C. In other words, a formal representative can represent several elements of a same equivalence class.

Let us illustrate the principle of formal representative with the program in Fig. 1, with $\mathsf{n} = 3$ scalar variables i, n, and p. Consider the equivalence class of a memory state at control point 4 which has not yet entered the loop, thus in which the predicate $\mathbf{zero}(u, v)$ is degenerate, and in which, for instance, $i = 0$, $n = 10$, and $p = 5$. It can be represented by the formal representative $R = (0, 10, 5, x, y)$ (written as a row vector for reason of space) and the set of valuations $V = \{\nu \mid \nu(x) > \nu(y)\}$: indeed, each representative $R\nu$ corresponds to a predicate $\mathbf{zero}(u, v)$ such that $u > v$. In that case, all the equivalent numerical configurations for the degenerate predicate $\mathbf{zero}(u, v)$ are represented in the formal representative.

Therefore, formal representatives allow keeping several representatives for a given class C instead on focusing on only one of them. In the following sections, we define *formal affine spaces*, which extend the affine equality domain to range over formal representatives. These formal affine spaces are combined with sets of valuations represented by affine inequality constraints over $\mathcal{X}$, giving the right values for the representatives. Besides, we describe how to compute the formal affine spaces, so as to automatically discover affine invariants on some representatives of distinct equivalence classes.

3 Formal Affine Spaces

We now formally introduce the abstract domain to represent sets of equivalence classes of array predicates. We follow the abstract interpretation methodology [1], by defining a concretization operator, and then abstract operators such as union.

Let Δ be the set of equivalence classes w.r.t the equivalence relation $\simeq$, and $\Delta(\mathcal{X})$ be the set of formal representatives. Formally, $\Delta(\mathcal{X})$ is isomorphic to the cartesian product of $\mathbb{R}^{\mathsf{n}}$, representing the set of memory states over scalar variables, with $\mathcal{X}^{\mathsf{p}}$. Given a formal representative M, $\pi_1(M)$ represent the n-tuple consisting in the n first coordinates. This element of $\mathbb{R}^{\mathsf{n}}$ is called the *real component* of M. Besides, the p last coordinates of M forms $\pi_2(M)$, called *formal component* of M. Similarly, the ith coordinate of M is said to be *real* (respectively *formal*) if $\mathsf{i} \leq \mathsf{n}$ (resp. $\mathsf{i} > \mathsf{n}$).

While the affine equality domain was initially introduced using conjunctions of equality constraints [3], affine spaces can be represented by means of generators as well [9]. An *affine generator system* $E + \Omega$ is given by a family $E = (e_i)_{1 \leq i \leq s}$ of linearly independent vectors of $\mathbb{R}^{\mathsf{n}}$, and a point $\Omega \in \mathbb{R}^{\mathsf{n}}$. It is associated to the affine space defined by:

$$\mathsf{Span}(E + \Omega) = \left\{ \Omega + \sum_{i=1}^{s} \lambda_i e_i \mid \lambda_1, \ldots, \lambda_s \in \mathbb{R} \right\} , \quad (1)$$

$$\begin{matrix} \pi_1 \left\{ \begin{matrix} \\ \\ \\ \end{matrix} \right. \\ \pi_2 \left\{ \begin{matrix} \\ \\ \end{matrix} \right. \end{matrix} \left[\begin{pmatrix} 0 \\ 1 \\ 0 \\ x_1 \\ x_2 \end{pmatrix}, \begin{pmatrix} 0 \\ 0 \\ 1 \\ y_1 \\ y_2 \end{pmatrix} \right] + \begin{pmatrix} 0 \\ 0 \\ 0 \\ z_1 \\ z_2 \end{pmatrix} \mathrel{|} V$$

where $V = \{x_1 = x_2 \wedge y_1 = y_2 \wedge z_1 > z_2\}$

$$\begin{matrix} \pi_1 \left\{ \begin{matrix} \\ \\ \\ \end{matrix} \right. \\ \pi_2 \left\{ \begin{matrix} \\ \\ \end{matrix} \right. \end{matrix} \left[\begin{pmatrix} 0 \\ 1 \\ 0 \\ x'_1 \\ x'_2 \end{pmatrix}, \begin{pmatrix} 0 \\ 0 \\ 1 \\ y'_1 \\ y'_2 \end{pmatrix} \right] + \begin{pmatrix} 1 \\ 0 \\ 0 \\ z'_1 \\ z'_2 \end{pmatrix} \mathrel{|} V'$$

where $V' = \{x'_1 = x'_2 = 0 \wedge y'_1 = y'_2 = 0 \wedge z'_1 = z'_2 = 0\}$

Fig. 3. Two formal affine spaces for $\mathsf{n} = 3$ and $\mathsf{p} = 2$

corresponding to the set of the points generated by the addition of linear combinations of the vectors e_i to the point Ω. Affine generator systems are equivalent to sets of affine constraints. Indeed, the elimination of the λ_i in the combinations given in Eq. (1) yields an equivalent set of affine constraints over the coordinates of the points.

Formal affine spaces are defined by extending affine generator systems of $\mathbb{R}^{\mathsf{n}}$ with p formal coordinates: generators are now elements of $\Delta(\mathcal{X})$, provided with a set of valuations.

Definition 1. *A* formal affine space $E + \Omega \mathrel{|} V$ *is given by a family* $E = (e_1, \ldots, e_s)$ *of vectors of* $\Delta(\mathcal{X})$*, a point* Ω *of* $\Delta(\mathcal{X})$ *verifying:*

- *the* $(\pi_1(e_i))_{1 \leq i \leq s}$ *are linearly independent,*
- *any two formal variables occurring in* $(\pi_2(e_i))_i$ *and* $\pi_2(\Omega)$ *are distinct,*

and an affine inequality constraint system V *over the formal variables occurring in* $(\pi_2(e_i))_i$ *and* $\pi_2(\Omega)$.

Figure 3 gives an example of formal affine spaces. We abusively denote by $\nu \in V$ the fact that the valuation ν satisfies the constraint system V. Similarly to "classic" affine generator systems, a formal affine space $E + \Omega \mathrel{|} V$ generates a set of formal representatives, written as combinations $\Omega + \sum_i \lambda_i e_i$. As explained in Sect. 2, each formal representative R, provided with the set of valuations satisfying V, represents a set of several representatives which belong to a same equivalence class C: for any $\nu \in V$, $C = [R\nu]$. Following these principles, the concretization operator γ maps any formal space $E + \Omega \mathrel{|} V$ to the set of the equivalence classes represented by the generated formal representatives:

$$\gamma(E + \Omega \mathrel{|} V) \stackrel{def}{=} \{C \mid R \in \mathsf{Span}(E + \Omega) \wedge \forall \nu \in V.\ C = [R\nu]\} \ , \qquad (2)$$

where $\mathsf{Span}(E + \Omega)$ consists of the combinations $\Omega + \sum_{i=1}^{s} \lambda_i e_i$, for $\lambda_i \in \mathbb{R}$.

Example 1. Consider the formal affine space $E + \Omega \mathrel{|} V$ on the left-hand side of Fig. 3. Any combination in $\mathsf{Span}(E + \Omega)$ is a formal representative R of the form $(0, \lambda, \mu, \lambda x_1 + \mu y_1 + z_1, \lambda x_2 + \mu y_2 + z_2)$ (written as a row vector for reason of space) where $\lambda, \mu \in \mathbb{R}$. Suppose that the dimensions respectively represent the scalar variables i, n, p, and the parameters u and v of a predicate **zero**(u, v).

Then R represents the equivalence classes of memory states in which $i = 0$, n and p have independent values, and for any valuation $\nu \in V$,

$$u = \lambda\nu(x_1) + \mu\nu(y_1) + \nu(z_1) > \lambda\nu(x_2) + \mu\nu(y_2) + \nu(z_2) = v \ , \quad (3)$$

or equivalently, the predicate $\mathbf{zero}(u, v)$ is degenerate. In particular, $E + \Omega \mid V$ allows abstracting the memory states at control point 4 in Fig. 1 which have not yet entered the loop. Besides, it represents several representatives for the degenerate predicate $\mathbf{zero}(u, v)$, while a "classic" affine invariant would select only one of them. Similarly, the formal affine space $F + \Omega' \mid V'$ on the right-hand side of Fig. 3 yields formal representatives R' corresponding to classes of memory states such that $i = 1$, n and p are arbitrary, and $u = v = 0$, since for $i \in \{1, 2\}$, $\lambda\nu'(x'_i) + \mu\nu'(y'_i) + \nu'(z'_i) = 0$ for any valuation $\nu' \in V'$. Then, it is an abstraction of the memory states after the first iteration of the first body loop in Fig. 1: the first element of the array t (index 0) contains the value 0. □

3.1 Joining Two Formal Spaces

We wish to define a union operator $\sqcup$ which provides an over-approximation of two formal affine spaces $E + \Omega \mid V$ and $F + \Omega' \mid V'$. Let us illustrate the intuition behind the definition of $\sqcup$ by sufficient conditions.

Suppose that $G + O \mid W$ is the resulting formal space. A good start is to require $\sqcup$ to be sound w.r.t. the underlying real affine generator systems: if $\pi_1(G + O)$ denotes the real affine generator system obtained by applying π_1 on each vector g_i of G and on the origin, then $\pi_1(G + O)$ has to represent a larger affine space than those generated by $\pi_1(E + \Omega)$ and $\pi_1(F + \Omega')$. To ensure this condition, let us build $G + O \mid W$ by extending the *sum system* of the two real systems $\pi_1(E + \Omega)$ and $\pi_1(F + \Omega')$.[2] More precisely, if $G_r + O_r$ denotes the sum system, we add p fresh formal variables to each vector of G_r and to O_r, which yields $G + O$.

Then, to ensure $\gamma(E + \Omega \mid V) \subseteq \gamma(G + O \mid W)$, we require $\mathsf{Span}(E + \Omega)$ to be "included" in $\mathsf{Span}(G + O)$. Although the inclusion already holds for their real components ($\mathsf{Span}(\pi_1(E+\Omega)) \subseteq \mathsf{Span}(\pi_1(G+O))$), $\mathsf{Span}(E+\Omega)$ and $\mathsf{Span}(G+O)$ can not be directly compared since they may contain different formal variables. Therefore, we build a substitution σ_P over the formal variables occurring in $\pi_2(E + \Omega)$, such that for any $R \in \mathsf{Span}(E + \Omega)$, we have $R\sigma_P \in \mathsf{Span}(G + O)$. This substitution is induced by the *change-of-basis matrix* P from $\pi_1(E + \Omega)$ to $\pi_1(G+O)$, which verifies $\mathsf{mat}(\pi_1(E+\Omega)) = \mathsf{mat}(\pi_1(G+O)) \times P$ ($\mathsf{mat}(\pi_1(E+\Omega))$ is the matrix whose columns are formed by the vectors $(\pi_1(e_i))_i$ and $\pi_1(\Omega)$). The matrix P expresses the coefficients of the (unique) decomposition of each $\pi_1(e_i)$ and $\pi_1(\Omega)$ in terms of the $\pi_1(O)$ and $(\pi_1(g_k))_k$. It allows to express the

[2] The *sum system* is obtained by extracting a free family G_r from the vectors $(\pi_1(e_i))_i$, $(\pi_1(f_i))_j$, and $\pi_1(\Omega') - \pi_1(\Omega)$, and choosing $O_r = \pi_1(\Omega)$. Then, $G_r + O_r$ generates the smallest affine space greatest than the affine spaces represented by both $\pi_1(E + \Omega)$ and $\pi_1(F + \Omega')$.

$$P = \begin{pmatrix} 0\,0\,0 \\ 1\,0\,0 \\ 0\,1\,0 \\ 0\,0\,1 \end{pmatrix} \quad Q = \begin{pmatrix} 0\,0\,1 \\ 1\,0\,0 \\ 0\,1\,0 \\ 0\,0\,1 \end{pmatrix} \quad \forall i \in \{1,2\}. \begin{cases} \sigma_P(x_i) \mapsto \mathbf{y}_i \\ \sigma_P(y_i) \mapsto \mathbf{z}_i \\ \sigma_P(z_i) \mapsto \mathbf{t}_i \end{cases} \begin{cases} \sigma_Q(x'_i) \mapsto \mathbf{y}_i \\ \sigma_Q(y'_i) \mapsto \mathbf{z}_i \\ \sigma_Q(z'_i) \mapsto \mathbf{t}_i + \mathbf{x}_i \end{cases}$$

Fig. 4. Change-of-basis matrices and their associated substitutions

$\pi_2(e_i)$ and $\pi_2(\Omega)$ in terms of the $\pi_2(O)$ and $(\pi_2(g_k))_k$ as well, by defining σ_P by $\sigma_P(\mathsf{mat}(\pi_2(E+\Omega))) \overset{def}{=} \mathsf{mat}(\pi_2(G+O)) \times P$.

Now, it suffices that W be a stronger system of constraints than $V\sigma_P$, the system obtained by applying the substitution σ_P on V. Indeed, for any class $C \in \gamma(E+\Omega \mid V)$, there exists $R \in \mathsf{Span}(E+\Omega)$ such that for any $\nu \in V$, $C = [R\nu]$. Then, for any $\nu' \in W$, we have $\nu' \in V\sigma_P$, so that there exists a valuation $\nu \in V$ such that $\forall x.(\sigma_P(x))\nu' = \nu(x)$. This implies $(R\sigma_P)\nu' = R\nu$, hence $C = [(R\sigma_P)\nu']$. A similar reasoning can be performed for $F+\Omega' \mid V'$, which leads to the following definition of $\sqcup$:

Definition 2. *The union $(E+\Omega \mid V) \sqcup (F+\Omega' \mid V')$ is defined as the formal space $G+O \mid W$ where $\pi_1(G+O)$ is the sum of $\pi_1(E+\Omega)$ and $\pi_1(F+\Omega')$, yielding two change-of-basis matrices P and Q respectively, and W is the conjunction of the two systems of constraints $V\sigma_P$ and $V'\sigma_Q$.*

The following proposition states that the union operator is sound.

Proposition 1. *The union $(E+\Omega \mid V) \sqcup (F+\Omega' \mid V')$ over-approximates the union of the sets of classes represented by $E+\Omega \mid V$ and $F+\Omega' \mid V'$.*

Example 2. Consider the formal spaces $E+\Omega \mid V$ and $F+\Omega' \mid V'$ introduced in Ex. 1. The sum of the two real affine generator systems $\pi_1(E+\Omega)$ and $\pi_1(F+\Omega')$ is a system in which i, n, and p are all independent, so that:

$$G+O \overset{def}{=} \begin{matrix} i \\ n \\ p \\ u \\ v \end{matrix} \left[\begin{pmatrix} 1 \\ 0 \\ 0 \\ \mathbf{x}_1 \\ \mathbf{x}_2 \end{pmatrix}, \begin{pmatrix} 0 \\ 1 \\ 0 \\ \mathbf{y}_1 \\ \mathbf{y}_2 \end{pmatrix}, \begin{pmatrix} 0 \\ 0 \\ 1 \\ \mathbf{z}_1 \\ \mathbf{z}_2 \end{pmatrix} \right] + \begin{pmatrix} 0 \\ 0 \\ 0 \\ \mathbf{t}_1 \\ \mathbf{t}_2 \end{pmatrix} . \tag{4}$$

The corresponding change-of-basis matrices P and Q are given in Fig. 4. In particular, these matrices represent the relation $\pi_1(\Omega') = \pi_1(O) + \pi_1(g_1)$, which generates the substitutions $z'_1 \mapsto \mathbf{t}_1 + \mathbf{x}_1$ and $z'_2 \mapsto \mathbf{t}_2 + \mathbf{x}_2$. The associated substitutions σ_P and σ_Q are then defined in Fig. 4. Applying them on the constraint systems V and V' yields: $V\sigma_P = \{\mathbf{y}_1 = \mathbf{y}_2 \wedge \mathbf{z}_1 = \mathbf{z}_2 \wedge \mathbf{t}_1 > \mathbf{t}_2\}$ and $V'\sigma_Q = \{\mathbf{y}_1 = \mathbf{y}_2 = 0 \wedge \mathbf{z}_1 = \mathbf{z}_2 = 0 \wedge \mathbf{t}_1 + \mathbf{x}_1 = \mathbf{t}_2 + \mathbf{x}_2 = 0\}$, so that:

$$W = \{\mathbf{x}_1 = -\mathbf{t}_1 \wedge \mathbf{x}_2 = -\mathbf{t}_2 \wedge \mathbf{y}_1 = \mathbf{y}_2 = 0 \wedge \mathbf{z}_1 = \mathbf{z}_2 = 0 \wedge \mathbf{t}_1 > \mathbf{t}_2\} . \tag{5}$$

It can be intuitively verified that $G+O \mid W$ contains the formal spaces $E+\Omega \mid V$ and $F+\Omega' \mid V'$:

- when $i = 0$, we have $u = \mathbf{t}_1 + \lambda \mathbf{y}_1 + \mu \mathbf{z}_1$ and $v = \mathbf{t}_2 + \lambda \mathbf{y}_2 + \mu \mathbf{z}_2$ for some $\lambda, \mu \in \mathbb{R}$, so that for any $\nu \in W$, $u\nu = \nu(\mathbf{t}_1) > \nu(\mathbf{t}_2) = v\nu$. Then the predicate $\mathbf{zero}(u, v)$ is degenerate.
- when $i = 1$, we have $u = \mathbf{t}_1 + \mathbf{x}_1 + \lambda \mathbf{y}_1 + \mu \mathbf{z}_1$ and $v = \mathbf{t}_2 + \mathbf{x}_2 + \lambda \mathbf{y}_2 + \mu \mathbf{z}_2$, hence $u\nu = v\nu = 0$ for any valuation $\nu \in W$. In that case, the predicate $\mathbf{zero}(u, v)$ ranges over the first element of the array.

The resulting formal space $G + O \mid W$ is an over-approximation of the memory states arising at control point 4 in Fig. 1, after at most one loop iteration.

We could show that joining $E + \Omega \mid V$ with the formal space resulting from the loop body execution on $G + O \mid W$, yields the affine space $G + O \mid W'$, where $W' = \{\mathbf{x}'_1 = 0 \wedge \mathbf{x}'_2 = 1 \wedge \mathbf{y}'_1 = \mathbf{y}'_2 = 0 \wedge \mathbf{z}'_1 = \mathbf{z}'_2 = 0 \wedge \mathbf{t}'_1 = 0 \wedge \mathbf{t}'_2 = -1\}$. It could be also verified that this affine space is a fixpoint of the loop transfer function. It represents the expected invariant $u = 0$ and $v = i - 1$. In particular, the computation automatically discovers the right representative $\mathbf{zero}(0, -1)$ (obtained with $i = 0$) among all the representatives $\mathbf{zero}(u, v)$ such that $u > v$ contained in $E + \Omega \mid V$. □

Definition 2 and Ex. 2 raise some remarks. Firstly, when considering increasing formal affine spaces, the underlying real affine generators are logically growing, while the sets of valuations become smaller (the constraint system becomes stronger). Intuitively, this corresponds to an increasing determinism in the choice of the representatives in the equivalence classes abstracted by the formal space. In particular, when considering formal spaces obtained by iterating an increasing transfer function to compute a global invariant, two cases (among possibly more) are singular: when the set of valuations is reduced to a singleton, and when this set is empty. In the former, the formal affine space coincide with an affine generator system over $\mathbb{R}^{\mathsf{n}+\mathsf{p}}$: in other words, some representatives in the over-approximated equivalence classes are bound with program variables by an affine invariant. This situation happens at the end of Ex. 2, in which $u = 0$ and $v = i - 1$ in the affine space over-approximating the loop invariant. In the latter case, the discovery of an affine invariant failed: by definition of γ, the concretization of the formal space is the entire set Δ.

Secondly, consider the two abstract memory states that we tried to join in Sect. 1 to compute an invariant of the first loop in Fig. 1: on the one hand, a degenerate predicate $\mathbf{zero}(u, v)$ with $i = 0$, and on the other hand, a non-degenerate one $\mathbf{zero}(u, v)$ with $u = 0$, $v = i - 1$, and $1 \leq i \leq n$. We could verify that joining the two representations by means of formal spaces, and in particular, computing the conjunction of the two corresponding constraint systems $V\sigma_P$ and $V'\sigma_Q$, exactly amounts to check whether the affine relations $u = 0$ and $v = i - 1$ match the degenerate condition $u > v$ when $i = 0$. More generally, when it succeeds, the approach based on matching degenerate condition coincides with the operations performed when joining two formal spaces. The major advantage of formal affine spaces is that it is adapted to any program or coding style, while matching degenerate conditions may fail. For example, let us consider the piece of program `i := n-1; if ... then t[i] := 0; i := i-1; fi;`. The matching approach would check if the non-degenerate invariant $\mathbf{zero}(u, v) \wedge u =$

$v = i + 1 = n - 1$ match the degenerate condition when $i = n - 1$, which is obviously false.

3.2 Precision and Further Abstract Operators

All usual abstract operators can be defined on formal affine spaces. For reason of space, we only give an enumeration. First, a partial order $\sqsubseteq$, defined in a similar way to the union operator, can be introduced. Then, the concretization γ can be shown to be monotonic, and the union $\sqcup$ is the best possible join operator w.r.t. the order $\sqsubseteq$. Furthermore, the definition of guard, constraint satisfiability, and assignment operations closely follows the definition of the same primitives on real affine generator systems [3,9], thus their design is simple. The main difference is that guards, satisfiability and assignments over predicate parameters involve operations on both the family of generators and the system of constraints representing the sets of valuations. For the latter, only usual operators, such as assignments or extracting a valuation satisfying the set of constraints, are necessary. All the operators on formal affine spaces are proven to be conservative. Moreover, exactness holds for guards, satisfiability, and invertible assignments, when they are applied to a formal affine space whose system of constraints representing the valuations is satisfiable.

4 Application to the Analysis of Array Manipulations

Formal affine spaces has been implemented to analyze array manipulation programs. The analysis computes abstract memory states consisting in a finite sequence of predicates, and a formal affine space over the program variables and the predicate parameters. Note that a reduced product of formal affine spaces with convex polyhedra [4] over scalar variables is used to increase precision, since affine generator systems do not precisely handle inequality guards.

Array assignments (*ie* assignments of the form `t[i] := e`) introduce new predicates in the abtract state (intuitively, non-degenerate predicates of the form $\mathbf{p}(u, v)$ with $u = v = i$). Then, some predicates may represent contiguous memory areas of a same array, and thus can be merged in a single predicate. The situations in which two predicates $\mathbf{p}$ and $\mathbf{q}$ can be merged correspond to simple geometric configurations. Two of these configurations for one- and two-dimensional are depicted respectively at the top and the bottom of Fig. 5.

All these situations can be expressed as conjunctions of affine equality constraints over the parameters of the two predicates. When these constraints are satisfied, a new predicate $\mathbf{p} \curlyvee \mathbf{q}$ is introduced in the abstract state. The statement $\mathbf{p} \curlyvee \mathbf{q}$ itself over-approximates $\mathbf{p}$ and $\mathbf{q}$: it expresses a property on the values of the array element which is weaker than those expressed by $\mathbf{p}$ and $\mathbf{q}$. And its parameters are initialized to fit the whole area obtained by concatenating the memory areas corresponding to $\mathbf{p}$ and $\mathbf{q}$. Finally, the predicates $\mathbf{p}$ and $\mathbf{q}$ and their parameters are removed from the abstract state.

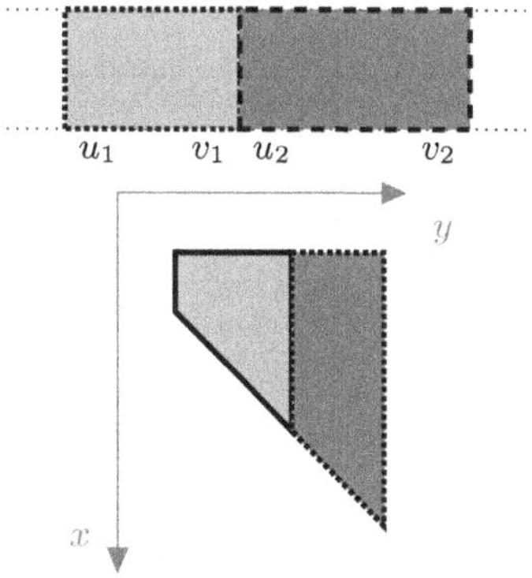

Fig. 5. Merging two contiguous predicates

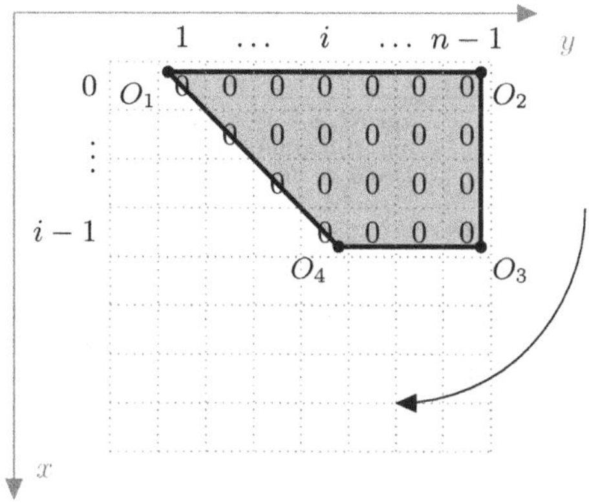

Fig. 6. Example of a two-dimensional predicate

One-dimensional Predicates. Two kinds of predicates are used to analyze array manipulations, depending on the type of arrays.

For arrays whose elements take their values in a finite set of cardinal K (such as booleans or C enumerations), we consider one predicate $\mathbf{c}$ per possible value. Then $\mathbf{c}(u, v)$ states that the array contains the value c between the indices u and v. We allow at most K pairwise distinct predicates $\mathbf{c}_1, \ldots, \mathbf{c}_K$ per array. The merging operations are applied only to predicates representing the same constant. Besides, if two predicates $\mathbf{c}(u_1, v_1)$ and $\mathbf{c}(u_2, v_2)$ ranging over the same array can not be merged, they are simply removed from the abstract state. Although this choice is very strict, it offers a tractable analysis, which is precise enough to handle the examples given in Figs. 1 and 2, as reported in Table 1.

For integer arrays, conjunctions of interval and bounded difference constraints (*ie* of the form $c_1 \leq x \leq c_2$ or $c_1 \leq x - y \leq c_2$) between the array content and the scalar variables are used. For instance, the predicate $\langle 0 \leq t \leq n-1 \rangle\,(u, v)$ represents the fact that the elements of the array t located between the indices u and v all contain values between 0 and $n - 1$ (n being a program scalar variable). Such predicates are implemented under the form of $\mathsf{n} + 1$ intervals: one to bound the array values in an interval, n to bound the differences with the n scalar variables. Then, the analysis allows at most one predicate per array. If a predicate associated to an array is introduced during the computation while this array already has a predicate, both are merged if possible, or simply removed if not. Moreover, to ensure termination, the statement $\mathbf{p} \curlyvee \mathbf{q}$ is obtained by pointwise widening the intervals contained in $\mathbf{p}$ and $\mathbf{q}$.

Two-dimensional Predicates. We use two-dimensional predicates which range over convex quadrilateral areas of two-dimensional arrays. Predicates are of the form $\mathbf{p}(O_1, O_2, O_3, O_4)$, and have now eight parameters, corresponding the x- and y-coordinates of the associated vertices O_1, O_2, O_3, and O_4. Degenerate and non-degenerate predicates are distinguished by the rotation direction of the

Table 1. Analysis benchmarks

Programs	Invariants (by default, at the end of the program)	Time
Fig. 1	$\mathbf{zero}(0, p-1) \wedge \mathbf{one}(p, n-1)$	~ 0.6 s
Fig. 2	outer loop invariant: $\mathbf{zero}(0, i-1) \wedge \mathbf{one}(i, n-1)$	~ 0.7 s
`full_init`	i. and d. $\langle 0 \le t \le n-1 \rangle\, (0, n-1)$	< 0.2 s
`range_init`	i. and d. $\langle p \le t \le q-1 \rangle\, (p, q-1)$	< 0.2 s
`partial_init`	i. $\langle 0 \le t \le n-1 \rangle\, (0, j-1)$ and d. $\langle 0 \le t \le n-1 \rangle\, (j, n-1)$	~ 0.2 s
`partition`	i. $\langle ge \ge 0 \rangle\, (0, gelen-1) \wedge \langle lt \le -1 \rangle\, (0, ltlen-1)$	~ 0.4 s
	d. $\langle ge \ge 0 \rangle\, (gelen, n-1) \wedge \langle lt \le -1 \rangle\, (ltlen, n-1)$	~ 0.5 s
`full_matrix`	r. $\langle m = 0 \rangle\, ((0,0), (0, n-1), (n-1, n-1), (n-1, 0))$	12.9 s
	c.. $\langle m = 0 \rangle\, ((n-1, 0), (0,0), (0, n-1), (n-1, n-1))$	13.4 s
`lower_triang`	r. $\langle m = 0 \rangle\, ((0,1), (0, n-1), (i-1, n-1), (i-1, i))$	12.6 s
(outer loop	c. $\langle m = 0 \rangle\, ((0,1), (0,1), (0, j-1), (j-2, j-1))$	14.7 s
invariants)	dg. $\langle m = 0 \rangle\, ((0,1), (0, k-1), (n-k, n-1), (n-2, n-1))$	11.3 s
`upper_triang`	r. $\langle m = 0 \rangle\, ((1,0), (1,0), (i-1, i-2), (i-1, 0))$	14.6 s
(outer loop	c. $\langle m = 0 \rangle\, ((n-1, 0), (1,0), (j, j-1), (n-1, j-1))$	13.1 s
invariants)	dg. $\langle m = 0 \rangle\, ((n-1, 0), (n-k+1, 0), (n-1, k-2), (n-1, 0))$	15.0 s

points O_1, O_2, O_3, and O_4. We use the convention that the interior of the polygon $O_1O_2O_3O_4$ is not empty if and only if O_1, O_2, O_3, and O_4 are ordered clockwise, as in Fig. 6. The shape of the polygons $O_1O_2O_3O_4$ is restricted by requirements, not fully detailed here, but implying in particular that the coordinates of the O_i are integer, and the lines (O_iO_{i+1}) are either horizontal, vertical, or diagonal. These requirements are weak enough to express the invariants used in the targeted algorithms. Moreover, they allow characterizing degenerate polygons by a condition consisting of several affine inequalities over the predicate parameters.

The analysis allows for each matrix at most two predicates: one is one-dimensional, while the other is two-dimensional. Indeed, the matrix algorithms we wish to analyze performs intermediate manipulations on rows, columns, or diagonals. Thus, the former predicate is used to represent the invariant on the current one-dimensional structure, while the latter collects the information on the older structures, which form a two-dimensional shape. The predicates propagate bounded difference constraints relative to the matrix content.

Benchmarks. Table 1 reports the invariants discovered by our analyzer, implemented in Objective Caml (5000 lines of code), and the time taken for each analysis on a 1 Gb RAM laptop using one core of a 2 GHz Intel Pentium Core Duo processor. The first six programs involve only one-dimensional arrays. The two first programs are successfully analyzed using constant predicates, and the right array shape is discovered. The third one, `full_init`, initializes each element `t[i]` of the array `t` of size `n` with the value `i`. It results in a fully initialized array with values ranging between 0 and $n-1$. The program `range_init` has a similar behavior, except that it performs the initialization between the indices `p` and `q` only. The programs `partial_init` and `partition` are taken from [7] and [10] respectively. The former copies the value `i` in `t[j]` when the values of two other arrays `a[i]` and `b[i]` are equal, and then increments `j`. The latter partitions the positive or null and strictly negative values of a source array `a` into the destination arrays `ge` and `lt` respectively. The three last programs involve matrices. The first one, `full_matrix`, fully initializes a matrix `m` of size $n \times n$. The two last ones only fill the upper- and lower-triangular part of the matrix with the value 0. Each program contains two nested loops. As an illustration, the invariant of the outer loop of the column-after-column version of `lower_triang` discovered by the analysis is given in Fig. 6. The reader can verify that the final invariant obtained for $i = n - 1$ corresponds to a lower-triangular matrix. Several versions of each program are analyzed: for one-dimensional array manipulation algorithms, incrementing (i.) or decrementing (d.) loops (except for the programs in Figs. 1 and 2 which already use both versions of loops), and for matrix manipulation loops, row-after-row (r.), column-after-column (c.), or diagonal-after-diagonal (dg.) matrix traversal.[3] All the examples involving one-dimensional arrays only are successfully analyzed in less than a second. Analysis time does not exceed 15 s on programs manipulating matrices, which is a good result, considering the complexity of the merge conditions for two-dimensional predicates, and the fact that these programs contain nested loops. These benchmarks show that the analysis is sufficiently robust to discover the excepted invariant for several stategies of array or matrix manipulations programs. In particular, the right representatives for degenerate predicates are automatically found out in various and complex situations. As an example, the degenerate predicates discovered for the programs `lower_triang` (obtained with $i = 0$, $j = 1$, and $k = 1$) and `upper_triang` (obtained with $i = 1$, $j = 0$, and $k = 1$) all represent different configurations of interior-empty quadrilateral shapes. Furthermore, although not reported in Table 1, the analysis handles simple transformations (such as loop unrolling) on the experimented programs, without any loss of precision. Finally, for one-dimensional predicates, we have experimented, with formal affine spaces, the manual substitution of the general degenerate condition $u > v$ by the right degenerate configurations for each program. In that case, operations on formal affine spaces roughly coincide with operations in a usual equality constraint domain. We have found that the additional cost in time due to formal affine spaces is small (between 8% and 30%), which suggests that this numerical abstract domain has good performance, while it automatically discovers the right representatives.

5 Related Work

Several static analyses use predicates to represent memory shape properties: among others, [11,12,13,14,15] infer elaborate invariants on dynamic memory structures, such as lists and trees. Most of these works do not involve a precise treatment of arrays. Some abstract interpretation based analyzers [16,17,18] precisely handle manipulations of arrays whose size is exactly known. Besides, [17] can represent all the array elements by a single abstract element (*array smashing*). Albeit not very precise, it could also represent an unbounded number of array elements.

To our knowledge, only [19,6,7,20,10,21] handle precise properties ranging over an unbounded number of one-dimensional array elements. Most of them involve the predicates presented in this paper, and some other expressing more properties on the values of the array elements, such as equality, sorting or pointer

[3] The source code of each program is available at `http://www.lix.polytechnique.fr/Labo/Xavier.Allamigeon`

aliasing properties. The approach of [19,20,10] differs ours in the use of a theorem prover in order to abstract reachable states in [19], and of counterexample-guided abstraction refinement in [20,10]. They share with our analysis common benchmarks: for example, [20,10] analyzes the program `full_init` in respectively 1.190 s and 0.27 s, and `partition` in 7.960 s and 3.6 s.[4] The returned invariants are the same as those given in Table 1. The other works [6,7,21] use the abstract interpretation framework. The analysis developed in [21] involves predicates on arrays and lists, and allows expressing invariants of the form $E \wedge \bigwedge_j \forall U_j (F_j \Rightarrow e_j)$, where E, F_j and e_j are quantifier-free facts. This approach is more general than ours, since it automatically discovers universally quantified predicates, while we explicitely define the family of predicates (uni- or two-dimensional) in our analysis. The drawback is that it requires under-approximation abstract domains and associated operators because of the universal quantification. In constrast, our concretization operator (defined in (2)) involves a universal quantifier over valuations $\nu \in V$, which can be shown to commute with the existential quantifier $\exists R \in \mathsf{Span}(E + \Omega)$. Then, *exact* operations on the inequality constraint systems representing the valuations, such as intersections or assignments, yield sound and precise results (see Sect. 3.2). In [21], `full_init` and `partition` are respectively analyzed in 3.2 s and 73.0 s on a 3 GHz machine, yielding the same invariants than with our analysis. In [6], semantic loop unrolling and introduction by heuristics of well-chosen degenerate predicates (called *tautologies*) are combined. It handles array initialization algorithm (the exact nature of the algorithm, partial, incrementing, decrementing, *etc*, is not mentionned), and bubble sort and QuickSort algorithms. In [7], array elements are distinguished according to their position w.r.t. to the current loop index (strictly before, equal to, or strictly after). This yields a partition of the memory configurations into distinct categories, which are characterized by the presence or the absence of array elements having a certain position w.r.t. to a loop index. The program `partial_init` is analyzed in 40 s on a 2.4 GHz machine, and yields a partition of four memory configurations corresponding to the invariant given in Table 1. Finally, as far as we know, no existing work reports any experiments on two-dimensional array manipulation programs.

6 Conclusion

We have introduced a numerical abstract domain which allows to represent sets of equivalence classes of predicates, by inferring affine invariants on some representatives of each class, without any heuristics. Combined with array predicates, it has been experimented in a sound static analysis of array and matrix manipulation programs. Experimental results are very good, and the approach is sufficiently robust to handle several array traversing stategies. Future work will focus on the extension of the abstraction to other systems of generators, such as convex polyhedra, in order to incorporate the reduced product implemented in the analysis into the abstraction of equivalence classes.

[4] A 1.7 GHz machine was used in both works.

References

1. Cousot, P., Cousot, R.: Abstract interpretation: a unified lattice model for static analysis of programs by construction or approximation of fixpoints. In: POPL1977, Los Angeles, California, ACM Press, New York (1977)
2. Miné, A.: The octagon abstract domain. In: AST 2001 in WCRE 2001. IEEE, pp. 310–319. IEEE CS Press, Los Alamitos (2001)
3. Karr, M.: Affine relationships among variables of a program. Acta Inf. 6 (1976)
4. Cousot, P., Halbwachs, N.: Automatic discovery of linear restraints among variables of a program. In: POPL 1978, Tucson, Arizona, USA, ACM Press, New York (1978)
5. Cousot, P., Cousot, R.: Abstract interpretation and application to logic programs. Journal of Logic Programming 13(2–3), 103–179 (1992)
6. Cousot, P.: Automatic Verification by abstract interpretation. In: Zuck, L.D., Attie, P.C., Cortesi, A., Mukhopadhyay, S. (eds.) VMCAI 2003. LNCS, vol. 2575, pp. 20–24. Springer, Heidelberg (2002)
7. Gopan, D., Reps, T., Sagiv, M.: A framework for numeric analysis of array operations. SIGPLAN Not. 40(1) (2005)
8. Mauborgne, L., Rival, X.: Trace Partitioning in Abstract Interpretation Based Static Analyzers. In: Sagiv, M. (ed.) ESOP 2005. LNCS, vol. 3444, Springer, Heidelberg (2005)
9. Müller-Olm, M., Seidl, H.: A Note on Karr's Algorithm. In: Díaz, J., Karhumäki, J., Lepistö, A., Sannella, D. (eds.) ICALP 2004. LNCS, vol. 3142, Springer, Heidelberg (2004)
10. Beyer, D., Henzinger, T.A., Majumdar, R., Rybalchenko, A.: Path invariants. In: PLDI 2007, ACM Press, New York (2007)
11. Sagiv, S., Reps, T.W., Wilhelm, R.: Parametric shape analysis via 3–valued logic. In: POPL 1999 (1999)
12. Ball, T., Majumdar, R., Millstein, T., Rajamani, S.K.: Automatic predicate abstraction of C programs. SIGPLAN Not. 36(5) (2001)
13. Distefano, D., O'Hearn, P.W., Yang, H.: A local shape analysis based on separation logic. In: Hermanns, H., Palsberg, J. (eds.) TACAS 2006. LNCS, vol. 3920, Springer, Heidelberg (2006)
14. Berdine, J., Calcagno, C., Cook, B., Distefano, D., O'Hearn, P., Wies, T., Yang, H.: Shape analysis for composite data structures. In: Damm, W., Hermanns, H. (eds.) CAV 2007. LNCS, vol. 4590, Springer, Heidelberg (to appear, 2007)
15. Beyer, D., Henzinger, T.A., Théoduloz, G.: Lazy shape analysis. In: Huang, D.-S., Li, K., Irwin, G.W. (eds.) ICIC 2006. LNCS (LNAI), vol. 4114, Springer, Heidelberg (2006)
16. Venet, A., Brat, G.: Precise and efficient static array bound checking for large embedded C programs. In: PLDI 2004, ACM Press, New York (2004)
17. Cousot, P., Cousot, R., Feret, J., Mauborgne, L., Miné, A., Monniaux, D., Rival, X.: The ASTRÉE Analyser. In: Sagiv, M. (ed.) ESOP 2005. LNCS, vol. 3444, Springer, Heidelberg (2005)
18. Allamigeon, X., Godard, W., Hymans, C.: Static Analysis of String Manipulations in Critical Embedded C Programs. In: Yi, K. (ed.) SAS 2006. LNCS, vol. 4134, Springer, Heidelberg (2006)
19. Flanagan, C., Qadeer, S.: Predicate abstraction for software verification. In: POPL 2002, ACM Press, New York (2002)
20. Jhala, R., McMillan, K.L.: Array abstractions from proofs. In: Damm, W., Hermanns, H. (eds.) CAV 2007. LNCS, vol. 4590, Springer, Heidelberg (2007)
21. Gulwani, S., McCloskey, B., Tiwari, A.: Lifting abstract interpreters to quantified logical domains. In: POPL 2008 (to appear, 2008)

Upper Adjoints for Fast Inter-procedural Variable Equalities

Markus Müller-Olm[1] and Helmut Seidl[2]

[1] Westf. Wilhelms-Universität Münster, Mathematik und Informatik, 48149 Münster, Germany
mmo@math.uni-muenster.de
[2] TU München, Informatik, I2, 85748 Garching, Germany
seidl@in.tum.de

Abstract. We present a polynomial-time algorithm which at the extra cost of a factor $\mathcal{O}(k)$ (k the number of variables) generalizes inter-procedural copy constant propagation. Our algorithm infers variable-variable equalities in addition to equalities between variables and constants. Like copy constant propagation, it tracks constant and copying assignments but abstracts more complex assignments and guards. The algorithm is based on the observation that, for the abstract lattice of consistent equivalence relations, the upper adjoints of summary functions can be represented much more succinctly than summary functions themselves.

1 Introduction

The key task when realizing inter-procedural analyses along the lines of the functional approach of Sharir/Pnueli [13,8], is to determine the *summary functions* for procedures which describe their effects on the abstract program state before the call. Given a complete lattice $\mathbb{D}$ for the abstract program states, the summary functions are taken from the set of monotonic or (if we are lucky) distributive functions $\mathbb{D} \to \mathbb{D}$. This set is often large (if not infinite), rendering it a nontrivial task to identify a representation for summary functions which is efficiently supports basic operations such as function composition or function application to values of $\mathbb{D}$. Examples for such efficient representations are pairs of sets in case of gen/kill bit-vector problems [6] or vector spaces of matrices in case of affine equality analyses [11].

In this paper we present one further analysis where efficient representations of summary functions exist, namely, the analysis of variable-variable together with variable-constant equalities. This analysis is a generalization of copy constant propagation [6]. Based on the new analysis, register allocation can be enhanced to additionally remove certain register-register assignments. The idea is to allow the allocator to assign variables $\mathbf{x}$ and $\mathbf{y}$ to the same register, given that $\mathbf{x} = \mathbf{y}$ holds at each program point where both variables are live. This technique is known as *register coalescing* [3].

Example 1. Consider the program from Fig. 1. In this program, the variables $\mathbf{x}_2$ and $\mathbf{x}_3$ are both live at program point 3. Since $\mathbf{x}_2 = \mathbf{x}_3$ definitively holds at this program point, we can coalesce $\mathbf{x}_2, \mathbf{x}_3$ into a variable $\mathbf{y}$. By doing so, the assignment $\mathbf{x}_3 \leftarrow \mathbf{x}_2$ becomes $\mathbf{y} \leftarrow \mathbf{y}$ and thus can be removed. □

S. Drossopoulou (Ed.): ESOP 2008, LNCS 4960, pp. 178–192, 2008.

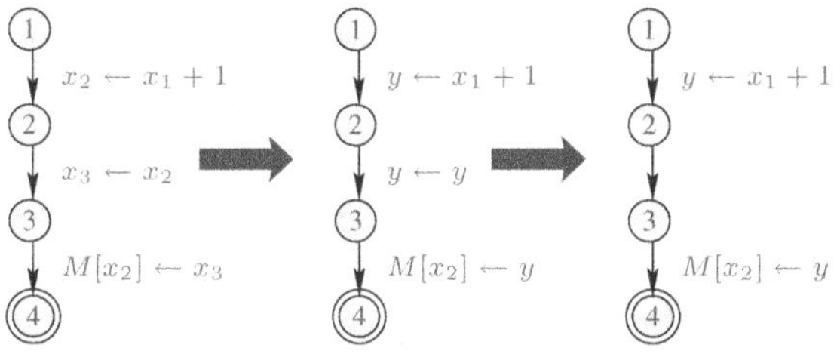

Fig. 1. A program with variable-variable assignments

The summary functions for inter-procedural equality analysis are completely distributive, i.e., commute with arbitrary least upper bounds. Also, the complete lattice of abstract values at program points is $\sqcup$-*atomic* (for a precise definition see below). Therefore, summary functions can (at least in principle) be represented through tabulation of their values for $\sqcup$-atoms. The number of these atoms, though, is exponential in the number of program variables — rendering this immediate idea as not practical.

In this paper, we report that summary functions for equality analysis can nonetheless be succinctly represented. The key idea is not to represent summary functions themselves, but their *upper adjoints* — a well-known construction from the theory of Galois connections which, for a completely $\sqcup$-distributive function, returns a completely $\sqcap$-distributive function. This construction has also been used for *demand-driven* program analyses [5,7]. It provides the solution in our application since the lattice in question has quadratically many $\sqcap$-atomic elements only, thus allowing for an efficient tabulation of upper adjoints. As a result, we obtain a fast inter-procedural equality analysis whose worst-case complexity is only one factor k (k the number of variables) slower than the fastest known algorithm for inferring copy constants [6].

Related work. Equality of variables can be considered as a particular case of a generalized analysis of availability of expressions, also called *value numbering* [1]. Originally, this analysis tracks for basic blocks the symbolic expressions representing the values of the variables assigned to. The key point is that operator symbols are left uninterpreted. The inferred equalities between variables and terms therefore are *Herbrand* equalities. Later, the idea of inferring Herbrand equalities was generalized to arbitrary control-flow graphs [14]. Only recently, this problem has attracted fresh attention. In [4], Gulwani and Necula show that the original algorithm of Steffen, Knoop and Rüthing can be turned into a polynomial time algorithm if one is interested in polynomially sized equalities between variables and terms only. Progress in a different direction was made in [10] and [12] where the authors generalize Herbrand equalities to deal with negative guards or side-effect free functions, respectively. Still, it is open whether full inter-procedural analysis of Herbrand equalities is possible.

On the other hand, when only assignments of variables and constants are tracked, the abstract domain can be chosen *finite* – thus implying computability of the analysis. The naive approach, however, results in an exponential-time algorithm. A less naive approach may interpret (or code) the constants as *numbers*. The problem then consists in inferring specific *affine* equalities between variables. The latter problem is known to

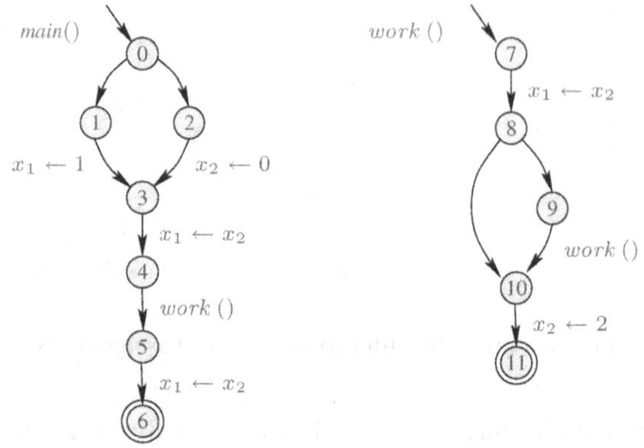

Fig. 2. An example program with procedures

be inter-procedurally decidable in polynomial time (given that each required arithmetic operation counts for $\mathcal{O}(1)$). The algorithm for this problem as presented in [11], however, has a factor k^8 in the worst-case complexity bound (k the number of variables). In the present paper we improve on this by reducing the exponent to 4 in the worst case — where sparse representations could be even more efficient.

This paper is organized as follows. After defining programs and their collecting semantics in Section 2, we introduce in Section 3 the complete lattice of consistent equivalence relations that is central for our approach. We discuss basic operations on this lattice and their complexity. Section 4 is concerned with representing summary functions as needed in our inter-procedural analysis. It turns out that in our scenario it is advantageous to represent summary functions not directly but by their upper adjoints. We then present in Section 5 our inter-procedural analysis. We extend our approach to local variables in Section 6. Section 7 summarizes and concludes.

2 Programs and Their Collecting Semantics

For this paper, we view programs as a finite collection of procedures f where each f is given by a finite control-flow graph as in Fig. 2. Each edge in the control-flow graphs is either labeled with a call $f()$ to a procedure f or with an assignment s. In pictures, we omit the label if it represents a skip operation $\mathbf{x}_i \leftarrow \mathbf{x}_i$. Let V denote the set of values the program uses in its computations. For technical reasons, we assume $|V| \geq 2$. Let $\mathbf{X} = \{\mathbf{x}_1, \ldots, \mathbf{x}_k\}$ be the set of global program variables. Later, we extend our approach to deal with local variables as well. In order to concentrate on the essentials of the analysis, we consider simplified programs only. So, we assume that conditional branching has already been abstracted to non-deterministic branching. Since our analysis only tracks variable-to-variable assignments and constant-to-variable assignments, we consider assignments $\mathbf{x}_i \leftarrow \mathbf{x}_j$, $\mathbf{x}_i \leftarrow c$ or $\mathbf{x}_i \leftarrow ?$ for variables $\mathbf{x}_i, \mathbf{x}_j \in \mathbf{X}$ and constants $c \in V$. Here the *non-deterministic* assignment $\mathbf{x}_i \leftarrow ?$ may assign *any* value to $\mathbf{x}_i$. This is used to abstract read operations which change the value of $\mathbf{x}_i$ in an unpredictable way or assignments of expressions that are not just a variable or constant. Note that the same class of programs is considered for *copy constant propagation* [6].

The *collecting semantics* of a program assigns to each program point v the set $\mathcal{C}[u]$ of program states which occur at u in an execution of the program. In our application, the variables $\mathbf{x}_1, \ldots, \mathbf{x}_k$ take values from the set V. Accordingly, an individual program state can be represented by a vector $(x_1, \ldots, x_k) \in V^k$ where x_i denotes the value of variable $\mathbf{x}_i$, and $\mathcal{C}[u]$ is a subset of V^k. The definition of the collecting semantics of a program is based on a specification of the effects $[\![s]\!]$ of assignments s onto the set of states in which s is to be executed. The effects of assignments are given by:

$$\begin{array}{ll} [\![\mathbf{x}_i \leftarrow ?]\!]\, Y &= \{x' \mid \exists x \in Y : \forall k \neq i : x'_k = x_k\} \\ [\![\mathbf{x}_i \leftarrow \mathbf{x}_j]\!]\, Y &= \{x' \mid \exists x \in Y : x'_i = x_j \wedge \forall k \neq i : x'_k = x_k\} \\ [\![\mathbf{x}_i \leftarrow c]\!]\, Y &= \{x' \mid \exists x \in Y : x'_i = c \wedge \forall k \neq i : x'_k = x_k\} \end{array}$$

A procedure f induces a transformation of the set of possible program states before the call to the set of program states that occur after the call if the procedure is called in any of these states. Here, we choose to collect this transformation *from the rear* and consider for each program point u of a procedure f, the transformation $\mathcal{S}[u] : 2^{V^k} \to 2^{V^k}$ induced by same-level program executions starting from u and reaching the procedure exit of f at the same level. Then, the transformation for procedure f is given by $\mathcal{S}[\mathsf{st}_f]$, where st_f is the entry point of f. The transformations $\mathcal{S}[u]$ are characterized as the least solution of the following system of in-equations:

$$\begin{array}{lll} \mathcal{S}[\mathsf{rt}_f] \supseteq \mathsf{Id} & & \mathsf{rt}_f \text{ exit point of procedure } f \\ \mathcal{S}[u] \supseteq \mathcal{S}[v] \circ \mathcal{S}[\mathsf{st}_f] & & (u, f(), v) \text{ a call edge, } \mathsf{st}_f \text{ entry point of } f \\ \mathcal{S}[u] \supseteq \mathcal{S}[v] \circ [\![s]\!] & & (u, s, v) \text{ an assignment edge} \end{array}$$

where $\mathsf{Id}\, X = X$ for every set of program states X and "$\supseteq$" is the pointwise extension of the superset relation to set-valued functions. Since the expressions on right-hand sides of all in-equations denote monotonic functions, the system of in-equations has a unique least solution by the Knaster-Tarski fixpoint theorem.

Assume that we are given the effects $\mathcal{S}[\mathsf{st}_f]$ of calls to the procedures f. Then these can be used to determine, for every program point u, the set of program states $\mathcal{C}[u] \subseteq V^k$ which possibly are attained when reaching u. These can be determined as the least solution of the following system of in-equations:

$$\begin{array}{lll} \mathcal{C}[\mathsf{st}_{main}] \supseteq V^k & & \\ \mathcal{C}[\mathsf{st}_f] \supseteq \mathcal{C}[u] & & (u, f(), \_) \text{ a call edge} \\ \mathcal{C}[v] \supseteq \mathcal{S}[\mathsf{st}_f]\,(\mathcal{C}[u]) & & (u, f(), v) \text{ a call edge} \\ \mathcal{C}[v] \supseteq [\![s]\!]\,(\mathcal{C}[u]) & & k = (u, s, v) \text{ an assignment edge}\,. \end{array}$$

3 The Abstract Domain

We are interested in equalities between variables and variables and between variables and constants. In order to express such properties, we introduce the complete lattice $\mathbb{E}(\mathbf{X}, V)$ (or $\mathbb{E}$ for short). Its least element $\bot$ describes the empty set of program states and represents that all conceivable equalities are valid. Thus, $\alpha(\emptyset) = \bot$ where $\alpha : 2^{V^k} \to \mathbb{E}$ is the function which maps sets of program states to their respective best description in $\mathbb{E}$. Every element $E \neq \bot$ in the lattice is an equivalence relation on $\mathbf{X} \cup V$ where constants are considered as pairwise distinct, i.e., non-equivalent. Let us call such an equivalence relation *consistent*. The consistent equivalence relation describing a set $\emptyset \neq X \subseteq 2^{V^k}$, is given by $\alpha(X)$ where $(\mathbf{x}_i, \mathbf{x}_j) \in \alpha(X)$ iff $x_i = x_j$ for all $(x_1, \ldots, x_k) \in X$ and $(\mathbf{x}_i, c) \in \alpha(X)$ for $c \in V$ iff $x_i = c$ for all $(x_1, \ldots, x_k) \in X$. Technically, we can represent a consistent equivalence relation E as an array (for simplicity also denoted by E) where $E[i] = c$ iff the equivalence class of $\mathbf{x}_i$ contains the constant $c \in V$ and $E[i] = \mathbf{x}_j$ for one representative variable $\mathbf{x}_j$ from the equivalence class of $\mathbf{x}_i$ if this class does not contain a constant. Then, two variables $\mathbf{x}_i$ and $\mathbf{x}_j$ belong to the same equivalence class iff $E[i] = E[j]$ and a variable $\mathbf{x}_i$ and a constant c belong to the same class iff $E[i] = c$. Logically, we can represent E by the conjunction of equalities $\mathbf{x}_i = E[i]$ for those $\mathbf{x}_i$ with $E[i] \neq \mathbf{x}_i$, i.e., by a conjunction of at most k equalities of the form $\mathbf{x}_i = \mathbf{x}_j$ or $\mathbf{x}_i = c$ for distinct variables $\mathbf{x}_i, \mathbf{x}_j$ and constants c.

On the set $\mathbb{E}$, we define an ordering $\sqsubseteq$ as implication, i.e., $E_1 \sqsubseteq E_2$ iff either $E_1 = \bot$ or E_1 is a consistent equivalence relation where every equality of E_2 is implied by the conjunction of equalities of E_1. Thus, the least upper bound of two consistent equivalence relations E_1, E_2 is the equivalence relation which is represented by the conjunction of all equalities implied by E_1 as well as by E_2. The greatest lower bound of two equivalence relations logically is given by their conjunction.

Not every two consistent equivalence relations have an other consistent equivalence relation as greatest lower bound. The conjunction of $\mathbf{x}_1 = 1$ and $\mathbf{x}_1 = 2$, e.g., equates the distinct constants 1 and 2. The greatest lower bound therefore is given by $\bot$ which thus logically denotes false. Note that the length h of a strictly increasing sequence:

$$\bot \sqsubset E_1 \sqsubset \ldots \sqsubset E_h$$

in $\mathbb{E}$ is bounded by $h \leq k + 1$ where k is the number of program variables.

Lemma 1. *1. The least upper bound $E_1 \sqcup E_2$ can be computed in time $\mathcal{O}(k)$.*
2. The greatest lower bound $E_1 \sqcap \ldots \sqcap E_n$ of n equivalence relations can be computed in time $\mathcal{O}((n + k) \cdot k)$.

Proof. W.l.o.g. assume that all E_i are different from $\bot$. The first assertion follows since we can determine, in linear time, for each variable $\mathbf{x}_i$, the pair $(E_1[i], E_2[i])$ giving us the pair of equivalence classes w.r.t. E_1 and E_2, respectively, to which $\mathbf{x}_i$ belongs. Then using bucket sort, the equivalence classes of $E = E_1 \sqcup E_2$ can be computed in time $\mathcal{O}(k)$. Let X denote a maximal set of variables all mapped to the same pair (t_1, t_2). If $t_1 = t_2 = c$ for a constant c, then $E[j] = c$ for all $\mathbf{x}_j \in X$. Otherwise, all variables in X are equal, but have unknown value. Therefore, we set, for each $\mathbf{x}_j \in X$, $E[j] = \mathbf{x}_i$ for some (e.g., the first) variable $\mathbf{x}_i \in X$.

An algorithm establishing the complexity bound of the second assertion works as follows. We start with one of the given equivalence relations $E = E_1$ and then successively add the at most $(n - 1) \cdot k$ equalities to represent the remaining equivalence relations. An algorithm for computing $(\mathbf{x}_i = t) \wedge E$ for (an array representation of) a consistent equivalence relation $E \neq \bot$ is presented in Fig. 3.

$$
\begin{array}{ll}
(\mathbf{x}_i = c) \wedge E & = \textbf{if } (E[i] = c' \in V) \ \textbf{if } (c = c') \ \textbf{return } E; \ \textbf{else return } \bot; \\
& \quad \textbf{else } \{ \quad /\!/ \ E[i] \text{ is a variable} \\
& \qquad X \leftarrow \{\mathbf{x}_j \mid E[j] = E[i]\}; \\
& \qquad \textbf{forall } (\mathbf{x}_j \in X) \ E[j] \leftarrow c; \\
& \qquad \textbf{return } E; \\
& \quad \} \\
(\mathbf{x}_i = \mathbf{x}_j) \wedge E & = \textbf{if } (E[i] = E[j]) \ \textbf{return } E; \\
& \quad \textbf{else if } (E[i] = c \in V) \ \textbf{if } (E[j] = c' \in V) \ \textbf{return } \bot; \\
& \qquad \textbf{else } \{ \quad /\!/ \ E[j] \text{ is a variable} \\
& \qquad\quad X \leftarrow \{\mathbf{x}_{j'} \mid E[j'] = E[j]\}; \\
& \qquad\quad \textbf{forall } (\mathbf{x}_{j'} \in X) \ E[j'] \leftarrow c; \\
& \qquad\quad \textbf{return } E; \\
& \qquad \} \\
& \quad \textbf{else } \{ \quad /\!/ \ E[i] \text{ is a variable} \\
& \qquad X \leftarrow \{\mathbf{x}_{i'} \mid E[i'] = E[i]\}; \\
& \qquad \textbf{forall } (\mathbf{x}_{i'} \in X) \ E[i'] \leftarrow E[j]; \\
& \qquad \textbf{return } E; \\
& \quad \}
\end{array}
$$

Fig. 3. The Implementation of conjunctions $\mathbf{x}_i = t \wedge E$ for $E \neq \bot$

Every test in this algorithm takes time $\mathcal{O}(1)$. If some update of E occurs, then either an equivalence class receives a constant value or two equivalence classes are merged. Both events can only occur $\mathcal{O}(k)$ times. Since each update can be executed in time $\mathcal{O}(k)$, the complexity estimation for the greatest lower bound computation follows. □

The mapping α is completely distributive, i.e., it commutes with arbitrary least upper bounds. Thus, it is the lower adjoint (*abstraction*) of a *Galois*-connection [9]. The counterpart to α, the *concretization* $\gamma : \mathbb{E} \to 2^{V^k}$ is given by $\gamma(E) = \{x \in V^k \mid x \models E\}$ for $E \neq \bot$ and $\gamma(\bot) = \emptyset$. Here, we write $x \models E$ for a vector x satisfying the equivalence relation E. For every assignment s, we define the abstract effect $[\![s]\!]^\sharp$ by:

$$
\begin{array}{l}
[\![\mathbf{x}_i \leftarrow ?]\!]^\sharp \, E = \exists^\sharp \mathbf{x}_i . \, E \\
[\![\mathbf{x}_i \leftarrow t]\!]^\sharp \, E = \begin{cases} (\mathbf{x}_i = t) \wedge \exists^\sharp \mathbf{x}_i . \, E, & \text{if } t \neq \mathbf{x}_i \\ E, & \text{if } t = \mathbf{x}_i \end{cases}
\end{array}
$$

for every $t \in \mathbf{X} \cup V$. Here, the abstract existential quantification $\exists^\sharp \mathbf{x}_i . \, E'$ is defined as $\bot$ if $E' = \bot$ and otherwise as the conjunction of all equalities implied by E' which do not contain $\mathbf{x}_i$. We note that $E' \mapsto \exists^\sharp \mathbf{x}_i . \, E'$ is completely distributive, i.e., commutes with arbitrary least upper bounds. Therefore, all abstract transformers $[\![s]\!]^\sharp$ are completely distributive. An implementation of the transformer $[\![\mathbf{x}_i \leftarrow ?]\!]^\sharp$ for consistent equivalence relations $E \neq \bot$ is provided in Fig. 4. According to this implementation, the result of $[\![\mathbf{x}_i \leftarrow ?]\!]^\sharp \, E$, i.e., $\exists^\sharp \mathbf{x}_i . \, E$ can be computed in time $\mathcal{O}(k)$. Therefore, all abstract transformers $[\![s]\!]^\sharp$ can be evaluated in linear time. The result of the analysis of the program from Fig. 1 is shown in Fig. 5. Note that we have listed only the non-trivial equalities. Also, the information is propagated in forward direction through the

$$
\begin{array}{ll}
[\![\mathbf{x}_i \leftarrow ?]\!]^\sharp\, E = & \textbf{if}\ (E[i] = c \in V)\ \{E[i] \leftarrow \mathbf{x}_i;\ \textbf{return}\ E;\} \\
& \textbf{else}\ \{\ X \leftarrow \{\mathbf{x}_j \mid j \neq i, E[j] = E[i]\}; \\
& \quad E[i] \leftarrow \mathbf{x}_i; \\
& \quad \textbf{if}\ (X \neq \emptyset)\ \{\textbf{choose}\ \mathbf{x}_j \in X;\ \ \textbf{forall}\ (\mathbf{x}_{j'} \in X)\ \ E[j'] \leftarrow \mathbf{x}_j;\} \\
& \quad \textbf{return}\ E; \\
& \}
\end{array}
$$

Fig. 4. The Implementation of the transformer $[\![\mathbf{x}_i \leftarrow ?]\!]^\sharp$ for $E \neq \bot$

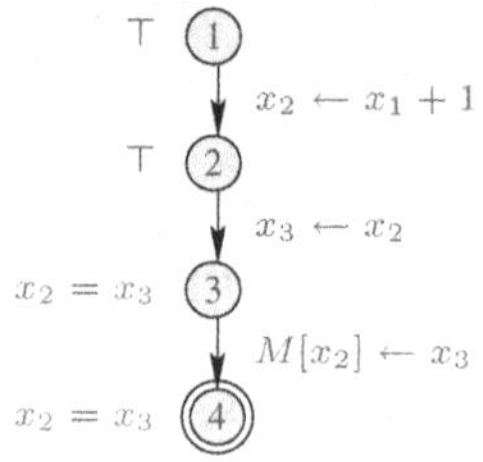

Fig. 5. The equalities between the variables in the program of Fig. 1

control-flow graph where at program start only trivial equalities between variables are assumed, i.e., $E_0[i] = \mathbf{x}_i$ for all i.

4 Representing Summary Functions

Let $g : \mathbb{E} \to \mathbb{E}$ denote a completely distributive function. As the lattice $\mathbb{E}$ is quite large, a direct representation of g, e.g., through a value table is not practical. Surprisingly, this is different for the *upper adjoint* g^- of g. For an arbitrary complete lattice $\mathbb{D}$ and $g : \mathbb{D} \to \mathbb{D}$, the function $g^- : \mathbb{D} \to \mathbb{D}$ is defined by:

$$g^-(d) = \bigsqcup\{d' \in \mathbb{D} \mid g(d') \sqsubseteq d\}$$

It is well-known from lattice theory that for completely distributive g, the pair of functions (g, g^-) forms a *Galois connection*. Thus, $g^- \circ g \sqsupseteq \mathsf{Id}$ and $g \circ g^- \sqsubseteq \mathsf{Id}$. In particular, the upper adjoint g^- is completely distributive as well – however, for the reverse ordering (see, e.g., [9]), i.e., for every $X \subseteq \mathbb{D}$, $g^-(\bigsqcap X) = \bigsqcap\{g^-(d) \mid d \in X\}$. For a distinction, we call g^- completely $\sqcap$-distributive. For completely distributive g, the function g^- is just another representation of the function g itself. In order to see this, we define for a completely $\sqcap$-distributive function $g : \mathbb{D} \to \mathbb{D}$ the *lower adjoint*:

$$g^+(d') = \bigsqcap\{d \in \mathbb{D} \mid d' \sqsubseteq g(d)\}$$

It is well-known that lower and upper adjoints determine each other uniquely. Thus, we have, for every completely distributive g, $(g^-)^+ = g$. Summarizing, we conclude that instead of computing with g, we as well might compute with its upper adjoint g^-. From an efficiency point of view, however, the functions g and g^- need not behave identical. Exactly this is the case for equality analysis.

An element $d \neq \bot$ of a complete lattice is *atomic* if $d_1 \sqsubseteq d$ implies that either $d_1 = \bot$ or $d_1 = d$. A lattice is *atomic* if every element x is the least upper bound of all atomic elements smaller or equal to x. Indeed, the set $\mathbb{E}$ ordered with "$\sqsubseteq$" is an atomic complete lattice — the number of atomic elements, though, is huge. A consistent equivalence relation E is atomic iff each equivalence class contains a distinct constant. Thus, the number of atomic elements in $\mathbb{E}$ equals m^k where k and m are the numbers of variables and constants, respectively.

Interestingly, the set $\mathbb{E}$ ordered with the reverse ordering "$\sqsupseteq$" is also an atomic complete lattice. For a distinction, we call the atomic elements of $(\mathbb{E}, \sqsubseteq)$ $\sqcup$-atomic and the atomic elements of the dual lattics $(\mathbb{E}, \sqsupseteq)$ $\sqcap$-atomic. For our lattice, the $\sqcap$-atomic elements are given by the single equalities $\mathbf{x}_i = \mathbf{x}_j$ and $\mathbf{x}_i = c$ for variables $\mathbf{x}_i, \mathbf{x}_j$ and constants c. Thus, the number of $\sqcap$-atomic elements is only $\mathcal{O}(k \cdot (k+m))$.

Over an atomic lattice, a completely distributive function g is given by its image on the atoms. In our case, this means that this representation for g^- is much more succinct than the corresponding representation for g. More specifically, it is of size $\mathcal{O}(k^2 \cdot (k+m))$ as the image of each of the $\mathcal{O}(k \cdot (k+m))$ $\sqcap$-atoms can be represented by a conjunction of at most k equalities. For computing the upper adjoints of the effects of procedures, we need the upper adjoints of the basic computation steps of the program. Thus, we define $[\![s]\!]^- = ([\![s]\!]^\sharp)^-$ for statements s and find:

$$\begin{aligned} [\![\mathbf{x}_i \leftarrow ?]\!]^- E &= \forall \mathbf{x}_i . E = \begin{cases} E & \text{if } \mathbf{x}_i \text{ does not occur in } E \\ \bot & \text{otherwise} \end{cases} \\ [\![\mathbf{x}_i \leftarrow t]\!]^- E &= E[t/\mathbf{x}_i] \end{aligned}$$

In case of the complete lattice $\mathbb{E}$, we realize that the upper adjoints of the abstract transformers of assignments in fact equal the *weakest pre-condition transformers* for these statements. An implementation of these abstract transformers for arguments $E \neq \bot$ (represented as an array) is given in Fig. 6. In particular, we find that each of these transformers can be evaluated in time $\mathcal{O}(k)$.

5 Inter-procedural Analysis

In the following, we present our inter-procedural analysis. For simplicity, we first consider global variables only. Assume that the set of global variables is given by $\mathbf{X} = \{\mathbf{x}_1, \ldots, \mathbf{x}_k\}$. The effect of a single edge is represented by a completely distributive function from $\mathbb{F} = \mathbb{E} \to \mathbb{E}$ where $\mathbb{E} = \mathbb{E}(\mathbf{X}, V)$. Again, we collect the abstract effects of procedures *from the rear*:

$$\begin{array}{lll} [\![\mathsf{rt}_f]\!]^- \sqsubseteq \mathsf{Id} & & \mathsf{rt}_f \text{ exit point of procedure } f \\ [\![u]\!]^- \sqsubseteq [\![\mathsf{st}_f]\!]^- \circ [\![v]\!]^- & & (u, f(), v) \text{ a call edge, } \mathsf{st}_f \text{ entry point of } f \\ [\![u]\!]^- \sqsubseteq [\![s]\!]^- \circ [\![v]\!]^- & & (u, s, v) \text{ an assignment edge} \end{array}$$

where $\mathsf{Id}\, E = E$ for every $E \in \mathbb{E}$. For a program point u of a procedure f, $[\![u]\!]^-$ describes the upper adjoint of the transformation induced by same-level program executions starting from u and reaching the procedure exit of f at the same level.

$$
\begin{array}{lll}
[\![\mathbf{x}_i \leftarrow ?]\!]^- E & = & \textbf{if } (E[i] \neq \mathbf{x}_i) \ \mathtt{return}\ \bot; \\
& & \textbf{else if } (\exists j \neq i.\ E[j] = E[i]) \ \mathtt{return}\ \bot; \\
& & \mathtt{else\ return}\ E; \\
[\![\mathbf{x}_i \leftarrow c]\!]^- E & = & \textbf{if } (E[i] = c' \in V) \ \textbf{if } (c \neq c') \ \mathtt{return}\ \bot; \\
& & \qquad \mathtt{else}\ \{E[i] \leftarrow \mathbf{x}_i; \mathtt{return}\ E;\} \\
& & \textbf{else} \ \{ \ // \ E[i] \text{ is a variable} \\
& & \quad X \leftarrow \{\mathbf{x}_j \mid j \neq i, E[j] = E[i]\}; \\
& & \quad E[i] \leftarrow \mathbf{x}_i; \ \textbf{forall}\,(\mathbf{x}_j \in X) \ E[j] \leftarrow c; \\
& & \quad \mathtt{return}\ E; \\
& & \} \\
[\![\mathbf{x}_i \leftarrow \mathbf{x}_j]\!]^- E & = & \textbf{if } (E[i] = c \in V) \ \textbf{if } (E[j] = c' \in V) \ \textbf{if } (c \neq c') \ \mathtt{return}\ \bot; \\
& & \qquad\qquad \mathtt{else}\ \{E[i] \leftarrow \mathbf{x}_i; \mathtt{return}\ E;\} \\
& & \qquad \textbf{else} \ \{ \ // \ E[j] \text{ is a variable} \\
& & \qquad\quad X \leftarrow \{\mathbf{x}_{j'} \mid E[j'] = E[j]\}; \\
& & \qquad\quad E[i] \leftarrow \mathbf{x}_i; \ \textbf{forall}\,(\mathbf{x}_{j'} \in X) \ E[j'] \leftarrow c; \\
& & \qquad\quad \mathtt{return}\ E; \\
& & \qquad \} \\
& & \textbf{else} \ \{ \ // \ E[i] \text{ is a variable} \\
& & \quad X \leftarrow \{\mathbf{x}_{i'} \mid i' \neq i, E[i'] = E[i]\}; \\
& & \quad E[i] \leftarrow \mathbf{x}_i; \ \textbf{forall}\,(\mathbf{x}_{i'} \in X) \ E[i'] \leftarrow E[j]; \\
& & \quad \mathtt{return}\ E; \\
& & \}
\end{array}
$$

Fig. 6. The Implementation of the transformers $[\![s]\!]^-$ for $E \neq \bot$

The crucial computation step here is the composition $h^- \circ g^-$ where $g^-, h^- \in \mathbb{F}$. In order to determine $h^-(g^-(e))$ for an equality e, we recall that $g^-(e)$ is represented by at most k equalities e'. We can determine $h^-(g^-(e))$ by computing the greatest lower bound of the values $h^-(e')$, i.e. of at most k equivalence relations. By Lemma 1 (2), the latter takes time $\mathcal{O}(k^2)$. For determining a representation of $h^- \circ g^-$, the values $h^-(g^-(e))$ need to be computed for $\mathcal{O}(k \cdot (k+m))$ equalities if m is the number of constants. We conclude that composition can be computed in time $\mathcal{O}(k^3 \cdot (k+m))$.

Since the expressions on right-hand sides of in-equations are monotonic, the system of in-equations has a unique *greatest* solution. Since the operations used in right-hand sides of the equation system are completely $\sqcap$-distributive, we obtain:

Theorem 1. *For every procedure f and every program point u of f,* $[\![u]\!]^- = (\bar{\alpha}(\mathcal{S}[u]))^-$.

Here, the abstraction function $\bar{\alpha} : (2^{V^k} \to 2^{V^k}) \to \mathbb{E} \to \mathbb{E}$ for summary functions is defined as the best abstract transformer, i.e., by $\bar{\alpha}(g) = \alpha \circ g \circ \gamma$. We observe that, during evaluation of a procedure, the values of constants will not change. Therefore, instead of analyzing the weakest pre-condition for every equation $\mathbf{x}_i = c$, $c \in V$, separately, we can as well determine the weakest pre-condition for the single equation $\mathbf{x}_i = \bullet$ for a distinguished fresh variable $\bullet$. The weakest pre-condition E_c for the specific equation $\mathbf{x}_i = c$ then can be determined from the weakest pre-condition E for $\mathbf{x}_i = \bullet$ by substituting c for $\bullet$, i.e., as $E_c = E[c/\bullet]$. The advantage is that now the size of the representation of a function is just $\mathcal{O}(k^3)$ and thus independent of the number of constants occurring in the program. Also, composition of function then can be executed in time $\mathcal{O}(k^4)$. Note that variables not assigned to during procedure evaluation can also be treated as constants and therefore be captured by $\bullet$ — thus allowing to shrink the representation of summary functions even further.

Example 2. Consider the program from Fig. 2. The set of variables is $\mathbf{X} = \{\mathbf{x}_1, \mathbf{x}_2\}$. The assignments $\mathbf{x}_1 \leftarrow \mathbf{x}_2$ and $\mathbf{x}_2 \leftarrow 2$ correspond to the functions h_1^-, h_2^- with

	h_1^-	h_2^-
$\mathbf{x}_1 = \mathbf{x}_2$	$\top$	$\mathbf{x}_1 = 2$
$\mathbf{x}_1 = \bullet$	$\mathbf{x}_2 = \bullet$	$\mathbf{x}_1 = \bullet$
$\mathbf{x}_2 = \bullet$	$\mathbf{x}_2 = \bullet$	$2 = \bullet$

In a first round of Round-Robin iteration, we obtain for program points $11, 10, 9, 8, 7$ of the procedure *work*:

	11	10	9	8	7
$\mathbf{x}_1 = \bullet$	$\mathbf{x}_1 = \bullet$	$\mathbf{x}_1 = \bullet$	$\top$	$\mathbf{x}_1 = \bullet$	$\mathbf{x}_2 = \bullet$
$\mathbf{x}_2 = \bullet$	$\mathbf{x}_2 = \bullet$	$2 = \bullet$	$\top$	$2 = \bullet$	$2 = \bullet$
$\mathbf{x}_1 = \mathbf{x}_2$	$\mathbf{x}_1 = \mathbf{x}_2$	$\mathbf{x}_1 = 2$	$\top$	$\mathbf{x}_1 = 2$	$\mathbf{x}_2 = 2$

In this example, the fixpoint is reached already after the second iteration. □

From the upper adjoint $[\![\mathsf{st}_f]\!]^-$, we obtain the abstract effect of procedure f by:

$$[\![f]\!]^\sharp(E) = ([\![\mathsf{st}_f]\!]^-)^+(E) = \bigsqcap\{E' \mid [\![\mathsf{st}_f]\!]^-(E') \sqsupseteq E\}$$

where the E' in the greatest lower bound are supposed to be $\sqcap$-atomic. The number of these elements is $\mathcal{O}(k \cdot (k+m))$. Using the trick with the extra variable $\bullet$, we can compute the application of $[\![f]\!]^\sharp$ to a given element E in time $\mathcal{O}(k^3)$ – independent of the number of constants occurring in the program.

The functions $[\![f]\!]^\sharp$ can be used to determine, for every program point u the conjunction of all equalities $\mathcal{E}[u] \in \mathbb{E}$ which definitely hold when the program point u is reached. For that, we put up the following system of in-equations whose unknowns $\mathcal{E}[v]$ (v program point) take values in $\mathbb{E}$:

$$\begin{array}{lll} \mathcal{E}[\mathsf{st}_{main}] \sqsupseteq \top & & \\ \mathcal{E}[\mathsf{st}_f] & \sqsupseteq \mathcal{E}[u] & (u, f(), \_) \text{ a call edge} \\ \mathcal{E}[v] & \sqsupseteq [\![f]\!]^\sharp(\mathcal{E}[u]) & (u, f(), v) \text{ a call edge} \\ \mathcal{E}[v] & \sqsupseteq [\![s]\!]^\sharp(\mathcal{E}[u]) & (u, s, v) \text{ an assignment edge} \end{array}$$

It should be noted that, during fixpoint iteration, we never must construct $[\![f]\!]^\sharp$ as a whole. Instead, we only need to evaluate these functions on argument values E. Since all right-hand sides are monotonic, this system of in-equations has a least solution.

Example 3. Consider again the program from Fig. 2. Then we obtain the following equalities for program points 0 through 11:

$1, 2, 3$	4	5	6	$7, 8, 9$	10	11
$\top$	$\mathbf{x}_1 = \mathbf{x}_2$	$\mathbf{x}_2 = 2$	$\mathbf{x}_1 = \mathbf{x}_2 = 2$	$\mathbf{x}_1 = \mathbf{x}_2$	$\top$	$\mathbf{x}_2 = 2$

□

Also for inter-procedural reachability, a precision theorem can be proven. We have:

Theorem 2. *The least solution $\mathcal{E}[v]$, v a program point, can be computed in time $\mathcal{O}(n \cdot k^4)$ where n is the size of the program and k is the number of variables in the program. Moreover, for every program point v, $\mathcal{E}[v] = \alpha(\mathcal{C}[v])$.* □

In order to compute the least solution within the stated running time, we first compute the values $[\![\mathsf{st}_f]\!]^-$ by applying *semi-naive* fixpoint iteration as in [2] to the system of in-equations characterizing the (upper adjoints of) summary functions. The key idea of semi-naive iteration is to propagate just the individual increments to attained values instead of abstract values as a whole. In our case, such an increment consists of a single equality $(\mathbf{x}_i = t)$ that is added as an additional conjunct to the pre-condition of some $\sqcap$-atomic element in the representation of some computed summary function. Thus, distributed over the fixpoint computation, the accumulated effort spent on a single in-equation is not bigger than the effort for a single complete evaluation of the right hand side on functions with a representation of maximum size. As mentioned, the most complex operation occuring in a right hand side, composition of functions, can be computed in time $\mathcal{O}(k^4)$ using the special variable $\bullet$. Given the values $[\![\mathsf{st}_f]\!]^-$, the fixpoint of the system of in-equations for $\mathcal{E}$ can be computed by standard fixpoint iteration: as the height of the lattice $\mathbb{E}$ is $\mathcal{O}(k)$ each right hand side is re-evaluated at most $\mathcal{O}(k)$ times and the most complex operation, application of $[\![f]\!]^\sharp$ takes time $\mathcal{O}(k^3)$. The total running time estimation given in Theorem 2 follows by summing up over all in-equations as their number is bounded by the size of the program.

The resulting bound is by a factor k larger than the best known upper bound for copy constant propagation [6] where no equalities between variables are tracked. On the other hand, instead of relying on equivalence relations, we could code variable equalities as specific linear dependences. The techniques from [11] then result in an algorithm with worst-case complexity $\mathcal{O}(n \cdot k^8)$ — which is a factor k^4 worse than the new bound.

6 Local Variables

In the following, we extend our inter-procedural analysis to local variables.

Example 4. Consider the program from Fig. 7. The local variable a_1 of procedure *work* can be coalesced with the global x_1 as both are equal throughout the body of *work*. □

In order to simplify notation, we assume that all procedures have the same set of local variables $\mathbf{A} = \{\mathbf{a}_1, \dots, \mathbf{a}_l\}$. The set of global variables is still $\mathbf{X} = \{\mathbf{x}_1, \dots, \mathbf{x}_k\}$. First of all, we extend the collecting semantics to local variables. A state is now described by a vector $(x_1, \dots, x_k, a_1, \dots, a_l) \in V^{k+l}$ which is identified with the pair (x, a) of vectors $x = (x_1, \dots, x_k) \in V^k$ and $a = (a_1, \dots, a_l) \in V^l$ of values for the global and local variables, respectively. The transformations $\mathcal{S}[u]$ now are taken from the set $\mathbb{T} = V^{k+l} \to V^{k+l}$. In order to avoid confusion between the values of the local variables of caller and callee the rules for call edges must be modified. For this purpose we introduce two transformations: The first, $\mathsf{enter} \in \mathbb{T}$, captures how a set of states propagates from the call to the start edge of the called procedure:

$$\mathsf{enter}(X) = \{(x, a) \mid \exists a' : (x, a') \in X\}$$

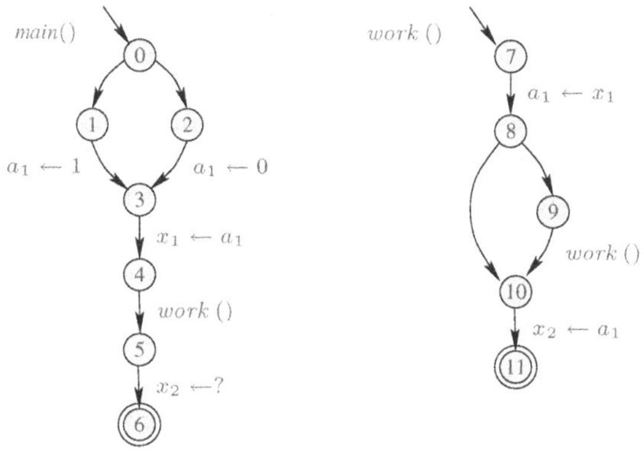

Fig. 7. An example program with local variable $\mathbf{a}_1$

Here, we assume that local variables have an arbitrary value at the beginning of their scope but other conventions can be described similarly. The second transformation $H : \mathbb{T} \to \mathbb{T}$ adjusts the transformation computed for a called procedure to the caller:

$$H(g)(X) = \{(x', a) \mid \exists x, a' : (x', a') \in g(\mathsf{enter}\,\{(x, a)\})\}$$

It ensures that local variables of the caller are left untouched by the call. The modified rules for call edges in the systems of in-equations for $\mathcal{S}$ and $\mathcal{C}$ look as follows:

$$\begin{array}{lll} \mathcal{S}[u] & \supseteq \mathcal{S}[v] \circ H(\mathcal{S}[\mathsf{st}_f]) & (u, f(), v) \text{ a call edge, } \mathsf{st}_f \text{ entry point of } f \\ \mathcal{C}[\mathsf{st}_f] & \supseteq \mathsf{enter}(\mathcal{C}[u]) & (u, f(), \_) \text{ a call edge} \\ \mathcal{C}[v] & \supseteq H(\mathcal{S}[\mathsf{st}_f])(\mathcal{C}[u]) & (u, f(), v) \text{ a call edge} \end{array}$$

In addition, V^k is replaced by $\mathsf{enter}(V^{k+l})$ in the in-equation for $\mathcal{C}[\mathsf{st}_{main}]$.

As for global variables alone, we first define the domain for the forward analysis whose summary functions then are represented through their upper adjoints. The extra complication is that now equalities may involve local variables of the procedures on the call stack which are not visible inside the called procedure. The solution is to allow *auxiliary variables* from a set $\mathbf{Y}$ (of cardinality k) for distinct local information of the caller which must be tracked by the callee, but not modified. Thus, the abstract forward semantics of procedures operates on conjunctions of equations over global variables $\mathbf{X}$, local variables $\mathbf{A}$, and auxiliary variables $\mathbf{Y}$, i.e., takes elements from $\mathbb{E}' = \mathbb{E}(\mathbf{X} \cup \mathbf{A} \cup \mathbf{Y}, V)$. Since at procedure exit, local variables of the procedure are no longer of interest, post-conditions are conjunctions just over global and auxiliary variables, i.e., summary functions should return elements from $\mathbb{E}'' = \mathbb{E}(\mathbf{X} \cup \mathbf{Y}, V)$. Thus, forward summary functions are completely distributive functions from $\mathbb{F}' = \mathbb{E}' \to \mathbb{E}''$ whereas their upper adjoints are completely $\sqcap$-distributive functions from $\mathbb{F}'' = \mathbb{E}'' \to \mathbb{E}'$. In this setting, the abstraction function $\tilde{\alpha} : (2^{V^{k+l}} \to 2^{V^{k+l}}) \to \mathbb{F}'$ takes the form:

$$\begin{array}{rcl} \tilde{\alpha}(F)(E) & = & \bigsqcap\{E' \mid \forall y, x', a' : \\ & & (x', a') \in F(\{(x, a) \mid (x, a, y) \models E\}) \Rightarrow (x', y) \models E'\}\,. \end{array}$$

As in Section 5, we aim at avoiding to treat each constant in post-conditions separately. Recall that auxiliary variables from $\mathbf{Y}$ are not modified during the execution of the call. We conclude that, for the sake of determining weakest pre-conditions, at most one auxiliary variable, say $\bullet$, suffices in single equality post-conditions. Since we have at most this single $\bullet$ in the post-condition, we also have at most one $\bullet$-variable in pre-conditions. Accordingly, we represent upper adjoints by completely $\sqcap$-distributive functions from:

$$\mathbb{F}_0 = \mathbb{E}(\mathbf{X} \cup \{\bullet\}, \emptyset) \to \mathbb{E}(\mathbf{X} \cup \mathbf{A} \cup \{\bullet\}, V)$$

Any such function $g \in \mathbb{F}_0$ is meant to represent the function $\mathsf{Ext}(g) \in \mathbb{F}''$ defined by:

$$\begin{array}{ll} \mathsf{Ext}(g)(\mathbf{x}_i = \mathbf{x}_j) & = g(\mathbf{x}_i = \mathbf{x}_j) \\ \mathsf{Ext}(g)(e) & = \begin{cases} e, & \text{if } g^-(\mathbf{x}_1 = \bullet) \neq \top \\ \top, & \text{if } g^-(\mathbf{x}_1 = \bullet) = \top \end{cases} \\ \mathsf{Ext}(g)(\mathbf{x}_i = t) & = g(\mathbf{x}_i = \bullet)[t/\bullet] \end{array}$$

where the equality e and the term t contain only constants, local variables or $\bullet$. The first clause exploits that g is special in that it does not introduce $\bullet$ for post-conditions not containing $\bullet$. The second clause deals with equalities between local variables and constants in presence of non-termination of the called procedure (identified through $g^-(\mathbf{x}_1 = \bullet) = \top$). In order to determine the representations from $\mathbb{F}_0$ for procedures, effects of control-flow edges are described by completely $\sqcap$-distributive functions from

$$\mathbb{F} = \mathbb{E}(\mathbf{X} \cup \{\bullet\} \cup \mathbf{A}, V) \to \mathbb{E}(\mathbf{X} \cup \{\bullet\} \cup \mathbf{A}, V)$$

If g^- is the (upper adjoint of the) effect of a procedure body, the (upper adjoint of the) effect of a call to this procedure is given by $H^-(g^-) \in \mathbb{F}$ where

$$\begin{array}{ll} H^-(g^-)(\mathbf{x}_i = \mathbf{x}_j) & = \forall \mathbf{a}_1 \ldots \mathbf{a}_l . \, g^-(\mathbf{x}_i = \mathbf{x}_j) \\ H^-(g^-)(e) & = \begin{cases} e, & \text{if } g^-(\mathbf{x}_1 = \bullet) \neq \top \\ \top, & \text{if } g^-(\mathbf{x}_1 = \bullet) = \top \end{cases} \\ H^-(g^-)(\mathbf{x}_i = t) & = (\forall \mathbf{a}_1 \ldots \mathbf{a}_l . \, g^-(\mathbf{x}_i = \bullet))[t/\bullet] \end{array}$$

Here, the equality e and the term t contain only constants, local variables or $\bullet$. Then summary functions can be characterized by the least solution of the constraint system:

$[\![\mathsf{rt}_f]\!]^- \sqsubseteq \mathsf{Id}$	rt_f exit point of procedure f
$[\![u]\!]^- \sqsubseteq H^-([\![\mathsf{st}_f]\!]^-) \circ [\![v]\!]^-$	$(u, f(), v)$ a call edge, st_f entry point of f
$[\![u]\!]^- \sqsubseteq [\![s]\!]^- \circ [\![v]\!]^-$	(u, s, v) an assignment edge

where $\mathsf{Id}\, E = E$ for every $E \in \mathbb{E}(\mathbf{X} \cup \{\bullet\}, \emptyset)$. For a program point u of a procedure f, $[\![u]\!]^- \in \mathbb{F}_0$ describes the upper adjoint of the transformation induced by program executions that start at u and reach the procedure exit of f at the same level.

The crucial computation step here is the composition $h^- \circ g^-$ for $g^- \in \mathbb{F}_0$ and $h^- \in \mathbb{F}$. In order to determine the value $h^-(g^-(e))$ for an equality e, we recall that every equivalence relation $g^-(e)$ is represented by at most $k + l + 1$ equalities e' for k global and l local variables. Thus, $h^-(g^-(e))$ can be computed as the greatest lower bound of the $\mathcal{O}(k + l)$ equivalence relations $h^-(e')$. By Lemma 1 (2), the latter can be done in time $\mathcal{O}((k + l)^2)$. For determining $h^- \circ g^-$, the values $h^-(g^-(e))$ must be computed for $\mathcal{O}(k^2)$ equalities. Thus, composition can be computed in time $\mathcal{O}(k^2(k + l)^2)$.

Example 5. Consider the program from Fig. 7. The assignments $\mathbf{a}_1 \leftarrow \mathbf{x}_1$ and $\mathbf{x}_2 \leftarrow \mathbf{a}_1$ correspond to the following functions:

	$\mathbf{a}_1 = \mathbf{x}_1$	$\mathbf{a}_1 = \mathbf{x}_2$	$\mathbf{x}_1 = \mathbf{x}_2$	$\mathbf{a}_1 = \bullet$	$\mathbf{x}_1 = \bullet$	$\mathbf{x}_2 = \bullet$
$[\![\mathbf{a}_1 \leftarrow \mathbf{x}_1]\!]^-$	$\top$	$\mathbf{x}_1 = \mathbf{x}_2$	$\mathbf{x}_1 = \mathbf{x}_2$	$\mathbf{x}_1 = \bullet$	$\mathbf{x}_1 = \bullet$	$\mathbf{x}_2 = \bullet$
$[\![\mathbf{x}_2 \leftarrow \mathbf{a}_1]\!]^-$	$\mathbf{a}_1 = \mathbf{x}_1$	$\top$	$\mathbf{a}_1 = \mathbf{x}_1$	$\mathbf{a}_1 = \bullet$	$\mathbf{x}_1 = \bullet$	$\mathbf{a}_1 = \bullet$

In a first round of Round-Robin iteration, we obtain for program points $11, 10, 9, 8, 7$:

	11	10	9	8	7
$\mathbf{x}_1 = \bullet$	$\mathbf{x}_1 = \bullet$	$\mathbf{x}_1 = \bullet$	$\top$	$\mathbf{x}_1 = \bullet$	$\mathbf{x}_1 = \bullet$
$\mathbf{x}_2 = \bullet$	$\mathbf{x}_2 = \bullet$	$\mathbf{a}_1 = \bullet$	$\mathbf{a}_1 = \bullet$	$\mathbf{a}_1 = \bullet$	$\mathbf{x}_1 = \bullet$
$\mathbf{x}_1 = \mathbf{x}_2$	$\mathbf{x}_1 = \mathbf{x}_2$	$\mathbf{x}_1 = \mathbf{a}_1$	$\top$	$\mathbf{x}_1 = \mathbf{a}_1$	$\top$

The second iteration changes the value for the postcondition $\mathbf{x}_1 = \mathbf{x}_2$ at program point 9 from $\top$ to $\mathbf{x}_1 = \mathbf{a}_1$. Here, the fixpoint is reached after the second iteration. □

Since the expressions on right-hand sides of in-equations are completely distributive, the system of in-equations has a unique greatest solution, and we find:

Theorem 3. *For every program point* u, $\mathsf{Ext}([\![u]\!]^-) = (\tilde{\alpha}(\mathcal{S}[u]))^-$.

The proof of this theorem is a generalization of the corresponding proof for Theorem 1. From $[\![\mathsf{st}_f]\!]^-$, we again obtain the abstract effect of a call to f, this time by

$$[\![f]\!]^\sharp(E) = (H^-([\![\mathsf{st}_f]\!]^-))^+(E)$$

where $g^+(E) = \bigwedge\{e \mid E \sqsubseteq g(e)\}$. According to the special structure of g, time $\mathcal{O}((k+l)^2 \cdot k)$ is sufficient to compute all equalities e with $E \sqsubseteq H^-([\![\mathsf{st}_f]\!]^-)(e)$.

The abstract effects $[\![f]\!]^\sharp$ allow to determine for every program point u, the conjunction of all equalities which hold when reaching u. These are characterized by:

$$\begin{array}{lll}
\mathcal{E}[\mathsf{st}_{main}] \sqsupseteq \mathsf{enter}^\sharp(\top) & & \\
\mathcal{E}[\mathsf{st}_f] & \sqsupseteq \mathsf{enter}^\sharp(\mathcal{E}[u]) & (u, f(), _) \text{ a call edge} \\
\mathcal{E}[v] & \sqsupseteq [\![f]\!]^\sharp(\mathcal{E}[u]) & (u, f(), v) \text{ a call edge} \\
\mathcal{E}[v] & \sqsupseteq [\![s]\!]^\sharp(\mathcal{E}[u]) & (u, s, v) \text{ an assignment edge}
\end{array}$$

where $\mathsf{enter}^\sharp(E)$ is the conjunction of all equalities e involving only globals and constants implied by E. The resulting consistent equivalence relation can be constructed in time $\mathcal{O}(k+l)$. This is also the case for $[\![s]\!]^\sharp(E)$, s an assignment (see Section 3).

Example 6. Consider the program from Fig. 7. We obtain the following equalities:

0, 1, 2, 3	4	5	6	7	8, 9, 10	11
$\top$	$\mathbf{x}_1 = \mathbf{a}_1$	$\mathbf{x}_1 = \mathbf{x}_2 = \mathbf{a}_1$	$\mathbf{x}_1 = \mathbf{a}_1$	$\top$	$\mathbf{x}_1 = \mathbf{a}_1$	$\mathbf{x}_1 = \mathbf{x}_2 = \mathbf{a}_1$

We conclude that inside the procedure *work*, we can coalesce $\mathbf{x}_1$ and $\mathbf{a}_1$ and thus avoid to intermediately move the value of the global $\mathbf{x}_1$ into the local $\mathbf{a}_1$. □

Theorem 4. *The system of in-equations for reachability in presence of local variables has a least solution* $\mathcal{E}[v]$, *v program point, where for every* v, $\mathcal{E}[v] = \alpha(\mathcal{C}[v])$.

Thus, the sets of valid equalities at all program points can be computed in time $\mathcal{O}(n \cdot k^2 \cdot (k+l)^2)$ *for programs of size n with k global and l local variables.* □

7 Conclusion

We have provided an algorithm for inter-procedurally inferring all valid variable-variable and variable-constant equalities — after abstracting from guards and complex assignments. Based on the succinct representation of summary functions through their upper adjoints, we constructed a polynomial time algorithm with worst-case complexity $\mathcal{O}(n \cdot k^4)$ (where k is the number of program variables and n is the size of the program). We then extended our approach to programs with local variables. The key observation is that upper adjoints allow very succinct representations of summary functions: on the one hand, the number of $\sqcap$-atomic elements is smaller than the number of $\sqcup$-atomic elements, on the other hand, we can avoid tracking each constant individually. Similar ideas may also help to speed up further inter-procedural program analyses. In future work, we also want to apply our analysis to inter-procedural register coalescing.

References

1. Alpern, B., Wegman, M., Zadeck, F.K.: Detecting Equality of Variables in Programs. In: 15th ACM Symp. on Principles of Programming Languages (POPL), pp. 1–11 (1988)
2. Fecht, C., Seidl, H.: Propagating Differences: An Efficient New Fixpoint Algorithm for Distributive Constraint Systems. Nordic Journal of Computing (NJC) 5(4), 304–329 (1998)
3. George, L., Appel, A.W.: Iterated Register Coalescing. ACM Transactions on Programming Languages and Systems (TOPLAS) 18(3), 300–324 (1996)
4. Gulwani, S., Necula, G.C.: A Polynomial-Time Algorithm for Global Value Numbering. In: Giacobazzi, R. (ed.) SAS 2004. LNCS, vol. 3148, pp. 212–227. Springer, Heidelberg (2004)
5. Horwitz, S., Reps, T.W., Sagiv, M.: Demand Interprocedural Dataflow Analysis. In: 3rd ACM Symp. on the Foundations of Software Engineering (FSE), pp. 104–115 (1995)
6. Horwitz, S., Reps, T.W., Sagiv, M.: Precise Interprocedural Dataflow Analysis via Graph Reachability. In: 22nd ACM Symp. on Principles of Programming Languages (POPL), pp. 49–61 (1995)
7. Knoop, J.: Parallel Data-Flow Analysis of Explicitly Parallel Programs. In: Chen, P.P., Akoka, J., Kangassalu, H., Thalheim, B. (eds.) Conceptual Modeling. LNCS, vol. 1565, pp. 391–400. Springer, Heidelberg (1999)
8. Knoop, J., Steffen, B.: The Interprocedural Coincidence Theorem. In: Barahona, P., Porto, A., Moniz Pereira, L. (eds.) EPIA 1991. LNCS, vol. 541, pp. 125–140. Springer, Heidelberg (1991)
9. Melton, A., Schmidt, D.A., Strecker, G.E.: Galois Connections and Computer Science Applications. In: Poigné, A., Pitt, D.H., Rydeheard, D.E., Abramsky, S. (eds.) Category Theory and Computer Programming. LNCS, vol. 240, pp. 299–312. Springer, Heidelberg (1986)
10. Müller-Olm, M., Rüthing, O., Seidl, H.: Checking Herbrand Equalities and Beyond. In: Cousot, R. (ed.) VMCAI 2005. LNCS, vol. 3385, pp. 79–96. Springer, Heidelberg (2005)
11. Müller-Olm, M., Seidl, H.: Precise Interprocedural Analysis through Linear Algebra. In: 31st ACM Symp. on Principles of Programming Languages (POPL), pp. 330–341 (2004)
12. Müller-Olm, M., Seidl, H., Steffen, B.: Interprocedural Herbrand Equalities. In: Sagiv, M. (ed.) ESOP 2005. LNCS, vol. 3444, pp. 31–45. Springer, Heidelberg (2005)
13. Sharir, M., Pnueli, A.: Two Approaches to Interprocedural Data Flow Analysis. In: Muchnick, S.S., Jones, N.D. (eds.) Program Flow Analysis: Theory and Applications, ch. 7, Program Flow Analysis: Theory and Applications, pp. 189–233. Prentice Hall, Englewood Cliffs (1981)
14. Steffen, B., Knoop, J., Rüthing, O.: The Value Flow Graph: A Program Representation for Optimal Program Transformations. In: Jones, N.D. (ed.) ESOP 1990. LNCS, vol. 432, pp. 389–405. Springer, Heidelberg (1990)

Cover Algorithms and Their Combination

Sumit Gulwani and Madan Musuvathi

Microsoft Research, Redmond, WA, 98052
{sumitg,madanm}@microsoft.com

Abstract. This paper defines the cover of a formula ϕ with respect to a set of variables V in theory T to be the strongest quantifier-free formula that is implied by $\exists V : \phi$ in theory T. Cover exists for several useful theories, including those that do not admit quantifier elimination. This paper describes cover algorithms for the theories of uninterpreted functions and linear arithmetic. In addition, the paper provides a combination algorithm to combine the cover operations for theories that satisfy some general condition. This combination algorithm can be used to compute the cover a formula in the combined theory of uninterpreted functions and linear arithmetic. This paper motivates the study of cover by describing its applications in program analysis and verification techniques, like symbolic model checking and abstract interpretation.

1 Introduction

Existential quantifier elimination is a core primitive used in several program analysis and verification techniques. Given a quantifier-free formula ϕ and a set of variables V, existentially quantifying away V involves computing a quantifier-free formula that is logically equivalent to $\exists V : \phi$. This operation is useful in practice to eliminate variables that are no longer necessary from a formula. For instance, the image computation in symbolic model checking [14] involves computing the quantifier-free formula equivalent to $\exists V : R(V) \wedge T(V, V')$. Here, $R(V)$ represents the current set of reachable states and $T(V, V')$ represents the transition relation between the current values of the state variables V and their new values V'.

Existential quantifier elimination can be performed, albeit with exponential complexity, for propositional formulas. However, this operation is not defined for formulas containing interpreted symbols from certain theories. For example, consider the formula $F(x) = 0$ in the theory of uninterpreted functions. There is no quantifier-free formula that is equivalent to $\exists x : F(x) = 0$ as it is not possible to state that 0 is in the range of function F without using quantifiers. This limits the application of techniques like symbolic model checking to systems described by formulas in these theories.

To address this problem, we introduce the notion of *cover*. Given a quantifier-free formula ϕ containing interpreted symbols from theory T and a set of variables V, we define $\mathbb{C}_T V : \phi$ (called the cover of ϕ with respect to V in T) as the strongest quantifier-free formula in T that is implied by $\exists V : \phi$. Formally, the cover operation satisfies the following constraints.

S. Drossopoulou (Ed.): ESOP 2008, LNCS 4960, pp. 193–207, 2008.

$$(\exists V: \phi) \quad \Rightarrow_T \quad (\mathbb{C}_T V: \phi)$$
$$((\exists V: \phi) \Rightarrow_T \gamma) \quad \text{iff} \quad ((\mathbb{C}_T V: \phi) \Rightarrow_T \gamma), \text{ for all quantifier-free formulas } \gamma$$

When the theory T is obvious from context, we drop the subscript T from the notation and refer to the cover simply as $\mathbb{C}V: \phi$.

Intuitively, applying the cover operation on a formula with respect to V eliminates all variables in V from the formula. However, the resulting formula only retains *quantifier-free* facts pertaining to other variables in the formula. For an example, let ϕ be the formula $y = \mathtt{Mem}(a+x) - \mathtt{Mem}(b+x)$, where Mem is an uninterpreted function. Using cover to eliminate the variable x, we get

$$(\mathbb{C}x: y = \mathtt{Mem}(a+x) - \mathtt{Mem}(b+x)) \quad \equiv \quad (a = b \Rightarrow y = 0)$$

Note that $\exists x: \phi$ implies the right hand side of the above equation. The results in this paper show that this is the most precise quantifier-free formula that is implied by ϕ and that does not involve x. Example 3 in Section 4 provides an algorithm to compute the cover of this formula, and Section 2.2 describes an application that requires computing the cover of such formulas. Finally, the reader should also note that applying cover does not retain *quantified* facts. For example, $\mathbb{C}x: \phi$ does not imply the fact $(\forall x: \mathtt{Mem}(a+x) = \mathtt{Mem}(b+x)) \Rightarrow y = 0$, while $\exists x: \phi$ does.

This distinguishing fact of cover allows us to define this operation even for theories that do not admit existential quantifier elimination. In Section 3, we describe the cover algorithm for the theory of uninterpreted functions. Note that cover is trivially defined for propositional formulas and theory of linear arithmetic, as cover, by definition, reduces to existential quantifier elimination when it exists.

In Section 4, we present a *combination* algorithm for computing cover for union of two theories that individually support cover operations and satisfy some general condition. Our combination algorithm is based on extension of Nelson-Oppen methodology for combining decision procedures [16]. However, in our combination framework, we also need to exchange *conditional* variable equalities (of the form $\gamma \Rightarrow v_1 = v_2$) and variable-term equalities (of the form $\gamma \Rightarrow v = t$) between component theories. Our combination algorithm works for theories that are convex, stably infinite, disjoint, and have a finite set of *simple terms* (Definition 1 in Section 4). The theories of linear arithmetic and uninterpreted functions, for example, satisfy these constraints.

We also describe how the cover operation can be used in program analysis and verification techniques that otherwise depend on existential quantifier elimination. In particular, this paper presents a modified symbolic model checking algorithm (Section 2.1) using the cover operation in the image computation step. This new algorithm can be used to reason about transition systems involving operations from the rich set of theories for which the cover operation is defined. Moreover, when the transition system can be described using quantifier-free formulas, we show that the symbolic model checking algorithm using cover is not only sound, but also *precise* (Theorem 1). In other words, when the checking algorithm terminates, any error reported is guaranteed to be a real error in the system. This is in stark contrast with other over-approximation based techniques [1,3,15], which only guarantee soundness. Precision is very important for *falsification* techniques. A similar application is in performing abstract interpretation of programs over abstractions whose elements are quantifier-free formulas describing program states.

In summary, this paper has the following main contributions.

- We introduce the notion of cover as the most precise quantifier-free over-approximation to existential quantifier elimination. We study this operation and present its useful properties.
- As a practical application, we present a new symbolic model checking algorithm using cover. This algorithm is both sound and *precise*, and can be used to reason about transition systems described using formulas in a rich set of theories.
- We show how to do a precise analysis of programs by performing abstract interpretation over abstract domains that describe program states using quantifier-free formulas.
- We show that cover can be computed for the theory of uninterpreted functions.
- We present an extension to the Nelson-Oppen combination framework that can be used to combine the cover operation of theories satisfying a general condition. We show that useful theories such as the theory of uninterpreted functions and linear arithmetic satisfy these conditions.

2 Applications of Cover

Before presenting cover algorithms for some theories, and a methodology for combining cover algorithms in the following sections, we first motivate the study of cover by describing some useful applications for the cover operation.

2.1 Symbolic Model Checking

Our main motivation for cover is to apply symbolic model checking to reason about transition systems that involve rich operations from the theory of uninterpreted functions, which naturally arise in program analysis and software verification.

A transition system can be described by the tuple $(V, I(V), T(V_{old}, V_{new}), E(V))$, where V represents the set of state variables, $I(V)$ is a formula describing the set of initial states, $T(V_{old}, V_{new})$ is a formula describing the transition relation between the old values V_{old} and new values V_{new} of the variables in V, and $E(V)$ is a formula describing the set of error states. For clarity, if $\phi(V)$ is a formula with variables from V, we will use $\phi(V')$ to be the formula obtained from ϕ by renaming each variable in V with the corresponding variable in V'.

Given a transition system, the symbolic model checking algorithm computes the set of reachable states $R(V)$ iteratively as follows.

$$R_0(V) \equiv I(V)$$
$$R_i(V) \equiv R_{i-1}(V) \vee (\exists V_{old}: R_{i-1}(V_{old}) \wedge T(V_{old}, V)) \quad \text{for } i > 0$$

This iteration reaches a fix point at n if and only if $R_n(V) \Rightarrow R_{n-1}(V)$. At this point, $R_n(V)$ is an inductive invariant of the transition system. Also, if $R_n(V) \Rightarrow \neg E(V)$ then the system does not reach an error state.

A transition system $(V, I(V), T(V_{old}, V_{new}), E(V))$ is quantifier-free when the formulas $I(V), T(V_{old}, V_{new})$, and $E(V)$ are all quantifier-free. In practice, transition systems arising from many software verification applications are quantifier-free. For such systems, we propose a new symbolic model checking algorithm that uses the cover operation instead of existential quantification. Also, we show that this new algorithm is sound and precise. Moreover, this algorithm terminates whenever the original model checking algorithm terminates.

In the discussion below, we assume that the transition system uses operations from a theory T, such as the union of the theory of reals and uninterpreted functions. We assume that the cover operations are performed with respect to this theory. (See Section 3 for the actual cover algorithms.)

The symbolic model checking algorithm using cover is as follows.
SMC-Cover Algorithm:

$$CR_0(V) \equiv I(V)$$
$$CR_i(V) \equiv CR_{i-1}(V) \vee (\mathbb{C}V_{old}: CR_{i-1}(V_{old}) \wedge T(V_{old}, V)) \quad \text{for } i > 0$$

In the equations above, $CR_i(V)$ determines the set of reachable states determined using the cover operation after i iterations. The fix point is reached, as before, at point n when $CR_n(V) \Rightarrow CR_{n-1}(V)$.

Lemma 1. *Given a quantifier-free transition system* $(V, I(V), T(V_{old}, V_{new}), E(V))$*,* $CR_n(V) \Rightarrow \phi$ *if and only if* $R_n(V) \Rightarrow \phi$ *for all quantifier-free formulas* ϕ*.*

Proof. The proof is by induction. The base case is trivial as $CR_0(V) \equiv I(V) \equiv R_0(V)$. For the induction, assume the lemma holds for all iterations up to $n-1$. Note, that by definition

$$R_n(V) \equiv \exists V_{old}: R_{n-1}(V_{old}) \wedge T(V_{old}, V) \vee R_{n-1}(V)$$

$$CR_n(V) \equiv \mathbb{C}V_{old}: CR_{n-1}(V_{old}) \wedge T(V_{old}, V) \vee CR_{n-1}(V)$$

Consider a quantifier-free formula ϕ that does not contain, without loss of generality, variables from V_{old}.[1] Now, if $R_n(V) \Rightarrow \phi$, then the following are true

$$R_{n-1}(V) \Rightarrow \phi$$
$$\exists V_{old}: R_{n-1}(V_{old}) \wedge T(V_{old}, V) \Rightarrow \phi$$

[1] The variables from V_{old}, if present, can be renamed.

From the first equation, we have $CR_{n-1}(V) \Rightarrow \phi$ by induction. Moreover from the second equation, we have

$$\begin{aligned}
R_{n-1}(V_{old}) \wedge T(V_{old}, V) &\Rightarrow \phi \quad \text{as } \phi \text{ does not contain variables in } V_{old} \\
R_{n-1}(V_{old}) &\Rightarrow (T(V_{old}, V) \Rightarrow \phi) \\
CR_{n-1}(V_{old}) &\Rightarrow (T(V_{old}, V) \Rightarrow \phi) \quad \text{by induction, as } T(V_{old}, V) \text{ is quantifier-free} \\
CR_{n-1}(V_{old}) \wedge T(V_{old}, V) &\Rightarrow \phi \\
\mathbb{C}V_{old} : CR_{n-1}(V_{old}) \wedge T(V_{old}, V) &\Rightarrow \phi \quad \text{by definition}
\end{aligned}$$

Thus, we have $CR_n(V) \Rightarrow \phi$, proving the *if* direction of the lemma. Proving the other direction is similar and follows from the property that cover over-approximates existential quantification.

Using Lemma 1 and the following properties of cover, we can prove the desired result stated in Theorem 1.

Property 1. $\mathbb{C}V : \mathbb{C}W : \phi(V, W) \equiv \mathbb{C}V, W : \phi(V, W)$

Property 2. $\mathbb{C}V : \exists W : \phi(V, W) \equiv \mathbb{C}V : \mathbb{C}W : \phi(V, W)$

Theorem 1. *Given a transition system $(V, I(V), T(V_{old}, V_{new}), E(V))$, where both $T(V_{old}, V_{new})$ and $E(V)$ are quantifier-free, then the symbolic model checking algorithm using cover is sound and precise.*

Proof. The proof follows from Lemma 1. Since $E(V)$ is quantifier-free, $R_n(V) \Rightarrow \neg E(V)$ if and only if $CR_n(V) \Rightarrow \neg E(V)$. Thus, the symbolic model checking algorithm using cover proves the absence of error whenever the original symbolic model checking algorithm proves the same. Also, when the former algorithm reports an error, the latter reports the error.

Theorem 2. *Given a transition system $(V, I(V), T(V_{old}, V_{new}), E(V))$, where both $T(V_{old}, V_{new})$ and $E(V)$ are quantifier-free, then the symbolic model checking algorithm using cover terminates whenever the symbolic model checking algorithm terminates.*

Proof. Say, the symbolic model checking algorithm terminates at step n, then $R_n(V) \Rightarrow R_{n-1}(V)$. Thus, by Lemma 1, we have $R_n(V) \Rightarrow CR_{n-1}(V)$. Since $CR_{n-1}(V)$ is a quantifier-free formula we have $CR_n(V) \Rightarrow CR_{n-1}(V)$. Thus the symbolic model checking algorithm using cover terminates.

Checking Infinite State Systems. The algorithm mentioned above is, in general, not guaranteed to terminate when the transition system describes an infinite state systems. To guarantee termination, this algorithm has to be combined with appropriate abstraction [15] or *widening* techniques [4] to selectively lose facts regarding the set of reachable states. Designing such algorithms is beyond the scope of this paper. However, the cover operation, as opposed to a less precise approximation to existential quantification, is still useful in this setting because it greatly simplifies the design of subsequent refinement [1,3] algorithms. In particular, refinement needs to be performed only at the 'widen' points where information is lost [6].

```
void foo(int a[], int b[]) {
    int y = 0; int x = ?;
    while(*) { y = y + a[x] - b[x]; x = ?; }
    if (y ≠ 0) { assert(a ≠ b); }
}
```

Fig. 1. An example program whose loop invariant (required to prove the assertion) can be generated using cover operation

2.2 Abstract Interpretation over Precise Abstractions

Abstract Interpretation is a well-known methodology to analyze programs over a given abstraction [4]. An abstract interpreter performs a forward analysis on the program computing invariants (which are elements of the underlying abstract lattice over which the analysis is being performed) at each program point. The invariants are computed at each program point from the invariants at the preceding program points in an iterative manner using appropriate transfer functions.

Most of the abstract interpreters that have been described in literature operate over an abstraction whose elements are usually conjunction of atomic predicates in some theory, e.g., linear arithmetic [5], uninterpreted functions [8,9]. These abstractions cannot reason about disjunctive invariants in programs and there is a loss of precision at join points in programs.

Abstractions whose elements are boolean combinations of atomic predicates in an appropriate theory can reason about disjunctive invariants in programs. The join operation (required to merge information at join points) for such an abstraction is simply disjunction, while the meet operation (required to gather information from conditional nodes) is simply conjunction. However, the strongest postcondition operation (required to compute invariants across assignment nodes) is non-trivial. In fact, it is exactly the cover operation for the underlying theory. Hence, a cover operation for a theory can be used to perform abstract interpretation of programs over an abstraction whose elements are quantifier-free formulas over that theory.

Consider, for example, the program shown in Figure 1. We do not know of any existing abstract interpreter that can prove the assertion in the program. For this, we need to do abstract interpretation over the abstraction of quantifier-free formulas in the combined theory of linear arithmetic and uninterpreted functions. Analyzing the first loop iteration involves computing the strongest postcondition of $y = 0$ with respect to the assignment $y := y + a[x] - b[x]$ (in the abstraction of quantifier-free formulas), which is equivalent to computing $\mathbb{C}x', y' : (y' = 0 \wedge y = y' + \texttt{Mem}(a + x') - \texttt{Mem}(b + x') \wedge x = *)$, where Mem denotes the deference operator and can be regarded as an uninterpreted function. This yields the formula $a = b \Rightarrow y = 0$, which also turns out to be the loop invariant and hence fixed point is reached in the next loop iteration.

Furthermore, the invariant computed at the end of the procedure can be turned into a procedure summary by eliminating the local variables of the procedure, again by using the cover operation. Procedure summaries are very useful in performing a context-sensitive reasoning of a program in a modular fashion.

2.3 Computation of Interpolants

Finally, the cover operation can be used to compute *quantifier-free interpolants*. Let $\phi_1(V_1, V)$ and $\phi_2(V_2, V)$ be quantifier-free formulas, such that ϕ_1 contains variables in $V_1 \cup V$, ϕ_2 contains variables in $V_2 \cup V$, $V_1 \cap V_2 = \emptyset$, and $\phi_1(V_1, V) \Rightarrow \phi_2(V_2, V)$. A quantifier-free interpolant $I(V)$ is a quantifier-free formula that contains only variables from V and satisfies $(\phi_1(V_1, V) \Rightarrow I(V)) \wedge (I(V) \Rightarrow \phi_2(V, V_2))$. We can see that $\mathbb{C}V_1 : \phi_1(V, V_1)$ and $\neg(\mathbb{C}V_2 : \neg\phi_2(V, V_2))$ are (respectively the strongest and weakest) quantifier-free interpolants. Such interpolants have recently been used in fix point computations [15] and to refine abstractions [11].

3 Cover Algorithm for the Theory of Uninterpreted Functions

The cover algorithm for theory of uninterpreted functions is given in Figure 3. The algorithm assumes that there are only binary uninterpreted functions, but it can be easily extended to handle uninterpreted functions of any arity.

Property 3. The cover operation distributes over disjunctions, i.e.,

$$(\mathbb{C}V : (\phi_1 \vee \phi_2)) \quad \equiv \quad (\mathbb{C}V : \phi_1) \vee (\mathbb{C}V : \phi_2)$$

Hence, without loss of any generality, the algorithm assumes that the input formula ϕ is a conjunction of atomic facts, where each atomic fact is either a positive or negative atom.

The reasoning behind the cover algorithm is as follows. Suppose $\phi(U, V) \Rightarrow \gamma(U, W)$ such that $U = \mathtt{Vars}(\phi) \cap \mathtt{Vars}(\gamma)$, $U \cap V = \emptyset$, and $W \cap U = \emptyset$. We require $\mathbb{C}V : \phi \Rightarrow \gamma$. By Craig's interpolant theorem, there exists a $\delta(U)$ such that $(\phi(U, V) \Rightarrow \delta(U)) \wedge (\delta(U) \Rightarrow \gamma(U, W))$. The fact that one can find a quantifier-free interpolant for formulas in the theory of uninterpreted functions follows from [15]. Without loss of generality, one can represent $\delta(U)$ (in conjunctive normal form) as a conjunction of clauses where each clause is of the form $(s_1 = t_1 \wedge \ldots \wedge s_a = t_a) \Rightarrow (s'_1 = t'_1 \vee \ldots \vee s'_b = t'_b)$, where the terms s_i, t_i, s'_j, t'_j only contain variables from U. Therefore, $\phi(U, V)$ implies each of the clauses individually. Finally, from the convexity of the theory of uninterpreted functions [16], whenever $\phi(U, V)$ implies $(s_1 = t_1 \wedge \ldots \wedge s_a = t_a) \Rightarrow (s'_1 = t'_1 \vee \ldots \vee s'_b = t'_b)$, there exists some $1 \leq i \leq b$ such that $\phi(U, V)$ implies $(s_1 = t_1 \wedge \ldots \wedge s_a = t_a) \Rightarrow s'_i = t'_i$. Lines 12 and 15 in the function $\mathtt{ComputeCover}_{\mathtt{uf}}(\phi)$ compute all such implied equalities. While there could be infinite such implied equalities, one only needs to consider equalities of the form $s_j = t_j$, $1 \leq j \leq a$ where s_j and t_j are terms in the congruence closure graph of ϕ. This is because equalities can only propagate "upwards" during congruence closure. Similarly, one only needs to consider the case in which s'_i and t'_i are in the congruence closure graph of ϕ. The formal correctness of the cover algorithm is presented in the full version of the paper [7].

Line 1 involves computing a congruence closed graph G that represents the equalities implied by ϕ. G is a set of congruence classes, and each congruence

$$\text{Formula } \phi \quad : \quad s_1 = F(z_1, v) \ \wedge \ s_2 = F(z_2, v) \ \wedge \ t = F(F(y_1, v), F(y_2, v))$$

$$\mathbb{C}v : \phi \quad : \quad z_1 = z_2 \Rightarrow s_1 = s_2 \ \wedge \ \bigwedge_{i,j \in \{1,2\}} y_1 = z_i \wedge y_2 = z_j \ \Rightarrow \ t = F(s_i, s_j)$$

Fig. 2. An example of cover operation for the theory of uninterpreted functions

class is a set of nodes n, where a node is either a variable y, or a F-node $F(c_1, c_2)$ for some congruence classes c_1 and c_2. Note that two nodes n_1 and n_2 in G are in the same congruence class iff ϕ implies $n_1 = n_2$. The function `Rep`(c) returns a representative term for class c that does not involve any variables in V, if any such term exists; otherwise it returns $\perp$.

Line 2 calls procedure `Mark` that takes a congruence closed graph G and a set of variables V as inputs, and sets $M[n]$ to 1 for F-nodes n iff node n in G becomes undefined if variables V are removed from G. An F-node $F(c_1, c_2)$ is undefined iff classes c_1 or c_2 are undefined. A class c is undefined iff it contains all undefined nodes. The function `AllMark` takes a congruence class c as an input and returns true iff all nodes in c are marked.

Lines 5 through 8 compute $W[n_1, n_2]$, which denotes the weakest constraint not involving variables in V and which along with ϕ implies $n_1 = n_2$. $W[n_1, n_2]$ is first initialized to `Init`(n_1, n_2), which returns a constraint not involving variables in V and which along with ϕ implies $n_1 = n_2$. $W[n_1, n_2]$ is then updated in a transitive closure style.

Line 4 initializes `result` to all equalities and disequalities that are implied by ϕ and that do not involve any variables in V. Lines 12 and 15 then update `result` by conjoining it with all implied equalities that are implied by ϕ and that do not involve any variable from V. Lines 11-12 can be treated as a special case of lines 13-15 when the context Z does not contain any holes (i.e., $k = 0$).

Example 1. Figure 2 shows an example of the cover operation over the theory of uninterpreted functions. For the formula ϕ in Figure 2, let n_1 be the node $F(y_1, v)$, n_2 be the node $F(y_2, v)$, and n be the node $F(n_1, n_2)$. The procedure `Mark` marks all the nodes in the congruence closed graph G, as every node depends on the variable v that needs to be eliminated. After executing lines 5 through 8, the algorithm computes $W[s_1, n_1]$, for instance, to be the constraint $z_1 = y_1$. Note, that an equality between z_1 and y_1 results in an equality between the nodes s_1 and n_1, and this is the weakest constraint to do so. Similarly, $W[s_1, n_2]$ is the constraint $z_2 = y_1$, and so on. For this example, the set N_e in Line 9 contains all the nodes in G. Consider the context $Z[n_1, n_2] = F(n_1, n_2)$. By choosing the node m_1 to be s_1 and m_2 to be s_1 in line 13, we obtain the formula $z_1 = y_1 \wedge z_2 = y_1 \Rightarrow t = F(s_1, s_1)$ in line 15, and so on. The result returned by the algorithm is shown in Figure 2.

Complexity: The complexity of the algorithm described in Figure 3 can be exponential in the size of the input formula ϕ. This is because there can be an exponential number of ways of choosing an appropriate sequence of k nodes $m_1, \ldots, m_k$ in line 13. Hence, the size of the cover can itself be exponential in

```
ComputeCover_uf(φ, V) =
1    Let G be the congruence closure of φ.
2    Mark(G,V);
3    let G' be the graph obtained from G after removing all nodes n s.t. M[n] = 1;
4    result ← all equalities and disequalities implied by G';
     // Compute W[n₁, n₂]
5    forall nodes n₁, n₂ ∈ G: W[n₁, n₂] ← Init(n₁, n₂);
6    forall nodes n ∈ G:
7        forall nodes n₁, n₂ ∈ G:
8            W[n₁, n₂] ← W[n₁, n₂] ∨ (W[n₁, n] ∧ W[n, n₂]);
     // Compute result
9    let N_e = {n | n ∈ G, M[n] = 1, CRep(n) ≠ ⊥};
10   forall nodes n ∈ N_e
11       forall nodes m ∈ G s.t. W[m, n] ≠ false:
12           result ← result ∧ (W[n, m] ⇒ CRep(n) = CRep(m));
13       forall contexts Z[n₁, .., n_k] s.t. n = Z[n₁, .., n_k], Vars(Z) ∩ V = ∅, n_i ∈ N_e for 1 ≤ i ≤ k
14           forall nodes m₁, .., m_k ∈ G s.t. W[n_i, m_i] ≠ false and CRep(m_i) ≠ ⊥ for 1 ≤ i ≤ k:
15               result ← result ∧ ((⋀_{i=1}^{k} W[c_i, d_i]) ⇒ CRep(n) = Z[CRep(m₁), ..., CRep(m_k)]);
16   return result;
```

```
// Marks those nodes n (M[n] = 1) which become undefined when variables in V are removed
Mark(G,V) =
    forall nodes n ∈ G: M[n] ← 1;
    forall variables y ∉ V: M[y] ← 0;
    while any change
        forall nodes F(c₁, c₂): if ¬AllMark(c₁) ∧ ¬AllMark(c₂), M[F(c₁, c₂)] ← 0;
```

```
// Returns true if every node in the equivalence class c is marked
AllMark(c) =
    forall nodes n in class c: if M[n] = 1, return true;
    return false;
```

```
// Initial candidate for the weakest constraint that implies n₁ = n₂
Init(n₁, n₂) =
    if Class(n₁) = Class(n₂), return true;
    if n₁ ≡ F(c₁, c₂) and n₂ ≡ F(c₁', c₂')
        if Rep(c₁) ≠ ⊥ ∧ Rep(c₁') ≠ ⊥ ∧ c₂ = c₂', return Rep(c₁) = Rep(c₁');
        if Rep(c₂) ≠ ⊥ ∧ Rep(c₂') ≠ ⊥ ∧ c₁ = c₁', return Rep(c₂) = Rep(c₂');
        return Init(c₁, c₁') ∧ Init(c₂, c₂');
    return false;
```

```
// Find a term in the equivalence class not containing a variable in V
Rep(c) =
    if AllMark(c) return ⊥;
    if c has a variable y s.t. M[y] = 0, return y;
    let F(c₁, c₂) be the node s.t. M[F(c₁, c₂)] = 0. return F(Rep(c₁), Rep(c₂));
```

```
// Find a representative term for n that does not contain a variable in V
CRep(n) =
    return Rep(Class(n));
```

Fig. 3. Cover Algorithm for Theory of Uninterpreted Functions

size of the input formula ϕ. The formula ϕ in Figure 2 can be easily generalized to obtain a formula of size $O(n)$ whose cover is of size $O(2^n)$.

Special Case of Unary Uninterpreted Functions. For the special case when the formula ϕ involves only unary uninterpreted functions, the cover algorithm simply involves erasing variables in V from congruence closure of ϕ. Equivalently, the algorithm only involves Lines 1 through 4 in the `ComputeCover` procedure described in Figure 3. The complexity of the cover algorithm for unary uninterpreted functions is thus $O(n \log n)$, where n is the size of the input formula.

4 Combination Algorithm for Cover

In this section, we show how to obtain a cover algorithm for combination of two theories $T_1 \cup T_2$ from the cover algorithms for the individual theories T_1 and T_2. Our combination methodology is based on extension of Nelson-Oppen methodology for combining decision procedures for two theories. As a result, the restrictions on theories that allow for efficient combination of their decision procedures (namely, convexity, stably infiniteness, and disjointness) also transfer to the context of combining cover algorithms for those theories.

The Nelson-Oppen methodology for combining decision procedures involves sharing variable equalities $v = u$ between the formulas in the two theories. For combining cover algorithms, we also need to share variable-term equalities (i.e., equalities between variables and terms) apart from variable equalities. Furthermore, these equalities may also be conditional on any predicate. More formally, the general form of equalities that we share between the two formulas in the two theories is $\gamma \Rightarrow v = t$, where γ is a formula that does not involve any variable to be eliminated, and either v and t are both variables (in which case we refer to it as a *conditional variable equality*) or v is a variable that needs to be eliminated and t is a term that does not involve any variable to be eliminated (in which case we refer it to as a *conditional variable-term equality*). The terms t are restricted to come from a set that we refer to as set of *simple terms* (Definition 1).

We now introduce some notation that is needed to describe the cover algorithm for combination of two theories.

Definition 1 (Set of Simple Terms). *A set S is a set of simple terms for variable v with respect to a formula ϕ in theory T (denoted by $\mathtt{SST}_T(v, \phi)$), if for all conjunctions of atomic predicates γ such that $v \not\in \mathtt{Vars}(\gamma)$, and all terms t that are distinct from v:*

$$
\begin{array}{rcl}
v \not\in \mathtt{Vars}(S) & \textit{and} & \mathtt{Vars}(S) \subseteq \mathtt{Vars}(\phi) \\
(\gamma \wedge \phi \Rightarrow_T v = t) & \Rightarrow & \exists t' \in S \ s.t. (\gamma \wedge \phi \Rightarrow_T v = t') \ \wedge \ (\gamma \wedge \phi \Rightarrow_T t = t')
\end{array}
$$

We refer to t' as $ST(S, \gamma, t)$.

The theories of linear arithmetic and uninterpreted functions admit a finite set of simple terms for their formulas. The following theorems describe how to compute a set of simple terms for a formula in the corresponding theory.

Theorem 3 (Set of Simple Terms for Linear Arithmetic). *Let ϕ be the formula $\bigwedge_{i=1}^{n} v \le a_i \wedge \bigwedge_{i=1}^{m} v \ge b_i \wedge \bigwedge_{i=1}^{n'} v < a'_i \wedge \bigwedge_{i=1}^{m'} v > b'_i \wedge \phi'$. where $v \notin \mathtt{Vars}(\phi'), v \notin \mathtt{Vars}(a_i)$ and $v \notin \mathtt{Vars}(b_i))$. Then, $\{a_i\}_{i=1}^{n}$ is $\mathtt{SST}_{\ell a}(v, \phi)$.*

Theorem 4 (Set of Simple Terms for Uninterpreted Functions). *Let ϕ be a formula over the theory of uninterpreted functions. Let G be the congruence closure of ϕ. Let t be any term in the congruence class of v in G that does not involve v (if any such term exists). Then, the singleton set containing t is $\mathtt{SST}_{\mathtt{uf}}(v, \phi)$ (if any such term exists). If no such term exists then, $\mathtt{SST}_{\mathtt{uf}}(v, \phi) = \emptyset$.*

The proofs of Theorem 3 and Theorem 4 are given in the full version of the paper [7].

We use the notation $WC_T(\phi, \delta, V)$ to denote $\neg \mathbb{C}_T V : \phi \wedge \neg\delta$. Intuitively, $WC_T(\phi, \delta, V)$ denotes the weakest constraint that together with ϕ implies δ and that does not involve any variable from set V.

The following property is useful in describing $\mathtt{Cover}_{T_1 \cup T_2}(\phi, V)$ in terms of $\mathtt{Cover}_{T_1}$ and $\mathtt{Cover}_{T_2}$.

Property 4. Let ϕ and ϕ' be quantifier-free formulas in theory T such that

$$\phi \Rightarrow_T \phi'$$
$$V \cap \mathtt{Vars}(\phi') \;=\; \emptyset$$
$$(V \cap \mathtt{Vars}(\gamma) = \emptyset \;\wedge\; \phi \Rightarrow_T \gamma) \;\Rightarrow\; (\phi' \Rightarrow_T \gamma)\,,\ \text{for all quantifier-free formulas } \gamma$$

Then, $\phi' \equiv \mathtt{Cover}_T(\phi, V)$.

We use the notation $\mathtt{Num}(T)$ for any theory T to denote the maximum number of variables that may occur in any atomic predicate in theory T. For example, $\mathtt{Num}(T) = 2$ for difference logic (theory of linear arithmetic with only difference constraints) as well as for theory of unary uninterpreted functions.

The procedure $\mathtt{ComputeCover}_{T_1 \cup T_2}$ in Figure 4 takes as input a formula ϕ and a set of variables V to be eliminated and computes $\mathbb{C}_{T_1 \cup T_2} V : \phi$ using the cover algorithms for theories T_1 and T_2. Line 1 performs purification of ϕ, which involves decomposing ϕ (which is a conjunction of atomic predicates in the combined theory $T_1 \cup T_2$) into conjunctions of atomic predicates that are either in theory T_1 or in T_2 by introducing a fresh variable for each *alien* term in ϕ. The set of all such fresh variables is referred to as U, while V' denotes the set of all variables that we need to eliminate from $\phi_1 \wedge \phi_2$. Lines 4 to 11 repeatedly exchange conditional variable equalities and conditional variable-term equalities between ϕ_1 and ϕ_2. Lines 13 and 14 call the procedure $\mathtt{ComputeSimpleCover}_{\mathrm{T}}$, which takes as inputs a set of variables V, a formula ϕ in theory T, and a formula F of the form $\bigwedge \gamma_i \Rightarrow_{T'} v_i = t_i$ (where $v_i \in V$ and T' is any theory) such that $V \cap (\mathtt{Vars}(\gamma_i) \cup \mathtt{Vars}(t_i)) = \emptyset$, and computes $\mathbb{C}_{T \cup T'} V : \phi \wedge F$.

The proof of correctness (including termination) of the combination algorithm in Figure 4 is non-trivial and is given in the full version of the paper [7]. We give a brief sketch of the proof here. Let γ_i's be some atomic predicates that do not

$\texttt{ComputeCover}_{T_1 \cup T_2}(V, \phi)$ =

  $\phi_1, \phi_2 = \texttt{Purify}(\phi)$; let U be the variables introduced during $\texttt{Purify}(\phi)$;

  let $V' = V \cup U$;

  $F_1 \leftarrow$ true; $F_2 \leftarrow$ true;

  repeat until no change:

    for $j = 1, 2$:

      let $\bigwedge_{i=1}^{n} \gamma_i \Rightarrow v_i = u_i$ be some conditional variable equalities implied by F_{3-j};

      let $\bigwedge_{i=1}^{m} \delta_i \Rightarrow w_i = t_i$ be some conditional variable-term equalities implied by F_{3-j};

      let $\psi = \bigwedge_{i=1}^{n} \gamma_i \wedge \bigwedge_{i=1}^{m} \delta_i$; let $E = \bigwedge_{i=1}^{k} v_i = u_i$; let $W = V' - \{w_i \mid 1 \leq i \leq m\}$;

      let $S_v \equiv \texttt{SST}_{T_j}(v, \mathbb{C}_{T_j} W - \{v\} : \phi_j \wedge E)$ for any variable v;

      $F_j \leftarrow F_j \wedge \bigwedge_{v_1, v_2 \in V'} \psi \wedge WC_{T_j}(\phi_j \wedge E, v_1 = v_2, W)[t_i/w_i] \Rightarrow v_1 = v_2$

        $\wedge \bigwedge_{v \in V', t \in S_v} \psi \wedge WC_{T_j}(\phi_j \wedge E, v = t, W)[t_i/w_i] \Rightarrow v = t$

  let F'_j be the conjunction of all implied variable-term equalities $\gamma_i \Rightarrow v_i = t_i$ implied by F_j s.t. $\texttt{Vars}(\gamma_i) \cap V' = \emptyset$ (for $j = 1, 2$);

  let $\alpha_1 = \texttt{ComputeSimpleCover}_{T_1}(V', \phi_1, F'_2)$;

  let $\alpha_2 = \texttt{ComputeSimpleCover}_{T_2}(V', \phi_2, F'_1)$;

  return $\alpha_1 \wedge \alpha_2$;

$\texttt{ComputeSimpleCover}_{\texttt{T}}(V, \phi, F)$ =

  result $\leftarrow \texttt{ComputeCover}(V, \phi)$;

  forall collections $\bigwedge_{i=1}^{m} \gamma_i \Rightarrow w_i = t_i$ of conditional variable-term equalities implied by F s.t. $m \leq \texttt{Num}(T)$ and w_i are all distinct variables:

    let $\gamma = \bigwedge_{i=1}^{n} \gamma_i$; let $W = V - \{w_i \mid 1 \leq i \leq m\}$;

    result $\leftarrow$ result $\wedge (\gamma \Rightarrow \texttt{ComputeCover}(W, \phi)[t_i/w_i])$;

  return result;

Fig. 4. Cover algorithm for combination of two theories $T_1 \cup T_2$

involve variables in V and furthermore $\phi \Rightarrow \gamma_1 \vee \ldots \vee \gamma_k$. We show that the formula $\texttt{ComputeCover}_{T_1 \cup T_2}(V, \phi) \wedge \neg\gamma_1 \wedge \ldots \wedge \neg\gamma_k$ is unsatisfiable by simulating the decision procedure for theory $T_1 \cup T_2$ based on Nelson-Oppen's combination methodology (with the knowledge of the Nelson-Oppen proof of unsatisfiability of the formula $\phi \wedge \neg\gamma_1 \wedge \ldots \wedge \neg\gamma_k$).

The complexity of the cover algorithm for combination of two theories is an exponential (in size of the input formula ϕ and cardinality of its set of simple terms) factor of the complexity of the cover algorithms for individual theories. For combination of difference logic (theory of linear arithmetic with only difference constraints) and unary uninterpreted functions, which is a useful combination that occurs in practice, the cover algorithm can be simplified and it runs in time polynomial in size of the input formula ϕ.

We now present some examples of computation of cover for the combined theory of linear arithmetic (ℓa) and uninterpreted functions (uf). Example 2 demonstrates the importance of sharing variable-term equalities, while Example 3 demonstrates the importance of sharing conditional equalities.

Example 2. Compute $\mathbb{C}_{\ell a \cup uf}\{v_1, v_2\} : \phi$, where ϕ is $(a \leq v_1 + 1 \wedge v_1 \leq a - 1 \wedge v_2 \leq b \wedge v_1 = F(v_3) \wedge v_2 = F(F(v_3)))$, for some uninterpreted function F.

We first decompose ϕ into pure formulas ϕ_1 and ϕ_2:

$$\phi_1 = (a \le v_1 + 1 \ \wedge \ v_1 \le a - 1 \ \wedge \ v_2 \le b)$$
$$\phi_2 = (v_1 = F(v_3) \ \wedge \ v_2 = F(F(v_3)))$$

We then share variable-term equalities between ϕ_1 and ϕ_2 as follows:

$$\phi_1 \xrightarrow{v_1=a-1} \phi_2 \xrightarrow{v_2=F(a-1)} \phi_1$$

We then compute $\mathbb{C}_{\ell a}\{v_1, v_2\} : \phi_1 \wedge v_2 = F(a-1)$ to obtain the result $F(a-1) \le b$. Note that the cover algorithm for linear arithmetic does not need to understand the term $F(a-1)$ and can just treat it as some fresh variable.

Example 3. Compute $\mathbb{C}_{\ell a \cup uf} x : \phi$, where ϕ is $(y = \mathtt{Mem}(a+x) - \mathtt{Mem}(b+x))$ for some uninterpreted function Mem.
Purifying ϕ, we obtain ϕ_1 and ϕ_2 by introducing new variables u_1, u_2, u_3, u_4.

$$\phi_1 = (y = u_1 - u_2 \ \wedge \ u_3 = a + x \ \wedge \ u_4 = b + x)$$
$$\phi_2 = (u_1 = \mathtt{Mem}(u_3) \ \wedge \ u_2 = \mathtt{Mem}(u_4))$$

We then share conditional equalities between ϕ_1 and ϕ_2 as follows:

$$\phi_1 \xrightarrow{a=b \Rightarrow u_3=u_4} \phi_2 \xrightarrow{a=b \Rightarrow u_1=u_2} \phi_1$$

We then compute $\mathbb{C}_{\ell a}\{x, u_1, u_2, u_3, u_4\} : \phi_1 \wedge a = b \Rightarrow u_1 = u_2$ to obtain the result $a = b \Rightarrow y = 0$.

5 Related Work

5.1 Discovering Invariants over Combination of Linear Arithmetic and Uninterpreted Functions

There has been some work on generating conjunctive invariants that involve combination of linear arithmetic and uninterpreted functions. [10] discovers invariants over a given set of terms, while generates invariants over programmer specified templates [2]. Our approach (extended with a suitable widening operation) can be used to discover (possibly disjunctive) invariants over the combination of theories without the need to provide any terms/templates.

5.2 Abduction

An important key idea used in the cover algorithms described in this paper is that of *abduction*. Abduction is reasoning from an observation to its best explanation. More formally, an abductive explanation of observation ψ given environment E in language L is a formula $\psi' = \mathtt{Abduct}(E, \psi, L)$ such that $\psi' \wedge E \Rightarrow \psi$, ψ' is in L, and ψ' is the weakest such formula. The notion of abduction is widely used in the artificial intelligence community [17] and in the logic programming community [12].

The array $W[n_1, n_2]$ (computed in lines 5 through 8 in Figure 3) used in the algorithm for computing cover of a formula ϕ with respect to variables V in the theory of uninterpreted functions is essentially $\mathtt{Abduct}(\phi, n_1{=}n_2, L)$, where L is the language of formulas over variables other than V. Similarly, the formula $WC(\phi, \delta, V)$ used in the combination cover algorithm is essentially $\mathtt{Abduct}(\delta, \phi, L)$.

5.3 Predicate Cover

The notion of cover discussed in this paper is similar to the *predicate cover* [13] operation used in predicate abstraction algorithms. For a formula ϕ, predicate cover is the weakest Boolean formula over a set of given predicates that implies ϕ. In contrast, the cover of ϕ is defined over a much richer language — the set of all quantifier-free formulas.

6 Conclusion and Future Work

This paper defines cover as the most precise quantifier-free over-approximation to existential quantifier elimination, and describes algorithms to compute the cover of formulas in the theories of uninterpreted functions and linear arithmetic. In addition, this paper provides a combination algorithm to combine the individual cover algorithms for these theories. This paper also describes how the cover operation can be used in program analysis and verification techniques that otherwise require existential quantifier elimination.

We hope to extend this study in future work. We are currently exploring the implementation of the symbolic model checking algorithm described in this paper. Also, the notion of cover can be parameterized by types of formulas that one is interested in. Instead of generating the most precise quantifier-free formula, one may be interested in formulas that are conjunctions of, say, atomic predicates, or at most k disjunctions of atomic predicates, or implications of the form $\phi_1 \Rightarrow \phi_2$, where ϕ_1 and ϕ_2 are conjunctions of atomic predicates in variables V_1 and V_2 respectively. The latter may be useful in computing procedure summaries, where V_1 and V_2 denote the set of input and output variables respectively.

References

1. Ball, T., Rajamani, S.K.: The SLAM project: Debugging system software via static analysis. In: 29th Annual Symposium on POPL, pp. 1–3 (2002)
2. Beyer, D., Henzinger, T., Majumdar, R., Rybalchenko, A.: Invariant synthesis for combined theories. In: Cook, B., Podelski, A. (eds.) VMCAI 2007. LNCS, vol. 4349, pp. 378–394. Springer, Heidelberg (2007)
3. Chaki, S., Clarke, E., Groce, A., Jha, S., Veith, H.: Modular verification of software components in C. Transactions on Software Engg. 30(6), 388–402 (2004)
4. Cousot, P., Cousot, R.: Abstract interpretation: A unified lattice model for static analysis of programs by construction or approximation of fixpoints. In: POPL (1977)
5. Cousot, P., Halbwachs, N.: Automatic discovery of linear restraints among variables of a program. In: 5th ACM Symposium on POPL, pp. 84–96 (1978)
6. Gulavani, B., Rajamani, S.: Counterexample driven refinement for abstract interpretation. In: Hermanns, H., Palsberg, J. (eds.) TACAS 2006. LNCS, vol. 3920, Springer, Heidelberg (2006)
7. Gulwani, S., Musuvathi, M.: Cover algorithms and their combination. Technical Report MSR-TR-2006-09, Microsoft Research (January 2006)

8. Gulwani, S., Necula, G.C.: Global value numbering using random interpretation. In: 31st Annual ACM Symposium on POPL (January 2004)
9. Gulwani, S., Necula, G.C.: A polynomial-time algorithm for global value numbering. In: Giacobazzi, R. (ed.) SAS 2004. LNCS, vol. 3148, pp. 212–227. Springer, Heidelberg (2004)
10. Gulwani, S., Tiwari, A.: Combining abstract interpreters. In: PLDI, pp. 376–386 (2006)
11. Henzinger, T.A., Jhala, R., Majumdar, R., McMillan, K.L.: Abstractions from proofs. In: 31st Annual ACM Symposium on POPL, pp. 232–244 (2004)
12. Kakas, A.C., Kowalski, R.A., Toni, F.: Abductive logic programming. Journal of Logic and Computation 2(6), 719–770 (1992)
13. Lahiri, S.K., Ball, T., Cook, B.: Predicate Abstraction via Symbolic Decision Procedures. In: Etessami, K., Rajamani, S.K. (eds.) CAV 2005. LNCS, vol. 3576, pp. 24–38. Springer, Heidelberg (2005)
14. McMillan, K.: Symbolic model checking: an approach to the state explosion problem. PhD thesis, Carnegie Mellon University (1992)
15. McMillan, K.: An Interpolating Theorem Prover. In: Jensen, K., Podelski, A. (eds.) TACAS 2004. LNCS, vol. 2988, pp. 16–30. Springer, Heidelberg (2004)
16. Nelson, G., Oppen, D.C.: Simplification by cooperating decision procedures. ACM TOPLAS 1(2), 245–257 (1979)
17. Paul, G.: Ai approaches to abduction, 35–98 (2000)

TAPIDO: Trust and Authorization Via Provenance and Integrity in Distributed Objects (Extended Abstract)*

Andrew Cirillo, Radha Jagadeesan, Corin Pitcher, and James Riely

School of CTI, DePaul University

Abstract. Existing web services and mashups exemplify the need for flexible construction of distributed applications. How to do so securely remains a topic of current research. We present TAPIDO, a programming model to address Trust and Authorization concerns via Provenance and Integrity in systems of Distributed Objects. Creation of TAPIDO objects requires (static) authorization checks and their communication provides fine-grain control of their embedded authorization effects. TAPIDO programs constrain such delegation of rights by using provenance information. A type-and-effect system with effect polymorphism provides static support for the programmer to reason about security policies. We illustrate the programming model and static analysis with example programs and policies.

1 Introduction

Web services, portlets, and mashups are collaborative distributed systems built by assembling components from multiple independent web applications. Building such systems requires programming abstractions that directly address service composition and content aggregation. From a security standpoint, such composition and aggregation involves subtle combinations of authentication, authorization, delegation, and trust.

The issues are illustrated by account aggregation services that provide centralized control of an individual's accounts held with one or more institutions. An individual first grants permission for an aggregator to access owned accounts located at various institutions. In a typical use case, the aggregator is asked to provide a summary balance of all registered accounts: the aggregator asks each institution for the relevant account balance; the institution then determines whether or not to grant access; with the accumulated balances, the aggregator returns a summary of registered accounts to the individual. This simple service already raises several security and privacy issues related to trust and authorization. To name just two:

- The account owner's intent to access their account should be established by the institution. Message integrity is required to verify such intent.
- Principals should establish that the flow of messages through the system complies with authorization, audit, and privacy policies for account access. Message provenance is required to verify that the message history does comply with such policies.

* Companion technical report available at `http://www.teasp.org/tapido/`. Andrew Cirillo and James Riely were supported by NSF Career 0347542. Radha Jagadeesan and Corin Pitcher were supported by NSF Cybertrust 0430175.

S. Drossopoulou (Ed.): ESOP 2008, LNCS 4960, pp. 208–223, 2008.

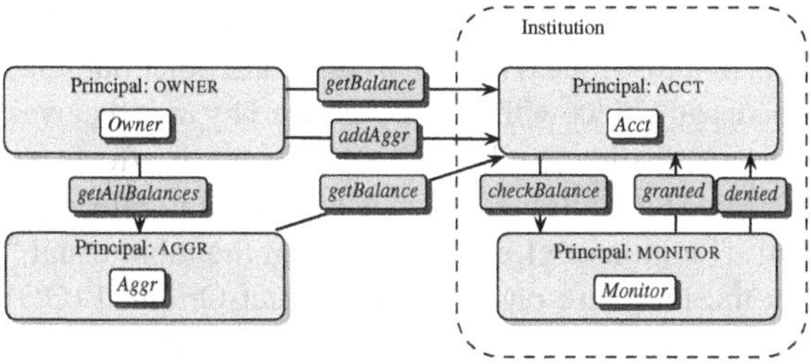

Fig. 1. Principals Involved in Account Aggregation

It has been said that "An application can be mashup-friendly or it can be secure, but it cannot be both." [1]. We disagree. In this paper, we describe the use of message provenance and integrity to achieve both security and flexibility aims in this general programming context. In this extended abstract, we focus on the expressive power of the programming model using examples. For a complete formal treatment of the static analysis, please see the companion technical report.

In the remainder of this section, we present an informal overview of our approach using the account aggregation example. The principals involved are the account owner, the aggregation service, and two principals for the institution holding the account. The institution uses two principals to distinguish privileged monitor code from public-facing, unprivileged code. The owner requests the balance from the public-facing account object, which in turn contacts a trusted monitor to determine whether access should be granted or denied. The flow of messages is summarized in Figure 1.

Object model. TAPIDO's object model is based upon Java's notion of remote objects. We locate objects at atomic principals. Examples of atomic principals are nodes on a distributed system, a user or a process. For an object p, the location is available to the programmer via p.loc. As with Java's remote objects, objects are immobile and rooted at the location where they are created. A method invocation on an object leads to code execution at the location of the callee object. Thus, when the caller and callee objects are located at different locations, method invocation leads to a change of location context. References to objects are mobile — they can be freely copied and they move around through the system as arguments to methods or return values. We do not address mobility of objects themselves; thus, we do not discuss serialization and code mobility.

TAPIDO assumes a communication model that guarantees the provenance and integrity of messages. Thus, TAPIDO focuses on semantic attacks on trust and authorization, rather than on attacks against the cryptographic techniques required to achieve this communication model. Thus, our approach assume an underlying network model in which the sender of the message can be reliably determined; this model is well-studied [2,3,4,5] and realizable [6,7,8]. Using a relatively high-level model permits us to concentrate on attacks that seek unauthorized access, rather than studying the underlying cryptographic protocols that facilitate the integrity assumption.

Statics. Effects are communicated through object references. The language of effects is a decidable monotonic fragment of first-order logic (e.g., Datalog) extended to work over authorization logics. The modalities of authorization logics [9,10,11,12] permit different participants of a distributed system to maintain potentially inconsistent world-views, e.g. if b receives an object with effect ϕ created by a, it receives the effect a *says* ϕ, rather than the more absolute truth ϕ. Our language of effects also includes logic variables to achieve ML-style polymorphism with respect to effects.

Our "object-centric" notion of effects differs from the more usual "method-centric" notions explored in the literature on effects in Object-Oriented (OO) languages. The effects on objects can only refer to the immutable data of the object — if the object is an authorization token, this effect can record the rights associated with these object. For honest agents, object effects are validated at the point of creation, effectively ensuring that the global policy permits the creation of the object. When such an object is received — e.g., as an argument to a method call — the effects are transferred as a benefit to the recipient. In any execution of a well-typed program, there is a *corresponding* [13] object creation validating such accrual of rights.

The attackers that we consider are untrustworthy atomic principals running *any* well-typed Java program. Following [14] and our own earlier work [15], they may "utter" anything whatsoever in terms of effects. For example, opponents may create authorization objects without actually having the rights to create them, aiming to subvert the global authorization policy. A program is *safe* [16] if every object creation at runtime is justified by the accumulated effects. Our type system ensures that well-typed programs remain safe under evaluation in the face of arbitrary opponent processes.

In the account aggregation example, consider when an individual requests their balance from the institution holding their account through the aggregator. The guarantee sought is that the institution may only respond with the account balance when the request is approved by the account owner. With a pre-arranged protocol, approval can be conveyed by a message passed from the account owner to the institution via the aggregator. The institution's code must be able to verify that it originates with the owner and not been modified en route. The code must also ensure that the integrity-verified message and the pre-arranged protocol entail the owner's approval in the past; even in the presence of attackers who (perhaps falsely) claim possession of rights.

We describe a program incorporating such a design in our model, and verify the required properties with our static analysis.

Programming Provenance. Provenance — the history of ownership of an object — has received much interest in databases, e.g., see [17] for a survey. Security-passing style implementations [18] of stack inspection are already reminiscent of such ideas in a security context, since the provenance of the extra security-token parameter can be viewed as encoding the current relevant security context.

Provenance plays a crucial role in both the privacy architecture and the security (access control and accountability) of the account aggregation example. Consider the request from the account owner to the institution via the aggregator. The institution may impose an access control policy on the provenance of the request, e.g., to restrict the aggregators that can be used with the institution's services. Such a policy is distinct from, but can be used in conjunction with, an access control policy based upon the originator of the request. Similarly, the institution's audit policy may require a record of the provenance of requests (including the identities of the owner and the aggregator) to support an accountability obligation, e.g., to explain why and to whom account information was provided should the institution be accused of dishonest behavior.

Finally, the account owner can demand security of the path traversed by the result of such a request to ensure data privacy. This is demonstrated to the account owner by returning the relevant snapshot of the history of their data along with their data.

In contrast to stack inspection and history-based access control (e.g., see [19]) that mandate the flow of the security token, and record in it the *full* history of information used to make a judgement, our "user-defined" approach relies on trust relationships between the principals that are recorded as part of the history to make judgements.

In the account aggregation example, the response from the institution to the account owner has full history that can be described with the regular expression $\text{ACCT} \cdot \textit{trusted}^* \cdot \text{AGGR} \cdot \textit{trusted}^* \cdot \text{OWNER}$, where *trusted* represents a collection of trusted principals. Our explicit programming of this path in the sequel maintains only a subsequence of the history that matches $\text{ACCT} \cdot \textit{trusted}^* \cdot \text{AGGR} \cdot \text{OWNER}$. Such abbreviations of the full history are codified in the security policy by assumptions on these principals — e.g., that the aggregator received the result from a trustworthy principal that can be relied upon to enforce the policy, *and* that the aggregator can be relied upon to report this information accurately.

We describe a program incorporating such a design in our model, and verify the required properties with our static analysis.

Related work. The study of effect systems was initiated in the context of functional languages (e.g., see Gifford and Lucassen [20,21], and Talpin and Jouvelot [22,23] amongst others). The ideas have since been applied broadly to OO languages; to name but a few, specifying the read/write behavior of methods [24,25], confinement [26,27], type reclassification [28], object protocols [29] and session types [30].

The most closely related papers are types for authorization, by Fournet, Gordon and Maffeis [31], a successor paper by the same authors [14] and our own earlier paper [15]. All of these papers (including this one) focus on authorization issues and so the work on information flow, e.g., see [32] for a survey, is not directly relevant. However, as in information flow based methods, TAPIDO global policy drives program design.

Fournet, Gordon and Maffeis [31] introduce an assume-guarantee reasoning framework with Datalog assertions for dealing with types for authorization. Both papers [31,14] are based in a pi-calculus formalism and view authorization as "a complex cryptographic protocol" [31] in the context of the traditional "network is the opponent" model. The successor paper uses dependency analysis on authorization logic to formalize a subtle notion of security despite compromise. Our object-centric effects adapt their static annotations to an OO setting. Our requirements on object creation (resp. transfer of effects to the callee) are analogous to their *expectation* (resp. *statement*) annotations.

Our prior paper [15] was inspired by [31]. It was also placed in a mobile process calculus, but diverged from [31,14] in assuming a model with explicit identities and a network that guaranteed integrity.

In this paper, we study imperative distributed objects by building on these intuitions. Our primary aim in this paper is to provide foundations of a programming methodology to ensure that distributed systems validate authorization and security policies; e.g., one of the aims of our examples is to illustrate the use of standard OO mechanisms to incrementally construct security guarantees. While the pi-calculus (with notions of keys) is expressive enough to code distributed objects (with explicit identities), such a translation is arguably inconsistent with our overall aims — just consider the complex encoding of state in the control of a pi-program. Such a translation based semantics approach obfuscates the simple (from an object standpoint) invariants that underlie our analysis. At any rate, the type systems in these three papers do not include the invariants of processes required to capture the type annotations of TAPIDO.

2 Language

We present the evaluation semantics for TAPIDO, a distributed class-based language with mutable objects. Our treatment of classes follows earlier direct semantics for class-based languages [33,34,24,35]. We do not address issues of genericity [36,34] or inner classes [37]. Our treatment of concurrency follows Gordon and Hankin's concurrent object calculus [38]. As in Cardelli's Obliq [39], our object references have distributed scope, rather than local scope [40]. Our treatment of locations borrows heavily from process algebras with localities (see [41] for a survey).

We first describe our naming conventions. Names for classes (c, d), methods (ℓ), fields (f, g), variables (x, y, z), objects (p, q) and principals (a, b) are drawn from separate namespaces, as usual. Predicate variables (α, β) and predicate constructors (γ) occur in static annotations used during type-checking.

The reserved words of the language include: the variable names "this" and "caller"; the binary predicate constructors "$\wedge$", representing conjunction, and "says", representing quoting; the ternary predicate constructor *Prov* is used to indicate that the first argument (an object) was received from the second argument (source principal) by the third argument (target principal). We write the binary constructors infix.

The language is explicitly typed. Object types ($c\texttt{<}\vec{\phi}\texttt{>}$) include the actual predicate parameters $\vec{\phi}$, which we treat formally as *extended values*. Value types include objects (C), principals (Prin) and Unit. Extended value types include predicate types (P), which are resolved during typechecking. The process type (Proc) has no values.

$C, D ::= c\texttt{<}\vec{\phi}\texttt{>}$	Object Types
$T, S ::= C \mid \mathsf{Prin} \mid \mathsf{Unit}$	Value Types
$P, Q ::= \mathsf{Pred}(\vec{\mathscr{T}})$	Predicate Types
$\mathscr{T}, \mathscr{S} ::= T \mid P \mid \mathsf{Proc}$	Types
$\mu ::= \mathsf{final} \mid \mathsf{mutable}$	Mutability Annotations
$\mathscr{D} ::= \mathsf{class}\ c\texttt{<}\vec{\alpha} : \vec{P}\texttt{>} \lhd D\{\vec{\mu}\ \vec{T}\ \vec{f};\ \vec{\mathscr{M}}\}\ [\theta]$	Classes ($\vec{\alpha}$ bound in D, θ, $\vec{T}$, $\vec{\mathscr{M}}$)
$\mathscr{M} ::= \texttt{<}\vec{\beta} : \vec{Q}\texttt{>} S\ \ell(\vec{T}\ \vec{x})\ \{M\}$	Methods ($\vec{\beta}$ bound in S, $\vec{T}$, M; $\vec{x}$ in M)

One may write classes and methods that are generic in the predicate variables, achieving ML-style polymorphism with respect to effects. Class declarations thus include the formal predicate parameters $\vec{\alpha}$, which may occur in the effect θ (see next table) associated with instances of the class. In addition to effects, class declarations include field and method declarations, but omit implicit constructor declarations. Fields include mutability annotations, which are used in the statics. The syntax of values and terms is as follows[1].

V,W,U,A,B,ϕ,ψ ::=	Open Extended Values
$\quad x \mid p \mid a \mid \mathsf{unit}$	Variable, Runtime Value
$\quad \alpha \mid \gamma \mid \phi(\vec{V}) \mid \cdots$	Predicates
M,N,L,θ ::=	Terms
$\quad V \mid \mathsf{new}\ c\texttt{<}\vec{\phi}\texttt{>}(\vec{V})$	Value, Object Creation
$\quad \mathsf{let}\ x = V.\ell\texttt{<}\vec{\phi}\texttt{>}(\vec{W});M \mid V.f \mid V.\mathsf{loc} \mid V.f := W$	Object Operations
$\quad \mathsf{if}\ V = W\ \mathsf{then}\ M\ \mathsf{else}\ N \mid \mathsf{let}\ x = N;M \mid N \mathbin{\Vert\!\ulcorner} M$	Control Flow
$\quad p{:}c\{\vec{f} = \vec{V}\} \mid (\nu p{:}C)\,M \mid a[M]$	Runtime Terms

We use the metavariables ϕ, ψ and θ to represent values and terms of predicate type, and the other metavariables to represent runtime values and terms, with A and B reserved for values of principal type. Predicates are static annotations used in type-checking, which do not play any role in the dynamics.

An *expectation* "expect θ" may be written as "new $\mathsf{Proof}\texttt{<}\theta\texttt{>}()$", where class Proof is defined "class $\mathsf{Proof}\texttt{<}\alpha:\mathsf{Pred}\texttt{>}\{\}\,[\alpha]$".

The syntax of terms includes standard OO primitives for object creation, method call, and field get/set. The let binder in method calls is necessary to describe the provenance of return values. Constructors and methods take predicate parameters that are used statically. The special "field" loc returns the location of an object. The conditional allows equality testing of values.

Concurrent composition ($\Vert\!\ulcorner$) is asymmetric. In $N \mathbin{\Vert\!\ulcorner} M$, the returned value comes from M; the term N is available only for side effects. In the sequential composition "let $x = N; M$", x is bound with scope M. We elide the let, writing simply "$N; M$" when x does not occur in M. We also use standard syntactic sugar in place of explicit sequencing. For example, we may write "$y.f.g$" to abbreviate "let $x = y.f; x.g$".

Heap elements ($p{:}c\{\cdots\}$), name restriction ((νp)) and frames ($a[M]$) are meant only to occur at runtime. The first two of these model the heap, whereas the last models the (potentially distributed) "call stack". We expect that these constructs do not occur in user code. An object name binder (ν) is separate from the associated denotation ($p{:}c\{\vec{f} = \vec{V}\}$), allowing arbitrary graphs of heap objects. (The preceding example indicates that p is located at a, with actual class c and fields $\vec{f} = \vec{V}$.) The frame $a[M]$ indicates that M is running under the authority of a.

Structural Congruence. Evaluation is defined using a structural congruence on terms. Let $\equiv$ be the least congruence on terms that satisfies the following axioms. The rules in the left column are from [38]. They capture properties of concurrent composition,

[1] When writing definitions using classes and methods, we often elide irrelevant bits of syntax, e.g., we leave out the parameters to classes when empty, such as writing Object rather than Object<·>. We identify syntax up to renaming of bound names, and write $M[x := V]$ for substitution of V for x in M (and similarly for other categories). We sometimes write extends for $\triangleleft$ for clarity. We often elide type information. We write "$S\ \ell\ (\vec{T}\ \vec{x});$" as shorthand for "$S\ \ell\ (\vec{T}\ \vec{x})\ \{\}$".

including semi-associativity and the interaction with let. The rules in the right column, inspired by [41], capture properties of distribution. The first of these states that the interpretation of a value is independent of the location at which it occurs. The second states that computation of a frame does not depend upon the location from which the frame was invoked.

Structural Congruence. $(M \equiv M')$ (where $p \notin fn(M)$)

$$(M \Vdash N) \Vdash L \equiv M \Vdash (N \Vdash L) \qquad a[V] \equiv V$$
$$(M \Vdash N) \Vdash L \equiv (N \Vdash M) \Vdash L \qquad a[b[M]] \equiv b[M]$$
$$((\nu p) N) \Vdash M \equiv (\nu p)(N \Vdash M) \qquad a[N \Vdash M] \equiv a[N] \Vdash a[M]$$
$$M \Vdash ((\nu p) N) \equiv (\nu p)(M \Vdash N) \qquad a[(\nu p) N] \equiv (\nu p)\, a[N]$$
$$\mathsf{let}\, x = (L \Vdash N); M \equiv L \Vdash (\mathsf{let}\, x = N; M) \qquad a[\mathsf{let}\, x = N; M] \equiv \mathsf{let}\, x = a[N]; a[M]$$
$$\mathsf{let}\, x = ((\nu p) N); M \equiv (\nu p)(\mathsf{let}\, x = N; M)$$

One may view interesting terms as *configurations*, which we now define. A *store* Σ is a collection of distributed heap terms, $b_1[p_1 : c_1\{\cdots\}] \Vdash \cdots \Vdash b_m[p_m : c_m\{\cdots\}]$, where each p_j is unique. A *thread* is either a value or a term $a[M]$ that does not contain occurrences of a name restriction or heap term. (A value represents a terminated thread.) An *initial* thread is a term $a[M]$ such that M additionally contains no blocks. A *configuration* is a term of the form $(\nu\vec{p})(\Sigma \Vdash M_1 \Vdash \cdots \Vdash M_n)$, where each M_i is a thread. A configuration is *initial* if each of its threads is initial. Evaluation preserves the shape of a configuration up to structural equivalence: If M is a configuration and $M \rightarrow M'$ then M' is structurally equivalent to a configuration.

Evaluation. The evaluation relation is defined with respect to an arbitrary fixed class table. The class table is referenced indirectly in the semantics through the lookup functions *fields* and *body*; we elide the standard definitions.

Evaluation is defined using the following axioms; we elide the standard inductive rules that lift structural equivalence to evaluation ($M \rightarrow M'$ if $M \equiv N \rightarrow N' \equiv M'$) and that describe computation in context (for example, $b[M] \rightarrow b[M']$ if $M \rightarrow M'$). We discuss the novelties below.

Term Evaluation. $(M \rightarrow M')$

$$\mathsf{new}\, c(\vec{V}) \rightarrow (\nu p)(p : c\{\vec{f} = \vec{V}\} \Vdash p)$$
$$\quad \text{if } \mathit{fields}(c) = \vec{f} \text{ and } |\vec{f}| = |\vec{V}|$$
$$b[p : c\{\cdots\}] \Vdash a[\mathsf{let}\, y = p.\ell(\vec{W}); L] \rightarrow b[p : c\{\cdots\}] \Vdash a[\mathsf{let}\, y = b[M']; L']$$
$$\quad \text{if } \mathit{body}(c.\ell) = (\vec{x})\{M\} \text{ and } |\vec{x}| = |\vec{W}|$$
$$\quad \text{where } M' = \mathit{Prov}(\vec{W}, a, b) \Vdash M[\mathsf{caller} := a][\mathsf{this} := p][\vec{x} := \vec{W}]$$
$$\quad \text{and } L' = \mathit{Prov}(y, b, a) \Vdash L$$
$$b[p : c\{\cdots\}] \Vdash p.\mathsf{loc} \rightarrow b[p : c\{\cdots\}] \Vdash b$$
$$b[p : c\{f = V \cdots\}] \Vdash p.f := W \rightarrow b[p : c\{f = W \cdots\}] \Vdash \mathsf{unit}$$
$$b[p : c\{f = V \cdots\}] \Vdash p.f \rightarrow b[p : c\{f = V \cdots\}] \Vdash V$$
$$\mathsf{if}\, V = V\, \mathsf{then}\, M\, \mathsf{else}\, N \rightarrow M$$
$$\mathsf{if}\, V = W\, \mathsf{then}\, M\, \mathsf{else}\, N \rightarrow N \quad \text{if } V \neq W$$
$$\mathsf{let}\, x = V; M \rightarrow M[x := V]$$

The rule for new creates an object and returns a reference to it; in the Gordon/Hankin formalism, the heap stays on the left, whereas the return value goes on the right. p.loc returns the location of p.

Method invocation happens at the callee site, and thus a new frame is introduced in the consequent $b\,[M']$. The provenance of the actual parameters is recorded in $Prov(\vec{W}, a, b)$, which is shorthand for $Prov(W_1, a, b), \ldots, Prov(W_n, a, b)$. In M', the special variable caller is bound to calling principal; there are also standard substitutions for this and the formal parameters. In L', the provenance of the return value is recorded in $Prov(y, b, a)$.

Effects. Effects play a crucial role in the statics, but are ignored by evaluation. In summary, trustworthy processes are required to justify object creation by validating the expectations associated with classes in terms of accumulated effects. Opponent processes, on the other hand, may ignore expectations but are otherwise well typed. We say that a term is *safe* if the expectations associated with object creation by trusted principals during evaluation are always justified by the accumulated effects. We establish the standard properties of Preservation and Progress. As a corollary, we deduce that well-typed trustworthy processes remain safe when composed with *arbitrary* opponents.

Our proof of type-safety identifies the key properties required of the logic of effects. Thus, the logic of effects has to support structural rules on the left, support transitivity via cut, and ensure closure of the equality predicate under substitution and reduction. In addition, typechecking of examples (such as the ones that follow) also requires closure of inference under the inference rules of affirmation in the authorization logic of [10], e.g., functoriality of *says*, distribution of *says* over conjunction, and $(\alpha \Rightarrow A\ says\ \beta) \Rightarrow (A\ says\ \alpha \Rightarrow A\ says\ \beta)$. In this extended abstract, we illustrate the type system using examples; full details can be found in the companion technical report.

3 Examples

In these examples, effects are described in a variant of Datalog extended to work over authorization logic. As with regular Datalog, a program is built from a set of Horn clauses without function symbols. In contrast to regular Datalog, the literals can also be in the form of quotes of principals. The well-formed user predicates are typed, with fixed arity. They are always instantiated with pure terms in a type-respecting fashion; pure terms are guaranteed to converge to a value without mutating the heap.

3.1 Workflow

In this stateful workflow pattern, a user submits data of type T by creating an object of class SubmittedCell. (For simplicity, we do not address generic types here.) The manager must subsequently approve the data by creating an object of class ApprovedCell.

```
class Celll<α,β:Pred(T)> { }
class SubmittedCell<α,β:Pred(T)> extends Celll<α,β> {
```

```
  final T data; final Prin user; final Prin manager;
} [this.user says α(this.data)]
class ApprovedCell<α,β:Pred(T)> extends CellI<α,β> {
  final T data; final Prin user; final Prin manager;
} [this.user says α(this.data) ∧ this.manager says β(this.data)]
class FailedCell<α,β:Pred(T)> extends CellI<α,β> { }
```

In CellI<α,β>, α is the predicate that the user establishes on the data in the submission. β is the predicate that the manager establishes on the data. The final effect on approved cells represents both approvals in the static types.

The submission and approval objects are generated by a CellFactory in response to receipt of a request object (of class CellReq<γ>). The submit method of CellFactory <α,β> receives the effect req.loc *says* α(req.data) on its req parameter. The resulting instance of SubmittedCell<α,β> carries this assumption, along with the name of a manager that must approve the request.

```
class CellReq<γ:Pred(T)> { final T data; } [γ(this.data)]
class CellFactory<α,β:Pred(T)> {
  SubmittedCell<α,β> submit(CellReq<α> req, Prin manager) {
    new SubmittedCell<α,β>(req.data, req.loc, manager)
  }
  CellI<α,β> approve(CellReq<β> req, SubmittedCell<α,β> cell) {
    if ((req.loc=cell.manager) && (req.data=cell.data) && (this.loc=cell.loc))
    then new ApprovedCell<α,β>(cell.data, cell.user, cell.manager)
    else  new FailedCell<α,β>()
}}
```

The approve method receives the effect req.loc *says* β(req.data). After checking that req.loc is the same as cell.manager, it may conclude that cell.manager *says* β(req.data). To establish the final effect on the ApprovedCell, the factory must establish that the data in the approval request is the same as the data in the initial request. Further, it must be the case that submit and approve are called upon factories located at the same principal, since the ApprovedCell vouches for both α and β, although these are validated at different times. If any of the equality tests are missing, the code fails to typecheck.

Visitors for typecases. The class CellI is an interface for cells. The visitor design pattern [42] provides a type-safe way to write code that is dependent on the actual dynamic type/subclass. Thus, we add methods such as visitApprovedCell to class CellV<α,β> (in general, one such visit method for each subclass). To dispatch to the visitor, the CellI interface is augmented with an accept method, implemented in each subclass; e.g., if S is the return type of the visitor, the implementation of ApprovedCell<α,β>.accept is:

```
S accept(CellV<α,β> v) { v.visitApprovedCell(this) }
```

Encoding Provenance. The submission and approval requests described above for the workflow cell do not track provenance. To accommodate provenance tracking, e.g., for the account balance requests discussed in Section 1, we develop an idiom for decorating such requests as they are passed from principal to principal. The decorations indicate the provenance of the transmitted data. As usual with a decorator design pattern [42], the Req<α> class is split into three classes: the interface ReqI<α>, the concrete class ReqC<α> (which corresponds to the original Req<α>), and the decorator ReqD<α>. We use a visitor to inspect the resulting object. Again, let T be the type of the request data and S be the arbitrary return type of the visitor.

```
class ReqV<α> { S visitReqC(ReqC<α> x); S visitReqD(ReqD<α> x); }
class ReqI<α> { S accept(ReqV<α> v); }
class ReqC<α> extends ReqI<α> { final T data;
  S accept(ReqV<α> v) { v.visitReqC(this) }
} [α(this)]
class ReqD<α> extends ReqI<α> { final ReqI<α> payload; final Prin src; final Prin tgt;
  S accept(ReqV<α> v) { v.visitReqD(this); }
} [Prov(this.payload, this.src, this.tgt)]
```

Significantly, it is the concrete class ReqC<α> that retains the original effect α(this). The decorator, instead, carries an effect concerning the provenance of the decorated data. The effect *Prov*, used here at type Pred(ReqI<α>,Prin,Prin), is a claim about the provenance of one hop of a request. It indicates that this.payload was received from this.src by this.tgt. Thus, the object creation **new** ReqD(p,A,B) typechecks only when the static semantics can deduce that p has been received by B from A.

To illustrate request decoration, consider the following trustworthy forwarder[2]:

```
class TrustworthyForwarder extends AggrI { mutable AggrI next;
  RespI getAllBalances(ReqI<SubmitBal> req) {
    let resp:RespI = next.approve(new ReqD<SubmitBal>(req, caller, this.loc));
    new RespD(resp, next.loc, this.loc); } }
```

The method body is typechecked in the context of the assertion *Prov*(req,caller,this.loc), thus permitting the construction of the ReqD object. Similarly, the *Prov*(resp,next.loc, this.loc) assertion established by the method invocation on next enables the typechecking of the construction of the new RespD object. In contrast, an untrustworthy forwarder might produce an inaccurate provenance decoration for the request, e.g., using **new** ReqD<*SubmitBal*>(req,FAKESRC,FAKETGT)). In the following account aggregation example, the principals trusted to provide accurate provenance decorations are specified via the θ_2 component of the global policy.

3.2 Account Aggregation

Recall, from Figure 1, a rough outline of the protocol: (1) OWNER informs ACCT that AGGR may aggregate its balances (using Acct.addAggr); (2) OWNER requests a summary of its balances from AGGR (using Aggr.getAllBalances); (3) AGGR requests the

[2] For reasons of space we omit definition of AggrI, an interface class with a single getAllBalances method, and classes RespI, RespC, RespD for responses by analogy with non-generic versions of request classes ReqI, ReqC, ReqD.

balance from ACCT using Acct.getBalance. Steps (1) and (3) involve communication between the public-facing ACCT and the private MONITOR. In addition, let the principal FORWARDER be trusted to relay messages using the decorator previously discussed. For simplicity, we use a single forwarder and account as well as a single class to represent the code running at each principal. (We follow the convention that field owner references an instance of class Owner located at principal OWNER.) Due to space limitations, we elide the code implementing step (1) of the protocol. We recall that Step (2) of the protocol is initiated by the OWNER, with a call to Aggr.getAllBalances.

The global security policy. The global system policy has the form $[\text{OWNER } \textit{says } (\theta_0)] \wedge [\text{AGGR } \textit{says } (\theta_1 \wedge \theta_2 \wedge \theta_3)] \wedge [\text{MONITOR } \textit{says } (\theta_4 \wedge \theta_5)] \wedge [\text{ACCT } \textit{says } \theta_6]$. The predicates $\theta_0 \ldots \theta_6$ are formalized shortly. Informally, θ_0 will ensure that the OWNER is authorized to submit balance requests. θ_1 and θ_2 will characterize the paths that are considered secure. θ_3 will ensure that the aggregator only creates requests that arrive from owner on secure paths. θ_4 and θ_5 will ensure that the MONITOR only accepts requests from owner or from aggregators certified by the owner. θ_6 will ensure that the account delegates authorization decisions to the monitor.

The design of the entire program that follows is driven by this global policy, i.e., our code is set up to satisfy the expectations of each principal. Our presentation of the formal policies piecemeal along with the associated classes is only for concise exposition.

Notation. To encode the policy, we use several predicate constructors, which we write in italics. *SubmitAggr*, with type Pred(Prin), indicates that an aggregator has been submitted for approval. Likewise *ApproveAggr* indicates that the request was approved. *SubmitBal*, with type Pred(ReqC<*SubmitBal*>), is a claim that a balance request has been submitted. *ApproveBal*, with type Pred(ReqI<*SubmitBal*>), is a claim that a balance request (perhaps with decorators) has been approved. As described previously, *Prov*, used here at type Pred(ReqI<*SubmitBal*>, Prin, Prin), is a claim about the provenance of one hop of a request. *CheckedProv*, with type Pred(ReqI<*SubmitBal*>), indicates that the provenance of a request has been checked, and is specified using reachability via *Prov*, incorporating trust in principals that report about each hop.

We assume that the field Monitor.cell is set appropriately. For simplicity, we have hard-coded AGGR and other principals throughout the example code; one may instead use a final field to store principals of interest, deferring the choice to instantiation-time.

Owner. We use some abbreviations and elide the code to check the response received back from the aggregator, which is similar to the visitor used by the aggregator, shown later below. Acct.addAggr expects arguments of type CellReq<*SubmitAggr*>, and Aggr.getAllBalances expects arguments of type ReqI<*SubmitBal*>.

```
class Owner { mutable AcctI acct; mutable AggrI aggr;  /* could be forwarders */
  Unit main() {
    acct.addAggr(new CellReq<SubmitAggr>(AGGR));
    let response:RespI = aggr.getAllBalances(new ReqC<SubmitBal>(this.loc));
    ... /* check response for compliance with privacy policy */ }
} [θ0]
```

where $\theta_0 = (\mathit{SubmitAggr}(\text{AGGR})) \wedge (\mathit{SubmitBal}(\mathbb{X})\,\text{:-}\,\mathbb{X}.\mathsf{data} = \mathbb{X}.\mathsf{loc} = \mathsf{this.loc})$. This effect indicates that the instantiator must be able to submit the aggregator request and that the instantiator must be able to submit any balance request that it creates, so long as the data field truthfully records its identity. The second requirement is expressed using a Datalog variable $\mathbb{X}$, ranging over values of type ReqC<*SubmitBal*>.

Aggregator. The code uses the following effects.

$$\begin{aligned}
\theta_1 &= \mathit{CheckedProv}(\mathbb{X}) \text{ :- } \mathit{Prov}(\mathbb{X},\, \mathbb{S},\, \mathsf{this.loc}),\ \mathbb{S} = \text{OWNER OR } \mathbb{S} = \text{FORWARDER} \\
\theta_2 &= \mathit{CheckedProv}(\mathbb{X}.\mathsf{payload}) \text{ :- } \text{FORWARDER } \mathit{says}\ \mathit{Prov}(\mathbb{X}.\mathsf{payload},\, \mathbb{S},\, \text{FORWARDER}), \\
&\qquad \mathit{CheckedProv}(\mathbb{X}) \\
\theta_3 &= \mathit{SubmitBal}(\mathbb{X}) \text{ :- } \text{OWNER } \mathit{says}\ \mathit{SubmitBal}(\mathbb{Y}),\ \mathbb{Y}.\mathsf{data}{=}\mathbb{X}.\mathsf{data}{=}\text{OWNER},\ \mathit{CheckedProv}(\mathbb{Y})
\end{aligned}$$

The first two of these deal with provenance. The base case θ_1 validates an object delivered to aggregator from forwarder or owner. θ_2 recurses down one level of the decorated object, making explicit the trust on trusted forwarders. Together θ_1 and θ_2 ensure that a request is deemed valid if it has passed through trusted intermediaries. θ_3 allows the aggregator to create new balance requests, if it has checked the provenance of the request: both the new request $\mathbb{X}$ and the old one $\mathbb{Y}$ must have the data field set to OWNER; further, the OWNER must avow that they created the old request.

```
class Aggr extends AggrI { final Acct acct;
  RespI getAllBalances(ReqI<SubmitBal> req) {
    if ((caller=FORWARDER) || (caller=OWNER)) then
      let req2:ReqI<SubmitBal> = req.accept(new AggrReqV(req));
      let resp:RespI = acct.getBalance(req2);
      new RespD(resp, acct.loc, this.loc) }
} [θ1 ∧ θ2 ∧ θ3]
```

The validation of the creation of req2 uses θ_1 to satisfy the effect of the the class AggrReqV. The auxiliary class AggrReqV is a visitor to typecase on the request being either a concrete request, or being a forwarded request.

```
class AggrReqV extends ReqV<SubmitBal> {
  final ReqI<SubmitBal> in;
  ReqI<SubmitBal> visitReqC(ReqC<SubmitBal> x) {
    if ((this.in=x) && (x.loc=x.data=OWNER)) then
      new ReqC<SubmitBal>(x.data)
    else ... /* error */ }
  ReqI<SubmitBal> visitReqD(ReqD<SubmitBal> x) {
    if ((this.in=x) && (x.loc=x.tgt=FORWARDER)) then
      x.payload.accept(new AggrReqV(x.payload))
    else ... /* error */ }
} [θ1 ∧ θ2 ∧ θ3 ∧ CheckedProv(this.in)]
```

As the visitor traverses the decorators, it maintains the invariant that *CheckedProv* is true of the object being visited. The visitor updates the effect each time it moves to a new element by creating (and using) a new visitor. On callback to visitReqC or visitReqD, the ReqI *should* be the same as the one with the effect; the type system ensures that this is explicitly checked. To type visitReqC requires θ_3, which allows us to create the new ReqC located at AGGR. To type visitReqD, we first deduce *CheckedProv*(x) from this.in = x and the class effect. Since x is a ReqD, we have x.loc *says Prov*(x.payload, x.src, x.tgt). Since x.loc = x.tgt = FORWARDER and *CheckedProv*(x), then θ_2 yields *CheckedProv*(x.payload), allowing creation of the new AggrReqV.

The enforcement of the privacy policy of the introduction by the OWNER can be achieved using similar techniques.

Account. Calls to Acct.getBalance are delegated to Monitor.checkBalance, which results in a call back to either Acct.granted or Acct.denied.

```
class Acct { mutable int Balance; mutable Monitor monitor; mutable RespI result;
  RespI getBalance(ReqI<SubmitBal> req) {
    monitor.checkBalance(req, this);
    this.result }
  Unit granted(ReqI<ApproveBal> req) {
    if (req.loc=MONITOR) then
      expect MONITOR says ApproveBal(req);
      this.result := new RespC(req)
    else ... /* error */ }
  Unit denied() { ... /* error */ } ...
} [θ6]
```

Here θ_6 = *ApproveBal*($\mathbb{X}$) :- MONITOR *says ApproveBal*($\mathbb{X}$). Thus, if the granted method is called back, then it must be the case that the monitor approved the request.

Monitor. The effects of the monitor code are expressed using the following predicates.

θ_4 = *ApproveBal*($\mathbb{X}$) :- OWNER *says SubmitBal*($\mathbb{X}$), $\mathbb{X}$.data=OWNER
θ_5 = *ApproveBal*($\mathbb{X}$) :- OWNER *says SubmitAggr*($\mathbb{Y}$), this.loc *says ApproveAggr*($\mathbb{Y}$), $\mathbb{Y}$ *says SubmitBal*($\mathbb{X}$), $\mathbb{X}$.data=OWNER

```
class Monitor { mutable CellI<SubmitAggr, ApproveAggr> cell;
  Unit checkBalance(ReqI<SubmitBal> req, Acct acct) {
    if (req.loc=req.data=OWNER)
    then /* audit the request */; acct.granted(new ReqC<ApproveBal>(req.data))
    else this.cell.accept(new MonitorCellV(req, acct)) }
} [θ4 ∧ θ5]
class MonitorCellV extends CellV<SubmitAggr, ApproveAggr> {
  final ReqI<SubmitBal> req; final Acct acct;
  Unit visitFailedCell(FailedCell<SubmitAggr, ApproveAggr> x) { this.acct.denied() }
  Unit visitSubmittedCell(SubmittedCell<SubmitAggr, ApproveAggr> x) { this.acct.denied() }
  Unit visitApprovedCell(ApprovedCell<SubmitAggr, ApproveAggr> x) {
    if ((x.loc=this.loc) && (OWNER=x.user) && (this.loc=x.manager)
        && (this.req.loc=x.data) && (this.req.data=OWNER))
    then /* audit the request */; this.acct.granted(new ReqC<ApproveBal>(this.req.data))
    else this.acct.denied() }
} [θ5]
```

In checkBalance, θ_4 establishes the safety of creating the ReqC, whereas θ_5 establishes the safety of creating the MonitorCellV.

4 Conclusion

TAPIDO is designed to counter the claim that "an application can be mashup-friendly or it can be secure, but it cannot be both." Our model of dynamics adds only two non-standard features, namely (a) the ability to detect the creator location, and (b) integrity of remote method invocation. We have shown that this suffices to code useful tracking of the provenance of an object reference. Our type system adds (polymorphic) object level effects to standard types. From a programming point of view, this style allows trust-based decisions that are validated by the policy context of the application.

References

1. Chess, B., O'Neil, Y.T., West, J.: Javascript hijacking. Technical report, Fortify Software (2007), `http://www.fortifysoftware.com/news-events/releases/2007/2007-04-02.jsp`
2. Lampson, B., Abadi, M., Burrows, M., Wobber, E.: Authentication in distributed systems: Theory and practice. ACM Trans. Comput. Syst. 10(4), 265–310 (1992)
3. Wobber, E., Abadi, M., Burrows, M., Lampson, B.: Authentication in the Taos operating system. ACM Trans. Comput. Syst. 12(1), 3–32 (1994)
4. Abadi, M., Fournet, C., Gonthier, G.: Authentication primitives and their compilation. In: POPL, pp. 302–315 (2000)
5. Landau, S.: Liberty ID-WSF security and privacy overview (2006), `http://www.projectliberty.org/`
6. Li, N., Mitchell, J.C., Tong, D.: Securing Java RMI-based distributed applications. In: ACSAC, pp. 262–271. IEEE Computer Society, Los Alamitos (2004)
7. Scheifler, B., Venners, B.: A conversation with Bob Scheifler, part I, by Bill Venners (2002), `http://www.artima.com/intv/jinisecu.html`
8. Gordon, A.D., Pucella, R.: Validating a web service security abstraction by typing. Formal Asp. Comput. 17(3), 277–318 (2005)
9. Abadi, M., Burrows, M., Lampson, B.W., Plotkin, G.D.: A calculus for access control in distributed systems. ACM Trans. Program. Lang. Syst. 15(4), 706–734 (1993)
10. Abadi, M.: Access control in a core calculus of dependency. In: ICFP, pp. 263–273. ACM, New York (2006)
11. Garg, D., Pfenning, F.: Non-interference in constructive authorization logic. CSFW 19, 283–296 (2006)
12. Garg, D., Bauer, L., Bowers, K.D., Pfenning, F., Reiter, M.K.: A linear logic of authorization and knowledge. In: Gollmann, D., Meier, J., Sabelfeld, A. (eds.) ESORICS 2006. LNCS, vol. 4189, pp. 297–312. Springer, Heidelberg (2006)
13. Woo, T.Y.C., Lam, S.S.: A semantic model for authentication protocols. In: IEEE Symposium on Research in Security and Privacy (1993)
14. Fournet, C., Gordon, A.D., Maffeis, S.: A type discipline for authorization in distributed systems. In: CSF, IEEE Computer Society Press, Los Alamitos (2007)
15. Cirillo, A., Jagadeesan, R., Pitcher, C., Riely, J.: Do As I SaY! programmatic access control with explicit identities. In: CSF, IEEE, Los Alamitos (2007)

16. Gordon, A.D., Jeffrey, A.: Authenticity by typing for security protocols. Journal of Computer Security 11(4), 451–520 (2003)
17. Buneman, P., Tan, W.C.: Provenance in databases. In: SIGMOD Conference, pp. 1171–1173. ACM, New York (2007)
18. Wallach, D.S., Appel, A.W., Felten, E.W.: SAFKASI: a security mechanism for language-based systems. ACM Trans. Softw. Eng. Methodol. 9(4), 341–378 (2000)
19. Abadi, M., Fournet, C.: Access control based on execution history. In: Proc. Network and Distributed System Security Symp. (2003)
20. Gifford, D.K., Lucassen, J.M.: Integrating functional and imperative programming. In: LISP and Functional Programming, pp. 28–38 (1986)
21. Lucassen, J.M., Gifford, D.K.: Polymorphic effect systems. In: POPL, pp. 47–57 (1988)
22. Talpin, J., Jouvelot, P.: Polymorphic type, region and effect inference. J. Funct. Program. 2(3), 245–271 (1992)
23. Talpin, J., Jouvelot, P.: The type and effect discipline. Inf. Comput. 111(2), 245–296 (1994)
24. Bierman, G., Parkinson, M., Pitts, A.: MJ: An imperative core calculus for Java and Java with effects. Technical Report 563, Cambridge University Computer Laboratory (2003)
25. Greenhouse, A., Boyland, J.: An object-oriented effects system. In: Guerraoui, R. (ed.) ECOOP 1999. LNCS, vol. 1628, pp. 205–229. Springer, Heidelberg (1999)
26. Grothoff, C., Palsberg, J., Vitek, J.: Encapsulating objects with confined types. In: TOPLAS (to appear, 2007)
27. Potanin, A., Noble, J., Clarke, D., Biddle, R.: Featherweight generic confinement. J. Funct. Program. 16(6), 793–811 (2006)
28. Damiani, F., Drossopoulou, S., Giannini, P.: Refined effects for unanticipated object re-classification: $Fickle_3$. In: Blundo, C., Laneve, C. (eds.) ICTCS 2003. LNCS, vol. 2841, pp. 97–110. Springer, Heidelberg (2003)
29. DeLine, R., Fähndrich, M.: Enforcing high-level protocols in low-level software. In: PLDI, pp. 59–69 (2001)
30. Dezani-Ciancaglini, M., Yoshida, N., Ahern, A., Drossopoulou, S.: A distributed object-oriented language with session types. In: De Nicola, R., Sangiorgi, D. (eds.) TGC 2005. LNCS, vol. 3705, pp. 299–318. Springer, Heidelberg (2005)
31. Fournet, C., Gordon, A.D., Maffeis, S.: A type discipline for authorization policies. In: Sagiv, M. (ed.) ESOP 2005. LNCS, vol. 3444, pp. 141–156. Springer, Heidelberg (2005)
32. Sabelfeld, A., Myers, A.C.: Language-based information-flow security. IEEE J. Selected Areas in Communications 21(1), 5–19 (2003)
33. Flatt, M., Krishnamurthi, S., Felleisen, M.: Classes and mixins. In: POPL, pp. 171–183 (1998)
34. Igarashi, A., Pierce, B., Wadler, P.: Featherweight Java: A minimal core calculus for Java and GJ. In: OOPSLA (1999)
35. Drossopoulou, S., Eisenbach, S., Khurshid, S.: Is the Java type system sound? Theory and Practice of Object Systems 5(11), 3–24 (1999)
36. Bracha, G., Odersky, M., Stoutamire, D., Wadler, P.: Making the future safe for the past: Adding genericity to the Java programming language. In: OOPSLA, pp. 183–200 (1998)
37. Igarashi, A., Pierce, B.C.: On inner classes. Information and Computation 177(1), 56–89 (2002)
38. Gordon, A.D., Hankin, P.D.: A concurrent object calculus: Reduction and typing. In: Proceedings HLCL'98, ENTCS (1998)
39. Cardelli, L.: A language with distributed scope. In: POPL, pp. 286–297. ACM Press, New York (1995)

40. Jeffrey, A.S.A.: A distributed object calculus. In: Proc. Foundations of Object Oriented Languages (2000)
41. Castellani, I.: Process algebras with localities. In: Handbook of Process Algebra, North-Holland, pp. 945–1045 (2001)
42. Gamma, E., Helm, R., Johnson, R., Vlissides, J.: Design Patterns. Addison-Wesley, Reading (1995)

Linear Declassification

Yûta Kaneko and Naoki Kobayashi

Graduate School of Information Sciences, Tohoku University
{kaneko,koba}@kb.ecei.tohoku.ac.jp

Abstract. We propose a new notion of declassification policy called *linear declassification*. Linear declassification controls not only which functions may be applied to declassify high-security values, but also *how often* the declassification functions may be applied. We present a linear type system which guarantees that well-typed programs never violate linear declassification policies. To state a formal security property guaranteed by the linear declassification, we also introduce *linear relaxed non-interference* as an extension of Li and Zdancewic's relaxed non-interference. An application of the linear relaxed non-interference to quantitative information flow analysis is also discussed.

1 Introduction

There have been extensive studies on policies and verification methods for information flow security [4,16,10,7,11,13]. The standard policy for secure information flow is the *non-interference* property, which means that low-security outputs cannot be affected by high-security inputs. A little more formally, a program e is secure if for any high inputs h_1 and h_2 and low input l, $e(h_1, l)$ and $e(h_2, l)$ are equivalent for low-level observers. The standard non-interference property is, however, too restricted in practice, since it does not allow any leakage of secret information. For example, a login program does leak information about the result of comparison of a string and a password.

To allow intentional release of secret information, a variety of notions of declassification have been proposed [7,12,13]. Sabelfeld and Myers [12] proposed delimited information release, where e is secure if, roughly speaking, whenever $d(h_1) = d(h_2)$ for the declassification function d, $e(h_1, l)$ and $e(h_2, l)$ are equivalent for low-level observers. As a similar criterion, Li and Zdancewic [7] proposed a notion of relaxed non-interference (relaxed NI, in short), where e is secure (i.e., satisfies relaxed NI) if $e(h, l)$ can be factorized into $e'(dh)$, where d is a declassification function and e' does not contain h. Both the frameworks guarantee that a program leaks only partial information $d(h)$ about the high-security value h. For example, if d is the function $\lambda x.x \,\mathbf{mod}\, 2$, then only the parity information can be leaked.

The above criteria alone, however, do not always guarantee desirable secrecy properties. For example, consider a declassification function $d \stackrel{\triangle}{=} \lambda x.\lambda s.(s = x)$, which takes a high-security value x, and returns a *function* that takes a string and returns whether s and x are equal. Declassifications through such a function

S. Drossopoulou (Ed.): ESOP 2008, LNCS 4960, pp. 224–238, 2008.

often occur in practice, for instance, in a login program, which compares a user's password with an input string. Note that $d(h) \equiv \lambda s.(s = h)$ and h contain the same quantity of information; In fact, even if e is h itself (so that it clearly leaks the entire information), it can be factorized into:

$$(\lambda g.\mathbf{let}\ test(s) = \mathbf{if}\ g(s)\ \mathbf{then}\ s\ \mathbf{else}\ test(s+1)\ \mathbf{in}\ test(0))\,(d(h)).$$

Thus, the relaxed NI guarantees nothing about the quantity of information declassified through the function d. (In the case of delimited information release [12], the problem can be avoided by choosing $\lambda x.(l = x)$ as d, instead of $\lambda x.\lambda s.(s = x)$; see more detailed discussion in Section 5.)

To overcome the problem mentioned above, we propose a new notion of declassification called *linear declassification*, which controls *how often* declassification functions can be applied to each high-security value, and how often a value (which may be a function) obtained by declassification may be used. We define a linear type system that ensures that any well-typed program satisfies a given linear declassification policy.

To formalize the security property guaranteed by the linear declassification, we also extend Li and Zdancewic's relaxed non-interference [7] to *linear relaxed non-interference*, which says that e is secure if e can be factorized into $e'(\lambda^u x.(dh))$, where e' does not contain h *and e' can call the function $\lambda x.(dh)$ at most u times to declassify the value of h.*

The linear relaxed non-interference is useful for quantitative information flow analysis [8,3,2]. For example, if a program e containing an n-bit password satisfies the linear relaxed non-interference under the policy that $\lambda x.\lambda s.(s = x)$ is used at most once, we know that one has to run e $O(2^n)$ times in average to get complete information about the password. On the other hand, if the declassification function is replaced by $\lambda x.\lambda s.(s > x)$, the password may be leaked by only n runs of the program. In the paper, we show (through an example) that the linear relaxed non-interference enables us to estimate the quantity of information leakage (per program run) by looking at only the security policy, not the program.

The rest of this paper is structured as follows. Section 2 introduces the language of programs and linear declassification policies. Section 3 introduces a linear type system which guarantees that a program adheres to linear declassification policies. Section 4 defines linear relaxed non-interference as an extension of Li and Zdancewic's relaxed non-interference. Section 4 also discusses an application of the linear relaxed non-interference to quantitative analysis of information flow. Section 5 discusses related work and Section 6 concludes.

2 Language

This section introduces the syntax and semantics of programs and declassification policies.

2.1 Syntax

Definition 1 (expressions). The set of *expressions*, ranged over by e, is defined by:

$$\begin{aligned}
e \text{ (expressions)} &::= x \mid n \mid \sigma \mid d\langle\!\langle e \rangle\!\rangle \mid e_1 \oplus e_2 \mid \textbf{if } e_1 \textbf{ then } e_2 \textbf{ else } e_3 \\
&\quad\mid \lambda^u x.e \mid \textbf{fix } x(y) = e \mid e_1 e_2 \mid \langle e_1, \ldots, e_n \rangle \mid \#_i(e) \\
u \text{ (uses)} &::= 0 \mid 1 \mid \omega \\
\oplus \text{ (operators)} &::= + \mid - \mid = \mid \cdots
\end{aligned}$$

Here, the meta-variables x and n range over the sets of variables and integers respectively. The meta-variable σ ranges over the set of special variables holding high-security integers, to which security policies (given below) are associated. For the sake of simplicity, we consider only integers as primitive values, and assume that $e_1 = e_2$ returns 1 if the values of e_1 and e_2 are the same, and returns 0 otherwise. **if** e_1 **then** e_2 **else** e_3 returns the value of e_3 if the value of e_1 is 0, and returns the value of e_2 otherwise. The expression $\lambda^u x.e$ denotes a function that can be used at most u times. If u is ω, the function can be used an arbitrary number of times.[1] Note that use annotations can be automatically inferred by standard usage analysis [17,6,9], so that programmers need not specify them (except for those in policies introduced below). The expression **fix** $x(y) = e$ denotes a recursive function that can be used an arbitrary number of times. The expression $e_1 e_2$ is an ordinary function application. The expression $d\langle\!\langle e \rangle\!\rangle$ is a special form of function application, where the meta-variable d ranges over the set $\mathcal{N}_D$ of special function variables (defined in a policy introduced below). The expression $\langle e_1, \ldots, e_n \rangle$ returns a tuple consisting of the values of $e_1, \ldots, e_n$. Note that n may be 0, in which case, the tuple is empty.

We write $[e'/x]e$ for the (capture-avoiding) substitution of e' for x in e. We write $\mathbf{SVar}(e)$ for the set of security variables occurring in e.

Definition 2 (policies). The set of *policies* is defined by:

$$\begin{aligned}
p \text{ (security levels)} &::= \mathbf{L} \mid \mathbf{H} \mid \{d_1 \mapsto u_1, \cdots, d_n \mapsto u_n\} \\
D \text{ (declassification environment)} &::= \{d_1 \mapsto \lambda^\omega x.e_1, \cdots, d_n \mapsto \lambda^\omega x.e_2\} \\
\Sigma \text{ (policy)} &::= \{\sigma_1 \mapsto p_1, \cdots, \sigma_n \mapsto p_n\}
\end{aligned}$$

A security level p expresses the degree of confidentiality of each value. If p is $\mathbf{L}$, the value may be leaked to low-security principals. If p is $\mathbf{H}$, no information about the value may be leaked. If p is $\{d_1 \mapsto u_1, \cdots, d_n \mapsto u_n\}$, then the value may be leaked only through declassification functions $d_1, \ldots, d_n$ and each declassification function d_i may be applied to the value at most u_i times. For example, if the security level of σ is $\{d_1 \mapsto 1, d_2 \mapsto \omega, d_3 \mapsto 0\}$, then $d_1\langle\!\langle \sigma \rangle\!\rangle + d_2\langle\!\langle \sigma \rangle\!\rangle + d_2\langle\!\langle \sigma \rangle\!\rangle$ is allowed, but neither $d_3\langle\!\langle \sigma \rangle\!\rangle$ nor $d_1\langle\!\langle \sigma \rangle\!\rangle + d_1\langle\!\langle \sigma \rangle\!\rangle$ is.

A declassification environment D defines declassification functions. A policy Σ maps σ_i to its security level. Note that the use of $D(d_i)$ is always ω. This is because how often d_i can be used is described in Σ for each security variable σ.

[1] For the sake of simplicity, we consider only $0, 1, \omega$ as uses. It is easy to extend the language and the type system given in the next section to allow $2, 3, \ldots$.

Example 1. Let $D = \{d \mapsto \lambda^{\omega}x.\lambda^1 y.x = y\}$ and $\Sigma = \{\sigma \mapsto \{d \mapsto 1\}\}$. This policy specifies that information about σ can be leaked by at most one application of d. Since the result of the application is a linear (use-once) function $\lambda^1 y.\sigma = y$, the policy means that σ may be compared with another integer only once.

Note that if $D(d)$ is $\lambda^{\omega}x.\lambda^{\omega}y.x = y$, then the declassification may be performed only once, but the resulting value $\lambda^{\omega}y.\sigma = y$ can be used an arbitrary number of times. Therefore, an attacker can obtain complete information about σ by applying the function to different values.

2.2 Operational Semantics

This section introduces an operational semantics to define the meaning of expressions and policies formally.

A run-time state is modeled by a pair $\langle H, e\rangle$, where H is a heap given below.[2]

Definition 3 (heap)

$$\begin{aligned} H \text{ (heap)} &::= \{f_1 \mapsto \lambda^{u_1}x_1.e_1, \ldots, f_n \mapsto \lambda^{u_n}x_n.e_n, \\ &\qquad \sigma_1 \mapsto (n_1, p_1), \ldots, \sigma_m \mapsto (n_m, p_m)\} \\ f \text{ (function pointer)} &::= x \mid d \end{aligned}$$

Here, f ranges over the set consisting of (ordinary) variables $(x, y, z, \ldots)$ and declassification function variables $(d_1, d_2, \ldots,)$.

A heap H keeps information about how often each function may be applied and how the value of each security variable may be declassified in the rest of the computation. For example, $H(\sigma) = (2, \{d \mapsto 1\})$ means that the value of σ is 2, and the value can be declassified only once through the declassification function d.

For a system (Σ, D, e), the initial heap is determined by Σ, D, and the actual values of the security variables. Let g be a mapping from $dom(\Sigma)$ to the set of integers. We write $H_{\Sigma,D,g}$ for the initial heap $D \cup \{\sigma_1 \mapsto (g(\sigma_1), \Sigma(\sigma_1)), \ldots, \sigma_k \mapsto (g(\sigma_k), \Sigma(\sigma_k))\}$ (where $dom(\Sigma) = \{\sigma_1, \ldots, \sigma_k\}$). We use evaluation contexts to define the operational semantics.

Definition 4 (evaluation context). The set of evaluation contexts, ranged over by E, is given by:

$$\begin{aligned} E \text{ (evaluation context)} &::= [\,] \mid [\,]e \mid x[\,] \mid d\langle\!\langle [\,] \rangle\!\rangle \mid \textbf{if } [\,] \textbf{ then } e_1 \textbf{ else } e_2 \\ &\quad\mid [\,] \oplus e \mid v \oplus [\,] \mid \langle v_1, \ldots, v_{k-1}, [\,], e_{k+1}, \ldots, e_n\rangle \mid \#_i([\,]) \\ v \text{ (values)} &::= f \mid n \mid \sigma \mid \langle v_1, \ldots, v_n\rangle \end{aligned}$$

The relation $\langle H, e\rangle \longrightarrow \langle H', e'\rangle$ is the least relation closed under the rules in Figure 1. In the figure, $F\{x \mapsto v\}$ is the mapping F' such that $F'(x) = v$, and $F'(y) = F(y)$ for any $y \in dom(F) \setminus \{x\}$. $val(H, v)$ is defined to be n if $v = n$, or $v = \sigma$ and $H(\sigma) = (n, p)$.

The key rules are E-App and E-Decl. In E-App, the use of the function y is decreased by one. Here, the subtraction $u - 1$ is defined by: $1 - 1 = 0$ and

[2] Note that unlike the usual heap-based semantics, tuples are *not* stored in a heap.

$$\frac{y \text{ fresh}}{\langle H, E[\lambda^u x.e]\rangle \longrightarrow \langle H\{y \mapsto \lambda^u x.e\}, E[y]\rangle} \quad \text{(E-Fun)}$$

$$\frac{H(d) = \lambda^\omega x.e}{\langle H\{\sigma \mapsto (n,p)\}, E[d\langle\langle\sigma\rangle\rangle]\rangle \longrightarrow \langle H\{\sigma \mapsto (n, p-d)\}, E[[n/x]e]\rangle\rangle} \quad \text{(E-Decl)}$$

$$\frac{H(d) = \lambda^\omega x.e}{\langle H, E[d\langle\langle n\rangle\rangle]\rangle \longrightarrow \langle H, E[[n/x]e]\rangle} \quad \text{(E-Decl2)}$$

$$\langle H\{y \mapsto \lambda^u x.e\}, E[yv]\rangle \longrightarrow \langle H\{y \mapsto \lambda^{u-1} x.e\}, E[[v/x]e]\rangle \quad \text{(E-App)}$$

$$\frac{val(H, v) \neq 0}{\langle H, E[\textbf{if } v \textbf{ then } e_1 \textbf{ else } e_2]\rangle \longrightarrow \langle H, E[e_1]\rangle} \quad \text{(E-IfT)}$$

$$\frac{val(H, v) = 0}{\langle H, E[\textbf{if } v \textbf{ then } e_1 \textbf{ else } e_2]\rangle \longrightarrow \langle H, E[e_2]\rangle} \quad \text{(E-IfF)}$$

$$\langle H, E[v_1 \oplus v_2]\rangle \longrightarrow \langle H, E[val(H, v_1) \underline{\oplus} val(H, v_2)]\rangle \quad \text{(E-Op)}$$

$$\frac{z \text{ fresh}}{\langle H, E[\textbf{fix } x(y) = e]\rangle \longrightarrow \langle H \cup \{z \mapsto \lambda^\omega y.[z/x]e\}, E[z]\rangle} \quad \text{(E-Fix)}$$

$$\langle H, E[\#_i\langle v_1, \ldots, v_n\rangle]\rangle \longrightarrow \langle H, E[v_i]\rangle \quad \text{(E-Proj)}$$

Fig. 1. Evaluation rules

$\omega - 1 = \omega$. Note that $0 - 1$ is undefined, so that if $H(y) = \lambda^0 x.e$, the function y can no longer be used (in other words, the evaluation of $E[yv]$ get stuck).

In E-Decl, the security level p for σ changes after the reduction. Here, $p - d$ is defined by:

$$\{d_1 \mapsto u_1, \ldots, d_n \mapsto u_n\} - d_i = \{d_1 \mapsto u'_1, \ldots, d_n \mapsto u'_n\}$$
$$\text{where } u'_j = \begin{cases} u_j - 1 \text{ if } j = i \\ u_j \quad\quad \text{otherwise} \end{cases}$$
$$\mathbf{L} - d_i = \mathbf{L}$$

For example, if the security level p of σ is $\{d \mapsto 1\}$, then after the declassification, the security level becomes $p - d = \{d \mapsto 0\}$, which means that the value of σ can no longer be declassified. Note that $\mathbf{H} - d_i$ is undefined, so that an integer of security level $\mathbf{H}$ can never be declassified. Rule E-Decl2 is for the case when a declassification function d is applied to an ordinary integer.

In rule E-Op, $\underline{\oplus}$ is the binary operation on integers denoted by the operator symbol $\oplus$. The remaining rules are standard.

Example 2. Recall the security policy in Example 1: $D = \{d \mapsto \lambda^\omega x.\lambda^1 y.(x = y)\}$ and $\Sigma = \{\sigma \mapsto \{d \mapsto 1\}\}$.
$\langle H_{\Sigma,D,\{\sigma\mapsto 3\}}, d\langle\langle\sigma\rangle\rangle 2\rangle$ is reduced as follows.

$$\begin{aligned} &\langle D \cup \{\sigma \mapsto (3, \{d \mapsto 1\})\}, d\langle\langle\sigma\rangle\rangle 2\rangle \\ \longrightarrow &\langle D \cup \{\sigma \mapsto (3, \{d \mapsto 0\})\}, (\lambda^1 y.(3 = y))2\rangle \\ \longrightarrow &\langle D \cup \{\sigma \mapsto (3, \{d \mapsto 0\}), z \mapsto \lambda^1 y.(3 = y)\}, z(2)\rangle \end{aligned}$$

$$\longrightarrow \langle D \cup \{\sigma \mapsto (3, \{d \mapsto 0\}), z \mapsto \lambda^0 y.(3 = y)\}, 3 = 2\rangle$$
$$\longrightarrow \langle D \cup \{\sigma \mapsto (3, \{d \mapsto 0\}), z \mapsto \lambda^0 y.(3 = y)\}, 0\rangle$$

On the other hand, both $\langle d\langle\!\langle \sigma \rangle\!\rangle, d\langle\!\langle \sigma \rangle\!\rangle\rangle$ and $(\lambda^\omega f.\langle f(1), f(2)\rangle)(d\langle\!\langle \sigma \rangle\!\rangle)$ get stuck. □

3 Type System

This section introduces a linear type system, which ensures that if $\langle \Sigma, D, e\rangle$ is well-typed, then e satisfies the security policy specified by Σ and D.

3.1 Types

Definition 5 (types). The set of types, ranged over by τ, is defined by:

$$\tau \text{ (types)} ::= int_p \mid \tau_1 \xrightarrow{\varphi}_u \tau_2 \mid \langle \tau_1, \ldots, \tau_n\rangle$$
$$\varphi \text{ (effects)} ::= \mathtt{t} \mid \mathtt{nt}$$

The integer type int_p describes integers whose security level is p. For example, $int_{\{d\mapsto 1\}}$ is the type of integers that can be declassified through the function d at most once. The function type $\tau_1 \xrightarrow{\varphi}_u \tau_2$ describes functions that can be used at most u times and that take a value of type τ_1 as an argument and return a value of type τ_2. The effect φ describes whether the function is terminating (when $\varphi = \mathtt{t}$) or it may not be terminating (when $\varphi = \mathtt{nt}$). The effect will be used for preventing leakage of information from the termination behavior of a program. The type $\langle \tau_1, \ldots, \tau_n\rangle$ describes tuples consisting of values of types $\tau_1, \ldots, \tau_n$.

The *sub-effect relation* $\leq$ on effects is the partial order defined by $\mathtt{t} \leq \mathtt{nt}$. The *sub-level relation* $\sqsubseteq$ on security levels and the subtyping relation $\tau_1 \leq \tau_2$ are the least relations closed under the rules in Figure 2. For example, $int_{\{d\mapsto 1\}} \xrightarrow{\mathtt{t}}_\omega int_{\{d\mapsto\omega\}}$ is a subtype of $int_{\{d\mapsto\omega\}} \xrightarrow{\mathtt{nt}}_1 int_{\{d\mapsto 1\}}$. We write $\varphi_1 \vee \varphi_2$ for the least upper bound of φ_1 and φ_2 (with respect to $\leq$), and $p_1 \sqcup p_2$ for the least upper bound of p_1 and p_2 with respect to $\sqsubseteq$.

$$\frac{}{\mathbf{L} \sqsubseteq p \sqsubseteq \mathbf{H}} \qquad \frac{u_i' \leq u_i \text{ for each } i \in \{1, \ldots, m\}}{\{d_1 \mapsto u_1, \ldots, d_m \mapsto u_m, \ldots\} \sqsubseteq \{d_1 \mapsto u_1', \ldots, d_m \mapsto u_m'\}}$$

$$\frac{p_1 \sqsubseteq p_2}{int_{p_1} \leq int_{p_2}} \qquad \frac{\tau_1' \leq \tau_1 \quad \tau_2 \leq \tau_2' \quad u' \leq u \quad \varphi \leq \varphi'}{\tau_1 \xrightarrow{\varphi}_u \tau_2 \leq \tau_1' \xrightarrow{\varphi'}_{u'} \tau_2'}$$

$$\frac{\tau_i \leq \tau_i' \text{ for each } i \in \{1, \ldots, n\}}{\langle \tau_1, \ldots, \tau_n\rangle \leq \langle \tau_1', \ldots, \tau_n'\rangle}$$

Fig. 2. Subtyping rules

3.2 Typing

A type environment is a mapping from a finite set consisting of extended variables (ordinary variables, security variables, and declassification function names) to types. We have two forms of type judgment: $\vdash \langle \Sigma, D, e\rangle$ for the whole system (consisting of a policy, a declassification environment, and an expression), and $\Gamma \vdash e : \tau \,\&\, \varphi$ for expressions. The judgment $\vdash \langle \Sigma, D, e\rangle$ means that e satisfies the security policy specified by Σ and D. $\Gamma \vdash e : \tau \,\&\, \varphi$ means that e evaluates to a value of type τ under an environment described by Γ. If $\varphi = \mathtt{t}$, then evaluation of e must terminate. If $\varphi = \mathtt{nt}$, then e may or may not terminate. For example, $\sigma : int_{\{d\mapsto 1\}}, f : int_{\{d\mapsto 1\}} \xrightarrow{\mathtt{t}}_{\omega} int_{\{d\mapsto 1\}} \vdash f\sigma : int_{\{d\mapsto 1\}} \,\&\, \mathtt{t}$ is a valid judgment, but neither $\sigma : int_{\{d\mapsto 1\}}, f : int_{\{d\mapsto \omega\}} \xrightarrow{\mathtt{t}}_{\omega} int_{\{d\mapsto 1\}} \vdash f\sigma : int_{\{d\mapsto 1\}} \,\&\, \mathtt{t}$ nor $\sigma : int_{\{d\mapsto 1\}}, f : int_{\{d\mapsto 1\}} \xrightarrow{\mathtt{nt}}_{\omega} int_{\{d\mapsto 1\}} \vdash f\sigma : int_{\{d\mapsto 1\}} \,\&\, \mathtt{t}$ is. (In the former, the security level of σ does not match that of the argument required by f. In the latter, the type of f says that f may not terminate, but the conclusion says that $f\sigma$ terminates.)

Figure 3 shows the typing rules. Two auxiliary judgments $\vdash \Sigma : \Gamma$ and $\vdash D : \Gamma$ are used for defining $\vdash \langle \Sigma, D, e\rangle$. The definitions of the operations used in the typing rules are summarized in Figure 4.

We explain some key rules below.

- T-Op: Suppose e_1 has type $int_{\{d\mapsto 1\}}$. Then, the value of e_1 can be declassified through the function d, but that does not necessarily imply that $e_1 \oplus e_2$ can be declassified through the function d. Therefore, we raise the security level of $e_1 \oplus e_2$ to $\mathbf{H}$ unless both of the security levels of e_1 and e_2 are $\mathbf{L}$.
- T-If: Since information about the value of e_0 indirectly flows to the value of the if-expression, the security level of the if-expression should be greater than or equal to the *ceil* of security level of e_0. For the sake of simplicity, we require that the values of if-expressions must be integers.
- T-Fun: The premise means that free variables are used according to Γ *each time* the function is applied. Since the function may be applied u times, the usage of free variables is expressed by $u \cdot \Gamma$ in total.
- T-Dcl: The premise ensures that e must have type $int_{d\mapsto 1}$, so that e can indeed be declassified through d.

Example 3. Let $\tau_d = int_{\mathbf{L}} \xrightarrow{\mathtt{t}}_{\omega} int_{\mathbf{L}} \xrightarrow{\mathtt{t}}_{1} int_{\mathbf{L}}$. $d\langle\!\langle\sigma\rangle\!\rangle 2$ is typed as follows.

$$\dfrac{\dfrac{\sigma : int_{\{d\mapsto 1\}} \vdash \sigma : int_{\{d\mapsto 1\}} \,\&\, \mathtt{t}}{d : \tau_d, \sigma : int_{\{d\mapsto 1\}} \vdash d\langle\!\langle\sigma\rangle\!\rangle : int_{\mathbf{L}} \xrightarrow{\mathtt{t}}_{1} int_{\mathbf{L}} \,\&\, \mathtt{t}} \quad \emptyset \vdash 2 : int_{\mathbf{L}} \,\&\, \mathtt{t}}{d : \tau_d, \sigma : int_{\{d\mapsto 1\}} \vdash d\langle\!\langle\sigma\rangle\!\rangle 2 : int_{\mathbf{L}} \,\&\, \mathtt{t}}$$

Example 4. Let e be $\mathbf{fix}\ f(x) = \mathbf{if}\ d\langle\!\langle\sigma\rangle\!\rangle x\ \mathbf{then}\ x\ \mathbf{else}\ f(x+1)$. Let $\Sigma_1 = \{\sigma \mapsto \{d \mapsto \omega\}\}$, $\Sigma_2 = \{\sigma \mapsto \{d \mapsto 1\}\}$, and $D = \{d \mapsto \lambda^{\omega} x.\lambda^{1} y.(x = y)\}$. Then, $\vdash \langle \Sigma_1, D, e(0)\rangle : int_{\mathbf{L}}$ holds but $\vdash \langle \Sigma_2, D, e(0)\rangle : int_{\mathbf{L}}$ does not.

$\Gamma \vdash e : \tau$

$$\Gamma, x : \tau \vdash x : \tau \,\&\, \mathtt{t} \quad \text{(T-VAR)}$$

$$\Gamma \vdash n : \mathit{int}_{\mathbf{L}} \,\&\, \mathtt{t} \quad \text{(T-CONST)}$$

$$\Gamma, \sigma : \mathit{int}_p \vdash \sigma : \mathit{int}_p \,\&\, \mathtt{t} \quad \text{(T-SVAL)}$$

$$\frac{\Gamma_1 \vdash e_1 : \mathit{int}_{p_1} \,\&\, \varphi \qquad \Gamma_2 \vdash e_2 : \mathit{int}_{p_2} \,\&\, \varphi}{\Gamma_1 + \Gamma_2 \vdash e_1 \oplus e_2 : \mathit{int}_{\lceil p_1 \rceil \sqcup \lceil p_2 \rceil} \,\&\, \varphi} \quad \text{(T-OP)}$$

$$\frac{\Gamma, x : \tau_1 \vdash e : \tau_2 \,\&\, \varphi}{u \cdot \Gamma \vdash \lambda^u x.e : \tau_1 \xrightarrow{\varphi}_u \tau_2 \,\&\, \mathtt{t}} \quad \text{(T-FUN)}$$

$$\frac{\Gamma, x : \tau_1 \xrightarrow{\mathtt{nt}}_\omega \tau_2, y : \tau_1 \vdash e : \tau_2 \,\&\, \varphi}{\omega \cdot \Gamma \vdash \mathbf{fix}\; x(y) = e : \tau_1 \xrightarrow{\varphi}_\omega \tau_2 \,\&\, \mathtt{t}} \quad \text{(T-FIX)}$$

$$\frac{\Gamma_1 \vdash e_1 : \tau_1 \xrightarrow{\varphi_0}_1 \tau_2 \,\&\, \varphi_1 \qquad \Gamma_2 \vdash e_2 : \tau_1 \,\&\, \varphi_2}{\Gamma_1 + \Gamma_2 \vdash e_1\; e_2 : \tau_2 \,\&\, \varphi_0 \vee \varphi_1 \vee \varphi_2} \quad \text{(T-APP)}$$

$$\frac{\Gamma \vdash e : \mathit{int}_{\{d \mapsto 1\}} \,\&\, \varphi_1}{(d : \mathit{int}_{\mathbf{L}} \xrightarrow{\varphi_0}_\omega \tau) + \Gamma \vdash d\langle\!\langle e \rangle\!\rangle : \tau \,\&\, \varphi_0 \vee \varphi_1} \quad \text{(T-DCL)}$$

$$\frac{\Gamma \vdash e : \tau' \,\&\, \varphi' \qquad \tau' \leq \tau \qquad \varphi' \leq \varphi}{\Gamma \vdash e : \tau \,\&\, \varphi} \quad \text{(T-SUB)}$$

$$\frac{\Gamma_1 \vdash e_0 : \mathit{int}_{p_0} \,\&\, \varphi_0 \qquad \Gamma_2 \vdash e_1 : \mathit{int}_{p_1} \,\&\, \varphi_1 \qquad \Gamma_2 \vdash e_2 : \mathit{int}_{p_2} \,\&\, \varphi_2 \qquad \varphi_1 = \varphi_2 = \mathtt{t} \text{ if } \lceil p_0 \rceil = \mathbf{H}}{\Gamma_1 + \Gamma_2 \vdash \mathbf{if}\; e_0\; \mathbf{then}\; e_1\; \mathbf{else}\; e_2 : \mathit{int}_{\lceil p \rceil \sqcup p_1 \sqcup p_2} \,\&\, \varphi_0 \vee \varphi_1 \vee \varphi_2} \quad \text{(T-IF)}$$

$$\frac{\Gamma_i \vdash e_i : \tau_i \,\&\, \varphi_i \text{ (for each } i \in \{1, \ldots, n\})}{\Gamma_1 + \cdots + \Gamma_n \vdash \langle e_1, \ldots, e_n \rangle : \langle \tau_1, \ldots, \tau_n \rangle \,\&\, \varphi_1 \vee \cdots \vee \varphi_n} \quad \text{(T-TUPLE)}$$

$\vdash \Sigma : \Gamma$

$$\vdash \{\sigma_1 \mapsto p_1, \ldots, \sigma_n \mapsto p_n\} : (\sigma_1 : \mathit{int}_{p_1}, \ldots, \sigma_n : \mathit{int}_{p_n}) \quad \text{(T-POLICY)}$$

$\vdash D : \Gamma$

$$\frac{\emptyset \vdash \lambda^\omega x.e_i : \tau_i \,\&\, \varphi_i \text{ for each } i \in \{1, \ldots, n\}}{\vdash \{d_1 \mapsto \lambda^\omega x.e_1, \cdots, d_n \mapsto \lambda^\omega x.e_n\} : (d_1 : \tau_1, \ldots, d_n : \tau_n)} \quad \text{(T-DENV)}$$

$\vdash \langle \Sigma, D, e \rangle$

$$\frac{\vdash \Sigma : \Gamma_1 \qquad \vdash D : \Gamma_2 \qquad \Gamma_1, \Gamma_2 \vdash e : \tau \,\&\, \varphi \qquad \text{all the security levels in } \Gamma_2 \text{ are } \mathbf{L}}{\vdash \langle \Sigma, D, e \rangle : \tau} \quad \text{(T-SYS)}$$

Fig. 3. Typing rules

3.3 (Partial) Type Soundness

The following theorem means that evaluation of a well-typed program never gets stuck. A proof is given in the extended version of this paper [5].

$$u_1 + u_2 = \begin{cases} 0 \text{ if } u_1 = u_2 = 0 \\ 1 \text{ if } (u_1, u_2) \in \{(0,1),(1,0)\} \\ \omega \text{ otherwise} \end{cases}$$

$$\mathit{int}_{\mathbf{L}} + \mathit{int}_{\mathbf{L}} = \mathit{int}_{\mathbf{L}} \qquad \mathit{int}_{\mathbf{H}} + \mathit{int}_{\mathbf{H}} = \mathit{int}_{\mathbf{H}}$$

$$\mathit{int}_{\{d_1 \mapsto u_1, \ldots, d_n \mapsto u_n\}} + \mathit{int}_{\{d_1 \mapsto u'_1, \ldots, d_n \mapsto u'_n\}} = \mathit{int}_{\{d_1 \mapsto (u_1 + u'_1), \ldots, d_n \mapsto (u_n + u'_n)\}}$$

$$(\tau_1 \xrightarrow{\varphi}_u \tau_2) + (\tau_1 \xrightarrow{\varphi}_{u'} \tau_2) = \tau_1 \xrightarrow{\varphi}_{(u+u')} \tau_2$$

$$\langle \tau_1, \ldots, \tau_n \rangle + \langle \tau'_1, \ldots, \tau'_n \rangle = \langle \tau_1 + \tau'_1, \ldots, \tau_n + \tau'_n \rangle$$

$$(\Gamma_1 + \Gamma_2)\ (x) = \begin{cases} \Gamma_1\ (x) & \text{if } x \in dom(\Gamma_1) \setminus dom(\Gamma_2) \\ \Gamma_2\ (x) & \text{if } x \in dom(\Gamma_2) \setminus dom(\Gamma_1) \\ \Gamma_1\ (x) + \Gamma_2\ (x) & \text{if } x \in dom(\Gamma_1) \cap dom(\Gamma_2) \end{cases}$$

$$u_1 \cdot u_2 = \begin{cases} 0 \text{ if } u_1 = 0 \text{ or } u_2 = 0 \\ 1 \text{ if } u_1 = u_2 = 1 \\ \omega \text{ otherwise} \end{cases}$$

$$u \cdot \mathit{int}_L = \mathit{int}_L \qquad u \cdot \mathit{int}_H = \mathit{int}_H$$

$$u \cdot \mathit{int}_{\{d_1 \mapsto u_1, \ldots, d_n \mapsto u_n\}} = \mathit{int}_{\{d_1 \mapsto u \cdot u_1, \ldots, d_n \mapsto u \cdot u_n\}}$$

$$u \cdot (\tau_1 \rightarrow_{u'} \tau_2) = \tau_1 \rightarrow_{u \cdot u'} \tau_2 \qquad u \cdot \langle \tau_1, \ldots, \tau_n \rangle = \langle u \cdot \tau_1, \ldots, u \cdot \tau_n \rangle$$

$$(u \cdot \Gamma)\ (x) = u \cdot \Gamma(x)$$

$$\lceil p \rceil = \begin{cases} \mathbf{L} \text{ if } p = \mathbf{L} \\ \mathbf{H} \text{ otherwise} \end{cases}$$

Fig. 4. Operations on policies, types, and type environments

Theorem 1. *Suppose that* $dom(\Sigma) = \{\sigma_1, \ldots, \sigma_k\}$.
If $\vdash \langle \Sigma, D, e \rangle$ *and* $\langle H_{\Sigma, D, \{\sigma_1 \mapsto n_1, \ldots, \sigma_k \mapsto n_k\}}, e \rangle \longrightarrow^* \langle H, e' \rangle \not\longrightarrow$, *then* e' *is a value.*

Note that Theorem 1 alone does not necessarily guarantee that e satisfies the security policy. In fact, the evaluation of $\langle H_{\emptyset, \emptyset, \{\sigma \mapsto 2\}}, \sigma + 1 \rangle$ does not get stuck (yields the value 3), but it does leak information about σ. The security property satisfied by well-typed programs is formalized in the next section.

4 Linear Relaxed Non-interference

In this section, we define *linear relaxed non-interference* (linear relaxed NI, in short) as a new criterion of information flow security, and prove that well-typed programs of our type system satisfy that criterion. Linear relaxed NI is an extension of relaxed NI [7]. We first review relaxed NI and discuss its weakness in Section 4.1. We then define linear relaxed NI and show that our type system guarantees linear relaxed NI. Section 4.3 discusses an application of linear relaxed NI to quantitative information flow analysis.

4.1 Relaxed Non-interference

Relaxed non-interference [7] is an extension of non-interference. Suppose that $\Sigma = \{\sigma \mapsto \{d \mapsto \omega\}\}$. Informally, an expression e satisfies relaxed NI under the policy Σ if e can be factorized (up to a certain program equivalence) into $e'(d\sigma)$, where e' does not contain σ. If d is a constant function $\lambda x.0$, then the relaxed NI degenerates into the standard non-interference.

As already discussed in Section 1, the relaxed NI does not always guarantee a desired secrecy property. For example, consider the case where $d = \lambda x.\lambda y.x = y$. Then, *any* expression containing σ can be factorized into $e'(d\sigma)$ up to the standard contextual equivalence. In fact, σ is contextually-equivalent to:[3]

$$(\lambda^{\omega} g.(\mathbf{fix}\ \mathit{test}(s) = \mathbf{if}\ g(s)\ \mathbf{then}\ s\ \mathbf{else}\ \mathit{test}(s+1))\ 0)(d\langle\!\langle \sigma \rangle\!\rangle)$$

4.2 Linear Relaxed Non-interference

We first define the notion of (typed) contextual equivalence. For the sake of simplicity, we consider only closed terms (thus, it suffices to consider only contexts of the form $e[\,]$). We write $\langle H, e\rangle \Downarrow n$ if $\langle H, e\rangle \longrightarrow^* \langle H', n\rangle$ for some n.

Definition 6 (contextual equivalence). Suppose that $\emptyset \vdash e_1 : \tau \,\&\, \varphi$ and $\emptyset \vdash e_2 : \tau \,\&\, \varphi$. e_1 and e_2 are *contextually equivalent*, written $e_1 \approx_{\tau,\varphi} e_2$, if, for any e such that $\emptyset \vdash e : \tau \xrightarrow{\mathtt{nt}}_{\omega} \mathit{int}_{\mathbf{L}}$, $\langle \emptyset, ee_1\rangle \Downarrow 0$ if and only if $\langle \emptyset, ee_2\rangle \Downarrow 0$.

Note that in the above definition, the initial heap is empty, so that neither security variables σ nor declassification functions are involved; thus, the contextual equivalence above should coincide with standard typed equivalence for linear λ-calculus.

We now define the linear relaxed non-interference.

Definition 7 (linear relaxed non-interference). Let $\Sigma = \{\sigma_1 \mapsto \{d_1 \mapsto u_{11}, \ldots, d_k \mapsto u_{1k}\}, \ldots, \sigma_m \mapsto \{d_1 \mapsto u_{m1}, \ldots, d_k \mapsto u_{mk}\}\}$. Suppose also that $\mathbf{SVar}(e) \subseteq \{\sigma_1, \ldots, \sigma_m\}$. $\langle \Sigma, D, e\rangle$ satisfies *linear relaxed non-interference* at τ if there exists e' such that the following equivalence holds for any integers $n_1, \ldots, n_m$:

$$\begin{aligned}[][n_1/\sigma_1, \ldots, n_m/\sigma_m]D(e) \approx_{\tau,\mathtt{nt}} e'\ &\langle \lambda^{u_{11}} x.(D(d_1)n_1), \ldots, \lambda^{u_{1k}} x.(D(d_k)n_1)\rangle \\ &\cdots \\ &\langle \lambda^{u_{m1}} x.(D(d_1)n_m), \ldots, \lambda^{u_{mk}} x.(D(d_k)n_m)\rangle\end{aligned}$$

Here $D(e)$ denotes the term obtained from e by replacing each occurrence of a declassification expression $d\langle\!\langle e \rangle\!\rangle$ with $D(d)e$.

Intuitively, the above definition means that if $\langle \Sigma, D, e\rangle$ satisfies *linear relaxed non-interference*, then e can leak information about the security variables $\sigma_1, \ldots, \sigma_m$ only by calling declassification functions at most the number of times specified by Σ. Note that in the above definition, e' cannot depend on the values of the security variables $n_1, \ldots, n_m$.

[3] Actually, Li and Zdancewic [7] uses a finer equivalence than the contextual equivalence, so that the above factorization is not valid. However, if σ ranges over a finite set, then a similar factorization is possible by unfolding the recursion: consider a program **if** $\sigma = 0$ **then** 0 **else if** $\sigma = 1$ **then** 1 **else if** $\sigma = 2$ **then** 2 **else** $\cdots$.

We now show that well-typed programs satisfy linear relaxed non-interference.

Theorem 2. *If* $\vdash \langle \Sigma, D, e\rangle : \tau$ *and all the security levels in* τ *are* $\mathbf{L}$*, then* $\langle \Sigma, D, e\rangle$ *satisfies the linear relaxed non-interference at* τ*.*

A proof of the above theorem is given in [5].

4.3 Application to Quantitative Information Flow Analysis

In this subsection, we discuss how linear relaxed NI can be applied to quantitative information flow analysis [8,2]. Unlike the classical information flow analysis, which obtains *binary* information of whether or not a high-security value is leaked to public, the quantitative analysis aims to estimate the *quantity* of the information leakage based. Recently, definitions and methods of the quantitative information flow analysis have been extensively studied by Malacaria et al. [8,2], based on Shannon's information theory [15]. The quantitative analysis is generally more expensive than the classical information flow analysis, and has not been fully automated. As discussed below, the linear relaxed NI enables us to estimate the quantity of information leakage per program run *by looking at only the security policy,* not the program itself. Since the security policy of a program is typically much smaller than the program itself, this reduces the cost of quantitative information flow analysis.

For the sake of simplicity, we consider below only a single high security variable σ and the declassification environment $D = \{d \mapsto \lambda^{\omega}x.\lambda^1 y.x \oplus y\}$, with the fixed security policy $\Sigma = \{\sigma \mapsto \{d \mapsto 1\}\}$.

Suppose that $\langle \Sigma, D, e\rangle$ satisfies linear relaxed NI at $int_{\mathbf{L}}$. Let us consider the *quantity* of information that flows from σ to the value of e. By Definition 7, there exists an e' such that for any n and n_1, $\langle \{\sigma \mapsto (n,p)\} \cup D, e\rangle \Downarrow n_1$ if and only if $\langle \{\sigma \mapsto (n,p)\} \cup D, e'\langle \lambda^1 x.d\langle\!\langle \sigma\rangle\!\rangle\rangle\rangle \Downarrow n_1$, where e' does not contain σ. Moreover, since $e'\langle \lambda^1 x.d\langle\!\langle \sigma\rangle\!\rangle\rangle$ is well-typed, if $\langle \{\sigma \mapsto (n,p)\} \cup D, e'\langle \lambda^1 x.d\langle\!\langle \sigma\rangle\!\rangle\rangle\rangle \longrightarrow^* \langle H, n_1\rangle$ and the value of σ is used during the reduction, then the reduction sequence must be of the following form:[4]

$$
\begin{array}{ll}
& \langle \{\sigma \mapsto (n, \{d \mapsto 1\})\} \cup D, e'\langle \lambda^1 x.d\langle\!\langle \sigma\rangle\!\rangle\rangle\rangle \\
\longrightarrow^* & \langle \{\sigma \mapsto (n, \{d \mapsto 1\})\} \cup H_1, E_1[\lambda^1 x.d\langle\!\langle \sigma\rangle\!\rangle]\rangle \\
\longrightarrow^* & \langle \{\sigma \mapsto (n, \{d \mapsto 1\}), z \mapsto \lambda^1 x.d\langle\!\langle \sigma\rangle\!\rangle\} \cup H_2, E_2[z\langle\,\rangle]\rangle \\
\longrightarrow^* & \langle \{\sigma \mapsto (n, \{d \mapsto 0\}), z \mapsto \lambda^0 x.d\langle\!\langle \sigma\rangle\!\rangle, w \mapsto \lambda^1 y.n \oplus y\} \cup H_3, E_3[w(m)]\rangle \\
\longrightarrow & \langle \{\sigma \mapsto (n, \{d \mapsto 0\}), z \mapsto \lambda^0 x.d\langle\!\langle \sigma\rangle\!\rangle, w \mapsto \lambda^0 y.n \oplus y\} \cup H_3, E_3[n \oplus m]\rangle \\
\longrightarrow & \langle \{\sigma \mapsto (n, \{d \mapsto 0\}), z \mapsto \lambda^0 x.d\langle\!\langle \sigma\rangle\!\rangle, w \mapsto \lambda^0 y.n \oplus y\} \cup H_3, E_3[m']\rangle \\
\longrightarrow^* & \langle \{\sigma \mapsto (n, \{d \mapsto 0\}), z \mapsto \lambda^0 x.d\langle\!\langle \sigma\rangle\!\rangle, w \mapsto \lambda^0 y.n \oplus y\} \cup H_4, n_1\rangle
\end{array}
$$

Here, since e' does not contain σ, H_i and E_i $(i = 1, 2, 3)$ are independent of the value n of σ.

---

[4] For the sake of simplicity, we consider only terminating programs. Non-terminating programs can be treated in a similar manner, by introducing a special value $\perp$ for representing non-termination.

Let $\mathtt{L}$ be a random variable representing e' above, $\mathtt{H}$ be a random variable representing the value n of σ, and $\mathtt{O}$ be a random variable representing the final value n_1. Then, by the reduction sequence above, $\mathtt{O}$ can be expressed as follows.

$$\mathtt{O} = f_O(f_1(\mathtt{L}), \mathtt{H}\underline{\oplus} f_2(\mathtt{L}))$$

Here, $f_1(\mathtt{L})$ corresponds to the pair (H_3, E_3) and $f_2(\mathtt{L})$ corresponds to m in the reduction step above. The function f_O represents the computation of n_1 from the configuration $\langle\{\sigma \mapsto (n, \{d \mapsto 0\}), \ldots\} \cup H_3, E_3[m']\rangle$.

According to [8,2], the leakage of information is expressed by:[5]

$$\mathcal{I}(\mathtt{O};\mathtt{H} \mid \mathtt{L}) = \mathcal{H}(\mathtt{O} \mid \mathtt{L}) = \mathcal{H}(\mathtt{O},\mathtt{L}) - \mathcal{H}(\mathtt{L})$$

Here, $\mathcal{H}(\vec{X})$ is defined as $\Sigma_{\vec{x}} P(\vec{X} = \vec{x}) \log \frac{1}{P(\vec{X}=\vec{x})}$ (and $P(\vec{X} = \vec{x})$ denotes the probability that the value of $\vec{X}$ is $\vec{x}$).

Using $\mathtt{O} = f_O(f_1(\mathtt{L}), \mathtt{H}\underline{\oplus} f_2(\mathtt{L}))$, $\mathcal{I}(\mathtt{O};\mathtt{H} \mid \mathtt{L})$ is estimated as follows.

$$\begin{aligned}
\mathcal{I}(\mathtt{O};\mathtt{H} \mid \mathtt{L}) &= \mathcal{H}(\mathtt{O},\mathtt{L}) - \mathcal{H}(\mathtt{L}) \\
&= \mathcal{H}(f_O(f_1(\mathtt{L}), \mathtt{H}\underline{\oplus} f_2(\mathtt{L})), \mathtt{L}) - \mathcal{H}(\mathtt{L}) \\
&\leq \mathcal{H}(f_1(\mathtt{L}), \mathtt{H}\underline{\oplus} f_2(\mathtt{L}), \mathtt{L}) - \mathcal{H}(\mathtt{L}) && \text{(by } \mathcal{H}(f(X)) \leq \mathcal{H}(X)\text{)} \\
&= \mathcal{H}(\mathtt{H}\underline{\oplus} f_2(\mathtt{L}), \mathtt{L}) - \mathcal{H}(\mathtt{L}) && \text{(by the definition of } \mathcal{H}\text{)} \\
&= \mathcal{H}(\mathtt{H}\underline{\oplus} f_2(\mathtt{L}) \mid \mathtt{L}) && \text{(by the definition of } \mathcal{H}(\mathtt{X} \mid \mathtt{Y})\text{)} \\
&\leq \mathcal{H}(\mathtt{H}\underline{\oplus} f_2(\mathtt{L}) \mid f_2(\mathtt{L}))
\end{aligned}$$

Thus, $\mathcal{I}(\mathtt{O};\mathtt{H} \mid \mathtt{L})$ is bound by the maximum information leakage by the operation $\underline{\oplus}$ (more precisely, the maximum value of $\mathcal{H}(\mathtt{H}\underline{\oplus}\mathtt{X} \mid \mathtt{X})$ obtained by changing the distribution for $\mathtt{X}$).

If $\underline{\oplus}$ is the equality test for k-bit integers, then

$$\begin{aligned}
\mathcal{H}(\mathtt{H}\underline{\oplus}\mathtt{X} \mid \mathtt{X}) &= P(\mathtt{H} = \mathtt{X}) \log \frac{1}{P(\mathtt{H}=\mathtt{X})} + P(\mathtt{H} \neq \mathtt{X}) \log \frac{1}{P(\mathtt{H}\neq\mathtt{X})} \\
&= \frac{1}{2^k} \log 2^k + \frac{2^k-1}{2^k} \log \frac{2^k}{2^k-1} \;\leq\; \frac{k+1}{2^k}
\end{aligned}$$

Thus, the maximum leakage is bound by $\frac{k+1}{2^k}$ (which is considered safe if k is sufficiently large).

On the other hand, if $\underline{\oplus}$ is the inequality test $<$, then, the maximum value of $\mathcal{H}(\mathtt{H}\underline{\oplus}\mathtt{X} \mid \mathtt{X})$ is obtained by letting $P(\mathtt{X} = 2^{k-1}) = 1$.

$$\mathcal{H}(\mathtt{H}\underline{\oplus}\mathtt{X} \mid \mathtt{X}) = P(\mathtt{H} < 2^{k-1}) \log \frac{1}{P(\mathtt{H}<2^{k-1})} + P(\mathtt{H} \geq 2^{k-1}) \log \frac{1}{P(\mathtt{H}\geq 2^{k-1})} = 1$$

Thus, we know that 1 bit of information about σ may be leaked by each run of the program.

Note that the above discussion, we used only the fact that $\langle \Sigma, D, e\rangle$ satisfies linear relaxed NI; the discussion applies to *any* program e that satisfies the policy Σ and D. Thus, the quantity of information leakage can be estimated only by looking at Σ and D.

[5] Note that we are considering deterministic programs. Note also that we do not consider timing attacks. It is possible to hide timing attacks to some extent, by using Agat's technique, for instance [1].

5 Related Work

There have been many studies on information flow security and declassification policies: see [11,13] for a general survey and comparison of declassification policies. Most closely related to our work is Sabelfeld and Myers' work on delimited information release [12], and Li and Zdancewic's work on relaxed NI [7]. They control *what* functions can be used for declassification, but not *how often* the declassification functions may be used. Controlling *what* declassification functions are used is sufficient if the declassification functions do not return functions. In fact, in delimited information release, one can use $\lambda x.(l = x)$ (where l is a low security variable) for the password example; No matter how often declassification is performed, the leaked information is the one bit information $h = l$. (In the relaxed NI [7], this is not allowed since policies must be closed terms.) If the declassification functions return functions (as in the password example in this paper), however, controlling *what* declassification functions are used is not sufficient for bounding the quantity of information leakage. In the case of the password example, if one wants to specify that the password can be compared with *some* string but does not to want to specify which string should be compared with the password, then one should use $\lambda x.\lambda s.(s = x)$ as the declassification function. We should therefore control *how often* functions are used to bound the quantity of information leakage.

Another approach to extending relaxed NI would be to replace the equivalence relation in the definition of relaxed NI with a complexity-preserving relation, as discussed in [13]. Let us write $e \succeq e'$ if e' is more efficient than e (see [14] for formal discussion of such a relation). Then, if $e \succeq e'(d\,h)$ holds for some e' that does not contain h, e cannot declassify information about h much faster than by calling the declassification function d. In the password example (where $d = \lambda x.\lambda s.(x = s)$), $e \succeq e'(d\,h)$ implies that it takes a time exponential in the bit length of h for e to leak the entire information about h. Thus, this approach is useful for estimating the speed of information leakage. The approach, however, sometimes gives too conservative estimation of the rate of information leakage. For example, PIN code for a bank account typically consists of only 4 digits, hence knowing that a program satisfies the complexity-preserving relaxed NI for the declassification function $\lambda x.\lambda s.(x = s)$ does not give enough security assurance (because calling the declassification function 10^4 times would not take a second). On the other hand, if the program satisfies the linear relaxed NI, the PIN code can be tested only once per program run, so that we can obtain reasonable security assurance by controlling how often the program can be run.

Li and Zdancewic's type system for relaxed NI [7] allows more flexible declassification than ours; for example, if a declassification function for σ is $\lambda x.((x{+}1) = 2)$, then declassification can be performed in two steps, by first applying $\lambda x.x{+}1$ and then $\lambda y.y = 2$. We think it is possible to extend our linear type system to allow such flexible declassification.

Quantitative analysis of information flow has been recently studied by Malacaria et al. [8,3,2] for imperative languages. As demonstrated in Section 4.3, the linear relaxed non-interference allows us to apply quantitative analysis only to declassification functions instead of the whole program, by which enabling a combination of traditional information flow analysis (with linearity analysis) and quantitative information flow analysis. A limitation of our approach is that only $0, 1, \omega$ uses are considered, so that if a declassification is performed inside a recursive function, the number of declassifications is always estimated as ω. To remove that limitation, we need to generalize uses, possibly using dependent types (for example, we can write $\Pi n : int_{\mathbf{L}}.int_{\{d \mapsto n\}} \rightarrow int_{\mathbf{L}}$ for the type of functions that takes an integer n and a high-security value x, and applies the declassification function d to x, n times).

Our type system can be considered an instance of linear type systems [17,6,9]. In the usual linear type systems, the type of an integer is annotated with how often the integer is accessed. In our type system, the type of an integer is annotated with how often each declassification function may be applied to the integer. We did not discuss a type inference algorithm in this paper, but a type inference algorithm (that is quadratic in the program size, provided that the number of declassification functions is constant) can be developed in a standard manner [9].

6 Conclusion

We introduced a new notion of declassification called *linear declassification*, which not only controls what functions can be used for declassifying high-security values but also *how often* the declassification functions may be applied. We have also introduced *linear relaxed non-interference* to formalize the property guaranteed by linear declassification. The linear relaxed non-interference enables integration of traditional type-based information flow analysis and quantitative information flow analysis, by allowing us to apply quantitative analysis locally to declassification functions.

In the paper, we used password checking as the motivating example. It is left for future work to study more applications of linear declassification. We used a static type system to guarantee linear relaxed NI. Combining our approach with dynamic analysis (for counting of how often functions are called) would also be an interesting direction for future work.

Acknowledgment. We would like to thank Andrei Sabelfeld and Eijiro Sumii for discussions on this work. We would also like to thank anonymous referees for useful comments.

References

1. Agat, J.: Transforming out timing leaks. In: Proc. of POPL, pp. 40–53 (2000)
2. Clark, D., Hunt, S., Malacaria, P.: Quantitative information flow, relations and polymorphic types. Journal of Logic and Computation 15(2), 181–199 (2005)
3. Clark, D., Hunt, S., Malacaria, P.: A static analysis for quantifying information flow in a simple imperative language. Journal of Computer Security 15(3), 321–371 (2007)

4. Denning, D.E., Denning, P.J.: Certification of programs for secure information flow. Communications of the ACM 20(7), 504–513 (1977)
5. Kaneko, Y., Kobayashi, N.: Linear declassification (2007), `http://www.kb.ecei.tohoku.ac.jp/~koba/papers/lindcl-full.pdf` (extended version)
6. Kobayashi, N.: Quasi-linear types. In: Proc. of POPL, pp. 29–42 (1999)
7. Li, P., Zdancewic, S.: Downgrading policies and relaxed noninterference. In: Proc. of POPL, pp. 158–170 (2005)
8. Malacaria, P.: Assessing security threats of looping constructs. In: Proc. of POPL, pp. 225–235 (2007)
9. Mogensen, T.: Types for 0, 1 or Many Uses. In: Clack, C., Hammond, K., Davie, T. (eds.) IFL 1997. LNCS, vol. 1467, pp. 112–122. Springer, Heidelberg (1998)
10. Pottier, F., Simonet, V.: Information flow inference for ML. In: Proc. of POPL, pp. 319–330 (2002)
11. Sabelfeld, A., Myers, A.C.: Language-based information-flow security. IEEE J. Selected Areas in Communications 21(1), 5–19 (2003)
12. Sabelfeld, A., Myers, A.C.: A Model for Delimited Information Release. In: Futatsugi, K., Mizoguchi, F., Yonezaki, N. (eds.) ISSS 2003. LNCS, vol. 3233, pp. 174–191. Springer, Heidelberg (2004)
13. Sabelfeld, A., Sands, D.: Declassification: Dimensions and principles. Journal of Computer Security (to appear). A preliminary version appeared in Proceedings of 18th IEEE Computer Security Foundations Workshop (CSFW-18), pp. 255-269 (2005)
14. Sands, D., Gustavsson, J., Moran, A.: Lambda Calculi and Linear Speedups. In: Mogensen, T.Æ., Schmidt, D.A., Sudborough, I.H. (eds.) The Essence of Computation. LNCS, vol. 2566, pp. 60–82. Springer, Heidelberg (2002)
15. Shannon, C.E.: A mathematical theory of communication. The Bell System Technical Journal 27, 379–423 (1948)
16. Smith, G., Volpano, D.: Secure information flow in a multi-threaded imperative language. In: Proc. of POPL, pp. 355–364 (1998)
17. Turner, D.N., Wadler, P., Mossin, C.: Once upon a type. In: Proceedings of Functional Programming Languages and Computer Architecture, pp. 1–11. San Diego, California (1995)

Just Forget It –
The Semantics and Enforcement of Information Erasure

Sebastian Hunt[1] and David Sands[2]

[1] City University, London
[2] Chalmers university of Technology, Sweden

Abstract. There are many settings in which sensitive information is made available to a system or organisation for a specific purpose, on the understanding that it will be erased once that purpose has been fulfilled. A familiar example is that of online credit card transactions: a customer typically provides credit card details to a payment system on the understanding that the following promises are kept: (i) Noninterference (NI): the card details may flow to the bank (in order that the payment can be authorised) but not to other users of the system; (ii) Erasure: the payment system will not retain any record of the card details once the transaction is complete. This example shows that we need to reason about NI and erasure in combination, and that we need to consider interactive systems: the card details are used in the interaction between the principals, and then erased; without the interaction, the card details could be dispensed with altogether and erasure would be unnecessary. The contributions of this paper are as follows. (i) We show that an end-to-end erasure property can be encoded as a "flow sensitive" noninterference property. (ii) By a judicious choice of language construct to support erasure policies, we successfully adapt this result to an interactive setting. (iii) We use this result to design a type system which guarantees that well typed programs are properly erasing. Although erasure policies have been discussed in earlier papers, this appears to be the first static analysis to enforce erasure.

1 Information Erasure

There are many settings in which sensitive information is made available to a system or organisation for a specific purpose, on the understanding that it will be erased once that purpose has been fulfilled. Common examples involve erasure of some authentication token, such as voter identity in e-voting, or biometric data in fingerprint-activated left-luggage lockers. A more everyday example is an online credit card transaction. A customer typically provides credit card details to a payment system on the understanding that the following promises are kept:

Noninterference (NI): the card details may flow to the bank (in order that the payement can be authorised) but not to other users of the system;

Erasure: the payment system will *not* retain any record of the card details once the transaction is complete.

In this case, erasure ensures that the transaction does not make the customer or bank vulnerable to breaches of security in the payment system which occur after the transaction is complete. Two aspects of erasure are illustrated by this example:

S. Drossopoulou (Ed.): ESOP 2008, LNCS 4960, pp. 239–253, 2008.

1. We need to be able to reason about NI and erasure in combination: we show that flow sensitive NI combined with erasure is equivalent to a re-classification of the erased input.
2. To give a satisfactory account of erasure, we need to consider *interactive* systems: the card details are used in the interaction between the customer, the payment system and the bank, and *then* erased; without the interaction, the card details could be dispensed with altogether and erasure would be unnecessary.

Background. The idea and motivations for studying erasure properties of programs come from recent work of Chong and Myers [CM05], and we borrow some notation from that paper. Their paper deals with expressive temporal information flow policies for program variables which include combinations of erasure and declassification. In their simplest form, erasure policies are written in the form $a \overset{c}{\nearrow} b$, and are used to describe a variable whose security level is initially a, but which is erased to level b as soon as condition c (in principle an arbitrary property of the computation) is satisfied. Policies as described in [CM05] are quite complex (expressive), and their semantics is necessarily quite involved. It is perhaps not surprising that they have not described an enforcement mechanism (e.g. a type system) for their policy language.

In this paper we take a fresh look at the erasure problem with a much less ambitious policy language. We focus on just erasure, independently from declassification concerns. We show how, together with a judicious choice of language construct to support erasure policies, we can take advantage of the close relationship between erasure semantics and noninterference to provide, to our knowledge, the first static analysis to enforce erasure policies.

Summary. We begin (Section 2) by considering what we call *end-to-end* erasure for non interactive programs. Consider the following trivial program: $y := y+1 \;;\; cc := 0$. This program erases (the initial value of) *cc*. On the other hand, $(\textbf{if}\ isVisa(cc)\ y := y+1) \;;\; cc := 0$ does not erase *cc*, since some information about *cc* is retained by y. More generally (following [CM05]) we talk about erasure of a variable *to a higher security level*. In this very simple setting we show that:

- an end-to-end erasure property can be encoded as a "flow sensitive" noninterference property (Proposition 1), and
- if we also require that the program is noninterfering, then this is a necessary and sufficient condition for erasure (Proposition 2).

End-to-end erasure is too simple to be useful in itself. In Section 3 we move on to the study of erasure in the presence of fresh inputs and program outputs. Consider for example the program to the right. Here the erasure property we might want is that no information about the input *cc* in the first line of the loop body can be observed after the transaction (the loop body) is complete. In this case the input is *not* erased because it is

$$
\begin{array}{l}
\textbf{while}\ serverUp\ \{\\
\quad \textbf{input}\ cc\ \textbf{from}\ user\\
\quad \textbf{input}\ details\ \textbf{from}\ user\\
\quad payment\ :=\ process(cc)\\
\quad \textbf{output}\ payment\ \textbf{to}\ bank\\
\quad custInfo\ :=\ custInfo \oplus details\\
\quad cc\ :=0\\
\}\ldots
\end{array}
$$

still present in *payment*, so if the server goes down the credit card information of the last transaction could be retrieved from this variable and output by the system.

Defining what it means for a program to erase data in the general case is potentially complex and, we suspect, correspondingly difficult to enforce. The key idea that we introduce in Section 3 is a simple language mechanism to specify a well behaved class of erasure policies. We introduce a block structured input command of the form **input** x **from** a **erased in** C (the exact syntactic form accommodates a more general notion than this and is written **input** $x : a \nearrow b$ **in** C) thereby tying the semantic lifetime of the input (from the point of view of certain observers) to code block C. This facilitates the subsequent development as follows:

- the definition of when a program correctly enforces such erasure policies (we call such a program *input erasing*) becomes easy to state (Definition 4)
- because of the block structured nature of the erasure policy, we can apply ideas from Section 2 to determine a local end-to-end style erasure condition (Definition 6) which, as for end-to-end erasure, can also be expressed as a reclassified noninterference property (Theorem 1)
- we can then show that the local erasure condition together with a suitable noninterference property is sufficient to guarantee that a program is input erasing (Theorem 2).

Our final contribution (Section 4) is to use this local characterisation of erasure to design a type system which guarantees that well typed programs are input erasing. The type system is a direct adaptation (extension) of a flow sensitive type system for noninterference described in [HS06].

Section 5 discusses some of the subtleties of erasure and the computation model. Section 6 concludes, revisiting related work and sketching some ideas for further work.

2 End-to-End Erasure

We start by considering erasure in its "purest" form. Consider programs which just transform some initial memory state to a final memory state. Concretely, we can consider a simple *while* language with no input or output commands (essentially the language described in Figure 2 with all the input-output machinery removed). The semantics of this language can be given as a small-step deterministic transition relation on configurations, where terminating computations have the form $\langle C, s\rangle \twoheadrightarrow \langle \mathbf{skip}, t\rangle$ (here C is a program and s, t are memory *states*: finite mappings from the set *Var* of variable names to values).

2.1 Flow Sensitive End-to-End Noninterference

As in [HS06] we consider a flow sensitive form of noninterference. Let Γ, Γ' be finite mappings from variable names to elements of $\langle \mathcal{L}, \sqsubseteq, \sqcup, \sqcap\rangle$ a lattice of security levels. We will call these *security type assignments*. We write $s =_X t$ to mean that states s and t agree on all variables in the set X. For $a \in \mathcal{L}$ we write $\Gamma \vdash s =_a t$ to mean that s and t are equal to all observers at or below security level a, with respect to the security type assignment Γ. That is: $\Gamma \vdash s =_a t$ iff $s =_X t$ where $X = \{x | \Gamma(x) \sqsubseteq a\}$.

Definition 1 (Noninterference (NI)). *A command C is noninterfering from Γ to Γ', written $\Gamma\ \{C\}\ \Gamma'$, iff, for all $a \in \mathcal{L}$, if $\Gamma \vdash s =_a t$ and $\langle C, s\rangle \twoheadrightarrow \langle \mathbf{skip}, s'\rangle$ then $\langle C, t\rangle \twoheadrightarrow \langle \mathbf{skip}, t'\rangle$ for some t' such that $\Gamma' \vdash s' =_a t'$.*

(Note that, since programs are deterministic, if t' exists - ie if the program terminates - it is unique.) In other words, noninterference says that if two initial states are indistinguishable to an observer at a (with respect to Γ) then the resulting states will also be indistinguishable (with respect to Γ'). Note that, unlike [HS06], this is a termination *sensitive* NI property, meaning that we do *not* allow information leaks through termination/nontermination behaviour. We chose this stronger variant because it is better suited to a computational model with input-output (Section 3).

2.2 End-to-End Erasure

In what follows we have chosen to model erasure of the information stored in individual variables. Our choice is essentially pragmatic: it allows us to express the key ideas in a simple way while supporting reasonably expressive erasure policies. Other choices are possible. For example we could model erasure of all information stored at a given security level, or, conversely, partial erasure of the information stored in a variable. To be more general still, one could model erasure of arbitrary projections on the program state – and such things could be done in the PER model [SS01] or using abstract noninterference [GM04]).

We define end-to-end erasure as a simple information flow property. In its simplest form, say that a program *completely erases* the information in variable x if varying (just) the information in x prior to execution has no effect on the final program state. In fact we want to be more general than this (following [CM05]). We will say that x is erased *to some level* b, if varying x leaves the final state unchanged from the viewpoint of all observers except those at level b or above. In what follows we write $\neg x$ for $Var - \{x\}$.

Definition 2 (End-to-End Erasure). *Command C erases x to b in Γ', written $C : x\nearrow b$ in Γ', iff, whenever $s =_{\neg x} t$ and $\langle C, s\rangle \twoheadrightarrow \langle \mathbf{skip}, s'\rangle$ then $\langle C, t\rangle \twoheadrightarrow \langle \mathbf{skip}, t'\rangle$, for some t' such that $\forall c \not\sqsupseteq b,\ \Gamma' \vdash s' =_c t'$.*

Note that we can recover complete erasure from the more general definition, in the form $C : x\nearrow\top$ in Γ, as long as we have some security level $\top$ such that, for all variables y, $\Gamma(y) \not\sqsupseteq \top$.

Consider the example programs in Figure 1. We have $P_1 : z_L \nearrow H$ in Γ, but P_2 does *not* erase $z_L\nearrow H$ because although z_L itself is physically overwritten, information about the initial value of z_L is still present in y_M. The same goes for P_3: it does not erase z_L to H, this time because of an indirect information flow to y_M.

Typically, we will wish to enforce policies in which erasure is required *in addition* to NI. The programs in Figure 1 satisfy $\Gamma\ \{P_i\}\ \Gamma\ (i = 1, 2, 3)$. If we replaced $z_L :=0$ with $z_L := y_M$ in P_1 the program would still erase z_L to H, but would not be noninterfering from Γ to Γ.

2.3 Relating End-to-End Erasure and NI

It is clear from the definitions that end-to-end erasure and noninterference are closely related. In later sections we exploit this relationship in both the design of an erasure

$P_1 : x_H := x_H + y_M + z_L$	$P_2 : x_H := x_H + y_M + z_L$	$P_3 : x_H := x_H + y_M + z_L$
$y_M := y_M + 2$	$y_M := y_M + z_L$	**if** $(z_L = 0)\ y_M := y_M{+}1$
$z_L := 0$	$z_L := 0$	$z_L := 0$

Fig. 1. Example programs, assuming security type assignment $\Gamma = [x_H{\mapsto}H, y_M{\mapsto}M, z_L{\mapsto}L]$ with respect to the three point lattice $L \sqsubseteq M \sqsubseteq H$

policy mechanism, and in the adaptation of the flow sensitive type system from [HS06] to produce a type system which also enforces erasure policies. The key observation is that every erasure property can be enforced by requiring a related NI property.

Proposition 1. *If* $\Gamma[x \mapsto b]\ \{C\}\ \Gamma'$ *then* $C : x \nearrow b$ *in* Γ'.

Proof. Assume lhs. Suppose $s =_{\neg x} t$ and $c \not\sqsupseteq b$. From the definitions and by assumption of lhs, it suffices to show that $\Gamma[x \mapsto b] \vdash s =_c t$: this is immediate from $s =_{\neg x} t$ and $\Gamma[x \mapsto b](x) = b \not\sqsubseteq c$. □

For example, the Proposition tells us that we can verify $P_1 : z_L \nearrow H$ (Figure 1) by showing that $\Gamma[x_L{\mapsto}H]\ \{P_1\}\ \Gamma$, and this can be done, for example, using the type system from [HS06].

While useful, this leaves open the possibility that the reclassified NI condition of Proposition 1 is too strong in general, requiring much more than is necessary to ensure erasure. In practice, however, we wish to enforce erasure *and* noninterference together. The following result shows that, if we already require the NI property $\Gamma\ \{C\}\ \Gamma'$, then the reclassified NI property $\Gamma[x \mapsto b]\ \{C\}\ \Gamma'$ is *precisely* what we need to ensure that x is erased to b.

Proposition 2. *If* $\Gamma\ \{C\}\ \Gamma'$ *then* $C : x \nearrow b$ *in* $\Gamma' \iff \Gamma[x \mapsto b]\ \{C\}\ \Gamma'$.

Proof. (Sketch) Assume $\Gamma\ \{C\}\ \Gamma'$ and consider the $\iff$. From right to left is immediate by Proposition 1. Now, for arbitrary sets of variables X, Y, let us write $C : X \Rightarrow Y$ to mean that, for all s, t such that $s =_X t$, if execution of $\langle C, s\rangle$ terminates in some state s' then $\langle C, t\rangle$ terminates in some state $t' =_Y s'$. It should be clear that both erasure and NI are conjunctions of properties of this form. The key step in the argument from left to right is to establish the lemma that $\bigwedge_i C : X_i \Rightarrow Y$ implies $C : \bigcap_i X_i \Rightarrow Y$ and hence that the conjunction of NI and erasure implies the rhs. We omit the details but note that the lemma does *not* hold in general for termination *insensitive* NI. □

3 Erasure in the Presence of Input-Output

The previous section showed how end-to-end erasure policies can be determined by using reclassification and noninterference. But end-to-end erasure is not the kind of policy we ultimately want to enforce. If all the attacker does is literally observe the final values of a computation then Proposition 2 really tells us that an erasure policy is just a way to fix a noninterference policy for which some data was assigned a level which is too low.

Our task now is to generalise the notion of erasure to make it more meaningful and more expressive. To do this we consider a system with inputs and outputs, and a notion of erasure at an intermediate program point. For simplicity, we will identify security levels with channels, thus for each $a \in \mathcal{L}$, we assume exactly one channel, also named a, which carries data at level a (c.f. [OCC06]).

It is tempting (and potentially expressive) to introduce separate constructs for input and erasure. But consider the example to the right. Clearly, x is literally overwritten with a constant in every run which passes the erasure assertion. Intuitively though, this program should be rejected, since an observer of outputs on a can still deduce something about the erased data. This is an example of one particular problem; there are potentially many such problems compounded by the interaction between different erasure operations and the deductions an observer can make though inputs and outputs.

$$\begin{array}{l}\textbf{input } x \textbf{ from } a\\ \textbf{if } (x = 0)(x := -1;\ \textbf{erased } x \textbf{ to } b)\\ \textbf{output } x \textbf{ on } a\end{array}$$

Our key idea is to avoid these problems by combining input and erasure into a single block structured command:

$$\textbf{input } x : a \nearrow b \textbf{ in } C$$

which can be read as the policy "input x on channel a then compute C, after which x will have been erased to level b". By associating the lifetime of the data with the erasure policy in a block-structured way we avoid some of the subtle problems of indirect information flow interacting with the erasure policy. More importantly, we will show that we can apply the end-to-end erasure definition locally to the command C to achieve a meaningful global erasure.

To show that this is really the case we must first extend our definitions of noninterference and erasure to take into account the fact that the language now has IO.

3.1 A Language with Input and Output

To be concrete let us take the simple *while* language and add input as an erasure declaration as above, and a simple output statement. For the operational semantics of this language we assume the existence of an infinite input stream for each security level. We let I denote the set of input streams and, for any level a, I_a denotes the stream of a-inputs, and $I_a(m), m > 0$ denotes the mth input on channel a.

We assume a small-step operational semantics with configurations of the form $\langle C, s, \mathbf{i}\rangle$, where C and s are as before and $\mathbf{i} \in \mathcal{L} \to \mathbb{N}$ is the input stream pointer which records how much of the input streams have been consumed so far.

Transitions are written in the form $I \vdash \langle C, s, \mathbf{i}\rangle \xrightarrow{\ell} \langle C', t, \mathbf{i}'\rangle$ where the label ℓ is either an input event $a?v$, a silent transition τ, or an output event $a!v$. We will often omit the label τ. The syntax and semantics are given in Figure 2. The input streams I are left implicit in the rules. We assume an expression evaluator $[\![E]\!]s$ which produces a value from an expression and an environment. We implicitly assume well-typedness for expressions.

A "vanilla" input command **input** x **from** a, i.e. one which is not associated with an erasure property, can be defined as a shorthand for the trivial erasure **input** x : $a \nearrow a$ **in skip** (it is trivially erasing because "after executing **skip** the value input on channel a will only be visible at level a or above").

$$\begin{array}{rl}\text{Expressions} & E ::= n \mid x \mid E\ op\ E' \\ \text{Commands} & C ::= \mathbf{skip} \mid x := E \mid C_1\ ;\ C_2 \mid \mathbf{if}\ E\ C_1\ C_2 \mid \mathbf{while}\ E\ C \\ & \quad \mid \mathbf{input}\ x : a \nearrow b\ \mathbf{in}\ C \mid \mathbf{output}\ E\ \mathbf{on}\ a \\ \text{Reduction Contexts} & R ::= [\cdot] \mid (R[\cdot]\ ;\ C)\end{array}$$

$$\frac{I_a(n) = v \qquad n = \mathbf{i}(a) + 1}{\langle \mathbf{input}\ x : a \nearrow b\ \mathbf{in}\ C, s, \mathbf{i}\rangle \overset{a?v}{\to} \langle C, s[x \mapsto v], \mathbf{i}[a \mapsto n]\rangle}$$

$$\frac{[\![E]\!]s = v}{\langle x := E, s, \mathbf{i}\rangle \overset{\tau}{\to} \langle \mathbf{skip}, s[x \mapsto v], \mathbf{i}\rangle} \qquad \frac{[\![E]\!]s = v}{\langle \mathbf{output}\ E\ \mathbf{on}\ a, s, \mathbf{i}\rangle \overset{a!v}{\to} \langle \mathbf{skip}, s, \mathbf{i}\rangle}$$

$$\frac{[\![E]\!]s = v \in \{\mathbf{true}, \mathbf{false}\}}{\langle \mathbf{if}\ E\ C_{\mathbf{true}}\ C_{\mathbf{false}}, s, \mathbf{i}\rangle \overset{\tau}{\to} \langle C_v, s, \mathbf{i}\rangle}$$

$$\frac{}{\langle \mathbf{while}\ E\ C, s, \mathbf{i}\rangle \overset{\tau}{\to} \langle \mathbf{if}\ E\ (C\ ;\ \mathbf{while}\ E\ C)\ \mathbf{skip}, s, \mathbf{i}\rangle}$$

$$\frac{}{\langle (\mathbf{skip}\ ;\ C), s, \mathbf{i}\rangle \overset{\tau}{\to} \langle C, s, \mathbf{i}\rangle} \qquad \frac{\langle C, s, \mathbf{i}\rangle \overset{\ell}{\to} \langle C', s', \mathbf{i}'\rangle}{\langle R[C], s, \mathbf{i}\rangle \overset{\ell}{\to} \langle R[C'], s', \mathbf{i}'\rangle}$$

Fig. 2. Syntax and Semantics

From the single step evaluation relation we define the zero-or-more-step relation $\overset{\alpha}{\twoheadrightarrow}$, labelled with a sequence of non-silent events, in the obvious way. We write $c_1 \twoheadrightarrow c_2$ to mean that $c_1 \overset{\alpha}{\twoheadrightarrow} c_2$ for some (possibly empty) α and $c_1 \overset{\alpha}{\twoheadrightarrow}$ to mean $\exists c_2 . c_1 \overset{\alpha}{\twoheadrightarrow} c_2$.

3.2 Noninterference and Input Erasure

We extend the equality relation $=_a$ to input streams (and input stream pointers) by saying $I =_a I'$ ($\mathbf{i} =_a \mathbf{j}$) whenever $I_c = I'_c$ ($\mathbf{i}(c) = \mathbf{j}(c)$) for all $c \sqsubseteq a$. We write $\alpha =_a \beta$ to mean equality of the projections of α and β to all labels on channel a or lower.

Definition 3 (Input-Output Noninterference). *We define a command C to be* input-output noninterfering *if for all $a \in \mathcal{L}$, and all input streams I and I', if $I =_a I'$ and $I \vdash \langle C, s, \mathbf{i}\rangle \overset{\alpha}{\twoheadrightarrow}$ then $I \vdash \langle C, s, \mathbf{i}\rangle \overset{\beta}{\twoheadrightarrow}$ for some β such that $\alpha =_a \beta$.*

Let us now turn to the definition of the erasure property that we want. It says that in any execution, once control has reached the end of the input block $\mathbf{input}\ x : a \nearrow b\ \mathbf{in}\ C$ – i.e. once we have finished executing C – then no information about x should be visible through subsequent input or output events except at level b or higher.

Definition 4 (Input Erasure). *We say that a command C_0 is* input erasing *if for all input streams I the following property holds. Suppose we have a computation of the following form:*

$$I \vdash \langle C_0, s_0, \mathbf{i}_0\rangle \twoheadrightarrow \langle R[\mathbf{input}\ x : a \nearrow b\ \mathbf{in}\ C], s, \mathbf{i}\rangle \twoheadrightarrow \langle R[\mathbf{skip}], s_1, \mathbf{i}_1\rangle \overset{\alpha}{\twoheadrightarrow}$$

where the computation $R[\mathbf{input}\ x : a \nearrow b\ \mathbf{in}\ C] \twoheadrightarrow R[\mathbf{skip}]$ is independent of $R[\cdot]$. Let I' be an input stream which only differs from I on channel a at input position

$\mathbf{i}(a)+1$. *Then the input erasing condition requires that there exists a computation of the following form:*

$$I' \vdash \langle C_0, s_0, \mathbf{i}_0\rangle \twoheadrightarrow \langle R[\mathbf{input}\ x : a \nearrow b\ \mathbf{in}\ C], s, \mathbf{i}\rangle \twoheadrightarrow \langle R[\mathbf{skip}], t_1, \mathbf{j}_1\rangle \overset{\beta}{\twoheadrightarrow}$$

such that $\forall c \not\sqsupseteq b$ *we have* $s_i =_c t_i$, $\mathbf{i}_i =_c \mathbf{j}_i$ $(i = 1, 2)$ *and* $\alpha =_c \beta$.

Note that the requirement that $I' \vdash \langle C_0, s_0, \mathbf{i}_0\rangle \twoheadrightarrow \langle R[\mathbf{input}\ x : a \nearrow b\ \mathbf{in}\ C], s, \mathbf{i}\rangle$ is actually vacuous since the computation has not yet reached the point at which I and I' differ. The start state s_0 and $\mathbf{i}_0$ in the above are universally quantified, but could be fixed. A natural choice for an initial input pointer would of course be $\lambda a.0$.

The following proposition formalises the sense in which the "vanilla" input is trivially erasing:

Proposition 3. *If C is input-output noninterfering and if each input command in C has the form* $\mathbf{input}\ x : a \nearrow a\ \mathbf{in}\ \mathbf{skip}$ *for some x and a then C is input erasing.*

3.3 Characterising Input Erasure with a Local Erasure Condition

In this section we develop a local characterisation of erasure – a generalisation of end-to-end erasure which we can apply locally to the command $\mathbf{input}\ x : a \nearrow b\ \mathbf{in}\ C$ – which will help us establish the "global" input erasure condition.

To do this we will need to work with a stronger notion of noninterference than input-output noninterference. Although the definition of input-output noninterference is a reasonable top level definition (for more discussion on this point see section 5) it is difficult to work with since it says nothing about the state. For example it is *not* compositional with respect to sequential composition: $C_1 = \mathbf{input}\ x\ \mathbf{on}\ H\ ;\ \mathbf{if}\ x\ \mathbf{then}\ y := 1$ is IO-noninterfering, and so is $C_2 = \mathbf{output}\ y\ \mathbf{on}\ L$, but $C_1\ ;\ C_2$ is not. It is convenient therefore to work with a stronger definition which also looks at the initial and terminal state (in the case that the program terminates).

Definition 5 (Stateful Input-Output Noninterference). *A command C is noninterfering from Γ to Γ', written $\Gamma\ \{C\}\ \Gamma'$, iff, for all $a \in \mathcal{L}$, and all input streams I, I', if $\Gamma \vdash s =_a t$, $I =_a I'$, $\mathbf{i} =_a \mathbf{j}$ then*

1. *if $I \vdash \langle C, s, \mathbf{i}\rangle \overset{\alpha}{\twoheadrightarrow}$ then $I' \vdash \langle C, t, \mathbf{j}\rangle \overset{\beta}{\twoheadrightarrow}$ for some β such that $\alpha =_a \beta$, and*
2. *if $I \vdash \langle C, s, \mathbf{i}\rangle \twoheadrightarrow \langle \mathbf{skip}, s', \mathbf{i}'\rangle$ then $I' \vdash \langle C, t, \mathbf{j}\rangle \twoheadrightarrow \langle \mathbf{skip}, t', \mathbf{j}'\rangle$ such that $\mathbf{i}' =_a \mathbf{j}'$ and $\Gamma' \vdash s' =_a t'$.*

Now we will define an extension of the end-to-end erasure property. The idea is that, when enforced locally on the erasing input command, the property will be sufficient to ensure the global erasure property.

The definition ensures that if a specific variable x is erased from a to b then it is neither "visible" in the state except at or above b (precisely as before) *nor* via the input pointer:

Definition 6 (Local Erasure). *Command C erases x to b in Γ', written $C : x \nearrow b$ in Γ', iff, whenever $s =_{\neg x} t$ and $I \vdash \langle C, s, \mathbf{i}_0\rangle \twoheadrightarrow \langle \mathbf{skip}, s', \mathbf{i}\rangle$ then $I \vdash \langle C, t, \mathbf{i}_0\rangle \twoheadrightarrow \langle \mathbf{skip}, t', \mathbf{j}\rangle$, for some t' and $\mathbf{j}$ such that $\forall c \not\sqsupseteq b$, $\Gamma' \vdash s' =_c t'$ and $\mathbf{i} =_c \mathbf{j}$.*

Note that in definitions 5 and 6 we have overload the terminology used in definitions 1 and 2 respectively. It is reasonable to do this because they are conservative extensions of the earlier definitions.

The local erasure condition ignores the input and outputs that take place before the computation is complete, but the condition nevertheless demands that $\mathbf{i} =_c \mathbf{j}$. This is motivated by the fact that the state of the input pointer can be used as a covert store to save information about the erased secret. Consider the command C defined as

$$\begin{array}{l}\mathbf{if}\ (x \neq 0)\ (\mathbf{input}\ y\ \mathbf{on}\ M);\\ x := 0; y := 0\end{array} \qquad \text{(where } L \sqsubseteq M \sqsubseteq H\text{)}$$

If we ignored the final value of the input pointers, then this command would be considered to erase x. This would be too weak for our purposes because after the erasure, information about x *will* be known to an observer at level M. To see this, consider using the command (C) in the program to the right. So for example if the M input stream has the value $0, 1 \ldots$ then the value of y output on M will be 0 if x was 0 and 1 otherwise.

$$\begin{array}{l} y := 0\ ;\\ \mathbf{input}\ x : L \nearrow H\ \mathbf{in}\ C;\\ \mathbf{input}\ y\ \mathbf{on}\ M\ ;\\ \mathbf{output}\ y\ \mathbf{on}\ M\end{array}$$

Reclassification. In the manner of Proposition 1, we will show that the local erasure property can be characterised in terms of noninterference. But since noninterference cares about the input output events that occur during a computation, and local erasure does not, we need a way to "turn a blind eye" to input output events. Towards this end it is useful – for specification purposes only – to introduce a language construct which "hides" inputs and outputs:

Definition 7. *We extend the language with commands of the form $\widehat{C}$ with semantics*

$$\frac{\langle C, s, \mathbf{i}\rangle \xrightarrow{\alpha} \langle C', s', \mathbf{i}'\rangle}{\langle \widehat{C}, s, \mathbf{i}\rangle \xrightarrow{\tau} \langle \widehat{C'}, s', \mathbf{i}'\rangle} \qquad \frac{}{\langle \widehat{\mathbf{skip}}, s, \mathbf{i}\rangle \xrightarrow{\tau} \langle \mathbf{skip}, s, \mathbf{i}\rangle}$$

This is essentially just like the hiding operation of CSP, and is commonly used in process calculi to specify noninterference properties (see e.g. [Ros95, FG95]), except that here we are hiding *all* events, so $\widehat{C}$ behaves like C but with every input or output label of C replaced by the silent action τ.

Theorem 1 (Local Erasure as Reclassification). *If $\Gamma\ \{C\}\ \Gamma'$ then*

$$C : x \nearrow b \text{ in } \Gamma' \iff \Gamma[x \mapsto b]\ \{\widehat{C}\}\ \Gamma'$$

The theorem says that to check noninterference and erasure for a command it is necessary and sufficient to check noninterference and a reclassified noninterference property but where input and output labels are ignored.

Proof (Omitted for space reasons. See extended version of this article).

3.4 From Local to Global Erasure

We have defined a local erasure condition for commands with IO. The purpose of the local condition is to provide sufficient conditions for input erasure. But in order to complete this picture we need some noninterference conditions: the local erasure property can only give input erasure if the rest of the program does not allow the erased information to flow back down to a lower level, i.e. it must have a noninterference property.

Annotations. To state the noninterference assumptions we need, we will use program annotations. Annotations will provide the link to compositional program analyses such as type systems. An annotation here is just a security type assignment. The operational semantics of an annotation is transparent (otherwise it would not be an annotation!): we extend the grammar of reduction contexts with the annotated context $(R[\cdot])^{\Gamma}$, and specify the rule $\langle \mathbf{skip}^{\Gamma}, s, \mathbf{i}\rangle \rightarrow \langle \mathbf{skip}, s, \mathbf{i}\rangle$. In an annotated subterm C^{Γ}, the annotation Γ is intended to describe the security levels of the state at the point in execution after C has been evaluated. This intuition is made concrete in the following definition which connects annotations to the noninterference property.

Definition 8 (Well-annotated Commands). *Command C_0 is* well annotated *iff:*

1. *every annotated input command* $(\mathbf{input}\ x : a \nearrow b\ \mathbf{in}\ C)^{\Gamma}$ *in C_0 has the local erasure property $C : x \nearrow b$ in Γ;*
2. *whenever a command of the form $R[\mathbf{skip}^{\Gamma}]$ is reached from any computation beginning with C_0, then $\Gamma\ \{R[\mathbf{skip}]\}\ \Gamma'$ for some Γ'.*

Theorem 2. *If C_0 is a well-annotated command such that every input command in C_0 is annotated, then C_0 is input erasing.*

Proof (Omitted for space reasons. See extended version of this article).

4 Erasure by Typing

In this section we use the results of the previous section to design a type system for erasure (and noninterference). The idea is that we use Theorem 1 to guide us in the treatment of the input erasure command, standard subject reduction and noninterference properties of the type system to establish a well-annotated version of the program, and Theorem 2 to prove that the type system guarantees input erasure.

Our type system is a simple extension of the flow sensitive system of [HS06] (alternative flow sensitive base systems, such as [AB04], could also be considered). We modify the system of [HS06] to be *termination sensitive*: the rules only allow while loops to be performed over the lowest security level ($\bot$), and these can only occur in the context $\bot$. This is of course a rather restrictive notion. A more liberal system would allow high loops when they can be shown to be terminating.

The type rules are shown in Figure 3. For a command C, judgements have the form $p \vdash \Gamma\ \{C\}\ \Gamma'$ where $p \in \mathcal{L}$, and Γ, Γ' are security type assignments. The idea is that if Γ gives the security levels of variables before execution of C, then Γ' will give their security levels afterwards. The type p represents the usual "program counter" level and

$$\text{Skip}\frac{}{p \vdash \Gamma\ \{\mathbf{skip}\}\ \Gamma} \qquad \text{Assign}\frac{\Gamma \vdash E : t}{p \vdash \Gamma\ \{x := E\}\ \Gamma[x \mapsto p \sqcup t]}$$

$$\text{Erase}\frac{p \vdash \Gamma[x \mapsto a]\ \{C\}\ \Gamma' \quad p \vdash \Gamma[x \mapsto b]\ \{C'\}\ \Gamma' \quad p \sqsubseteq a \quad C' = \text{deleteOutput}(C)}{p \vdash \Gamma\ \{\mathbf{input}\ x : a \nearrow b\ \mathbf{in}\ C\}\ \Gamma'}$$

$$\text{Output}\frac{\Gamma \vdash E : b \qquad p \sqcup b \sqsubseteq a}{p \vdash \Gamma\ \{\mathbf{output}\ E\ \mathbf{on}\ a\}\ \Gamma} \qquad \text{Annotate}\frac{p \vdash \Gamma\ \{C\}\ \Gamma'}{p \vdash \Gamma\ \{C^{\Gamma'}\}\ \Gamma'}$$

$$\text{Seq}\frac{p \vdash \Gamma\ \{C_1\}\ \Gamma' \quad p \vdash \Gamma'\ \{C_2\}\ \Gamma''}{p \vdash \Gamma\ \{C_1\ ;\ C_2\}\ \Gamma''} \qquad \text{If}\frac{\Gamma \vdash E : t \quad p \sqcup t \vdash \Gamma\ \{C_i\}\ \Gamma' \quad i = 1,2}{p \vdash \Gamma\ \{\mathbf{if}\ E\ C_1\ C_2\}\ \Gamma'}$$

$$\text{While}\frac{\Gamma \vdash E : \bot \quad \bot \vdash \Gamma\ \{C\}\ \Gamma}{\bot \vdash \Gamma\ \{\mathbf{while}\ E\ C\}\ \Gamma} \qquad \text{Sub}\frac{p_1 \vdash \Gamma_1\ \{C\}\ \Gamma_1'}{p_2 \vdash \Gamma_2\ \{C\}\ \Gamma_2'} \quad p_2 \sqsubseteq p_1, \Gamma_2 \sqsubseteq \Gamma_1, \Gamma_1' \sqsubseteq \Gamma_2'$$

Fig. 3. Type System

serves to eliminate indirect information flows: the rules ensure that only variables with final types (in Γ') greater than or equal to p may be changed by C. Similarly, input and output is only permitted on channels greater than or equal to p.

The purpose of the type system is to guarantee noninterference and input erasure. Here we provide explanation of the rules for input and output, since they are the new ones. The rule for input commands follows Theorem 1 rather directly, making use of a command transformer deleteOutput(C) which simply replaces every output command in its argument with **skip**. This is the means by which we ignore outputs when checking the local erasure requirement. We cannot however ignore inputs, since we still need to ensure that there are no covert channels via the input pointers. Output is simply treated like an assignment to a variable of a fixed security type. One can note that if we specialise the typing rules to "vanilla" inputs, as represented by commands of the form $\mathbf{input}\ x : a \nearrow a\ \mathbf{in\ skip}$, then we get what appears to be a flow sensitive version of the deterministic part of the type system from [OCC06].

Example. Let us reconsider the credit-card transaction server loop from the introduction. Let us suppose that $\bot \sqsubseteq \mathit{user} \sqsubseteq \mathit{bank} \sqsubseteq \top$. To represent the intention that the credit card data is erased by the end of each loop iteration, the code can be rewritten as shown to the right. For the purpose of typing we assume that $\mathit{process}(\mathit{cc})$ is just some expression involving cc. Since $\top$ is used to model the level of data that is no longer physically present, no variables should be given a final type of $\top$. With this restriction there is (thankfully) no typing for this program. The body of the erasure statement C is, in fact, suitably noninterfering, as shown by the typing $\bot \vdash \Gamma\ \{C\}\ \Gamma$ where $\Gamma(\mathit{serverUp}) = \bot$ and $\Gamma(x) = \mathit{user}$ for all other variables x. But to type the enclosing erasure input we also need the typing $\bot \vdash \Gamma[\mathit{cc} {\mapsto} \top]\ \{\text{eraseOutput}(C)\}\ \Gamma$. This is

$$\begin{array}{l}
\mathbf{while}\ \mathit{serverUp}\ \{\\
\quad \mathbf{input}\ \mathit{cc} : \mathit{user} \nearrow \top\ \mathbf{in}\ \{\\
\quad\quad \left.\begin{array}{l}
\mathbf{input}\ \mathit{details}\ \mathbf{from}\ \mathit{user}\\
\mathit{payment} := \mathit{process}(\mathit{cc})\\
\mathbf{output}\ \mathit{payment}\ \mathbf{to}\ \mathit{bank}\\
\mathit{custInfo} := \mathit{custInfo} \oplus \mathit{details}\\
\mathit{cc} := 0
\end{array}\right\} C\\
\quad \}\\
\}\ldots
\end{array}$$

not possible because $payment := process(cc)$ forces $payment$ to type $\top$ instead of $user$. By appending $payment := 0$ to the end of C the program becomes typeable.

4.1 Type Correctness

In this section we sketch the main milestones in the correctness argument. For reasons of space, details of proofs are not included. In what follows, we say that C is *well-typed* if, for some p, Γ, Γ', there exists a derivation of $p \vdash \Gamma \; \{C\} \; \Gamma'$.

Before verifying the motivating semantic properties of the type system, we show that it is well behaved with respect to reduction by establishing the obvious subject reduction property.

Theorem 3 (Subject Reduction). *If C is well-typed and $I \vdash \langle C, s, \mathbf{i} \rangle \twoheadrightarrow \langle C', s', \mathbf{i}' \rangle$, then C' is well-typed.*

The two fundamental semantic properties we require of the type system are:

NI Type Correctness: that it guarantees the stateful input-output NI property, Definition 5 (and thus the top level input-output NI property, Definition 3).
Erasure Type Correctness: that it can be used to establish the premises of Theorem 2 (and thus to guarantee input erasure).

Theorem 4 (NI Type Correctness). *If $p \vdash \Gamma \; \{C\} \; \Gamma'$ then $\Gamma \; \{C\} \; \Gamma'$.*

The proof, an induction on the computation steps, makes use (as usual) of the subject reduction property and an auxiliary property that C does not modify store or perform any inputs or outputs on channels below level p.

Corollary 1. *Well-typed programs are input-output noninterfering.*

Theorem 5 (Erasure Type Correctness). *If C is well-typed then C is well-annotated.*

Proof. (Sketch) The proof of the theorem is in two parts, corresponding to the two parts of the definition of well-annotation. For the first part we rely on Theorem 1, which shows that well-annotation of input commands is a corollary of the following lemma:

Lemma 1. *If $p \vdash \Gamma \; \{(\mathbf{input}\; x : a \nearrow b \;\mathbf{in}\; C)^{\Gamma'}\} \; \Gamma''$ then $\Gamma[x \mapsto b] \; \{\widehat{C}\} \; \Gamma'$.*

For the second part, we rely on the following lemma:

Lemma 2. *If $p \vdash \Gamma_0 \; \{R[\mathbf{skip}^{\Gamma}]\} \; \Gamma'$ then $\Gamma \; \{R[\mathbf{skip}]\} \; \Gamma'$.*

– which is proved by induction on $R[\cdot]$. The second part of well-annotation then follows by subject reduction. □

Corollary 2. *Well-typed programs are input erasing.*

Proof. By inspection of the type system, any derivation of a typing for a program must include a sub-derivation $p \vdash \Gamma \; \{\mathbf{input}\; x : a \nearrow b \;\mathbf{in}\; C\} \; \Gamma'$ for every input command, and we can use each such Γ' to annotate the corresponding input command. By inserting uses of Annotate into the original type derivation we can clearly recover a derivation for the annotated program. By Theorem 5 the annotated program is well-annotated and hence, by Theorem 2, is input erasing. Since the annotated program is semantically equivalent to the original, it follows that the original is input erasing. □

5 On the Adequacy of the Input-Output Model

We have adopted a simple stream-based model of input-output. In a general nondeterministic setting, such a model does not adequately model a "high" attacker who is trying to pass information to "low" through the program, and it becomes necessary to quantify over all possible *strategies* adopted by the principals. This is a well known problem in the noninterference literature [WJ90]. See [OCC06] for a recent language-based take on the issue. Fortunately, since we deal with deterministic programs, it turns out that simple stream models *are* nevertheless adequate, as shown recently by Clark and Hunt [CH07].

What about erasure? Are there potential problems that arise from not modelling an active attacker's strategy? In fact the problem here is that we *cannot* reasonably model inputs as coming from an attacker with an arbitrary strategy, because it only makes sense to promise to erase data if the supplier is *not* an adversary. A payment system typically promises, on completion of a transaction, to erase the credit card data but to retain the shipping address. The system will not succeed in erasing the credit card data if the user's strategy is to re-input the credit card data as a response to a subsequent request for the shipping address, but clearly we do not want to admit such strategies.

There are more subtle cases which show that we must assume even more about the data supplier's behaviour. Suppose that, before the credit card is erased, the program sends back to the user a special offer code *"zahojasf23"* with the promise "present this code when you next shop with us for a 10% discount". What if this code is simply an encryption of the credit card number? The program in this case may well have erased the credit card number by the end of the transaction, but if the user re-inputs this code then the program will have reconstructed the credit card number.

What assumptions are reasonable for the data supplier? We assume, from a noninterference perspective, that attackers can make arbitrarily accurate semantic deductions based on their observations and complete knowledge of the program. For a non attacker it seems reasonable to assume the opposite – the honest user sees the program as a black box. How then can we solve the problem from the example above if the user cannot be relied upon to *know* whether *"zahojasf23"* contains their credit card information? Our proposed solution is to:

- assume that the user is aware of the erasure "contract"; they know that they are providing an input which is scheduled for erasure, and they are notified when the erasure is complete, and
- assume that the user treats any outputs from the program (at their level) as potentially tainted with data currently scheduled for erasure.

We believe that the stream model that we have used here correctly captures these assumptions, but it is beyond the scope of this paper to explicitly model such user strategies in order to *prove* that the stream model is indeed correct in this sense.

6 Conclusions and Further Work

We have studied the semantics of erasure and shown its connection to noninterference. We have introduced a particular idiom for expressing erasure policies in code, and shown that a natural global erasure property can be enforced by a combination of noninterference and a local erasure property, which in turn can also be established by a noninterference property. This leads to a fairly direct definition of a type system for which well typed programs correctly erase their data. We conclude here by returning to the related work, before finishing with some remarks about further work.

Related work. In addition to Chong and Myers work [CM05], Hansen and Probst [HP06] describe what they call *simple erasure policies* which correspond to a specific instance of our end-to-end erasure policies, but stated in terms of the erasure of a whole level rather than a single variable. Neither of these works describe an implementation of erasure, either by encoding into standard noninterference or developing a specific program analysis.

There are several fundamental differences between the *definition* of erasure developed here and that of Chong and Myers. Ignoring the fact that [CM05] also deals with declassification policies, we note the following differences. Firstly, [CM05] does not consider a system with interaction, something that we feel is central to making notions of erasure meaningful. Secondly, in the abstract system model in [CM05] the state of the system is *just* a store. The obvious way to encode an imperative program as such a system would be to use a *program counter* variable, but there is no suitable *policy* in their language which one could attach to such a program counter. Thus their model might not be suitable for modelling imperative programs – at least not with a straightforward encoding. Thirdly, they require a "physical erasure" condition which says that at the point where a variable is erased it should contain a predefined constant. This is stronger than necessary. Although we can *satisfy* erasure properties in that way, there is nothing to stop us from erasing data to level b by e.g. overwriting it with something else from a lower level. Lastly, since erasure can be thought of as a dual to declassification (since it is used to strengthen as opposed to weaken NI) we can see that their erasure condition and ours tackle different *dimensions* of erasure: using the terminology of [SS05], their erasure properties deal with *when* erasure takes place, whereas our input-centric erasure determines *where* (in the code) erasure takes place.

Finally, we note that our use of a block structured erasure command is similar in spirit to Almeida Matos and Boudol's [AB05] block structured declassification construct, **flow** F **in** C, which locally extends the global information flow policy with flows F for the duration of C.

Further Work. There are several obvious avenues for further work.

We can follow the "dimensions" and consider, for example, refinement of *what* is erased. For example, erasure of all except the first four digits of a credit card number. Work on corresponding "what" declassification policies [SS05] can be applied directly.

The input erasure construct used here can be generalised in a number of potentially useful ways. One possibility is to introduce an erasure region – a code block in which all subsequent inputs are erased.

A naive implementation of the type system as presented is potentially exponential in the depth of nesting of erasure statements, because the body of the erasure statement appears twice in the premise of the Erase rule. By building on results from [HS06], we are hopeful that this behaviour can be avoided by obtaining the two typings for the body of an erasure input as specialisations of a single principal type.

On the theoretical side we noted at the end of the previous section the need for further work on modelling attacker strategies and "honest" participants. A process calculus setting may prove more suitable to conduct such an investigation.

Acknowledgements. Thanks to various members of the ProSec group at Chalmers for helpful comments, to Steve Chong and to the anonymous referees for numerous helpful comments and suggestions. This work was partly supported by EPSRC research grant EP/C009746/1 Quantitative Information Flow, the Swedish research agencies Vinnova, SSF, VR and by the Information Society Technologies programme of the European Commission under the IST-2005-015905 MOBIUS project.

References

[AB04] Amtoft, T., Banerjee, A.: Information Flow Analysis in Logical Form. In: Giacobazzi, R. (ed.) SAS 2004. LNCS, vol. 3148, pp. 100–115. Springer, Heidelberg (2004)

[AB05] Almeida Matos, A., Boudol, G.: On declassification and the non-disclosure policy. In: Proc. IEEE Computer Security Foundations Workshop (June 2005)

[CH07] Clark, D., Hunt, S.: Observation, nondeterminism and nondeducability on strategies. In: Workshop presentation at PLID 2007, 3rd International Workshop on Programming Language Dependence and Independence (August 2007)

[CM05] Chong, S., Myers, A.C.: Language-based information erasure. In: Proc. IEEE Computer Security Foundations Workshop (June 2005)

[FG95] Focardi, R., Gorrieri, R.: A classification of security properties for process algebras. J. Computer Security 3(1), 5–33 (1995)

[GM04] Giacobazzi, R., Mastroeni, I.: Abstract non-interference: parameterizing non-interference by abstract interpretation. In: Proc. ACM Symp. on Principles of Programming Languages, pp. 186–197 (2004)

[HP06] Hansen, R.R., Probst, C.W.: Non-interference and erasure policies for java card bytecode. In: 6th International Workshop on Issues in the Theory of Security (WITS 2006) (2006)

[HS06] Hunt, S., Sands, D.: On flow-sensitive security types. In: POPL 2006, Proceedings of the 33rd Annual. ACM SIGPLAN - SIGACT. Symposium. on Principles of Programming Languages (January 2006)

[OCC06] O'Neill, K.R., Clarkson, M.R., Chong, S.: Information-flow security for interactive programs. In: Proc. IEEE Computer Security Foundations Workshop, pp. 190–201. IEEE Computer Society, Los Alamitos (2006)

[Ros95] Roscoe, A.W.: CSP and determinism in security modeling. In: Proc. IEEE Symp. on Security and Privacy, May 1995, pp. 114–127 (1995)

[SS01] Sabelfeld, A., Sands, D.: A per model of secure information flow in sequential programs. Higher-Order and Symbolic Computation 14(1), 59–91 (2001)

[SS05] Sabelfeld, A., Sands, D.: Dimensions and principles of declassification. In: Proceedings of the 18th IEEE Computer Security Foundations Workshop, pp. 255–269. IEEE Computer Society Press, Los Alamitos (2005)

[WJ90] Wittbold, J.T., Johnson, D.M.: Information flow in nondeterministic systems. In: IEEE Symposium on Security and Privacy, pp. 144–161 (1990)

Open Bisimulation for the Concurrent Constraint Pi-Calculus*

Maria Grazia Buscemi[1] and Ugo Montanari[2]

[1] IMT Lucca Institute for Advanced Studies, Italy
m.buscemi@imtlucca.it
[2] Dipartimento di Informatica, University of Pisa, Italy
ugo@di.unipi.it

Abstract. The concurrent constraint pi-calculus (cc-pi-calculus) has been introduced as a model for concluding Service Level Agreements. The cc-pi calculus combines the synchronous communication paradigm of process calculi with the constraint handling mechanism of concurrent constraint programming. While in the original presentation of the calculus a reduction semantics has been proposed, in this work we investigate the abstract semantics of cc-pi processes. First, we define a labelled transition system of the calculus and a notion of open bisimilarity *à la* pi-calculus that is proved to be a congruence. Next, we give a symbolic characterisation of bisimulation and we prove that the two semantics coincide. Essentially, two processes are open bisimilar if they have the same stores of constraints - this can be statically checked - and if their moves can be mutually simulated. A key idea of the symbolic transition system is to have 'contextual' labels, i.e. labels specifying that a process can evolve only in presence of certain constraints. Finally, we show that the polyadic Explicit Fusions calculus introduced by Gardner and Wischik can be translated into monadic cc-pi and that such a transition preserves open bisimilarity. The mapping exploits fusions and tuple unifications as constraints.

1 Introduction

Service Oriented Computing is an emerging paradigm that builds upon the notion of services as interoperable elements that can be described, published, searched and composed. Services may expose both functional properties (i.e. what they do) and non-functional properties (i.e. the way they are supplied). A Service Level Agreement (SLA) is a contract between two parties, usually a service provider and a customer, that records non-functional properties about a service like performance, availability, and cost.

The concurrent constraint pi-calculus (cc-pi calculus) [5] is a model of SLA negotiations that combines two main programming paradigm: name-passing calculi (see e.g. [9]) and concurrent constraint programming [14,13]. On the one side, cc-pi inherits from the Pi-F calculus [16] a symmetric, synchronous mechanism of interaction between senders and receivers, where the sent name is 'fused' (i.e. identified) to the received name and such *explicit fusion* allows to use interchangeably the two names.

* Research supported by the EU IST-FP6 16004 Integrated Project SENSORIA.

S. Drossopoulou (Ed.): ESOP 2008, LNCS 4960, pp. 254–268, 2008.

On the other side, cc-pi generalises explicit fusions to be arbitrary constraints and introduces primitives for creating, removing and making logical checks on constraints. For instance, a cc-pi process $P = c \,|\, \texttt{tell}\; c'.Q$ can place a constraint c' corresponding to a certain SLA parameter and then evolve to the parallel composition of $c \otimes c'$ and Q, if $c \otimes c'$ is *consistent*. A process $P = c \,|\, \texttt{ask}\; c'.Q$ makes a transition to Q if the constraint c' is *entailed* by c. As another example, a process $P = (x = v \otimes v = y) \,|\, \overline{x}\langle z \rangle.P' \,|\, y\langle w \rangle.Q'$, with $\overline{x}\langle z \rangle$ an output action, $y\langle w \rangle$ an input action and $(x = v \otimes v = y)$ a combination of constraints, can make a synchronisation because the identification of the names x and y is entailed by the constraints in parallel. Moreover, such an interaction yields the name fusion $z = w$, which is consistent with the other constraints. In fact, we can think about this synchronisation as a simultaneous execution of an $\texttt{ask}\; x = y$ action and a $\texttt{tell}\; z = w$ action. From this viewpoint, cc-pi calculus combines primitives borrowed from different paradigms in a coherent way. Another feature of the cc-pi calculus is to include a restriction operation (x) *à la* pi-calculus that allows for local stores of constraints. Synchronisations may have the effect of combining local stores of interacting processes into a global store.

The constraint systems adopted in cc-pi rely on *named c-semirings*, i.e. c-semirings [3] enriched with a notion of *support* to express the relevant names of a constraint. These structures can specify networks of constraints for defining constraint satisfaction problems and to model fuzzy or probabilistic values, as well as Herbrand unifications.

A main contribution of this work is to characterise cc-pi processes that have the same behaviours. Not surprisingly, as a notion of behavioural equivalence we take *bisimulation*, which is a key idea in the context of process calculi. Roughly, two processes are bisimilar if they are able to match each other's moves. A desirable property of behavioural equivalences is that two processes are equivalent in all contexts. Indeed, this feature allows for compositional reasoning about complex interactive systems. Nevertheless, the universal quantification over all contexts makes this definition of a little use in practice. Open bisimulation [12] has been introduced on the pi-calculus as a behavioural equivalence that has a coinductive definition and is guaranteed to be a congruence. In fact, the term 'open' is meant to emphasise that in this bisimulation names can be identified at any time and, so, the relation is preserved by name substitutions.

In this paper we show that open bisimulation naturally transfers to cc-pi processes and it is still a congruence. In our setting, constraints running in parallel with a process have an effect on the names of that process as they can allow or disallow transitions. Hence, the parallel contexts consisting of constraints are as discriminating as arbitrary contexts and the natural adaptation of open bisimilarity to cc-pi is to replace substitutions with constraints in parallel. For instance, the process $\overline{x}\langle z \rangle.\mathbf{0} \,|\, y\langle w \rangle.\mathbf{0}$ that tries to synchronise on channels with different names and the inert process $\mathbf{0}$ are not bisimilar since, in the context $x = y \,|\, \_$, the first one can make a move while the second one is stuck. Beside the dynamic behaviour of processes, the present open bisimilarity takes into account the knowledge exposed by a process to its environment, that is expressed by the store of constraints of the process. This notion reminds the definition of *static equivalence* that has been defined for the applied pi-calculus [1] and it generalises to constraints a similar concept used for open bisimulation in Pi-F [15]. Note that checking whether two processes have the same static behaviour can be performed at compile-time. As an example, consider the processes $c\,|\,\mathbf{0}$ and $\mathbf{0}$. They are both inert but, in the context ask $c\,|\,\_$, the first process can make a transition while the second one cannot.

Checking open bisimilarity is hard since it involves a universal quantification over constraints. We provide an efficient version of open bisimulation and we prove that the two notions coincide. The main idea behind *symbolic bisimulations* [8,4,12] is to define specialised transition systems, whose labels specify the minimum conditions that must hold in order for a transition to take place. We adapt this concept to our framework by defining a transition system whose labels represent the 'least restrictive' constraints that allow process moves. We exploit the division operator over c-semiring values [2], which is well defined under mild assumptions. According to the symbolic semantics, e.g., the process $c\,|\,\texttt{ask}\ d.\mathbf{0}$ can make a transition labelled by a constraint $c' = d \div c$, which is the weakest constraint such that the combination $c \otimes c'$ entails d.

The results of this work generalise to constraints analogous achievements proved for the Pi-F calculus [15]. To highlight this connection, we translate polyadic Pi-F calculus into monadic cc-pi and we prove that such a translation is fully abstract with respect to open bisimulation. This amounts to say that open bisimilarity over the instance of cc-pi corresponding to Pi-F coincides with the analogous equivalence over Pi-F processes. Note that the encoding of polyadicity exploits the fact that name tuples can be expressed as Herbrand constraints and that tuple matching corresponds to term unification.

Diaz Frias *et al.* [6] introduce the pi$^+$-calculus, an extension of the pi-calculus with constraint agents that can perform `tell` and `ask` actions, and they define a barbed bisimulation for the calculus. In contrast to our model, the constraint systems are first-order theories rather than algebraic structures and they do not support local stores. Gilbert and Palamidessi [7] address the interplay between mobility and constraints. Unlike our approach, they enrich concurrent constraint programming with the notion of localities and process migration rather than adding a channel-based communication mechanism *à la* pi-calculus.

2 Named Constraints

Let $\mathcal{N}$ be an infinite, countable set of *names* and let $x, y, z\ldots$ range over names. We define *(name) fusions* as total equivalence relations on $\mathcal{N}$ with only finitely many non-singular equivalence classes. By $x{=}y$ we denote the fusion with a unique non-singular equivalence class containing x and y. bA *substitution* is a function $\sigma : \mathcal{N} \to \mathcal{N}$. We denote by $[y/x]$ the substitution that maps x into y. A *permutation* ρ is a bijective substitution. The *kernel* $K(\rho)$ of a permutation ρ is the set of names that are changed by ρ. A *permutation algebra* A is defined by a carrier set and by a function defining how states are transformed by the finite-kernel permutations. In our case, A characterises the set of 'relevant' names of each element c of the c-semiring as the support $\mathsf{supp}(c)$ in A.

We now recall basic concepts about semirings and c-semirings. We refer to [11,3,2] for a more detailed treatment. A *commutative semiring* is a tuple $\langle A, \oplus, \otimes, 0, 1\rangle$ such that: (i) A is a set and $0, 1 \in A$, and $\oplus, \otimes : A \times A \to A$ are binary operators making the triples $\langle A, \otimes, 1\rangle$ and $\langle A, \oplus, 0\rangle$ commutative monoids (semigroups with identity), satisfying the following axioms.

$$a \otimes (b \oplus c) = (a \otimes b) \oplus (a \otimes c)\ \forall a, b, c \in A \qquad a \otimes 0 = 0\ \forall a \in A$$

A *constraint semiring (c-semiring)* $\langle A, \oplus, \otimes, 0, 1\rangle$ is a commutative semiring such that $\oplus$ is idempotent and such that $a \oplus 1 = 1$ for all $a \in A$ (i.e. with top element). Typical examples are the c-semiring for classical constraint satisfaction problems $\langle\{\mathsf{False}, \mathsf{True}\}, \vee, \wedge, \mathsf{False}, \mathsf{True}\rangle$, the c-semiring for fuzzy constraint satisfaction problems $\langle [0,1], \mathsf{max}, \mathsf{min}, 0, 1\rangle$, and the c-semiring of weighted constraint satisfaction problems $\langle \mathbb{R}^+ \cup \{+\infty\}, \mathsf{min}, +, +\infty, 0\rangle$. Note that the Cartesian product of two c-semirings is a c-semiring, hence this framework is also suited to model multicriteria optimization.

Commutative semirings with top element are also known in the literature as *absorptive*. Absorptiveness implies that the sum operator is idempotent. Semirings that satisfy this last property are often called *tropical*. Hence, c-semirings are tropical semirings with top element. Next, we briefly overview some classical notions and results on absorptive and tropical semirings that we rephrase for c-semirings.

Let $\preceq$ be a relation over A such that $a \preceq b$ iff $a \oplus b = b$. This relation gives us a way to compare semiring values and constraints. Assume a c-semiring $C = \langle A, \oplus, \otimes, 0, 1\rangle$. Then: (i) $\preceq$ is a partial order; (ii) $\oplus$ and $\otimes$ are monotone on $\preceq$; (iii) $a \otimes b \preceq a, b$, for all a, b; (iv) 0 is its minimum and 1 its maximum; and (v) for all $a, b \in A$, $a \oplus b$ is the least upper bound of a and b. Moreover, if $\otimes$ is idempotent, $a \otimes b$ is the greatest lower bound of a and b. C is *invertible* if there exists an element $c \in A$ such that $b \otimes c = a$ for all elements $a, b \in A$ such that $a \preceq b$; C is *complete* if it is closed with respect to infinite sums, and the distributivity law holds also for an infinite number of summands. It can be proved that if C is complete then the set $\{x \in A \mid b \otimes x \preceq a\}$ admits a maximum for all elements $a, b \in A$, denoted $a \div b$. Note that the idempotency of $\otimes$ implies that the invertibility property holds. However, for the purpose of this paper, we simply require invertibility and completeness while not imposing idempotency of $\otimes$.

2.1 Named c-Semirings

A named c-semiring is a complete and invertible c-semiring enriched with a notion of name fusions, a permutation algebra A and a hiding operator $(\nu x.)$ that makes a name x local in c. Note that in certain named c-semirings the hiding operator coincides with the homologous operator $\exists x$ defined in cc programming. Formally, a *named c-semiring* $C = \langle C, \oplus, \otimes, \nu x., \rho, 0, 1\rangle$ is a tuple where: (i) $x{=}y \in C$ for all x and y in $\mathcal{N}$; (ii) $\langle C, \oplus, \otimes, 0, 1\rangle$ is a complete and invertible c-semiring; (iii) $\langle C, \rho\rangle$ is a finite-support permutation algebra such that every permutation ρ distributes over $\otimes$ and $\oplus$ and is inactive on 0 and 1 ; (iv) $\forall x$, $\nu x. : C \to C$ is a unary operation; (v) for all $c, d \in C$ and for all ρ the following axioms hold.

$$
\begin{array}{lll}
x{=}y \otimes c \;=\; x{=}y \otimes [y/x]c & & \rho(\nu x. c) = \nu x. (\rho c) \text{ if } x \notin K(\rho) \\
\nu x.\, 1 = 1 & \nu x. \nu y. c = \nu y. \nu x. c & \nu x.\, c = \nu y. [y/x]c \quad \text{if } y \notin \mathsf{supp}(c) \\
\nu x. (c \otimes d) = c \otimes \nu x. d \quad \text{if } x \notin \mathsf{supp}(c) & & \nu x. (c \oplus d) = c \oplus \nu x. d \quad \text{if } x \notin \mathsf{supp}(c)
\end{array}
$$

The top left axiom above accounts for combining fusions and generic elements of c-semirings According to the top right axiom, the order of ρ and ν can be changed if x is not affected by ρ. The remaining axioms rule how the ν operation interacts with the operations of the c-semiring and they are inspired by the analogous structural congruence axioms for restriction in process calculi. Note that the notion of support $\mathsf{supp}(c)$ associated with permutation algebras recalls the concept of free names in process calculi.

Given $C = \langle A, \oplus, \otimes, \rho, \nu x., 0, 1\rangle$, a *(named) constraint* c is an element of A. For $C \subseteq A$, C is *consistent* if $(\otimes C) \neq 0$; moreover, for $c \in A$, C *entails* c if $(\otimes C) \leq c$.

Herbrand constraints. A *Herbrand constraint system* can be defined by considering a signature Σ along with an equational theory $=_E$ on the term algebra $T_\Sigma(\mathcal{N})$ plus the additional rules:

$$(\text{SUB-TERM}) \frac{f(t_1,\ldots,t_n) =_E f(t'_1,\ldots,t'_n)}{t_i =_E t'_i}\ i = 1,\ldots,n \quad (\text{REPLACE}) \frac{x =_E t \quad t_1 =_E t_2}{[t/x]t_1 =_E [t/x]t_2}$$

and with the restrictions that $x \neq_E t(x)$ and $f(t_1,\ldots,t_n) \neq_E g(t_1,\ldots,t_m)$, where $t(x)$ is any term different than x which contains x and $f \neq g$. Axiom (SUB-TERM) above allows to reduce the unification of two terms to the unification of their sub-terms provided that the outer function symbols are the same. Axiom (REPLACE) reduces the unification of two terms containing a term t such that $t =_E x$ to the unification of the terms with x in place of t. The restrictions prevents from unifying, respectively, a variable with terms containing that variable, and two terms containing a distinct outer function symbols.

We let C_H be the tuple $C_H = \langle C, \oplus, \otimes, \nu x., \rho, 0, 1\rangle$ where: (i) C is the set of the above-defined equational theories plus a bottom element $\perp$; (ii) $E_1 \oplus E_2 = E_1 \cap E_2$; (iii) $E_1 \otimes E_2$ is the unification of E_1 and E_2, i.e. it is the smallest equational theory largest than or equal to $E_1 \cup E_2$, if it exists, otherwise $\perp$; (iv) $\nu x.\, E = E \cap \bar{E}$, where $t_1 =_{\bar{E}} t_2$ if $t_1 =_E t_2$ or x does not occur in t_1, t_2; (v) $\rho t_1 =_{\rho E} \rho t_2$ if $t_1 =_E t_2$; (vi) $0 = \perp$ and $1 = \{(t,t) \,|\, t \in T_\Sigma(\mathcal{N})\}$. C_H can be proved to be a named c-semiring with idempotent product $\otimes$.

Example 1 (pairs, tuples). Pairs of names can be expressed as elements of the named c-semiring C_H by assuming two sorts, names and lists, and by taking the signature $\Sigma = \{(\_,\_), \text{nil}\}$, where nil is a constant of sort '$\rightarrow$ lists' and $(\_,\_)$ is a binary operation of sort 'names $\times$ lists $\rightarrow$ lists'. A tuple of arity n can be defined as $\langle x_1,\ldots,x_n\rangle = (x_1,(x_2,(\ldots(x_{n-1},\text{nil}))\ldots)$. Notice that, for instance, the unification of two theories of different arities $\langle x_1,x_2\rangle$ and $\langle y_1,y_2,y_3\rangle$ reduces to unifying the subterms nil and (y_3,nil) hence leading to $\perp$, since the outer functions are distinct. On the other hand, the unification of $\langle x_1,x_2,x_3\rangle$ and $\langle y_1,y_2,y_3\rangle$ yields the identification of the components $x_i = y_i$.

Soft constraints. Given a domain D of interpretation for the set of names $\mathcal{N}$ and a c-semiring $S = \langle A, \oplus, \otimes, 0, 1\rangle$, a *soft* constraint c can be represented as a function $c = (\mathcal{N} \rightarrow D) \rightarrow A$ associating to each variable assignment $\eta = \mathcal{N} \rightarrow D$ (i.e. instantiation of the variables occurring in it) a value in A, which can be interpreted e.g. as a set of preference values or costs. Soft constraints can be combined by means of the operators of S. Assume C_{soft} is the tuple $C_{\text{soft}} = \langle C, \oplus', \otimes', \nu x., \rho, 0', 1'\rangle$ such that: (i) C is the set of all soft constraints over $\mathcal{N}$, D and S; (ii) name equalities $x{=}y$ are defined as $(x = y)\eta = 1$ if $\eta(x) = \eta(y)$, $(x = y)\eta = 0$ otherwise; (iii) $(c_1 \oplus' c_2)\eta = c_1\eta \oplus c_2\eta$; (iv) $(c_1 \otimes' c_2)\eta = c_1\eta \otimes c_2\eta$; (v) $(\nu x.c)\eta = \sum_{d \in D}(c\eta\{^d/_x\})$, where $\sum_{d \in D}$ denotes the c-semiring sum operator and the assignment $\eta\{^d/_x\}$ is defined, as usual, as $\eta\{^d/_x\}(y) = d$ if $x = y$, $\eta(y)$ otherwise; (vi) $(\rho c)\eta = c\bar{\eta}$ with $\bar{\eta}(x) = \eta(\rho(x))$; (vii) $0'\eta = 0$ and $1'\eta = 1$ for all η. It is possible to prove that C_H is indeed a named c-semiring and that the product $\otimes'$ is idempotent provided that $\otimes$ is idempotent. Remark that for $S = \langle\{\mathsf{False}, \mathsf{True}\}, \vee, \wedge, \mathsf{False}, \mathsf{True}\rangle$, the named constraints of $\mathcal{C}_{\text{soft}}$ leads to solutions consisting of the set of tuples of legal domain values.

3 The cc-pi Calculus

The concurrent constraint calculus (cc-pi calculus) features symmetric non-binding input and output actions like in Pi-F calculus along with primitives for constraint handling. The syntax and reduction semantics of the calculus are defined in Fig. 1. Unlike the original presentation of cc-pi [5], here we give a monadic version of the calculus. Moreover, we disregard the `check` and `retract` operators. In fact, `check` is irrelevant for the purpose of this paper but it could be easily included; by contrast, adding `retract` would not be trivial since it would require dealing with a more complex constraint theory. The cc-pi calculus is parametric with respect to named constraints. We let $c, d, e \ldots$ range over constraints of an arbitrary named c-semiring $\mathcal{C}$. The notions of *bound names*, *free names*, and α-conversion of a process are as usual apart that the occurrence of the name y in a process with an input prefix $x\langle y\rangle.U$ is free and that the set of free names is extended to constraints by adding the following clauses:

$$\mathrm{fn}(\pi.U) = \mathsf{supp}(c) \cup \mathrm{fn}(U) \ \text{ if } \pi = \mathtt{tell}\ c, \mathtt{ask}\ c \qquad \mathrm{fn}(c) = \mathsf{supp}(c)$$

The last three structural axioms in Fig. 1 state the correspondence between parallel composition and semiring product, restriction and constraint hiding, the inert process $\mathbf{0}$ and the top element of c-semiring 1, respectively. Using structural congruence, every process P can be rewritten into the *normal form* $P \equiv (\widetilde{x})\,(c\,|\,U)$, where c is a constraint, U can only contain restrictions under prefixes, i.e. $U \not\equiv (\widetilde{y})U'$, and if $x_i \in \mathsf{supp}(c)$ then $x_i \in \mathrm{fn}(U)$. Roughly, the rules move each name $x \notin \mathrm{fn}(U)$ close to c and then apply $\nu x.$ to c.

The idea behind the reduction relation is to proceed as follows. First, to put processes into the normal form by applying the rule for structural congruent processes. Next, applying the rules for dealing with primitives on constraints or for synchronising processes. Afterward, closing with respect to summation, parallel composition of unconstrained processes, and restriction. For instance, the parallel composition $x = z\,|\,\overline{x}\langle y\rangle.U\,|\,z\langle w\rangle.V$ can evolve to $x = z \otimes y = w\,|\,U\,|\,V$ since the equality of the names x and z is entailed by the constraint $x = z$ and the store $x = z \otimes y = w$ is consistent. Remark that it is legal to treat name equalities as constraints c over $\mathcal{C}$ because, by definition, named c-semirings contain fusions. Note also that the rule for parallel composition intentionally allows to add only unconstrained process. For this reason, several rules like those for τ's and summation must include the constraint c in parallel.

4 A Labelled Semantics for cc-pi

We now come to the first contribution of this work. We propose a labelled semantics that coincides with the reduction semantics when restricting to closed processes. We start by introducing the notion of *store* of constraints of processes, that represents the static knowledge exposed by a process to its environment. Roughly, $\mathsf{store}(P)$ is the constraint which is obtained by replacing each unconstrained process occurring in P with $\mathbf{0}$ and by

The syntax of *prefixes* π, *unconstrained processes* U and *constrained processes* P is:

$$\begin{array}{lcllllll} \pi & ::= & \tau & \mid \bar{x}\langle y\rangle & \mid x\langle y\rangle & \mid \texttt{tell}\ c & \mid \texttt{ask}\ c \\ U & ::= & \mathbf{0} & \mid U|U & \mid \Sigma_i \pi_i.U_i & \mid (x)U & \mid I(\tilde{y}) \\ P & ::= & U & \mid c & \mid P|P & \mid (x)P & \end{array}$$

The *structural congruence*, $\equiv$, is the smallest congruence over processes closed with respect to α-conversion and satisfying the following axioms:

$$P|Q \equiv Q|P \quad (P|Q)|R \equiv P|(Q|R) \quad (x)(y)P \equiv (y)(x)P \quad P|(x)Q \equiv (x)(P|Q) \ \textit{if}\ x \notin \mathrm{fn}(P)$$
$$I(\tilde{y}) \equiv [\tilde{y}/\tilde{x}]U \quad \textit{if}\ I(\tilde{x}) \stackrel{\mathrm{def}}{=} U \qquad c|d \equiv c \otimes d \qquad (x)c \equiv \nu x.c \qquad \mathbf{0} \equiv 1$$

The *reduction relation* over processes $\mapsto$ is the smallest relation satisfying the following rules:

$$c\,|\,\tau.U \mapsto c\,|\,U \qquad c\,|\,\texttt{tell}\ d.U \mapsto c\otimes d\,|\,U \ \ \text{if}\ c\otimes d \neq 0 \qquad c\,|\,\texttt{ask}\ d.U \mapsto c\,|\,U\ \text{if}\ c \preceq d$$

$$c\,|\,(\bar{x}\langle y\rangle.U + \Sigma\pi_i.U_i)\,|\,(z\langle w\rangle.V + \Sigma\pi'_j.V_j) \longrightarrow c\otimes(y=w)\,|\,U\,|\,V \quad \text{if}\ c\otimes(y=w)\neq 0 \wedge c \preceq x=z$$

$$\frac{c\,|\,\pi_i.U_i \mapsto P}{c\,|\,\Sigma\pi_i.U_i \mapsto P} \qquad \frac{P \mapsto P'}{P\,|\,U \mapsto P'\,|\,U} \qquad \frac{P \mapsto P'}{(x)P \mapsto (x)P'} \qquad \frac{P \equiv P' \quad P' \mapsto Q' \quad Q' \equiv Q}{P \mapsto Q}$$

Fig. 1. The cc-pi calculus

applying the structural axioms on constraints to compute the resulting constraint. More formally, for P a process, store(P) is inductively defined as follows:

$$\mathsf{store}(c) = c \quad \mathsf{store}(P\,|\,Q) = \mathsf{store}(P)\otimes\mathsf{store}(Q) \quad \mathsf{store}(U) = 1 \quad \mathsf{store}((x)P) = \nu x.\mathsf{store}(P)$$

For example, if $P = (x)(y = x\,|\,x = z\,|\,c(x,v)\,|\,(w)y\langle w\rangle.U)$, $\mathsf{store}(P) = y = z\otimes c(y,v)$. Note that the concept of store is close to the notion of 'frame' given in applied pi-calculus [1] and it generalises to constraints the equivalence relation that characterises the explicit fusions of a process in Pi-F calculus [15].

Assume a set of actions $\mathcal{A} = \{\tau, \bar{x}\langle y\rangle, x\langle y\rangle, \bar{x}(z), x(z)\}$, where τ is a silent action, $\bar{x}\langle y\rangle$ and $x\langle y\rangle$ are *free actions*, and $\bar{x}(z)$ and $x(z)$ are *bound actions*. We let α, β range over $\mathcal{A}$. The labelled transition semantics of processes is the smallest relation $P \xrightarrow{\alpha} Q$, defined by the rules in Fig. 2 plus a rule (OPEN-O) for output and the symmetric counterpart of rule (COMM). The operational rules that deal with τ-transitions are analogous to the reduction rules given in the previous section. The additional rules are standard apart that the usual side condition $x \neq z$ of the rule (OPEN-I) is replaced by the condition that $x = z$ cannot be entailed by the store of constraints of the process. By $\xrightarrow{\tau}^{\star}$ we refer to a sequence of transitions $\xrightarrow{\tau}$.

Proposition 1. *Let P be a process. $P \mapsto Q$ iff $P \xrightarrow{\tau} Q$.*

4.1 Example: Modelling Service Level Agreements

We now consider a variant of an example introduced in [5] that does not include `retract` operations. Consider a service that offers computing resources like units of

(PREF)
$$c\,|\,\pi.U \xrightarrow{\pi} c\,|\,U \quad \pi = \tau, \bar{x}\langle y\rangle, x\langle y\rangle$$

(TELL)
$$c\,|\,\texttt{tell}\ d.U \xrightarrow{\tau} c\otimes d\,|\,U \ \text{ if } c\otimes d \neq 0$$

(ASK)
$$c\,|\,\textsf{ask}\ d.U \xrightarrow{\tau} c\,|\,U \quad \text{if } c \preceq d$$

(SUM)
$$\frac{c\,|\,\pi_i.U_i \xrightarrow{\alpha} U'}{c\,|\,\sum \pi_i.U_i \xrightarrow{\alpha} U'}$$

(PAR)
$$\frac{P \xrightarrow{\alpha} P' \quad \text{bn}(\alpha)\cap \text{fn}(U) = \emptyset}{P\,|\,U \xrightarrow{\alpha} P'\,|\,U}$$

(COMM)
$$\frac{c\,|\,U \xrightarrow{x\langle y\rangle} c\,|\,U' \quad c\,|\,V \xrightarrow{\bar{z}\langle w\rangle} c\,|\,V' \quad c\otimes(y=w)\neq 0 \quad c\preceq x=z}{c\,|\,U\,|\,V \xrightarrow{\tau} c\otimes(y=w)\,|\,U'\,|\,V'}$$

(RES)
$$\frac{P \xrightarrow{\alpha} P' \quad x \notin \text{n}(\alpha)}{(x)\,P \xrightarrow{\alpha} (x)\,P'}$$

(OPEN-I)
$$\frac{P \xrightarrow{z\langle x\rangle} P' \quad \textsf{store}(P) \not\preceq x = z}{(x)\,P \xrightarrow{z(x)} P'}$$

(STRUCT)
$$\frac{P \equiv P' \quad P' \xrightarrow{\alpha} Q' \quad Q' \equiv Q}{P \xrightarrow{\alpha} Q}$$

Fig. 2. Labelled Transition System of the cc-pi calculus

CPUs of a given power and suppose the service provider and a client want to reach a SLA. The provider and the client can be described by the following cc-pi processes.

$$\begin{aligned}
\textsf{Client}_{\textsf{req}}(r) &\equiv (y)\,(\texttt{tell}\ c_{\textsf{req}}(y).\bar{r}\langle y\rangle)\\
\textsf{Provider}_{\textsf{off},\textsf{N}}(r) &\equiv (x_0)\,(\texttt{tell}\ (x_0 = \textsf{N}).\textsf{Ac_Req}_{\textsf{off}}(x_0, r))\\
\textsf{Ac_Req}_{\textsf{off}}(x,r) &\equiv (v)\,(x')\,(\texttt{tell}\ (x' = x - v \otimes x' \geq 0).\texttt{tell}\ d_{\textsf{off}}(v)).r\langle v\rangle.\textsf{Ac_Req}_{\textsf{off}}(x', r))
\end{aligned}$$

The client starts by placing a constraint $c_{\textsf{req}}(y)$ that specifies that the requested resources y must be at least req, then it contacts the provider on channel r. If the synchronisation succeeds, the negotiation is concluded. On the other side, the provider initially fixes the maximum number of total available resources N, then starts to accept requests by imposing two constraints on the number of resources v that will be allocated to each client: $(x' = x - v) \otimes x' \geq 0$ states that v must be less than the total available resources (x is initially N) and that the remaining resources are $x' \geq 0$; $d_{\textsf{off}}(v)$ specifies that v must be less than a fixed maximum number of resources off that are offered to every client. Finally, the provider tries to reach an agreement with a client over channel r and, in case of success, is ready to offer the remaining resources x' to other clients. The negotiation between a client $\textsf{Client}_{\textsf{req}}(r)$ and a provider $\textsf{Provider}_{\textsf{off},\textsf{N}}(r)$ can be modelled in cc-pi as follows. First, each party consumes its `tell` prefixes:

$$\begin{aligned}
(r)\,(\textsf{Provider}_{\textsf{off},\textsf{N}}(r)\,|\,\textsf{Client}_{\textsf{req}}(r)) \xrightarrow{\tau}{}^{\star}\ &(r)\,(y)\,(x_0)\,(v)\,(x')\,(c_{\textsf{req}}(y)\otimes d_{\textsf{off}}(v)\otimes(x_0=\textsf{N})\otimes\\
&(x' = x_0 - v\otimes x' \geq 0)\,|\,\bar{r}\langle y\rangle\,|\,r\langle v\rangle.\textsf{Ac_Req}_{\textsf{off}}(x', r))
\end{aligned}$$

If the fusion $y = v$ yields a consistent store of constraint, the synchronisation on r can take place and the two parties have reached an agreement expressed by the constraint

$$c_{\textsf{req}}(y)\otimes d_{\textsf{off}}(v)\otimes(x_0=\textsf{N})\otimes(x' = x_0 - v)\otimes(x'\geq 0)\otimes(y=v) \qquad (1)$$

As mentioned in the previous section, the cc-pi calculus is parametric with respect to named constraints. Hence, in cc-pi we can capture different constraint satisfaction problems by changing the underlying named c-semiring of a given process while keeping the same process specification. To highlight this feature, we now consider two instantiations of the constraint system adopted in the above negotiation scenario and we show that they lead to different solutions. In both cases, we assume an assignment $\eta : \mathcal{N} \to \mathbb{N}$ of names to non-negative integers and we take the constraints to be functions $c : (\mathcal{N} \to \mathbb{N}) \to A$ that map each name assignment to a value of a c-semiring $S = \langle A, \oplus, \otimes, 0, 1 \rangle$. Constraints are combined by using the operations of S, as shown in §2.1. The two cases below correspond to different choices of the c-semiring S.

Crisp constraint interpretation. Consider $S = \langle \{\mathsf{False}, \mathsf{True}\}, \vee, \wedge, \mathsf{False}, \mathsf{True} \rangle$ that leads to solutions consisting of the set of tuples of legal domain values. For instance, the interpretation of the constraint $c = (\mathsf{a} \geq x) \otimes (y \geq \mathsf{b})$, where x, y are names, a and b are in $\mathbb{N}$, and $\geq$ stands for 'greater than or equal' over $\mathbb{N}$, is that $c\eta = \mathsf{True}$ if $\mathsf{a} \geq \eta(x)$ and $\eta(y) \geq \mathsf{b}$, while $c\eta = \mathsf{False}$ otherwise. We define the constraints c_{req} and d_{off} as follows:

$$c_{\mathsf{req}}(y) \stackrel{\text{def}}{=} y \geq \mathsf{req} \qquad d_{\mathsf{off}}(v) \stackrel{\text{def}}{=} \mathsf{off} \geq v.$$

Assuming the interpretation of name equalities is as expected, the store of constraints (1) has a solution if $\min\{\mathsf{off}, \mathsf{N}\} \geq \mathsf{req}$. For instance, $\mathsf{Provider}_{7,15}$ can reach an agreement with Client_5, but not with Client_8. Moreover, the constraint system resulting from the negotiation between a provider and n clients has a solution if

$$\mathsf{req_i} \leq \mathsf{off} \quad \text{and} \quad \sum_{\mathsf{i}} \mathsf{req_i} \leq \mathsf{N} \quad \text{for} \quad \mathsf{i} = 1, \ldots, n.$$

For example, if there are three clients and each of them requests at least 6 units of resources, a provider $\mathsf{Provider}_{7,15}$ can only reach an agreement with two of them.

Weighted constraint interpretation. Consider the c-semiring of weighted constraint satisfaction problems $S_W = \langle \mathbb{R}^+ \cup \{+\infty\}, \min, +, 0, +\infty \rangle$, which associates a cost to each domain tuple. In our example, this c-semiring allows to model the viewpoint of the client that wishes to minimise the total cost of the proposed solution. Note that in this case the associated ordering $\preceq$ over constraints reduces to $\geq$ over reals, i.e. a value is preferred to another if it is smaller. The interpretation of a named constraint $c = (x = y)$ is that, for η an assignment of names to non-negative integers, $c\eta = 0$ if $\eta(x) = \eta(y)$, while $c\eta = +\infty$ otherwise. The constraints $y = 0$, $x_0 = \mathsf{N}$, $x' = x_0 - v$, and $y = v$, where 0 and N are values in the domain $\mathbb{N}$, can be interpreted similarly. We define the constraints d_{off} and c_{req} as below.

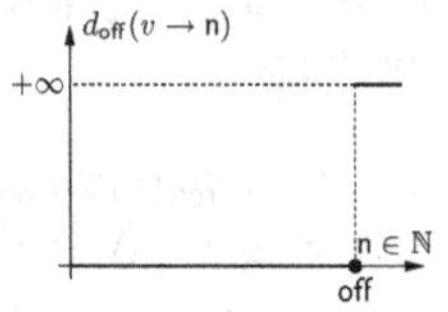

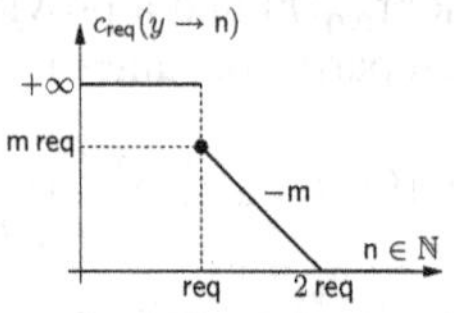

The constraint d_{off} is a simple translation of the analogous constraint given in the crisp case, i.e. $d_{\mathsf{off}}(v \to \mathsf{n}) = 0$ if $\mathsf{off} \geq \mathsf{n}$, while $d_{\mathsf{off}}(v \to \mathsf{n}) = +\infty$ otherwise. On the other side, the constraint $c_{\mathsf{req}}(y)$ specifies that: (i) if y assumes a value that is less than req, then the cost is maximum; (ii) if the value of y is between req and 2req, the cost decreases according to the slope $-\mathsf{m}$; (iii) for every value that is greater than 2req the cost is minimum, meaning that the client has no additional benefit in acquiring more than 2req resources. The possible solutions of the constraint system (1) are as follows.

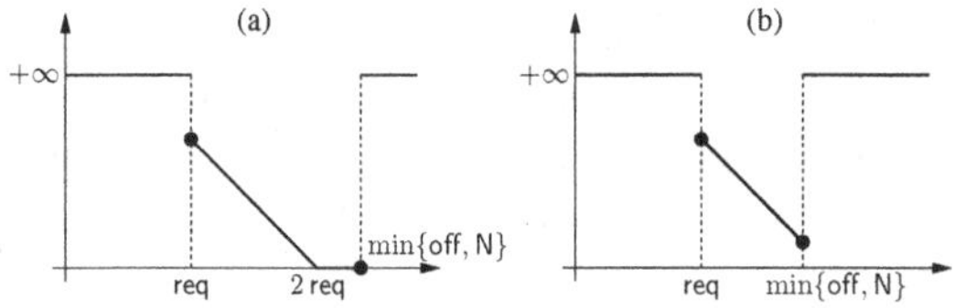

If $\min\{\mathsf{off}, \mathsf{N}\} < \mathsf{req}$, the system has no solution. If $\min\{\mathsf{off}, \mathsf{N}\} \geq 2\mathsf{req}$ the system yields a set of solutions which all have the maximum level of preference 0 (case (a)). Finally, if $\mathsf{req} \leq \min\{\mathsf{off}, \mathsf{N}\} < 2\mathsf{req}$ the solution is selected by means of the c-semiring $\oplus$ operation (min over reals) in that interval, thus leading to $\min\{\mathsf{off}, \mathsf{N}\}$ (case (b)).

Remark 1. The present semantics does not specify how to solve the constraint system generated at each step. In fact, the consistency check performed when placing new constraints, either through a `tell` action or by a synchronisation, only requires that the resulting constraint is different from the bottom element of the c-semiring 0. While in the crisp case this choice amounts to take optimal solutions (i.e., name instantiations that lead to constraint evaluating to the top element 1), in the more general setting of soft constraints this semantics does not provide a way to discard non-optimal solutions.

5 Open Bisimulation

We now define a process equivalence *à la* open pi-calculus bisimulation. In our setting, the obvious counterpart of closing with respect to substitutions is to close with respect to constraints in parallel. We require that two equivalent processes have the same static and dynamic behaviour. Hereafter, by $c \preceq (\alpha = \beta)$ we abbreviate: (i) $c \preceq (x = y) \otimes (w = z)$, if $\alpha = \overline{x}\langle w\rangle$ and $\beta = \overline{y}\langle z\rangle$ (and analogously for input actions), (ii) $c \preceq (x = y)$, if $\alpha = \overline{x}(w)$ and $\beta = \overline{y}(w)$, where $\preceq$ and $\otimes$ are the partial order and the product operations of c-semirings; $c \preceq \tau = \tau$ stands for $c \preceq 1$.

Definition 1 (open bisimilarity). Open bisimilarity *($\sim^o$) is the largest symmetric relation S between processes such that PSQ implies:*

1. $\mathsf{store}(P) = \mathsf{store}(Q)$*;*
2. *If* $P \xrightarrow{\alpha} P'$ *with* $\mathrm{bn}(\alpha) \cap \mathrm{fn}(Q) = \emptyset$ *then* $Q \xrightarrow{\beta} Q'$ *and* $P'\ S\ Q'$*, for some* Q' *and* β *such that* $\mathsf{store}(P) \preceq \alpha = \beta$*;*
3. $c\,|\,P\ S\ c\,|\,Q$*, for all constraints* $c \neq 0$*.*

The first item above states that two processes must expose the same stores. This requirement does not take dynamic behaviours of processes into account. From this viewpoint, the equivalence of stores is a generalisation to constraints of the *static equivalence* defined in applied pi-calculus [1]. The condition $\mathsf{store}(P) \preceq \alpha = \beta$ in the second item intuitively means that the label identification must be entailed by the constraints of P, i.e. the labels must coincide in the 'context' $\mathsf{store}(P)$. For instance, $x = y\,|\,\overline{x}\langle z\rangle$ and $x = y\,|\,\overline{y}\langle z\rangle$ satisfy this requirement. Finally, the third item of the above definition is the counterpart of closing with respect to substitutions in open bisimulation for pi-calculus processes. As an example, the processes `ask` $c.U$ and $\mathbf{0}$ are not bisimilar because $c\,|$ `ask` $c.U$ can make a move while $c\,|\,\mathbf{0}$ is stuck. In fact, it is possible to show that $\sim^o$ coincides with a classical notion of contextual equivalence. We now state that $\sim^o$ is preserved by every operator of the calculus. The proof is a generalisation of the proofs of the analogous results on open pi-calculus without restriction and Pi-F calculus.

Theorem 1. *$\sim^o$ is a congruence.*

Example 2. Consider the example depicted in § 4.1. Suppose there are two providers $\mathsf{Provider}_{4,40}$ and $\mathsf{Provider}_{3,40}$ that have the same amount of available resources but that offer different units of resources to each client. Obviously, these two providers behave differently when interacting with other processes. For instance, only the first provider can reach an agreement with a client that requires at least 4 resources, i.e. $\mathsf{Client}_4\,|\,\mathsf{Provider}_{4,40}$ can make a τ-transition while $\mathsf{Client}_4\,|\,\mathsf{Provider}_{3,40}$ is stuck. It can be easily shown that the two processes are not open bisimilar. After $\mathsf{Provider}_{4,40}$ and $\mathsf{Provider}_{3,40}$ place their own constraints, they both evolve to the processes

$$(r)\,(x_0)\,(v)\,(x')\,(x_0 = 40 \otimes x' = x_0 - v \otimes x' \geq 0 \otimes v \leq \mathsf{off_i}\,|\,r\langle v\rangle.\mathsf{Ac\_Req_{off_i}}(x', r))$$

where $\mathsf{off_i}$ are 4 and 3, respectively. Since the names are all bound, the stores are both empty and, hence, the target processes cannot be distinguished. However, after the processes 'extrude' the name v over r, their respective stores become

$$(r)\,(x_0)\,(x')\,(x_0 = 40 \otimes x' = x_0 - v \otimes x' \geq 0 \otimes v \leq \mathsf{off_i})$$

which are equal to $v \leq \min\{40, \mathsf{off_i}\}$. Thus, the stores of the two processes are now distinguished and the first condition of Def. 1 does not hold. Similarly, we can show that the processes $\mathsf{Provider}_{4,40}$ and $\mathsf{Provider}_{4,32}$ are not bisimilar.

5.1 Symbolic Characterisation

We now give an efficient version of open bisimulation and we prove that the two notions coincide. For lack of space, we omit the proof of this result. Let $\mathcal{L} = \mathcal{A} \cup \{c\,|\,c \text{ is a named constraint}\}$, ranged over by λ, be a set of labels, and assume the label τ coincides with the top element of the named c-semiring 1.

We define a transition system whose transitions are of the form $P \overset{\lambda}{\rightarrowtail} Q$, where λ can be either a standard label or a constraint e that is the *maximal* element (according to $\preceq$) such that $e\,|\,\mathsf{store}(P)$ allows P to evolve to Q. Recall that $c \preceq d$ intuitively means that d is 'less restrictive' than c. Hence, transitions that are labelled by maximal constraints specify minimal conditions.

The *symbolic transition semantics* of processes is the smallest relation $P \overset{\lambda}{\rightarrowtail} Q$, defined by the rules in Fig. 3 plus a rule (S-OPEN-O) for output and the symmetric version of rule (S-COMM). The symbolic transition system is the same as its 'concrete' counterpart but for rules (S-ASK) and (S-COMM). According to rule (S-ASK), a process $\mathtt{ask}\ d.U$ in parallel with a constraint c can make a transition labelled by the least restrictive constraint whose combination with c entails d, i.e. by the maximal element of the set $\{x \in A\,|\,c \otimes x \preceq d\}$. The assumption on the completeness of c-semirings ensures that such an element, noted $d \div c$, exists and is unique (see § 2). Remark that, in general, it does not hold that $d \div c \otimes c = d$. Rule (S-COMM) follows the same intuition, though in this case the condition that must be entailed is $x = z$.

(S-PREF)
$$c\,|\,\pi.U \overset{\pi}{\rightarrowtail} c\,|\,U \quad \pi = \tau, \bar{x}\langle y\rangle, x\langle y\rangle$$

(S-TELL)
$$c\,|\,\mathtt{tell}\ d.U \overset{\tau}{\rightarrowtail} c\otimes d\,|\,U \ \text{ if } c\otimes d \neq 0$$

(S-ASK)
$$c\,|\,\mathtt{ask}\ d.U \overset{d\div c}{\rightarrowtail} c\,|\,U$$

(S-SUM)
$$\frac{c\,|\,\pi_i.U_i \overset{\lambda}{\rightarrowtail} U'}{c\,|\,\sum \pi_i.U_i \overset{\lambda}{\rightarrowtail} U'}$$

(S-PAR)
$$\frac{P \overset{\lambda}{\rightarrowtail} P' \quad \mathrm{bn}(\lambda)\cap\mathrm{fn}(U)=\emptyset}{P\,|\,U \overset{\lambda}{\rightarrowtail} P'\,|\,U}$$

(S-COMM)
$$\frac{c\,|\,U \overset{x\langle y\rangle}{\rightarrowtail} c\,|\,U' \quad c\,|\,V \overset{\bar{z}\langle w\rangle}{\rightarrowtail} c\,|\,V' \quad c\otimes(y=w)\neq 0}{c\,|\,U\,|\,V \overset{(x=z)\div c}{\rightarrowtail} c\otimes(y=w)\,|\,U'\,|\,V'}$$

(S-RES)
$$\frac{P \overset{\lambda}{\rightarrowtail} P' \quad x\notin \mathrm{n}(\lambda)}{(x)P \overset{\lambda}{\rightarrowtail} (x)P'}$$

(S-OPEN-I)
$$\frac{P \overset{z\langle x\rangle}{\rightarrowtail} P' \quad \mathsf{store}(P)\not\preceq x=z}{(x)P \overset{z(x)}{\rightarrowtail} P'}$$

(S-STRUCT)
$$\frac{P\equiv P' \quad P' \overset{\lambda}{\rightarrowtail} Q' \quad Q'\equiv Q}{P \overset{\lambda}{\rightarrowtail} Q}$$

Fig. 3. Symbolic Semantics of the cc-pi calculus

Definition 2 (symbolic bisimilarity). Symbolic (open) bisimilarity *($\sim^s$) is the largest symmetric relation $\mathcal{S}$ between processes such that $P\mathcal{S}Q$ implies:*

1. $\mathsf{store}(P) = \mathsf{store}(Q)$*;*
2. *If* $P \overset{\alpha}{\rightarrowtail} P'$ *with* $\alpha\neq\tau$ *and* $\mathrm{bn}(\alpha)\cap\mathrm{fn}(Q)=\emptyset$ *then* $Q \overset{\beta}{\rightarrowtail} Q'$ *and* $P'\ \mathcal{S}\ Q'$*, for some* Q' *and* β *such that* $\mathsf{store}(P)\preceq\alpha=\beta$*;*
3. *If* $P \overset{c}{\rightarrowtail} P'$ *then* $Q \overset{d}{\rightarrowtail} Q'$ *and* $c\,|\,P'\ \mathcal{S}\ c\,|\,Q'$*, for some* Q' *and* d *such that* $c\preceq d$*.*

The last condition above reminds the analogous clause of symbolic open pi-calculus in which a process that can evolve under a certain condition can be simulated by another process that can make a transition labelled with a weaker condition.

Example 3. Consider again the example shown in § 4.1. Assume two providers $\mathsf{Provider}_{10,8}$ and $\mathsf{Provider}_{15,8}$ that offer different amounts of resources to each client but that have the same number of remaining resources. Trivially, these two processes are equivalent, because they can only satisfy clients that require maximum 8 resources. However, proving that the two processes are open bisimilar requires checking their behaviour in presence of any constraint. Let us see why they are symbolically bisimilar. Initially, the two processes place their own constraints and evolve to processes that have the same empty store of constraints. Next, when the number of offered resources v is communicated the stores of constraints of the processes become $v\leq\min\{\mathsf{off}_\mathsf{i},8\}$, which admit the same solutions regardless off_i is 15 or 10.

Theorem 2. *Symbolic bisimilarity* $\sim^s$ *and open bisimilarity* $\sim^o$ *coincide.*

6 Embedding Polyadic Pi-F Calculus

We start by recalling the Pi-F calculus. For better relating the calculus with cc-pi, we present the Pi-F in the standard pi-calculus fashion rather than in the 'commitment' style [16]. Assume the set of labels $\mathcal{M} = \{\tau, z\langle\tilde{y}\rangle, \bar{z}\langle\tilde{y}\rangle, (\tilde{x})z\langle\tilde{w}\rangle, (\tilde{x})\bar{z}\langle\tilde{w}\rangle \mid \tilde{x} \subseteq \tilde{w}\}$ and let μ range over $\mathcal{M}$. The syntax, structural congruence and labelled transition system of Pi-F processes are shown in Figure 4. The syntax (Fig. 4(a)) is similar to the syntax of cc-pi processes but for the fact that in Pi-F input and output prefixes are polyadic, that summation, `tell`, `ask` are missing, and that explicit fusions $\tilde{x} = \tilde{y}$ replace constraints c. Despite the original presentation of the calculus, this syntax rules out processes containing name fusions under prefixes. This choice follows the analogous restriction applied in cc-pi, which avoids that two processes synchronise and, simultaneously, add some constraints to the store, thus possibly yielding an inconsistency. However, we can release this restriction in both calculi if we consider the fragment of cc-pi with explicit fusions rather than arbitrary constraints. To emphasise this syntactical analogy with cc-pi, we have chosen also in this case to distinguish between processes U and P. The structural axioms (Fig. 4(b)) are the same as in cc-pi but for the fact that the axioms dealing with constraints are replaced by the axioms for explicit fusions. The definition of equivalence relation $\mathsf{Eq}(P)$ (Fig 4(c)) specifies the explicit fusions of a process P. We write $\varphi \cup \psi$ for the equivalence-closed union of the equivalence relations φ and ψ, $\varphi \setminus x$ for when x is a singleton class and all other names are related as in φ, and Id for the identity relation. In [15] several bisimulations for the Pi-F calculus are proposed, including a symbolic bisimulation, and they are all proved equivalent. For convenience, here we consider the *inside-outside* bisimulation that is the closest to open bisimulation.

$$\pi ::= \tau \mid \bar{x}\langle\tilde{y}\rangle \mid x\langle\tilde{y}\rangle \quad U ::= \mathbf{0} \mid U|U \mid \pi.U \mid (x)U \mid I(\tilde{y}) \quad P ::= U \mid \tilde{x} = \tilde{y} \mid P|P \mid (x)P$$

(a) syntax

$$P \mid \mathbf{0} \equiv_F P \qquad P \mid Q \equiv_F Q \mid P \qquad (P \mid Q) \mid R \equiv_F P \mid (Q \mid R) \qquad (x)(y)P \equiv_F (y)(x)P$$
$$P|(x)Q \equiv_F (x)(P|Q) \quad \textit{if } x \notin \mathrm{fn}(P) \qquad I(\tilde{y}) \equiv_F [\tilde{y}/\tilde{x}]U \quad \textit{if } I(\tilde{x}) \stackrel{\mathrm{def}}{=} U$$
$$x{=}x \equiv_F \mathbf{0} \quad (x)\,(x{=}y) \equiv_F \mathbf{0} \qquad x{=}y \equiv_F y{=}x \qquad x{=}y \mid y{=}z \equiv_F x{=}z \mid y{=}z$$
$$x{=}y \mid x\langle\tilde{z}\rangle.P \equiv_F x{=}y \mid y\langle\tilde{z}\rangle.P \qquad w{=}y \mid x\langle\tilde{z}\rangle.P \equiv_F w{=}y \mid x\langle\tilde{z}\rangle[y/w].P \quad \textit{if } w \in \tilde{z}$$
$$x{=}y \mid \bar{x}\langle\tilde{z}\rangle.P \equiv_F x{=}y \mid \bar{y}\langle\tilde{z}\rangle.P \qquad w{=}y \mid \bar{x}\langle\tilde{z}\rangle.P \equiv_F w{=}y \mid \bar{x}\langle\tilde{z}\rangle[y/w].P \quad \textit{if } w \in \tilde{z}$$

(b) structural congruence

$$\mathsf{Eq}(\mathbf{0}) = \mathsf{Id} \qquad \mathsf{Eq}(x = y) = \{(x,y),(y,x)\} \cup \mathsf{Id} \qquad \mathsf{Eq}(\pi.U) = \mathsf{Id}$$
$$\mathsf{Eq}(P \mid Q) = \mathsf{Eq}(P) \cup \mathsf{Eq}(Q) \quad \mathsf{Eq}((x)P) = \mathsf{Eq}(P) \setminus x \quad \mathsf{Eq}(I(\tilde{y})) = \mathsf{Eq}([\tilde{y}/\tilde{x}]U) \quad \textit{if } I(\tilde{x}) \stackrel{\mathrm{def}}{=} U$$

(c) equivalence relation $\mathsf{Eq}(P)$

(PREF) $$\pi.U \xrightarrow{\pi}_{\mathsf{f}} U$$

(COMM) $$\frac{P \xrightarrow{x\langle\tilde{y}\rangle}_{\mathsf{f}} P' \quad Q \xrightarrow{\bar{x}\langle\tilde{w}\rangle}_{\mathsf{f}} Q' \quad |\tilde{y}| = |\tilde{w}|}{P \mid Q \xrightarrow{\tau}_{\mathsf{f}} P' \mid Q' \mid \tilde{y} = \tilde{w}}$$

(PAR) $$\frac{P \xrightarrow{\mu}_{\mathsf{f}} P' \quad \mathrm{bn}(\mu) \cap \mathrm{fn}(Q) = \emptyset}{P \mid Q \xrightarrow{\mu}_{\mathsf{f}} P' \mid Q}$$

(RES) $$\frac{P \xrightarrow{\mu}_{\mathsf{f}} P' \quad x \notin \mathrm{n}(\mu)}{(x)\,P \xrightarrow{\mu}_{\mathsf{f}} (x)\,P'}$$

(OPEN-I) $$\frac{P \xrightarrow{(\tilde{w})z\langle\tilde{y}\rangle}_{\mathsf{f}} P' \quad (x,z) \notin \mathsf{Eq}(P),\ x \in \tilde{y} \setminus \tilde{w}}{(x)\,P \xrightarrow{(x\tilde{w})z\langle\tilde{y}\rangle}_{\mathsf{f}} P'}$$

(STRUCT) $$\frac{P \equiv_F P' \xrightarrow{\mu}_{\mathsf{f}} Q' \equiv_F Q}{P \xrightarrow{\mu}_{\mathsf{f}} Q}$$

(d) operational semantics (omitting a rule (OPEN-O) for output)

Fig. 4. Pi-F calculus

Definition 3 (inside-outside bisimilarity). Inside-outside bisimilarity *($\sim^{io}$) is the largest symmetric relation S between Pi-F processes such that PSQ implies:*

- $\mathtt{Eq}(P) = \mathtt{Eq}(Q)$;
- *If* $P \xrightarrow{\mu}_{\mathsf{f}} P'$ *with* $\mathrm{bn}(\mu) \cap \mathrm{fn}(Q) = \emptyset$ *then* $Q \xrightarrow{\mu}_{\mathsf{f}} Q'$ *and* $P'\ S\ Q'$;
- $P\,|\,x = y \ \ S \ \ Q\,|\,x = y$, *for all fusions* $x = y$.

We give below a translation of Pi-F processes into cc-pi where we take the underlying named c-semiring to be the named c-semiring of Herbrand constraint systems with a signature including the operations for tupling, as shown in Example 1. Remark that in this case $x = \langle y_1, \ldots, y_n \rangle$ denotes the unification of the name x with the term $\langle y_1, \ldots, y_n \rangle$ and that a name equality $\widetilde{x} = \widetilde{y}$, with $\widetilde{x}$ and $\widetilde{y}$ of the same arity n, can be modelled as the constraint $z = \langle x_1, \ldots, x_n \rangle \otimes w = \langle y_1, \ldots, y_n \rangle \otimes z = w$. We abbreviate $\langle x_1, \ldots, x_n \rangle$ by $\widetilde{x}$.

Definition 4. *Let* $[\![\_]\!]$ *be the following translation of Pi-F agents:*

$$[\![\tau.U]\!] = \tau.[\![U]\!] \quad [\![\overline{x}\langle\widetilde{y}\rangle.U]\!] = (z)(\overline{x}\langle z\rangle.[\![U]\!]\,|\,z = \widetilde{y}) \quad [\![x\langle\widetilde{y}\rangle.U]\!] = (z)(x\langle z\rangle.[\![U]\!]\,|\,z = \widetilde{y})$$

$$[\![\mathbf{0}]\!] = \mathbf{0} \quad [\![P\,|\,Q]\!] = [\![P]\!]\,|\,[\![Q]\!] \quad [\![(x)P]\!] = (x)[\![P]\!] \quad [\![I(\widetilde{y})]\!] = [\![[\widetilde{y}/\widetilde{x}]U]\!] \quad \text{if } I(\widetilde{x}) \stackrel{\text{def}}{=} U$$

Theorem 3. $P \sim^{io} Q$ *iff* $[\![P]\!] \sim^{o} [\![Q]\!]$.

Proof (Hint). By theorem 2 and by an analogous result proved in [15] for the Pi-F calculus, the theorem can be restated by replacing $\sim^{o}$ and $\sim^{io}$ with their respective symbolic versions. This fact greatly simplifies the proof. Another key point is that the instance of cc-pi that we consider includes more contexts that Pi-F, i.e. the contexts $\widetilde{x} = \widetilde{y}$, where the arity of $\widetilde{x}$ and $\widetilde{y}$ is non-null and it is the same for both tuples. In fact, the cc-pi processes that belong to the inverse image $[\![\_]\!]^{-1}$ of the translation cannot be discriminated by these contexts. To see this point, note that checking equivalence over the above contexts corresponds to taking the symbolic transitions $[\![P]\!]^{-1} \overset{x=y\otimes c}{\rightarrowtail} [\![Q]\!]^{-1}\,|\,c$ where $[\![P]\!]^{-1} \overset{x=y}{\rightarrowtail} [\![Q]\!]^{-1}$ also holds. The first kind of transition is not maximal and it can be discarded since there is another transition that is maximal.

7 Conclusions

In general our labelled transition system takes any name instantiation that leads to constraints not evaluating to the bottom element of the c-semiring and it does not provide a way to discard non-optimal solutions. We plan to generalise the notion of consistency to α-consistency, where α is a strictly non-negative threshold. Accordingly, we could study a variant of the present semantics in which, for instance, the consistency check in the rules for placing constraints is substituted by an α-consistency check. We also intend to enrich our semantics in order to model non-deterministic timed behaviours and to compare it to paradigms such as timed concurrent constraint programming [10].

It would also be interesting to further explore the expressiveness of cc-pi by providing fully abstract encodings of other calculi, such as the applied pi-calculus and the pi-calculus. The main idea behind embedding applied pi-calculus would be to characterise a variant of the named c-semiring for Herbrand constraints that models a generic signature along with an equational theory. On the other side, translating the pi-calculus into cc-pi seems harder. The main challenge in translating the pi-calculus would be to express in terms of named constraints the concept of distinctions, which are used to define open bisimulation on the cc-pi calculus with restriction operator.

Acknowledgments. We thank Fabio Gadducci, Magnus Johansson and Bjorn Victor for fruitful discussions.

References

1. Abadi, M., Fournet, C.: Mobile values, new names, and secure communication. In: POPL 2001: Proceedings of the 28th ACM SIGPLAN-SIGACT Symposium on Principles of Programming Languages, pp. 104–115. ACM Press, New York (2001)
2. Bistarelli, S., Gadducci, F.: Enhancing constraints manipulation in semiring-based formalisms. In: ECAI, pp. 63–67. IOS Press, Amsterdam (2006)
3. Bistarelli, S., Montanari, U., Rossi, F.: Semiring-based constraint satisfaction and optimization. Journal of the ACM 44(2), 201–236 (1997)
4. Boreale, M., De Nicola, R.: A symbolic semantics for the pi-calculus. Inf. Comput. 126(1), 34–52 (1996)
5. Buscemi, M.G., Montanari, U.: Cc-pi: A constraint-based language for specifying service level agreements. In: De Nicola, R. (ed.) ESOP 2007. LNCS, vol. 4421, pp. 18–32. Springer, Heidelberg (2007)
6. Diaz, J.F., Rueda, C., Valencia, F.: A calculus for concurrent processes with constraints. CLEI Electronic Journal 1(2) (1998)
7. Gilbert, D., Palamidessi, C.: Concurrent Constraint Programming with Process Mobility. In: Palamidessi, C., Moniz Pereira, L., Lloyd, J.W., Dahl, V., Furbach, U., Kerber, M., Lau, K.-K., Sagiv, Y., Stuckey, P.J. (eds.) CL 2000. LNCS (LNAI), vol. 1861, pp. 463–477. Springer, Heidelberg (2000)
8. Hennessy, M., Lin, H.: Symbolic bisimulations. Theor. Comp. Sci. 138, 353–389 (1995)
9. Milner, R., Parrow, J., Walker, J.: A calculus of mobile processes, I and II. Inform. and Comput., 100(1), 1–40,41–77 (1992)
10. Palamidessi, C., Valencia, F.: A Temporal Concurrent Constraint Programming Calculus. In: Walsh, T. (ed.) CP 2001. LNCS, vol. 2239, pp. 302–316. Springer, Heidelberg (2001)
11. Rudeanu, S., Vaida, D.: Semirings in operations research and computer science. Fundam. Inf. 61(1), 61–85 (2004)
12. Sangiorgi, D.: A theory of bisimulation for the π-calculus. Acta Inform. 33, 69–97 (1996)
13. Saraswat, V.: Concurrent Constraint Programming. PhD thesis, Carnegie Mellon University (1993)
14. Saraswat, V., Rinard, M.: Concurrent constraint programming. In: Proc. POPL 1990. ACM Press (1990)
15. Wischik, L., Gardner, P.: Strong Bisimulation for the Explicit Fusion Calculus. In: Walukiewicz, I. (ed.) FOSSACS 2004. LNCS, vol. 2987, pp. 484–498. Springer, Heidelberg (2004)
16. Wischik, L., Gardner, P.: Explicit fusions. Theoret. Comput. Sci. 340(3), 606–630 (2005)

The Conversation Calculus: A Model of Service-Oriented Computation

Hugo T. Vieira, Luís Caires, and João C. Seco

CITI / Departamento de Informática, Universidade Nova de Lisboa, Portugal

Abstract. We present a process-calculus model for expressing and analyzing service-based systems. Our approach addresses central features of the service-oriented computational model such as distribution, process delegation, communication and context sensitiveness, and loose coupling. Distinguishing aspects of our model are the notion of conversation context, the adoption of a context sensitive, message-passing-based communication, and of a simple yet expressive mechanism for handling exceptional behavior. We instantiate our model by extending a fragment of the π-calculus, illustrate its expressiveness by means of many examples, and study its basic behavioral theory; in particular, we establish that bisimilarity is a congruence.

1 Introduction

Web services have emerged mainly as a toolkit of technological and methodological solutions for building open-ended collaborative software systems on the Internet. Many concepts that are frequently put forward as distinctive of service-oriented computing, namely, object-oriented distributed programming, long duration transactions and compensations, separation of workflow from service instances, late binding and discovery of functionalities, are certainly not new, at least when considered in isolation. What is certainly new about services is that they are contributing to physically realize (on the Internet) a global, interaction-based, loosely-coupled, model of computation. We would like to better understand in what sense service orientation is to be seen as a new paradigm to build and reason about distributed systems.

The main contributions of this work are the development of a process calculus for service-oriented computing based on a novel notion of conversation context, and the study of its basic behavioral theory. In particular, we establish that bisimilarity is a congruence, thus asserting the proper status of the proposed constructions as operators at the level of the behavioral semantics; we believe that such a result has not yet been provided for other related service calculi. Our starting point is an attempt to isolate and clarify essential characteristics of the service-oriented model, in order to propose a motivation from "first principles" of a reduced set of general abstractions for expressing and analyzing service-based systems. We then instantiate our model by modularly extending the static fragment of the π-calculus with conversation contexts, message-passing communication primitives, and an exception handling mechanism.

1.1 Some Key Aspects of Service-Oriented Computing

We identify as key aspects of the service-oriented computational model: *distribution*, process *delegation*, communication and *context* sensitiveness, and *loose coupling*.

S. Drossopoulou (Ed.): ESOP 2008, LNCS 4960, pp. 269–283, 2008.

Distribution. The purpose of a service relationship is to allow the incorporation of certain activities in a given system, without having to engage *local* resources and capabilities to support or implement such activities. By delegating activities to an external service provider, which will perform them using its own *remote* resources and capabilities, a computing system may concentrate on those tasks for which it may autonomously provide convenient solutions. Thus, the notion of service makes particular sense when the service provider and the service client are separate entities, with access to separate sets of resources and capabilities. This understanding of the service relationship between provider and client assumes an underlying distributed computational model, where client and server are located at least in distinct (operating system) processes, more frequently in distinct sites of a network.

Process Delegation versus Operation Invocation. The primitive remote communication mechanism in distributed computing is message passing. On top of this basic mechanism, the only one really implementable, more sophisticated abstractions may be represented, namely remote procedure call (passing first-order data) and remote method invocation (also passing remote object references). Along these lines, we see service invocation as a still higher level mechanism, allowing the service client to delegate to a remote server not just a single operation or task, but the execution of a whole interactive activity (technically, a process). This emphasis on the remote delegation of *interactive processes* is, in our view, a distinguishing feature of service-oriented computing, as opposed to the remote delegation of individual operations.

Invocation of a service by a client results in the creation of a new service instance. A service instance is composed by a pair of endpoints, one endpoint located in the server site, where the service is defined, the other endpoint in the client site, where the request for instantiation took place. From the viewpoint of each partner, the respective endpoint acts as a local process, with potential direct access to local resources and capabilities. Thus, we do not consider an endpoint to be a name, a port address, or channel, but an interactive process. Dual endpoints work together in a tightly coordinated way, by exchanging data and control information through a private communication tunnel.

Contexts and Context Sensitiveness. A context is a space where computation and communication happens. A context may have a spatial meaning, e.g., as a *site* in a distributed system, but also a behavioral meaning, e.g., as a *context of conversation* between two or more parties. In the latter situation, remote parties may well talk under the same context of conversation, so that contexts of conversation need not be localized, but accessible at different points. Moreover, the same message may appear in two different contexts, with different meanings – web services technology has introduced artifacts such as "correlation" to determine the appropriate context for otherwise indistinguishable messages. Thus, the notion of context of conversation seems to be a convenient abstraction mechanism to structure the interactions between several entities collaborating in a service-oriented system.

A context is also a natural abstraction to publish together closely related services. Typically, services published by the same entity are expected to share common resources; we notice that such sharing is common at several scales of granularity. Extreme examples are: a "small" object, where the service definitions are the methods and the shared context is the object internal state, and an ISP such as, e.g., Amazon, that publishes many services for many different purposes; such services certainly share internal resources in the Amazon context, such as databases, payment gateways, and so on.

Loose Coupling. A service-based computation usually consists in an collection of remote partner service instances, in which functionality is to be delegated, some locally implemented processes, and one or more control (or orchestration) processes. The flexibility and openness of a service-based design, or at least an aimed feature, results from a loose coupling between these various components. For instance, an orchestration describing a "business process", should be specified in a quite independent way of the particular subsidiary service instances used, paving the way for dynamic binding and dynamic discovery of service providers. In the orchestration language `WSBPEL` [2], loose coupling to external services is enforced to some extent by the separate declaration of "partner links" and "partner roles" in processes. In the modeling language SRML [11], the binding between service providers and clients is mediated by "wires", which describe plugging constraints between otherwise hard to match interfaces. These are two instances of the same general principle.

To avoid tight coupling of services, the interface between a service instance (at each of its several endpoints) and the context of instantiation should be mediated by appropriate connecting processes, in order to hide and/or adapt the endpoint communication protocol (which is in some sense dependent of the particular implementation or service provider chosen) to the abstract behavioral interface expected by the context of instantiation. All computational entities cooperating in a service task should then be encapsulated (delimited inside a conversation context), and able to communicate between themselves and the outer context only via some general message passing mechanism.

Communication. Computations interacting in a context may offer essentially three forms of communication capabilities. First, they may communicate within the context, corresponding to regular internal computations in the context. Second, an endpoint must be able to send messages to and receive messages from the other (dual) endpoint of the context, reflecting interactions between the client and the server roles of a service instance. Third, internally to a context it must be possible to send messages to and receive messages from the enclosing context, thus allowing for a context to be seen as a regular process by its peers at the upper level. Contexts as the one described may be nested at many levels, corresponding to subsidiary service instances, processes, etc.

In the next Section, we present the conversation calculus, a process model crafted to incorporate the several key aspects just discussed; we explain the various primitives of the calculus, and define its syntax and operational semantics. In Section 3 we further motivate our model and calculus by means of several examples. In Section 4 we define the behavioral semantics and present related technical results. We compare our approach with related work in Section 5 and conclude in Section 6.

2 The Conversation Calculus

In this section, we motivate and present in detail the primitives of our calculus. After that, we present the syntax of our calculus, and formally define its operational semantics, by means of a labeled transition system.

Context. A key contribution of this paper is the notion of conversation context. A conversation context is a medium where related interactions can take place. A conversation context can be distributed in many pieces, and processes inside any piece can seamlessly talk to any other piece of the same context. Each context has a unique name (cf., a URI), and is partitioned in two endpoints, which we will refer by "initiator" (◀), or "responder" (▶). We use the endpoint access construct $n \blacktriangleleft [P]$ to say that the process P is placed at the initiator endpoint of context n, and the (dual) construct $n \blacktriangleright [P]$ to say that the process P is placed at the responder endpoint of context n. Potentially, each endpoint access will be placed at a different enclosing context. On the other hand, any such endpoint access will necessarily be placed at a single enclosing context. The relationship between the enclosing context and such an endpoint may be seen as a call/callee relationship, but where both entities may interact continuously.

Communication. Communication between subsystems is realized by means of message passing. Internal computation is related to communications between subsystems inside a given context. First, we denote the output and the input of messages to/from the current context by the constructs $\mathtt{out} \downarrow \mathit{label}(\widetilde{v}).P$ and $\mathtt{in} \downarrow \mathit{label}(\widetilde{x}).P$. In the output case, the terms v_i represent message arguments, values to be sent, as expected. In the input case, the variables x_i represent message parameters and are bound in P, as expected. The direction symbol $\downarrow$ (read "here") says that the corresponding communication actions must interact in the current endpoint.

Second, we denote the output and the input of messages to/from the enclosing endpoint by the constructs $\mathtt{out} \uparrow \mathit{label}(\widetilde{v}).P$ and $\mathtt{in} \uparrow \mathit{label}(\widetilde{x}).P$. The direction symbol $\uparrow$ (read "up") says that the corresponding communication actions must interact in the (uniquely determined) enclosing endpoint.

Third, we denote the output and the input of messages to/from the dual endpoint by the constructs $\mathtt{out} \leftarrow \mathit{label}(\widetilde{v}).P$ and $\mathtt{in} \leftarrow \mathit{label}(\widetilde{x}).P$ The direction symbol $\leftarrow$ (read "other") says that the corresponding communication action must interact with the dual endpoint, relative to the context where the $\mathtt{out} \leftarrow$ or $\mathtt{in} \leftarrow$ process is running.

Service Publication and Service Instantiation. A context may publish one or more service definitions. Service definitions are stateless entities, pretty much as function definitions in a functional programming language. A service definition may be expressed by the construct $\mathtt{def}\ \mathit{serviceName} \Rightarrow \mathit{ServiceBody}$ where $\mathit{serviceName}$ is the service name, and $\mathit{ServiceBody}$ is the process that is to be executed at the service endpoint (responder) for each service instance, in other words the service body. In order to be published, such a definition must be inserted into a context, e.g.,

$$\mathit{serviceProvider} \blacktriangleright [\mathtt{def}\ \mathit{serviceName} \Rightarrow \mathit{ServiceBody} \mid \cdots]$$

Such a published service may be instantiated by means of the construct

$$\mathtt{instance}\ n\, \rho\, \mathit{serviceName} \Leftarrow \mathit{ClientProtocol}$$

where $n\,\rho$ describes the context (n) and the endpoint role (ρ) where the service is published. For instance, the service defined above may be instantiated by

$$\mathtt{instance}\ \mathit{serviceProvider} \blacktriangleright \mathit{serviceName} \Leftarrow \mathit{ClientProtocol}$$

The *ClientProtocol* describes the process that will run inside the initiator endpoint. The outcome of a service instantiation is the creation of a new globally fresh context identity (a hidden name), and the creation of two dual endpoints of a context named by this fresh identity. The responder endpoint will contain the *ServiceBody* process and will be placed at the *serviceProvider* context. The initiator endpoint will contain the *ClientProtocol* process and will be placed at the same context as the **instance** expression that requested the service instantiation. The newly created endpoints appear to their enclosing contexts as a local process, and may interact continuously by means of $\uparrow$ communication.

Context Awareness. A process running inside a given context is able to dynamically access its identity, by means of the construct **here**$(x).P$. The variable x will be replaced inside the process P by the name n of the current context. The computation will proceed as $P\{x{\leftarrow}n\}$. This primitive bears some similarity with the **self** or **this** of object-oriented languages, even if it has a different semantics.

Exception Handling. We introduce primitives to model exceptional behavior, in particular fault signaling, fault detection, and resource disposal. These aspects are orthogonal to the introduced communication mechanisms, but need to be tackled in any model of service-oriented computation. The primitive to signal exceptional behavior is **throw**.$Exception$. This construct throws an exception with continuation the process $Exception$, and has the effect of forcing the termination of all other processes running in all enclosing contexts, up to the point where a **try** − **catch** block is found (if any). The continuation $Exception$ will be activated when (and if) the exception is caught by such an exception handler. The exception handler construct **try** P **catch** $Handler$ actively allows a process P to run until some exception is thrown inside P. At that moment, all of P is terminated, and the $Handler$ handler process, which is guarded by **try**−**catch**, is activated, concurrently with the continuation $Exception$ of the **throw**.$Exception$ that originated the exception, in the context of a given **try** − **catch**− block. By exploiting the interaction potential of the $Handler$ and $Exception$ processes, one may represent many adequate recovery and resource disposal protocols.

2.1 Syntax and Semantics of the Calculus

We may now formally introduce the syntax and semantics of the conversation calculus. We assume given an infinite set of names Λ, an infinite set of variables $\mathcal{V}$, and an infinite set of labels $\mathcal{L}$. We abbreviate $a_1, \ldots, a_k$ by $\widetilde{a}$. We use dir for the communication directions, α for directed message labels, and ρ for the endpoint roles ($\rho = \blacktriangleleft$, the initiator role, or $\rho = \blacktriangleright$, the responder role). We denote by $\overline{\rho}$ the dual role of ρ, for instance $\overline{\blacktriangleright} = \blacktriangleleft$. Notice that message and service identifiers (from $\mathcal{L}$) are plain labels, not subject to restriction or binding. The syntax of the calculus is defined in Fig. 1.

The static core of our language is derived from the π-calculus [19]. We thus have **stop** for the inactive process, $P \mid Q$ for the parallel composition, (**new** $a)P$ for name restriction, and $!P$ for replication. Then we have context-oriented polyadic communication primitives: **out** $\alpha(\widetilde{v}).P$ for output and **in** $\alpha(\widetilde{x}).P$ for input. In the communication primitives, α denotes a pair of name and direction, as explained before. We then have the context endpoint access construct $n\,\rho\,[P]$, the context awareness primitive **here**$(x).P$,

$$
\begin{array}{llll}
a, b, c, \ldots & \in & \Lambda & (\textit{Names}) \\
x, y, z, \ldots & \in & \mathcal{V} & (\textit{Variables}) \\
n, v, \ldots & \in & \Lambda \cup \mathcal{V} & \\
l, s \ldots & \in & \mathcal{L} & (\textit{Labels}) \\
\mathit{dir} & ::= & \downarrow \mid \leftarrow \mid \uparrow & (\textit{Directions}) \\
\alpha & ::= & \mathit{dir}\ l & \\
\rho & ::= & \blacktriangleright \mid \blacktriangleleft & (\textit{Endpoint Roles})
\end{array}
\qquad
\begin{array}{lll}
P, Q ::= & & \\
 & \mathtt{stop} & \mid n\,\rho\,[P] \\
\mid & P \mid Q & \mid \mathtt{here}(x).P \\
\mid & (\mathtt{new}\ a)P & \mid \mathtt{instance}\ n\,\rho\,s \Leftarrow P \\
\mid & \mathtt{out}\ \alpha(\tilde{v}).P & \mid \mathtt{def}\ s \Rightarrow P \\
\mid & \mathtt{in}\ \alpha(\tilde{x}).P & \mid \mathtt{try}\ P\ \mathtt{catch}\ Q \\
\mid & !P & \mid \mathtt{throw}.P
\end{array}
$$

Fig. 1. The Conversation Calculus

the service invocation and service definition primitives $\mathtt{instance}\ n\,\rho\,s \Leftarrow P$ and $\mathtt{def}\ s \Rightarrow P$, respectively. The primitives for exception handling are the $\mathtt{try}\ P\ \mathtt{catch}\ Q$ and the $\mathtt{throw}.P$. The distinguished occurrences of a, $\tilde{x}$, and x are binding occurrences in $(\mathtt{new}\ a)P$, $\mathtt{in}\ \alpha(\tilde{x}).P$, and $\mathtt{here}(x).P$, respectively. The sets of free ($\mathit{fn}(P)$) and bound ($\mathit{bn}(P)$) names and variables in a process P are defined as usual, and we implicitly identify α-equivalent processes.

We define the semantics of the conversation calculus using a labeled transition system. We introduce transition labels λ. We use *act* to range over actions, defined as

$$\mathit{act} ::= \tau \mid \alpha(\tilde{a}) \mid \mathtt{here} \mid \mathtt{throw} \mid \mathtt{def}\ s$$

Then, a transition label λ is an expression as given by $\lambda ::= c\,\rho\,\mathit{act} \mid \mathit{act} \mid (\nu a)\lambda$. In $(\nu a)\lambda$ the distinguished occurrence of a is bound with scope λ (cf., the π-calculus bound output and bound input actions). A transition label containing $c\,\rho$ is said to be *located at* $c\,\rho$ (or just *located*), otherwise is said to be *unlocated*. We write $(\widetilde{\nu a})$ to abbreviate a (possibly empty) sequence $(\nu a_1)\ldots(\nu a_k)$.

We adopt a few conventions and notations. We note by λ^{dir} a transition label λ^{dir} containing the direction dir ($\uparrow, \leftarrow, \downarrow$). Then we denote by $\lambda^{dir'}$ the label obtained by replacing dir by dir' in λ^{dir}. Given an unlocated label λ, we represent by $c\,\rho \cdot \lambda$ the label obtained by locating λ at $c\,\rho$, so that e.g., $c\,\rho \cdot (\widetilde{\nu a})\mathit{act} = (\widetilde{\nu a})c\,\rho\,\mathit{act}$. We assert $\mathit{loc}(\lambda)$ if λ is not located and does not contain $\mathtt{here}$.

The set of transition labels is polarized and equipped with an injective involution $\overline{\lambda}$ (such that $\overline{\overline{\lambda}} = \lambda$). The involution, used to define synchronizing (matching) transition labels, is defined such that $\overline{\mathit{act}} \neq \mathit{act}'$ for all $\mathit{act}, \mathit{act}'$, and

$$\overline{c\,\rho\,\mathtt{def}\ s} \triangleq c\,\rho\,\overline{\mathtt{def}\ s} \qquad \overline{c\,\rho\,\downarrow\alpha} \triangleq c\,\rho\downarrow\overline{\alpha} \qquad \overline{c\,\rho\leftarrow\alpha} \triangleq c\,\overline{\rho}\leftarrow\overline{\alpha}$$

We define $\mathit{out}(\lambda)$ as $\tilde{a} \setminus (\tilde{b} \cup \{c\})$, if $\lambda = (\widetilde{\nu b})\overline{c\,\rho\,\alpha(\tilde{a})}$ or $\lambda = (\widetilde{\nu b})\overline{\alpha(\tilde{a})}$. We use $\mathit{fn}(\lambda)$ and $\mathit{bn}(\lambda)$ to denote (respectively) the free and bound names of a transition label.

In Figs. 2, 3 and 4 we present the labeled transition system for the calculus. The rules presented in Fig. 2 closely follow the π-calculus labeled transition system (see [20]). In (vii) the unlocated $\leftarrow$ label is excluded (to synchronize it must first get located in some context). We omit the rule symmetric to (vi).

We briefly review the rules presented in Fig. 3: (i) service instantiation request; (ii) service instantiation; (iii) after going through a context boundary, an $\uparrow$ message becomes $\downarrow$; (iv) an unlocated $\downarrow$ message gets located at the context identity in which it originates, analogously (v) for a $\leftarrow$ message and (vi) for service instantiation; (vii) a

$$\mathtt{out}\ \alpha(\tilde{v}).P \xrightarrow{\overline{\alpha(\tilde{v})}} P \quad (i) \qquad \mathtt{in}\ \alpha(\tilde{x}).P \xrightarrow{(\nu\tilde{n})\alpha(\tilde{v})} P\{\tilde{x}{\leftarrow}\tilde{v}\} \ \ (\tilde{n} \subseteq \tilde{v}) \quad (ii)$$

$$\frac{P \xrightarrow{\lambda} Q \quad n \notin fn(\lambda)}{(\mathbf{new}\ n)P \xrightarrow{\lambda} (\mathbf{new}\ n)Q}(iii) \qquad \frac{P \xrightarrow{\lambda} Q \quad n \in out(\lambda)}{(\mathbf{new}\ n)P \xrightarrow{(\nu n)\lambda} Q}(iv) \qquad \frac{P \mid !P \xrightarrow{\lambda} Q}{!P \xrightarrow{\lambda} Q}(v)$$

$$\frac{P \xrightarrow{\lambda} Q \quad \lambda \neq \mathtt{throw}}{P \mid R \xrightarrow{\lambda} Q \mid R}(vi) \qquad \frac{P \xrightarrow{(\nu\tilde{n})\lambda} P' \quad Q \xrightarrow{(\nu\tilde{n})\overline{\lambda}} Q' \quad \lambda \neq \leftarrow l(\tilde{a})}{P \mid Q \xrightarrow{\tau} (\mathbf{new}\ \tilde{n})(P' \mid Q')}(vii)$$

Fig. 2. Basic Operators

$$\mathtt{instance}\ n\,\rho\,s \Leftarrow P \xrightarrow{\overline{(\nu c)n\rho\ \mathtt{def}\ s}} c \blacktriangleleft [P] \quad (i) \qquad \mathtt{def}\ s \Rightarrow P \xrightarrow{(\nu c)\mathtt{def}\ s} c \blacktriangleright [P] \quad (ii)$$

$$\frac{P \xrightarrow{\lambda^{\uparrow}} Q}{n\,\rho\,[P] \xrightarrow{\lambda^{\downarrow}} n\,\rho\,[Q]}(iii) \qquad \frac{P \xrightarrow{\lambda^{\downarrow}} Q}{n\,\rho\,[P] \xrightarrow{n\rho\cdot\lambda^{\downarrow}} n\,\rho\,[Q]}(iv) \qquad \frac{P \xrightarrow{\lambda^{\leftarrow}} Q}{n\,\rho\,[P] \xrightarrow{n\rho\cdot\lambda^{\leftarrow}} n\,\rho\,[Q]}(v)$$

$$\frac{P \xrightarrow{(\nu c)\mathtt{def}\ s} Q}{n\,\rho\,[P] \xrightarrow{(\nu c)n\rho\ \mathtt{def}\ s} n\,\rho\,[Q]}(vi) \qquad \frac{P \xrightarrow{n\rho\ \mathtt{here}} Q}{n\,\rho\,[P] \xrightarrow{\tau} n\,\rho\,[Q]}(vii) \qquad \mathtt{here}(x).P \xrightarrow{n\rho\ \mathtt{here}} P\{x{\leftarrow}n\} \quad (viii)$$

$$\frac{P \xrightarrow{\lambda} Q \quad loc(\lambda)}{n\,\rho\,[P] \xrightarrow{\lambda} n\,\rho\,[Q]}(ix) \qquad \frac{P \xrightarrow{\tau} Q}{n\,\rho\,[P] \xrightarrow{\tau} n\,\rho\,[Q]}(x) \qquad \frac{P \xrightarrow{(\nu\tilde{n})act} P' \quad Q \xrightarrow{(\nu\tilde{n})\overline{c\rho\ act}} Q'}{P \mid Q \xrightarrow{c\rho\ \mathtt{here}} (\mathbf{new}\ \tilde{n})(P' \mid Q')}(xi)$$

Fig. 3. Service and Context Operators

$$\mathtt{throw}.P \xrightarrow{\mathtt{throw}} P \quad (i) \qquad \frac{P \xrightarrow{\mathtt{throw}} R}{P \mid Q \xrightarrow{\mathtt{throw}} R}(ii) \qquad \frac{P \xrightarrow{\mathtt{throw}} R}{n\,\rho\,[P] \xrightarrow{\mathtt{throw}} R}(iii)$$

$$\frac{P \xrightarrow{\lambda} Q \quad \lambda \neq \mathtt{throw}}{\mathtt{try}\ P\ \mathtt{catch}\ R \xrightarrow{\lambda} \mathtt{try}\ Q\ \mathtt{catch}\ R}(iv) \qquad \frac{P \xrightarrow{\mathtt{throw}} R}{\mathtt{try}\ P\ \mathtt{catch}\ Q \xrightarrow{\tau} Q \mid R}(v)$$

Fig. 4. Exception Handling Operators

`here` label matches the enclosing context; $(viii)$ a `here` label reads the context identity; (ix) a non-`here` located label transparently crosses the context boundary, likewise (x) for a τ label; (xi) an unlocated label synchronizes with a part (the unlocated part) of a located label, originating a `here` label, thus requiring the interaction to occur inside the given context. We omit the rule symmetric to (xi).

As for the rules in Fig. 4: (i) signals an exception; (ii) and (iii) terminate enclosing computations, (iv) a non-`throw` transition crosses the handler block, (v) an exception is caught by the handler block. We omit the rule symmetric to (ii).

Notice that the presentation of the transition system is fully modular: the rules for each operator are independent, so that one may easily consider several fragments of the calculus (e.g., without exception handling primitives). The operational semantics of closed systems, usually represented by a reduction relation, is here specified by $\xrightarrow{\tau}$.

3 Examples

In this section, we illustrate the expressiveness of our calculus through a sequence of simple, yet illuminating examples. For the sake of commodity, we informally extend the language with some auxiliary primitives, e.g., **if** − **then** − **else**, etc, and recursion **rec** $X.P$ (that may be represented using replication).

3.1 Reading a Remotely Generated Value

A provider *antarctica* provides a service *temperature*. Whenever invoked, such service reads the current value of a sensor at the provider site, and sends it to the caller endpoint.

$$antarctica \blacktriangleright [Sensor \mid \mathbf{def}\ temperature \Rightarrow \mathbf{in} \uparrow measure(x).\mathbf{out} \leftarrow value(x)]$$

By *Sensor* we denote some process running in the $antarctica \blacktriangleright [\cdots]$ context, and that is able to send $measure(t)$ messages inside that context, where t is the current temperature. To use the service in "one shot", a remote client may use the code

$$\mathbf{instance}\ antarctica \blacktriangleright temperature \Leftarrow \mathbf{in} \leftarrow value(x).\mathbf{out} \uparrow temp(x)$$

The effect of this code would be to send a $temp(t)$ message to the client context, where t is the temperature as read at the *antarctica* site. A service delegation as the one just shown resembles a plain remote method call in a distributed object system.

3.2 Service Composition and Orchestration

Our next example, depicted in in Fig. 5, illustrates a familiar service composition and orchestration scenario (inspired by a tutorial example on BPEL published in the Oracle website [15]). Any instance of the *travelApproval* service is expected to receive a *TravelRequest* message and return a *clientCallBack* message after finding a suitable flight. The implementation of the service relies on subsidiary services provided by *americanAirlines* and *deltaAirlines* in order to identify the most favorable price.

Notice how the service instance interacts with service side resources in order to find the *travelClass* associated to each *employee*, by means of the *employeeTravelStatusRequest* and *employeeTravelStatusResponse* messages to and from the server context.

Notice also that the service endpoint is used to pass around control messages with the requests and responses to and from the two airline services involved – *flightRequestAA*, *flightRequestDA* and *flightResponseAA*, *flightResponseDA*, respectively. These message exchanges form a loosely-coupled interaction between the orchestration code and the subsidiary service endpoints. There is thus a clear separation between the partner service instances, that adapt the remote endpoint functionalities (or protocols) to the particular roles performed by the instances in this local process, and the orchestration script, that is a process communicating with the several instances via messages. In our view, this separation captures the essence of BPEL's partner links and partner roles, introduced with the motivation of decoupling the description of the business process (the workflow) from the identification and binding to the actual partners involved in the particular service instances.

We discuss an interesting variation of the previous example. We would now like to instantiate the *flightAvailability* services independently (e.g., at site setup time), in the

```
def travelApproval ⇒ (
    instance americanAirlines ▶ flightAvailability ⇐          % Partner americanAirlines
        in ↑ flightRequestAA(flightData, travelClass).
        out ← flightDetails(flightData, travelClass).
        in ← flightTicketCallBack(response, price).
        out ↑ flightResponseAA(response, price)
    |
    instance deltaAirlines ▶ flightAvailability ⇐             % Partner deltaAirlines
        in ↑ flightRequestDA(flightData, travelClass).
        out ← flightDetails(flightData, travelClass).
        in ← flightTicketCallBack(response, price).
        out ↑ flightResponseDA(response, price)
    |
    in ← travelRequest(employee, flightData).                  % Orchestration
    out ↑ employeeTravelStatusRequest(employee).
    in ↑ employeeTravelStatusResponse(travelClass).(
        out ↓ flightRequestAA(flightData, travelClass) |
        out ↓ flightRequestDA(flightData, travelClass))
    |
    in ↓ flightResponseAA(flightAA, priceAA).
    in ↓ flightResponseDA(flightDA, priceDA).
    if (priceAA < priceDA) then
        out ← clientCallBack(flightAA)
    else
        out ← clientCallBack(flightDA)
)
```

Fig. 5. The Travel Approval Service

service provider context, rather than creating new instances for each instantiation of the *travelApproval* service. In other words, the service *deltaAirlines* ▶ *flightAvailability* and the service *americanAirlines* ▶ *flightAvailability* will be used by the orchestration script in the same way as the *employeeTravelStatus* already was, by means of loosely coupled message exchanges. We depict the solution in Fig. 6. Since many concurrent instantiations of the *travelApproval* service may be outstanding at any given moment, the need arises to explicitly keep track of the messages relative to each instance (establish a correlation mechanism, in web services terminology). Correlation is achieved by passing the name of the current context (accessed by the **here**(*context*) primitive) in the request messages to the services instantiated in the shared context (e.g., as in the message *flightRequestAA*(*context*, ⋯)), allowing the replies associated with the requests to be placed directly in the corresponding contexts.

3.3 Orc

The Orc language [16] is frequently cited as an interesting general model of service orchestration. This example is also relevant to our discussion because Orc also seems to present a mechanism of process delegation, although in a more restricted sense than we are introducing here. In fact, calling a site in Orc causes a persistent process to be

$$
\begin{array}{l}
\textbf{instance}\ \mathit{americanAirlines} \blacktriangleright \mathit{flightAvailability} \Leftarrow \\
\quad !\ \textbf{in} \uparrow \mathit{flightRequestAA}(r, \mathit{flightData}, \mathit{travelClass}). \\
\quad\ \ \textbf{out} \leftarrow \mathit{flightDetails}(\mathit{flightData}, \mathit{travelClass}). \\
\quad\ \ \textbf{in} \leftarrow \mathit{flightTicketCallBack}(\mathit{response}, \mathit{price}). \\
\quad\ \ r \blacktriangleright [\textbf{out} \downarrow \mathit{flightResponseAA}(\mathit{response}, \mathit{price})] \\
| \\
\textbf{instance}\ \mathit{deltaAirlines} \blacktriangleright \mathit{flightAvailability} \Leftarrow \\
\quad !\ \textbf{in} \uparrow \mathit{flightRequestDA}(r, \mathit{flightData}, \mathit{travelClass}). \\
\quad\ \ \textbf{out} \leftarrow \mathit{flightDetails}(\mathit{flightData}, \mathit{travelClass}). \\
\quad\ \ \textbf{in} \leftarrow \mathit{flightTicketCallBack}(\mathit{response}, \mathit{price}). \\
\quad\ \ r \blacktriangleright [\textbf{out} \downarrow \mathit{flightResponseDA}(\mathit{response}, \mathit{price})] \\
| \\
!\ \textbf{def}\ \mathit{travelApproval} \Rightarrow (\\
\quad \textbf{in} \leftarrow \mathit{travelRequest}(\mathit{employee}, \mathit{flightData}). \\
\quad \textbf{here}(\mathit{context}). \\
\quad \textbf{out} \uparrow \mathit{employeeTravelStatusRequest}(\mathit{context}, \mathit{employee}). \\
\quad \textbf{in} \downarrow \mathit{employeeTravelStatusResponse}(\mathit{travelClass}).(\\
\quad\quad \textbf{out} \uparrow \mathit{flightRequestAA}(\mathit{context}, \mathit{flightData}, \mathit{travelClass})\ | \\
\quad\quad \textbf{out} \uparrow \mathit{flightRequestDA}(\mathit{context}, \mathit{flightData}, \mathit{travelClass})) \\
\quad | \\
\quad \textbf{in} \downarrow \mathit{flightResponseAA}(\mathit{flightAA}, \mathit{priceAA}). \\
\quad \textbf{in} \downarrow \mathit{flightResponseDA}(\mathit{flightDA}, \mathit{priceDA}). \\
\quad \cdots \%\ \textit{respond to client as before})
\end{array}
$$

Fig. 6. Correlating concurrent conversations

spawned, consisting the observable behavior of such a process in streaming a sequence of values to the caller context.

We present an encoding of Orc in Fig. 7. To simplify presentation, we introduce anonymous contexts defined as $[P] \triangleq (\textbf{new}\ n)(n \blacktriangleright [P])$ where n is not used in P. We denote by $[\![O]\!]_{out}$ the encoding of an Orc process O into a conversation calculus process. The *out* parameter identifies the message label used to output the stream of values generated by the Orc process. So, for instance, in the encoding of Orc's sequential composition $f \gg x \gg g$ each value produced by f (and hence emitted by $[\![f]\!]_{out_1}$ in out_1) will replace x in a new copy of g. The anonymous context guarantees non interference, being the values produced by g forwarded to the upper environment as values produced by $f \gg x \gg g$.

The operational correspondence property between the encoding presented in Fig. 7 and the formal semantics presented in [16] is shown in the technical report [8], where an encoding of a distributed object calculus [7] is also developed.

3.4 Exceptions

We illustrate a few usage idioms for our exception handling primitives in Fig. 8. In Fig. 8 (a) and (b) we show how exceptions can be used to program conversation interruption. As shown in (a) any remote endpoint instance of the *interruptible* service may be interrupted by the service protocol *ServiceProto* by dropping a *stop*() message inside the endpoint context. Such a message causes the endpoint to send a *stop*() message to

$$
\begin{array}{ll}
[\![n.S(x)]\!]_{out} & \triangleq \mathbf{instance}\ n \blacktriangleright S \Leftarrow \\
& \quad (\mathbf{out} \leftarrow args(x).!\mathbf{in} \leftarrow result(x).\mathbf{out} \uparrow out(x)) \\
[\![n.S(x) = e]\!] & \triangleq n \blacktriangleright [!\ \mathbf{def}\ S \Rightarrow (\mathbf{in} \leftarrow args(x).[\![e]\!]_{out} \mid \\
& \quad\quad !\mathbf{in} \downarrow out(x).\mathbf{out} \leftarrow result(x))] \\
[\![f \gg x \gg g]\!]_{out} & \triangleq [[\![f]\!]_{out_1} \mid \\
& \quad !\mathbf{in} \downarrow out_1(x).([\![g]\!]_{out_2} \mid \mathbf{in} \downarrow out_2(x).\mathbf{out} \uparrow out(x))] \\
[\![f\ \mathbf{where}\ x :\in g]\!]_{out} & \triangleq [(\mathbf{new}\ x)(\\
& \quad [\![f]\!]_{out} \mid \\
& \quad !\mathbf{in} \downarrow out(x).\mathbf{out} \uparrow out(x) \mid \\
& \quad \mathbf{try} \\
& \quad\quad [\![g]\!]_{out_2} \mid \mathbf{in} \downarrow out_2(y).\mathbf{throw}\ x \blacktriangleright [\mathbf{out} \leftarrow val(y)] \\
& \quad \mathbf{catch}\ \mathbf{0})] \\
[\![x]\!]_{out} & \triangleq x \blacktriangleleft [\mathbf{in} \leftarrow val(y).\mathbf{out} \uparrow out(y)] \\
[\![f \mid g]\!]_{out} & \triangleq [\![f]\!]_{out} \mid [\![g]\!]_{out} \\
[\![\mathbf{0}]\!]_{out} & \triangleq \mathbf{0}
\end{array}
$$

Fig. 7. An embedding of Orc

$$
(a)\quad
\begin{array}{l}
server \blacktriangleright [\\
\quad \mathbf{def}\ interruptible \Rightarrow \\
\quad\quad \mathbf{in} \downarrow stop().\mathbf{out} \leftarrow stop().\mathbf{throw} \\
\quad\quad \mid ServiceProto\ ]
\end{array}
\qquad
(b)\quad
\begin{array}{l}
\mathbf{instance} \\
\quad server \blacktriangleright interruptible \Leftarrow \\
\quad\quad \mathbf{in} \leftarrow stop().\mathbf{throw} \\
\quad\quad \mid ClientProto
\end{array}
$$

$$
(c)\quad
\begin{array}{l}
\mathbf{rec}\ Restart. \\
\quad \mathbf{try} \\
\quad\quad \mathbf{instance} \\
\quad\quad\quad server \blacktriangleright interruptible \Leftarrow \ldots \\
\quad \mathbf{catch}\ Restart
\end{array}
\qquad
(d)\quad
\begin{array}{l}
server \blacktriangleright [\\
\quad \mathbf{def}\ timeBound \Rightarrow \\
\quad\quad \mathbf{in} \uparrow timeAllowed(delay). \\
\quad\quad \mathbf{wait}(delay).\mathbf{throw} \\
\quad\quad \mid ServiceProto\ ]
\end{array}
$$

Fig. 8. Exception handling

the other (client side) endpoint, and then throwing an exception, which will cause abortion of the service endpoint. On the other hand, the service invocation protocol, shown in (*b*), will throw an exception at the client endpoint upon reception of *stop*(). Notice that this behavior will possibly happen concurrently with ongoing interactions between *ServiceProto* and *ClientProto*. In Fig. 8 (*c*) we show a pattern for a client that allows for the recovery of a failure by repeatedly re-launching the service. In Fig. 8 (*d*) we show a time-aware service definition. Any invocation of the *TimeBound* service will be allocated no more than *delay* time units before being interrupted, where *delay* is a dynamic parameter value read from the current server side context (we assume a possible extension of our sample language with a $\mathbf{wait}(t)$ primitive).

Somehow related to exceptional behavior is the notion of compensation (see [12]), of particular relevance to service-oriented computing. In the technical report [8] we exhibit an encoding into the conversation calculus of a core fragment of the Compensating CSP calculus [6].

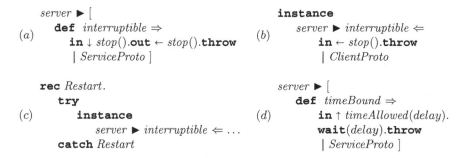

4 Behavioral Semantics

We define a compositional behavioral semantics of the conversation calculus by means of strong bisimulation. The main technical result of this section is a proof that strong bisimilarity is a congruence for all the primitives of our calculus. This further ensures that our syntactically defined constructions induce properly defined behavioral operators at the semantic level. Detailed proofs may be found in the technical report [8].

Definition 4.1. *A (strong) bisimulation is a symmetric binary relation $\mathcal{R}$ on processes such that, for all processes P and Q, if $P\mathcal{R}Q$, we have:*

If $P \xrightarrow{\lambda} P'$ and $bn(\lambda) \cap fn(Q) = \emptyset$ then there is Q' such that $Q \xrightarrow{\lambda} Q'$ and $P'\mathcal{R}Q'$.

We denote by $\sim$ (strong bisimilarity) the largest strong bisimulation.

Theorem 4.2. *Strong bisimilarity is a congruence for all operators.*

N.B. Here we consider for input prefix the universal instantiation congruence principle: if $P\{x{\leftarrow}n\} \sim Q\{x{\leftarrow}n\}$ for all n then $\mathtt{in}\ \alpha(x).P \sim \mathtt{in}\ \alpha(x).Q$ (cf., [20] Theorem 2.2.8(2)). We may also prove several other behavioral equations of interest.

Proposition 4.3. *The following equations hold up to strong bisimilarity.*

1. $n \blacktriangleright [P] \mid n \blacktriangleright [Q] \sim n \blacktriangleright [P \mid Q]$.
2. $m \blacktriangleright [n \blacktriangleright [o \blacktriangleright [P]]] \sim n \blacktriangleright [o \blacktriangleright [P]]$.
3. $n \blacktriangleright [\mathtt{out} \uparrow m(\widetilde{v}).R] \sim \mathtt{out} \downarrow m(\widetilde{v}).n \blacktriangleright [R]$.
4. $m \blacktriangleright [n \blacktriangleright [\mathtt{out} \downarrow l(\widetilde{v}).P]] \sim n \blacktriangleright [\mathtt{out} \downarrow l(\widetilde{v}).m \blacktriangleright [n \blacktriangleright [P]]]$.
5. $m \blacktriangleright [n \blacktriangleright [\mathtt{out} \leftarrow l(\widetilde{v}).P]] \sim n \blacktriangleright [\mathtt{out} \leftarrow l(\widetilde{v}).m \blacktriangleright [n \blacktriangleright [P]]]$.
6. $m \blacktriangleright [n \blacktriangleright [\mathtt{def}\ s \Rightarrow P]] \sim n \blacktriangleright [\mathtt{def}\ s \Rightarrow P]$
7. $m \blacktriangleright [n \blacktriangleright [\mathtt{instance}\ n \rho\, s \Leftarrow P]] \sim n \blacktriangleright [\mathtt{instance}\ n \rho\, s \Leftarrow P]$

For instance, Proposition 4.3(2) captures the local character of message-based communication in our model. The behavioral identities stated in Proposition 4.3 allow us to prove an perhaps surprising normal form property, that contributes to illuminate the spatial structure of conversation calculus systems. A guarded process is a process of the form $\mathtt{out}\ \alpha(\widetilde{v}).P$ or $\mathtt{in}\ \alpha(\widetilde{x}).P$, $\mathtt{here}(x).P$, $\mathtt{instance}\ n\,\rho\,s \Leftarrow P$, or $\mathtt{def}\ s \Rightarrow P$. We use G to range over parallel compositions of guarded processes. We then have the following

Proposition 4.4. *Let P be a process in the finite exception-free fragment. Then there exist sets of guarded processes $\widetilde{G}, \widetilde{G'}, \widetilde{G''}$, sets of names $\widetilde{a}, \widetilde{b}, \widetilde{c}, \widetilde{d}$, and roles $\widetilde{\rho}, \widetilde{\rho'}, \widetilde{\rho''}$ such that*

$$P \sim (\mathtt{new}\ \widetilde{a})(\, G_1 \mid \ldots \mid G_t \mid b_1\, \rho_1\, [G_1'] \mid \ldots \mid b_j\, \rho_j\, [G_j'] \\ \mid c_1\, \rho_1'\, [d_1\, \rho_1''\, [G_1'']] \mid \ldots \mid c_k\, \rho_k'\, [d_k\, \rho_k''\, [G_k'']])$$

and where the sequences $b_i \rho_i$ and $c_i \rho_i' d_i \rho_i''$ are all pairwise distinct.

Intuitively, Proposition 4.4 states that any process (of the finite exception-free fragment of the calculus) is behaviorally equivalent to a process where the maximum nesting of contexts is two. The restriction to finite (replication-free) and exception-free processes is sensible, if one just wants to focus on the communication topology.

We may interpret the normal form existence result as follows. A system is composed by several conversation contexts. The set of upward ($\uparrow$) communication paths of a system may be seen as a graph, where the nodes are processes and contexts, and arcs connect processes to their call-ancestor contexts. As each such arc is uniquely defined by its two terminal nodes, so is the communication structure of an arbitrary process defined (up to bisimilarity) by a system where the (syntactic) nesting of contexts is of at most depth two (see [8]). Intuitively, the structure suggested here represents the join-subconversation relation of concurrently ongoing conversations. Then, the normal form of Proposition 4.4 is analogous to a flattened representation of such a graph.

5 Related Work

Various calculi have been recently proposed with the aim to capture aspects of service-oriented computation. At the root of each one, one finds different motivations and methodological approaches. Some intend to model artifacts of the web services technology, in order to develop applied verification techniques (e.g., COWS [18], SOCK [13]), others were introduced in order to demonstrate analysis techniques (e.g., [7,9]), yet others have the goal of isolating primitives for formalizing and programming service-oriented applications (SCC [3], SSCC [17], CaSPiS [4]) just to refer a few.

The inspiration for the work presented here was motivated by previous developments around SCC [3], a process calculus designed to model service-oriented computing introduced within the Sensoria Project [1]. Our proposal inherits from [14] and SCC the presence of client-server session establishment primitives. However, we end up following a fresh approach, based on the notion of conversation context, and on a simple and flexible message-passing communication. Our development of the concept of conversation context was initially motivated by the concept of session (see [14]). We see conversation contexts as being more general than sessions, in the same sense that coroutining may be seen as a generalization of the stricter procedure (stack-oriented) call discipline. Moreover, the fact that in our model endpoint accesses may appear as arbitrary interacting processes to their enclosing contexts makes them quite different from the more familiar data streaming session endpoints.

Our up ($\uparrow$) communication primitive was introduced with the aim of expressing the interaction between nested conversation contexts, in particular, between service instances endpoints and their callers, with loose-coupling in mind. Similar primitives have been already introduced in ambient calculi, namely Seal [10], Boxed Ambients [5] and Box π [21]. Our computation model is very different from those models (which are targeted at modeling migration and mobility), as witnessed by Proposition 4.4. Hence, even if formally related to some primitives introduced in [5,10], at least when their reaction rules are considered in isolation, our communication primitives have very different consequences at the semantic level (for example, two $\uparrow$ messages can synchronize, just as long as they originate in subcontexts of the same context).

Primitives to deal with exceptional behavior (for example, closing sessions) are present in several service calculi. Perhaps surprisingly, our exception mechanism, although clearly based on the classical construct for functional languages, does not seem to have been much explored in process calculi; we believe that it allows us to express many interesting exceptional behavior situations.

We have demonstrated that our approach is expressive enough to capture Orc's composition operators; we expect that similar results may be established for calculi with related constructs, such as streams and pipelines [17,4], at least in the absence of types.

6 Concluding Remarks

We have presented a model for service-oriented computation, building on the identification of some general aspects of service-based systems. We have instantiated our model by proposing the conversation calculus, which incorporates abstractions of the several aspects involved by means of carefully chosen programming language primitives. We have focused our presentation on a detailed justification of the concepts involved, on examples that illustrate the expressiveness of our model, and on the semantic theory for our calculus, based on a standard strong bisimilarity. Our examples demonstrate how our calculus may express many service-oriented idioms in a rather natural way. The behavioral semantics allowed us to prove several interesting behavioral identities. Some of these identities suggested a normal form result that clarifies the spatial communication topology of conversation calculus systems.

Conversation contexts are natural subjects for typing disciplines, in terms of the message interchange patterns that may happen at their borders. We expect types specifying various properties of interfaces, service contracts, endpoint session protocols, security policies, resource usage, and service level agreements, to be in general assigned to context boundaries. One of the most interesting challenges to be addressed by type systems for the conversation calculus is then to discipline the delegation of conversation contexts according to quite strict usage disciplines, allowing for the static verification of systems where several (not just two) partners join and leave dynamically a conversation in a coordinated way.

Acknowledgments. We thank our colleagues of the Sensoria Project for many discussions about programming language concepts and core calculi for service based computing. We also acknowledge the anonymous referees for their detailed and useful comments and suggestions.

References

1. IP Sensoria Project: `http://www.sensoria-ist.eu/`
2. Alves, A., et al.: Web Services Business Process Execution Language Version 2.0. Technical report, OASIS (2006)
3. Boreale, M., Bruni, R., Caires, L., De Nicola, R., Lanese, I., Loreti, M., Martins, F., Montanari, U., Ravara, A., Sangiorgi, D., Vasconcelos, V., Zavattaro, G.: SCC: A Service Centered Calculus. In: Bravetti, M., Núñez, M., Zavattaro, G. (eds.) WS-FM 2006. LNCS, vol. 4184, Springer, Heidelberg (2006)

4. Boreale, M., Bruni, R., De Nicola, R., Loreti, M.: A Service Oriented Process Calculus with Sessioning and Pipelining. Technical report, Draft (2007)
5. Bugliesi, M., Castagna, G., Crafa, S.: Access Control for Mobile Agents: The Calculus of Boxed Ambients. ACM Transactions on Programming Languages and Systems 26(1), 57–124 (2004)
6. Butler, M.J., Hoare, C.A.R., Ferreira, C.: A Trace Semantics for Long-Running Transactions. In: Abdallah, A.E., Jones, C.B., Sanders, J.W. (eds.) Communicating Sequential Processes. LNCS, vol. 3525, pp. 133–150. Springer, Heidelberg (2005)
7. Caires, L.: Spatial-Behavioral Types for Distributed Services and Resources. In: Montanari, U., Sanella, D. (eds.) Proceedings of the Second International Symposium on Trustworthy Global Computing. LNCS, vol. 4661, pp. 98–115. Springer, Heidelberg (2006)
8. Caires, L., Vieira, H.T., Seco, J.C.: A Model of Service Oriented Computation. TR-DI/FCT/UNL 6/07, Universidade Nova de Lisboa (2007)
9. Carbone, M., Honda, K., Yoshida, N.: Structured Communication-Centred Programming for Web Services. In: De Nicola, R. (ed.) ESOP 2007. LNCS, vol. 4421, pp. 2–17. Springer, Heidelberg (2007)
10. Castagna, G., Vitek, J., Nardelli, F.Z.: The Seal Calculus. Information and Computation 201(1), 1–54 (2005)
11. Fiadeiro, J.L., Lopes, A., Bocchi, L.: A Formal Approach to Service Component Architecture. In: Bravetti, M., Núñez, M., Zavattaro, G. (eds.) WS-FM 2006. LNCS, vol. 4184, pp. 193–213. Springer, Heidelberg (2006)
12. Gray, J., Reuter, A.: Transaction Processing: Concepts and Techniques. Morgan Kaufmann, San Francisco (1993)
13. Guidi, C., Lucchi, R., Gorrieri, R., Busi, N., Zavattaro, G.: SOCK: A Calculus for Service Oriented Computing. In: Dan, A., Lamersdorf, W. (eds.) ICSOC 2006. LNCS, vol. 4294, pp. 327–338. Springer, Heidelberg (2006)
14. Honda, K., Vasconcelos, V.T., Kubo, M.: Language Primitives and Type Discipline for Structured Communication-Based Programming. In: Hankin, C. (ed.) ESOP 1998. LNCS, vol. 1381, pp. 122–138. Springer, Heidelberg (1998)
15. Juric, M.B.: A Hands-on Introduction to BPEL, Oracle (white paper) (2006)
16. Kitchin, D., Cook, W.R., Misra, J.: A Language for Task Orchestration and Its Semantic Properties. In: Baier, C., Hermanns, H. (eds.) CONCUR 2006. LNCS, vol. 4137, pp. 477–491. Springer, Heidelberg (2006)
17. Lanese, I., Vasconcelos, V.T., Martins, F., Ravara, A.: Disciplining Orchestration and Conversation in Service-Oriented Computing. In: 5th International Conference on Software Engineering and Formal Methods, pp. 305–314. IEEE Computer Society Press, Los Alamitos (2007)
18. Lapadula, A., Pugliese, R., Tiezzi, F.: A Calculus for Orchestration of Web Services. In: De Nicola, R. (ed.) ESOP 2007. LNCS, vol. 4421, pp. 33–47. Springer, Heidelberg (2007)
19. Milner, R., Parrow, J., Walker, D.: A Calculus of Mobile Processes, Part I + II. Information and Computation 100(1), 1–77 (1992)
20. Sangiorgi, D., Walker, D.: The π-calculus: A Theory of Mobile Processes. Cambridge University Press, Cambridge (2001)
21. Sewell, P., Vitek, J.: Secure Composition of Untrusted Code: Box π, Wrappers, and Causality. Journal of Computer Security 11(2), 135–188 (2003)

Inferring Channel Buffer Bounds Via Linear Programming

Tachio Terauchi[1] and Adam Megacz[2]

[1] Tohoku University
terauchi@ecei.tohoku.ac.jp
[2] University of California, Berkeley
megacz@cs.berkeley.edu

Abstract. We present a static analysis for inferring the maximum amount of buffer space used by a program consisting of concurrently running processes communicating via buffered channels. We reduce the problem to linear programming by casting the analysis as a fractional capability calculus system. Our analysis can reason about buffers used by multiple processes concurrently, and runs in time polynomial in the size of the program.

1 Introduction

We consider programs consisting of concurrently running processes communicating via buffered channels. Each process runs sequentially at its own speed, and synchronizes by communicating over channels. Communications are buffered in the sense that the messages may not be immediately sent to the receiver, but are held at some place. But holding messages costs buffer resources. If the buffers have a predetermined maximum size, unwanted behavior may happen if a process tries to send over a channel whose buffer is full. If the buffer is lossy, messages could get lost. Otherwise, it could block or change the sender process's control flow. This paper presents a static analysis for obtaining a conservative bound on channel buffers so that such behavior never happens, that is, channel buffers are used within their bounds. Such an analysis has application in determining a program's resource usage bound.

We cast our analysis as a *capability calculus*. The capability calculus is a static system originally proposed for reasoning about resources in sequential computation [2]. We use the extension of the capability calculus to channel communicating concurrent programs to allow capabilities to be passed at synchronization points [6]. We also use fractional capabilities [1,5,6] so that we can efficiently infer capabilities via linear programming.

Our analysis can automatically discover some non-trivial buffer bounds. For example, consider the program in Figure 1 consisting of two concurrently running processes communicating via the channels `foo` and `bar`, used to transmit integer values. The variables `i, j, m, n` are assumed to be initialized to some positive integers. Process 1 reads from the channel `bar` and stores the read value in

S. Drossopoulou (Ed.): ESOP 2008, LNCS 4960, pp. 284–298, 2008.

```
Process 1            Process 2
while i < m          while j < n
   bar?(x);             bar!(j);
   foo!(1);             foo?(y);
   foo!(i);             foo?(z);
   i := i + x           j := j + y + z
```

Fig. 1. Example

variable `x`, writes twice to `foo`, and then updates the variable `i` and repeats if the loop condition is met. Process 2 writes once to `bar` and reads twice from `foo`, and then repeats if the loop condition is met. Buffer space to store only one integer is needed for the channel `bar`. This is because when process 2 is about to write to `bar` for the second time, process 1 must have already read the first integer from `bar` as process 2's write is preceded by the two reads from `foo` in the previous iteration, which in turn were written by process 1 after the read from `bar`. The same argument holds by induction for the subsequent iteration of the loop. Similarly, the program only needs buffer space to store two integers for the channel `foo`. Our analysis is able to automatically infer these optimal bounds.

The rest of the paper is organized as follows. Section 2 introduces the syntax of the simple concurrent language we use to describe the analysis. Section 3 defines the operational semantics of the language and formally defines what it means for a program to run within a buffer bound. Section 4 presents the capability calculus which statically guarantees that a program runs within a buffer bound. Section 5 presents the analysis algorithm as a type inference algorithm for the capability calculus. Section 6 discusses limitations of our work. Section 7 discusses related work. Section 8 concludes.

2 The Simple Concurrent Language

We focus on the simple concurrent language shown in Figure 2. The language is essentially the simple imperative language WHILE extended with concurrency primitives. Formally, a program, p, is a parallel composition of finitely many processes. A process, $i.s$, is a sequential statement s prefixed by a process index i. A sequential statement consists of the usual imperative features as well as primitives for buffered communications. Here, $e_1!(e_2)$ means writing the value of e_2 to the buffered channel e_1, and $e?(x)$ means storing the value read from the channel e in variable x. The variables are process-local, and so the only means of communication are channel reads and writes. We use meta-variables x, x', etc. for variables and c, c', etc. for channels. Channels are first class and can be used as values, that is, they can be assigned to variables or written to channels. Binary integer operations such as $+, -, \times, \leq$, etc., are ranged over by the symbol op.

To keep the presentation to the novel features of the analysis, this simple language lacks the ability to create processes and channels dynamically, but it is

$$
\begin{array}{lll}
p ::= i.s & & (\textit{process}) \\
\quad \mid p_1 \mid\mid p_2 & & (\textit{parallel composition}) \\
s ::= s_1 ; s_2 & & (\textit{sequential composition}) \\
\quad \mid \texttt{skip} & & (\textit{skip}) \\
\quad \mid \texttt{if}\ e\ \texttt{then}\ s_1\ \texttt{else}\ s_2 & & (\textit{branch}) \\
\quad \mid \texttt{while}\ e\ \texttt{do}\ s & & (\textit{loop}) \\
\quad \mid x \texttt{ := } e & & (\textit{assignment}) \\
\quad \mid e_1 \texttt{!}(e_2) & & (\textit{channel write}) \\
\quad \mid e\texttt{?}(x) & & (\textit{channel read}) \\
e ::= c & & (\textit{channel constant}) \\
\quad \mid x & & (\textit{local variable}) \\
\quad \mid n & & (\textit{integer constant}) \\
\quad \mid e_1\ op\ e_2 & & (\textit{integer operation})
\end{array}
$$

Fig. 2. The syntax of the simple concurrent language

easy to extend the analysis to handle dynamic creation of processes and channels by borrowing the techniques from [3,6].

3 Operational Semantics

We define the following mathematical convention. Given a mapping (i.e., a set-theoretic function) f, $f[a \mapsto b]$ is a mapping such that $f[a \mapsto b](a) = b$ and $f[a \mapsto b](a') = f(a')$ for $a' \neq a$.

The operational semantics of the language is defined as a series of reductions from states to states. A state is represented by the triple (B, S, p) where B is a *buffer* and S is a *store*.

A store is a mapping from process index to process store. A *process store* a mapping from variables to values. We use symbols h, h', etc. to denote a process store. Values are subset of expressions (e) defined as follows.

$$v ::= c \mid n$$

Figure 3 shows the evaluation rules. Expressions are evaluated entirely locally. Their evaluation relation are of the form $(h, e) \Downarrow v$ and defined by the rules **Chan**, **Int**, **Var**, and **Op**. Here, $[\![op]\!]$ is the standard semantics of the binary operator *op*. The sequential composition operator ; is associative. Also, we let `skip` be a ; identity, that is, $s = s; \texttt{skip} = \texttt{skip}; s$. The parallel composition operator $\mid\mid$ is commutative and associative, e.g., $p_1 \mid\mid p_2 \mid\mid p_3 = p_2 \mid\mid p_3 \mid\mid p_1$. Note that the process reduction rules only reduce the left-most process, and so we rely on process re-ordering to reduce other processes. We assume that the process indices are disjoint in any program p. **If1**, **If2**, **While1**, and **While2** do not involve channel communication and are self-explanatory. **Assign** is also a process-local reduction because variables are local.

Write and **Read** handle communications over channels. We write $B.\mathit{write}(c, v)$ for the buffer B after v is written to the channel c, and $B.\mathit{read}(c)$

$$\frac{}{(h,c) \Downarrow c}\ \textbf{Chan} \qquad \frac{}{(h,n) \Downarrow n}\ \textbf{Int}$$

$$\frac{}{(h,x) \Downarrow h(x)}\ \textbf{Var} \qquad \frac{(h,e_1) \Downarrow n_1 \qquad (h,e_2) \Downarrow n_2}{(h, e_1\ op\ e_2) \Downarrow n_1 \ [\![op]\!]\ n_2}\ \textbf{Op}$$

$$\frac{(S(i),e) \Downarrow n \qquad n \neq 0}{(B,S,i.(\texttt{if}\ e\ \texttt{then}\ s_1\ \texttt{else}\ s_2);s \mid\mid p) \rightarrow (B,S,i.s_1;s \mid\mid p)}\ \textbf{If1}$$

$$\frac{(S(i),e) \Downarrow 0}{(B,S,i.(\texttt{if}\ e\ \texttt{then}\ s_1\ \texttt{else}\ s_2);s \mid\mid p) \rightarrow (B,S,i.s_2;s \mid\mid p)}\ \textbf{If2}$$

$$\frac{(S(i),e) \Downarrow n \qquad n \neq 0}{(B,S,i.(\texttt{while}\ e\ \texttt{do}\ s_1);s \mid\mid p) \rightarrow (B,S,i.s_1;(\texttt{while}\ e\ \texttt{do}\ s_1);s \mid\mid p)}\ \textbf{While1}$$

$$\frac{(S(i),e) \Downarrow 0}{(B,S,i.(\texttt{while}\ e\ \texttt{do}\ s_1);s \mid\mid p) \rightarrow (B,S,i.s \mid\mid p)}\ \textbf{While2}$$

$$\frac{(S(i),e) \Downarrow v \qquad S' = S[i \mapsto S(i)[x \mapsto v]]}{(B,S,i.x \texttt{ := } e;s \mid\mid p) \rightarrow (B,S',i.s \mid\mid p)}\ \textbf{Assign}$$

$$\frac{(S(i),e_1) \Downarrow c \qquad (S(i),e_2) \Downarrow v \qquad B' = B.\mathit{write}(c,v)}{(B,S,i.e_1\,!\,(e_2);s \mid\mid p) \rightarrow (B',S,i.s \mid\mid p)}\ \textbf{Write}$$

$$\frac{(S(i),e) \Downarrow c \qquad (B',v) = B.\mathit{read}(c) \qquad S' = S[i \mapsto S(i)[x \mapsto v]]}{(B,S,i.e?(x);s \mid\mid p) \rightarrow (B',S',i.s \mid\mid p)}\ \textbf{Read}$$

Fig. 3. The operational semantics of the simple concurrent language

for the pair (B', v) where v is the value read from channel c and B' is the buffer after the read.

Formally, a buffer B is a mapping from channels to buffer contents. We model buffer contents as a bag of values. Buffer writes and reads are defined as follows.

$$\begin{array}{ll} B.\mathit{write}(c,v) = B[c \mapsto B(c) \uplus \{v\}] & \\ B.\mathit{read}(c) = (B[c \mapsto S], v) & \text{if } B(c) = S \uplus \{v\} \end{array}$$

Here, $\uplus$ denotes bag union, e.g., $\{v\} \uplus \{v\} = \{v, v\}$. Note that we are not concerned about the order of values written/read to/from a buffer, and so to allow maximum generality, we model a buffer as a bag of values from which an arbitrary value can be read at a channel read provided that the bag is non-empty.

The operational semantics allows arbitrary many values to be stored in a buffer. In practice, buffers may be bounded due to physical resource constraints. Exactly what happens if a sender tries to write to a full buffer is outside of the scope of the paper. The goal of the analysis is to infer buffer bounds to ensure that such behavior never occurs. In contrast, a receiver is allowed to wait on an empty buffer, allowing the processes to synchronize over a channel.

For simplicity, we assume that every value has the same size and occupies the same amount of space in the buffers. We write $P \rightarrow^* Q$ for zero or more reduction steps from the state P to the state Q. We now formally define what it means for a program to run within a buffer bound.

Definition 1. *We say that the buffer bound of* c *in* P *is within* n *if for any* (B, S, p) *such that* $P \rightarrow^* (B, S, p)$, $|B(c)| \leq n$.

4 The Capability Calculus

Our analysis returns a buffer bound for each channel in the program. To this end, we design a capability calculus such that given a state P, we can obtain a buffer bound for each channel in P from the derivation for P in the calculus.

The capability calculus is a kind of a type system. The types are defined as follows.

$$\begin{array}{rll} \tau ::= & ch(\rho, \tau, \Psi) & (channels) \\ | & int & (integers) \end{array}$$

The type $ch(\rho, \tau, \Psi)$ denotes a type of a channel used to send and receive values of the type τ. Here, ρ is the *handle* of the channel. Let **Handles** be the set of channel handles. Symbols Ψ, Ψ', etc. represent *capability mappings.* A capability mapping is a function from **Handles** to non-negative rational numbers augmented with ∞, that is, $\mathbb{Q}^+ \cup \{0, \infty\}$. We use the ordering $q \leq \infty$ for all $q \in \mathbb{Q}^+ \cup \{0, \infty\}$, and the following arithmetic relation: $q + \infty = \infty$, $q \times \infty = \infty$ for $q \neq 0$, and $0 \times \infty = 0$.

We say that Ψ such that $\Psi(\rho) = q$ has q amount of ρ. We often refer to Ψ itself as "capabilities", with the understanding that we mean the amount of capabilities in Ψ. Capabilities are conceptual, that is, capabilities only exist in the static type system world and do not appear in the dynamic semantics. Conceptually, each process holds some amount of capabilities representing the amount of buffer space available for its use. For instance, a process holding capabilities Ψ may write $\Psi(\rho)$ many values to the buffers for channels with the handle ρ. The capability mapping appearing in a channel type represent the capabilities that are passed when communicating over that channel. That is, when two processes communicate over a channel having the type $ch(\rho, \tau, \Psi)$, the sender process passes the capabilities Ψ to the receiver process.

We define arithmetic operations over capabilities. The addition and subtraction of capability mappings are defined point-wise as $\Psi + \Psi' = \lambda\rho.\Psi(\rho) + \Psi'(\rho)$ and $\Psi - \Psi' = \lambda\rho.\Psi(\rho) - \Psi'(\rho)$. Because capabilities must be non-negative, $\Psi - \Psi'$ is undefined if $\Psi(\rho) < \Psi'(\rho)$ for some ρ. We define the relation $\Psi \leq \Psi'$ point-wise as $\forall\rho \in \textbf{Handles}.\Psi(\rho) \leq \Psi'(\rho)$. For convenience, we let 0 denote a constant capability mapping that maps all handles to 0, that is, $0 = \lambda\rho.0$. Therefore, for example, $0[\rho \mapsto 1]$ is a capability mapping that maps ρ to 1 and ρ' to 0 for all $\rho' \neq \rho$.

Figure 4 shows the type checking rules. The judgements for expressions are of the form $\Gamma \vdash e : \tau$, where Γ is a type environment mapping variables and channels to their types. The rules **VAR**, **CHAN**, **INT**, and **OP** type expressions and are self-explanatory.

$$\frac{}{\Gamma \vdash c : \Gamma(c)}\ \textbf{CHAN} \qquad \frac{}{\Gamma \vdash n : \mathit{int}}\ \textbf{INT}$$

$$\frac{}{\Gamma \vdash x : \Gamma(x)}\ \textbf{VAR} \qquad \frac{\Gamma \vdash e_1 : \mathit{int} \quad \Gamma \vdash e_2 : \mathit{int}}{\Gamma \vdash e_1\ op\ e_2 : \mathit{int}}\ \textbf{OP}$$

$$\frac{}{\Gamma, \Psi \vdash \texttt{skip} : \Psi}\ \textbf{SKIP} \qquad \frac{\Gamma \vdash e : \Gamma(x)}{\Gamma, \Psi \vdash x \texttt{ := } e : \Psi}\ \textbf{ASSIGN}$$

$$\frac{\Gamma, \Psi \vdash s_1 : \Psi_1 \quad \Gamma, \Psi_1 \vdash s_2 : \Psi_2}{\Gamma, \Psi \vdash s_1; s_2 : \Psi_2}\ \textbf{SEQ}$$

$$\frac{\Gamma \vdash e : \mathit{int} \quad \Psi' \leq \Psi_1 \quad \Psi' \leq \Psi_2 \quad \Gamma, \Psi \vdash s_1 : \Psi_1 \quad \Gamma, \Psi \vdash s_2 : \Psi_2}{\Gamma, \Psi \vdash \texttt{if}\ e\ \texttt{then}\ s_1\ \texttt{else}\ s_2 : \Psi'}\ \textbf{IF}$$

$$\frac{\Gamma \vdash e : \mathit{int} \quad \Gamma, \Psi' \vdash s : \Psi'' \quad \Psi' \leq \Psi \quad \Psi' \leq \Psi''}{\Gamma, \Psi \vdash \texttt{while}\ e\ \texttt{do}\ s : \Psi'}\ \textbf{WHILE}$$

$$\frac{\Gamma \vdash e : \mathit{ch}(\rho, \Gamma(x), \Psi')}{\Gamma, \Psi \vdash e?(x) : \Psi + \Psi' + \mathit{0}[\rho \mapsto 1]}\ \textbf{READ}$$

$$\frac{\Gamma \vdash e : \mathit{ch}(\rho, \tau, \Psi') \quad \Gamma \vdash e' : \tau}{\Gamma, \Psi \vdash e!(e') : \Psi - \Psi' - \mathit{0}[\rho \mapsto 1]}\ \textbf{WRITE}$$

Fig. 4. The type checking rules

The type judgements for the statements are of the form $\Gamma, \Psi \vdash s : \Psi'$, where Ψ is the capabilities before the execution of s, and Ψ' is the capabilities after the execution of s. **SKIP**, **SEQ**, and **ASSIGN** are self-explanatory. **IF** ensures that the capabilities at the branch join point cannot exceed the capabilities after the then branch or the else branch. **WHILE** is similar to **IF**.

In **READ**, the hypothesis ensures that type of the received value agrees with the type of the variable where the value is going to be stored. In the conclusion of **READ**, the capabilities Ψ' passed from the sender is added to the capabilities held by the process. In addition, because a read frees a buffer space, we gain a single buffer space, and so we add the capability $\mathit{0}[\rho \mapsto 1]$.

WRITE passes Ψ' to the receiver, and thus the capabilities Ψ' is subtracted in the conclusion of the rule. The subtraction of capabilities is defined as $\Psi_1 - \Psi_2 = \Psi_3$ iff $\Psi_3 + \Psi_2 = \Psi_1$. In addition, because a write uses a buffer space, we express this by subtracting $\mathit{0}[\rho \mapsto 1]$ in the conclusion. Note that the non-negativity assumption of capabilities implies that $\Psi(\rho) \geq 1$.

We define some notational shortcuts. Let $\mathit{writeSend}(\mathit{ch}(\rho, \tau, \Psi)) = \Psi$ and $\mathit{hdl}(\mathit{ch}(\rho, \tau, \Psi)) = \rho$. Let $HC_B(\rho, \Gamma)$ be the subset of the domain of B having the handle ρ, that is,

$$HC_B(\rho, \Gamma) = \{c \in \mathit{dom}(B) \mid \mathit{hdl}(\Gamma(c)) = \rho\}$$

Note that $|HC_B(\rho, \Gamma)| > 1$ means that multiple channels have the same handle ρ.

We write $\Gamma \vdash B(c)$ to mean that the buffer $B(c)$ is well-typed, that is, for each $v \in B(c)$, $\Gamma \vdash v : \tau$, where $\Gamma(c) = ch(\rho, \tau, \Psi)$ for some ρ, Ψ. We write $\Gamma \vdash h$ to mean that the process store h is well-typed, that is, $\Gamma \vdash h(x) : \Gamma(x)$ for each $x \in dom(h)$. Because variables are process local, without loss of generality, we assume that each process uses a disjoint set of variables.

Definition 2 (Well-typed State). *We write*

$$\Gamma, \Psi_1, \ldots, \Psi_n, \Psi_B \vdash (B, S, i_1.s_1 || \ldots || i_n.s_n)$$

if

(1) For each channel $c \in dom(B)$, $\Gamma \vdash B(c)$.
(2) For each i_j, $\Gamma \vdash S(i_j)$.
(3) For each s_j, $\Gamma, \Psi_j \vdash s_j : \Psi'_j$ for some Ψ'_j.
(4) $\Psi_B = \sum_{c \in dom(B)} |B(c)| \times writeSend(\Gamma(c))$.

In (4), $m \times \Psi$ is defined as $\lambda\rho.m \times \Psi(\rho)$.

For simplicity, we have used simple types so that some programs are untypable (for instance, a program that uses integers as channels). But it is easy to extend the system with sum types and recursive types so that all programs become typable [4].

We now state the main result of this section which says that a well-typed program runs within buffer bounds that can be obtained from its type derivation.

Theorem 1. *Suppose $\Gamma, \Psi_1, \ldots, \Psi_n, \Psi_B \vdash (B, S, p)$. Suppose $hdl(\Gamma(c)) = \rho$. Let $\Psi_p = \Psi_B + \sum_{j=1}^{n} \Psi_j$. Then the buffer bound of c in (B, S, p) is within $\Psi_p(\rho) + \sum_{c' \in HC_B(\rho, \Gamma)} |B(c')|$.*

The key steps of the proof appear in the appendix.

4.1 Example

Recall the following program from Section 1. Let us call this program p.

$$\begin{array}{l} 1.\texttt{while i} < \texttt{m do (bar?(x); foo!(1); foo!(i); i := i + x)} \,||\\ 2.\texttt{while j} < \texttt{n do (bar!(j); foo?(y); foo?(z); j := j + y + z)} \end{array}$$

Let B be an empty buffer, that is, $B(\texttt{foo}) = B(\texttt{bar}) = \emptyset$. Let S be a store such that $S(1)$ maps $\texttt{i}, \texttt{m}, \texttt{x}$ to some integer and $S(2)$ maps $\texttt{j}, \texttt{n}, \texttt{y}, \texttt{z}$ to some integer. Let

$$\begin{aligned} \Gamma = \{&\texttt{i} \mapsto int, \texttt{j} \mapsto int, \texttt{m} \mapsto int, \texttt{n} \mapsto int,\\ &\texttt{x} \mapsto int, \texttt{y} \mapsto int, \texttt{z} \mapsto int,\\ &\texttt{foo} \mapsto ch(\rho_{foo}, int, 0[\rho_{bar} \mapsto 0.5]),\\ &\texttt{bar} \mapsto ch(\rho_{bar}, int, 0[\rho_{foo} \mapsto 2])\} \end{aligned}$$

$$\begin{aligned} \Psi_1 &= \Psi_B = 0\\ \Psi_2 &= 0[\rho_{foo} \mapsto 2][\rho_{bar} \mapsto 1] \end{aligned}$$

Then, we have $\Gamma, \Psi_1, \Psi_2, \Psi_B \vdash (B, S, p)$. The type of `foo` indicates that whenever process 2 reads from `foo`, 0.5 amount of capability for `bar` is passed to process 2. Therefore, by reading `foo` twice, process 2 gains $0.5 + 0.5 = 1$ buffer space for `bar`. Likewise, `bar`'s type says that reading `bar` once begets two buffer space for `foo`.

Let $\Psi_p = \Psi_1 + \Psi_2 + \Psi_B$. Note that $\Psi_p(\rho_{foo}) = 2$ and $\Psi_p(\rho_{bar}) = 1$, indicating that the buffer bound of `foo` is 2 in (B, S, p) and the buffer bound of `bar` is 1 in (B, S, p). As argued in Section 1, these are the optimal bounds for the program.

5 Analysis Algorithm

Intuitively, the analysis algorithm is a type inference algorithm for the type system presented in Section 4. Because there are multiple type derivations possible for a program, we would like to obtain a derivation that gives the smallest buffer bound for each channel. Our strategy is to reduce the problem to linear programming such that the buffer bound appears as the objective function to be minimized.

The analysis is separated in two phases. Informally, the first phase infers everything about the type derivation except for the amount of capabilities. The second phase uses linear programming to find the minimum amount of capabilities required to complete the type derivation.

5.1 Phase 1

The first phase is mostly a standard type-based analysis based on unification constraints, generating capability constraints on the side. Figure 5 shows the constraint generation rules. Here, α's are type variables, ϱ's are channel handle variables, and φ's are capability mapping variables. The inference rules are straightforward constraint-based implementation of the type checking rules in Figure 4.

The inference judgement for expressions, $\Delta \vdash e : \alpha; C$, is read "given the environment Δ, e is inferred to have the type α with the set of constraints C." The inference judgement for statements, $\Delta, \varphi \vdash s : \varphi'; C$ is read "given environment Δ, s is inferred to have the *pre-capability* φ and the *post-capability* φ' with the set of constraints C."

We initialize Δ such that each $\Delta(x)$ and each $\Delta(c)$ is a fresh type variable. We visit each AST node (expressions and statements) in a bottom up manner to build the set of constraints.

The resulting set of constraints contains two kinds of constraints:

(a) Type unification constraints: $\sigma = \sigma'$
(b) Capability inequality constraints: $\phi \leq \phi'$

where

$$\sigma ::= \alpha \mid ch(\varrho, \alpha, \varphi) \mid int$$
$$\phi ::= \varphi \mid 0[\varrho \mapsto 1] \mid \phi + \phi \mid \phi - \phi$$

$$\frac{\alpha, \varrho, \varphi \text{ fresh}}{\Delta \vdash c : \Delta(c); \{ch(\varrho, \alpha, \varphi) = \Delta(c)\}} \textbf{ CHAN}$$

$$\frac{\alpha \text{ fresh}}{\Delta \vdash n : \alpha; \{\alpha = int\}} \textbf{ INT} \qquad \frac{}{\Delta \vdash x : \Delta(x); \emptyset} \textbf{ VAR}$$

$$\frac{\Delta \vdash e_1 : \alpha_1; C_1 \qquad \Delta \vdash e_2 : \alpha_2; C_2 \qquad \alpha_3 \text{ fresh}}{\Delta \vdash e_1 \; op \; e_2 : \alpha_3; C_1 \cup C_2 \cup \{\alpha_1 = \alpha_2 = \alpha_3 = int\}} \textbf{ OP}$$

$$\frac{\varphi \text{ fresh}}{\Delta, \varphi \vdash \texttt{skip} : \varphi; \emptyset} \textbf{ SKIP}$$

$$\frac{\Delta \vdash e : \alpha; C \qquad \varphi \text{ fresh}}{\Delta, \varphi \vdash x \; \texttt{:=} \; e : \varphi; C \cup \{\alpha = \Delta(x)\}} \textbf{ ASSIGN}$$

$$\frac{\Delta, \varphi_1 \vdash s_1 : \varphi_1'; C_1 \qquad \Delta, \varphi_2 \vdash s_2 : \varphi_2'; C_2}{\Delta, \varphi_1 \vdash s_1; s_2 : \varphi_2'; C_1 \cup C_2 \cup \{\varphi_1' = \varphi_2\}} \textbf{ SEQ}$$

$$\frac{\Delta \vdash e : \alpha; C \qquad \Delta, \varphi_1 \vdash s_1 : \varphi_1'; C_1 \qquad \Delta, \varphi_2 \vdash s_2 : \varphi_2'; C_2 \qquad \varphi, \varphi' \text{ fresh}}{\begin{array}{l}\Delta, \varphi \vdash \texttt{if } e \texttt{ then } s_1 \texttt{ else } s_2 : \varphi'; \\ \qquad C \cup C_1 \cup C_2 \cup \{\alpha = int, \varphi_1 = \varphi_2 = \varphi, \varphi' \leq \varphi_1', \varphi' \leq \varphi_2'\}\end{array}} \textbf{ IF}$$

$$\frac{\Delta \vdash e : \alpha; C \qquad \Delta, \varphi' \vdash s : \varphi''; C' \qquad \varphi \text{ fresh}}{\Delta, \varphi \vdash \texttt{while } e \texttt{ do } s : \varphi'; C \cup C' \cup \{\alpha = int, \varphi' \leq \varphi, \varphi' \leq \varphi''\}} \textbf{ WHILE}$$

$$\frac{\Delta \vdash e : \alpha; C \qquad \varrho, \varphi, \varphi', \varphi'' \text{ fresh}}{\Delta, \varphi \vdash e?(x) : \varphi''; C \cup \{\alpha = ch(\varrho, \Delta(x), \varphi'), \varphi'' = \varphi + \varphi' + 0[\varrho \mapsto 1]\}} \textbf{ READ}$$

$$\frac{\Delta \vdash e : \alpha; C \qquad \Delta \vdash e' : \alpha'; C' \qquad \varrho, \varphi, \varphi', \varphi'' \text{ fresh}}{\begin{array}{l}\Delta, \varphi \vdash e!(e') : \varphi''; \\ \qquad C \cup C' \cup \{\alpha = ch(\varrho, \alpha', \varphi'), \varphi'' = \varphi - \varphi' - 0[\varrho \mapsto 1]\}\end{array}} \textbf{ WRITE}$$

Fig. 5. The type inference rules

Note that an equality constraint $\phi = \phi'$ can expressed by inequality constraints $\phi \leq \phi'$ and $\phi' \leq \phi$. The constraints of the kind (a) can be resolved by the standard unification algorithm, which may create more constraints of the kind (b). In addition, it creates constraints of the form $\varrho = \varrho'$, which can also be resolved by the standard unification algorithm. This leaves us with a set of constraints of the kind (b).

5.2 Phase 2

The second phase of the algorithm finds a satisfying solution to the remaining constraints generated in the first phase. In general, there can be more than one solution to these constraints. We find the minimum solution as follows. Let $p = i_1.s_1 \mid\mid \ldots \mid\mid i_n.s_n$ be the program being analyzed. Phase 1 returns pre-capability φ_j for each process s_j such that $\Delta, \varphi_j \vdash s_j : \varphi_j'; C_j$. We create a fresh capability mapping variable φ_p and add the constraint $\varphi_p = \sum_{j=1}^{n} \varphi_j$.

Next, for each ϱ (that is, its equivalence class obtained via the unification in phase 1), we instantiate a linear programming problem using the remaining constraints together with the constraint $\varphi_p = \sum_{i=1}^{n} \varphi_i$. More precisely, each constraint mapping variable φ is instantiated as a linear programming variable $\varphi(\varrho)$, and $0[\varrho' \mapsto 1]$ is replaced by 1 if $\varrho' = \varrho$ and by 0 otherwise. We also add constraints $\varphi(\varrho) \geq 0$ to ensure that each capability mapping is non-negative. The objective function to minimize is $\varphi_p(\varrho)$. For any solution to the set of constraints, $\varphi_p(\varrho)$ is a valid buffer bound on the channel with the handle ϱ, and so minimizing $\varphi_p(\varrho)$ gives us the best possible buffer bound for the analysis.

We state the correctness of the analysis algorithm. We use the symbol η to denote a *constraint solution*, which is a sorted substitution mapping type variables to types, channel handle variables to channel handles, and capability mapping variables to capability mappings. A constraint solution becomes a mapping from σ, Δ, and ϕ in the obvious way (we let $\eta(0[\varrho \mapsto 1]) = 0[\eta(\varrho) \mapsto 1]$).

Definition 3. *We write $\eta \models C$ ("η solves C") if*

- *for each $\sigma = \sigma' \in C$, $\eta(\sigma) = \eta(\sigma')$.*
- *for each $\phi \leq \phi' \in C$, $\eta(\phi) \leq \eta(\phi')$.*

Lemma 1

- *If $\Delta \vdash e : \alpha; C$ and $\eta \models C$, then $\eta(\Delta) \vdash e : \eta(\alpha)$.*
- *If $\Delta, \varphi \vdash s : \varphi'; C$ and $\eta \models C$, then $\eta(\Delta), \eta(\varphi) \vdash s : \eta(\varphi)$.*

Proof By induction on the type derivation.

Theorem 2 (Soundness). *Let $p = i_1.s_1 \mid\mid \ldots \mid\mid i_n.s_n$. Suppose*

$$\eta \models \{\varphi_p = \sum_{j=1}^{n} \varphi_j\} \cup \bigcup_{j=1}^{n} C_j$$

where $\Delta, \varphi_j \vdash s_j : \varphi'_j; C_j$ for each s_j. Let $P = (B, S, p)$ such that B is an empty buffer (i.e., $B(c) = \emptyset$ for all channels c) and S is a store such that $\eta(\Delta) \vdash S(i_j)$ for each i_j, then the buffer bound of c in P is within $\eta(\varphi_p)(\rho)$, where $\rho = hdl(\eta(\Delta)(c))$.

Proof. Straightforward from Lemma 1 and Theorem 1.

We have implemented a prototype of the analysis algorithm, available at http://research.cs.berkeley.edu/project/cccd-impl.

5.3 Analysis of the Algorithm

Linear programming is one of the most well studied problems in computer science. Algorithms with both good theoretical complexity and practical running times are known. The instance of linear programming problem in phase 2 can be solved in time polynomial in the size of the constraints by algorithms such as interior points methods.

Therefore, the complexity of the algorithm is bound by the time phase 1 takes to generate the capability constraints, which is polynomial for our simple concurrent language. In general, the complexity will increase if we include more complex programming constructs such as data structures and functions if we stick with the simple types. But this can be avoided by incorporating sum types and recursive types [4].

5.4 Example

We demonstrate the algorithm on the running example.

$$\begin{array}{l}1.\texttt{while i} < \texttt{m do } (\texttt{bar?(x)}; \texttt{foo!(1)}; \texttt{foo!(i)}; \texttt{i := i + x}) \parallel \\ 2.\texttt{while j} < \texttt{n do } (\texttt{bar!(j)}; \texttt{foo?(y)}; \texttt{foo?(z)}; \texttt{j := j + y + z})\end{array}$$

Suppose that the following environment Δ was inferred in the first phase.

$$\begin{array}{l}\Delta(\texttt{i}) = \Delta(\texttt{j}) = \Delta(\texttt{m}) = \Delta(\texttt{n}) = int \\ \Delta(\texttt{x}) = \Delta(\texttt{y}) = \Delta(\texttt{z}) = int \\ \Delta(\texttt{foo}) = ch(\varrho_{foo}, int, \varphi_{foo}) \\ \Delta(\texttt{bar}) = ch(\varrho_{bar}, int, \varphi_{bar})\end{array}$$

The capability constraints generated from analyzing process 1 are as follows (after some simplification).

$$\begin{array}{l}\varphi_{entr1} \leq \varphi_{exit1} \\ \varphi_{temp11} = \varphi_{entr1} + \varphi_{bar} + 0[\varrho_{bar} \mapsto 1] \\ \varphi_{temp12} = \varphi_{temp11} - \varphi_{foo} - 0[\varrho_{foo} \mapsto 1] \\ \varphi_{exit1} = \varphi_{temp12} - \varphi_{foo} - 0[\varrho_{foo} \mapsto 1]\end{array}$$

Here, φ_{entr1} is the capabilities at the while loop entry, φ_{exit1} is the capabilities at the loop exit, φ_{temp11} is the capabilities after the read `bar?(x)`, and φ_{temp12} is the capabilities after the write `foo!(1)`. The capability constraints generated from analyzing process 2 are as follows (after some simplification).

$$\begin{array}{l}\varphi_{entr2} \leq \varphi_{exit2} \\ \varphi_{temp21} = \varphi_{entr2} - \varphi_{bar} - 0[\varrho_{bar} \mapsto 1] \\ \varphi_{temp22} = \varphi_{temp21} + \varphi_{foo} + 0[\varrho_{foo} \mapsto 1] \\ \varphi_{exit2} = \varphi_{temp22} + \varphi_{foo} + 0[\varrho_{foo} \mapsto 1]\end{array}$$

Here, φ_{entr2} is the capabilities at the while loop entry, φ_{exit2} is the capabilities at the loop exit, φ_{temp21} is the capabilities after `bar!(j)`, and φ_{temp22} is the capabilities after `foo?(y)`.

The capabilities to minimize is $\varphi_p = \varphi_{entr1} + \varphi_{entr2}$, or more precisely, $\varphi_p(\varrho_{foo})$ and $\varphi_p(\varrho_{bar})$. For $\varphi_p(\varrho_{bar})$, this reduces to solving the following linear programming instance.

$$\text{minimize } entr_1 + entr_2$$

$$\begin{array}{ll}exit_1 \geq entr_1 & exit_2 \geq entr_2 \\ temp_{11} = entr_1 + bar + 1 & temp_{21} = entr_2 - bar - 1 \\ temp_{12} = temp_{11} - foo & temp_{22} = temp_{21} + foo \\ exit_1 = temp_{12} - foo & exit_2 = temp_{22} + foo\end{array}$$

We also add the constraint $a \geq 0$ for each linear programming variable a appearing above. The minimum solution is attained at

$$\{entr_1 = 0, entr_2 = 1, bar = 0, foo = 0.5,\\ temp_{11} = 1, temp_{12} = 0.5, exit_1 = 0,\\ exit_2 = 1, temp_{21} = 0, temp_{22} = 0.5\}$$

This gives us the bound $entr_1 + entr_2 = 1$. Similarly, solving for the minimum $\varphi_p(\varrho_{foo})$ gives us the bound 2 for `foo`.

6 Limitations

Our analysis cannot infer a finite buffer bound for channels written in a (reachable) loop whose capabilities cannot be "balanced" at the loop exit. Consider the following program.

$$1.\mathtt{i} := 0; \mathtt{while}\ \mathtt{i} < 3\ \mathtt{do}\ (\mathtt{c!}(0); \mathtt{i} := \mathtt{i} + 1)$$

Clearly, the buffer bound for the channel `c` is 3. But note that the **WHILE** rule in Figure 4 requires the capabilities at the end of the loop to be greater than that of the start, and this is not possible for this loop due to `c!`(0). This manifests in the analysis as ∞ returned as the bound (that is, there exists no finite solution to the linear programming instance). This implies that any loop that makes an "unbalanced send" must be unrolled prior to the analysis. This is actually an instance of the analysis's insensitivity to branch conditions. The issue just becomes most pronounced for loops.

Also, because of its simple flow&path-insensitive unification-based nature, our analysis may equate different channels when channels are used as values (e.g., stored in variables and passed as messages). This leads to different channels sharing the same buffer in the analysis. For example, analyzing the program below, the analysis equates the channels `c` and `d`, and thus infers the bound 2 for both `c` and `d` even though the ideal bound is 1.

$$1.\mathtt{x} := \mathtt{c}; \mathtt{x} := \mathtt{d} \;||\; 2.\mathtt{c!}(0) \;||\; 3.\mathtt{d!}(0)$$

Hence, the analysis may need to be coupled with a more powerful alias analysis to analyze programs that extensively use channels as values.

7 Related Work

Closely related work is Kobayashi et al.'s type and effect system [3] for inferring the upper bound on the number of pending inputs and outputs on rendezvous channels. There are several differences from our work with theirs. One is that their system relies more on the syntactic structure of the program to determine who is responsible to send and receive capabilities (viewing their effect constraints as capability sends and receives). For instance, if there are multiple reads in a succession then the last read is responsible for receiving all the necessary capabilities. In contrast, our analysis allows more freedom on who can send and receive capabilities, and lets linear programming choose the optimal amount of capabilities to send and receive. For example, in the program below, the optimum buffer space for the channel c is 1, which our analysis is able to infer.

$$1.\texttt{c!}(0) \mid\mid 2.\texttt{b?}(\texttt{x}); \texttt{a?}(\texttt{x}); \texttt{c!}(1) \mid\mid 3.\texttt{c?}(\texttt{y}); \texttt{b!}(0) \mid\mid 4.\texttt{a!}(0)$$

But because c!(1) is preceded immediately by a?(x), Kobayashi et al.'s system infers the bound 2 instead. Another difference is the use of fractions (i.e., rational arithmetic) that allows our system to have a polynomial time type inference via linear programming. Also, some programs (e.g., the running example) require fractions to infer the optimal buffer bound.

The main technique used in our analysis, passing of fractional capabilities, was used for the purpose of checking determinism of concurrent programs [6]. Fractional capabilities were invented for the purpose of allowing concurrent reads of reference cells [1,5], and capability calculus was originally proposed for reasoning about resources in sequential programs [2]. In previous applications of fractional capabilities, linear programming was used only to find a satisfying solution to a set of linear inequality constraints, whereas our work makes use of the objective function to find the minimum solution.

8 Conclusions

We have presented a static analysis for inferring the buffer bound of concurrent programs communicating via buffered channels. We have cast the analysis as a capability calculus with fractional capabilities where capabilities can be passed at channel communication point. Our analysis reduces the problem to linear programming and runs in time polynomial in the size of the program.

References

1. Boyland, J.: Checking interference with fractional permissions. In: Static Analysis, Tenth International Symposium, San Diego, CA, June 2003, pp. 55–72 (2003)
2. Crary, K., Walker, D., Morrisett, G.: Typed memory management in a calculus of capabilities. In: Proceedings of the 26th Annual ACM SIGPLAN-SIGACT Symposium on Principles of Programming Languages, January 1999, pp. 262–275. San Antonio, Texas (1999)
3. Kobayashi, N., Nakade, M., Yonezawa, A.: Static analysis of communication for asynchronous concurrent programming languages. In: Static Analysis, Second International Symposium, Glasgow, Scotland, September 1995, pp. 225–242 (1995)
4. Steensgaard, B.: Points-to analysis in almost linear time. In: Proceedings of the 23rd Annual ACM SIGPLAN-SIGACT Symposium on Principles of Programming Languages, January 1996, pp. 32–41. St. Petersburg Beach, Florida (1996)
5. Terauchi, T., Aiken, A.: Witnessing side-effects. In: 10th ACM SIGPLAN International Conference on Functional Programming, Tallinn, Estonia, September 2005, pp. 105–115 (2005)

6. Terauchi, T., Aiken, A.: A Capability Calculus for Concurrency and Determinism. In: Baier, C., Hermanns, H. (eds.) CONCUR 2006. LNCS, vol. 4137, pp. 218–232. Springer, Heidelberg (2006)

A Proof of Theorem 1

Lemma 2. *Suppose* $\Gamma \vdash e : \tau$, $\Gamma \vdash h$, *and* $(h, e) \Downarrow v$. *Then* $\Gamma \vdash v : \tau$.

Proof. By induction on the type derivation.

Lemma 3. *Suppose* $\Gamma, \Psi_1, \ldots, \Psi_n, \Psi_B \vdash (B, S, p_1)$ *and* $(B, S, p_1) \rightarrow (B', S', p_2)$. *Then there exist* $\Psi'_1, \ldots, \Psi'_n, \Psi'_B$ *such that*

(a) $\Gamma, \Psi'_1, \ldots, \Psi'_n, \Psi'_B \vdash (B', S', p_2)$
(b) Let $\Psi_p = \Psi_B + \sum_{j=1}^n \Psi_j$ *and* $\Psi'_p = \Psi'_B + \sum_{j=1}^n \Psi'_j$. *Then, for each channel* c, $\Psi'_p(\rho) + \sum_{c' \in HC_{B'}(\rho, \Gamma)} |B'(c')| \leq \Psi_p(\rho) + \sum_{c' \in HC_B(\rho,\Gamma)} |B(c')|$ *where* $\rho = \mathit{hdl}(\Gamma(c))$.

Proof. The proof is by case analysis on $(B, S, p_1) \rightarrow (B', S', p_2)$. We just show the key cases. First, note that (b) can be restated so that the statement is "for each ρ, ..." instead of "for each c, ... where $\rho = \mathit{hdl}(\Gamma(c))$." We use this form as it is more convenient.

Consider the case $(B, S, p_1) \rightarrow (B', S', p_2)$ is an instance of **Write**, that is,

$$\frac{(S(i_j), e_1) \Downarrow c \qquad (S(i_j), e_2) \Downarrow v \qquad B' = B.\mathit{write}(c, v)}{(B, S, i_j.e_1\,!(e_2); s \mid\mid p) \rightarrow (B', S, i_j.s \mid\mid p)}$$

Without loss of generality, let $j = 1$. We have

$$\frac{\Gamma \vdash e_1 : \mathit{ch}(\rho, \tau, \Psi') \qquad \Gamma \vdash e_2 : \tau}{\Gamma, \Psi_1 \vdash e_1\,!(e_2) : \Psi_1 - \Psi' - \mathit{0}[\rho \mapsto 1]}$$

Let $\Psi'_1 = \Psi_1 - \Psi' - \mathit{0}[\rho \mapsto 1]$. Let $\Psi'_j = \Psi_j$ for $j \neq 1$. Let $\Psi'_B = \sum_{c \in \mathit{dom}(B')} |B'(c)| \times \mathit{writeSend}(\Gamma(c))$. Then we have $\Gamma, \Psi'_1, \ldots, \Psi'_n, \Psi'_B \vdash (B', S, i_j.s \mid\mid p)$. Thus (a) holds.

By Lemma 2, $\mathit{hdl}(\Gamma(c)) = \rho$. Let $\Psi'_p = \Psi'_B + \sum_{j=1}^n \Psi'_j$ and $\Psi_p = \Psi_B + \sum_{j=1}^n \Psi_j$. Clearly, for $\rho' \neq \rho$,

$$\Psi'_p(\rho') + \sum_{c' \in HC_{B'}(\rho', \Gamma)} |B'(c')| = \Psi_p(\rho') + \sum_{c' \in HC_B(\rho', \Gamma)} |B(c')|$$

Also, because $\Psi'_B + \Psi'_1 = \Psi_B + \Psi_1 - \mathit{0}[\rho \mapsto 1]$ and $|B'(c)| = |B(c)| + 1$,

$$\Psi'_p(\rho) + \sum_{c' \in HC_{B'}(\rho, \Gamma)} |B'(c')| = \Psi_p(\rho) + \sum_{c' \in HC_B(\rho, \Gamma)} |B(c')|$$

Thus (b) holds.

Consider the case $(B, S, p_1) \to (B', S', p_2)$ is an instance of **Read**, that is,

$$\frac{(S(i_j), e) \Downarrow c \qquad (B', v) = B.\mathit{read}(c) \qquad S' = S[i_j \mapsto S(i_j)[x \mapsto v]]}{(B, S, i_j.e?(x); s \parallel p) \to (B', S', i_j.s \parallel p)}$$

Without loss of generality, let $j = 1$. We have

$$\frac{\Gamma \vdash e : \mathit{ch}(\rho, \Gamma(x), \Psi')}{\Gamma, \Psi_1 \vdash e?(x) : \Psi_1 + \Psi' + 0[\rho \mapsto 1]}$$

Let $\Psi'_1 = \Psi_1 + \Psi' + 0[\rho \mapsto 1]$. Let $\Psi'_j = \Psi_j$ for $j \neq 1$. Let $\Psi'_B = \sum_{c \in \mathit{dom}(B')} |B'(c)| \times \mathit{writeSend}(\Gamma(c))$. Then we have $\Gamma, \Psi'_1, \ldots, \Psi'_n, \Psi'_B \vdash (B', S', i_j.s \parallel p)$. Thus (a) holds.

By Lemma 2, $\mathit{hdl}(\Gamma(c)) = \rho$. Let $\Psi'_p = \Psi'_B + \sum_{j=1}^{n} \Psi'_j$ and $\Psi_p = \Psi_B + \sum_{j=1}^{n} \Psi_j$. Clearly, for $\rho' \neq \rho$,

$$\Psi'_p(\rho') + \sum_{c' \in HC_{B'}(\rho', \Gamma)} |B'(c')| = \Psi_p(\rho') + \sum_{c' \in HC_B(\rho', \Gamma)} |B(c')|$$

Also, because $\Psi'_B + \Psi'_1 = \Psi_B + \Psi_1 + 0[\rho \mapsto 1]$ and $|B'(c)| = |B(c)| - 1$,

$$\Psi'_p(\rho) + \sum_{c' \in HC_{B'}(\rho, \Gamma)} |B'(c')| = \Psi_p(\rho) + \sum_{c' \in HC_B(\rho, \Gamma)} |B(c')|$$

Thus (b) holds.

Theorem 1. *Suppose* $\Gamma, \Psi_1, \ldots, \Psi_n, \Psi_B \vdash (B, S, p)$. *Suppose* $\mathit{hdl}(\Gamma(c)) = \rho$. *Let* $\Psi_p = \Psi_B + \sum_{j=1}^{n} \Psi_j$. *Then the buffer bound of* c *in* (B, S, p) *is within* $\Psi_p(\rho) + \sum_{c' \in HC_B(\rho, \Gamma)} |B(c')|$.

Proof. Straightforward from Lemma 3.

Verification of Higher-Order Computation: A Game-Semantic Approach

C.-H.L. Ong

Oxford University Computing Laboratory
users.comlab.ox.ac.uk/luke.ong/

Abstract. We survey recent developments in an approach to the verification of higher-order computation based on game semantics. Higher-order recursion schemes are in essence (programs of) the simply-typed lambda calculus with recursion, generated from uninterpreted first-order symbols. They are a highly expressive definitional device for infinite structures such as word languages and infinite ranked trees. As applications of a representation theory of innocent strategies based on *traversals*, we present a recent advance in the model checking of trees generated by recursion schemes, and the first machine characterization of recursion schemes (by a new variant class of higher-order pushdown automata called *collapsible pushdown automata*). We conclude with some speculative remarks about reachability checking of functional programs. A theme of the work is the fruitful interplay of ideas between the neighbouring fields of semantics and verification.

Game semantics has emerged as a powerful paradigm for giving semantics to a variety of programming languages and logical systems. It has been used to construct the first syntax-independent fully abstract models for a spectrum of programming languages ranging from purely functional languages to languages with non-functional features such as control operators and locally-scoped references [3,26,4,5,25,2,30] etc. In this extended abstract, we present in brief recent developments in *algorithmic game semantics*, which is concerned with applying game semantics to computer-assisted verification and program analysis [22,19,36,33,34].

Game semantics has several features which make it very promising for such applications. It provides a very *concrete* way of building *fully abstract* models. It has a clear operational content, which admits *compositional methods* in the style of denotational semantics. The basic objects studied in game semantics are games (between two players, called P and O), and strategies on games. As strategies can be seen as certain kinds of highly-constrained processes, they admit the same kind of automata-theoretic representations central to model checking and allied methods in computer-assisted verification [43,14]. Moreover games and strategies naturally form themselves into intricate mathematical structures that give very accurate models of advanced high-level programming languages, as the various full abstraction results show. For an introduction to game semantics, see for example [6].

S. Drossopoulou (Ed.): ESOP 2008, LNCS 4960, pp. 299–306, 2008.

Traversal: A Representation Theory of Innocent Strategies

In game semantics, programs are modelled as P-strategies. Strategies, which are certain sets of *plays* (or *legal positions*), are typically composed by *parallel composition plus hiding*, in the sense of the process algebra CSP [24]. The starting point of our work is a *representation theory* of the game semantics of higher-type programs (such as recursion schemes, PCF and Idealized Algol) that is very concrete, involving combinatorics over infinite structures defined by the abstract syntax trees of the programs being modelled. Take a program M which may be open. In this approach the strategy-denotation of M, written $[\![M]\!]$, is represented by a set $\mathcal{T}r(M)$ of *traversals* over a possibly infinite tree – called the *computation tree* of M – which is generated from (a souped up version of) the abstract syntax tree of M. (Formally a traversal over a tree is a sequence of nodes starting from the root; quite unlike a path in the tree, a traversal can "jump" all over the tree, and may visit certain nodes infinitely often.) A traversal over the computation tree of M does not correspond to a play in $[\![M]\!]$, but rather to an *interaction sequence* that is obtained by *uncovering* [26] a play in $[\![M]\!]$ in a hereditary fashion; and a suitable projection of $\mathcal{T}r(M)$ – corresponding to the operation of hiding – gives the strategy-denotation $[\![M]\!]$. We call such a result a *Path-Traversal Correspondence Theorem.* (Denoting programs by sets of interaction sequences obtained by hereditary uncovering was first considered by Greenland in his DPhil thesis [20], which he has called *revealed semantics.*) The set $\mathcal{T}r(M)$ is defined by recursion over the syntax of M and by rule induction. Intuitively these formation rules define what amounts to the composition algorithm of innocent strategies (less the hiding) but expressed in a setting in which moves (of the innocent game) are mapped to nodes of the computation tree. In [12] (see also Blum's forthcoming DPhil thesis [10]) we give a self-contained account of the traversal-based representation theory and establish Path-Traversal Correspondence Theorems for a number of higher-order languages including recursion schemes and PCF.

In the following we consider (higher-order) recursion schemes as a definitional device for infinite structures (mainly ranked trees, but also word languages and directed graphs). We sketch two applications of a Path-Correspondence Theorem for recursion schemes: the first concerns the verification of (possibly infinite) ranked trees generated by recursion schemes, and the second is a machine characterization of recursion schemes.

Recursion schemes of order 1, originally known as *recursive program schemes*, were first formalized and studied in the early 70's [17,35] (although the basic ideas of program schemes and fixpoint theory go further back to David Park in the late 60's); they were an influential formalism for the semantical analysis of both imperative and functional programs [35,15]. We fix a (ranked) alphabet Σ. *Types* are generated from a base type o using the arrow constructor $\rightarrow$. A (higher-order) *recursion scheme* is a finite set of equations of the form $F\, x_1 \cdots x_n = e$, where $F : A_1 \rightarrow \cdots \rightarrow A_n \rightarrow o$ is a typed non-terminal, each $x_i : A_i$ is a typed variable, and e is an applicative term of type o constructed from the non-terminals (which include a distinguished *start symbol*), terminals (which are the Σ-symbols), and variables $x_1, \cdots, x_n$. The scheme is said to be *order-k* if the highest order of the non-terminals is k. We use (deterministic) recursion schemes here as generators of possibly infinite term-trees. The *tree* generated by a recursion scheme is defined to be the (possibly infinite) term-tree built up from the first-order terminal symbols by applying the (equations *qua*) rewrite rules *ad infinitum*, replacing the formal parameters by the actual parameters, starting from the start symbol. Note that in essence, recursion schemes are programs of the *simply-typed lambda calculus with recursion* (generated from uninterpreted 1st-order symbols).

Model-Checking Trees Generated by Recursion Schemes

In a FOSSACS'02 paper [28], Knapik, Niwiński and Urzyczyn studied the infinite hierarchy of term-trees generated by higher-order recursion schemes that are *homogeneously typed* and satisfy a syntactic constraint called *safety*[1]. They showed that for every $n \geq 0$, the trees that are generated by order-n safe schemes have decidable monadic second-order (MSO) theories. Later in the year at MFCS'02 [13], Caucal introduced a tree hierarchy and a graph hierarchy that are defined by mutual recursion, using a pair of powerful transformations that preserve decidability of MSO theories. Caucal's tree hierarchy coincides with the hierarchy of trees generated by higher-order safe recursion schemes. In [28] Knapik *et al.* asked if the safety assumption is really necessary for their MSO decidability result. A partial answer was subsequently obtained by Aehlig, de Miranda and Ong; in a TLCA'05 paper [7], they showed that trees that are generated by order-2 recursion schemes, whether safe or not, have decidable MSO theories. Independently, Knapik, Niwiński, Urzyczyn and Walukiewicz obtained a sharper result: in an ICALP'05 paper [29], they proved that the modal mu-calculus model-checking problem for trees generated by order-2 recursion schemes (whether safe or not) is 2-EXPTIME complete. A year later in a LICS'06 paper [37], we gave a complete answer to the question:

Theorem 1 (Decidability). *The modal mu-calculus model-checking problem for trees generated by order-n recursion schemes (whether safe or not, and whether homogeneously typed or not) is n-EXPTIME complete, for every $n \geq 0$. Thus these trees have decidable MSO theories.*

Our approach to the decidability result is to transfer the algorithmic analysis from the tree generated by a recursion scheme, which we call *value tree*, to the *computation tree*, which is itself a tree generated by a related order-0 recursion scheme (equivalently, a regular tree). The computation tree recovers useful intensional information about the computational process behind the construction of the value tree. Paths in the value tree correspond exactly to plays in the game

[1] The *safety condition* may be presented as a set of rules that determine where a variable may occur as a subterm of a term, depending on both the order of the variable and the order of the term (see [11,10]).

semantics of the recursion scheme; a traversal is then (a representation of) the *uncovering* of such a play. By appealing to the Path-Traversal Correspondence Theorem, we prove that a given alternating parity tree automaton (APT) [18] has an accepting run-tree over the value tree if and only if it has an accepting *traversal-tree* over the computation tree. Our problem is then reduced to finding an effective way of recognizing a set of infinite traversals (over a given computation tree) that satisfy the parity condition. This requires a new idea as a traversal is most unlike a path. Our solution again exploits the game-semantic connection. It is a property of traversals that their *P-views* are paths (in the computation tree). This allows us to simulate a traversal over a computation tree by (the P-views of its prefixes, which are) annotated paths of a certain kind in the same tree. The simulation is made precise in the notion of *traversal-simulating* APT. We establish the correctness of the simulation by proving that a given *property*[2] APT has an accepting traversal-tree over the computation tree if and only if the associated *traversal-simulating* APT has an accepting run-tree over the computation tree. Note that the decidability of the modal mu-calculus model-checking problem for trees generated by recursion schemes follows at once since computation trees are regular, and the APT acceptance problem for regular trees is decidable [40,18].

A Machine Characterization of Higher-Order Recursion Schemes

Another application of the Path-Traversal Correspondence Theorem concerns a fundamental question about higher-order recursion schemes: *Can we characterize their expressivity by a class of machine models?* Knapik, Niwiński and Urzyczyn [28] have shown that as generators of ranked trees, higher-order *safe* recursion schemes are equi-expressive with *higher-order pushdown automata* [31]. Their result and an earlier result by Damm and Goerdt [16] may be viewed as attempts to answer the question; they both had to impose somewhat unnatural syntactic constraints (of safety and derived types respectively) on recursion schemes in order to establish their characterizations.

A partial answer was recently obtained by Knapik, Niwiński, Urzyczyn and Walukiewicz. In an ICALP'05 paper [29], they proved that order-2 homogeneously-typed (but not necessarily safe) recursion schemes are equi-expressive with a variant class of order-2 pushdown automata called *panic automata*. In a preprint [21], we give a complete answer to the question. We introduce a new kind of higher-order pushdown automata (which generalize *pushdown automata with links* [8], or equivalently panic automata, to all finite orders), called *collapsible pushdown automata* (CPDA), in which every symbol in the stack has a link to a (necessarily lower-ordered) stack situated somewhere below it. In addition to the higher-order stack operations $push_i$ and pop_i, CPDA have an important operation called *collapse*, whose effect is to "collapse" a stack s to the prefix as indicated by the link from the top_1-symbol of s. In [21] we prove the following result:

[2] *Property* APT because the APT corresponds to the property described by a given modal mu-calculus formula.

Theorem 2 (Equi-Expressivity). *CPDA are equi-expressive with* recursion schemes *as generators of (possibly infinite) ranked trees.*

In one direction, we give a simple algorithm that transforms an order-n CPDA to an order-n recursion scheme that generates the same tree, uniformly for all $n \geq 0$. In the other direction, using ideas from game semantics, we give an effective transformation of order-n recursion schemes (not assumed to be *homogeneously typed*, and hence not necessarily *safe*) to order-n CPDA that compute *traversals* over the computation tree of the scheme, and hence paths in the tree generated by the scheme. Our equi-expressivity result is the first automata-theoretic characterization of higher-order recursion schemes. Thus CPDA are also a characterization of the *simply-typed lambda calculus with recursion* (generated from uninterpreted 1st-order symbols) and of (pure) *innocent strategies*.

Verifying PCF Programs: Reachability Checking

As a further direction (and a possible application of path-traversal correspondence), we consider the problem of reachability checking of higher-order computation. In the simplest form, reachability is the problem: Given a state of a transition system, is it reachable from the start state? Reachability is arguably the most important test in the computer-assisted verification of computing systems. Reachability (in its various forms) is expressible in standard temporal logics such as EF, LTL, CTL, etc., but it is typically computationally more tractable than the model checking of any of these logics (e.g. for pushdown systems, reachability is polytime [1], whereas EF-, LTL- and CTL-model checking are respectively PSPACE-complete, EXPTIME-complete and EXPTIME-complete [27]). In recent years, reachability checkers (such as SLAM [9], Blast [23], etc.) for first-order imperative programs have had a major impact in the verification community. Perhaps because of its simplicity and ease of use, reachability is now a standard approach to checking safety properties in the industry. It is therefore somewhat surprising that no reachability checker has been developed for higher-order programming languages such as Ocaml, Haskell and $F\#$. Indeed, to our knowledge, reachability of higher-order computation does not appear to have been studied in the literature.

The simplest (though already challenging) setting is PCF (generated from finite base types). We propose the following decision problem:

> PCF-Reachability: *Given a (possibly open) PCF term M and a subterm N of M, is there a program context $C[\,]$ such that the evaluation of $C[M]$ entails the evaluation of N? (Precisely, is there a program context $C[\,]$ such that $C[M] \longrightarrow^* E[N]$ for some evaluation context $E[\,]$?)*

For which fragment of PCF is the problem decidable? If there are positive answers, it would be interesting to consider the "global version" of the problem i.e. is it possible to compute a finite description of the set of contexts $C[\,]$ for a given pair of M and N?

An approach that seems promising is to appeal to the Path-Traversal Theorem for PCF [10], and consider traversals over the computation tree of M. The idea is to use appropriate alternating tree automata to "guess" a set of paths in the computation tree simulating traversals that witness yes-instances of the problem (see [37]). If this works out, it would be interesting to present the algorithm in terms that functional programmers can readily understand and appreciate.

Remark 1. (i) It is not clear if there is any connection between reachability (in our sense) and control flow analysis (e.g. [42]) of functional programs. In the past couple of years there have been several interesting developments in the verification and flow analysis of functional language. Xu and Peyton Jones have studied contract checking in Haskell (see Xu's forthcoming PhD thesis). A recent project of Shivers *et al.* [32] used abstract interpretation (specifically *abstract counting*) to build more precise flow analysers by garbage collecting "dead" environment structure in the abstract state space traversed by the functional programs.

(ii) When restricted to *finitary* (i.e. recursion-free) PCF, the problem is related to the atoms case of the Interpolation Problem, which is decidable [38]. (The Interpolation Problem is equivalent to the Higher-Order Matching Problem [41,39].)

References

1. Bouajjani, A., Esparza, J., Maler, O.: Reachability analysis of pushdown automata: Application to model-checking. In: International Conference on Concurrency Theory, pp. 135–150 (1997)
2. Abramsky, S., Honda, K., McCusker, G.: Fully abstract game semantics for general reference. In: Proceedings of IEEE Symposium on Logic in Computer Science, 1998, Computer Society Press (1998)
3. Abramsky, S., Jagadeesan, R., Malacaria, P.: Full abstraction for PCF. Information and Computation 163 (2000)
4. Abramsky, S., McCusker, G.: Linearity, sharing and state: A fully abstract game semantics for Idealized Algol with active expressions. In: O'Hearn, P.W., Tennent, R.D. (eds.) Algol-like languages, Birkhäuser (1997)
5. Abramsky, S., McCusker, G.: Call-by-value games. In: Nielsen, M. (ed.) CSL 1997. LNCS, vol. 1414, Springer, Heidelberg (1998)
6. Abramsky, S., McCusker, G.: Game semantics. In: Schwichtenberg, H., Berger, U. (eds.) Logic and Computation: Proceedings of the 1997 Marktoberdorf Summer School, Springer, Heidelberg (1998)
7. Aehlig, K., de Miranda, J.G., Ong, C.-H.L.: The monadic second order theory of trees given by arbitrary level two recursion schemes is decidable. In: Urzyczyn, P. (ed.) TLCA 2005. LNCS, vol. 3461, pp. 39–54. Springer, Heidelberg (2005)
8. Aehlig, K., de Miranda, J.G., Ong, C.-H.L.: Safety is not a restriction at level 2 for string languages. In: Proceedings of the 8th International Conference on Foundations of Software Science and Computational Structures (FOSSACS 2005). LNCS, vol. 3411, pp. 490–501. Springer, Heidelberg (2005)
9. Ball, T., Rajamani, S.K.: The SLAM Project: Debugging system software via static analysis. In: Proc. POPL, pp. 1–3. ACM Press, New York (2002)

10. Blum, W.: The Safe Lambda Calculus. PhD thesis, University of Oxford (in preparation, 2008)
11. Blum, W., Ong, C.-H.L.: Safe lambda calculus. In: Della Rocca, S.R. (ed.) TLCA 2007. LNCS, vol. 4583, pp. 39–53. Springer, Heidelberg (2007)
12. Blum, W., Ong, C.-H.L.: Path-correspondence theorems and their applications (preprint, 2008)
13. Caucal, D.: On Infinite Terms Having a Decidable Monadic Theory. In: Diks, K., Rytter, W. (eds.) MFCS 2002. LNCS, vol. 2420, pp. 165–176. Springer, Heidelberg (2002)
14. Clarke, E.M., Grumberg, O., Peled, D.: Model Checking. MIT Press, Cambridge (1999)
15. Damm, W.: The IO- and OI-hierarchy. Theoretical Computer Science 20, 95–207 (1982)
16. Damm, W., Goerdt, A.: An automata-theoretical characterization of the OI-hierarchy. Information and Control 71, 1–32 (1986)
17. de Roever, W.-P., de Bakker, J.W.: A calculus for recursive program schemes. In: Nivat, M. (ed.) Proc. IRIA symposium on Automata, Languages and Programming, North-Holland, Amsterdam (1972)
18. Emerson, E.A., Jutla, C.S.: Tree automata, mu-calculus and determinacy. In: Proceedings of FOCS 1991, pp. 368–377 (1991)
19. Ghica, D.R., McCusker, G.: Reasoning about Idealized ALGOL Using Regular Languages. In: Welzl, E., Montanari, U., Rolim, J.D.P. (eds.) ICALP 2000. LNCS, vol. 1853, pp. 103–116. Springer, Heidelberg (2000)
20. Greenland, W.: Game semantics for region analysis. PhD thesis, Oxford University Computing Laboratory (2005)
21. Hague, M., Murawski, A.S., Ong, C.-H.L., Serre, O.: Collapsible pushdown automata and recursion schemes. Technical report, Oxford University Computing Laboratory, p. 59 (preprint, 2007), `http://users.comlab.ox.ac.uk/luke.ong/`
22. Hankin, C., Malacaria, P.: A new approach to control flow analysis. In: Koskimies, K. (ed.) CC 1998. LNCS, vol. 1383, pp. 95–108. Springer, Heidelberg (1998)
23. Henzinger, T.A., Jhala, R., Majumdar, R., Sutre, G.: Software verification with BLAST. In: Proc. 10th SPIN Workshop (2003)
24. Hoare, C.A.R.: Communicating Sequential Processes. Prentice-Hall, Englewood Cliffs (1985)
25. Honda, K., Yoshida, N.: Game-theoretic analysis of call-by-value computation (extended abstract). In: Degano, P., Gorrieri, R., Marchetti-Spaccamela, A. (eds.) ICALP 1997. LNCS, vol. 1256, Springer, Heidelberg (1997)
26. Hyland, J.M.E., Ong, C.-H.L.: On Full Abstraction for PCF: I. Models, observables and the full abstraction problem, II. Dialogue games and innocent strategies, III. A fully abstract and universal game model. Information and Computation 163, 285–408 (2000)
27. Walukiewicz, I.: Model Checking CTL Properties of Pushdown Systems. In: Kapoor, S., Prasad, S. (eds.) FST TCS 2000. LNCS, vol. 1974, Springer, Heidelberg (2000)
28. Knapik, T., Niwiński, D., Urzyczyn, P.: Higher-Order Pushdown Trees Are Easy. In: Nielsen, M., Engberg, U. (eds.) ETAPS 2002. LNCS, vol. 2303, pp. 205–222. Springer, Heidelberg (2002)
29. Knapik, T., Niwiński, D., Urzyczyn, P., Walukiewicz, I.: Unsafe Grammars and Panic Automata. In: Caires, L., Italiano, G.F., Monteiro, L., Palamidessi, C., Yung, M. (eds.) ICALP 2005. LNCS, vol. 3580, pp. 1450–1461. Springer, Heidelberg (2005)

30. Laird, J.: A semantic analysis of control. PhD thesis, University of Edinburgh (1998)
31. Maslov, A.N.: Multilevel stack automata. Problems of Information Transmission 12, 38–43 (1976)
32. Might, M., Chambers, B., Shivers, O.: Model Checking Via ΓCFA. In: Cook, B., Podelski, A. (eds.) VMCAI 2007. LNCS, vol. 4349, pp. 59–73. Springer, Heidelberg (2007)
33. Murawski, A., Walukiewicz, I.: Third-Order Idealized Algol with Iteration Is Decidable. In: Sassone, V. (ed.) FOSSACS 2005. LNCS, vol. 3441, pp. 202–218. Springer, Heidelberg (2005)
34. Murawski, A.S., Ong, C.-H.L., Walukiewicz, I.: Idealized Algol with ground recursion and DPDA equivalence. In: Caires, L., Italiano, G.F., Monteiro, L., Palamidessi, C., Yung, M. (eds.) ICALP 2005. LNCS, vol. 3580, pp. 917–929. Springer, Heidelberg (2005)
35. Nivat, M.: On the interpretation of recursive polyadic program schemes. Symp. Math. XV, 255–281 (1975)
36. Ong, C.-H.L.: Observational equivalence of third-order Idealized Algol is decidable. In: Proceedings of IEEE Symposium on Logic in Computer Science, Copenhagen, Denmark, July 22-25, 2002, pp. 245–256. Computer Society Press (2002)
37. Ong, C.-H.L.: On model-checking trees generated by higher-order recursion schemes. In: Proceedings 21st Annual IEEE Symposium on Logic in Computer Science, Seattle, pp. 81–90. Computer Society Press (2006), `users.comlab.ox.ac.uk/luke.ong/`
38. Padovani, V.: Decidability of all minimal models. In: Berardi, S., Coppo, M. (eds.) TYPES 1995. LNCS, vol. 1158, pp. 201–215. Springer, Heidelberg (1996)
39. Padovani, V.: Decidability of fourth-order matching. Math. Struct. in Comp. Science 10, 361–372 (2000)
40. Rabin, M.O.: Decidability of second-order theories and automata on infinite trees. Trans. Amer. Maths. Soc. 141, 1–35 (1969)
41. Schubert, A.: A linear interpolation for the higher-order matching problem. In: Bidoit, M., Dauchet, M. (eds.) CAAP 1997, FASE 1997, and TAPSOFT 1997. LNCS, vol. 1214, pp. 441–452. Springer, Heidelberg (1997)
42. Shivers, O.: Control-flow analysis of higher-order languages. PhD thesis, Carnegie-Mellon University (1991)
43. Vardi, M., Wolper, P.: An automata-theoretic approach to automatic program verification. In: Proc. IEEE Annual Symposium on Logic in Computer Science, IEEE Computer Society Press (1986)

Verification of Equivalent-Results Methods

K. Rustan M. Leino and Peter Müller

Microsoft Research, Redmond, WA, USA
{leino,mueller}@microsoft.com

Abstract. Methods that query the state of a data structure often return identical or equivalent values as long as the data structure does not change. Program verification depends on this fact, but it has been difficult to specify and verify such equivalent-results methods and their callers.

This paper presents an encoding from which one can determine equivalent-results methods to be deterministic modulo a user-defined equivalence relation. It also presents a technique for checking that a query method returns equivalent results and enforcing that the result depends only on a user-defined influence set.

The technique is general, for example it supports user-defined equivalence relations based on *Equals* methods and it supports query methods that return newly allocated objects. The paper also discusses the implementation of the technique in the context of the Spec# static program verifier.

Introduction

Computer programs contain many methods that query the state of a data structure and return a value based on that state. As long as the data structure remains unchanged, one expects different invocations of the query method to produce equivalent return values. For methods returning scalar values, the return values are expected to be the same. For methods returning object references, the most interesting equivalences are reference equality and equivalence based on the *Equals* method.

A simple and common example of a query method is the *Count* method of a collection class, like *List* in Fig. 0, where for a given collection the method returns the number of elements stored in the collection. Obviously, one expects *Count* to return identical values when called twice on the same collection. Another example is shown in the *Calendar* class in Fig. 2, where invocations of the *GetEarliestAppointment* will yield equivalent results as long as the state of the calendar does not change. However, since *GetEarliestAppointment* returns a newly allocated object, the results will not be identical. Due to object-allocation, query methods cannot be expected to be deterministic. Nevertheless, their results are expected to be equivalent. Therefore, we shall refer to such query methods as *equivalent-results methods*.

Query methods (also called *pure methods*) are particularly important in assertion languages such as JML [16] or Spec# [2] because they allow assertions to be expressed in an abstract, implementation-independent way. For instance, *Count* is used in the precondition of *GetItem* (Fig. 0) to refer to the number of elements in the list without revealing any implementation details. However, reasoning about assertions that contain query methods is difficult. The client program in Fig. 1 illustrates the problem. It uses a

S. Drossopoulou (Ed.): ESOP 2008, LNCS 4960, pp. 307–321, 2008.

```
class List ⟨T⟩ {
  int Count()
    ensures 0 ⩽ result;
  { ... }

  T GetItem(int n)
    requires 0 ⩽ n < Count();
  { ... }
  ⋮
}
```

Fig. 0. A *List* class whose *Count* method returns the number of elements in a given list and whose *GetItem* method returns a requested element of the list. The postcondition of *Count* promises the return value to be non-negative, and the precondition of *GetItem* requires parameter n to be less than the value returned by *Count*.

```
List ⟨T⟩ list;
⋮
if (n < list.Count()) {
  S  // some statement that changes the state, but not the list
  t = list.GetItem(n);
}
```

Fig. 1. A code fragment that uses the *List* class from Fig. 0. The if statement guards the invocation of *GetItem* to ensure that *GetItem* 's precondition is met. To verify the correctness of this code, one needs to be able to determine that the two invocations of *Count* return the same value.

conditional statement to establish the precondition of *GetItem*. We assume that statement S does not change the list structure. Therefore, we expect that the condition still holds when *GetItem* is called, that is, that the two calls to *Count* yield the same result. There are essentially three approaches for a program verifier to conclude this fact.

The first approach is to require that the postcondition of the query method is strong enough for a caller to determine exactly what value is returned. Typically, this can be achieved by having a postcondition of the form $result = E$. In our example, this postcondition would allow the verifier to compare the state affected by S to the state read by E to determine whether the two calls to *Count* return the same result. However, requiring such strong postconditions may entail a dramatic increase in the complexity of the specification. For *Count*, one would have to axiomatize mathematical lists and use that mathematical abstraction in the specification of the *List* class. We consider this burden too high, in particular for the verification of rather simple properties.

The second approach is to define the return value of the method to be a function of the program state. If the program state has not changed by the time the method is invoked again, this approach allows one to conclude the return value is the same as before. But this approach is too brittle, for two reasons. First, it treats state changes too coarsely. For example, statement S in Fig. 1 may change the program state, but as long as it does not change the state of the list, we want to be able to conclude that the result

```
class Appointment {
  int time;
  // ... more fields here

  pure override bool Equals(object o)
    ensures GetType() = typeof(Appointment) ⇒
        (result ⟺
            o ≠ null ∧ GetType() = o.GetType() ∧
            time = ((Appointment)o).time ∧ ... more comparisons here);
  { ... }
}

class Calendar {
  pure Appointment GetEarliestAppointment(int day) {
    Appointment a;
    // find earliest appointment on day day
    ...
    return a.Clone();
  }

  void ScheduleMorningMeeting(int day, List⟨Person⟩ invitees)
    requires 10 ⩽ GetEarliestAppointment(day).time;
  { ... }
}

class Person {
  void Invite(Calendar c, ...) {
    if (10 ⩽ c.GetEarliestAppointment(5).time) {
      // compute invitees
      List⟨Person⟩ invitees = new List⟨Person⟩();
      while (...) {
        ...
        invitees.Add(p);
      }
      // schedule those invitees
      c.ScheduleMorningMeeting(5, invitees);
    }
  }
}
```

Fig. 2. A *Calendar* program whose *GetEarliestAppointment* method returns an equivalent value as long as the calendar does not change. The correctness of the code fragment at the bottom of the figure depends on that the call to *GetEarliestAppointment* in the precondition of *ScheduleMorningMeeting* returns a value that is equivalent to the one returned by the call to *GetEarliestAppointment* in the guard of the if statement.

of *Count* is unchanged. Second, this approach is too precise about the return value. For example, the object references returned by two calls to *GetEarliestAppointment* in Fig. 2 are not identical, yet the data they reference are equivalent. Queries that return newly allocated objects are very common, especially in JML's model classes [17].

The third approach is to require that all query methods used in specifications are equivalent-results methods whose results depend only on certain heap locations. We call this set of locations the *influence set* of a query method. With this approach, the code in Fig. 1 can be verified by showing that the locations modified by S are not in the influence set of $Count$. From the equivalent-results property and the fact that $Count$ returns an integer, we can conclude that the two calls to $Count$ yield the same results.

Existing program verifiers such as the Spec# static program verifier Boogie [1] and ESC/Java2 [15] apply the third approach. However, these systems do not enforce that query methods actually are equivalent-results methods and that their result actually depends only on the declared influence set. Blindly assuming these two properties is unsound. Checking the properties is not trivial, even for methods that return scalar values. For instance, $GetHashCode$ is an equivalent-results method and should be permitted in assertions, but returning the hash code of a newly allocated object leads to non-determinism and must be prevented.

In this paper, we present a simple technique to check that a query method is an equivalent-results method and that its result depends only on its parameters and the declared influence set. This technique supports user-defined equivalence relations based on, for instance, $Equals$ methods. We use self-composition [3,21] to simulate two executions of the method body from start states that coincide in the influence set and to prove that the respective results are indeed equivalent. We also present axioms that enable reasoning about equivalent-results methods and argue why they are sound. Our technique is very general: it supports user-defined equivalence relations, it does not require a particular way of specifying influence sets, and it uses a relaxed notion of purity. In particular, implementations of query methods may use non-deterministic language features and algorithms, and may return newly allocated objects. We plan to implement our technique for pure methods in Boogie, but our results do not rely on the specifics of Spec#. Therefore, they can be adopted by other program verifiers.

Outline. Section 1 provides the background on program verification that is needed in the rest of this paper. Section 2 presents an encoding of equivalent-results methods that enables the kind of reasoning discussed above. Section 3 explains our technique for checking the equivalence of results. Section 4 discusses the application of our technique to Spec#. The remaining sections summarize related work and offer conclusions.

1 Background on Program Verification

In this section, we review details of program verification relevant to our paper. For a more comprehensive and tutorial account of this material, we refer to some recent Marktoberdorf lecture notes [20].

Architecture of Program Verifiers. To verify a program, the program's proof obligations (*e.g.*, that preconditions are met) are encoded as logical formulas called *verification conditions*. The verification conditions are valid formulas if and only if the program is correct with respect to the properties being verified. Each verification condition is fed

```
class C {
  int y;
  int M(int x)
    requires 0 ⩽ x;
    modifies this.y;
    ensures result + x ⩽ this.y;
  { ... }
```

Fig. 3. An example class in the source language, showing an instance field y and a method M with a method specification

to a theorem prover, such as an SMT solver or an interactive proof assistant, which attempts to ascertain the validity of the formula or construct counterexample contexts that may reveal errors in the source program. As has been noted by several state-of-the-art verifiers, it is convenient to generate verification conditions in two steps: first encode the source program in an intermediate verification language, and then generate input for the theorem prover from the intermediate language [1,12,5]. Since the second step concerns issues that are orthogonal to our focus in this paper, we look only at the first step. The notation we will use for the intermediate verification language is BoogiePL [1,11]. A BoogiePL program consists of a first-order logic theory, which in particular specifies the heap model of the source language, and an encoding of the source program. We explain these two parts in the following subsections.

Heap Model. We model the heap as a two-dimensional array that maps object identities and field names to values [24], so a field selection expression $o.f$ is modeled as $\$Heap[o,f]$. By making the heap explicit, we correctly handle object aliases, as is well known [4,24]. In the encoding, we use a boolean field $\$alloc$ in each object to model whether or not the object has been allocated. The subtype relation is denoted by $<:$.

For any set S of locations (that is, of object-field pairs), we define a relation $\equiv_S$ that relates two heaps if they have the same values for all locations in S. More precisely:

$$(\forall H, K, S \bullet (H \equiv_S K \iff (\forall o, f \bullet (o,f) \in S \Rightarrow H[o,f] = K[o,f])))$$

Note that $\equiv_S$ is an equivalence relation: it is reflexive, symmetric, and transitive. If $H \equiv_S K$, we say that H and K are *equivalent modulo* S.

We assume that pure methods do not modify the state of any object that is allocated in the pre-state of the method execution. This definition allows a pure method to allocate and modify new objects such as iterators [25]. More precisely, if $H0$ and $H1$ denote the heaps immediately before and after the call to a pure method, and S is a set of locations of objects that are allocated in $H0$, the following property holds:

$$H0 \equiv_S H1 \qquad (0)$$

Encoding of Source Programs. Each source-language method is encoded as a procedure in the intermediate verification language. To understand the basic encoding, consider a method M in a class C with a field y, shown in Fig. 3.

The specification of M has a precondition that obligates the callers of M to pass a non-negative argument value. In turn, the precondition lets the implementation of M

$$
\begin{array}{l}
\textbf{procedure } C.M(\mathit{this},\ x) \textbf{ returns } (\mathit{result});\\
\quad \textbf{requires } \mathit{this} \neq \textbf{null};\\
\quad \textbf{free requires } \$\mathit{Heap}[\mathit{this}, \$\mathit{alloc}] \land \$\mathit{typeof}(\mathit{this}) <: C;\\
\quad \textbf{ensures } \mathit{result} + x \leqslant \$\mathit{Heap}[\mathit{this}, C.y];\\
\quad \textbf{ensures } (\forall\, o, f \bullet\ o \neq \mathit{this} \land \textbf{old}(\$\mathit{Heap})[o, \$\mathit{alloc}] \Rightarrow\\
\qquad\qquad \$\mathit{Heap}[o, f] = \textbf{old}(\$\mathit{Heap})[o, f] \lor (o = \mathit{this} \land f = y)\ );\\
\quad \textbf{free ensures } (\forall\, o \bullet\ \textbf{old}(\$\mathit{Heap})[o, \$\mathit{alloc}] \Rightarrow \$\mathit{Heap}[o, \$\mathit{alloc}]\ );
\end{array}
$$

Fig. 4. A BoogiePL procedure declaration that encodes the signature and specification of the example method $C.M$

assume x to be non-negative on entry. The specification also has a modifies clause and a postcondition that obligate the implementation to make sure that its return value, parameter x, and the y field of the method's receiver object are related as specified, and to modify only $\mathtt{this}.y$. A caller can assume these properties upon return of a call.

A representative encoding of M as a BoogiePL procedure is shown in Fig. 4. The procedure declaration makes the implicit receiver parameter $\mathtt{this}$ explicit, and the anonymous return value is encoded as a named out-parameter. The types in BoogiePL are more coarse-grained than those in the source language, and for the purposes of this paper, they are only a distraction, so we omit them altogether. Three things are worth noting about the procedure specification.

First, method M's pre- and postconditions have direct analogs in the BoogiePL procedure, where the implicit dereferencing of the heap in a field selection expression is made explicit in the BoogiePL encoding.

Second, the method's modifies clause is encoded as a BoogiePL postcondition that dictates which locations in the heap are allowed to change. The latter says that for any non-null object o allocated on entry to the method and for any field f, the heap at location $o.f$ is unchanged except possibly at location $\mathtt{this}.y$.

Third, to verify a program, one often needs to know some properties that are guaranteed by the source language. For example, the static type of the receiver parameter of method M is C and the source-language type checker thus guarantees that the allocated type of the receiver is some subtype of C. The source language also guarantees that all object references in use by a program are allocated and (thanks to the fiction created by the garbage collector) remain allocated forever. To incorporate these guaranteed conditions in the encoding, BoogiePL conveniently offers *free pre- and postconditions* as part of a procedure declaration. Free preconditions are assumed on entry to a procedure implementation, but not checked at call sites, and analogously for free postconditions.

Proof Obligations and Soundness. Proving the correctness of a BoogiePL program amounts to statically verifying that the program does not abort due to a violated assertion (such as a precondition or postcondition). To do that, each assertion is turned into a proof obligation. One can then use an appropriate program logic to show that the assertions hold. For the proof, one may assume the conditions expressed as free preconditions, free postconditions, and explicit **assume** statements. The verification is sound if all of these assumptions actually hold.

2 Encoding of Equivalent-Results Methods

Our idea is to define an equivalence class of return values for each equivalent-results method. We define the equivalence class via a programmer-defined *similarity relation*. Typical choices for the similarity relation are reference equality and the *Equals* method. Rather than letting the similarity relation be the equivalence relation, we define the equivalence class to be those values that are related by the similarity relation to a particular element, called the *anchor element*. This has the advantage that the similarity relation need not be symmetric and transitive, which in practice the *Equals* method often is not [26]. Another advantage is that using an anchor element allows us to state axioms that are handled more efficiently by the theorem prover.

In this section, we explain similarity relations, anchor elements, and the influence sets that define the dependencies of method results.

Similarity Relations. For a method M, we let $\mathcal{R}_M(H, r, H', r')$ denote M's similarity relation, relating r whose state is evaluated in heap H and r' whose state is evaluated in heap H'. For example, if $\mathcal{R}_M$ denotes equality of scalar values or reference equality for object values, we have:

$$\mathcal{R}_M(H, r, H', r') \iff r = r' \tag{1}$$

and if $\mathcal{R}_M$ uses the *Equals* method, we have:

$$\mathcal{R}_M(H, r, H', r') \iff @\mathit{Equals}(H, r, H', r') \tag{2}$$

where $@\mathit{Equals}$ is a function automatically generated from the specification of *Equals*. Value r is always a return value of the method; r' is either a return value, in which case $H = H'$ or the anchor element, in which case H' is a special heap $\mathit{AnchorHeap}_M(p)$ where we evaluate anchor elements. The similarity relation defines an equivalence class of values that are related to the anchor element.

For the *Appointment.Equals* method in Fig. 2, the following axiom is automatically generated for function $@\mathit{Equals}$:

$$\begin{array}{l}(\forall\, H, \mathit{this}, K, o \bullet \\ \quad \mathit{this} \neq \mathbf{null} \wedge \$\mathit{typeof}(\mathit{this}) <: \mathit{Appointment} \wedge \$\mathit{typeof}(o) <: \mathit{Object} \Rightarrow \\ \qquad (@\mathit{Equals}(H, \mathit{this}, K, o) \iff \\ \qquad\quad o \neq \mathbf{null} \wedge \$\mathit{typeof}(\mathit{this}) = \$\mathit{typeof}(o) \wedge \\ \qquad\quad H[\mathit{this}, \mathit{time}] = K[o, \mathit{time}] \wedge \ldots \text{more comparisons here}))\end{array} \tag{3}$$

where, here and throughout, quantifications over H and K range over well-formed heaps. It is not the subject of our paper to describe how axioms for pure methods are described, but see our previous work with Ádám Darvas [10,9]; the difference is that here we use one heap argument for each of the two parameters to *Equals*.

Influence Sets. The influence set is a set of locations in the heap. Let $\mathcal{F}_M(H, p)$ denote the influence set of M as computed for parameters p in a heap H. Note that the computation of the influence set may depend on the heap. For example, consider a class *Schedule* with an *Appointment* field a. Suppose the influence set for some method applied to a schedule s is given by the set of path expressions $\{s.a,\ s.a.time\}$. Viewed in the intermediate-language notation, these path expressions denote the following object-field pairs: (s, a), $(\$Heap[s, a], time)$.

We require every influence set to be *self-protecting* [14], which means that any two heaps equivalent modulo the influence set compute the influence set the same way:

$$(\forall H, K, p \bullet\ H \equiv_{\mathcal{F}_M(H,p)} K \ \Rightarrow\ \mathcal{F}_M(H,p) = \mathcal{F}_M(K,p)\ ) \quad (4)$$

Self-protection can be enforced by requiring the set of path expressions that specify the influence set to be prefix closed: if it contains a path expression $E.x.y$, then it must also contain the path expression $E.x$. Therefore, the expression $E.x.y$ denotes the same location in heaps H and K.

The influence set specifies which parts of the program state are allowed to influence the return value. To a first order of approximation, the influence set is the *read set* or *read effect* of the method [6], but, technically, we actually allow methods to read any part of the state, as long as the values of things outside the influence set have no bearing on the return value.

Anchor Elements. The encoding of equivalent-results methods has to allow us to prove that two calls to an equivalent-results method M return equivalent results if the two heaps before the calls are equivalent modulo the influence set of M. We reach this conclusion in two steps. First, we encode by an axiom that the anchor element remains the same as long as the program state indicated by the influence set does not change. Second, we encode by a free postcondition that the actual return value of M is related to the anchor element by the similarity relation. Hence, the results of the two calls to M are in the same equivalence class.

Step A: In our intermediate-language encoding, we introduce a function $Anchor_M$ that yields an anchor element for the equivalence class of the return values of M. We axiomatize $Anchor_M$ as follows:

$$(\forall p, H, K \bullet\ H \equiv_{\mathcal{F}_M(H,p)} K \ \Rightarrow\ Anchor_M(H,p) = Anchor_M(K,p)\ ) \quad (5)$$

The axiom says that we pick the same anchor element whenever M is invoked with the same arguments p in two heaps H and K that are equivalent modulo $\mathcal{F}_M(H,p)$. In other words, the anchor element is a function of the program state projected onto the influence set.

Step B: We add to our encoding the following free postcondition:

$$\textbf{free ensures}\ \mathcal{R}_M(\$Heap, result, AnchorHeap_M(p), Anchor_M(\$Heap, p)); \quad (6)$$

To make sure the anchor object always denotes the same equivalence class, we evaluate its state in a special, constant heap $AnchorHeap_M$. We postpone until Section 3 how to justify this free postcondition.

```
H0 := $Heap;
call r := GetEarliestAppointment(c, 5);
H1 := $Heap;
if (10 ⩽ $Heap[r, time]) {
  // code to compute invitees ...
  K0 := $Heap;
  call r' := GetEarliestAppointment(c, 5);
  K1 := $Heap;
  assert 10 ⩽ $Heap[r', time];
  ...
}
```

Fig. 5. A sketch of the code fragment from the bottom of Fig. 2, giving the names $H0$, $H1$, $K0$, and $K1$ to the intermediate values of the heap, and giving the names r and r' to the return values of the two calls to *GetEarliestAppointment*. The assert statement at the end shows the condition that we want to prove.

Example. To prove the correctness of method *Invite* in Fig. 2, it suffices to show that the two invocations of *GetEarliestAppointment* return equivalent values. Recall, the second invocation takes place during the evaluation of the precondition of *ScheduleMorningMeeting*. Fig. 5 shows a BoogiePL encoding of that fragment. As illustrated by the assert statement in Fig. 5, we wish to prove that $H1[r, \mathit{time}]$ equals $K1[r', \mathit{time}]$.

The influence set of *GetEarliestAppointment* contains the fields that make up the representation of the *Calendar* object. Let $H0$ and $H1$ denote the heaps immediately before and after the first call to *GetEarliestAppointment*, and let $K0$ and $K1$ denote the heaps immediately before and after the second call.

Since *GetEarliestAppointment* is pure, it does not change the values of any previously allocated locations (see condition (0)), so $H0$ and $H1$ are equivalent modulo $\mathcal{F}(H0, c, 5)$, and $K0$ and $K1$ are equivalent modulo $\mathcal{F}(K0, c, 5)$ (we drop the subscript *GetEarliestAppointment* in this example). Assuming that the code that computes *invitees* has no effect on the values of the locations in the influence set, we also have that $H1$ and $K0$ are equivalent modulo $\mathcal{F}(H1, c, 5)$. By self-protection (4), we know that the three influence sets are equal. Thus, we can conclude by transitivity:

$$H1 \equiv_{\mathcal{F}(H1,c,5)} K1 \tag{7}$$

By axiom (5) and equation (7), we conclude that the anchor elements for the two calls are the same:

$$\mathit{Anchor}(H1, c, 5) = \mathit{Anchor}(K1, c, 5) \tag{8}$$

Now let r and r' denote (as indicated in Fig. 5) the values returned by the two calls to *GetEarliestAppointment*. The similarity relation is given by the *Equals* method. Thus, we conclude from postcondition (6):

$$@\mathit{Equals}(H1,\ r,\ \mathit{AnchorHeap}(c, 5), \mathit{Anchor}(H1, c, 5)) \quad \text{and}$$
$$@\mathit{Equals}(K1,\ r',\ \mathit{AnchorHeap}(c, 5), \mathit{Anchor}(K1, c, 5))$$

$$
\begin{array}{l}
\textbf{procedure } M(p) \textbf{ returns } (\mathit{result}) \\
\quad \textbf{requires } \mathcal{P}(\$\mathit{Heap}, p); \\
\quad \textbf{free requires } \mathcal{Q}(\$\mathit{Heap}, p); \\
\quad \textbf{ensures } \mathcal{S}(\textbf{old}(\$\mathit{Heap}), \$\mathit{Heap}, p, \mathit{result}); \\
\quad \textbf{free ensures } \mathcal{T}(\textbf{old}(\$\mathit{Heap}), \$\mathit{Heap}, p, \mathit{result}); \\
\quad \textbf{free ensures } \mathcal{R}_M(\$\mathit{Heap}, \mathit{result}, \mathit{AnchorHeap}_M(p), \mathit{Anchor}_M(\$\mathit{Heap}, p)); \\
\{ \\
\quad \textbf{var } \mathit{locals}; \\
\quad \mathit{Body} \\
\}
\end{array}
$$

Fig. 6. A procedure in the intermediate verification language, illustrating the general form of the procedure into which the method translates

By axiom (3) and property (8), we have

$$
\begin{array}{l}
H1[r, \mathit{time}] = \mathit{AnchorHeap}(c, 5)[\mathit{Anchor}(H1, c, 5), \mathit{time}] \ \wedge \\
K1[r', \mathit{time}] = \mathit{AnchorHeap}(c, 5)[\mathit{Anchor}(H1, c, 5), \mathit{time}]
\end{array}
$$

from which we conclude $H1[r, \mathit{time}] = K1[r', \mathit{time}]$, as required to establish the precondition of the call to $\mathit{ScheduleMorningMeeting}$.

3 Verifying Equivalence of Results

As we mentioned in Section 1, soundness of a verification system comes down to justifying every assumption that the proof system allows a proof to make use of. In the previous section, we introduced three conditions that we used as assumptions in the proof. The first assumption is the axiom of self-protection (4). It can be justified by a syntactic check on the path expressions used to define the influence set. The second assumption is the axiom about Anchor_M (5). It is justified on the basis that there exists a function Anchor_M that satisfies the axiom, for example any constant function. The third assumption is the free postcondition (6). In this section, we present a proof technique based on self-composition that justifies this assumption.

Ordinarily, a method M gives rise to a verification condition prescribed by a BoogiePL procedure implementation like procedure M in Fig. 6, where p denotes the in-parameters, $\mathcal{P}$ and $\mathcal{S}$ denote some checked pre- and postconditions, $\mathcal{Q}$ and $\mathcal{T}$ denote some free pre- and postconditions (*cf.* Fig. 4), locals are local variables, and Body is the BoogiePL encoding of the implementation of method M.

For every equivalent-results method M, we will now prescribe a second BoogiePL procedure, whose validity will justify the free postcondition (6). The key idea is to execute the method body twice starting in states that agree on the values of the in-parameters and all objects in the influence set. We then prove that the two executions yield equivalent results. This second procedure has the form shown by M' in Fig. 7 and is described as follows:

- The body of M' starts off with $\$\mathit{Heap}$, locals, and result set to arbitrary values, saves the value of $\$\mathit{Heap}$ in $\$\mathit{oldHeap}$, and assumes the preconditions $\mathcal{P}$ and $\mathcal{Q}$.

```
procedure M'(p) returns (result) {
  var locals;

  var $oldHeap := $Heap;
  assume P($Heap, p) ∧ Q($Heap, p);
  Body'
  assume S($oldHeap, $Heap, p, result) ∧ T($oldHeap, $Heap, p, result);

  assume Anchor_M($Heap, p) = result ∧ AnchorHeap_M(p) = $Heap;    // L0

  havoc $Heap, locals, result;
  assume $Heap ≡_{F_M($oldHeap,p)} $oldHeap;

  $oldHeap := $Heap;
  assume P($Heap, p) ∧ Q($Heap, p);
  Body'
  assume S($oldHeap, $Heap, p, result) ∧ T($oldHeap, $Heap, p, result);

  assert R_M($Heap, result, AnchorHeap_M(p), Anchor_M($Heap, p));    // L1
}
```

Fig. 7. A procedure that checks by assertion (L1) that M satisfies its free postcondition (6)

- It then performs $Body'$, which is $Body$ with occurrences of $\mathbf{old}(\$Heap)$ replaced by $\$oldHeap$ and occurrences of assert statements (*i.e.*, checked conditions) replaced by assume statements. These assume statements are justified by the fact that procedure M already prescribes checks for them, so if the conditions do not hold, the program verifier will generate appropriate errors when attempting to verify M.
- Upon termination of $Body'$, the postconditions $\mathcal{S}$ and $\mathcal{T}$ are assumed. Again, $\mathcal{S}$ can be assumed here because it is checked by M.
- We explain the assume statement (L0) below.
- Next, the code prepares for another execution of $Body'$. The second execution of $Body'$ is to start in a state where all locations of the influence set have the same values as in the first execution. Thus, $\$Heap$, $locals$, and $result$ are set to arbitrary values (using a **havoc** statement) and the value of $\$Heap$ is constrained (using an assume statement) to be equivalent to $\$oldHeap$ modulo the influence set.
- The preconditions are assumed, $Body'$ is executed a second time, and the postconditions are assumed.
- We explain the assert statement (L1) below.

The first half of M' culminates in assume statement (L0), which has the effect of defining $Anchor_M(\$Heap, p)$ and $AnchorHeap_M(p)$ to be the result value and result heap of an arbitrary execution of the method (namely, the first execution of $Body'$). In fact, by axiom (5), (L0) defines $Anchor_M(\$Heap, p)$ for all heaps that are equivalent to $\$Heap$ modulo the influence set. The second half of M' checks that (6) is indeed a postcondition of the method for all those equivalent heaps.

With that, we have justified all the assumptions that our technique introduces, and thus we have established that our technique is sound.

4 Application to Spec#

In verifying Spec# programs, we have run across scores of examples like the one in Fig. 0, where in Spec# the *Count* method tends to be a *property getter*, which is a form of parameter-less method. By default, property getters are treated as pure methods that read only the ownership cone of the receiver object. The *ownership cone* of an object is the set of locations that make up the object's representation [7]. Previously, our best solution for dealing with this situation in the Spec# program verifier was to introduce an axiom that says the return value of the method is a function of the ownership cone. But such an axiom is not sound if a pure method returns newly allocated object or values that are derived from such objects. Our technique in this paper gives a sound solution to the problem, and we intend to implement it. In this section, we describe some issues that pertain to the practical implementation of equivalent-results methods in Spec#.

We intend to restrict the choices for $\mathcal{R}_M$ in Spec# to support only the two choices (1) and (2). This will simplify the implementation while supporting the most common similarity relations. (The only other useful similarity we found puts all non-null references in one equivalence class.) To select between the two choices, we will introduce a default choice and a method annotation (a *custom attribute*) that can override the default.

For the influence set, we will only support the union of the ownership cones for some subset of the parameters. Ownership provides a form of abstraction, allowing one to specify influence sets without being specific about implementation details. There is already a notion of *confined* in Spec# that says that a pure method reads the ownership cone of a parameter. Moreover, the Spec# program verifier already has an encoding that lets one deduce, for *valid* objects, whether or not the ownership cone of the object has changed. The encoding is simply to inspect the object's ghost field *snapshot* [9]. An object is valid when its object invariant holds [19]. Since this is the precondition of almost all methods, we will not attempt to prove ownership cones to be the same other than via the *snapshot* field. Because of the snapshot encoding, we can write axiom (5) as:

$$
\begin{aligned}
(\forall\, p, H, K \bullet\ & H[p, \mathit{valid}] \wedge K[p, \mathit{valid}] \wedge H[p, \mathit{snapshot}] = K[p, \mathit{snapshot}] \\
& \Rightarrow \mathit{Anchor}_M(H, p) = \mathit{Anchor}_M(K, p)\ )
\end{aligned}
$$

(We have abused notation slightly: by $H[p, \mathit{valid}]$ and $H[p, \mathit{snapshot}]$, we really mean to refer to the *valid* and *snapshot* fields of all the parameters in p that contribute to the influence set, and likewise for K.) In fact, there is an alternative way to encode this property that is significantly more efficient for the SMT solver because it avoids quantification over pairs of heaps. The alternative encoding [9] introduces an uninterpreted function A_M and uses it to more directly say that $\mathit{Anchor}_M(H, p)$ is a function of p and $H[p, \mathit{snapshot}]$:

$$
(\forall\, p, H \bullet\ H[p, \mathit{valid}] \ \Rightarrow\ \mathit{Anchor}_M(H, p) = A_M(p, H[p, \mathit{snapshot}])\ )
$$

With the restriction to influence sets based on ownership cones and our focus on reasoning about these via snapshots, axiom (4) becomes trivial, so we omit it.

5 Related Work

The Java Modeling Language (JML) requires pure methods to be deterministic [18]. This requirement is not practical since pure methods often need to return newly allocated objects, which is illustrated by many pure methods in JML's model library [17]. Our notion of equivalent-results methods allows pure methods to return newly allocated objects. Since our axioms are based on a user-defined similarity relation such as an *Equals* method, determinism is not required for soundness.

The axiomatization of pure methods consists of two groups of axioms: method-specific axioms that specify the behavior of each individual method and general axioms that describe common properties of all pure methods. Previous work by Darvas and Müller [10] focuses on the method-specific axioms, but does not discuss the general axioms that we provide in this paper. Their axiomatization is sound, but too weak for many interesting examples. Darvas and Leino [9] present general axioms that are used in the Spec# verifier Boogie. Some of their work assumes that a pure method is deterministic and that its result depends only on a specified influence set, but these assumptions are not checked. Therefore, their axiomatization is unsound for pure methods that return newly allocated objects or whose result depends on locations outside the influence set. Our work eliminates both sources of unsoundness.

Jacobs developed SpecLeuven, a variant of Spec# for multi-threaded programs. In his work [13], *inspector methods* are syntactically enforced to be deterministic, which is sound but overly restrictive. Influence sets are checked by an extension of the Boogie methodology [19], which requires an object to be unpacked before its state is read. Our verification technique based on self-composition does not require any particular methodology.

ESC/Java2 [15,8] also operates under the unchecked assumption that pure methods are deterministic, which is unsound if they are not. Moreover, since JML specifications typically do not declare an influence set, ESC/Java2 has but limited support for reasoning about the effect of a heap modification on the result of a pure method.

The influence sets we use in this paper are similar to read effects. However, read effects constrain the whole execution of a method, whereas our influence sets only constrain the method result. We allow methods to read arbitrary locations as long as the result depends only on the declared influence set. Clarke and Drossopoulou [6] show how to declare and check read effects in an ownership type system. We use self-composition to verify influence sets, which is in general more fine-grained than type checking and does not require a particular ownership scheme.

Self-composition has been applied to prove secure information flow [3,21]. In fact, proving that a method result depends only on a specified influence set can be seen as an instance of secure information flow, where the method result, the method parameters, and the locations in the influence set have a low security level and all other locations have a high security level. In addition to information flow, we use self-composition to prove that two executions of a method yield equivalent results.

Separation logic [22] provides a powerful and elegant way to reason about the effects of heap modifications. The effect of pure methods can be achieved by introducing abstract predicates [23]. The influence set of a pure method corresponds to the footprint of the predicate. The frame rule can be used to show that certain heap modifications do not affect the truth value of the abstract predicate. However, even if pure methods are not used in contracts, the correctness of some programs relies on the equivalent-results property. We believe that our verification technique is also applicable to separation logic in order to verify such programs.

6 Conclusions

In this paper, we introduced the notion of equivalent-results methods and explained their usefulness for program specification: equivalent-results methods are expressive, for instance, they may return newly-allocated objects, and they permit an axiomatization that is sound and strong enough to verify interesting programs. We showed that the equivalent-results property can be checked by an automatic program verifier using self-composition. Our technique is very flexible: it does not require a particular programming methodology, uses a relaxed notion of purity, and even handles non-deterministic language features and algorithms. As future work, we plan to implement our technique in the Spec# verifier Boogie.

Acknowledgments. The idea of using self-composition was inspired by a discussion with Anindya Banerjee. We thank David Naumann and the anonymous reviewers for helpful comments, one of which led to a simplification of Fig. 7.

References

1. Barnett, M., Chang, B.-Y.E., DeLine, R., Jacobs, B., Leino, K.R.M.: Boogie: A Modular Reusable Verifier for Object-Oriented Programs. In: de Boer, F.S., Bonsangue, M.M., Graf, S., de Roever, W.-P. (eds.) FMCO 2005. LNCS, vol. 4111, pp. 364–387. Springer, Heidelberg (2006)
2. Barnett, M., Leino, K.R.M., Schulte, W.: The Spec# Programming System: An Overview. In: Barthe, G., Burdy, L., Huisman, M., Lanet, J.-L., Muntean, T. (eds.) CASSIS 2004. LNCS, vol. 3362, pp. 49–69. Springer, Heidelberg (2005)
3. Barthe, G., D'Argenio, P.R., Rezk, T.: Secure information flow by self-composition. In: Computer Security Foundations (CSFW), pp. 100–114. IEEE Computer Society Press, Los Alamitos (2004)
4. Burstall, R.M.: Some techniques for proving correctness of programs which alter data structures. Machine Intelligence 7, 23–50 (1972)
5. Chatterjee, S., Lahiri, S.K., Qadeer, S., Rakamarić, Z.: A Reachability Predicate for Analyzing Low-Level Software. In: Grumberg, O., Huth, M. (eds.) TACAS 2007. LNCS, vol. 4424, pp. 19–33. Springer, Heidelberg (2007)
6. Clarke, D.G., Drossopoulou, S.: Ownership, encapsulation and the disjointness of type and effect. In: OOPSLA. SIGPLAN Notices, vol. 37(11), pp. 292–310. ACM Press, New York (2002)
7. Clarke, D.G., Potter, J.M., Noble, J.: Ownership types for flexible alias protection. In: OOPSLA. SIGPLAN Notices, vol. 33(10), pp. 48–64. ACM Press, New York (1998)
8. Cok, D.: Reasoning with specifications containing method calls and model fields. Journal of Object Technology 4(8), 77–103 (2005)

9. Darvas, Á., Leino, K.R.M.: Practical Reasoning About Invocations and Implementations of Pure Methods. In: Dwyer, M.B., Lopes, A. (eds.) FASE 2007. LNCS, vol. 4422, pp. 336–351. Springer, Heidelberg (2007)
10. Darvas, Á., Müller, P.: Reasoning about method calls in interface specifications. Journal of Object Technology 5(5), 59–85 (2006)
11. DeLine, R., Leino, K.R.M.: BoogiePL: A typed procedural language for checking object-oriented programs. Technical Report MSR-TR-2005-70, Microsoft Research (March 2005)
12. Filliâtre, J.-C.: Why: a multi-language multi-prover verification tool. Research Report 1366, LRI, Université Paris Sud (March 2003)
13. Jacobs, B.: A Statically Verifiable Programming Model for Concurrent Object-Oriented Programs. PhD thesis, Katholieke Universiteit Leuven (2007)
14. Kassios, I.T.: Dynamic Frames: Support for Framing, Dependencies and Sharing Without Restrictions. In: Misra, J., Nipkow, T., Sekerinski, E. (eds.) FM 2006. LNCS, vol. 4085, pp. 268–283. Springer, Heidelberg (2006)
15. Kiniry, J.R., Cok, D.R.: ESC/Java2: Uniting ESC/Java and JML. In: Barthe, G., Burdy, L., Huisman, M., Lanet, J.-L., Muntean, T. (eds.) CASSIS 2004. LNCS, vol. 3362, pp. 108–128. Springer, Heidelberg (2005)
16. Leavens, G.T., Baker, A.L., Ruby, C.: JML: A notation for detailed design. In: Behavioral Specifications of Businesses and Systems, pp. 175–188. Kluwer Academic Publishers, Dordrecht (1999)
17. Leavens, G.T., Cheon, Y., Clifton, C., Ruby, C., Cok, D.R.: How the design of JML accommodates both runtime assertion checking and formal verification. Science of Computer Programming 55(1–3), 185–208 (2005)
18. Leavens, G.T., Poll, E., Clifton, C., Cheon, Y., Ruby, C., Cok, D., Müller, P., Kiniry, J.: JML reference manual. Dept. Comp. Sci., Iowa State University (2007), `http://www.jmlspecs.org`
19. Leino, K.R.M., Müller, P.: Object Invariants in Dynamic Contexts. In: Odersky, M. (ed.) ECOOP 2004. LNCS, vol. 3086, pp. 491–516. Springer, Heidelberg (2004)
20. Leino, K.R.M., Schulte, W.: A verifying compiler for a multi-threaded object-oriented language. In: 2006 Marktoberdorf Summer School on Programming Methodology, Springer, Heidelberg (to appear, 2007), `research.microsoft.com/~leino/papers.html`
21. Naumann, D.A.: From Coupling Relations to Mated Invariants for Checking Information Flow. In: Gollmann, D., Meier, J., Sabelfeld, A. (eds.) ESORICS 2006. LNCS, vol. 4189, pp. 279–296. Springer, Heidelberg (2006)
22. O'Hearn, P.W., Yang, H., Reynolds, J.C.: Separation and information hiding. In: POPL, pp. 268–280 (2004)
23. Parkinson, M.J., Bierman, G.M.: Separation logic and abstraction. In: POPL, pp. 247–258. ACM Press, New York (2005)
24. Poetzsch-Heffter, A., Müller, P.: Logical foundations for typed object-oriented languages. In: Programming Concepts and Methods (PROCOMET), pp. 404–423 (1998)
25. Salcianu, A., Rinard, M.: Purity and Side Effect Analysis for Java Programs. In: Cousot, R. (ed.) VMCAI 2005. LNCS, vol. 3385, pp. 199–215. Springer, Heidelberg (2005)
26. Stevenson, D.E., Phillips, A.T.: Implementing object equivalence in Java using the template method design pattern. SIGCSE Bulletin 35(1), 278–282 (2003)

Semi-persistent Data Structures

Sylvain Conchon and Jean-Christophe Filliâtre

LRI, Univ Paris-Sud, CNRS, Orsay F-91405
INRIA Futurs, ProVal, Orsay, F-91893

Abstract. A data structure is said to be *persistent* when any update operation returns a new structure without altering the old version. This paper introduces a new notion of persistence, called *semi-persistence*, where only ancestors of the most recent version can be accessed or updated. Making a data structure semi-persistent may improve its time and space complexity. This is of particular interest in backtracking algorithms manipulating persistent data structures, where this property is usually satisfied. We propose a proof system to statically check the valid use of semi-persistent data structures. It requires a few annotations from the user and then generates proof obligations that are automatically discharged by a dedicated decision procedure.

1 Introduction

A data structure is said to be *persistent* when any update operation returns a new structure without altering the old version. In purely applicative programming, data structures are automatically persistent [16]. Yet this notion is more general and the exact meaning of persistent is *observationally immutable.* Driscoll et al. even proposed systematic techniques to make imperative data structures persistent [9]. In particular, they distinguish *partial* persistence, where all versions can be accessed but only the newest can be updated, from *full* persistence where any version can be accessed or updated. In this paper, we study another notion of persistence, which we call *semi-persistence.*

One of the main interests of a persistent data structure shows up when it is used within a *backtracking* algorithm. Indeed, when we are back from a branch, there is no need to undo the modifications performed on the data structure: we simply use the old version, which persisted, and start a new branch. One can immediately notice that full persistence is not needed in this case, since we are reusing *ancestors* of the current version, but never *siblings* (in the sense of another version obtained from a common ancestor). We shall call *semi-persistent* a data structure where only ancestors of the newest version can be updated. Note that this notion is different from partial persistence, since we need to update ancestors, and not only to access them.

A semi-persistent data structure can be more efficient than its fully persistent counterpart, both in time and space. An algorithm using a semi-persistent data structure may be written as if it was operating on a fully persistent data structure, *provided that we only backtrack to ancestor versions.* Checking the

S. Drossopoulou (Ed.): ESOP 2008, LNCS 4960, pp. 322–336, 2008.

correctness of a program involving a semi-persistent data structure amounts to showing that

– first, the data structure is *correctly used*;
– second, the data structure is *correctly implemented*.

This article only addresses the former point. Regarding the latter, we simply give examples of semi-persistent data structures. Proving the correctness of these implementations is out of the scope of this paper (see Section 5).

Our approach consists in annotating programs with user pre- and postconditions, which mainly amounts to expressing the validity of the successive versions of a semi-persistent data structure. By validity, we mean being an ancestor of the newest version. Then we compute a set of proof obligations which express the correctness of programs using a weakest precondition-like calculus [8]. These obligations lie in a decidable logical fragment, for which we provide a sound and complete decision procedure. Thus we end up with an almost automatic way of checking the legal use of semi-persistent data structures.

Related work. To our knowledge, this notion of semi-persistence is new. However, there are several domains which are somehow connected to our work, either because they are related to some kind of stack analysis, or because they provide a decision procedure for reachability issues. First, works on escape analysis [12,4] address the problem of stack-allocating values; we may think that semi-persistent versions that become invalid are precisely those which could be stack-allocated, but it is not the case (as illustrated in Section 3.5). Second, works on stack analysis to ensure memory safety [14,18,19] provide methods to check the consistent use of push and pop operations. However, these approaches are not precise enough to distinguish between two sibling versions (of a given semi-persistent data structure). Regarding the decidability of our proof obligations, our approach is similar to other works regarding reachability in linked data structures [15,3,17]. However, our logic is much simpler and we provide a specific decision procedure. Finally, we can mention Knuth's *dancing links* [13] as an example of a data structure specifically designed for backtracking algorithms; but it is still a traditional imperative solution where an explicit undo operation is performed in the main algorithm.

This paper is organized as follows. First, Section 2 gives examples of semi-persistent data structures and shows the benefits of semi-persistence with some benchmarks. Then our formalization of semi-persistence is presented in two steps: Section 3 introduces a small programming language to manipulate semi-persistent data structures, and Section 4 defines the proof system which checks the valid use of semi-persistent data structures. Section 5 concludes with possible extensions. A long version of this paper, including proofs, is available online [7].

2 Examples of Semi-persistent Data Structures

We explain how to implement semi-persistent arrays, lists and hash tables and we present benchmarks to show the benefits of semi-persistence.

Arrays. Semi-persistent arrays can be implemented by modifying the persistent arrays introduced by Baker [1]. The basic idea is to use an imperative array for the newest version of the persistent array and indirections for old versions. For instance, starting with an array a_0 initialized with all zeros, and performing the successive updates $a_1 = \mathtt{set}(a_0, 1, 7)$, $a_2 = \mathtt{set}(a_1, 2, 8)$ and $a_3 = \mathtt{set}(a_2, 5, 3)$, we end up with the following situation:

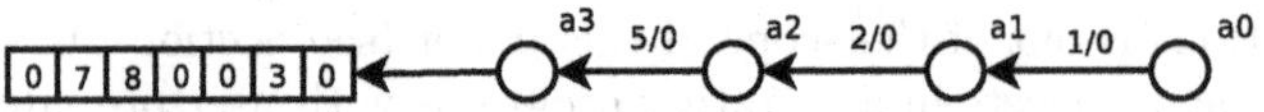

When accessing or updating an old version, e.g. a_1, Baker's solution is to first perform a *rerooting* operation, which makes a_1 point to the imperative array by reversing the linked list of indirections:

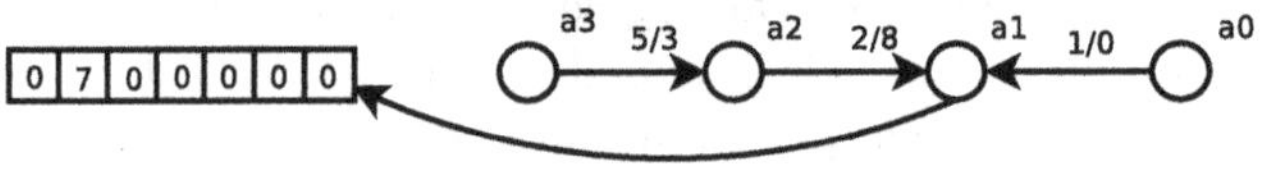

But if we know that we are not going to access a_2 and a_3 anymore, we can save this list reversal. All we need to do is to perform the assignments contained in this list (leaving a_2 and a_3 unchanged):

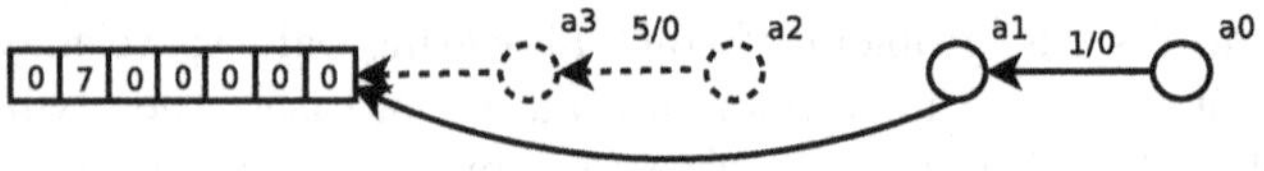

Thus it is really easy to turn these persistent arrays into a semi-persistent data structure, which is more efficient since we save some pointer assignments. This example is investigated in more detail in [6].

Lists. As a second example, we consider an immutable data structure which we make semi-persistent. The simplest and most popular example is the list data structure. To make it semi-persistent, the idea is to reuse *cons* cells between successive conses to the same list. For instance, given a list `l`, the cons operation `1::l` allocates a new memory block to store `1` and a pointer to `l`. Then a successive operation `2::l` could reuse the same memory block if the list is used in a semi-persistent way. Thus we simply need to replace `1` by `2`. To do this, we must maintain for each list the previous cons, if any.

Hash Tables. Combining (semi-)persistent arrays with (semi-)persistent lists, one easily gets (semi-)persistent hash tables.

Benchmarks. We present some benchmarks to show the benefits of semi-persistence. Each of the previous three data structures has been implemented in Ocaml[1]. Each data structure is tested the same way and compared to its fully persistent counterpart. The test consists in simulating a backtracking algorithm with branching degree 4 and depth 6, operating on a single data structure. N

[1] The full code is available in the long version of this paper [7].

successive update operations are performed on the data structure between two branching points.

The following table gives timings for various values of N. The code was compiled with the Ocaml native-code compiler (`ocamlopt -unsafe`) on a dual core Pentium 2.13GHz processor running under Linux. The timings are given in seconds and correspond to CPU time obtained using the UNIX `times` system call.

N	200	1000	5000	10000
persistent arrays	0.21	1.50	13.90	30.5
semi-persistent arrays	0.18	1.10	7.59	17.3
persistent lists	0.18	2.38	50.20	195.0
semi-persistent lists	0.11	0.76	8.02	31.1
persistent hash tables	0.24	2.15	19.30	43.1
semi-persistent hash tables	0.22	1.51	11.20	28.2

As we can see, the speedup ratio is always greater than 1 and almost reaches 7 (for semi-persistent lists). Regarding memory consumption, we compared the total number of allocated bytes, as reported by Ocaml's garbage collector. For the tests corresponding to the last column ($N = 10000$) semi-persistent data structures always used much less memory than persistent ones: 3 times less for arrays, 575 times less for lists and 1.5 times less for hash tables. The dramatic ratio for lists is easily explained by the fact that our benchmark program reflects the best case regarding memory allocation (allocation in one branch is reused in other branches, which all have the same length).

3 Programming with Semi-persistent Data Structures

This section introduces a small programming language to manipulate semi-persistent data structures. In order to keep it simple, we assume that we are operating on the successive versions of a single, statically allocated, data structure. Multiple data structures and dynamic allocation are discussed in Section 5.

3.1 Syntax

The syntax of our language is as follows:

$$
\begin{aligned}
e &::= x \mid c \mid p \mid f\ e \mid \texttt{let}\ x = e\ \texttt{in}\ e \\
&\quad \mid \texttt{if}\ e\ \texttt{then}\ e\ \texttt{else}\ e \\
d &::= \texttt{fun}\ f\ (x : \iota) = \{\phi\}\ e\ \{\psi\} \\
\iota &::= \texttt{semi} \mid \delta \mid \texttt{bool}
\end{aligned}
$$

A program expression is either a variable (x), a constant (c), a pointer (p), a function call, a local variable introduced by a `let` binding, or a conditional. The set of function names f includes some primitive operations (introduced in the next section). A function definition d introduces a function f with exactly one argument x of type ι, a precondition ϕ, a body and a postcondition ψ. A type ι is either the type `semi` of the semi-persistent data structure, the type δ of the values it contains, or the type `bool` of booleans. The syntax of pre- and postconditions will be given later in Section 4. A program Δ is a finite set of mutually recursive functions.

3.2 Primitive Operations

We may consider three kinds of abstract operations on semi-persistent data structures: *update* operations backtracking to a given version and creating a new successor, which becomes the newest version; *destructive access* operations backtracking to a given version, which becomes the newest version, and then accessing it; and *non-destructive access* operations accessing a *valid* version, that is an ancestor of the newest version, without modifying the data structure.

Since update and destructive access operations both need to backtrack, it is convenient to design a language based on the following three primitives: `backtrack`, which backtracks to a given version, making it the newest version; `branch` which builds a new successor of a given version, assuming it is the newest version; and `acc`, which accesses a given version, assuming it is a valid version. Then update and destructive access operations can be rephrased in terms of the above primitives:

$$\begin{aligned} \texttt{upd}\ e &= \texttt{branch}\ (\texttt{backtrack}\ e) \\ \texttt{dacc}\ e &= \texttt{acc}\ (\texttt{backtrack}\ e) \end{aligned}$$

3.3 Operational Semantics

We equip our language with a small step operational semantics, which is given in Figure 1. One step of reduction is written $e_1, S_1 \rightarrow e_2, S_2$ where e_1 and e_2 are program expressions and S_1 and S_2 are states. A value v is either a constant c or a pointer p. Pointers represent versions of the semi-persistent data structure. A state S is a stack $p_1, \ldots, p_m$ of pointers, p_m being the top of the stack. The semantics is straightforward, except for primitive operations. Primitive `backtrack` expects an argument p_n designating a valid version of the data structure, that is an element of the stack. Then all pointers on top of p_n are popped from the stack and p_n is the result of the operation. Primitive `branch` expects an argument p_n being the top of the stack and pushes a fresh value p, which is also the result of the operation. Finally, primitive `acc` expects an argument p_n designating a valid version, leaves the stack unchanged and returns some value for version p_n, represented by $\mathcal{A}(p_n)$. (We leave $\mathcal{A}$ uninterpreted since we are not interested in the values contained in the data structure.)

Note that reduction of `backtrack` p_n or `acc` p_n is blocked whenever p_n is not an element of S, which is precisely what we intend to prevent.

3.4 Type System with Effect

We introduce a type system to characterize well-formed programs. Our language is simply typed and thus type-checking is immediate. Meanwhile, we infer the

$$\begin{aligned} E &::= [] \mid f\ E \mid \texttt{let}\ x = E\ \texttt{in}\ e \mid \texttt{if}\ E\ \texttt{then}\ e\ \texttt{else}\ e \\ v &::= c \mid p \\ S &::= p \cdots p \end{aligned}$$

$$\begin{array}{rcll} \texttt{if true then}\ e_1\ \texttt{else}\ e_2, S & \rightarrow & e_1, S & \\ \texttt{if false then}\ e_1\ \texttt{else}\ e_2, S & \rightarrow & e_2, S & \\ \texttt{let}\ x = v\ \texttt{in}\ e, S & \rightarrow & e\{x \leftarrow v\}, S & \\ f\ v, S & \rightarrow & e\{x \leftarrow v\}, S & \text{if}\ \texttt{fun}\ f\ (x : \iota) = \{\phi\}\ e\ \{\psi\} \in \Delta \\ \texttt{backtrack}\ p_n, p_1 \cdots p_n p_{n+1} \cdots p_m & \rightarrow & p_n, p_1 \cdots p_n & \\ \texttt{branch}\ p_n, p_1 \cdots p_n & \rightarrow & p, p_1 \cdots p_n p & p\ \text{fresh} \\ \texttt{acc}\ p_n, p_1 \cdots p_n p_{n+1} \cdots p_m & \rightarrow & \mathcal{A}(p_n), p_1 \cdots p_n p_{n+1} \cdots p_m & \\ E[e_1], S_1 & \rightarrow & E[e_2], S_2 & \text{if}\ e_1, S_1 \rightarrow e_2, S_2\ \text{and}\ E \neq [] \end{array}$$

Fig. 1. Operational Semantics

effect ϵ of each expression, as an element of the boolean lattice $(\{\bot, \top\}, \wedge, \vee)$. This boolean indicates whether the expression modifies the semi-persistent data structure ($\bot$ meaning no modification and $\top$ a modification). Effects will be used in the next section to simplify constraint generation. Each function is given a type τ, as follows:

$$\tau ::= (x : \iota) \rightarrow^{\epsilon} \{\phi\}\ \iota\ \{\psi\}$$

The argument is given a type and a name (x) since it is bound in both precondition ϕ and postcondition ψ. Type τ also indicates the latent effect ϵ of the function, which is the effect resulting from the function application.

A typing environment Γ is a set of type assignments for variables $(x : \iota)$, constants $(c : \iota)$ and functions $(f : \tau)$. It is assumed to contain at least type declarations for the primitives, as follows:

$$\begin{array}{rcl} \texttt{backtrack} & : & (x : \texttt{semi}) \rightarrow^{\top} \{\phi_{\texttt{backtrack}}\}\ \texttt{semi}\ \{\psi_{\texttt{backtrack}}\} \\ \texttt{branch} & : & (x : \texttt{semi}) \rightarrow^{\top} \{\phi_{\texttt{branch}}\}\ \texttt{semi}\ \{\psi_{\texttt{branch}}\} \\ \texttt{acc} & : & (x : \texttt{semi}) \rightarrow^{\bot} \{\phi_{\texttt{acc}}\}\ \delta\ \{\psi_{\texttt{acc}}\} \end{array}$$

where pre- and postcondition are given later. As expected, both `backtrack` and `branch` modify the semi-persistent data structure and thus have effect $\top$, while the non-destructive access `acc` has effect $\bot$.

Given a typing environment Γ, the judgment $\Gamma \vdash e : \iota, \epsilon$ means "e is a well-formed expression of type ι and effect ϵ" and the judgment $\Gamma \vdash d : \tau$ means "d is a well-formed function definition of type τ". Typing rules are given in Figure 2. They assume judgments $\Gamma \vdash \phi$ pre and $\Gamma \vdash \psi$ post ι for the well-formedness of pre- and postconditions respectively, to be defined later in Section 4.1. Note that there is no typing rule for pointers, to prevent their explicit use in programs.

A program $\Delta = d_1, \ldots, d_n$ is well-typed if each function definition d_i can be given a type τ_i such that $d_1 : \tau_1, \ldots, d_n : \tau_n \vdash d_i : \tau_i$ for each i. The types τ_i can easily be obtained by a fixpoint computation, starting with all latent effects set to $\bot$, since effect inference is clearly a monotone function.

$$\text{VAR}\ \frac{x : \iota \in \Gamma}{\Gamma \vdash x : \iota, \bot} \qquad \text{CONST}\ \frac{c : \iota \in \Gamma}{\Gamma \vdash c : \iota, \bot}$$

$$\text{APP}\ \frac{f : (x : \iota_1) \rightarrow^{\epsilon_2} \{\phi\}\, \iota_2\, \{\psi\} \in \Gamma \qquad \Gamma \vdash e : \iota_1, \epsilon_1}{\Gamma \vdash f\ e : \iota_2, \epsilon_1 \vee \epsilon_2}$$

$$\text{ITE}\ \frac{\Gamma \vdash e_1 : \texttt{bool}, \epsilon_1 \qquad \Gamma \vdash e_2 : \iota, \epsilon_2 \qquad \Gamma \vdash e_3 : \iota, \epsilon_3}{\Gamma \vdash \texttt{if}\ e_1\ \texttt{then}\ e_2\ \texttt{else}\, e_3 : \iota, \epsilon_1 \vee \epsilon_2 \vee \epsilon_3}$$

$$\text{LET}\ \frac{\Gamma \vdash e_1 : \iota_1, \epsilon_1 \qquad \Gamma, x : \iota_1 \vdash e_2 : \iota_2, \epsilon_2}{\Gamma \vdash \texttt{let}\ x = e_1\ \texttt{in}\, e_2 : \iota_2, \epsilon_1 \vee \epsilon_2}$$

$$\text{FUN}\ \frac{x : \iota_1 \vdash \phi\ \mathsf{pre} \qquad x : \iota_1 \vdash \psi\ \mathsf{post}\ \iota_2 \qquad \Gamma, x : \iota_1 \vdash e : \iota_2, \epsilon}{\Gamma \vdash \texttt{fun}\, f\ (x : \iota_1) = \{\phi\}\, e\, \{\psi\} : (x : \iota_1) \rightarrow^{\epsilon} \{\phi\}\, \iota_2\, \{\psi\}}$$

Fig. 2. Typing Rules

3.5 Examples

Let us consider the following two functions f and g:

$\texttt{fun}\ f\ (x_0 : \texttt{semi}) = \{\texttt{valid}(x_0)\}$	$\texttt{fun}\ g\ (x_0 : \texttt{semi}) = \{\texttt{valid}(x_0)\}$
$\quad \texttt{let}\ x_1 = \texttt{upd}\ x_0\ \texttt{in}$	$\quad \texttt{let}\ x_1 = \texttt{upd}\ x_0\ \texttt{in}$
$\quad \texttt{let}\ x_2 = \texttt{upd}\ x_0\ \texttt{in}$	$\quad \texttt{let}\ x_2 = \texttt{upd}\ x_0\ \texttt{in}$
$\quad \texttt{acc}\ x_2$	$\quad \texttt{acc}\ x_1$

Each function expects a valid version x_0 of the data structure as argument and successively build two successors x_1 and x_2 of x_0. Then f accesses x_2, which is valid, and g accesses x_1, which is illegal since x_1 is not an ancestor of the newest version x_2. Let us check this on the operational semantics. Let S be a state composed of a single pointer p. The reduction of $f\ p$ in S runs as follows:

$$\begin{aligned} f\ p, p &\rightarrow \texttt{let}\ x_1 = \texttt{upd}\ p\, \texttt{in}\, \texttt{let}\ x_2 = \texttt{upd}\ p\, \texttt{in}\, \texttt{acc}\ x_2, p \\ &\rightarrow \texttt{let}\ x_1 = p_1\, \texttt{in}\, \texttt{let}\ x_2 = \texttt{upd}\ p\, \texttt{in}\, \texttt{acc}\ x_2, pp_1 \\ &\rightarrow \texttt{let}\ x_2 = \texttt{upd}\ p\, \texttt{in}\, \texttt{acc}\ x_2, pp_1 \\ &\rightarrow \texttt{let}\ x_2 = p_2\, \texttt{in}\, \texttt{acc}\ x_2, pp_2 \\ &\rightarrow \texttt{acc}\ p_2, pp_2 \\ &\rightarrow \mathcal{A}(p_2), pp_2p_3 \end{aligned}$$

and ends on the value $\mathcal{A}(p_2)$. On the contrary, the reduction of $g\ p$ in S blocks on $g\ p, p \rightarrow \ldots \rightarrow \texttt{acc}\ p_1, pp_2$.

4 Proof System

This section introduces a theory for semi-persistence and a proof system for this theory. First we define the syntax and semantics of logical annotations. Then we compute a set of constraints for each program expression, which is proved to express the correctness of the program with respect to semi-persistence. Finally we give a decision procedure to solve the constraints.

4.1 Theory of Semi-persistence

The syntax of annotations is as follows:

$$\begin{aligned} \text{term } t &::= x \mid p \mid \texttt{prev}(t) \\ \text{atom } a &::= t = t \mid \texttt{path}(t,t) \\ \text{postcondition } \psi &::= a \mid \psi \wedge \psi \\ \text{precondition } \phi &::= a \mid \phi \wedge \phi \mid \psi \Rightarrow \phi \mid \forall x.\, \phi \end{aligned}$$

Terms are built from variables, pointers and a single function symbol `prev`. Atoms are built from equality and a single predicate symbol `path`. A postcondition ψ is restricted to a conjunction of atoms. A precondition is a formula ϕ built from atoms, conjunctions, implications and universal quantifications. A negative formula (i.e. appearing on the left side of an implication) is restricted to a conjunction of atoms. We introduce two different syntactic categories ψ and ϕ for formulae but one can notice that ϕ actually contains ψ. This syntactic restriction on formulae is justified later in Section 4.5 when introducing the decision procedure. In the remainder of the paper, a "formula" refers to the syntactic category ϕ. Substitution a of term t for a variable x in a formula ϕ is written $\phi\{x \leftarrow t\}$. We denote by $\mathcal{S}(A)$ the set of all subterms of a set of atoms A.

The typing of terms and formulae is straightforward, assuming that `prev` has signature `semi` $\rightarrow$ `semi`. Function postconditions may refer to the function result, represented by the variable *ret*. Formulae can only refer to variables of type `semi` (including variable *ret*). We write $\Gamma \vdash \phi$ to denote a well-formed formula ϕ in a typing environment Γ.

We now give the semantics of program annotations. The main idea is to express that a given version is valid if and only if it is an ancestor of the newest version. To illustrate this idea, the following figure shows the successive version trees for the sequence of declarations $x_1 =$ `upd` x_0, $x_2 =$ `upd` x_1, $x_3 =$ `upd` x_1 and $x_4 =$ `upd` x_0:

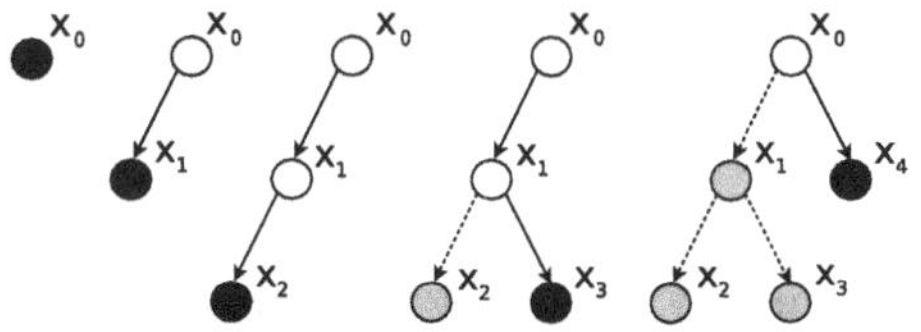

The newest version is pictured as a black node, other valid versions as white nodes and invalid ones as gray nodes.

The meaning of `prev` and `path` is to define the notion of ancestor: $\texttt{prev}(x)$ is the immediate ancestor of x and $\texttt{path}(x,y)$ holds whenever x is an ancestor of y. The corresponding theory can be axiomatized as follows:

Definition 1. *The theory $\mathcal{T}$ is defined as the combination of the theory of equality and the following axioms:*

$$\begin{aligned} &(A_1)\ \forall x.\, \texttt{path}(x,x) \\ &(A_2)\ \forall xy.\, \texttt{path}(x,\texttt{prev}(y)) \Rightarrow \texttt{path}(x,y) \\ &(A_3)\ \forall xyz.\, \texttt{path}(x,y) \wedge \texttt{path}(y,z) \Rightarrow \texttt{path}(x,z) \end{aligned}$$

We write $\models \phi$ if ϕ is valid in any model of $\mathcal{T}$.

The three axioms (A_1)–(A_3) exactly define `path` as the reflexive transitive closure of $\texttt{prev}^{-1}$, since we consider validity in all models of $\mathcal{T}$ and therefore in those where `path` is the smallest relation satisfying axioms (A_1)–(A_3). Antisymmetry is not needed (the absence of cycle in the version tree is related to the implementation of a semi-persistent data structure, not to its use). Note that `prev` is a total function and that there is no notion of "root" in our logic. Thus a version always has an immediate ancestor, which may or may not be valid.

To account for the modification of the newest version as program execution progresses, we introduce a "mutable" variable *cur* to represent the newest version. This variable does not appear in programs: its scope is limited to annotations. The only way to modify its contents is to call the primitive operations `backtrack` and `branch`. We are now able to give the full type expressions for the three primitive operations:

$$\begin{aligned}
\texttt{backtrack} : (x : \texttt{semi}) &\rightarrow^{\top} \{\texttt{path}(x, cur)\}\, \texttt{semi}\, \{ret = x \wedge cur = x\} \\
\texttt{branch} : (x : \texttt{semi}) &\rightarrow^{\top} \{cur = x\}\, \texttt{semi}\, \{ret = cur \wedge \texttt{prev}(cur) = x\} \\
\texttt{acc} : (x : \texttt{semi}) &\rightarrow^{\perp} \{\texttt{path}(x, cur)\}\, \delta\, \{\texttt{true}\}
\end{aligned}$$

As expected, effect $\top$ for the first two reflects the modification of *cur*. The validity of function argument x is expressed as $\texttt{path}(x, cur)$ in operations `backtrack` and `acc`. Note that `acc` has no postcondition (written `true` and which could stand for the tautology $cur = cur$) since we are not interested in the values contained in the data structure.

We are now able to define the judgements used in Section 3.4 for pre- and postconditions. We write $\Gamma \vdash \phi\ \textsf{pre}$ as syntactic sugar for $\Gamma, cur : \texttt{semi} \vdash \phi$. Similarly, $\Gamma \vdash \psi\ \textsf{post}\ \iota$ is syntactic sugar for $\Gamma, cur : \texttt{semi}, ret : \iota \vdash \psi$ when return type ι is `semi` and for $\Gamma, cur : \texttt{semi} \vdash \psi$ otherwise. Note that since Γ only contains the function argument x in typing rule FUN, the function precondition may only refer to x and *cur*, and its postcondition to x, *cur* and *ret*.

4.2 Constraints

We now give an algorithm to compute a formula expressing that a given program is correct. This is mostly a weakest precondition calculus, which is greatly simplified here since we have only one mutable variable (namely *cur*). For a program expression e and a formula ϕ we write this weakest precondition $\mathcal{C}(e, \phi)$. This is a formula expressing the conditions under which ϕ will hold after the evaluation of e. Note that *cur* may appear in ϕ, denoting the result of e, but does not appear in $\mathcal{C}(e, \phi)$ anymore. For a function definition d we write $\mathcal{C}(d)$ the formula expressing its correctness, that is the fact that the function precondition implies the weakest precondition obtained from the function postcondition, for any function argument and any initial value of *cur*. The definition for $\mathcal{C}(e, \phi)$ is given in Figure 3. This is a standard weakest precondition calculus, except for the conditional rule. Indeed, one would expect a rule such as

$$\begin{aligned}
&\mathcal{C}(\texttt{if}\ e_1\ \texttt{then}\ e_2\ \texttt{else}\, e_3, \phi) = \\
&\qquad \mathcal{C}(e_1, (ret = \texttt{true} \Rightarrow \mathcal{C}(e_2, \phi)) \wedge (ret = \texttt{false} \Rightarrow \mathcal{C}(e_3, \phi)))
\end{aligned}$$

$$\texttt{frame}_f(\phi) = \phi_f\{x \leftarrow ret\} \wedge \forall ret'.\, \psi_f\{ret \leftarrow ret', x \leftarrow ret\} \Rightarrow \phi\{ret \leftarrow ret'\}$$
$$\text{if } f : (x : \iota) \rightarrow^{\bot} \{\phi_f\}\, \iota'\, \{\psi_f\}$$
$$\texttt{frame}_f(\phi) = \phi_f\{x \leftarrow ret\} \wedge \forall ret'\, cur'.\ \psi_f\{ret \leftarrow ret', x \leftarrow ret, cur \leftarrow cur'\} \Rightarrow \phi\{ret \leftarrow ret', cur \leftarrow cur'\}$$
$$\text{if } f : (x : \iota) \rightarrow^{\top} \{\phi_f\}\, \iota'\, \{\psi_f\}$$

$$\begin{aligned}
\mathcal{C}(v, \phi) &= \phi\{ret \leftarrow v\} \\
\mathcal{C}(\texttt{if}\ e_1\ \texttt{then}\ e_2\ \texttt{else}\ e_3, \phi) &= \mathcal{C}(e_1, \mathcal{C}(e_2, \phi) \wedge \mathcal{C}(e_3, \phi)) \\
\mathcal{C}(\texttt{let}\ x = e_1\ \texttt{in}\ e_2, \phi) &= \mathcal{C}(e_1, \mathcal{C}(e_2, \phi)\{x \leftarrow ret\}) \\
\mathcal{C}(f\ e_1, \phi) &= \mathcal{C}(e_1, \texttt{frame}_f(\phi)) \\
\mathcal{C}(\texttt{fun}\, f\ (x : \iota) = \{\phi\}\, e\, \{\psi\}) &= \forall x.\, \forall cur.\, \phi \Rightarrow \mathcal{C}(e, \psi)
\end{aligned}$$

Fig. 3. Constraint synthesis

but since ϕ cannot test the result of condition e_1 (ϕ may only refer to variables of type `semi`), the conjunction above simplifies to $\mathcal{C}(e_2, \phi) \wedge \mathcal{C}(e_3, \phi)$.

The constraint synthesis for a function call, $\mathcal{C}(f\ e_1, \phi)$, is the only nontrivial case. It requires precondition ϕ_f to be valid and postcondition ψ_f to imply the expected property ϕ. Universal quantification is used to introduce f's results and side-effects. We use the effect in f's type to distinguish two cases: either the effect is $\bot$ which means that *cur* is not modified and thus we only quantify over f's result (hence we get for free the invariance of *cur*); or the effect is $\top$ and we quantify over an additional variable cur' which stands for the new value of *cur*. To simplify this definition, we introduce a formula transformer $\texttt{frame}_f(\phi)$ which builds the appropriate postcondition for argument e_1. Note that primitive operations are particular cases of function calls.

4.3 Examples

Simple Example. Let us consider again the two functions f and g from Section 3.5, $\texttt{valid}(x_0)$ being now expressed as $\texttt{path}(x_0, cur)$ and primitive operation `upd` having type

$$\texttt{upd} : (x : \texttt{semi}) \rightarrow^{\top} \{\texttt{path}(x, cur)\}\, \texttt{semi}\, \{ret = cur \wedge \texttt{prev}(cur) = x\}$$

We compute the associated constraints for an empty postcondition `true`. The constraint $\mathcal{C}(f)$ is

$$\begin{array}{l}
\forall x_0.\, \forall cur.\, \texttt{path}(x_0, cur) \Rightarrow \\
\quad \texttt{path}(x_0, cur)\ \wedge \forall x_1.\, \forall cur_1.\, (\texttt{prev}(x_1) = x_0 \wedge cur_1 = x_1) \Rightarrow \\
\quad\quad \texttt{path}(x_0, cur_1)\ \wedge \forall x_2.\, \forall cur_2.\, (\texttt{prev}(x_2) = x_0 \wedge cur_2 = x_2) \Rightarrow \\
\quad\quad\quad \texttt{path}(x_2, cur_2)\ \wedge \forall ret.\, \texttt{true} \Rightarrow \texttt{true}
\end{array}$$

It can be split into three proof obligations, which are the following universally quantified sequents:

$$\texttt{path}(x_0, cur) \vdash \texttt{path}(x_0, cur)$$
$$\texttt{path}(x_0, cur), \texttt{prev}(x_1) = x_0, cur_1 = x_1 \vdash \texttt{path}(x_0, cur_1)$$
$$\begin{array}{r}\texttt{path}(x_0, cur), \texttt{prev}(x_1) = x_0, \\ cur_1 = x_1, \texttt{prev}(x_2) = x_0, cur_2 = x_2 \vdash \texttt{path}(x_2, cur_2)\end{array}$$

The three of them hold in theory $\mathcal{T}$ and thus f is correct. Similarly, the constraint $\mathcal{C}(g)$ can be computed and split into three proof obligations. The first two are exactly the same as for f but the third one is slightly different:

$$\begin{array}{r}\texttt{path}(x_0, cur), \texttt{prev}(x_1) = x_0, \\ cur_1 = x_1, \texttt{prev}(x_2) = x_0, cur_2 = x_2 \vdash \texttt{path}(x_1, cur_2)\end{array}$$

In that case it does not hold in theory $\mathcal{T}$.

Backtracking Example. As a more complex example, let us consider a backtracking algorithm. The pattern of a program performing backtracking on a persistent data structure is a recursive function bt looking like

$$\texttt{fun}\ bt\ (x : \texttt{semi})\ = \dots\ bt\ (\texttt{upd}\ x)\ \dots\ bt\ (\texttt{upd}\ x)\ \dots$$

Function bt takes a data structure x as argument and makes recursive calls on several successors of x. This is precisely a case where the data structure may be semi-persistent, as motivated in the introduction. To capture this pattern in our framework, we simply need to consider two successive calls $bt(\texttt{upd}\ x)$, which can be written as follows:

$$\texttt{fun}\ bt\ (x : \texttt{semi})\ = \texttt{let}\ \_ = bt\ (\texttt{upd}\ x)\ \texttt{in}\ bt\ (\texttt{upd}\ x)$$

Function bt obviously requires a precondition stating that x is a valid version of the semi-persistent data structure. This is not enough information to discharge the proof obligations: the second recursive call $bt(\texttt{upd}\ x)$ requires x to be valid, which possibly could no longer be the case after the first recursive call. Therefore a postcondition for bt is needed to ensure the validity of x:

$$\begin{array}{l}\texttt{fun}\ bt\ (x : \texttt{semi})\ = \\ \quad \{\ \texttt{path}(x, cur)\ \}\ \texttt{let}\ \_ = bt\ (\texttt{upd}\ x)\ \texttt{in}\ bt\ (\texttt{upd}\ x)\ \{\ \texttt{path}(x, cur)\ \}\end{array}$$

Then it is straightforward to check that constraint $\mathcal{C}(bt)$ is valid in theory $\mathcal{T}$.

4.4 Soundness

In the remainder of this section, we consider a program $\Delta = d_1, \dots, d_n$ whose constraints are valid, that is $\models \mathcal{C}(d_1) \wedge \dots \wedge \mathcal{C}(d_n)$. We are going to show that the evaluation of this program will not block.

For this purpose we first introduce the notion of validity with respect to a state of the operational semantics:

Definition 2. *A formula* ϕ *is valid in a state* $S = p_1, \dots, p_n$*, written* $S \models \phi$*, if it is valid in any model* $\mathcal{M}$ *for* $\mathcal{T}$ *such that*

$$\begin{cases} \mathtt{prev}(p_{i+1}) = p_i & \text{for all } 1 \leq i < n \\ cur = p_n \end{cases}$$

Then we show that this validity is preserved by the operational semantics. To do this, it is convenient to see the evaluation contexts as formula transformers, as follows:

E	$E[\phi]$
$[]$	ϕ
$\mathtt{let}\ x = E_1\ \mathtt{in}\ e_2$	$E_1[\mathcal{C}(e_2, \phi)\{x \leftarrow ret\}]$
$\mathtt{if}\ E_1\ \mathtt{then}\ e_2\ \mathtt{else}\ e_3$	$E_1[\mathcal{C}(e_2, \phi) \wedge \mathcal{C}(e_3, \phi)]$
$f\ E_1$	$E_1[\mathtt{frame}_f(\phi)]$

There is a property of commutation between contexts for programs and contexts for formulae:

Lemma 1. $S \models \mathcal{C}(E[e], \phi)$ *if and only if* $S \models \mathcal{C}(e, E[\phi])$.

We now want to prove preservation of validity, that is if $S \models \mathcal{C}(e, \phi)$ and $e, S \rightarrow e', S'$ then $S' \models \mathcal{C}(e', \phi)$. Obviously, this does not hold for any state S, program e and formula ϕ. Indeed, if $S \equiv p_1 p_2$, $e \equiv \mathtt{upd}\ p_1$ and $\phi \equiv \mathtt{prev}(p_2) = p_1$, then $\mathcal{C}(e, \phi)$ is

$$\mathtt{path}(p_1, cur)\ \wedge \forall ret'\, cur'.\, (\mathtt{prev}(ret') = p_1 \wedge cur' = ret') \Rightarrow \mathtt{prev}(p_2) = p_1$$

which holds in S. But $S' \equiv p_1 p$ for a fresh p, $e' \equiv p$, and $\mathcal{C}(e', \phi)$ is $\mathtt{prev}(p_2) = p_1$ which does not hold in S' (since p_2 does not appear in S' anymore). Fortunately, we are not interested in the preservation of $\mathcal{C}(e, \phi)$ for any formula ϕ, but only for formulae which arise from function postconditions. As pointed out in Section 4.1, a function postcondition may only refer to x, cur and ret. Therefore we are only considering formulae $\mathcal{C}(e, \phi)$ where x is the only free variable (cur and ret do not appear in formulae $\mathcal{C}(e, \phi)$ anymore). This excludes the formula $\mathtt{prev}(p_2) = p_1$ in the example above.

We are now able to prove preservation of validity:

Lemma 2. *Let* S *be a state,* ϕ *be a formula and* e *a program expression. If* $S \models \mathcal{C}(e, \phi)$ *and* $e, S \rightarrow e', S'$ *then* $S' \models \mathcal{C}(e', \phi)$.

Finally, we prove the following progress property:

Theorem 1. *Let* S *be a state,* ϕ *be a formula and* e *a program expression. If* $S \models \mathcal{C}(e, \phi)$ *and* $e, S \rightarrow^* e', S' \not\rightarrow$*, then* e' *is a value.*

4.5 Decision Procedure

We now show that constraints are decidable and we give a decision procedure. First, we notice that any formula ϕ is equivalent to a conjunction of formulae of the form $\forall x_1. \ldots \forall x_n. a_1 \wedge \cdots \wedge a_m \Rightarrow a$, where the a_i's are atoms. This results from the syntactic restrictions on pre- and postconditions, together with the weakest preconditions rules which are only using postconditions in negative positions. Therefore we simply need to decide whether a given atom is the consequence of other atoms.

We denote by $H^\star$ the congruence closure of a set H of hypotheses $\{a_1, \ldots, a_m\}$. Obviously $\mathcal{S}(H^\star) = \mathcal{S}(H)$ since no new term is created. $H^\star$ is finite and can be computed as a fixpoint.

Algorithm 1. *For any atom a such that $\mathcal{S}(\{a\}) \subseteq \mathcal{S}(H)$, the following algorithm,* `decide`(H, a)*, decides whether $H \models a$.*

1. *First we compute the congruence closure $H^\star$.*
2. *If a is of the form $t_1 = t_2$, we return **true** if $t_1 = t_2 \in H^\star$ and **false** otherwise.*
3. *If a is of the form* `path`(t_1, t_2)*, we build a directed graph G whose nodes are the subterms of $H^\star$, as follows:*
   (a) for each pair of nodes t and `prev`(t) *we add an edge from* `prev`(t) *to t;*
   (b) for each `path`$(t_1, t_2) \in H^\star$ *we add an edge from t_1 to t_2;*
   (c) for each $t_1 = t_2 \in H^\star$ we add two edges between t_1 and t_2.
4. *Finally we check whether there is a path from t_1 to t_2 in G.*

Obviously this algorithm terminates since $H^\star$ is finite and thus so is G. We now show soundness and completeness for this algorithm.

Theorem 2. `decide`(H, a) *returns true if and only if $H \models a$.*

Note: the restriction $\mathcal{S}(\{a\}) \subseteq \mathcal{S}(H)$ can be easily met by adding to H the equalities $t = t$ for any subterm t of a; it was only introduced to simplify the proof above.

4.6 Implementation

We have implemented the whole framework of semi-persistence. The implementation relies on an existing proof obligations generator, Why [10]. This tool takes annotated first-order imperative programs as input and uses a traditional weakest precondition calculus to generate proof obligations. The language we use in this paper is actually a subset of Why's input language. We simply use the imperative aspect to make *cur* a mutable variable. Then the resulting proof obligations are *exactly* the same as those obtained by the constraint synthesis defined in Section 4.2.

The Why tool outputs proof obligations in the native syntax of various existing provers. In particular, these formulas can be sent to Ergo [5], an automatic prover for first-order logic which combines congruence closure with various built-in decision procedures. We first simply axiomatized theory $\mathcal{T}$ using (A_1)–(A_3), which proved to be powerful enough to verify all examples from this paper and several other benchmark programs. Yet it is possibly incomplete (automatic theorem provers use heuristics to handle quantifiers in first-order logic). To achieve completeness, and to assess the results of Section 4.5, we also implemented theory $\mathcal{T}$ as a new built-in decision procedure in Ergo. Again we verified all the benchmark programs.

5 Conclusion

We have introduced the notion of *semi-persistent* data structures, where update operations are restricted to ancestors of the most recent version. Semi-persistent data structures may be more efficient than their fully persistent counterparts, and are of particular interest in implementing backtracking algorithms. We have proposed an almost automatic way of checking the legal use of semi-persistent data structures. It is based on light user annotations in programs, from which proof obligations are extracted and automatically discharged by a decision procedure.

There is a lot of remaining work to be done. First, the language introduced in Section 3, in which we check for legal use of semi-persistence, could be greatly enriched. Beside the missing features such as polymorphism or recursive datatypes, it would be of particular interest to consider simultaneous use of several semi-persistent data structures and dynamic creation of semi-persistent data structures. Regarding the former, one would probably need to express disjointness of version subtrees, and thus to enrich the logical fragment used in annotations with disjunctions and negations; we may lose decidability of the logic, though. Regarding the latter, it would imply to express in the logic the freshness of the allocated pointers and to maintain the newest versions for each data structures.

Another interesting direction would be to provide systematic techniques to make data structures semi-persistent as previously done for persistence [9]. Clearly what we did for lists could be extended to tree-based data structures. It would be even more interesting to formally verify semi-persistent data structure *implementations*, that is to show that the contents of any ancestor of the version being updated is preserved. Since such implementations are necessarily using imperative features (otherwise they would be fully persistent), proving their correctness requires verification techniques for imperative programs. This could be done for instance using verification tools such as SPEC# [2] or Caduceus [11]. However, we would prefer verifying Ocaml code, as given in the long version of this paper [7] for instance, but unfortunately there is currently no tool to handle such code.

References

1. Baker, H.G.: Shallow binding makes functional arrays fast. SIGPLAN Not. 26(8), 145–147 (1991)
2. Mike Barnett, K., Leino, R.M., Schulte, W.: The Spec# programming system: An overview. In: Barthe, G., Burdy, L., Huisman, M., Lanet, J.-L., Muntean, T. (eds.) CASSIS 2004. LNCS, vol. 3362, Springer, Heidelberg (2005)
3. Benedikt, M., Reps, T.W., Sagiv, S.: A decidable logic for describing linked data structures. In: European Symposium on Programming, pp. 2–19 (1999)
4. Blanchet, B.: Escape analysis: Correctness proof, implementation and experimental results. In: Symposium on Principles of Programming Languages, pp. 25–37 (1998)
5. Conchon, S., Contejean, E.: Ergo: A Decision Procedure for Program Verification, `http://ergo.lri.fr/`

6. Conchon, S., Filliâtre, J.-C.: A Persistent Union-Find Data Structure. In: ACM SIGPLAN Workshop on ML, Freiburg, Germany (October 2007)
7. Conchon, S., Filliâtre, J.-C.: Semi-Persistent Data Structures. Research Report 1474, LRI, Université Paris Sud (September 2007), `http://www.lri.fr/~filliatr/ftp/publis/spds-rr.pdf`
8. Dijkstra, E.W.: A discipline of programming. Series in Automatic Computation. Prentice Hall Int., Englewood Cliffs (1976)
9. Driscoll, J.R., Sarnak, N., Sleator, D.D., Tarjan, R.E.: Making Data Structures Persistent. Journal of Computer and System Sciences 38(1), 86–124 (1989)
10. Filliâtre, J.-C.: The Why verification tool, `http://why.lri.fr/`
11. Filliâtre, J.-C., Marché, C.: The Why/Krakatoa/Caduceus Platform for Deductive Program Verification (Tool presentation). In: Damm, W., Hermanns, H. (eds.) CAV 2007. LNCS, vol. 4590, Springer, Heidelberg (to appear, 2007)
12. Hannan, J.: A type-based analysis for stack allocation in functional languages. In: Mycroft, A. (ed.) SAS 1995. LNCS, vol. 983, pp. 172–188. Springer, Heidelberg (1995)
13. Knuth, D.E.: Dancing links. In: Davies, B.R.J., Woodcock, J. (eds.) Millennial Perspectives in Computer Science, Palgrave, pp. 187–214 (2000)
14. Morrisett, J.G., Crary, K., Glew, N., Walker, D.: Stack-based typed assembly language. In: Types in Compilation, pp. 28–52 (1998)
15. Nelson, G.: Verifying reachability invariants of linked structures. In: POPL 1983: Proceedings of the 10th ACM SIGACT-SIGPLAN symposium on Principles of programming languages, pp. 38–47. ACM Press, New York (1983)
16. Okasaki, C.: Purely Functional Data Structures. Cambridge University Press, Cambridge (1998)
17. Ranise, S., Zarba, C.: A theory of singly-linked lists and its extensible decision procedure. In: SEFM 2006: Proceedings of the Fourth IEEE International Conference on Software Engineering and Formal Methods, Washington, DC, USA, pp. 206–215. IEEE Computer Society, Los Alamitos (2006)
18. Spalding, F., Walker, D.: Certifying compilation for a language with stack allocation. In: Proceedings of the 20th Annual IEEE Symposium on Logic in Computer Science (LICS 2005), Washington, DC, USA, pp. 407–416. IEEE Computer Society, Los Alamitos (2005)
19. Tofte, M., Talpin, J.-P.: Implementation of the typed call-by-value lambda-calculus using a stack of regions. In: Symposium on Principles of Programming Languages, pp. 188–201 (1994)

A Realizability Model for Impredicative Hoare Type Theory

Rasmus Lerchedahl Petersen[1], Lars Birkedal[1], Aleksandar Nanevski[2], and Greg Morrisett[2]

[1] IT University of Copenhagen
{rusmus,birkedal}@itu.dk
[2] Harvard University
{aleks,greg}@eecs.harvard.edu

Abstract. We present a denotational model of impredicative Hoare Type Theory, a very expressive dependent type theory in which one can specify and reason about mutable abstract data types.

The model ensures soundness of the extension of Hoare Type Theory with impredicative polymorphism; makes the connections to separation logic clear, and provides a basis for investigation of further sound extensions of the theory, in particular equations between computations and types.

1 Introduction

Dependent types provide a powerful form of specification for higher-order, functional languages. For example, using dependency, one can specify the signature of an array subscript operation as $\texttt{sub} : \forall\, \alpha\, .\, \Pi\, x\!:\!\alpha\, \texttt{array}.\Pi\, y\!:\!\{i\!:\!\texttt{nat} \mid i < x.\texttt{size}\}\, .\, \alpha$, where the type of the third argument, y, refines the underlying type nat using a predicate that ensures that y is a valid index for the array x.

Dependent types have long been used in formal mathematics, but their use in practical programming languages has proven challenging. One of the main reasons is that the presence of any computational effects, including non-termination, exceptions, access to store, or I/O – all of which are indispensable in practical programming – can quickly render a dependent type system unsound.

This can be addressed by restricting dependencies to only effect-free terms (e.g. as in DML [27]). But the goal of our work is to realize the full power of dependent types for specification of effectful programs. We have been developing the foundations of a language that we call *Hoare Type Theory* or HTT [18,17], which we intend to be an expressive, explicitly annotated internal language, providing a semantic framework for elaborating more practical external languages.

HTT starts with a pure, dependently typed core language and augments it with an indexed monadic type of the form $\{P\}x{:}A\{Q\}$. This type encapsulates effectful computations that may diverge or access a mutable store. The type can be read as a Hoare-like partial correctness specification, asserting that if the computation is run in a heap satisfying the pre-condition P, then if it terminates,

S. Drossopoulou (Ed.): ESOP 2008, LNCS 4960, pp. 337–352, 2008.

it will return a value x of type A and leave a heap described by Q. Through Hoare types, the system can enforce soundness in the presence of effects. The Hoare type admits small footprints as in separation logic [23,19], where the pre- and postconditions only describe the part of the store that the program actually uses; the unspecified part is automatically assumed invariant.

The most distinguishing feature of HTT in comparison with other recent proposals for Hoare- and separation logics for higher-order languages [4,14,28,15] is that specifications in HTT are *integrated with types.* In Hoare logic, it is not possible to abstract over specifications in the source programs, aggregate the logical invariants of the data structures with the data itself, compute with such invariants or nest the specifications into larger specifications or types. These features are essential ingredients for data abstraction and information hiding, and a number of works have been proposed towards integrating Hoare-like reasoning with type checking. Examples include tools and languages like Spec# [2], SPLint [12], ESC/Java [11], and JML [10].

Our prior work on HTT [18,17] addresses several of the main challenges for languages for integrated programming and verification [10]: (1) we allow effectful code in specifications by granting such code first-class status, via the monad for Hoare triples; (2) we control pointer aliasing, by employing the small footprint approach of separation logic; and (3) we use higher-order logic to allow for a uniform approach to programming and verification of imperative modules (aka mutable abstract data types), as suggested for separation logic in [5,6]. In our earlier work on HTT we proved soundness of the type theory via mostly operational methods, by proving progress and type preservation results. The operational proof was combined with a very crude denotational model, which just served to show that the assertion logic of HTT was sound. To deal with dependent types the operational proofs relied heavily on sophisticated techniques involving so-called hereditary substitutions [26].

In this paper we define a realizability model for an extension of Hoare Type Theory with impredicative polymorphism. Apart from the inherent interest in obtaining a denotational model, which provides an alternative more abstract conceptual understanding of the theory, the model serves the following purposes:

- Using the model we can prove soundness / consistency of an extension of Hoare Type Theory with *impredicative* polymorphism. Impredicative polymorphism is important for data abstraction (we show an example below) and for representing certain compiler transformations, such as closure conversion [16], in HTT. It is well-known that the operational methods involving hereditary substitutions mentioned above do not easily scale to impredicative polymorphism. We emphasize that it is highly non-trivial to devise a model of dependent type theory combining an impredicative universe of types with a classical logic and with computation types supporting fixed point induction. We summarize the key challenges involved later on in this introduction.
- The model allows us to use syntax and typing rules that have a more natural reading; in earlier presentations of HTT the operational techniques forced clunkier terms (in order to get the theorems to go through). In particular,

the syntax for computations is fairly close to the one employed in separation logic. Our impredicative HTT is the first model of separation logic for such an expressive language (higher types and impredicative polymorphism).
- We can finally introduce some non-trivial equations on computations. The operational approach we took before largely precluded this.

It is non-trivial to construct sound models of sophisticated dependent type theories such as HTT. Models for various fragments of dependent type theories have been studied intensively in categorical type theory; see, e.g., [13] and the references therein. Thus we shall make use of results from categorical type theory to *prove* that we construct a sound model of impredicative HTT, but we shall always write out the definitions in explicit terms so as to make the paper reasonably self contained. We now give an intuitive overview of the development.

Overview of HTT. HTT is a dependent type theory with types and kinds, where types are included in the kinds, and where types and kinds can both depend on kinds (and thus types). Thus contexts Γ assign kinds to variables and there are judgments $\Gamma \vdash \tau : \mathrm{Type}$ and $\Gamma \vdash A : \mathrm{Kind}$ to conclude that τ is a well-formed type in context Γ and that A is a well-formed kind in context Γ. Type and kind formers include dependent product (Π) and dependent sum (Σ). In the extension with impredicative polymorphism that we consider in this paper, we have that Type is a kind. Thus this part of pure impredicative HTT is (weak) Full Higher-order Dependent Type Theory (FhoDTT) [13].

In addition to types and kinds, HTT also includes a logic for reasoning about terms in context. Thus there is a judgment $\Gamma \vdash P : \mathrm{Prop}$ for concluding that P is a well-formed proposition and a judgment $\Gamma \mid P_1, \ldots, P_n \vdash P$ for logical entailment. The logic is higher-order, so Prop is a kind. In Jacobs's terminology we thus have a Higher-order Dependent Predicate Logic over (weak) Full Higher-order Dependent Type Theory [13]. The extra feature of HTT is that it includes a type for computations $\Gamma \vdash \{P\}\ x{:}\tau\ \{Q\} : \mathrm{Type}$. Here P and Q are propositions in context Γ and $\Gamma, x : \tau$, respectively. The intuition is that elements of this type consist of computations, which, given a heap satisfying P either diverges or produces a value of type τ and a heap in Q. Note that computations can diverge; term formers for computations include a fixed point term.

The great benefit of impredicative polymorphism is that for any type τ, $\Pi\ \alpha : \mathrm{Type}\ .\ \tau$ is also a type, even if τ depends on α. Thus terms of this polymorphic type can be returned by computations and stored in memory. Prop is also a kind. So again $\Pi P{:}\mathrm{Prop}\ .\ \tau$ is a type where τ may depend on P. This enables us to abstract over predicates in computation types. Using that $\Sigma P{:}\mathrm{Prop}\ .\ \tau$ is a type, we can pack computations with abstract invariants and hide implementation details. As an illustration of both of these features consider the following type of abstract stacks:

$$
\begin{array}{l}
\mathsf{stacktype} = \Pi\alpha{:}\mathrm{Type}\ .\ \Sigma\beta{:}\mathrm{Type}.\Sigma\ \mathit{inv}{:}\beta \times \alpha\,\mathrm{list} \to \mathrm{Prop}\ . \\
\quad /*\,\mathtt{new}\,*/\quad (-).\{\mathrm{emp}\}s{:}\beta\{\mathit{inv}(s,[])\} \times \\
\quad /*\,\mathtt{push}\,*/\ \Pi s{:}\beta\ .\ \Pi x{:}\alpha\ .\ (l{:}\alpha\,\mathrm{list}).\{\mathit{inv}(s,l)\}u{:}1\{\mathit{inv}(s,x::l)\} \times \\
\quad /*\,\mathtt{pop}\,*/\ \ \Pi s{:}\beta\ .\ (x{:}\alpha, l{:}\alpha\,\mathrm{list})\ .\ \{\mathit{inv}(s,x::l)\}y{:}\alpha\{\mathit{inv}(s,l) \wedge y =_\alpha x\} \times \\
\quad /*\,\mathtt{del}\,*/\ \ \Pi s{:}\beta\ .\ (l{:}\alpha\,\mathrm{list}).\{\mathit{inv}(s,l)\}u{:}1\{\mathrm{emp}\}
\end{array}
$$

The contexts before the precondition in the computation types, e.g., $(l:\alpha\,\text{list})$ for push, universally binds auxiliary / logical variables used in the specifications. A term of type stacktype accepts a type α and produces a stack of elements of this type. Such a stack consists of

- β, an abstract type to be thought of as α stack.
- inv, an abstract invariant that expresses that objects of type β represent functional stacks (as described by α list).
- Operations new, push, pop, and del. Notice, that push, pop, and del require an element of type β, and that the only way to obtain one such is via new.

Since stacktype is by impredicativity itself a type, we can have stacks of stacks. More generally, we can compose first-class abstract data types (i.e., objects) without needing to artificially stratify them which is necessary in modern programming. Note that in separation logic parlance the types are *tight*. For instance, the precondition for new is simply emp, so new does not rely on the input heap; the frame rule ensures that new can also be used with the following type $(-).\{\text{emp} * R\}s{:}\beta\{inv(s,[\,]) * R\}$, for any R. Further observe that implementors of the above abstract stack type are free to choose both the representation type β and the representation predicate inv. For example, an implementation using linked lists could take β to be Nat (since we use Nat as the type of locations) and $inv(s,l)$ to be the predicate that holds if s points to a linked list representation of l. A simple example client that creates a new Nat stack, pushes 4, pops it again to return it and deletes the stack would then look like this:

$$\begin{aligned}C = \lambda S{:}\texttt{stacktype}\ .\ &\texttt{do}\ S_{\text{Nat}} \leftarrow \texttt{ret}\ S(\text{Nat})\ \texttt{in}\\ &\texttt{unpack}\ S_{\text{Nat}}\ \texttt{as}\ (\beta, inv, \texttt{new}, \texttt{push}, \texttt{pop}, \texttt{del})\ \texttt{in}\\ &\quad \texttt{do}\ s \leftarrow \texttt{new}\ \texttt{in}\ \texttt{push}(s)(4); \texttt{do}\ n_4 \leftarrow \texttt{pop}(s)\ \texttt{in}\ \texttt{del}(s); \texttt{ret}\ n_4\end{aligned}$$

Then C has type $\Pi S{:}\texttt{stacktype}\ .\ (-).\{\text{emp}\}n{:}\text{Nat}\{\text{emp} \wedge n =_{\text{Nat}} 4\}$. We often (as in C) abbreviate $\texttt{do}\ y \leftarrow M\ \texttt{in}\ N$ to $M; N$ when y does not occur in N.

Computations are not only needed for accessing the store but also for non-termination as the pure fragment does not include fixed points. As an example of a simple fixed point computation (not using the store), consider the factorial function $fac : T$, where $T = \Pi n{:}\text{Nat}\ .\ (-).\{\text{emp}\}m{:}\text{Nat}\{\text{emp} \wedge m =_{\text{Nat}} n!\}$:

$$\begin{aligned}fac = \texttt{fix}\ f(n)\ \texttt{in}\ &\texttt{case}\ n\ \texttt{of}\\ &\quad\texttt{zero} \Rightarrow \texttt{ret}\ 1\ \texttt{or}\\ &\quad\texttt{succ}\ y \Rightarrow \texttt{do}\ m \leftarrow f(y)\ \texttt{in}\ \texttt{ret}\ m \times \texttt{succ}\ y\end{aligned}$$

We can implement another version of factorial using the store but with the same type, in the following manner. First we define a term $fac_S : T_S$, where $T_S = \Pi l{:}\text{Nat}\ .\ (n{:}\text{Nat}).\{l \mapsto_{\text{Nat}} n\}u{:}1\{l \mapsto_{\text{Nat}} n!\}$:

$$\begin{aligned}fac_S = \texttt{fix}\ f(l)\ \texttt{in}\ &\texttt{do}\ t \leftarrow !_{\text{Nat}}\ l\ \texttt{in}\ \texttt{case}\ t\ \texttt{of}\\ &\texttt{zero} \Rightarrow l :=_{\text{Nat}} 1\ \texttt{or}\\ &\texttt{succ}\ y \Rightarrow \texttt{do}\ l_y \leftarrow \texttt{alloc}_{\text{Nat}}\ y\ \texttt{in}\\ &\qquad f(l_y); \texttt{do}\ t_y \leftarrow !_{\text{Nat}}\ l_y\ \texttt{in}\ l :=_{\text{Nat}} t_y \times \texttt{succ}\ y; \texttt{dealloc}\ l_y\end{aligned}$$

Given this we can implement the factorial function as

$$fac' = \lambda n{:}\text{Nat}\ .\ \texttt{do}\ l \leftarrow\ \texttt{alloc}_{\text{Nat}}\ n\ \texttt{in}\ fac_S(l); \texttt{do}\ r \leftarrow !_{\text{Nat}}\ l\ \texttt{in}\ \texttt{dealloc}\ l; \texttt{ret}\ r$$

Now fac' has the same type T as fac. Using the model, we can prove that $fac =_T fac'$, so we can use them interchangeably when reasoning in the logic. This could not be done in earlier versions of HTT.

Overview of Model. Our model is a realizability model, built over a universal domain V, which is sufficiently rich to model divergent computations. The domain V also includes a subdomain of computations, called $\mathrm{T}(V)$.

The model for the weak FhoDTT part of HTT is mostly standard (see, e.g.,[13, Examples 11.6.5 and 11.6.7]): types are interpreted as chain-complete partial equivalence relations (complete pers) over V and kinds are interpreted as so-called assemblies (aka ω-sets) over V. The category of assemblies is an extension of the category of sets and functions which contains the category of complete pers as a full subcategory. The latter ensures that we soundly model that types are included among kinds. Moreover, the collection of all complete pers form a set and hence an assembly, and thus we model that Type is a Kind. Terms with type $\Pi x : \tau.\sigma$ are modeled as set-theoretic functions between the set of equivalence classes for the pers interpreting τ and σ which are *realized* by an element in V. That is, there is a continuous function from V to V that maps related elements in the first per to related elements in the second per. In reality, the model is a bit more complicated since we have to deal with *families* of types and kinds to model that types and kinds depend on kinds. Hence everything is indexed/fibred over the category of assemblies.

The propositions in HTT correspond to what is often called assertions in Hoare and separation logic. We model our classical propositions using the power set of heaps. Formally, we prove that the standard BI-hyperdoctrine [5] over Set can be extended to one over assemblies, and this guarantees that we get a sound model of the higher-order assertion logic (now for dependent types and kinds).

Finally, computation types are modeled roughly as follows. A computation type $\Gamma \vdash (\Delta).\{P\}x{:}\tau\{Q\}{:}\mathrm{Type}$ is modeled as an *admissible* per of continuous functions from Heap to $V \times$ Heap (or, rather, as a family of such, indexed over the interpretation of Γ). A per is admissible if it relates the bottom element to itself and is complete. Admissibility is needed for interpreting fixed points. An interesting issue is what per one should use on heaps. We have decided to use a per which equates two heaps if they have the same domain. This ensures that allocation of new heap cells, modeled here as taking the least unallocated address, will preserve the partial equivalence relation. This description is a bit rough for the following reasons. First, the interpretation ensures that computations can only access memory that is either described by the precondition P or allocated during the computation. Second, the interpretation uses the chain-complete closure of the post-condition Q. This ensures that the computation type really is interpreted as an admissible per. Taking the admissible closure is an alternative to restricting propositions to a fragment that always generates admissible pers or using test-functions/biorthogonality [9] to force admissibility. Third, the interpretation builds in the frame rule from separation logic, essentially by interpreting $\Gamma \vdash (\Delta).\{P\}x{:}\tau\{Q\}{:}\mathrm{Type}$ as $\Gamma \vdash \forall R{:}\mathrm{Prop}.(\Delta).\{P * R\}x{:}\tau\{Q * R\}{:}\mathrm{Type}$, at the modeling level. This idea comes from [8,9]; type theoretically the idea was also used in the earlier formulations of HTT [18,17].

In HTT every pure term can also be viewed as a computation. In the model this holds because pure terms are modeled via *continuously realized* functions, and such can be extended to continuous computations. Note that in a cruder set-theoretic model of the pure fragment of HTT, with types as sets with bounded cardinality and kinds as all sets, we would not be able to extend every pure term (any function, not necessarily continuous) to a continuous computation.

Let us summarize our informal overview of the model by mentioning what the key technical challenges are in constructing a model: First, note that our impredicative HTT combines a *classical* logic with an impredicative universe of types. Consistency, the very existence of a non-trivial model, is therefore highly non-trivial. It hinges on the fact that impredicative HTT does *not* include full subset types or the axiom of unique choice (that every functional relation determines a term). Second, note that we need to model types as some kind of domains in order to accomodate fixed points for the computation types, and, at the same time, types should form an impredicative universe. That is why we use chain-complete pers and not the more standard model of FhoDTT using all pers, and thus we need to prove that we actually do get a model of HTT using such pers. Third, we need to find chain-complete pers for modelling the computation types. Finally, since the logic is over dependent types we need to prove that we can get a model of separation logic over dependent types.

Related Work. In the previous section we have given some pointers to related work on models of separation logic and categorical models of dependent type theory. Other very related work includes the recent step-indexed model by Appel et. al. [1], where they describe a model that can be used for the types of imperative languages. However, their model is for a much simpler type system than the one we consider since we deal with dependent types involving pre- and postconditions. Appel et. al. do, however, include a treatment of recursive types; we have left that for future work. It is more challenging in our setting, since our types are much more expressive. (Recursive types should exist, though, since admissible pers do accomodate a wide range of recursive types [7].) In contrast with Appel et. al. we further include a logic to reason about terms; so far it is not well-understood how to model logics in step-indexed models.

Let us also emphasize the relation to the work of Honda, Yoshida, and Berger on Hoare logics for higher-order languages (see [28] and the references therein). One of the differences between the two approaches is that Honda et. al. do not allow for equational reasoning among functions (as we do in dependent type theory). Instead they make use of an evaluation predicate. Intuitively, the evaluation predicate of Honda et. al. can be used to represent in the logic the distinction between pure terms and computations that we instead capture using the monadic language. Honda et. al. have so far focused on total correctness and have thus avoided the need for admissibility, which we have to deal with as we consider partial correctness and have a rule for fixed point induction.

Honda et. al. are able to deal with recursion through the store, but do not cover impredicative polymorphism.

The remainder of the paper is organized as follows: In Section 2 we present the language of impredicative HTT, and in Section 3 the model. In Section 4 we conclude and describe future work. For reasons of space the formal treatment is brief, please see the accompanying technical report [20] for more details.

2 Language

The grammar for types, kinds, propositions, terms and computations is as follows:

$$
\begin{array}{lll}
\text{Types} & \tau,\sigma,\rho ::= & \mathrm{Nat} \mid 1 \mid \Pi^T\ x{:}A\,.\,\tau \mid \Sigma^T\ x{:}A\,.\,\tau \mid (\Gamma).\{P\}x{:}\tau\{P\} \\
\text{Kinds} & A,B ::= & \tau \mid \mathrm{Type} \mid \mathrm{Prop} \mid \Pi^K\ x{:}A\,.\,A \mid \Sigma^K\ x{:}A\,.\,A \\
\text{Prop's} & P,Q,R ::= & \top \mid \bot \mid M =_A M \mid P \wedge P \mid P \vee P \mid P \supset P \mid \neg P \mid \\
 & & \forall\, x{:}A\,.\,P \mid \exists\, x{:}A\,.\,P \mid \mathrm{emp} \mid M \mapsto_\tau M \mid P * P \mid P -\!\!* P \\
\text{Terms} & M,N ::= & x \mid \mathtt{zero} \mid \mathtt{succ}\ M \mid \mathtt{rec}_{\mathrm{Nat}}(M,M) \mid () \mid \lambda^K\ x{:}A.M \mid \\
 & & \lambda^T\ x{:}A.M \mid M\ M \mid (M,M)^K \mid (M,M)^T \mid \mathtt{fst}\ M \mid \\
 & & \mathtt{snd}\ M \mid \mathtt{unpack}\ M\ \mathtt{as}\ (x,y)\ \mathtt{in}\ M \mid \mathtt{ret}\ M \mid \\
 & & \mathtt{case}\ M\ \mathtt{of}\ \mathtt{zero} \Rightarrow M\ \mathtt{or}\ \mathtt{succ}\ x \Rightarrow M \mid \mathtt{fix}\ f(x)\ \mathtt{in}\ M \mid \\
 & & !_\tau\ M \mid M :=_\tau M \mid \mathtt{do}\ x \leftarrow M\ \mathtt{in}\ M \mid \mathtt{alloc}_\tau\ M \mid \mathtt{dealloc}\ M
\end{array}
$$

and there are the following judgments:

$$
\begin{array}{cccc}
\Gamma \vdash A{:}\mathrm{Kind} & \Gamma \vdash A = A : \mathrm{Kind} & \Gamma \vdash \tau{:}\mathrm{Type} & \Gamma \vdash P{:}\mathrm{Prop} \\
\Gamma \vdash M{:}A & \Gamma \vdash M = M : A & \Gamma \mid \Theta \vdash P &
\end{array}
$$

The external equality rules include β- and η-equalities and monadic laws for computations.

To express the pre- and post conditions of computations in terms of propositions, we often write $M \mapsto_\tau -$ as a shorthand for $\exists x{:}\tau.M \mapsto_\tau x$. The model that we present in the Section 3 also accommodates coproducts of types and kinds, but we have omitted these from this paper.

Given the explanation in the Introduction, most of the rules are standard except for those for the computation fragment, which we include below. There are two kinds of sums: $\Sigma^T\ x{:}A\,.\,\sigma$ (a type) is used for weak sums over families of types, and $\Sigma^K\ x{:}A\,.\,B$ (a kind) is used for strong sums over families of kinds. Because of the distinction between weak and strong sums, there are two sets of elimination rules for sums (one with $\mathtt{unpack}\ M\ \mathtt{as}\ (x,y)\ \mathtt{in}\ M$ and one with `fst` and `snd`), as is standard. In the following section describing the model we explain why we get these different kinds of elimination rules when we show the concrete interpretation of sums.

Here are the non-structural rules for computations. Most of them are unsurprising for a tight interpretation of separation logic. The *fix* rule is used to define recursive functions and captures reasoning via fixed-point induction.

$$\frac{\Gamma \vdash M\!:\!(\Delta).\{P\}y\!:\!\sigma\{S\} \quad \Gamma, \Delta, x\!:\!\tau \vdash Q\!:\!\mathrm{Prop} \quad \Gamma, y\!:\!\sigma \vdash N\!:\!(\Delta).\{S\}x\!:\!\tau\{Q\}}{\Gamma \vdash \mathtt{do}\ y \leftarrow M\ \mathtt{in}\ N\!:\!(\Delta).\{P\}x\!:\!\tau\{Q\}}\ \mathit{seq}$$

$$\frac{\Gamma, \Delta \vdash \tau\!:\!\mathrm{Type} \quad \Gamma \vdash M\!:\!\tau}{\Gamma \vdash \mathtt{ret}\ M\!:\!(\Delta).\{\mathrm{emp}\}x\!:\!\tau\{\mathrm{emp} \wedge x =_\tau M\}}\ \mathit{dia}$$

$$\frac{\Gamma \vdash \tau\!:\!\mathrm{Type} \quad \Gamma \vdash M\!:\!\mathrm{Nat}}{\Gamma \vdash\ !_\tau\ M\!:\!(y\!:\!\tau).\{M \mapsto_\tau y\}x\!:\!\tau\{M \mapsto_\tau y \wedge x =_\tau y\}}\ \mathit{lookup}$$

$$\frac{\Gamma \vdash \tau\!:\!\mathrm{Type} \quad \Gamma \vdash M\!:\!\mathrm{Nat} \quad \Gamma \vdash N\!:\!\tau}{\Gamma \vdash M :=_\tau N\!:\!(-).\{M \mapsto_\sigma -\}x\!:\!1\{M \mapsto_\tau N\}}\ \mathit{update}$$

$$\frac{\Gamma \vdash \tau\!:\!\mathrm{Type} \quad \Gamma \vdash M\!:\!\tau}{\Gamma \vdash \mathtt{alloc}_\tau\ M\!:\!(-).\{\mathrm{emp}\}x\!:\!\mathrm{Nat}\{x \mapsto_\tau M\}}\ \mathit{alloc}$$

$$\frac{\Gamma \vdash \tau\!:\!\mathrm{Type} \quad \Gamma \vdash M\!:\!\mathrm{Nat}}{\Gamma \vdash \mathtt{dealloc}\ M\!:\!(-).\{M \mapsto_\tau -\}x : 1\{\mathrm{emp}\}}\ \mathit{dealloc}$$

$$\frac{\begin{array}{c}\Gamma \vdash M_1\!:\!(\Delta).\{P \wedge M =_{\mathrm{Nat}} \mathtt{zero}\}x\!:\!\tau\{Q\} \quad \Gamma \vdash M\!:\!\mathrm{Nat} \\ \Gamma, y\!:\!\mathrm{Nat} \vdash M_2\!:\!(\Delta).\{P \wedge M =_{\mathrm{Nat}} \mathtt{succ}\ y\}x\!:\!\tau\{Q\}\end{array}}{\Gamma \vdash \mathtt{case}\ M\ \mathtt{of}\ \mathtt{zero} \Rightarrow M_1\ \mathtt{or}\ \mathtt{succ}\ y \Rightarrow M_2\!:\!(\Delta).\{P\}x\!:\!\tau\{Q\}}\ \mathit{case}$$

$$\frac{\Gamma, f\!:\!\Pi^T\ y\!:\!A\ .\ (\Delta).\{P\}x\!:\!\tau\{Q\}, y\!:\!A \vdash M\!:\!(\Delta).\{P\}x\!:\!\tau\{Q\}}{\Gamma \vdash \mathtt{fix}\ f(x)\ \mathtt{in}\ M\!:\!\Pi^T\ y\!:\!A\ .\ (\Delta).\{P\}x\!:\!\tau\{Q\}}\ \mathit{fix}$$

The structural rules for computations include the frame rule and the rule of consequence, see [20] for details.

3 Model

Universe of Realizers. Let $Cppo_\perp$ denote the category of chain-complete pointed partial orders and strict continuous functions. Recall that one can solve recursive domain equations in $Cppo_\perp$ for locally continuous bifunctors on $Cppo_\perp$. We take our universe of realizers to be a domain V satisfying the following recursive domain equation in $Cppo_\perp$:

$$V \cong 1_\perp \oplus \mathbb{N}_\perp \oplus (V \times V)_\perp \oplus (V \to V)_\perp \oplus \mathrm{T}(V)_\perp,$$

where $1_\perp$ is the lift of the one-element set, $\mathbb{N}_\perp$ is lift of the flat natural numbers, $\oplus$ is smash sum, $\times$ is cartesian product, $V \to V$ is the set of continous functions from V to V, and $\mathrm{T}(V)$ is the domain of computations:

$$\mathrm{T}(V) = \mathrm{H}(V)_\perp \multimap ((V \otimes \mathrm{H}(V)_\perp) \oplus \mathbb{E}),$$

in which $\multimap$ denotes strict function space, $\otimes$ is smash product, $\mathbb{E} = \{\mathtt{err}\}_\perp$ and $\mathrm{H}(V)$ is the domain of heaps: $\{h \in \mathrm{Cppo}_\perp(\mathbb{N}_\perp, V) \mid \mathrm{supp}(h) \text{ is finite}\}$, where $\mathrm{supp}(h)$ is the set $\{x \in \mathrm{dom}(h) \mid h(x) \neq \perp\}$, ordered in the following way:

$h \leq h' \Leftrightarrow \mathrm{supp}(h) = \mathrm{supp}(h') \wedge \forall n \in \mathrm{supp}(h).h(n) \leq h'(n)$. Note that H is a locally continous functor whose functorial action is given by composition.

To denote elements in V we use the following injections, mapping elements into the appropriate summand and then, via the above isomorphism, into V.

$$in_1 : 1 \to V \qquad in_{\mathbb{N}} : \mathbb{N} \to V \qquad in_{\times} : (V \times V) \to V$$
$$in_{\to} : (V \to V) \to V \qquad in_{\mathrm{T}} : \mathrm{T}(V) \to V$$

Semantic Operations on Heaps. Elements of $\mathrm{H}(V)$ are total functions with finite support. We wish to think of them as partial functions in order to model separation logic. This is accomplished by interpreting $h(n) = \bot$ as "n is not allocated in h". This works because two heaps are only related in the partial order if they have the *same* support (and, moreover, are also pointwise ordered). Here we describe some definitions reflecting this interpretation.

Firstly, for $h, h' \in \mathrm{H}(V)$ we define $h \overset{\downarrow}{=} h'$ as h and h' having the same support. We can then define the $*$-operator on "disjoint" heaps. For heaps $h_1, h_2 \in \mathrm{H}(V)$ such that $\mathrm{supp}(h_1) \cap \mathrm{supp}(h_2) = \emptyset$, we define $h_1 * h_2$ as the heap with support $\mathrm{supp}(h_1) \cup \mathrm{supp}(h_2)$ satisfying $(h_1 * h_2)|_{\mathrm{supp}(h_1)} = h_1 \wedge (h_1 * h_2)|_{\mathrm{supp}(h_2)} = h_2$. In other words, $h_1 * h_2$ is the (disjoint) amalgamation of h_1 and h_2.

For $h \in \mathrm{H}(V)$, it makes sense to ask for "the least unallocated cell of h". $\mathtt{leastfree}(h)$ is defined as $\min\{n \in \mathbb{N} \mid h(n) = \bot\}$.

Updating the heap cell n is by redefining the value at n. For $h \in \mathrm{H}(V)$, $n \in \mathbb{N}$ and $d \in V$, we define the heap $h[n \mapsto d]$ by $\lambda m \in \mathbb{N}\,.\,\mathtt{if}\ m = n\ \mathtt{then}\ d\ \mathtt{else}\ h(m)$. Allocation is then by updating a cell that was previously unallocated with an element different from $\bot$ and deallocation of cell n in h results in $h[n \mapsto \bot]$.

Types and Kinds. We now describe the FhoDTT structure needed for interpreting types and kinds, beginning with the category $\mathrm{Asm}(V)$ of assemblies over V, which will be used for modeling contexts:

Definition ($\mathrm{Asm}(V)$):

Objects: (X, E), where X is a set, and $E \colon X \to \mathsf{P}(V)$, such that for all $x \in X$, $E(x) \neq \emptyset$.
Morphisms: $f \colon (X, E) \to (X', E')$, where $f \colon X \to X'$ is a set-theoretic function, such that there exists a realizer α for it, i.e

$$\exists\, \alpha : V \to V\ .\ \forall x \in X\ .\ \forall d \in E(x)\ .\ \alpha(d) \in E(f(x))$$

Note that $\mathrm{Asm}(V)$ is an extension of the category of sets and functions: there is a full and faithful functor $\nabla : \mathrm{Set} \to \mathrm{Asm}(V)$, which maps a set X to (X, E) with $E(x) = V$. Functor ∇ is right adjoint to $\Gamma : \mathrm{Asm}(V) \to \mathrm{Set}$, defined by $\Gamma(X, E) = X$, that is, there is a one-to-one correspondence between morphisms $(X, E) \to \nabla(Y)$ in $\mathrm{Asm}(V)$ and functions $X \to Y$ in Set.

Kinds in context are interpreted as families of assemblies indexed over assemblies. Formally, the structure is a fibration $\mathrm{UFam}(\mathrm{Asm}(V)) \to \mathrm{Asm}(V)$, defined as in [13]. The fibration of uniform families of assemblies is equivalent to the standard codomain fibration over assemblies, denoted $\mathrm{Asm}(V)^{\to} \to \mathrm{Asm}(V)$.

Types in context are modelled as families of chain-complete per's indexed over assemblies. We denote the category of chain-complete per's by CPer(V). The indexing is captured via a fibration UFam(CPer(V)) $\to$ Asm(V), defined similarly to the one for all pers (not only chain-complete pers).

Any complete per R can be seen as an assembly $(V/R, E)$, where V/R is the set of equivalence classes of R and E is the identity function. This will be used to model that types are included among the kinds. This inclusion of complete pers into assemblies extends to families and the extension has a left adjoint:

Lemma 1. *The fibred inclusion of* UFam(CPer(V)) *into* UFam(Asm(V)) *has a fibred left adjoint given by chain completion.*

We now present the formal statement which ensures that we can model soundly the pure type and kind fragment of HTT. After that, we explain how types and kinds are modeled concretely.

Theorem 1. *The categories and functors in the diagram*

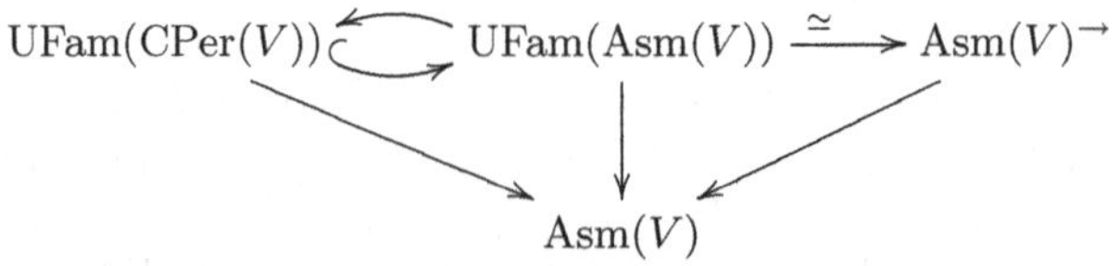

constitute a split weak FhoDTT with a fibred natural numbers object in UFam (CPer(V)), *which is also a fibred natural numbers object in* UFam(Asm(V)).

Corollary 1. *The pure type and kind fragment (excluding computation types) of HTT is sound wrt. the interpretation in the above FhoDTT.*

The empty context is interpreted as the terminal object in Asm(V): $[\![\emptyset]\!]^{\text{Ctxs}} = 1 = (\{*\}, * \mapsto V)$, and if $[\![\Gamma]\!]^{\text{Ctxs}} = (X, E)$ and $[\![\Gamma \vdash A : \text{Kind}]\!]^{\text{Kinds}} = ((A_x, E_{A_x}))_{x \in X}$ (a family of assemblies indexed over the assembly (X, E)), then $[\![\Gamma, x\!:\!A]\!]^{\text{Ctxs}}$ is

$$(\Sigma_{x \in X} A_x, (x, a) \mapsto \{(d, d') \in V \times V \mid d \in E(x) \wedge d' \in E_{A_x}(a)\})$$

Thus context formation is modeled by dependent sum. We now describe parts of the interpretation of kinds:

- the inclusion of types into kinds is modeled via the inclusion from complete pers into assemblies
- Type is modeled as an object in the fibre UFam(Asm(V))$_1$ over the terminal object 1 in Asm(V), i.e., as an object in Asm(V), namely $\nabla(Obj(\text{CPer}(V))$, where $Obj(\text{CPer}(V))$ is the set of all chain-complete pers over V.
- Prop is modeled by $\nabla\mathsf{P}(\mathsf{H}(V))$ (see the next subsection).
- Π^K is modeled by dependent product: If $[\![\Gamma \vdash A\!:\!\text{Kind}]\!]^{\text{Kinds}} = ((A_x, E_{A_x}))_{x \in X}$ and $[\![\Gamma, x : A \vdash B : \text{Kind}]\!]^{\text{Kinds}} = ((B_{(x,a)}, E_{B_{(x,a)}}))_{(x,a) \in \Sigma\ x:X\ .\ A_x}$ then $[\![\Gamma \vdash \Pi^K\ x\!:\!A\ .\ B\!:\!\text{Kind}]\!]^{\text{Kinds}}$ is given by

$$(\{f \in \Pi_{a \in A_x} B_{(x,a)} \mid E_{\Pi_x}(f) \neq \emptyset\}, E_{\Pi_x})_{x \in X},$$

where E_{Π_x} is given by

$$f \mapsto \{in_{\rightarrow}(g) \mid \forall a \in A_x.e \in E_{A_x}(a) \Rightarrow g\ e \in E_{B_{(x,a)}}(f(a))\}.$$

- Σ^K is modeled by dependent sum.
- External equality of kinds is interpreted by equality in the model.

We now describe the interpretation of the pure types:

- Nat is modeled by the flat naturals, i.e $(\{(in_{\mathbb{N}}(n), in_{\mathbb{N}}(n)) \mid n \in \mathbb{N}\})$
- 1 is modeled by the terminal object in CPer(V), i.e., as $(\{(in_1(*), in_1(*))\})$.
- Π^T is modeled by dependent product.
- Σ^T is modeled by dependent sum: If $[\![\Gamma \vdash A\!:\!\mathrm{Kind}]\!]^{\mathrm{Kinds}} = ((A_x, E_{A_x}))_{x \in X}$ and $[\![\Gamma, x : A \vdash \tau : \mathrm{Type}]\!]^{\mathrm{Types}} = (R_{(x,a)})_{(x,a) \in \Sigma\ x:X\ .\ A_x}$ then $[\![\Gamma \vdash \Sigma^T\ x : A\ .\ \tau\!:\!\mathrm{Type}]\!]^{\mathrm{Types}}$ is given by $(B_x)_{x \in X}$, where B_x is

$$\mathcal{CC}(\{(in_{\times}(d,e), in_{\times}(d',e')) \mid \exists a \in A_x.d, d' \in E_{A_x}(a) \wedge e\ R_{(x,a)} e'\}).$$

  Here $\mathcal{CC}(R)$ denotes the chain completion of R (the reflection into UFam (CPer(V)), cf. Lemma 1). We need to use the chain-completion to get a chain-complete per and the elements in the chain-completion are not necessarily pairs of realizers for the constituent types. This is why these sums are only weak. Indeed, if we try to apply the first-projection realizer to a realizer for an element of the above sum, then we will not be sure to end up with a realizer for A (we only know that we'll get something in the chain-completion of A).

An external equality judgment of kinds $\Gamma \vdash A = B$: Kind *holds* if A and B are interpreted as the same objects in the fibre over the interpretation of Γ. Likewise for external equality of types $\Gamma \vdash \tau = \sigma$: Type. The soundness corollary 1 means that any external equality judgment that can be derived holds.

The following lemma shows that any well-typed term corresponds to a proper value in the model, even the diverging computation. The computation types relate the least element of T(V) to itself.

Lemma 2. *For any type $\Gamma \vdash \sigma\!:\!\mathrm{Type}$, no per in the family $[\![\Gamma \vdash \sigma\!:\!\mathrm{Type}]\!]^{\mathrm{Types}}$ relates $\bot$ to itself.*

We omit the description of the interpretation of pure terms. Suffice it to say that lambda abstractions in the calculus really are interpreted via continuous functions (realizers from $V \to V$).

We say that an external equality judgment of terms $\Gamma \vdash M = N : A$ *holds* if M and N are interpreted as the same morphism. The soundness corollary 1 means that any derivable external equality judgment of terms holds.

Logic. As in separation logic, we really have a logic of heaps and hence propositions will be modeled as subsets of H(V). We obtain the structure needed for interpreting the logic as follows. The power set of heaps $\mathsf{P}(\mathrm{H}(V))$ ordered by inclusion is a BI-algebra [21] in Set. We embed it into Asm(V) via the functor ∇ to get $\nabla(\mathsf{P}(\mathrm{H}(V)))$. One can show that the object is an internally complete BI-algebra in Asm(V). Hence, as explained in [5], there is a canonical BI-hyperdoctrine $P = \mathrm{Asm}(\_, \nabla(\mathsf{P}(\mathrm{H}(V))))$, which soundly models classical higher-order separation logic. Note that the fibre over an object (X, E) in P is the set of morphisms in Asm(V) from (X, E) to $\nabla(\mathsf{P}(\mathrm{H}(V)))$, which, as mentioned earlier, is in one-to-one correspondence with functions from X to $\mathsf{P}(\mathrm{H}(V))$ in Set. Hence, a proposition in context $\Gamma \vdash P : \mathrm{Prop}$ is interpreted as follows: Suppose Γ is interpreted as the assembly (X, E). Then P is interpreted as a function from X to $\mathsf{P}(\mathrm{H}(V))$. The propositional connectives are all interpreted in the standard way from separation logic. For instance, $[\![\Gamma \vdash P * Q : \mathrm{Prop}]\!]^{\mathrm{Props}}_x$ is $\{h \mid \exists h_1 \in [\![\Gamma \vdash P : \mathrm{Prop}]\!]^{\mathrm{Props}}_x, h_2 \in [\![\Gamma \vdash Q : \mathrm{Prop}]\!]^{\mathrm{Props}}_x \;.\; h = h_1 * h_2\}$. The quantifiers are also interpreted in the standard way. For instance,

$$[\![\Gamma \vdash \forall y : A.P : \mathrm{Prop}]\!]^{\mathrm{Props}}_x = \{h \mid \forall y \in [\![\Gamma \vdash A : \mathrm{Kind}]\!]^{\mathrm{Kinds}}_x \;.\; h \in [\![\Gamma, y : A \vdash P]\!]^{\mathrm{Props}}_{(x,y)}\}$$

In the display above, note that $[\![\Gamma \vdash A : \mathrm{Kind}]\!]^{\mathrm{Kinds}}$ is a uniform family of assemblies over (X, E), so $[\![\Gamma \vdash A : \mathrm{Kind}]\!]^{\mathrm{Kinds}}_x$ is an assembly (Y, E_Y). When we write $y \in [\![\Gamma \vdash A : \mathrm{Kind}]\!]^{\mathrm{Kinds}}_x$, we mean that $y \in Y$. Note that y may *depend* on x (we have a separation logic for a *dependent* type theory).

Now it should also be clear why the kind Prop is interpreted as $\nabla(\mathsf{P}(\mathrm{H}(V)))$.

Computations. As mentioned in Section 1, a computation type $(\Delta).\{P\}x : \tau\{Q\}$ is modeled as an admissible per of realizers in T(V), which given heaps satisfying the precondition P do not produce error and upon termination leaves a heap satisfying the postcondition Q. The context Δ is implicitly quantified, so that this behaviour should be adhered to for all instantiations of Δ. Formally it looks like this. Assume $[\![\Gamma]\!]^{\mathrm{Ctxs}} = (X, E)$ and $[\![\Gamma, \Delta]\!]^{\mathrm{Ctxs}} = (\Sigma_{x \in X} Y_x, F)$. Then $[\![\Gamma \vdash (\Delta).\{P\}x : \tau\{Q\} : \mathrm{Type}]\!]^{\mathrm{Types}}$ is the family of pers $(S_x)_{x \in X}$ with fields given by $d \in |S_x|$ iff $d = in_{\mathrm{T}}(f)$ and

$$\begin{aligned} &\forall y \in Y_x. \forall E \in \mathrm{Prop}_{\Gamma,\Delta}. \forall h \in [\![\Gamma, \Delta \vdash (P \;*\; E)]\!]^{\mathrm{Props}}_{(x,y)}.(f(h) \neq \mathtt{err}) \wedge \\ &\Big(f(h) = (v_f, h_f) \Rightarrow \quad v_f \in |[\![\Gamma, \Delta \vdash \tau : \mathrm{Type}]\!]^{\mathrm{Types}}_{(x,y)}| \wedge \\ &\qquad\qquad\qquad h_f \in \mathcal{CC}([\![\Gamma, \Delta, x : \tau \vdash (Q \;*\; E)]\!]^{\mathrm{Props}}_{(x,y,v_f)})\Big) \end{aligned}$$

So suitable realizers are elements of T(V) that for any extension $P \;*\; E$ of P takes heaps satisfying $P \;*\; E$ to heaps satisfying the chain-completion of $Q \;*\; E$ and do not produce error. Thus the frame rule is baked into the interpretation of computations. This does not support the law of conjunctivity. The actual per is then given by $in_{\mathrm{T}}(f) \; S_x \; in_{\mathrm{T}}(g)$ iff $in_{\mathrm{T}}(f), in_{\mathrm{T}}(g) \in |S_x|$ and

$$\begin{aligned} &\forall y \in Y_x. \forall E \in \mathrm{Prop}_{\Gamma,\Delta}. \forall h, h' \in [\![\Gamma, \Delta \vdash (P \;*\; E)]\!]^{\mathrm{Props}}_{(x,y)}. h \stackrel{\downarrow}{=} h' \Rightarrow \\ &f(h) \downarrow \Leftrightarrow g(h') \downarrow \wedge \Big(f(h) = (v_f, h_f) \wedge g(h') = (v_g, h_g) \Rightarrow \\ &\qquad\qquad v_f \; [\![\Gamma, \Delta \vdash \tau : \mathrm{Type}]\!]^{\mathrm{Types}}_{(x,y)} \; v_g \;\wedge\; h_f \stackrel{\downarrow}{=} h_g\Big) \end{aligned}$$

So two realizers denote the same computation if they both fulfill the specification and on heaps with equal support gives results related in the interpretation of the return type and heaps with equal support.

Lemma 3. *Let* $[\![\Gamma]\!]^{\mathrm{Ctxs}} = (X, E)$ *and* $[\![\Gamma \vdash (\Delta).\{P\}x : \tau\{Q\} : \mathrm{Type}]\!]^{\mathrm{Types}} = (S_x)_{x \in X}$. *Then for all* $x \in X$, S_x *is a chain-complete per with its field inside* T(V), *relating* $in_{\mathrm{T}}(\lambda h \;.\; \bot)$ *to itself. As such it is an admissible per over* T(V).

As mentioned in the introduction, we require that computations should produce heaps with equal support (given suitable heaps with equal support) so that allocation can be modeled by taking the least unallocated address (see the semantics of `alloc` below). An unfortunate consequence of this choice is that two computations that intuitively behave in the same way but allocate cells in different order may *not* be equated by the model. We believe that the model can be refined by using realizers in FM-domains [25,24,3], such that support would then be up to a permutation of the locations in the heap. (Indeed, FM-domains have already been applied in a recent parametric model for separation logic [9].) We leave this refinement for future work, however.

We now describe how terms of computation types are interpreted in the model. Recall that for a computation type $(\Delta).\{P\}x\!:\!\tau\{Q\}$, we can give the interpretation of $\Gamma \vdash M\!:\!(\Delta).\{P\}x\!:\!\tau\{Q\}$ by giving the realizer α.

We first consider the structural rules for computations. We begin with the frame rule. Assume $[\![\Gamma]\!]^{\mathrm{Ctxs}} = (X, E)$ and that $[\![\Gamma \vdash M : (\Delta).\{P\}x : \tau\{Q\}]\!]^{\mathrm{Terms}}$ is realized by α. Then $[\![\Gamma \vdash M : (\Delta).\{P * R\}x : \tau\{Q * R\}]\!]^{\mathrm{Terms}}$ is also realized by α since, for all $x \in X$, the field of $[\![\Gamma \vdash (\Delta).\{P\}x : \tau\{Q\} : \mathrm{Type}]\!]^{\mathrm{Types}}_x$ is included in the field of $[\![\Gamma \vdash (\Delta).\{P * R\}x\!:\!\tau\{Q * R\} : \mathrm{Type}]\!]^{\mathrm{Types}}_x$ (here we use that the frame rule is baked into the interpretation of computation types). The remaining structural rules are also interpreted by using the same realizer. For the consequence rule we use that the chain-completion operation is monotone.

Now for the non-structural rules: Assume $[\![\Gamma]\!]^{\mathrm{Ctxs}} = (X, E)$ and that $[\![M]\!]$ is given by α and $[\![N]\!]$ is given by β when they are of computation types and m and n otherwise. Then

$$
\begin{aligned}
&[\![\Gamma \vdash \mathtt{do}\ y \leftarrow M\ \mathtt{in}\ N\!:\!(\Delta).\{P\}x\!:\!\tau\{Q\}]\!]^{\mathrm{Terms}}\\
&\quad = \lambda e\ .\ \lambda h\ .\ \mathtt{if}\ \alpha(e)(h) = (v_M, h_M)\ \mathtt{then}\ \beta(e, v_M)(h_M)\ \mathtt{else}\ \alpha(e)(h)\\
&[\![\Gamma \vdash \mathtt{ret}\ M\!:\!(\Delta).\{\mathrm{emp}\}x\!:\!\tau\{\mathrm{emp} \wedge x =_\tau M\}]\!]^{\mathrm{Terms}} = \lambda e\ .\ \lambda h.(m(e), h)\\
&[\![\Gamma \vdash\ !_\tau\ M\!:\!(y\!:\!\tau).\{M \mapsto_\tau y\}x\!:\!\tau\{M \mapsto_\tau y \wedge x =_\tau y\}]\!]^{\mathrm{Terms}}\\
&\quad = \lambda e\ .\ \lambda h\ .\ \mathtt{if}\ h(m(e)) = \bot\ \mathtt{then\ err\ else}\ (h(m(e)), h)\\
&[\![\Gamma \vdash M :=_\tau N\!:\!(-).\{M \mapsto -\}x\!:\!1\{M \mapsto_\tau N\}]\!]^{\mathrm{Terms}} = \lambda e\ .\ \lambda h.(*, h[m \mapsto n])\\
&[\![\Gamma \vdash \mathtt{alloc}_\tau\ M\!:\!(-).\{\mathrm{emp}\}x\!:\!\mathrm{Nat}\{x \mapsto_\tau M\}]\!]^{\mathrm{Terms}}\\
&\quad = \lambda e\ .\ \lambda h\ .\ \mathtt{let}\ l = \mathtt{leastfree}(h)\ \mathtt{in}\ (l, h[l \mapsto m])\\
&[\![\Gamma \vdash \mathtt{dealloc}\ M\!:\!(-).\{M \mapsto_\tau -\}x : 1\{\mathrm{emp}\}]\!]^{\mathrm{Terms}}\\
&\quad = \lambda e\ .\ \lambda h.\mathtt{if}\ h(m) = \bot\ \mathtt{then\ err\ else}\ (*, h[m \mapsto \bot])\\
&[\![\Gamma \vdash \mathtt{case}\ M\ \mathtt{of\ zero} \Rightarrow M_1\ \mathtt{or\ succ}\ y \Rightarrow M_2\!:\!(\Delta).\{P\}x\!:\!\tau\{Q\}]\!]^{\mathrm{Terms}}\\
&\quad = \lambda e\ .\ \lambda h\ .\ \mathtt{if}\ m(e) = in_{\mathbb{N}}(0)\ \mathtt{then}\ \alpha_1(e)(h)\ \mathtt{else}\ \alpha_2(e, m-1)(h)\\
&[\![\Gamma \vdash \mathtt{fix}\ f(x)\ \mathtt{in}\ M\!:\!\Pi^T\ y\!:\!\sigma\ .\ (\Delta).\{P\}x\!:\!\tau\{Q\}]\!]^{\mathrm{Terms}}\\
&\quad = \lambda e\ .\ \mathtt{fixedpointof}\ \lambda f\ .\ \lambda y\ .\ \alpha(e, f, y))
\end{aligned}
$$

Note that the realizers for computations are as one would hope. Consider, for example, lookup $!M$, whose realizer is $\lambda e\ .\ \lambda h\ .\ \mathtt{if}\ h(m(e)) = \bot\ \mathtt{then\ err\ else}$ $(h(m(e)), h)$. Given a realizer e in $E_X(x)$ (intuitively, a realizer for Γ), it produces a computation that when given a heap h yields error if the location $m(e)$ is not allocated in h and otherwise the value stored in h at $m(e)$, along with h. The realizer e is needed, as always, because the type theory is dependent.

For fixed points, the realizer is obtained by the usual least fixed point construction, which applies since $\lambda f\ .\ \lambda y\ .\ \alpha(e, f, y)$ is indeed an endofunction of the pointed domain $V \to T(V)$, when α is the realizer for $[\![\Gamma, f\!:\!\Pi^T\ y\!:\!\sigma\ .\ (\Delta).\{P\}x\!:\!\tau\{Q\}, y\!:\!\sigma \vdash M\!:\!(\Delta).\{P\}x\!:\!\tau\{Q\}]\!]^{\mathrm{Terms}}$.

Theorem 2. *The interpretation of computations is well-defined, i.e., any well-typed computation term* $\Gamma \vdash M : (\Delta).\{P\}x : \tau\{Q\}$ *is interpreted as a morphism* $1 \to [\![\Gamma \vdash (\Delta).\{P\}x : \tau\{Q\} : \mathrm{Type}]\!]^{\mathrm{Types}}$ *in the fibre over* $[\![\Gamma]\!]^{\mathrm{Ctxs}}$. *Moreover, the external equality rules for computations hold.*

Notice that the above theorem expresses that *well-typed programs do not produce error*: If $[\![\Gamma]\!]^{\mathrm{Ctxs}} = (X, E_X)$ and $[\![\Gamma \vdash M : (\Delta).\{P\}x : \tau\{Q\}]\!]^{\mathrm{Terms}} = m$ then, for all $x \in X$, all $e \in E_X(x)$, m(e) is in $[\![\Gamma \vdash (\Delta).\{P\}x : \tau\{Q\} : \mathrm{Type}]\!]^{\mathrm{Types}}_x$. Thus $m(e)$ is a realizer in $\mathrm{T}(V)$, which given a heap satisfying P does not produce `err`. If $m(e)$ then terminates (does not give $\bot$), it returns a value and a heap in the chain-completion of Q. For a discussion of the use of the chain-completion, please see the accompanying technical report.

4 Conclusion and Future Work

We have developed a realizability model for impredicative Hoare Type Theory, a very expressive dependent type theory in which one can specify and reason about mutable abstract data types. The model is used to establish the soundness of the type theory. Moreover, the model can be used to discover new equations between terms and types.

Our model also accommodates certain kinds of subset kinds and types. For a kind A we can model the subset kind $\{x : A \mid P\}$, for all propositions P. For a type τ we can model the subset kind $\{x : \tau \mid P\}$, for all *chain-complete* propositions P; it also seems possible to model subset types $\{x : \tau \mid P\}$, for all propositions P by using the chain-completion. The subset kinds / types will not be *full* subset kinds / types, however, for the same reason that we do not have full subset types for the standard separation logic BI-hyperdoctrine over Set [5]. Future work includes investigating how to model recursive types, as needed for the specification of programs that recurse through the store [22]. It would also be interesting to refine the model using, e.g., FM-domains to get a more abstract model of allocation leading to more equalities among terms. Another avenue for future work is to explore the soundness of higher-order frame rules [8]. This seems to involve a further level of indexing over a Kripke structure similar to the one in [8]. Finally, it would also be interesting to investigate relational parametricity for the impredicative polymorphism.

References

1. Appel, A., Melliès, P.-A., Richards, C., Vouillon, J.: A very modal model of a modern, major, general type system. In: POPL 2007 (2007)
2. Barnett, M., Leino, K.R.M., Schulte, W.: The Spec# programming system: An overview. In: Barthe, G., Burdy, L., Huisman, M., Lanet, J.-L., Muntean, T. (eds.) CASSIS 2004. LNCS, vol. 3362, Springer, Heidelberg (2005)
3. Benton, N., Leperchey, B.: Relational reasoning in a nominal semantics for storage. In: Urzyczyn, P. (ed.) TLCA 2005. LNCS, vol. 3461, pp. 88–101. Springer, Heidelberg (2005)

4. Berger, M., Honda, K., Yoshida, N.: A logical analysis of aliasing in imperative higher-order functions. In: Danvy, O., Pierce, B.C. (eds.) ICFP 2005, Tallinn, Estonia, September 2005, pp. 280–293 (2005)
5. Biering, B., Birkedal, L., Torp-Smith, N.: Bi hyperdoctrines and higher-order separation logic. In: Sagiv, M. (ed.) ESOP 2005. LNCS, vol. 3444, pp. 233–247. Springer, Heidelberg (2005)
6. Biering, B., Birkedal, L., Torp-Smith, N.: BI hyperdoctrines, Higher-Order Separation Logic, and Abstraction. In: TOPLAS 2007 (to appear, 2007)
7. Birkedal, L., Møgelberg, R., Petersen, R.: Domain-theoretic models of parametric polymorphism. In: TCS (to appear, 2007)
8. Birkedal, L., Torp-Smith, N., Yang, H.: Semantics of separation-logic typing and higher-order frame rules for algol-like languages. LMCS 2(5:1), 1–33 (2006)
9. Birkedal, L., Yang, H.: Relational parametricity and separation logic. In: Seidl, H. (ed.) FOSSACS 2007. LNCS, vol. 4423, Springer, Heidelberg (2007)
10. Burdy, L., Cheon, Y., Cok, D., Ernst, M., Kiniry, J., Leavens, G.T., Leino, K.R.M., Poll, E.: An overview of JML tools and applications. International Journal on Software Tools for Technology Transfer 7(3), 212–232 (2005)
11. Detlefs, D.L., Leino, K.R.M., Nelson, G., Saxe, J.B.: Extended static checking. Compaq Systems Research Center, Research Report 159 (December 1998)
12. Evans, D., Larochelle, D.: Improving security using extensible lightweight static analysis. IEEE Software 19(1), 42–51 (2002)
13. Jacobs, B.: Categorical Logic and Type Theory. Studies in Logic and the Foundations of Mathematics, vol. 141. Elsevier, Amsterdam (1999)
14. Krishnaswami, N.: Separation logic for a higher-order typed language. In: SPACE 2006, pp. 73–82 (2006)
15. Krishnaswami, N., Aldrich, J., Birkedal, L.: Modular verification of the subject-observer pattern via higher-order separation logic. In: FTfJP (2007)
16. Morrisett, G., Walker, D., Crary, K., Glew, N.: From System F to typed assembly language. ACM TPLS 21(3), 527–568 (1999)
17. Nanevski, A., Ahmed, A., Morrisett, G., Birkedal, L.: Abstract Predicates and Mutable ADTs in Hoare Type Theory. In: De Nicola, R. (ed.) ESOP 2007. LNCS, vol. 4421, pp. 189–204. Springer, Heidelberg (2007)
18. Nanevski, A., Morrisett, G., Birkedal, L.: Polymorphism and separation in Hoare Type Theory. In: ICFP 2006, Portland, Oregon, pp. 62–73 (2006)
19. O'Hearn, P.W., Yang, H., Reynolds, J.C.: Separation and information hiding. In: POPL 2004, pp. 268–280 (2004)
20. Petersen, R., Birkedal, L., Nanevski, A., Morrisett, G.: A realizability model of impredicative hoare type theory. Technical report, IT University of Copenhagen (2007), `http://www.itu.dk/people/birkedal/papers/httmodel-tr.pdf`
21. Pym, D.: The Semantics and Proof Theory of the Logic of Bunched Implications. Applied Logics Series, vol. 26. Kluwer, Dordrecht (2002)
22. Reus, B., Schwinghammer, J.: Separation Logic for Higher-Order Store. In: Ésik, Z. (ed.) CSL 2006. LNCS, vol. 4207, pp. 575–590. Springer, Heidelberg (2006)
23. Reynolds, J.C.: Separation logic: A logic for shared mutable data structures. In: LICS 2002, pp. 55–74 (2002)
24. Shinwell, M.: The Fresh Approach: Functional Programming with Names and Binders. PhD thesis, Computer Laboratory, Cambridge University (December 2004)
25. Shinwell, M.R., Pitts, A.M.: On a monadic semantics for freshness. TCS 342, 28–55 (2005)

26. Watkins, K., Cervesato, I., Pfenning, F., Walker, D.: A concurrent logical framework: The propositional fragment. In: Filliâtre, J.-C., Paulin-Mohring, C., Werner, B. (eds.) TYPES 2004. LNCS, vol. 3839, pp. 355–377. Springer, Heidelberg (2006)
27. Xi, H., Pfenning, F.: Dependent types in practical programming. In: POPL 1999, San Antonio, pp. 214–227 (1999)
28. Yoshida, N., Honda, K., Berger, M.: Local state in hoare logic for imperative higher-order functions. In: Seidl, H. (ed.) FOSSACS 2007. LNCS, vol. 4423, Springer, Heidelberg (2007)

Oracle Semantics for Concurrent Separation Logic

Aquinas Hobor[1,⋆], Andrew W. Appel[1,⋆], and Francesco Zappa Nardelli[2,⋆⋆]

[1] Princeton University
[2] INRIA

Abstract. We define (with machine-checked proofs in Coq) a modular operational semantics for Concurrent C minor—a language with shared memory, spawnable threads, and first-class locks. By *modular* we mean that one can reason about sequential control and data-flow knowing almost nothing about concurrency, and one can reason about concurrency knowing almost nothing about sequential control and data-flow constructs. We present a Concurrent Separation Logic with first-class locks and threads, and prove its soundness with respect to the operational semantics. Using our modularity principle, we proved the sequential C.S.L. rules (those inherited from sequential Separation Logic) simply by adapting Appel & Blazy's machine-checked soundness proofs. Our Concurrent C minor operational semantics is designed to connect to Leroy's optimizing (sequential) C minor compiler; we propose our modular semantics as a way to adapt Leroy's compiler-correctness proofs to the concurrent setting. Thus we will obtain end-to-end proofs: the properties you prove in Concurrent Separation Logic will be true of the program that actually executes on the machine.

1 Introduction

In recent years there has been substantial progress in building machine-checked correctness proofs: for a compiler front-end [8], for a nonoptimizing subset-Pascal compiler [9], and for a multistage optimizing compiler from C to assembly language [10]. These efforts, though they are remarkable and inspiring, do not address the problem of concurrency. Reasoning about concurrent programs, and compiling concurrent shared-memory programs with an optimizing compiler, can be very difficult. The model of computation that programmers might expect does not correspond to what is provided by the machine.

Can we adapt the sequential-language compilers and correctness proofs to the concurrent case by adding threads and locks to their source languages? Not easily. As Boehm explains, "Threads cannot be implemented as a library." [3] An optimizing compiler must be aware of the concurrency model or it might inadvertently break the locking discipline by, for example, changing the order of loads and stores to shared data. Boehm "point[s] out the important issues,

⋆ Supported in part by NSF Grants 0540914 and 0627650.

⋆⋆ Supported in part by ANR (project ParSec ANR-06-SETI-010-02).

S. Drossopoulou (Ed.): ESOP 2008, LNCS 4960, pp. 353–367, 2008.

and argue[s] that they lie almost exclusively with the compiler and the language specification itself, not with the thread library or its specification." But Boehm does not present a formal semantics: he just explains what can go wrong without one. In this paper we provide the formal semantics that Boehm called for. And we do it in such a way that sequential compilers and proofs preserve their sequential flavor: we will add threads as a kind of *semantic* library.

Contributions. **First** we show that "C + threads" can be specified modularly, by presenting an operational semantics of Extensible C minor. This language is sufficient for compiling C, ML, Java, and other high-level languages. Appel and Blazy [1] have demonstrated a (sequential) Separation Logic, with a machine-checked soundness proof in Coq w.r.t. the small-step operational semantics of *any possible extension* of Extensible C minor.

Second, we present a powerful and expressive Concurrent Separation Logic (CSL) that goes beyond O'Hearn's [11] by permitting dynamic lock and thread creation and by permitting ordinary assertions to describe lock invariants, which are in turn ordinary assertions. Our CSL is very similar to one that Gotsman *et al.* [5] independently developed, demonstrating that it must be *the* natural generalization of O'Hearn's CSL to first-class threads and locks.[1]

Third, we construct the operational semantics of Concurrent C minor, formed by extending Extensible C minor with threads and locks. A novel component of this semantics is a *modal substructural logic* for reasoning about separation in space and evolution in time. Our operational semantics is for well-synchronized programs without data races: any access to a memory location must be performed while holding a lock that gives *ownership* of that location: at least shared ownership for a read and full ownership for a write. Access without ownership causes the operational semantics to get stuck, meaning that the program has no semantics. One can use CSL (using a proof assistant, or via automatic flow analysis [6]) to prove that source programs are well synchronized.

Fourth, from the concurrent operational semantics we will construct a pseudosequential *oracle semantics* for Concurrent C minor. When a sequential thread peforms a concurrent operation such as lock or unlock, the oracle calculates the effect of running all the other threads before resuming back into this thread. We show the correctness of the oracle semantics w.r.t. the concurrent semantics.

The oracle semantics is ideal for reasoning about individual threads—for compilation and flow analysis, and for reusing proofs about the sequential language. Footprint annotations prevent unsound optimizations across lock/unlock operations but are minimally restrictive across sequential operations. The oracle is silent when any of the core sequential control- and data-flow operations are executed, and the operational semantics is deterministic. Therefore, adapting

[1] Our semantic model for CSL is more powerful than Gotsman's in several ways: our model permits assertions to be embedded directly into source code, permits function pointers, recursive assertions, and impredicative quantification; and (unlike Gotsman's) ours connects directly to a small-step sequential operational semantics for a verified-compilable intermediate representation, C minor.

existing machine-checked correctness proofs of the C minor compiler to Oracular C minor should be straightforward.

Fifth, we present a *shallow embedding* of CSL in the Calculus of Inductive Constructions (Coq). A shallow embedding, because it has no induction over CSL syntax, permits new CSL operators to be constructed as needed in a modular way. Our shallow embedding is independent of C-minor statement syntax, thus permitting the insertion of semantic CSL preconditions as annotations in C minor programs.

Finally, we demonstrate that CSL is sound with respect to our oracle semantics, and the oracle semantics is sound w.r.t. the concurrent operational semantics. Thus, properties proved of concurrent C programs will actually hold in machine-language execution.

2 Extensible C Minor

Appel and Blazy [1] describe some changes to Leroy's original C minor [10] that make it more suitable for Hoare-Logic reasoning. Expressions can read from the heap but have no side effects. Expression evaluation $\Psi; \sigma \vdash e \Downarrow v$ is with respect to a program Ψ and a *sequential state* $\sigma = (\rho; w; m)$, where ρ is the local-variable environment of the current function activation; and m is the global shared memory. The world w specifies the permissions that this thread has to access memory addresses in m. Worlds enable separation-logic-like reasoning: our semantics gets stuck on loads/stores outside the world. In this presentation we elide many details of C minor; see the full technical report [7] for details.

The sequential small-step relation $\Psi \vdash (\Omega, \sigma, \kappa) \longmapsto (\Omega', \sigma', \kappa')$ operates on *continuations* (Ω, σ, κ) where Ω is an *oracle*, σ is a sequential state, and κ is a control stack:

$$\kappa : \mathsf{control} \ ::= \ \mathsf{Kstop} \mid s \cdot \kappa \mid \ldots$$

Kstop is the empty control stack, $s \cdot \kappa$ means "execute the statement s, then continue with κ." C minor has other control operators for function return and nonlocal exit from loops. However, the concurrent semantics is parametric over any syntax of control with at least Kstop and $\cdot$.

Our C minor has a fixed set of control-flow constructs (e.g., if, loop, function call) and straight-line commands (e.g., assign, store, skip). To build an extension, one instantiates *syntax* of additional straight-line commands (e.g. lock, unlock). Then one provides a model of *oracles* to help interpret the additional commands. The oracle contains the state of all the other threads (and the schedule) and calculates what they do when control is yielded. Since our programs are (proved) race-free, preemptive schedules will yield equivalent results. For purely sequential C minor, oracles can be *unit*.

3 Concurrent C Minor

We extend C minor with five more statements to make *Concurrent C minor*:

$$s : \mathsf{stmt} \ ::= \ldots \mid \mathsf{lock}\, e \mid \mathsf{unlock}\, e \mid \mathsf{fork}\, e\,(\vec{e}) \mid \mathsf{make\_lock}\, e\, R \mid \mathsf{free\_lock}\, e$$

The lock (e) statement evaluates e to an address v, then waits until it acquires lock v. The unlock (e) statement releases a lock. A lock at location v is *locked* when the memory contains a 0 at v.

Each lock comes with a *resource invariant* R which is a predicate on world and memory. The invariants serve as a kind of "induction hypothesis" for a correctness or safety proof in CSL, and in particular they tell our operational semantics what addresses are owned by each thread and by each lock, and what addresses are transferred when locking or unlocking. This is standard in CSL [11]; but we go farther and use the invariants at a crucial point in our operational semantics to guarantees the absence of race conditions.

As usual in CSL [11] in order that the resource invariant R will be supported by a unique set of memory addresses in any given memory—these addresses constitute the memory ownership that a thread gains when acquiring a lock or loses when releasing it—the invariant R must be *precise*. The world ($\sim$ set of memory locations) controlled by a lock need not be static; it can change over time depending on the state of memory (one could say, "this lock controls that variable-sized linked list"). When a thread locks a lock, it joins the lock's world with its own; when it later unlocks the lock, it gives up the (possibily different) world satisfying R. This protocol ensures the absence of read/write or write/write race conditions.

The statement make_lock $e\,R$ takes an address e and a lock invariant R, and declares e to be a lock with the associated invariant. The address is turned back into an ordinary location by free_lock e. Both instructions are thread-local (don't synchronize with other threads or any global lock-controller). It is illegal to apply lock or unlock to nonlock addresses, or to apply ordinary load or store to locks.

The fork statement spawns a new thread, which calls function e on arguments $\vec{e}$. No variables are shared between the caller and callee except through the function parameters. The parent passes the child a portion of its world, implicitly specified by the (precise) precondition of the forked function. This portion typically contains visibility (partial ownership) of some locks—then the two threads can communicate. A thread exits by returning from its top-level function call.

We have not added a join operator, since this can be accomplished by the Concurrent C minor programmer by the use of a lock passed from parent to child, unlocked by the child just before exiting.

The concurrent operational semantics checks the truth of lock invariants when unlocking a lock, and checks the truth of function pre- and postconditions when spawning or exiting a thread. Failure of this check causes the operational semantics to get stuck. The language of these conditions contains the full power of logical propositions (Coq's `Prop`), so the operational semantics is nonconstructive: it is given by a classical relation.[2] The lock invariants and the function pre/postconditions can be taken directly from a program proof in concurrent separation logic.

For an example program in Concurrent C minor, see the technical report.

[2] We use a small, consistent set of classical axioms in Coq: extensionality, proposition extensionality, dependent unique choice, relational choice.

4 Concurrent Separation Logic

We define the usual operators of Separation Logic: **emp**, separating conjunction $*$, disjunction $\vee$, conjunction $\wedge$, and quantifiers $\exists, \forall$. Bornat *et al.* [4] explain the utility of fractional permissions for reasoning statically about alternating concurrent read with exclusive write access, so singleton "maps-to" is extended to support fractional permissions $e_1 \overset{\pi}{\mapsto} e_2$. A share can always be split: $e_1 \overset{\pi_1}{\mapsto} e_2 * e_1 \overset{\pi_2}{\mapsto} e_2 \Leftrightarrow e_1 \overset{\pi_1 \oplus \pi_2}{\mapsto} e_2$.

In fact we go beyond fractions, building on the share models presented by Parkinson [12, ch. 5] (see [7]). This permits correctness proofs of sophisticated visibility management schemes. But here we will simplify the presentation by just writing 100%, 50%, et cetera. 100% gives permission to read, write, or dispose. Owning $0 < \pi < 100\%$ gives read-only access.

We introduce a new assertion $e \overset{\pi}{\bullet\!\!\rightarrow} R$, which means that the expression e evaluates to a memory location containing a lock with resource-invariant R. We write resource(l, R) to mean that R is precise and closed (w.r.t. local variables). A location is either used as a lock or as a mutable reference: a lock assertion $e \overset{\pi}{\bullet\!\!\rightarrow} \_$ does not separate from a maps-to assertion $e \overset{\pi'}{\mapsto} \_$. Any nonempty ownership π gives the right to (attempt to) lock the lock. An auxiliary assertion, $\mathsf{hold}\ e\, R$, means that lock e with invariant R is locked by "this" thread.

To unlock a lock, the thread must "hold" it: another thread cannot unlock the lock unless the hold has been transferred. Therefore a lock invariant R for lock l must claim the hold of l, in addition to other claims S. That is, $R \Leftrightarrow \mathsf{hold}\ l\, R\ *\ S$, where $\Leftrightarrow$ means equivalence of assertions. We achieve this with a recursive assertion $\mu R.(\mathsf{hold}\ l\, R\ *\ S)$, using the μ operator of our CSL.

The assertion that some value f is a function with precondition P and postcondition Q is written $f : \{P\}\{Q\}$. A function can be either called (within this thread) or spawned (as a new thread); but to be spawned, its precondition must be precise: the precondition must specify uniquely the part of the world that the parent passes to the spawned thread.

To handle functions we extend the traditional Hoare triples with an extra context to become $\Gamma \vdash \{P\}s\{Q\}$. The concurrent extension of the logic is

$$\frac{\text{resource}(e, R) \qquad R \Leftrightarrow (\mathsf{hold}\ e\, R\ *\ S)}{\Gamma \vdash \{e \overset{100\%}{\mapsto} 0\}\mathsf{make\_lock}\ e\, R\{e \overset{100\%}{\bullet\!\!\rightarrow} R\ *\ \mathsf{hold}\ e\, R\}}$$

$$\frac{}{\Gamma \vdash \{e \overset{100\%}{\bullet\!\!\rightarrow} R\ *\ \mathsf{hold}\ e\, R\}\mathsf{free\_lock}\ e\{e \overset{100\%}{\mapsto} 0\}}$$

$$\frac{}{\Gamma \vdash \{e \overset{\pi}{\bullet\!\!\rightarrow} R\}\mathsf{lock}\ e\{e \overset{\pi}{\bullet\!\!\rightarrow} R\ *\ R\}} \qquad \frac{R \Leftrightarrow (\mathsf{hold}\ e\, R\ *\ S)}{\Gamma \vdash \{R\}\mathsf{unlock}\ e\{\mathbf{emp}\}}$$

$$\frac{\text{precise}\ (R)}{\Gamma \vdash \{e : \{R\}\{S\}\ *\ R(\vec{e})\}\mathsf{fork}\ e\, \vec{e}\{e : \{R\}\{S\}\}}$$

Fig. 1. Concurrent Separation Logic

$P * Q$	separating conjunction
$P \Rightarrow Q \quad P \wedge Q \quad P \vee Q$	implication, (nonseparating) conjuction, disjunction
$\forall v.Q \quad \exists v.Q$	quantification over values, shares, or predicates
$v \overset{\pi}{\mapsto} v'$	v is the address of readable data (writable if $\pi = 100\%$)
$v \overset{\pi}{\bullet\!\!\rightarrow} R$	v is a lock with resource invariant R
$\mathsf{hold}\ v\, R$	the token for "I currently hold the lock v"
$v : \{P\}\{Q\}$	v is a function with precondition P, postcondition Q
μF	recursive: $\mu F = F(\mu F)$
$e \Downarrow v$	the C minor expression e evaluates to v
$[A]_{\mathsf{Coq}}$	formula A in the underlying logic is true
resource(l, R)	R is a valid resource invariant (precise, closed) for lock l
world w	the current state's world is equal to w
$\triangleright Q$	"later": $Q(\rho, w', m)$ holds in all worlds w' strictly later than w
$\Box Q$	"necessarily": $Q \wedge \triangleright Q$
$\bigcirc Q$	"fashionably": $Q(\rho, w', m)$ holds in all worlds w' the same age as w
$!Q$	"everywhere": $Q(\rho', w, m')$ holds on all ρ', m' in the current world
safe(Ψ, κ)	with current state σ, for all oracles Ω, stepping $\Psi \vdash (\Omega, \sigma, \kappa) \longmapsto^* ...$ cannot get stuck.

Fig. 2. A selection of assertion operators

independent of the sequential operators and we refer to Appel and Blazy [1] for a description of the sequential logic, in which Γ specifies pre/postconditions of global functions. The concurrent rules are presented in figure 1; the full technical report [7] shows our logic applied to an example program.

Impredicativity. Our logic supports both recursive assertions and impredicative polymorphism: one can quantify not only over values and shares, but also assertions. We will use this when describing the lock invariants of object-oriented and higher-order-functional programs, in the same way that impredicative polymorphism is needed in the typed assembly languages of such programs. We also support recursive value-parameterized lock invariants that can describe, for example, "sorted list of lockable cells."

Our CSL does not reason about liveness, and cannot guarantee the absence of memory leaks. Resources can be sent down a black hole by deadlocks, by infinite loops, or by unlocking all of a lock's visibility into its own resource, or by a thread exiting with a nonempty postcondition.

5 A Modal Model of Joinable Worlds

Consider the assertion $P = (e \overset{\pi}{\bullet\!\!\rightarrow} R)$; here one assertion P describes another assertion R; and maybe R itself describes yet another assertion Q. This makes first-class locks difficult to model semantically. Intuitively, the solution is that P

is really a series of increasingly good approximations to the "true" invariant; the kth approximation of P can describe only the $k-1$ approximation of R, which in turn describes only the $k-2$ approximation of S. Then we can do induction on k to reason about the program.

To structure this in a clean way that avoids explicit mention of k, we adapt the "very modal model" of Appel, Melliès, Richards, and Vouillon [2]. They use modal logic to reason about the decrease of k as time advances through the storing and fetching of mutable references. Henceforth we will not mention k explicitly, but it will be implicit in the concept of the *age* of a world.

Our new model advances time as locks are acquired and released. But in addition, now we also reason modally about separation in space. From **machine states** we build a **Kripke model**, which we hide underneath a **modal logic**, which we hide underneath the user view of **Concurrent Separation Logic**.

The Kripke model: $\sigma \Vdash Q$ means that assertion Q holds in a state σ. The forcing relation $\Vdash$ is simple: $Q\sigma$ with Q simply a predicate on states. The world w in $\sigma = (\rho; w; m)$ plays the same role (granting permissions to read/write locations) as did the "footprints" ϕ in Appel & Blazy's Coq proof of sequential-Separation-Logic soundness, which makes it easy to use their proof techniques. The predicates Q of the modal logic are exactly the assertions of the Separation Logic.

Worlds map locations to permissions. Inside the Kripke model (not in the modal logic) we write Val_w^π to describe a nonempty fractional permission π to access a value-cell in world w. The permission $\text{Lock}_w^\pi R$ says that location l is a lock in world w with (nonempty) fractional visibility π. (The subscript w is needed to distinguish the "age" of the Lock permission, as $\text{Lock}_{w'}^\pi R$ in a later world w' has a more approximate semantic meaning.) Fractional visibility of a lock is enough to lock it; 100% visibility (so no other thread can see the lock) is required to deallocate the lock. To model that the locking thread "holds" the lock, and no other thread can unlock it (unless the "hold" is explicitly transferred), we require that R imply (at least) 50% visibility of the lock itself. That is, part of the "visibility" of a lock is really modeling "holding" the lock. The permission $\text{Fun}_w^\pi PQ$ is a function with precondition P and postcondition Q.

Worlds contain lock-permissions; lock-permissions carry assertions; and assertions are predicates on worlds. We resolve this (contravariant) circularity with a stratified construction as shown in the technical report [7].

A world describes the *domain* of the heap, where the *contents* of the heap reside in the global memory m. We write $w_1 \oplus w_2$ for the disjoint union of two worlds (where there may be overlap at an address l if the permissions agree and the shares do not exceed 100%). However, $w_1 \oplus w_2$ is only defined if w_1 and w_2 are of the same age; every world in the system ages one tick whenever any thread does a lock, unlock, or fork.

The operators above the line in Fig. 2 are what one might expect in a model of Concurrent Separation Logic. Below the line we have some new modal operators, useful in constructing the semantics but not to be seen by the end user of the Concurrent Separation Logic. *The modalities are contained within our CSL soundness proof.*

Why a modal logic. Suppose we are in world w, and we expect that the current memory m will satisfy predicate Q after *one or more* communications. We write $\rho, w, m \Vdash \triangleright Q$. A lock invariant is an example of a predicate we can only establish "later." To implement higher-order locks, we use the modal logic to keep track of approximations of assertions. We weaken Q every time the clock ticks (i.e., when a thread communicates), and we use $\triangleright$ to keep track of this weakening.

Suppose we lock l that controls world w_l, so our world goes from w to $w' \oplus w'_l$, where primes indicate ticking the clock. By "later" we do *not* refer to the fact that we gain w_l; the modal operator $\triangleright$ talks only about $w \to w'$ or $w_l \to w'_l$. The operator $*$ talks about the $\oplus$ joining. See the technical report[7] for further explanation.

6 Concurrent Operational Semantics

We specify a concurrent operational semantics to justify the claim that we have a reasonable model of conventional concurrency that corresponds to real machines. The semantics is "world-aware", that is, it gets stuck if a thread attempts to read data for which it has no permission. This means that it must also be "resource-invariant-aware", so that it can transfer the appropriate worlds when locking or unlocking a lock. Therefore, the operational semantics uses the modal logic.

The semantics has two distinct parts. The first part, called the "sequential submachine," executes all instructions that do not depend on other threads, such as call, store, and loop. The second part is fully concurrent; it schedules threads for execution by the sequential part and also handles the explicit synchronization commands: lock, unlock, and fork. Although make_lock and free_lock are new instructions, they do not require synchronization and can be executed by the sequential part of the machine.

This two-part design supports the first half of our modularity principle by hiding the complexities of sequential control- and data-flow from concurrent reasoning. Oracle semantics (section 7) supports the other half by hiding the complexities of concurrent computation from sequential reasoning.

6.1 Sequential Submachine

To build the internal sequential submachine, we extend Extensible C minor with the full syntax of all the concurrent instructions and rules for evaluating make_lock and free_lock. The computational result of both of these statements is straightforward, so we use the null oracle $\not{\Omega}$: unit.

To execute make_lock $e\, R$, the machine evaluates e, ensures that that location is fully owned and currently contains a zero, and updates the world to treat the location as a lock with invariant R. The lock is created with 100% visibility and is held 100% as well.

$$\frac{\begin{array}{cc}\Psi; (\rho; w; m) \vdash e \Downarrow v & \rho, w, m \Vdash (v \overset{100\%}{\mapsto} 0) \ * \ \text{world}\, w_{\text{core}} \\ \rho, w', m \Vdash \text{resource}(v, R) & \rho, w', m \Vdash (v \overset{100\%}{\bullet\!\!\rightarrow} R) * \mathsf{hold}\, v\, R \ * \ \text{world}\, w_{\text{core}}\end{array}}{\Psi \vdash (\not{\Omega}, (\rho; w; m), \mathsf{make\_lock}\, e\, R \cdot \kappa) \longmapsto (\not{\Omega}, (\rho; w'; m), \kappa)}$$

$\mathsf{free\_lock}\, e$ does the opposite, turning a wholly-owned lock back into a regular location [7]. At the truly concurrent operations – lock, unlock, fork – the sequential submachine is simply stuck.

6.2 Threads and Concurrent Machine State

The point of a concurrent machine is to execute several threads of control. We define a *thread* θ to be the tuple $(\rho, w, \hat{\kappa})$ with local variables ρ, a private world w, and a *concurrent control-descriptor* $\hat{\kappa}$, defined as follows:

$$\hat{\kappa} : \mathsf{concurrent\ control} \ ::= \mathsf{Krun}\, \kappa \mid \mathsf{Klock}\, v\, \kappa$$

$\mathsf{Krun}\, \kappa$ means the thread is in a runnable state, with κ as the next sequential control to execute. $\mathsf{Klock}\, v\, \kappa$ means that the thread is waiting on a lock at address v; after acquiring the lock, it will continue with κ. A list of threads we denote by $\vec{\theta}$, and we indicate the ith thread by θ_i.

A *concurrent machine state* $S = (\mho; \vec{\theta}; \mathcal{L}; m)$ has a schedule $\mho$, a (finite) list of thread-ids (natural numbers); a list of threads $\vec{\theta}$; a lock pool $\mathcal{L}$, which is a partial function that associates addresses of *unlocked* locks with the worlds they control; and a memory m. We will be quantifying over all schedules; once given a schedule, C minor executes deterministically, which greatly simplifies reasoning about sequential control-flow [1].

A concurrent machine state also carries with it a set of consistency requirements, ensuring the threads' private worlds are disjoint (among other things [7]). In Coq we ensure consistency of concurrent states with a dependently typed record. For this presentation, any concurrent machine state given should be considered consistent.

6.3 Concurrent Step Relation

The concurrent small-step relation $\Psi \vdash S \Longrightarrow S'$ describes how one concurrent state steps to another in the context of a program Ψ. The full concurrent step relation is given in the technical report[7], but the two critical features are a coroutine interleaving model and a nonconstructive semantics.

Coroutine Interleaving. The concurrent machine context-switches only for fully concurrent operations (lock, unlock, and fork). When executing a series of sequential instructions, the concurrent machine does so without interleaving (thread-number i is not removed from the head of the schedule):

$$\frac{\begin{array}{c}\Psi \vdash (\wp, (\rho; w; m), \kappa) \longmapsto (\wp, (\rho'; w'; m'), \kappa') \\ \vec{\theta}' = [\theta_1, \ldots, \theta_{i-1}, (\rho', w', \mathsf{Krun}\, \kappa'), \theta_{i+1}, \ldots, \theta_n]\end{array}}{\Psi \vdash (i :: \mho; [\theta_1, \ldots, \theta_{i-1}, (\rho, w, \mathsf{Krun}\, \kappa), \theta_{i+1}, \ldots, \theta_n]; \mathcal{L}; m) \Longrightarrow (i :: \mho; \vec{\theta}'; \mathcal{L}; m')}$$

This coroutine model of concurrency may seem strange: it is true that in general it is not equivalent to execution on a real machine. However, our operational semantics permits only well-synchronized programs to execute, so we can reason at the source level in a coroutine semantics and execute in an interleaving semantics or even a weakly consistent memory model. Of course, this claim will require proof: but the proof must be done w.r.t. the machine-language program in a machine-language version of our concurrent operational semantics; this is future work.

Nonconstructive semantics. The noncomputability of our operational semantics arises from the unlock rule:

$$\frac{\begin{array}{ccc} \Psi; (\rho; w; m) \vdash e \Downarrow v & m(v) = 0 & \rho, w, m \Vdash (\mathsf{hold}\ v\, P) * \mathbf{true} \\ w' \oplus w_{\text{lock}} = w & & \boxed{\rho, w_{\text{lock}}, m \Vdash \rhd P} \\ \mathcal{L}' = v : w_{\text{lock}}, \mathcal{L} & \multicolumn{2}{c}{\vec{\theta'} = [\theta_1, \ldots, \theta_{i-1}, (\rho, w', \mathsf{Krun}\ \kappa), \theta_{i+1}, \ldots, \theta_n]} \\ m' = [v \mapsto 1]m & \multicolumn{2}{c}{\text{ContextSwitch } (i :: \mho; \vec{\theta'}; \mathcal{L}'; m') = S} \end{array}}{\Psi \vdash (i :: \mho; [\theta_1, \ldots, \theta_{i-1}, (\rho, w, \mathsf{Krun\ unlock}\, e \cdot \kappa), \theta_{i+1}, \ldots, \theta_n]; \mathcal{L}; m) \Longmapsto S}$$

When a lock is unlocked, the semantics checks to make sure that its invariant will hold later ($\rho, w_{\text{lock}}, m \Vdash \rhd P$) – that is, after the unlock operation ticks the clock. If the invariant will not hold, the semantics gets stuck. However, assertions P may contain arbitrary predicates in classical logic—there is no decison procedure for assertions. We are saved by two things: first, if we are executing a program for which we have a proof in CSL, we will know that this check will succeed. Second, if one actually wished to execute a program to see the result, one could execute it on the fully constructive *erased* machine.

An erased machine is simply one that has had all of the worlds and oracles removed, leading to the following much simpler and constructive unlock rule:

$$\frac{\Psi; (\rho, m) \vdash e \Downarrow v \qquad m(v) = 0 \qquad \theta_i = (\rho, \mathsf{Krun\ unlock}\, e \cdot \kappa) \quad \theta_i' = (\rho, \mathsf{Krun}\ \kappa)}{\Psi \vdash (i :: \mho, [\theta_1, \ldots, \theta_i, \ldots, \theta_n], m) \Longmapsto (\mho, [\theta_1, \ldots, \theta_i', \ldots, \theta_n], [v \mapsto 1]m)}$$

This is a useful sanity check: the *real* machine takes no decisions based on erasable information; the erased semantics simply approves of fewer executions than the real machine.

When to erase. One could imagine (1) prove safety of a concurrent program w.r.t. the unerased semantics; (2) erase; (3) compile. But this would be a mistake: as explained by Boehm [3], the compiler may do concurrency-unsafe optimizations. Instead, we must preserve the worlds in the semantics in both source- and machine-language. This gives the compiler a specification of concurrency-safe optimizations. We erase the worlds last, after full compilation.

7 Oracle Semantics

A compiler, or a triple $\{P\}c\{Q\}$ in separation logic, considers a single thread at a time. Thus we want a semantics of single-thread computation. The sequential submachine of section 6.1 is single-threaded, but it is incomplete: it gets stuck at concurrent operations. The compiler (and its correctness proof) wants to compile code uniformally even around the concurrent operations. Similarly, in

$$\text{projection}\ \frac{\Omega = (\mho, \vec{\theta}, \mathcal{L}) \qquad \vec{\theta} = [\theta_1, \ldots, \theta_{i-1}, \theta_{i+1}, \ldots, \theta_n] \qquad \vec{\theta}' = [\theta_1, \ldots, \theta_{i-1}, (\rho, w, \hat{\kappa}), \theta_{i+1}, \ldots, \theta_n]}{(\Omega, (\rho; w; m), \hat{\kappa}) \overset{i}{\propto} (\mho; \vec{\theta}'; \mathcal{L}; m)}$$

$$\text{Ready}\ \frac{\theta_i = (\rho, w, \mathsf{Krun}\,\kappa)}{\text{Ready } i\ (i :: \mho; [\theta_1, \ldots, \theta_n]; \mathcal{L}; m)} \qquad \text{SO-done}\ \frac{\text{Ready } i\ S}{\Psi \vdash \text{StepOthers } i\ S\ S}$$

$$\text{SO-step}\ \frac{\neg(\text{Ready } i\ S) \qquad \Psi \vdash S \Longrightarrow S' \qquad \Psi \vdash \text{StepOthers } i\ S'\ S''}{\Psi \vdash \text{StepOthers } i\ S\ S''}$$

$$\Omega\text{-Invalid}\ \frac{\Omega = (i :: \_, \_, \_) \qquad \nexists S. (\Omega, \sigma, \mathsf{Krun}\,(s_c \cdot \kappa)) \overset{i}{\propto} S}{\Psi \vdash (\Omega, \sigma, s_c \cdot \kappa) \mapsto\!\!\!\!\longmapsto (\Omega, \sigma, s_c \cdot \kappa)}$$

Note: s_c ranges over only the concurrent instructions.

$$\Omega\text{-Diverges}\ \frac{\Omega = (i :: \_, \_, \_) \qquad (\Omega, \sigma, \mathsf{Krun}\,(s_c \cdot \kappa)) \overset{i}{\propto} S \qquad \Psi \vdash S \Longrightarrow S' \qquad \nexists S''. \Psi \vdash \text{StepOthers } i\ S'\ S''}{\Psi \vdash (\Omega, \sigma, s_c \cdot \kappa) \mapsto\!\!\!\!\longmapsto (\Omega, \sigma, s_c \cdot \kappa)}$$

$$\Omega\text{-Steps}\ \frac{\Omega = (i :: \_, \_, \_) \qquad (\Omega, \sigma, \mathsf{Krun}\,(s_c \cdot \kappa)) \overset{i}{\propto} S \qquad \Psi \vdash S \Longrightarrow S' \qquad \Psi \vdash \text{StepOthers } i\ S'\ S'' \qquad (\Omega', \sigma', \kappa) \overset{i}{\propto} S''}{\Psi \vdash (\Omega, \sigma, s_c \cdot \kappa) \mapsto\!\!\!\!\longmapsto (\Omega', \sigma', \kappa)}$$

Fig. 3. Oracle reduction relation $\mapsto\!\!\!\!\longmapsto$

a CSL proof, the commands c_1 and c_2 in $\{P\}c_1;c_2\{Q\}$ may contain concurrent operations, but a soundness proof for the sequence rule of separation logic is complicated enough (because of C minor's nonlocal exits) without adding to it the headaches involved in concurrency. Thus we want a deterministic sequential operational semantics that knows how to handle concurrent communications.

To build the desired semantics, we will build an *oracular machine* using our C minor extension system. As in Section 6.1, we provide the syntax of concurrent C minor. Instead of providing the empty oracle $\not\Omega$, however, we define a more meaningful oracle as follows:

$$\Omega : oracle := (\mho, \vec{\theta}, \mathcal{L})$$

An oracle now contains a schedule $\mho$, a list of threads $\vec{\theta}$, and a lock pool $\mathcal{L}$.

We generalize a sequential continuation (Ω, σ, κ) to a concurrent continuation $(\Omega, \sigma, \hat{\kappa})$ whose concurrent control $\hat{\kappa}$ may be ready ($\mathsf{Krun}\,\kappa$) or blocked on a lock ($\mathsf{Klock}\,v\,\kappa$). An oracle allows one to build a concurrent machine S from a thread number i and a concurrent continuation. The precise relationship is given by $(\Omega, \sigma, \hat{\kappa}) \overset{i}{\propto} S$, pronounced "$(\Omega, \sigma, \hat{\kappa})$ is the ith projection of S" (Figure 3).

To execute the extended statements, we use the rules given in Figure 3. For clarity, we use the symbol $\mapsto\!\!\!\!\longmapsto$ for the sequential step in oracular C minor, to distinguish from $\longmapsto$ which is the sequential step in the submachine (section 6.1).

However, both machines are built with the same C minor extension functors (applied to different oracle types) and therefore have much in common.

When the oracular machine gets to a concurrent instruction, there are several possibilities. The first is that there is no concurrent machine that can be built from the situation given (the rule Ω-Invalid). In this case, the machine loops endlessly, thereby becoming safe. In our proofs we quantify over all oracles—not just valid ones—and this rule allows us to gracefully handle invalid oracles.

In the remaining two cases, we are able to construct a concurrent machine S, and take at least one concurrent step: makelock, freelock, block on a lock (become Klock and context switch), or release a lock (and context switch), or fork (and context switch). After taking this step, the machine decides (classically) if the current thread will ever have control returned to it, by branching on the StepOthers judgement. If the schedule is unfair, if another thread executes an illegal instruction, or if the current thread is deadlocked, then the current thread might never have control returned to it. Rule Ω-Diverges models this by having the machine loop endlessly. The final case is when control returns (rule Ω-Steps); in this case the step proceeds with the new memory, world, and so forth that came from running the concurrent machine.

Classical reasoning in this system is unavoidable: first, the concurrent machine itself requires classical reasoning to find a world satisfying an unlock assertion; second, determining if control will return to a given thread reduces the halting problem. The nonconstructivity of our operational semantics is not a bug: we are not building an interpreter, we are building a specification for correctness proofs of compilers and program logics.

We use the oracular step to keep "unimportant" details of the concurrent machine from interfering with proofs about the sequential language. The key features of the oracular step are: 1) It is deterministic (proof in the t.r.[7]), 2) When it encounters a synchonization operation, it is able to make progress using the oracle, whereas the regular step relation gets stuck, 3) It composes with itself, whereas the regular step relation does not (because memory will change "between steps" due to other threads), and 4) In the cases where control would never return, such as deadlock, we will be safe.

8 Soundness of CSL on the Oracle Semantics

In this section we prove that Concurrent Separation Logic is sound with respect to the oracular step. In the next section we prove that the oracular step is sound with respect to the concurrent operational semantics.

A concurrent machine S is *concurrently safe* if, for any S' reachable by $S \Longmapsto^* S'$, either S' can step or its schedule is empty (S' is not stuck). We define $\sigma \Vdash \mathbf{safe}(\Psi, \kappa)$ for a single thread of the oracular machine to mean that $\Psi \vdash (\Omega, \sigma, \kappa) \longmapsto^*$ does not get stuck with any oracle Ω. We call this thread (Ω, σ, κ) *sequentially safe*, written $\Psi \vdash \mathrm{safe}(\Omega, \sigma, \kappa)$. That is, $\mathbf{safe}(\Psi, \kappa)$ is a modal assertion that quantifies over all oracles; $\mathrm{safe}(\Omega, \sigma, \kappa)$ is a predicate on a particular thread with a particular oracle.

Appel and Blazy [1] explain how to model the Hoare tuple $\Gamma \vdash \{P\}c\{Q\}$ in a continuation-passing style. We improve over Appel and Blazy in that our assertions are not predicates over programs. Our global assertion $\Gamma = f_1 : \{P_1\}\{Q_1\} * \cdots * f_n : \{P_n\}\{Q_n\}$ characterizes pre-and post-conditions of global function-names, while theirs characterized function bodies (i.e., syntax). This means that we can embed semantic assertions in program syntax without circularity. However, we are in danger of a different circularity: $\Gamma \vdash \{P\}c\{Q\}$ means "provided that for every $f_i : \{P_i\}\{Q_i\}$ in Γ, the judgment $\Gamma \vdash \{P_i\}\ \Psi(f_i)\ \{Q_i\}$ holds, then command c satisfies its pre- and postcondition," where $\Psi(f_i)$ is the body of function f_i. We solve this problem by defining the Hoare judgment as a recursive assertion. We use the later operator $\triangleright$ to achieve contractiveness, and we tick the clock at function calls. Because of this tick, by the time the caller actually enters a function body, it *will* be later.

$$\begin{aligned}\Gamma \vdash \{P\}c\{Q\} \quad \approx \quad \forall F, \Psi, \kappa.\ & (\triangleright \text{ function pre/postconditions in } \Gamma \text{ relate to } \Psi) \Rightarrow \\ & F \text{ closed w.r.t. modified vars of } c \Rightarrow \\ & (\Box \bigcirc !(Q * \Gamma * F \ \Rightarrow\ \mathbf{safe}(\Psi, \kappa))) \Rightarrow \\ & (\Box \bigcirc !(P * \Gamma * F \ \Rightarrow\ \mathbf{safe}(\Psi, c \cdot \kappa)))\end{aligned}$$

The continuation-passing interpretation of the Hoare triple is, for any frame F, if $Q * F$ is enough to guard κ, then $P * F$ is enough to guard $c \cdot \kappa$. We say $Q * F$ guards κ when any state σ that satisfies $Q * F$ is safe to execute with control κ. Each rule of sequential separation logic is proved as a derived lemma from this definition of the Hoare tuple.

Lemmas: The rules of CSL are proved as derived lemmas from the definition of the Hoare triple. For sequential statement rules, see [1]; for a proof of a concurrent rule, see [7].

Definition. We write $\Psi \vdash \Gamma$ to mean that for every function mentioned in Γ, its body in Ψ satisfies pre/postconditions of its function declarations. The end-user will prove this using the rules of CSL.

Theorem. Suppose $\Psi \vdash \Gamma$, and $\Gamma \Rightarrow \mathit{main} : \{\mathbf{true}\}\{\mathbf{true}\}$. Then for any n one can construct w_n and a consistent Ω such that $(\Omega, (\rho_0; w_n; m), \mathsf{call}\ \mathit{main}\ () \cdot \mathsf{Kstop})$ is safe to run for at least n communications+function calls.

Corollary. If a program is provable in CSL, then $\mathsf{call}\ \mathit{main}$ is sequentially safe.

9 Concurrent Safety from Oracular Safety

Now we connect the notions of sequential safety and concurrent safety. We say that a concurrent continuation $(\Omega, \sigma, \hat{\kappa})$ is "safe-as i" if, supposing it is the ith thread of the (unique) concurrent machine consistent with its oracle, then if this thread is ever ready and selected then it will be sequentially safe:

$$\frac{(\Omega, \sigma, \hat{\kappa}) \overset{i}{\propto} S \qquad \nexists S'.(\Psi \vdash \text{StepOthers } i\ S\ S')}{\Psi \vdash \text{safe-as } i\ (\Omega, \sigma, \hat{\kappa})} \qquad \frac{(\Omega, \sigma, \hat{\kappa}) \overset{i}{\propto} S \quad \Psi \vdash \text{StepOthers } i\ S\ S' \qquad (\Omega', \sigma', \mathsf{Krun}\,\kappa) \overset{i}{\propto} S' \quad \Psi \vdash \mathsf{safe}\,(\Omega', \sigma', \kappa)}{\Psi \vdash \text{safe-as } i\ (\Omega, \sigma, \hat{\kappa})}$$

Progress. All-threads-safe(S) means that each projection of S will be sequentially safe the next time it is ready and selected; this is enough for progress:

$$\frac{\forall i, \Omega, \sigma, \hat{\kappa}.\ (\Omega, \sigma, \hat{\kappa}) \overset{i}{\propto} S \ \rightarrow\ \Psi \vdash \text{safe-as } i\ (\Omega, \sigma, \hat{\kappa})}{\Psi \vdash \text{all-threads-safe}(S)}$$

Lemma. If $\Psi \vdash$ all-threads-safe(S), then S is not stuck. Proof: see [7].

Preservation. The preservation theorem is more complex due to the existence of forks: we need to know that the child will be safe if its function-precondition is satisfied. To handle this issue, we make the following definition:

$$\frac{\begin{array}{c}\exists \Gamma.\ \forall \rho, w.\ (w \in \vec{\theta}\ \vee\ w \in \mathcal{L}) \rightarrow \\ \rho, w, m \Vdash (\Psi \vdash \Gamma)\ \wedge\ (\forall v, P, Q.\ v : \{P\}\{Q\}\ \Rightarrow\ \Box \bigcirc !(\Gamma\ \Rightarrow\ v : \{P\}\{Q\}))\end{array}}{\Psi \vdash \text{all-funs-spawnable}(\mho, \vec{\theta}, \mathcal{L}, m)}$$

Lemma. If $\Psi \vdash$ all-threads-safe(S), $\Psi \vdash$ all-funs-spawnable(S), and $\Psi \vdash S \Longmapsto S'$, then $\Psi \vdash$ all-threads-safe(S') and $\Psi \vdash$ all-funs-spawnable(S').

Theorem. If each thread is sequentially safe and all functions are spawnable, the concurrent machine is safe.

Corollary. For any schedule $\mho$, if the initial thread call *main* () is sequentially safe and all functions are spawnable, then the concurrent machine is safe.

10 Conclusion

An implementation of C-threads comprises an optimizing C compiler and a threads library implemented in assembly language to handle lock/unlock/fork. From our oracle semantics, we can derive some very simple axioms that the proof of correctness of the optimizing compiler can use. For example, the compiler may wish to hoist loads and stores from one place to another, as dataflow and thread-safety permit. Thread-safety can be captured by simple axioms such as,

$$\frac{\Psi; (\rho; w; m) \vdash e \Downarrow v \qquad w \subset w'}{\Psi; (\rho; w'; m) \vdash e \Downarrow v}$$

That is, a bigger world doesn't hurt expression evaluation. To prove $w \subset w'$, we can provide the compiler with rules such as,

$$\frac{\begin{array}{c} c\ =\ \mathsf{loop}\, c'\ \vee\ c = \mathsf{exit}\, n\ \vee\ c = (x{:=}e)\ \vee\ c = \mathsf{if}\, e\, \mathsf{then}\, c_1\, \mathsf{else}\, c_2 \\ \Psi \vdash (\Omega, (\rho; w; m), c \cdot \kappa)\ \longmapsto\ (\Omega', (\rho'; w'; m'), \kappa') \end{array}}{w = w'}$$

For the extended instructions, the compiler may choose to use no rules at all (so that it cannot hoist loads/stores across calls to functions which may contain lock/unlock), or it may use rules that the world can only grow at a lock or shrink at an unlock. This allows hoisting loads/stores down past lock or up past unlock. All of these rules can be proved sound for our operational semantics.

Our goal in this research has been to provide the compiler with this simple and usable (and proved sound) operational semantics, which in turn is a basis for machine-checked compiler correctness proofs that connect end-to-end (via soundness of CSL) to correctness proofs of concurrent source programs. In future work we hope to connect (at the top) to flow analyses that can produce safety proofs witnessed in CSL, and (at the bottom) to formally prove that machines with weakly consistent memory operations will correctly execute a world-aware machine-level operational semantics that is the output of the compiler. Ideally these should be machine-checked proofs that connect to our Coq proofs of the CSL soundness that we have described here.

All definitions and claims have been fully machine-checked, except that the Coq proofs for Sections 8 and 9 are incomplete; these sections have been proved by hand at the level of rigor traditional for this conference. The concurrent and oracle machines (excluding core C minor) are specified in 1,331 lines; the proofs are 14,430 lines; total *including* sequential C minor and the sequential separation logic soundness proofs is 42,277 lines.

Acknowledgments. We thank Peter O'Hearn and Matthew Parkinson for many interesting and useful discussions.

References

1. Appel, A.W., Blazy, S.: Separation Logic for Small-Step CMINOR. In: Schneider, K., Brandt, J. (eds.) TPHOLs 2007. LNCS, vol. 4732, pp. 5–21. Springer, Heidelberg (2007)
2. Appel, A.W., Melliès, P.-A., Richards, C.D., Vouillon, J.: A very modal model of a modern, major, general type system. In: Proc. 34th Annual ACM Symposium on Principles of Programming Languages (POPL 2007), January 2007, pp. 109–122 (2007)
3. Boehm, H.-J.: Threads cannot be implemented as a library. In: PLDI 2005: ACM SIGPLAN Conf. on Prog. Language Design and Implementation, pp. 261–268 (2005)
4. Bornat, R., Calcagno, C., O'Hearn, P., Parkinson, M.: Permission accounting in separation logic. In: POPL 2005, pp. 259–270 (2005)
5. Gotsman, A., Berdine, J., Cook, B., Rinetzky, N., Sagiv, M.: Local reasoning for storable locks and threads. In: Shao, Z. (ed.) APLAS 2007. LNCS, vol. 4807, Springer, Heidelberg (2007)
6. Gotsman, A., Berdine, J., Cook, B., Sagiv, M.: Thread-modular shape analysis. In: PLDI 2007: ACM SIGPLAN Conf. on Prog. Lang. Design and Implementation (2007)
7. Hobor, A., Appel, A.W., Zappa Nardelli, F.: Oracle semantics for concurrent separation logic (extended version). Tech. report, Princeton University (January 2008)
8. Klein, G., Nipkow, T.: A machine-checked model for a Java-like language, virtual machine and compiler. ACM Trans. on Prog. Lang. and Systems 28, 619–695 (2006)
9. Leinenbach, D., Paul, W., Petrova, E.: Towards the formal verification of a C0 compiler: Code generation and implementation correctness. In: IEEE Conference on Software Engineering and Formal Methods (2005)
10. Leroy, X.: Formal certification of a compiler back-end, or: programming a compiler with a proof assistant. In: POPL 2006, pp. 42–54 (2006)
11. O'Hearn, P.W.: Resources, concurrency and local reasoning. Theoretical Computer Science 375(1), 271–307 (2007)
12. Parkinson, M.J.: Local Reasoning for Java. PhD thesis, Univ. of Cambridge (2005)

Certificate Translation in Abstract Interpretation

Gilles Barthe and César Kunz

INRIA Sophia Antipolis-Méditerranée, France
{Gilles.Barthe,Cesar.Kunz}@inria.fr

Abstract. A certificate is a mathematical object that can be used to establish that a piece of mobile code satisfies some security policy. Since in general certificates cannot be generated automatically, there is an interest in developing methods to reuse certificates. This article formalises in the setting of abstract interpretation a method to transform certificates of program correctness along program transformations.

1 Introduction

A certificate c is a mathematical object that can be checked automatically against some property ϕ it intends to prove; certificates arise naturally in logic, in the context of proof checking (via the Curry-Howard isomorphism) and of result checking. Certificates are also used to carry evidence of innocuousness of components in mobile code: in a typical Proof Carrying Code (PCC) scenario [11], a piece of mobile code is downloaded together with a certificate that shows its adherence to the consumer policy. While certificate checking is reasonably understood, certificate generation remains a challenging problem: while it is possible to generate certificates automatically for properties that are enforceable by automated program analyses, and in particular type systems, certificate generation remains necessarily interactive in the general case. It is therefore of interest to develop methods that simplify the construction of certificates.

In this paper, we use the setting of abstract interpretation [8,9] to describe a method for transforming certificates along program transformations. We provide sufficient conditions for transforming a certificate of a program G into a certificate of a program G', where G' is derived from G by a semantically justified program transformation, typically a program optimization. These results provide substantial leverage on our earlier work on certificate translation [3].

Certificate Translation. The primary goal of certificate translation is to extend the scope of PCC to complex policies, by supporting the generation of certificates from interactive source code verification. The scenario is of interest in situations where the functional correctness of the downloaded code is essential, and where certificate issues such as size or checking time are not relevant, e.g. in wholesale PCC, where one code verifier checks the certificate prior to distributing a cryptographically signed version to code consumers.

Certificate translation is tightly bound to the compilation infrastructure: for compilers that do not perform any optimization, proof obligations are preserved

S. Drossopoulou (Ed.): ESOP 2008, LNCS 4960, pp. 368–382, 2008.

(up to syntactic equality), and hence it is possible to reuse directly certificates of source code programs for their compilation; see e.g. [4].

In contrast, program optimizations make certificate translation more challenging. In [3], we show in a simplified setting that one can define certificate transformers for common program optimizations, provided one can infer automatically certificates of correctness for the underlying program analyses, by means of certifying analyzers. The existence of certifying analyzers and certificate translators is shown individually for each optimization.

Comparison with our previous work. The lack of a framework in which to formulate the basic concepts of certificate translation was a clear limitation of our earlier work, and made it difficult to assess the generality of certificate translation. The present article overcomes this limitation: we capture the essence of certificate translation in an algebraic setting that abstracts away from the specifics of programming languages, program transformations, and of verification methods. In fact, our results provide a means to generate, for given verification settings and program transformations, a set of proof obligations that guarantee the existence of certificate translators. The results of [3,4] can then be recovered by discharging these proof obligations.

2 Certified Solutions

This section extends the basic framework of abstract interpretation with certificate infrastructures, in order to introduce formally the notion of certified solution. Definition 7 provides a general definition of certified solution that is of independent interest from certificate transformation, and provides a unifying framework for existing *ad hoc* definitions, see Section 5. For the purpose of this article, one can think about certified solutions as:

- programs annotated with logical assertions, and bundled with a certificate of the correctness of the verification conditions, or;
- programs annotated with abstract values (or types), and bundled with a certificate that the program is correct with respect to the interpretation of the abstract values.

We view programs as flow graphs. Thus, programs are directed pointed graphs with a distinguished set of output nodes, from which execution may not flow.

Definition 1 (Programs). *A program is a pointed directed graph* $G = \langle \mathcal{N}, \mathcal{E}, l_{\mathsf{sp}} \rangle$*, where* $\mathcal{N}$ *is a set of nodes,* $l_{\mathsf{sp}} \in \mathcal{N}$ *is a distinguished initial node, and* $\mathcal{E} \subseteq \mathcal{N} \times \mathcal{N}$ *a finitely branching relation; elements of* $\mathcal{E}$ *are called edges. We let* $\mathcal{O}$ *be the set of nodes without successors.*

Throughout this section, we let $G = \langle \mathcal{N}, \mathcal{E}, l_{\mathsf{sp}} \rangle$ be a program.

The semantics of programs is specified as a transition relation between states. Although more general definitions could be used, we choose to model states as pairs consisting of a program point and of an environment.

```
c := 1
x' := x
y' := y
while (y' ≠ 1) do
  if (y' mod 2 = 1) then
    c := c × x'
  fi
done
x' = x' × c
```

Fig. 1. Fast exponentiation algorithm

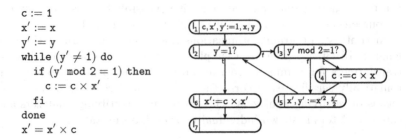

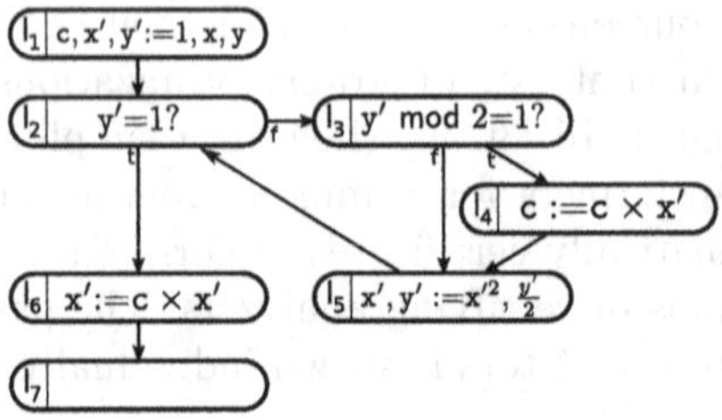

Fig. 2. Graph representation

Definition 2 (States, semantics). *Let* Env *be an abstract set of environments. The set of states is defined as* State $= \mathcal{N} \times$ Env. *The semantics of program G is given by an abstract relation* $\rightsquigarrow \subseteq$ State × State.

Example. Consider as a running example (Fig. 1) a fast exponentiation algorithm. Its representation as a (labeled) graph is given in Figure 2; labels are either assignments of the form $x{:=}e$, in which case the node has exactly one successor, or conditional statements of the form $b?$, in which case the node has exactly two successor nodes, respectively corresponding to the true and false branch of the condition.

Both the analysis and verification frameworks are viewed as abstract interpretations. Note that, in contrast to standard abstract interpretation, our domains are pre-orders, rather than partial orders[1].

Definition 3 (Abstract interpretation). *Let $G = \langle \mathcal{N}, \mathcal{E}, l_{\mathsf{sp}} \rangle$ be a program. An abstract interpretation of G is a triple $I = \langle A, \{T_e\}_{e \in \mathcal{E}}, f \rangle$, where*

- *A is a pre-lattice*[2] *$\langle D_A, \sqsubseteq_A, \sqsupseteq_A, \sqcup_A, \sqcap_A, \top_A, \bot_A \rangle$ of abstract states. By abuse of notation, we write A instead of D_A;*
- *f is the flow sense, either forward ($f = \downarrow$), or backward ($f = \uparrow$);*
- *$\{T_e\}_{e \in \mathcal{E}} : A \to A$ is a family of monotone transfer functions.*

Thus, an abstraction of the program consists of an abstract domain, e.g. assertions or types, and a set of transfer functions, e.g. weakest precondition transformers.

[1] A binary relation $\sqsubseteq$ on a set A is a pre-order if it is reflexive and transitive. A pre-order is a partial order if it is also antisymmetric. One natural domain for the verification infrastructure is that of propositions; we do not want to view it as a partial order since it would later imply (in Definition 6) that any formulas ϕ_1 and ϕ_2, if logically equivalent (i.e. if $\phi_1 \sqsubseteq \phi_2$ and $\phi_2 \sqsubseteq \phi_1$), by antisymmetry will have the same certificates (since $\phi_1 = \phi_2$), which is not desirable.

[2] Although it is sufficient to consider meet or join semi-lattices, depending on the flow of the interpretation, we find it more convenient to require our domains to be pre-lattices, since we deal both with forward and backwards analyses.

Furthermore, for every abstract domain A, we assume that $\models_A \subseteq \mathsf{Env} \times A$ is a satisfaction relation, s.t. $\sqsubseteq$ is an approximation order, i.e., that for all $\eta \in \mathsf{Env}$, $a_1, a_2 \in A$, if $\models_A \eta : a_1$ and $a_1 \sqsubseteq a_2$ then $\models_A \eta : a_2$. In the following, we simply write $\models$ omitting the subscript A.

Definition 4 (Consistency). *We say that I is consistent with the semantics of G w.r.t. $\models$ iff for all states $\langle l, \eta \rangle, \langle l', \eta' \rangle \in \mathsf{State}$ such that $\langle l, \eta \rangle \rightsquigarrow \langle l', \eta' \rangle$, and for all $a \in A$:*

- *if $f = \downarrow$ and $\models \eta : a$, then $\models \eta' : T_e(a)$;*
- *if $f = \uparrow$ and $\models \eta : T_e(a)$, then $\models \eta' : a$.*

A common means to verify program properties is to consider (pre- or post-) fixpoints of the transfer functions.

Definition 5 (Solution). *A labeling $S : \mathcal{N} \to A$ is a solution of I if*

- *$f = \uparrow$ and for every l in $\mathcal{N}$, $S(l) \sqsubseteq \bigsqcap_{\langle l,l' \rangle \in \mathcal{E}} T_{\langle l,l' \rangle}(S(l'))$;*
- *$f = \downarrow$ and for every node l in $\mathcal{N}$, $S(l) \sqsupseteq \bigsqcup_{\langle l',l \rangle \in \mathcal{E}} T_{\langle l',l \rangle}(S(l'))$.*

Lemma 1. *Let S be a solution of the abstract interpretation $I = \langle A, \{T_e\}, f \rangle$ and assume I consistent with the semantics of G. Then, if $\langle l, \eta \rangle \rightsquigarrow^\star \langle l', \eta' \rangle$ and $\models \eta : S(l)$ then $\models \eta' : S(l')$.*

In order to capture the notion of certified solution at an appropriate level of abstraction, we rely on a general notion of certificate infrastructure.

Definition 6 (Certificate infrastructure). *A certificate infrastructure for G consists of an abstract interpretation $I = \langle A, \{T_e\}_{e \in \mathcal{E}}, f \rangle$ for G, and a proof algebra $\mathcal{P}$ that assigns to every $a, a' \in A$ a set of certificates $\mathcal{P}(\vdash a \sqsubseteq a')$ s.t.:*

- *$\mathcal{P}$ is closed under the operations of Figure 3, where $a, b, c \in A$;*
- *$\mathcal{P}$ is sound, i.e. for every $a, a' \in A$, if $a \not\sqsubseteq a'$, then $\mathcal{P}(\vdash a \sqsubseteq a') = \emptyset$.*

In the sequel, we write $c :\vdash a \sqsubseteq a'$ or $c :\vdash a' \sqsupseteq a$ instead of $c \in \mathcal{P}(\vdash a \sqsubseteq a')$.

In the context of standard proof carrying code, the underlying pre-lattice is that of logical assertions, with logical implication $\Rightarrow$ as pre-order, and the transfer functions are the predicate transformers (based on weakest precondition or strongest postcondition) induced by instructions at any given program point. The particular form of certificates is irrelevant for this paper. It may nevertheless be helpful for the reader to think about certificates in terms of the Curry-Howard isomorphism and consider that $\mathcal{P}$ is given by the typing judgment in a dependently typed λ-calculus, i.e. $\mathcal{P}(\phi) = \{e \in \mathcal{E} \mid \langle\rangle \vdash e : \phi\}$, where $\mathcal{E}$ is the set of expressions of the type theory. Under such assumptions, one can provide an obvious type-theoretical interpretation to the functions of Figure 3; for example, $\mathsf{intro}_\sqcap$ is given by the λ-term $\lambda f.\ \lambda g.\ \lambda a.\ \langle fa, ga \rangle$.

In the sequel, we let $I = \langle A, \{T_e\}, f \rangle$ be a certificate infrastructure for G.

Definition 7 (Certified solution). *A certified solution for I is a pair $\langle S, \mathbf{c} \rangle$, where $S : \mathcal{N} \to A$ is a labeling and $\mathbf{c} = (c_l)_{l \in \mathcal{N}}$ is a family of certificates s.t. for every $l \in \mathcal{N}$,*

$$\begin{array}{lll}
\mathsf{axiom} & : & \mathcal{P}(\vdash a \sqsubseteq a) \\
\mathsf{weak}_{\sqcap} & : & \mathcal{P}(\vdash a \sqsubseteq b) \rightarrow \mathcal{P}(\vdash a \sqcap c \sqsubseteq b) \\
\mathsf{weak}_{\sqcup} & : & \mathcal{P}(\vdash a \sqsubseteq b) \rightarrow \mathcal{P}(\vdash a \sqsubseteq b \sqcup c) \\
\mathsf{elim}_{\sqcap} & : & \mathcal{P}(\vdash c \sqcap a \sqsubseteq b) \rightarrow \mathcal{P}(\vdash c \sqsubseteq a) \rightarrow \mathcal{P}(\vdash c \sqsubseteq b) \\
\mathsf{intro}_{\sqcup} & : & \mathcal{P}(\vdash a \sqsubseteq c) \rightarrow \mathcal{P}(\vdash b \sqsubseteq c) \rightarrow \mathcal{P}(\vdash a \sqcup b \sqsubseteq c) \\
\mathsf{intro}_{\sqcap} & : & \mathcal{P}(\vdash a \sqsubseteq b) \rightarrow \mathcal{P}(\vdash a \sqsubseteq c) \rightarrow \mathcal{P}(\vdash a \sqsubseteq b \sqcap c)
\end{array}$$

Fig. 3. Proof Algebra

– *if* $f = \uparrow$ *then* $c_l :\vdash S(l) \sqsubseteq \bigsqcap_{\langle l,l'\rangle \in \mathcal{E}} T_{\langle l,l'\rangle}(S(l'))$;
– *if* $f = \downarrow$ *then* $c_l :\vdash \bigsqcup_{\langle l',l\rangle \in \mathcal{E}} T_{\langle l',l\rangle}(S(l')) \sqsubseteq S(l)$.

It follows that S is a solution for I.

Many techniques, including lightweight bytecode verification and abstraction carrying code, do not bundle code with a full (certified) solution, but with a partial labeling (and some certificates) from which a full (certified) solution can be reconstructed. The remaining of this section relates the construction of a (certified) solution from a partial labeling.

Definition 8 (Labeling). *A partial labeling is a partial function $S : \mathcal{N} \rightharpoonup A$ s.t. entry and output nodes are annotated, i.e. $\mathcal{O} \cup \{l_{\mathsf{sp}}\} \subseteq \mathsf{dom}(S)$, and such that the program is sufficiently annotated, i.e. the restriction $G_{\mathcal{N}\setminus\mathsf{dom}(S)}$ of G to nodes that are not annotated is acyclic. A labeling S is total if $\mathsf{dom}(S) = \mathcal{N}$.*

In a partial labeling annot, annotations on entry and output nodes serve as specification, whereas we need sufficient annotations to reconstruct a total labeling $\overline{\mathsf{annot}}$ from the partial one.

Definition 9. *[Annotation propagation, verification condition] Let* annot *be a partial labeling. The labeling* $\overline{\mathsf{annot}}$ *is defined by the clause:*

– *if* $f = \uparrow$, $\overline{\mathsf{annot}}(l) = \begin{cases} \mathsf{annot}(l) & \text{if } l \in \mathsf{dom}(\mathsf{annot}) \\ \bigsqcap_{\langle l,l'\rangle \in \mathcal{E}} T_{\langle l,l'\rangle}(\overline{\mathsf{annot}}(l')) & \text{otherwise} \end{cases}$

– *if* $f = \downarrow$, $\overline{\mathsf{annot}}(l) = \begin{cases} \mathsf{annot}(l) & \text{if } l \in \mathsf{dom}(\mathsf{annot}) \\ \bigsqcup_{\langle l',l\rangle \in \mathcal{E}} T_{\langle l',l\rangle}(\overline{\mathsf{annot}}(l')) & \text{otherwise} \end{cases}$

For every $l \in \mathsf{dom}(\mathsf{annot})$, the verification condition $\mathsf{vc}(l)$ is defined by the clause

– $\mathsf{vc}(l) := \mathsf{annot}(l) \sqsubseteq \bigsqcap_{\langle l,l'\rangle \in \mathcal{E}} T_{\langle l,l'\rangle}(\overline{\mathsf{annot}}(l'))$ *if* $f = \uparrow$;
– $\mathsf{vc}(l) := \bigsqcup_{\langle l',l\rangle \in \mathcal{E}} T_{\langle l',l\rangle}(\overline{\mathsf{annot}}(l')) \sqsubseteq \mathsf{annot}(l)$ *if* $f = \downarrow$.

Given a partial labeling annot, one can build a certificate for $\overline{\mathsf{annot}}$ from certificates for the verification conditions on $\mathsf{dom}(\mathsf{annot})$.

Lemma 2. *Let* annot *be a partial labeling for I and assume given $c_l :\vdash \mathsf{vc}(l)$ for every $l \in \mathsf{dom}(\mathsf{annot})$. Then there exists $\mathbf{c}'$ s.t. $\langle \overline{\mathsf{annot}}, \mathbf{c}'\rangle$ is a certified solution.*

In the sequel, we shall abuse language and speak about certified solutions of the form $\langle \mathsf{annot}, \boldsymbol{c}\rangle$ where annot is a partial labeling and $\boldsymbol{c}$ is an indexed family of certificates that establish all verification conditions of annot.

Corollary 1. *Let $\langle \mathsf{annot}, \boldsymbol{c}\rangle$ be a certified partial labeling of $\langle I, \mathcal{P}\rangle$ and assume I consistent with the semantics of G. Then, if $\langle l_{\mathsf{sp}}, \eta\rangle \rightsquigarrow^* \langle l_o, \eta'\rangle$ with $l_o \in \mathcal{O}$ and $\models \eta : \mathsf{annot}(l_{\mathsf{sp}})$ then $\models \eta' : \mathsf{annot}(l_o)$.*

Example. The verification infrastructure to certify the running example is built from a weakest precondition calculus over first-order formulae. That is, the backward transfer functions are defined, for any assertion ϕ, as $T_{\langle l,l'\rangle}(\phi) = \phi[{}^{e}/_{x}]$ in case the node l contains the assignment $x{:=}e$, and as $b \Rightarrow \phi$ or $\neg b \Rightarrow \phi$ respectively for the positive and negative branch of a jump statement conditioned by the boolean expression b. We assume given a certificate of functional correctness for the program, i.e. we assume given a certified solution $\langle \mathsf{annot}, \boldsymbol{c}\rangle$ of $I = \langle A, \{T_e\}, \uparrow\rangle$, where annot (as shown in Figure 5) is the partial labeling s.t. the precondition is trivial, i.e. $\mathsf{annot}(l_1) = \mathsf{true}$, the invariant is $\mathsf{annot}(l_2) = c \times x'^{y'} = x^y$ and the postcondition is $\mathsf{annot}(l_7) = x'{=}x^y$.

3 Certifying Analyzers

The certificate transformations studied in the next section require that the analyzers upon which the program transformation is based are certifying, i.e. produce certificates which justify their results. In this section, we thus provide sufficient conditions under which every solution may be certified. Proposition 1 below generalizes a previous result of Chaieb [7], who only considered the case where $f = \uparrow$ and $f^\sharp = \downarrow$.

Let G be a program, $I^\sharp = \langle A^\sharp, \{T_e^\sharp\}, f^\sharp\rangle$ be an abstract interpretation, $I = \langle A, \{T_e\}, f\rangle$ a certificate infrastructure of program G, and $\gamma : A^\sharp \to A$ a concretization function.

Proposition 1 (Existence of certifying analyzers). *For every solution S of $I^\sharp$, one can compute $\boldsymbol{c}$ s.t. $\langle \gamma \circ S, \boldsymbol{c}\rangle$ is a certified solution for I, provided there exist:*

- *for every $a, a' \in A^\sharp$ s.t. $a \sqsubseteq^\sharp a'$, a certificate $\mathsf{monot}_\gamma(a, a') :\vdash \gamma(a) \sqsubseteq \gamma(a')$;*
- *for every $x \in A^\sharp$, a certificate $\mathsf{cons}(x) :\vdash \phi(x)$, where $\phi(x)$ is defined in Figure 4 according to the flows of the interpretations.*

Proof. For space reasons, we only show how to construct a certificate for the analysis in case $f = f^\sharp = \downarrow$. Let hyp stand for $T^\sharp_{\langle l',l\rangle}(S(l')) \sqsubseteq S(l)$ in

$$
\begin{array}{l}
p_1{:=}\mathsf{monot}_\gamma(\mathsf{hyp}) :\vdash \gamma(T^\sharp_{\langle l',l\rangle}(S(l'))) \sqsubseteq \gamma(S(l)) \\
p_2{:=}\mathsf{cons}(S(l')) :\vdash T_{\langle l',l\rangle}(\gamma(S(l'))) \sqsubseteq \gamma(T^\sharp_{\langle l',l\rangle}(S(l'))) \\
p_3{:=}\mathsf{weak}_\sqcap(-, p_1) :\vdash \gamma(T^\sharp_{\langle l',l\rangle}(S(l'))) \sqcap T_{\langle l',l\rangle}(\gamma(S(l'))) \sqsubseteq \gamma(S(l)) \\
p_4{:=}\mathsf{elim}_\sqcap(p_3, p_2) :\vdash T_{\langle l',l\rangle}(\gamma(S(l'))) \sqsubseteq \gamma(S(l)) \\
c_l{:=}\mathsf{intro}_\sqcup(\{p_4\}_{\langle l',l\rangle\in\mathcal{E}}) :\vdash \bigsqcup_{\langle l',l\rangle\in\mathcal{E}} T_{\langle l',l\rangle}(\gamma(S(l'))) \sqsubseteq \gamma(S(l))
\end{array}
$$

While Proposition 1 provides a means to construct certifying analyzers, it is sometimes of interest to rely on more direct methods to generate certificates: in [3], we show how to construct compact certificates for constant propagation and common sub-expression elimination in an intermediate language.

$f = f^\sharp = \downarrow$	$T_e(\gamma(x)) \sqsubseteq \gamma(T_e^\sharp(x))$
$f = f^\sharp = \uparrow$	$T_e(\gamma(x)) \sqsupseteq \gamma(T_e^\sharp(x))$
$f = \uparrow,\ f^\sharp = \downarrow$	$T_e(\gamma(T_e^\sharp(x))) \sqsupseteq \gamma(x)$
$f = \downarrow,\ f^\sharp = \uparrow$	$T_e(\gamma(T_e^\sharp(x))) \sqsubseteq \gamma(x)$

Fig. 4. Definition of $\phi(x)$

4 Certificate Translation

In this section, we provide sufficient conditions for the existence for certificate translators, that map certificates of a program G into certificates of another program G', derived from G by a program transformation. Rather than attempting to prove a general result where G and G' are related in some complex manner, we establish three existence results that can be used in combination to cover many cases of interest.

In a first instance, Section 4.1 generalizes program transformations by allowing G' to contain additional nodes that arise from duplicating fragments of G, as is the case for transformations such as loop unrolling. In a second instance, certificate transformation as defined in Section 4.2 requires that the transformed program G' is a subgraph of the original program G. This is the case, for example, when G' is derived from G by applying optimizations such as constant propagation or common sub-expression elimination. In a third instance, in Section 4.3, we provide a notion of program skeleton, which abstracts away some of the structure of the program, to deal with transformations that do not preserve so tightly the structure of programs, such as code motion. Finally, in Section 4.4 we generalize certificate translation, covering optimizations such as dead variable elimination.

Throughout this section, we assume given two programs: an initial program $G = \langle \mathcal{N}, \mathcal{E}, l_{\mathsf{sp}} \rangle$ and a transformed program $G' = \langle \mathcal{N}', \mathcal{E}', l_{\mathsf{sp}} \rangle$. Furthermore, we assume given the required infrastructure to certify these programs; more concretely, consider the two abstract interpretations $I = \langle A, \{T_e\}_{e \in \mathcal{E}}, f \rangle$ and $I' = \langle A, \{T'_e\}_{e \in \mathcal{E}'}, f \rangle$ over G and G', and a proof algebra $\mathcal{P}$ over A. Note that the abstract interpretations share the same underlying domain and flow sense.

4.1 Code Duplication

In this section, we consider the case where some subgraphs of the initial program are duplicated in the transformed program, with the aim to trigger further program optimizations. Typical cases of code duplication are loop unrolling and function inlining.

Definition 10 (Node replication). *A program $G^+ = \langle \mathcal{N} \cup \mathcal{N}^+, \mathcal{E}^+, l_{\mathsf{sp}} \rangle$ is a result of replicating nodes of program $G = \langle \mathcal{N}, \mathcal{E}, l_{\mathsf{sp}} \rangle$ if $\mathcal{N}^+ \subseteq \{l^+ \mid l \in \mathcal{N}\}$ and $\mathcal{E} = \{\langle l_1, l_2 \rangle \mid \langle l, l' \rangle \in \mathcal{E}^+ \wedge \langle l, l' \rangle \in \{l_1, l_1^+\} \times \{l_2, l_2^+\}\}$.*

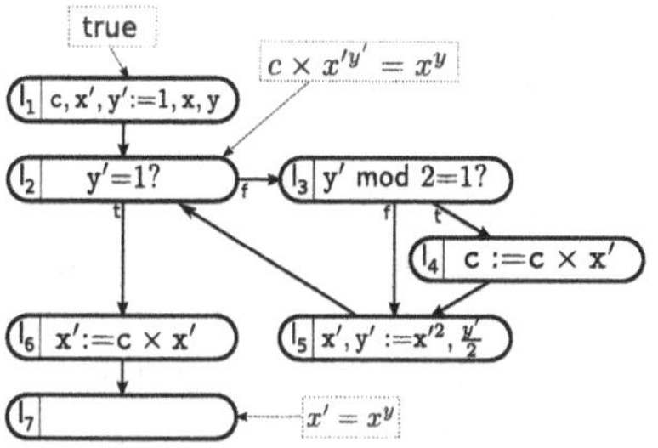

Fig. 5. Annotated program

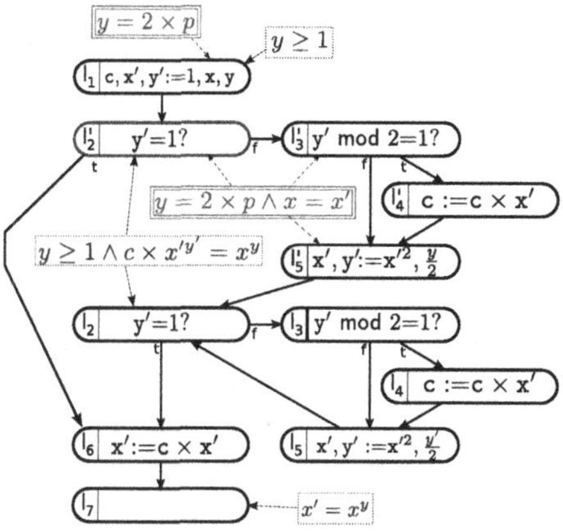

Fig. 6. Program after loop unrolling

Let $\langle I, \mathcal{P}\rangle$ be a certificate infrastructure with $I = \langle A, \{T_e\}_{e\in\mathcal{E}}, f\rangle$. Then, we define an extended certificate infrastructure $I^+ = \langle A, \{T_e\}_{e\in\mathcal{E}^+}, f\rangle$ for program G^+, the transfer functions T_e for $e \in \mathcal{E}^+ \setminus \mathcal{E}$ being such that for all $\langle \bar{l}_1, \bar{l}_2\rangle \in \mathcal{E}^+$, with $\bar{l}_i \in \{l_i, l_i^+\}$, $T_{\langle l_1,l_2\rangle} = T_{\langle \bar{l}_1,\bar{l}_2\rangle}$.

Proposition 2. *Assume the certificates of Fig. 7 exist for every* $a_1, a_2, b_1, b_2 \in A$. *Then every certified solution* $\langle S, \mathbf{c}\rangle$ *for* G *can be transformed into a certified solution* $\langle S^+, \mathbf{c}'\rangle$ *for* G^+, *s.t.* $S^+(l^+) = S(l)$ *for all* $l \in \mathsf{dom}(S)$.

Example. Figure 6 shows the result of applying loop unrolling. Formally, it consists in duplicating a subset of nodes as defined in Section 4.1. In the graph, nodes l_2, l_3, l_4 and l_5 are respectively duplicated into the nodes l_2', l_3', l_4', l_5' and a new subset of edges is defined accordingly. A certified labeling $\langle \mathsf{annot}^+, \mathbf{c}^+\rangle$, where $\mathsf{annot}^+(l_2') = \mathsf{annot}(l_2)$, is generated for the program in Figure 6, by application of Proposition 2.

4.2 Subgraph Transformation

In this section, we assume that G' is a subgraph of G, i.e. $\mathcal{N}' \subseteq \mathcal{N}$ and $\mathcal{E}' \subseteq \mathcal{E}$. Furthermore, we assume given an abstract interpretation $I = \langle A, \{T_e\}_{e\in\mathcal{E}}, f\rangle$ of G and a labelling S that justifies the transformation from G to G'.

Proposition 3 (Existence of certificate translators). *Let* $\langle S, \mathbf{c}^S\rangle$ *be a certified solution for* I *such that for every* $\langle l_1, l_2\rangle \in \mathcal{E}'$ *and* $a \in A$:

- *if* $f = \uparrow$ *then* $\mathsf{justif}(l_1, l_2) : \vdash S(l_1) \sqcap T_{\langle l_1,l_2\rangle}(a) \sqsubseteq T'_{\langle l_1,l_2\rangle}(a)$;
- *if* $f = \downarrow$ *then* $\mathsf{justif}(l_1, l_2) : \vdash T'_{\langle l_1,l_2\rangle}(a) \sqsubseteq S(l_2) \sqcap T_{\langle l_1,l_2\rangle}(a)$

Then, provided the certificates in Fig. 7 are given for every $a_1, a_2, b_1, b_2 \in A$, *one can transform every certified labeling* $\langle \mathsf{annot}, \mathbf{c}\rangle$ *for* G *into a certified labeling* $\langle \mathsf{annot}', \mathbf{c}'\rangle$ *for* G', *where* $\mathsf{annot}'(l) = \mathsf{annot}(l) \sqcap S(l)$ *for every node* l *in* $\mathsf{dom}(\mathsf{annot}') = \mathsf{dom}(\mathsf{annot}) \cap \mathcal{N}'$.

$$\begin{array}{l}
\mathsf{monot}_T : \mathcal{P}(\vdash a_1 \sqsubseteq a_2) \to \mathcal{P}(\vdash T(a_1) \sqsubseteq T(a_2)) \\
\mathsf{distr}_{\overleftarrow{(T,\sqcap)}} : \vdash T(a_1) \sqcap T(a_2) \sqsubseteq T(a_1 \sqcap a_2) \\
\mathsf{distr}_{\overrightarrow{(T,\sqcap)}} : \vdash T(a_1 \sqcap a_2) \sqsubseteq T(a_1) \sqcap T(a_2) \\
\mathsf{assoc}_{\overleftarrow{\sqcap}} : \mathcal{P}(\vdash a_1 \sqcap (b_1 \sqcap b_2) \sqsubseteq (a_1 \sqcap b_1) \sqcap b_2) \\
\mathsf{assoc}_{\overrightarrow{\sqcap}} : \mathcal{P}(\vdash (a_1 \sqcap b_1) \sqcap b_2 \sqsubseteq a_1 \sqcap (b_1 \sqcap b_2)) \\
\mathsf{commut}_{\sqcap} : \mathcal{P}(\vdash a_1 \sqcap a_2 \sqsubseteq a_2 \sqcap a_1)
\end{array}$$

Fig. 7. Requirements for certificate translation.

Using the results of Proposition 1, Proposition 3 can be instantiated to prove the existence of certificate transformers for many common optimizations, including constant propagation and common sub-expression elimination. In a nutshell, one first runs the certifying analyzer, which provides the solution S, then performs the optimization, and finally one provides a justification $\mathsf{justif}(l_1, l_2)$ for each edge (instruction) that has been modified by the optimization. This process is further illustrated in the following example.

Example. Suppose that we know (e.g. from the execution context) that the program is called with an even y; such knowledge is formalized by a precondition $y = 2 \times p$. Then, one can consider a forward abstract interpretation that analyses parity of variables and which variables are modified. A certifying analyzer for such an abstract interpretation exists by Proposition 1 and will produce a certified solution $\langle S, \mathbf{c}^S \rangle$ such that S (shown inside double squared boxes in Fig. 6) associates the assertion $y = 2 \times p$ to the node l_1, the assertion $y' = 2 \times p \wedge x = x'$ to the nodes $\{l'_2, l'_3, l'_5\}$ and true to any other node.

Figure 8 contains an optimized version of the program of Figure 6, where jump statements whose conditions can be determined statically have been eliminated (nodes l'_2 and l'_3) and unreachable nodes have been removed (node l'_4), and where assignments have been simplified by propagating the results of the analysis (node l'_5). By Proposition 3, one can build a certificate for the optimized program, with labeling $\mathsf{annot}'(l) = \mathsf{annot}(l) \sqcap S(l)$ for all nodes $l \in \mathsf{dom}(\mathsf{annot})$ (in squared boxes in the figure), provided there exists, for every $a \in A$ and for every modified edge, i.e. for every $\langle l, l' \rangle \in \{\langle l'_2, l'_3 \rangle, \langle l'_3, l'_5 \rangle, \langle l'_5, l_2 \rangle\}$, a certificate:

$$\mathsf{justif}_{\langle l,l' \rangle} : \vdash y' = 2 \times p \wedge x = x' \sqcap T_{\langle l,l' \rangle}(a) \sqsubseteq T'_{\langle l,l' \rangle}(a)$$

The remaining certificates $\mathsf{justif}(l, l')$ for $\langle l, l' \rangle \notin \{\langle l'_2, l'_3 \rangle, \langle l'_3, l'_5 \rangle, \langle l'_5, l_2 \rangle\}$ are trivially generated since $T'_{\langle l,l' \rangle} = T_{\langle l,l' \rangle}$.

We conclude this section with a proof sketch of the existence of certificate transformers in the case of a backward certificate infrastructure. The idea is to build for every l in $\mathcal{N}'$ the certificate

$$\mathsf{goal}(l) : \vdash S(l) \sqcap \overline{\mathsf{annot}}(l) \sqsubseteq \overline{\mathsf{annot}}'(l)$$

from which the existence of a certificate for annot' follows. We proceed by induction, using the principle derived from the fact that annot is a sufficient annotation. More concretely, one can attach to every node a weight that corresponds to

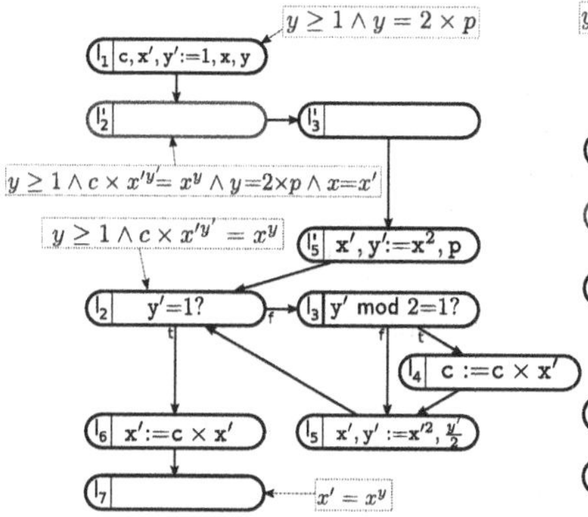

Fig. 8. Program after optimizing transformations

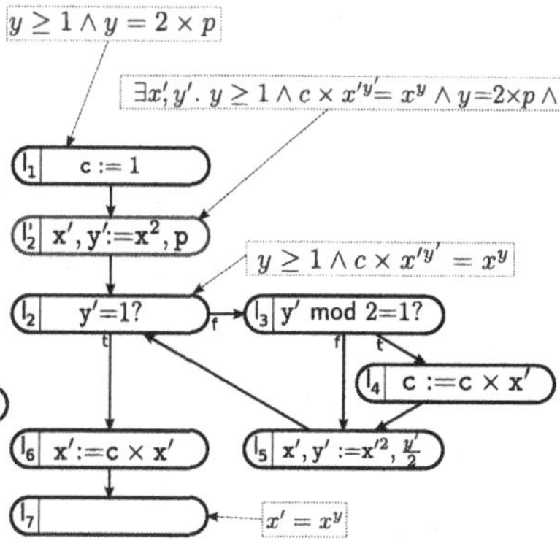

Fig. 9. Node coalescing and dead assignment elimination

the length of the longest path to an annotated node, i.e. a node $l \in \mathsf{dom}(\mathsf{annot})$. In the base case, where $l \in \mathsf{dom}(\mathsf{annot}')$, the certificate $\mathsf{goal}(l)$ is defined trivially, since $\overline{\mathsf{annot}}'(l) = S(l) \sqcap \overline{\mathsf{annot}}(l)$. For the inductive step, where $l \notin \mathsf{dom}(\mathsf{annot}')$, the proof is given in Figure 10, where the application of certificates $\mathsf{assoc}_{\sqcap}^{\leftarrow}$, $\mathsf{assoc}_{\sqcap}^{\rightarrow}$ and $\mathsf{commut}_{\sqcap}$ is omitted for readability.

4.3 Program Skeletons

Proposition 3 requires that the transformation is justified for each edge of the program; this rules out several well known optimizations such as instruction swapping or code motion, whose justification involves more than one instruction. To overcome this limitation, one can abandon the intuitive representation of programs, where each edge represents one instruction, and cluster several instructions into a single edge. The purpose of this section is to capture formally this idea of clustering, and use it to strengthen our basic result.

Throughout this section, we assume that $\mathcal{N}_0 \subseteq \mathcal{N}$ is a set of nodes such that $G_{|\mathcal{N}\setminus\mathcal{N}_0}$ and $G'_{|\mathcal{N}'\setminus\mathcal{N}_0}$ are acyclic. We define $\mathcal{E}_0 = \mathcal{E}^\star \cap \mathcal{N}_0 \times \mathcal{N}_0$ where $\mathcal{E}^\star$ denote the transitive closure of $\mathcal{E}$. Let $\langle I, \mathcal{P}\rangle$ be a certificate infrastructure with $I = \langle A, \{T_e\}, f\rangle$. The transfer functions $\hat{T}$ are defined for every $\langle l, l'\rangle \in \mathcal{E}^0$ and $a \in A$ as $\check{T}_{\langle l,l'\rangle}(a)$, where $\check{T}_e$ is defined for every $e \in \mathcal{E}$ as:

– if $f = \uparrow$, $\begin{cases} \check{T}_{\langle l,l'\rangle} = T_{\langle l,l'\rangle} & \langle l,l'\rangle \in \mathcal{E} \\ \check{T}_{\langle l,l'\rangle}(a) = \bigsqcap_{\{\langle l,l''\rangle \in \mathcal{E} \mid \mathsf{reaches}(l'',l')\}} T_{\langle l,l''\rangle}(\check{T}_{\langle l'',l'\rangle}(a)) & \langle l,l'\rangle \notin \mathcal{E} \end{cases}$

– if $f = \downarrow$, $\begin{cases} \check{T}_{\langle l',l\rangle} = T_{\langle l',l\rangle} & \langle l',l\rangle \in \mathcal{E} \\ \check{T}_{\langle l',l\rangle}(a) = \bigsqcup_{\{\langle l'',l\rangle \in \mathcal{E} \mid \mathsf{reaches}(l',l'')\}} T_{\langle l'',l\rangle}(\check{T}_{\langle l',l''\rangle}(a)) & \langle l',l\rangle \notin \mathcal{E} \end{cases}$

where the condition $\mathsf{reaches}(l, l')$ stands for the existence of a sequence of labels $l_1, \ldots, l_k$ with $l_1 = l$ and $l_k = l'$ s.t. $\langle l_i, l_{i+1}\rangle \in \mathcal{E}$, for all $i \in \{1, \ldots, k-1\}$. The set $\mathcal{E}'_0$ and the transfer functions $\hat{T}'$ are defined in a similar fashion.

The results of the previous sections extend immediately to program skeletons.

Let $a = S(l)$, $a' = S(l')$, $T = T_{\langle l,l' \rangle}$ and $T' = T'_{\langle l,l' \rangle}$ in:

$$\begin{array}{l}
\mathsf{hyp}_1{:=}\mathsf{monot}_T : \mathcal{P}(\vdash b_1 \sqsubseteq b_2) \rightarrow \mathcal{P}(\vdash T(b_1) \sqsubseteq T(b_2)) \\
\mathsf{hyp}_2{:=}\mathsf{distrib}_T : \mathcal{P}(\vdash T(b_1) \sqcap T(b_2) \sqsubseteq T(b_1 \sqcap b_2)) \\
\quad p_1{:=}\mathsf{goal}(l') :\vdash a' \sqcap \overline{\mathsf{annot}}(l') \sqsubseteq \overline{\mathsf{annot}}'(l') \\
\quad p_2{:=}\mathsf{hyp}_1(p_1) :\vdash T'(a' \sqcap \overline{\mathsf{annot}}(l')) \sqsubseteq T'(\overline{\mathsf{annot}}'(l')) \\
\quad p_3{:=}\mathsf{justif}(l,l') :\vdash a \sqcap T(a' \sqcap \overline{\mathsf{annot}}(l')) \sqsubseteq T'(a' \sqcap \overline{\mathsf{annot}}(l')) \\
\quad p_5{:=}\mathsf{elim}_\sqcap(\mathsf{weak}_\sqcap(-,p_2),p_3) :\vdash a \sqcap T(a' \sqcap \overline{\mathsf{annot}}(l')) \sqsubseteq T'(\overline{\mathsf{annot}}'(l')) \\
\quad p_6{:=}\mathsf{hyp}_2 :\vdash T(a') \sqcap T(\overline{\mathsf{annot}}(l')) \sqsubseteq T(a' \sqcap \overline{\mathsf{annot}}(l')) \\
\quad p_7{:=}\mathsf{axiom} :\vdash a \sqsubseteq a \\
\quad p_8{:=}\mathsf{weak}_\sqcap(p_6) :\vdash a \sqcap T(a') \sqcap T(\overline{\mathsf{annot}}(l')) \sqsubseteq T(a' \sqcap \overline{\mathsf{annot}}(l')) \\
\quad p_9{:=}\mathsf{intro}_\sqcap(p_8,\mathsf{weak}_\sqcap(p_6)) :\vdash{:}\sqsubseteq a \sqcap T(a') \sqcap T(\overline{\mathsf{annot}}(l'))a \sqcap T(a' \sqcap \overline{\mathsf{annot}}(l')) \\
\quad p_{10}{:=}\mathsf{elim}_\sqcap(\mathsf{weak}_\sqcap(p_5),p_9) :\vdash a \sqcap T(a') \sqcap T(\overline{\mathsf{annot}}(l')) \sqsubseteq T'(\overline{\mathsf{annot}}'(l')) \\
\quad p_{11}{:=}\mathbf{c}_l^S :\vdash a \sqsubseteq T(a') \\
\quad p_{12}{:=}\mathsf{elim}_\sqcap(p_{10},p_{11}) :\vdash a \sqcap T(\overline{\mathsf{annot}}(l')) \sqsubseteq T'(\overline{\mathsf{annot}}'(l')) \\
\quad p_{13}{:=}\mathsf{weak}_\sqcap(p_{12}) :\vdash a \sqcap \bigsqcap_{\langle l,l' \rangle \in \mathcal{E}} T(\overline{\mathsf{annot}}(l')) \sqsubseteq T'(\overline{\mathsf{annot}}'(l')) \\
\mathsf{goal}(l){:=}\mathsf{intro}_\sqcap(\{p_{12}\}_{\langle l,l' \rangle \in \mathcal{E}}) :\vdash a \sqcap \bigsqcap_{\langle l,l' \rangle \in \mathcal{E}} T(\overline{\mathsf{annot}}(l')) \sqsubseteq \bigsqcap_{\langle l,l' \rangle \in \mathcal{E}} T'(\overline{\mathsf{annot}}'(l'))
\end{array}$$

Fig. 10. Definition of $\mathsf{goal}(l)$ for certificate translation (case $f = \uparrow$)

Lemma 3. *Let $\langle S, \mathbf{c}_I \rangle$ be a certified solution for I s.t $\mathsf{dom}(S) \subseteq \mathcal{N}_0$. Then $\langle \hat{S}, \hat{\mathbf{c}}_{\hat{I}} \rangle = \langle S, \mathbf{c}_{I|\mathcal{N}_0} \rangle$ is a certified solution of $\hat{I} = \langle A, \hat{T}_e, f \rangle$.*

Proposition 4. *Let $\langle \hat{S}, \hat{\mathbf{c}}_{\hat{I}} \rangle = \langle S, \mathbf{c}_{I|\mathcal{N}_0} \rangle$ be a certified solution of $\hat{I} = \langle A, \hat{T}_e, f \rangle$. Suppose that for every $\langle l_1, l_2 \rangle \in \mathcal{E}'_0$ and $a \in A$:*

- *if $f = \uparrow$ then $\mathsf{justif}(l_1,l_2) :\vdash \hat{S}(l_1) \sqcap \hat{T}_{\langle l_1,l_2 \rangle}(a) \sqsubseteq \hat{T'}_{\langle l_1,l_2 \rangle}(a)$;*
- *if $f = \downarrow$ then $\mathsf{justif}(l_1,l_2) :\vdash \hat{T'}_{\langle l_1,l_2 \rangle}(a) \sqsubseteq \hat{S}(l_2) \sqcap \hat{T}_{\langle l_1,l_2 \rangle}(a)$*

Then every certified labeling $\langle \mathsf{annot}, \mathbf{c} \rangle$ for G such that $\mathsf{dom}(\mathsf{annot}) \subseteq \mathcal{N}_0$ can be transformed into a certified labeling $\langle \mathsf{annot}', \mathbf{c}' \rangle$ for G', where $\mathsf{annot}'(l)$ is defined as $\mathsf{annot}(l) \sqcap S(l)$ for all $l \in \mathsf{dom}(\mathsf{annot}') = \mathsf{dom}(\mathsf{annot}) \cap \mathcal{N}'$.

Example. A further simple transformation consists of coalescing the nodes l'_2, l'_3 and l'_5 to simplify the graph representation. Formally, we use the program skeletons to cluster the sub-graph constituted by the nodes l'_2, l'_3 and l'_5 into a single node l'_2. Then, we define the transfer function $\hat{T}_{\langle l'_2,l_2 \rangle} = T'_{\langle l'_5,l_2 \rangle}$ (formally, one should have $T_{\langle l'_2,l_2 \rangle} = T'_{\langle l'_2,l'_3 \rangle} \circ T'_{\langle l'_3,l'_5 \rangle} \circ T'_{\langle l'_5,l_2 \rangle}$ but $T'_{\langle l'_2,l'_3 \rangle}$ and $T'_{\langle l'_3,l'_5 \rangle}$ are the identity function). Hence, by a trivial application of Proposition 4, there exists a certified solution $\langle \hat{\mathsf{annot}}, \hat{\mathbf{c}} \rangle$, for the collapsed program representation $\langle \mathcal{N}_0, \mathcal{E}_0, l_{\mathsf{sp}} \rangle$, s.t. $\hat{\mathsf{annot}}(l) = \mathsf{annot}(l)$ for all $l \in \mathcal{N}_0$.

Proposition 4 can be used to prove preservation of proof obligations for non-optimizing compilers. Indeed, non-optimizing compilation transforms a graph representation of a program by splitting each node into a subgraph of more basic nodes, preserving the overall program structure. Thus, one can coalesce back the generated subgraphs into a skeleton structure similar to the source program. If we assume that transfer functions of the skeleton representation are equal to those of the source program (it is not sufficient that the functions are equivalent w.r.t. $\sqsubseteq$; equality is essential), then proof obligations are preserved and certificates can be reused without modification.

4.4 Second-Order Analysis-Based Optimizations

Proposition 3 does not cover optimizations that rely on analyses such as variable liveness to justify their result. This motivates the following mild generalization, in which the transformation is justified w.r.t. a composition operator.

Proposition 5. *Let* $\bullet : A \times A \to A$ *be a composition operator s.t. for every* $a_1, a_2, b_1, b_2 \in A$ *there exists a certificate*

$$\mathsf{monot}_\bullet : \mathcal{P}(\vdash a_1 \sqsubseteq a_2) \to \mathcal{P}(\vdash b_1 \sqsubseteq b_2) \to \mathcal{P}(\vdash a_1 \bullet b_1 \sqsubseteq a_2 \bullet b_2)$$

Let $\langle S, \mathbf{c}^S \rangle$ *be a certified solution for* I *s.t. for every* $\langle l_1, l_2 \rangle \in \mathcal{E}'$ *and* $a \in A$*:*

- *if* $f = \uparrow$ *then* $\mathsf{justif}(l_1, l_2) : \vdash S(l_1) \bullet T_{\langle l_1, l_2 \rangle}(a) \sqsubseteq T'_{\langle l_1, l_2 \rangle}(a \bullet S(l_2))$*;*
- *if* $f = \downarrow$ *then* $\mathsf{justif}(l_1, l_2) : \vdash T'_{\langle l_1, l_2 \rangle}(a \bullet S(l_1)) \sqsubseteq S(l_2) \bullet T_{\langle l_1, l_2 \rangle}(a)$

Then, provided the certificate monot_T *defined in Fig. 7 exist for all* $a_1, a_2 \in A$*, every certified labeling* $\langle \mathsf{annot}, \mathbf{c} \rangle$ *for* G *can be transformed into a certified labeling* $\langle \mathsf{annot}', \mathbf{c}' \rangle$ *for* G'*, where* $\mathsf{annot}'(l) = \mathsf{annot}(l) \bullet S(l)$ *for every node* l *in* $\mathsf{dom}(\mathsf{annot}') = \mathsf{dom}(\mathsf{annot}) \cap \mathcal{N}'$.

Example. Finally, we perform liveness analysis on program variables and remove assignments to dead variables. The resulting program is given in Figure 9. The remaining of this subsection is devoted to an explanation of the analysis, and to a justification of the transformation.

Assuming a standard program semantics, we say that a variable is live at a certain program point if its value will be needed in the future. An intensional definition classifies a variable x as live at a program node l if there is a path from l that reaches an expression referring to x, without traversing an assignment to x. We prefer to use a more extensional interpretation of liveness, inspired by Benton's Relational Hoare Logic [5], identifying a declaration of a set of live variables as a relational proposition. To this end, we generalize the abstract domain A of the certificate infrastructure to include relational propositions. An abstract domain A is relational if the associated satisfaction relation $\models_A$ is a subset of $(\mathsf{Env} \times \mathsf{Env}) \times A$. Hence, a relational proposition will be interpreted as a relation on execution environments. Formally, the extension consists on partitioning the domain of variables by attaching to each of them an index $_{\langle 1 \rangle}$ or $_{\langle 2 \rangle}$. The set of transfer functions is also modified accordingly; for instance, the substitution $\phi[^e/_x]$ corresponding to the assignment $x{:=}e$ at node l, is replaced by the substitution $\phi[^{e_{\langle 1 \rangle}}/_{x_{\langle 1 \rangle}}][^{e_{\langle 2 \rangle}}/_{x_{\langle 2 \rangle}}]$, where $e_{\langle i \rangle}$ is the result of indexing every variable occurring at e with $_{\langle i \rangle}$.

Then, we define $\gamma(X) = \bigwedge_{v \in X} v_{\langle 1 \rangle} = v_{\langle 2 \rangle}$ as an interpretation of the fact that all variables in X are live. In order to generate a certificate for the optimized program, we apply Proposition 5, using as composition operator over relational propositions the function $\centerdot$ defined as

$$\phi \centerdot \psi = \exists x^1, \ldots, x^k.\ \phi[{}^{x^1_{\langle 2 \rangle}}/_x] \ldots [{}^{x^k_{\langle 2 \rangle}}/_x] \wedge \psi[{}^{x^1_{\langle 1 \rangle}}/_x] \ldots [{}^{x^k_{\langle 1 \rangle}}/_x]$$

where $\{x^1, \ldots, x^k\}$ are the set of variables in ϕ or ψ. The interpretation of the composition operator is that if X declares the set of live variables, then $\gamma(X) \centerdot \phi$ is the result of existentially quantifying away from ϕ the variables that are not live.

By Proposition 1, we know that a certified solution $\langle \gamma \circ \mathsf{live}, \mathbf{c}'' \rangle$ exists s.t. $\mathsf{live}(l_1) = \{x, y\}$, $\mathsf{live}(l'_2) = \{x, y, c\}$ and $\mathsf{live}(l) = \{x, y, c, x', y'\}$ for $l \notin \{l_1, l'_2\}$. Since node l_1 contains an assignment to variables x' and y' and these variables are not live in node l'_2, we may safely simplify the statement by removing such assignments. From Proposition 5 we can transform the current certified solution by assuming the certificate

$$\mathsf{justif}(l_1, l'_2) : \vdash \gamma(\mathsf{live}(l_1)) \centerdot T_{\langle l_1, l'_2 \rangle}(\phi) \sqsubseteq T'_{\langle l_1, l'_2 \rangle}(\gamma(\mathsf{live}(l'_2)) \centerdot \phi) \ .$$

For readability, if ϕ is a non-relational proposition, $\gamma(X) \centerdot \phi$ is equivalently denoted $\exists y_1, \ldots, y_m.\ \phi$ where $\{y_1, \ldots, y_m\} = \mathsf{Var} - X$. Then, the goal of the certificate $\mathsf{justif}(l_1, l'_2)$ can be interpreted as $\vdash \phi[{}^1/_c][{}^x/_{x'}][{}^y/_{y'}] \sqsubseteq (\exists x', y'.\ \phi)[{}^1/_c]$.

5 Related Work

Certified solutions. Abstraction Carrying Code (ACC) is an instance of PCC where programs come with a solution in an abstract interpretation that can be used to specify the consumer policy [1]. ACC is closely related to our notion of certified solution; in fact, one may view the latter as a natural extension of ACC to settings where the pre-order relation is either undecidable, or expensive to compute, and where the use of certificates is required in order to check solutions. Besson *et al* [6] have recently developed a program analysis framework in which certificates are used to verify inclusions between elements of the abstract domain of polyhedra. Their analysis is also an instance of a certified solution. Rival [12,13] proposed a method to translate the result of a static analysis along program compilation. Result validation is restricted to post-fixpoint checking, i.e. there is no notion of certificate.

Certifying analyzers. We are aware of two previous works on certifying, or proof-producing, program analyses. Both consider the backwards case. Seo, Yang and Yi [15] consider a generic backwards abstract interpretation for a simple imperative language and provide an algorithm that automatically constructs safety proofs in Hoare logic from abstract interpretation results. Chaieb [7] considers a flow chart language equipped with a weakest precondition calculus, and provides sufficient conditions of the existence of certificates for solutions of backwards abstract interpretations. The technique was applied in the context of a certified PCC infrastructure [16].

Certificate translation. Müller and co-workers [2,10] define a proof transforming compiler for sequential Java. They consider Hoare logics for source and bytecode programs, and transform a correct derivation for a Java program into a correct derivation for the JVM program obtained by non-optimizing compilation.

Saabas and Uustalu [14] develop type-based methods to establish the existence of certifying analyzers and certificate transformers. They illustrate the feasibility of their method by explaining in detail two particular transformations: common subexpression elimination and dead variable elimination. They demonstrate the correctness of both transformations, by derivability of Hoare logic proofs, and provide an algorithm to transform a Hoare proof of the original program to a Hoare proof of the transformed program.

6 Conclusion

We have provided a crisp formalization of certificate translation in a mild extension of abstract interpretation in which solutions carry a certificate of their correctness. Our formalization allows us to give a rational reconstruction of our earlier work, and to establish the scalability of certificate translation. In order to further demonstrate the benefits of our framework, we show that certificate translation scales to concurrent languages, to relational program logics, which have been used to prove information flow properties, and that similar techniques can be used to justify hybrid certificates, that combine simultaneously several verification methods.

Acknowledgments. We are grateful to David Pichardie, Tamara Rezk and the referees for their constructive comments. This work is partially supported by the EU project MOBIUS.

References

1. Albert, E., Puebla, G., Hermenegildo, M.V.: Abstraction-carrying code. In: Baader, F., Voronkov, A. (eds.) LPAR 2004. LNCS (LNAI), vol. 3452, pp. 380–397. Springer, Heidelberg (2005)
2. Bannwart, F.Y., Müller, P.: A program logic for bytecode. In: Spoto, F. (ed.) Electronic Notes in Theoretical Computer Science, vol. 141, pp. 255–273. Elsevier, Amsterdam (2005)
3. Barthe, G., Grégoire, B., Kunz, C., Rezk, T.: Certificate translation for optimizing compilers. In: Yi, K. (ed.) SAS 2006. LNCS, vol. 4134, Springer, Heidelberg (2006)
4. Barthe, G., Rezk, T., Saabas, A.: Proof obligations preserving compilation. In: Dimitrakos, T., Martinelli, F., Ryan, P.Y.A., Schneider, S. (eds.) FAST 2005. LNCS, vol. 3866, pp. 112–126. Springer, Heidelberg (2006)
5. Benton, N.: Simple relational correctness proofs for static analyses and program transformations. In: Jones, N.D., Leroy, X. (eds.) Principles of Programming Languages, pp. 14–25. ACM Press, New York (2004)
6. Besson, F., Jensen, T., Pichardie, D., Turpin, T.: Result certification for relational program analysis. Technical report, IRISA (2007)

7. Chaieb, A.: Proof-producing program analysis. In: Barkaoui, K., Cavalcanti, A., Cerone, A. (eds.) ICTAC 2006. LNCS, vol. 4281, pp. 287–301. Springer, Heidelberg (2006)
8. Cousot, P., Cousot, R.: Abstract interpretation: A unified lattice model for static analysis of programs by construction or approximation of fixpoints. In: Principles of Programming Languages, pp. 238–252 (1977)
9. Cousot, P., Cousot, R.: Systematic design of program analysis frameworks. In: Principles of Programming Languages, pp. 269–282 (1979)
10. Müller, P., Nordio, M.: Proof-transforming compilation of programs with abrupt termination. Technical Report 565, ETH Zurich (2007)
11. Necula, G.C.: Proof-carrying code. In: Principles of Programming Languages, pp. 106–119. ACM Press, New York (1997)
12. Rival, X.: Abstract Interpretation-Based Certification of Assembly Code. In: Zuck, L.D., Attie, P.C., Cortesi, A., Mukhopadhyay, S. (eds.) VMCAI 2003. LNCS, vol. 2575, pp. 41–55. Springer, Heidelberg (2002)
13. Rival, X.: Symbolic Transfer Functions-based Approaches to Certified Compilation. In: Principles of Programming Languages, pp. 1–13. ACM Press, New York (2004)
14. Saabas, A., Uustalu, T.: Type systems for optimizing stack-based code. In: Huisman, M., Spoto, F. (eds.) Bytecode Semantics, Verification, Analysis and Transformation. Electronic Notes in Theoretical Computer Science, vol. 190(1), pp. 103–119. Elsevier, Amsterdam (2007)
15. Seo, S., Yang, H., Yi, K.: Automatic Construction of Hoare Proofs from Abstract Interpretation Results. In: Ohori, A. (ed.) APLAS 2003. LNCS, vol. 2895, pp. 230–245. Springer, Heidelberg (2003)
16. Wildmoser, M., Chaieb, A., Nipkow, T.: Bytecode analysis for proof carrying code. In: Spoto, F. (ed.) Bytecode Semantics, Verification, Analysis and Transformation. Electronic Notes in Theoretical Computer Science, vol. 141, Elsevier, Amsterdam (2005)

A Formal Implementation of Value Commitment

Cédric Fournet[2,1], Nataliya Guts[1], and Francesco Zappa Nardelli[3,1]

[1] MSR-INRIA Joint Centre
[2] Microsoft Research
[3] INRIA

Abstract. In an optimistic approach to security, one can often simplify protocol design by relying on audit logs, which can be analyzed a posteriori. Such auditing is widely used in practice, but no formal studies guarantee that the log information suffices to reconstruct past runs of the protocol, in order to reliably detect (and provide evidence of) any cheating. We formalize audit logs for a sample optimistic scheme, the value commitment. It is specified in a pi calculus extended with committable locations, and compiled using standard cryptography to implement secure logs. We show that our distributed implementation either respects the abstract semantics of commitments or, using information stored in the logs, detects cheating by a hostile environment.

1 A Cautiously Optimistic Approach to Security

Mutual distrust in distributed computing makes enforcing system-wide security assurances particularly challenging. Common protocols perform an important number of mandatory runtime checks and allow only legal computations to progress: in session-establishment protocols, for instance, a strong security invariant is usually enforced at every step of the run of the protocol. These runtime checks have a cost, in terms of cryptographic and networking operations; they may also conflict with other goals of the protocol, such as confidentiality.

A different approach, which we call optimistic, presumes instead that all involved principals are honest and well-behaved, and thus omits some runtime checks. Traces of protocol runs are stored in a secure log and can be used a posteriori to verify the compliance of each principal to its role: principals who attempt non-compliant actions will be blamed using the logged evidence. The security invariant is weaker than those achieved by more conservative protocols, but adequate for many non-critical applications.

Some protocols inherently rely on logs to establish their security properties. These protocols are often based on a *commitment* scheme. A principal commits to a value kept hidden; other principals of a system cannot read this value, but have a procedure to detect any change to the value after the commitment. Distant coin flipping is a simple protocol that illustrates commitments: suppose that A and B are not physically at the same place and want to toss a coin. Both A and B flip their own coin, exchange commitments on their results, then reveal and compare these results; A wins the toss if the two results are the same. For fairness, A's commitment should neither reveal any information to B, nor enable A to change her committed result after receiving B's.

Commitment is a building block for many protocols such as mental poker [3], sealed bid auctions, e-voting [6,5], and online games [12]. For instance, mental poker relies

S. Drossopoulou (Ed.): ESOP 2008, LNCS 4960, pp. 383–397, 2008.

on commitment to build a fair shuffling of the deck, then gradually reveal cards as the game proceeds. At the end of the game, the deck permutations used by each player can be revealed for auditing purposes.

Secure logging is not only an essential component of optimistic schemes, but is also widely used in standard practice. Much research effort has been devoted to techniques for implementing logs so as to guarantee properties such as *correctness*, *forward integrity*, and *forward secrecy* [15,18,17]. Still, which data should be logged? and why? Between general recommendations such as "an audit trail should include sufficient information to establish what events occurred and who (or what) caused them" [14,11] and efficient implementation techniques, we are not aware of any formal studies that characterize and verify the security properties achieved by protocols relying of logs.

In this paper, we give a formal answer to this question for the commitment scheme. We extend a simple distributed language, the applied pi calculus [1], with commitment datatypes and primitives, and we illustrate this extension by programming an online game. To abstract away from the possible misbehaviors of the environment, we propose a trustful and strong operational semantics for our commitment primitives. We show that our language can be compiled to the applied pi calculus, using standard cryptographic primitives, with adequate protection against an arbitrary, possibly hostile environment. We obtain an important security property stating that, for any source systems, our distributed implementation either respects the semantics of commitments or, using information stored in the logs, detects (and proves) cheating by a hostile environment.

Related work. Value commitments appear in formal models of protocols (e.g. [13]) and implementations of language abstractions (e.g. [19]). More closely related to our work, Etalle et al. [10,4] advocate the usage of logs for optimistic security enforcement. They formalize audit-based discretionary access control in collaborative work environments, and develop a logical framework for user accountability; they also design cryptographic support for communication evidence in a decentralized setting [8].

Contents. Section 2 presents our source language with value commitment. Section 3 illustrates the use of commitment for programming online games. Section 4 describes the language implementation, as a cryptographic translation to the applied pi calculus. Section 5 develops a labeled semantics and an extended translation to keep track of source-program invariants. Section 6 states our main results. Section 7 reports on our prototype implementation. Section 8 discusses future work.

Additional details appear online, at `http://www.msr-inria.inria.fr/projects/sec/logs`, including complete definitions for the source and target semantics and all proofs.

2 A Language with Value Commitment

The applied pi calculus is a process language parametrized by an equational theory on terms, which provides flexible support for modeling symbolic cryptographic primitives and data structures. We refer to [1] for a general presentation of its semantics.

To express the value commitment scheme, we extend an instance of applied pi with *committable cells*. The grammar for terms (M, V), processes (P), and systems (A) is given below. Our extensions to the standard syntax appear in grey boxes .

$M, V ::=$	$P ::=$	$A ::=$
$\mid u$	$\mid 0$	$\mid 0$
$\mid \mathit{func}(\widetilde{M})$	$\mid P_1 \mid P_2$	$\mid A_1 \mid A_2$
$\mid u.\mathbf{Idu}$	$\mid \nu c . P$	$\mid \nu u . A$
$\mid u.\mathbf{Idc}(p)$	$\mid u?(x).P$	$\mid \{ M / x \}$
$\mid u.\mathbf{Rd}(p\ M)$	$\mid u!\langle M \rangle.P$	$\mid p[P]$
	$\mid \mathsf{if}\ M = M'\ \mathsf{then}\ P\ \mathsf{else}\ P'$	$\mid u.(p)$
	$\mid \mathsf{repl}\ P$	$\mid u.(p\ M)$
	$\mid \mathsf{newloc}\,(x, y).P$	
	$\mid \mathsf{commit}\ M\ u\,(x).P$	

Terms are built from variables (denoted $x, y, \ldots$), names (denoted $c, l, s, \ldots$), function applications, and capabilities (described below). We assume that functions include at least a pairing function, denoted $+$, with associated projections $+_1, +_2$ and equations $+_i(x_1 + x_2) = x_i$ for $i = 1, 2$. (Our results extend to arbitrary data structures; we use integer constants in examples.) The metavariable u ranges over names and variables. Among names, we distinguish the set of *principals*, denoted p, a, e, and the set of *location names*, ranged over by l. Contrarily to standard applied pi, each process P runs under the control of a principal p, denoted $p[P]$.

Committable cells and capabilities. A cell is a memory location owned by a principal who can, once, commit its content to a value of its choice. In addition, the owner can pass capabilities to other principals, thereby granting these principals partial read access to the cell.

Our language features three kinds of capabilities. The *read capability* $l\,.\,\mathbf{Rd}\,(p\ \ M)$ is created by the owner p of the location l when it commits to a value M. Any principal can use a read capability to read the content of the location associated to the capability. The *identity capabilities* instead partially disclose the state of a cell without actually revealing the value possibly committed. So the *committed id capability* $l\,.\,\mathbf{Idc}\,(p\ )$ proves that the location l is committed and reveals the owner p of the location. The *uncommitted id capability* $l\,.\,\mathbf{Idu}$ just asserts the identity l of the location.

The language of terms is sorted: we distinguish *marshallable values*, that include all the terms except location and channel names, and *committable values*, that include all marshallable values except those that mention committed id and read capabilities.

The state of each committable cell is represented by a process: $l.(p\ )$ denotes an uncommitted cell named l owned by p; $l.(p\ M)$ denotes the same cell once it has been committed to the committable value M. Two new kinds of processes manipulate cells. The newloc process creates a fresh, uncommitted location and binds both its unique identifier l (from $\mathcal{L}$) and its uncommitted capability in its continuation:

$$a[\mathsf{newloc}\,(x, y).P] \longrightarrow \nu\, l\,.\,(l.(a\ ) \mid a[P\{^{l}/_{x}\}\{^{l\,.\,\mathbf{Idu}}/_{y}\}])$$

where l is fresh for P. The unique identifier l can then be used to commit an uncommitted cell to some committable value M:

$$l.(a\ ) \mid a[\mathsf{commit}\ M\ l\,(x).P] \longrightarrow l.(a\ M) \mid a[P\{^{l\,.\,\mathbf{Rd}\,(a\ M)}/_{x}\}]$$

The commit process yields a read capability for the newly-committed cell. The sort system does not allow to communicate or store in another location the cell name l: hence, only the principal that created the cell can commit a value into it. The abbreviation newcommit creates a new committed location (where x', x'' are fresh for P):

$$p[\mathsf{newcommit}\ M\ (x).P] \stackrel{\text{def}}{=} p[\mathsf{newloc}\ (x', x'').\mathsf{commit}\ M\ x'\ (x).P]$$

Capabilities can be communicated over channels; they can also be manipulated using special functions, according to the equational theory below.

$$\mathsf{read}(x\,.\,\mathbf{Rd}\ (p\ \ v)) = v \qquad \mathsf{get\_idc}(x\,.\,\mathbf{Rd}\ (p\ \ v)) = x\,.\,\mathbf{Idc}\ (p\ )$$
$$\mathsf{get\_idu}(x\,.\,\mathbf{Idc}\ (p\ )) = x\,.\,\mathbf{Idu} \qquad \mathsf{get\_prin}(x\,.\,\mathbf{Idc}\ (p\ )) = p$$
$$\mathsf{is\_idu}(x\,.\,\mathbf{Idu}) = \mathsf{ok} \qquad \mathsf{is\_idc}(x\,.\,\mathbf{Idc}\ (p\ )) = \mathsf{ok} \qquad \mathsf{is\_rd}(x\,.\,\mathbf{Rd}\ (p\ \ v)) = \mathsf{ok}$$

The read function yields the value from read capabilities. Since the read capability is generated when committing the cell, the semantics of the source language guarantees that all reads for a given cell always return the same value. The get_prin function yields the principal that owns the cell from committed capabilities. (We could also provide get_prin from uncommitted capabilities, at some additional cost in the cryptographic implementation.) The get_idu and get_idc functions downgrade capabilities, yielding a more restrictive capability for the same cell. Hence, get_idu yields an uncommitted capability, which can be used only to identify the cell, whereas get_idc takes a read capability and hides its committed value. The language finally has functions that support dynamic typechecking of capabilities. In particular, $\mathsf{is\_idc}(x) = \mathsf{ok}$ or $\mathsf{is\_rd}(x) = \mathsf{ok}$ implies that the cell associated with x is committed.

3 Example: An Online Game

Our example describes a game run by a server a_0, between n players $a_1, \ldots, a_n$. The game is played in one turn, with all players revealing their moves simultaneously. (A simple instance of the game with $n = 2$ is Rock, Paper, Scissors.) The players and the server are willing to cooperate, but with minimal trust assumptions between them; however, it is deemed sufficient to detect any dishonest principal at the end of the game. Similar examples include multiparty protocols for online auctions, voting, or partial-information games [16,3,6].

The protocol has three exchange rounds between the server and each player, using channels c_i for $i = 1..n$: (1) the server sets up the game, distributes the details to the players, and collects their sealed moves; (2) the server distributes all the players' sealed moves and collects their actual moves; (3) the server distributes the result of the game.

We begin with the server code, given below. For simplicity, the code does not provide any error handling—execution stops when a test fails.

$$\begin{aligned} A_0 = a_0[&\mathsf{newloc}\ (l, \mathit{result}_{id}).\mathsf{newcommit}\ \mathit{result}_{id} + \mathit{details}\ (\mathit{challenge}).\\ &(c_i!\langle \mathit{challenge}\rangle.c_i?(\mathit{promise}_i).\mathsf{if}\ \mathsf{get\_prin}(\mathit{promise}_i) = a_i\ \mathsf{then}\ )_{i=1..n}\\ &\mathsf{newcommit}\ \mathit{challenge} + \widetilde{\mathit{promise}}\ (\mathit{game}).\\ &(c_i!\langle \mathit{game}\rangle.c_i?(\mathit{move}_i).\mathsf{if}\ \mathsf{get\_idc}(\mathit{move}_i) = \mathit{promise}_i\ \mathsf{then}\ )_{i=1..n}\\ &\mathsf{commit}\,\mathsf{winner}(\widetilde{\mathit{move}}, \mathit{challenge})\ l\ (\mathit{result}).(c_i!\langle \mathit{result}\rangle.0)_{i=1..n}] \end{aligned}$$

In round (1), the server creates an uncommitted cell l for storing the outcome of the game, and a readable cell *challenge* that provides the identifier for l and the (unspecified) details of the game. Upon receiving each player's response, the server authenticates it as a committed capability from that player. In round (2), the server creates a second committed cell that binds the challenge to the received commitments from all players. Upon receiving each player's second response, the server correlates it as the read capability associated with their first response. In round (3), the server has all the players' information: it resolves the game and finally commits the cell l to the published result of the game (which may include, for instance, selected information from the players' moves). We omit the code for the function winner that computes this result.

The code for the players performs symmetric operations:

$$\begin{aligned} A_i = a_i[&c_i?(\mathit{challenge}).\mathsf{if}\ \mathsf{get\_prin}(\mathsf{get\_idc}(\mathit{challenge})) = a_0\ \mathsf{then} \\ &\mathsf{newcommit}\ z_i\ (\mathit{move}_i).c_i!\langle \mathsf{get\_idc}(\mathit{move}_i)\rangle. \\ &c_i?(\mathit{game}).\mathsf{if}\ \mathsf{valid\_game}(\mathit{game}, \mathit{challenge}, \mathit{move}_i)\ \mathsf{then} \\ &\quad c_i!\langle \mathit{move}_i\rangle.c_i?(\mathit{result}_i).\mathsf{if}\ \mathsf{no\_cheat}(\mathit{result}_i, \mathsf{read}(\mathit{game}))\ \mathsf{then}\ P_i] \end{aligned}$$

In round (1), after receiving the challenge, each player confirms its validity, for instance by checking that it is a genuine readable capability from a_0, then it selects a move and sends back its commitment. In round (2), after receiving all commitments, the player correlates them to the challenge and verifies that its own commitment is recorded (using for instance valid_game) then it releases its move in clear. In round (3), the player checks the outcome of the game and verifies a posteriori that the server followed the rules (using for instance no_cheat). The tests are defined as follows:

$$\begin{aligned} \mathsf{valid\_game}(x_1, x_2, x_3) &\stackrel{\text{def}}{=} +_1(\mathsf{read}(x_1)) = x_2\ \mathsf{and}\ \mathsf{get\_idc}(x_3) \in +_2(\mathsf{read}(x_1)) \\ \mathsf{no\_cheat}(x, y) &\stackrel{\text{def}}{=} \mathsf{get\_idu}(\mathsf{get\_idc}(x)) = +_1(y)\ \mathsf{and}\ \mathsf{get\_idc}(x) \in +_2(y) \end{aligned}$$

Guarantees offered to the players. We distinguish *language level* guarantees, enforced by the abstract semantics of locations, and *application level* guarantees, relying on high-level, application-specific checks on top of the language semantics. For each kind of guarantees, we also distinguish between immediate (conservative) and deferred (optimistic) enforcement. For instance, enforcement may be deferred until the content of a cell becomes readable.

As an illustration of immediate language-level checks, committed values offer basic authentication guarantees to the participants. For instance, each player has the privilege to choose its moves, and the move is securely attributed to the player even if the communication channels c_i are unprotected; participants can also check this attribution later.

To protect application integrity, the code must perform sufficient checks before proceeding with the game. Systematic testing of the owner identities for the received capabilities avoids unauthorized, possibly non-accountable, participants. Some checks are immediate, e.g. testing if two capabilities are associated to the same location; other checks that depend on the commitment semantics are delayed. In the example, players are guaranteed that they all get the same result (if any) for any given game, since they must get the same location read capability, but it is up to the application code to correlate the received read capability to the initial uncommitted capability.

At the same time, the applicative logic of our protocol guarantees that, even if the server is willing to leak information to the other players, those players cannot get that information before committing to their own moves.

4 Distributed Cryptography Implementation

The target language is an instance of applied pi, with standard (symbolic) cryptographic primitives and data structures but without ad-hoc rules or constructs for locations.

We rely on a cryptographic hash function, denoted h, and a public-key signature mechanism satisfying the equation $\mathsf{verify}(v\,,\,\mathsf{sign}(v\,,\,\mathsf{sk}(m))\,,\,\mathsf{pk}(m)) = \mathsf{ok}$. The functions $\mathsf{sk}(m)$ and $\mathsf{pk}(m)$ generate a pair of secret/public keys from a nonce m. All other data constructors admit a projection function $\mathit{func}_i(\mathit{func}(x_1\,,\,\ldots\,,\,x_n)) = x_i$.

To every principal p, we associate a keypair and export its public key tagged with constructor prin using an active substitution of the form $\{\,\mathsf{prin}(\mathsf{pk}(m_p))\,/\,p\,\}$.

Cryptographic implementation of capabilities. We compile the capabilities associated to a location $l.(p\ V)$ as follows:

$$
\begin{array}{ll}
l\,.\,\textbf{Rd}\,(p\ \ V) & \mathsf{rd}(p\,,\,s\,,\,[\![V]\!]\,,\,w) \\
l\,.\,\textbf{Idc}\,(p\,) & \mathsf{idc}(p\,,\,\mathsf{h}(s)+\mathsf{h}(s+[\![V]\!])\,,\,w) \\
l\,.\,\textbf{Idu} & \mathsf{idu}(\mathsf{h}(p+\mathsf{h}(s)))
\end{array}
$$

where $p = \mathsf{prin}(\mathsf{pk}(m_p))$ is the owner's public key, s is a fresh value used as a seed, and $w = \mathsf{sign}(\mathsf{h}(s)+\mathsf{h}(s+[\![V]\!])\,,\,\mathsf{sk}(m_p))$ signs the committed value $[\![V]\!]$.

A read capability is a tagged tuple that includes these elements. A committed id capability is a tagged tuple that provides p and verifiable evidence of the commitment without actually revealing $[\![V]\!]$. To this end, it includes both a hash of the committed value, first concatenated with the seed s, to protect against brute force attacks, yielding $\mathsf{h}(s+[\![V]\!])$, and the hash $\mathsf{h}(s)$, to enable the receiver to correlate the owner and signature with a previously-received uncommitted id capability by recomputing the identifier $\mathsf{h}(p+\mathsf{h}(s))$. An uncommitted id capability just includes this unique location identifier, which may be compared to other capabilities and, later, associated with p and s. The receiver can compute committed capabilities from read capabilities, and uncommitted capabilities from committed capabilities, but not the converse.

The signature w authenticates read and committed id capabilities, binding their content to the owner's key $\mathsf{sk}(m_p)$. Their receiver can extract p and $\mathsf{h}(s)+\mathsf{h}(s+[\![V]\!])$ from these tagged tuples and use them to verify w. When the signature is valid, the public key identifies the owner of the location associated to the capability.

Detection of multiple commitments. In a typical run, an honest principal receives a commitment to some value from the principal p, say $\mathsf{idc}(p\,,\,v_1+v_2\,,\,w)$, and later the value itself, say $\mathsf{rd}(p\,,\,s\,,\,z\,,\,w')$. The receiver can easily check that the two capabilities refer to the same location, by testing $\mathsf{h}(s) = v_1$, and verify the two signatures $w = \mathsf{sign}(v_1+v_2\,,\,\mathsf{sk}(m_p))$ and $w' = \mathsf{sign}(\mathsf{h}(s)+\mathsf{h}(s+z)\,,\,\mathsf{sk}(m_p))$. If these tests succeed, then the receiver can check whether $v_2 = \mathsf{h}(s+M)$: if the test fails, the principal p can be convicted of multiply committing the location identified by $\mathsf{h}(p+\mathsf{h}(s))$.

In preparation for the translation, we introduce functions that operate on tuples representing capabilities in the target language. For instance, the function read implements source-language reads as a projection, and check_idc verifies the seal of committed ids.

$$\begin{aligned}
\mathsf{read}(x) &\stackrel{\text{def}}{=} \mathsf{rd}_3(x)\\
\mathsf{get_idc}(x) &\stackrel{\text{def}}{=} \mathsf{idc}(\mathsf{rd}_1(x)\,,\ \mathsf{h}(\mathsf{rd}_2(x)) + \mathsf{h}(\mathsf{rd}_2(x) + \mathsf{rd}_3(x))\,,\ \mathsf{rd}_4(x))\\
\mathsf{check_idc}(x) &\stackrel{\text{def}}{=} \mathsf{verify}(\mathsf{idc}_2(x)\,,\ \mathsf{idc}_3(x)\,,\ \mathsf{prin}_1(\mathsf{idc}_1(x))) = \mathsf{ok}\\
\mathsf{get_idu}(x) &\stackrel{\text{def}}{=} \mathsf{idu}(\mathsf{h}(\mathsf{idc}_1(x) + (+_1\ \mathsf{idc}_2(x))))
\end{aligned}$$

In general, inconsistent capabilities may be scattered in the whole system. To detect such inconsistencies and reliably blame cheating principals, a compiled system logs all the committed capabilities generated or received by honest principals by sending them over the channel *log* to the following resolution process R:

$$\begin{aligned}
R = \mathsf{repl}\ &log?(y_1).log?(y_2).\\
&\mathsf{if}\ \mathsf{check_idc}(y_1)\ \mathsf{and}\ \mathsf{check_idc}(y_2)\ \mathsf{then}\\
&\mathsf{if}\ \mathsf{get_idu}(y_1) = \mathsf{get_idu}(y_2)\ \mathsf{and}\ \mathsf{idc}_2(y_1) \neq \mathsf{idc}_2(y_2)\ \mathsf{then}\ bad!\langle \mathsf{get_prin}(y_1)\rangle
\end{aligned}$$

This resolution process repeatedly reads pairs of Idc capabilities over the *log* channel and tests them for inconsistencies, as described above. If cheating is detected, the principal is blamed on channel *bad*. The resolution process acts as an external judge auditing the compiled system, and the data sent over the channel *log* as a secure audit trail. Since all messages on *log* are replicated, log entries cannot be erased or modified by a malicious principal, and every principal may run its own copy of process R. At the same time, a malicious principal cannot forge capabilities that would accuse an honest principal, as it cannot produce a valid seal associated with the honest principal.

Translation of initial configurations. Protocol descriptions can be expressed as initial configurations of a source system that do not contain, or refer to, locations and capabilities; these are created later, during the run of the protocol. We describe the translation of such configurations; a full treatment of capabilities and locations is deferred to Section 5. Our translation is a homomorphism over terms and over most systems.

$$[\![x]\!] = x \qquad [\![c]\!] = c \qquad [\![func(M_1\,,\ \ldots\,,\ M_n)]\!] = func([\![M_1]\!]\,,\ \ldots\,,\ [\![M_n]\!])$$

$$[\![A]\!] = [A] \mid R \mid E \qquad [a[P]] = \nu\, m_a\,.\,([\![P]\!]_a \mid \{\, \mathsf{prin}(\mathsf{pk}(m_a))\ /\ a\,\})$$

$$[A_1 \mid A_2] = [A_1] \mid [A_2] \qquad [\nu\, u\,.\,A] = \nu\, u\,.\,[A] \qquad [\{\, M\,/\,x\,\}] = \{\, [\![M]\!]\,/\,x\,\}$$

Let $\mathcal{A}$ the set of principals running a process in the system and $\mathcal{E}$ the set of other (possibly dishonest) principals whose names occur in the system ($\mathcal{E} = \mathcal{P} \cap \text{fn}(A) \setminus \mathcal{A}$).

For each principal $a \in \mathcal{A}$, the translation creates a secret seed m_a used to generate the pair of secret/public keys of the principal. The public key is published using an active substitution, while the process run by the principal is compiled within the scope of the private seed m_a used for signing. Similarly, the translation includes active substitutions $E = \prod_{e\in\mathcal{E}}(\{\, \mathsf{prin}(\mathsf{pk}(m_e))\ /\ e\,\} \mid \{\, H_e\ /\ m_e\,\})$ that records, for each principal $e \in \mathcal{E}$, a public key $\mathsf{pk}(m_e)$ and an associated secret H_e. The translation also spawns a replicated resolution server R.

The translation of processes is given next. (We omit the homomorphic clauses for 0, $P_1 \mid P_2$, $\mathsf{repl}\ P$, and $\nu\, c\,.\,P$).

$$\llbracket \mathsf{newloc}\,(x,y).P \rrbracket_a = \nu\, s'_l\,.\,\nu\, c_l\,.\,(c_l!\langle \mathsf{None}\rangle \mid \llbracket P \rrbracket_a \{{}^{c_l}/_{c_x}\}\{{}^{s'_l}/_{s_x}\}\{{}^{\mathsf{idu}(\mathsf{h}(a+\mathsf{h}(s'_l)))}/_y\})$$

$$\llbracket \mathsf{commit}\ V\ x\,(x').P \rrbracket_a = c_x?(y).(\llbracket P \rrbracket_a \mid \mathsf{repl}\ log!\langle \mathsf{idc}(a\,,\,v_x\,,\,w_x)\rangle)$$
$$\{{}^{\mathsf{h}(s_x)+\mathsf{h}(s_x+\llbracket V \rrbracket)}/_{v_x}\}\{{}^{\mathsf{sign}(v_x\,,\,\mathsf{sk}(m_a))}/_{w_x}\}\{{}^{\mathsf{rd}(a\,,\,s_x\,,\,\llbracket V \rrbracket\,,\,w_x)}/_{x'}\}$$

$$\begin{array}{l}
\mathsf{parse}\ x\ P = \\
\quad \mathsf{if\ is_rd}(x) = \mathsf{ok\ then} \\
\qquad \mathsf{if\ check_idc(get_idc}(x))\ \mathsf{then\ parse\ read}(x)\ (P \mid \mathsf{repl}\ log!\langle \mathsf{get_idc}(x)\rangle)\ \mathsf{else}\ r!\langle \mathsf{None}\rangle \\
\quad \mathsf{else\ if\ is_idc}(x) = \mathsf{ok\ then\ if\ check_idc}(x)\ \mathsf{then}\ P \mid \mathsf{repl}\ log!\langle x\rangle\ \mathsf{else}\ r!\langle \mathsf{None}\rangle \\
\qquad \mathsf{else\ if\ is_prin}(x) = \mathsf{ok\ or\ is_idu}(x) = \mathsf{ok\ then}\ P \\
\qquad\quad \mathsf{else\ if\ is_pair}(x) = \mathsf{ok\ then\ parse}\ (+_1\ x)\ (\mathsf{parse}\ (+_2\ x)\ P)\ \mathsf{else}\ r!\langle \mathsf{None}\rangle
\end{array}$$

$$\llbracket c!\langle M\rangle.P \rrbracket_a = c!\langle \llbracket M \rrbracket\rangle.\llbracket P \rrbracket_a$$

$$\llbracket c?(x).P \rrbracket_a = \nu\, r\,.\,(c?(x).\mathsf{parse}\ x\ \llbracket P \rrbracket_a \mid \mathsf{repl}\ (r?(\_).c?(x).\mathsf{parse}\ x\ \llbracket P \rrbracket_a))$$

$$\llbracket \mathsf{if}\ M = M'\ \mathsf{then}\ P_1\ \mathsf{else}\ P_2 \rrbracket_a = \mathsf{if}\ \llbracket M \rrbracket = \llbracket M' \rrbracket\ \mathsf{then}\ \llbracket P_1 \rrbracket_a\ \mathsf{else}\ \llbracket P_2 \rrbracket_a$$

The translation of newloc creates a fresh location seed s'_l and a local channel c_l (with a message None, recording that the location is uncommitted), and substitutes c_l for c_x, s'_l for s_x and the idu capability for y in the continuation.

The translation of commit can proceed only if the location has not been previously committed (the message on c_x provides mutual exclusion); it then substitutes the rd capability for x' in the continuation code. It also generates the corresponding idc capability for the location and logs it by sending it to the resolution protocol.

The parse function filters any received value received over channels. If the value is tagged with rd or idc, then it might (or not) be a valid capability, depending on the validity of its embedded signature: valid capabilities are passed to the continuation, while the associated idc is sent to the resolution protocol. If the value is tagged as a principal or an uncommitted capability, it is always passed to the continuation. For compound data, here pairs, each element is separately parsed. Other values, as well as non-valid committed capabilities, are silently discarded. In the translation of an input, we assume that the channel r is fresh for $\llbracket P \rrbracket_a$, and use this channel to loop after discarding such values.

5 Model and Translation of Environment Interactions

We define a labeled source semantics that explicitly captures all possible interactions between a system composed of honest principals and an abstract environment composed of potentially hostile principals. To maintain the committable-cell invariants, this semantics keeps track of the capabilities exported to the environment and of the partial knowledge acquired when receiving capabilities from the environment. We then extend our translation from initial configurations to any such reachable configuration.

Extended location states and capabilities. We use overlapping syntaxes for capabilities appearing in values, in transition labels, and in the processes representing the state of the cells. Their general form is $l\,.\,Cap\,([\,p\,]\,[\,H\,]\,[\,V\,])$, where l is the location identifier; $Cap \in \{0, \mathbf{Idu}, \mathbf{Idc}, \mathbf{Rd}\}$ is a capability tag; p is a principal name; H ranges over terms of the target language; and V is a value of the source language.

(This syntaxes extend those given in Section 2 for capabilities and location states, with $l.(a\ M) = l\,.\,0\,(a\ M)$). The fields p, H, and V are optional. The presence of a value V indicates that the location is committed to this value. The term H plays no role in the source language, but is technically convenient in its translation: it enables us to represent any reachable state of our implementation as the translation of a source system.

The interpretation of Cap depends on the principal p that owns the location. If a location is owned by $a \in \mathcal{A}$, then Cap represents the most permissive capability *sent to* the environment (and H is omitted), with $Cap = 0$ when no capabilities have been exported so far. If a location is owned by $e \notin \mathcal{A}$, then Cap represents the most permissive capability *received from* the environment (and H records some opaque cryptographic value in its received representation).

Ordering capabilities. We formalize the notion of "more permissive capability" by defining a preorder $\preceq$ on capabilities. Intuitively, $C \preceq C'$ holds if C and C' have compatible contents and C can be derived from C' using the equational theory. We also introduce a special capability $\bot$ that represents the absence of knowledge on a location. The order is defined by the axioms below:

$$\bot \preceq 0\ ct \qquad 0\ ct \preceq \mathbf{Idu}\ ct \qquad \mathbf{Idu}\ \mathsf{f}_u\,(ct) \preceq \mathbf{Idc}\ ct \qquad \mathbf{Idc}\ \mathsf{f}_c\,(ct) \preceq \mathbf{Rd}\ ct$$

$$Cap\,(p\ H) \preceq Cap\,(p\ H\ V)$$

where ct is any fixed contents and f_u and f_c are fixed functions that rewrite H in ct. We write $C \curlyvee C'$ for the sup of C and C' with respect to $\preceq$, when it exists.

Normal form. We say that a system is in *normal form* when it is of the form

$$S \;=\; \nu\mathcal{N}\,(\textstyle\prod_{l\in\mathcal{L}} l\,.\,C_l \mid \prod_{a\in\mathcal{A}} a[P_a] \mid \phi)$$

for some finite sets of names $\mathcal{N}$, $\mathcal{L}$, and $\mathcal{A}$ and active substitutions ϕ. Every initial configuration can be written in normal form (with $\mathcal{L} = \emptyset$) using structural equivalence. A system S is *well-formed* when it is structurally equivalent to a normal form such that if l is a location name within S then $l \in \mathcal{L}$ and l occurs only

1. in terms $l.C$ such that: (a) if $\mathsf{get\_prin}(l\,.\,C_l) \in \mathcal{A}$, then C and C_l are owned by the same principal and if C has a value, then C_l has the same value; and (b) if $\mathsf{get\_prin}(l\,.\,C_l) \notin \mathcal{A}$, then $C \preceq C_l$ (informally, for a cell owned by the environment, the system cannot have capabilities more permissive than those received);
2. in subprocesses $\mathsf{commit}\ M\ l\,(x).P$ of P_a when $a = \mathsf{get\_prin}(l\,.\,C_l)$;
3. in $\mathcal{N}$ when $\mathsf{get\_prin}(l\,.\,C_l) \in \mathcal{A}$ and $C_l = 0\ ct$.

In the labeled semantics below, we require that the initial and final systems and the label be well-formed. We define labeled transitions $A \xrightarrow{\alpha} A'$ between source systems on top of an auxiliary relation $C \xrightarrow{\gamma} C'$ between capabilities.

Labeled transitions on capabilities. Input/output actions with the environment can affect the state of memory cells. To model these updates compositionally we define a labeled transition semantics between capabilities.

$$\frac{}{C \xrightarrow{!\,C'} C \curlyvee C'} \qquad \frac{C' \preceq C \quad \mathsf{prin}(C') \in \mathcal{A}}{C \xrightarrow{?C'} C} \qquad \frac{\mathsf{prin}(C') \notin \mathcal{A}}{C \xrightarrow{?C'} C \curlyvee C'}$$

The label $!\,C'$ records that the capability C' is exported to the environment: the outcome of the transition $C \curlyvee C'$ is an updated record of the most permissive exported capability. The label $?\,C'$ records that the capability C' is imported from the environment. There are two import rules, depending on the owner of C'. If the owner is in $\mathcal{A}$, then the capability refers to a location which is part of the system, so the environment can send back at most capabilities that can be derived from those exported by the system, hence the $C' \preceq C$ condition. On the contrary, if the owner is not in $\mathcal{A}$, the environment can send any capability, provided that the capability is compatible with the partial knowledge that the system already has, i.e. that $C \curlyvee C'$ exists.

Labeled transitions on systems. The labeled semantics for systems is adapted from the one for the applied pi calculus. We point out the novelties, and refer to the companion paper for the full semantics.

The labeled semantics has silent steps for all system reductions, including the location-specific reductions described in Section 2. The axioms for input and output are recalled below. (We refer to [1] for a discussion of admissible output values when the equational theory includes cryptographic primitives.)

$$a[c!\langle M\rangle.P] \xrightarrow{c\,!\,M} a[P] \qquad a[c?(x).P] \xrightarrow{c?M} a[P\{^{M^\sharp}/_x\}]$$

When a capability is received, the rule substitutes in a capability value $M^\sharp$ obtained from the capability label M by erasing information used only to update the cell state.

The context rules below ensure that the communication of capabilities is reflected in the state of the cells of the system; the condition $l.C$ in M checks whether the cell $l.C$ occurs in the transmitted capability (possibly within another capability).

$$\frac{A \xrightarrow{c\,!\,M} A' \quad C_0 \xrightarrow{!\,C} C_1 \quad l.C \;\mathsf{in}\; M}{l\,.\,C_0 \mid A \xrightarrow{c\,!\,M} l\,.\,C_1 \mid A'} \qquad \frac{A \xrightarrow{c?M} A' \quad C_0 \xrightarrow{?C} C_1 \quad l.C \;\mathsf{in}\; M}{l\,.\,C_0 \mid A \xrightarrow{c?M} l\,.\,C_1 \mid A'}$$

$$\frac{A \xrightarrow{\alpha} A' \quad l.C \;\mathsf{not\ in}\; \alpha}{l\,.\,C_0 \mid A \xrightarrow{\alpha} l\,.\,C_0 \mid A'}$$

We equate $l\,.\,\bot \mid A$ to A, so that the input rule covers the case of an input carrying fresh, unknown locations from the environment. (The resulting configuration must be well-formed, which excludes the introduction of a fresh location state for l if one already exists in the system.) We impose the following well-formedness conditions on labels: (1) in every label, a location name occurs at most in a single, well-formed capability, plus possibly in the label restriction—this excludes e.g. pairs of simultaneous, incompatible commitments; and (2) the target term H, the principal in uncommitted capabilities, and the value in committed capabilities, appear iff the transition is an input and the capability is owned by $e \notin \mathcal{A}$.

Example of transitions in the source language. Consider the third round of the game of Section 3, with two honest players a_1 and a_2 and an external, untrusted principal $e_0 \notin \mathcal{A}$ running the server. A simplified configuration of this system can be written

$$A' = l\,.\,\mathbf{Idu}\,(e_0\ H)\ \mid\ a_1[c_1?(x_1).P_1]\ \mid\ a_2[c_2?(x_2).P_2]$$

where l is the uncommitted cell pre-allocated by e_0 to store the winning move. (Here $H = \mathsf{h}(e_0 + \mathsf{h}(s))$ for some secret s created by e_0.) We have possible input transitions on channels c_1 and c_2, to notify the winning move to each of the players. The first transition may be:

$$A' \xrightarrow{c_1?l\,.\,\mathbf{Rd}\,(e_0\ s\ 11)} l\,.\,\mathbf{Rd}\,(e_0\ s\ 11)\ \mid\ a_1[P_1\{^{l\,.\,\mathbf{Rd}\,(e_0\ 11)}/_{x_1}\}]\ \mid\ a_2[c_2?(x_2).P_2]$$

which triggers the final process P_1 with a read capability for l substituted for x_1, carrying the game result (here 11). At the same time, the state for l is updated by the third capability-transition rule, since $\mathbf{Idu}\,(e_0\ H) \curlyvee \mathbf{Rd}\,(e_0\ s\ 11) = \mathbf{Rd}\,(e_0\ s\ 11)$. Conversely, for instance, transitions with a label that attributes l to a_1 instead of e_0 are disabled. At this stage, the configuration records the commitment on l, so the only subsequent input transition $A'' \xrightarrow{c_2?l\,.\,C'} A'''$ carrying a read capability C' for l must be such that $\mathbf{Rd}\,(e_0\ s\ 11) \preceq C'$ (by the third capability-transition rule), that is, $C' = \mathbf{Rd}\,(e_0\ s\ 11)$. This guarantees that the second player gets exactly the same result as the first one.

Relating the reduction-based and labeled semantics for the source language. The labeled semantics precisely characterizes the interactions between a system and an arbitrary environment. Given two systems A and E consisting of principals in $\mathcal{A}$ and $\mathcal{E}$, respectively, if $E \mid A \longrightarrow^* S$ then there exist two such systems A' and E' and transitions $A \xrightarrow{\phi} A'$ such that $S \equiv \nu\mathcal{N}.(E' \mid A')$, where $\mathcal{N}$ is the set of names exported in the labels of ϕ. Conversely, for all systems A and transitions $A \xrightarrow{\phi} A'$, there exists a system E' and reductions $E \mid A \longrightarrow^* \nu\mathcal{N}.(E' \mid A')$.

Translation of extended location states and capabilities. We extend the translation of Section 4 to cover all configurations reachable by transitions from initial configurations. This extended translation is inductively defined for all well-formed configurations in normal form, using the clauses of Section 4 plus the rules below for location states and capabilities.

We extensively rely on active substitutions [1] with the following naming conventions: for a location l, c_l denotes the local channel that contains the state of the location, s_l the secret seed, v_l the hidden value, and w_l the seal. We define two extended processes that compute and log identifiers, commitment values, and seals for a location owned by a given principal p using active substitutions.

$$\varphi(M_1, M_2)_p = \{\,\mathsf{h}(p + M_1)\,/\,l\,\} \mid \varsigma(M_1, M_2)_p$$
$$\varsigma(M_1, M_2)_p = \{\,M_1 + M_2\,/\,v_l\,\} \mid \{\,\mathsf{sign}(v_l\,,\,\mathsf{sk}(m_p))\,/\,w_l\,\} \mid \mathsf{repl}\ log!\langle \mathsf{idc}(p\,,\,v_l\,,\,w_l)\rangle$$

We first translate locations owned by honest principals $a \in \mathcal{A}$. The translation implements these locations by sending the location state on the local channel c_l, activating the relevant substitutions, creating a fresh secret and, for committed locations only, running a replicated log entry:

$$[\![l\,.\,0\,(a\,)]\!] = [\![l\,.\,\mathbf{Idu}\,(a\,)]\!] = c_l!\langle\mathsf{None}\rangle \mid \{\,\mathsf{h}(a + \mathsf{h}(s_l))\,/\,l\,\} \mid \nu\,s\,.\,\{\,s\,/\,s_l\,\}$$
$$[\![l\,.\,0\,(a\ V)]\!] = [\![l\,.\,\mathbf{Idc}\,(a\ V)]\!] = [\![l\,.\,\mathbf{Rd}\,(a\ V)]\!] = \varphi(\mathsf{h}(s_l), \mathsf{h}(s_l + [\![V]\!]))_a \mid \nu\,s\,.\,\{\,s\,/\,s_l\,\}$$

We also translate locations owned by principals $e \notin \mathcal{A}$ whose capabilities have been previously received by some principals in $\mathcal{A}$. The translation records partial knowledge of these locations, in the form of active substitutions plus, for committed locations only, a replicated log entry. The form of the terms in these substitutions reflect the test that processes in $\mathcal{A}$ have successfully performed before accepting these values, e.g. that the seal is well-formed signature from e.

$$\begin{aligned}
&[\![l\,.\,\mathbf{Idu}\,(e\ H)]\!] = \{\, H \,/\, l \,\} \\
&[\![l\,.\,\mathbf{Idc}\,(e\ (\ M' \ + \ M''\ )\ V)]\!] = \varphi(M', M'')_e \\
&[\![l\,.\,\mathbf{Rd}\,(e\ M\ V)]\!] = \{\, M \,/\, s_l \,\} \mid \varphi(\mathsf{h}(M), \mathsf{h}(M + [\![V]\!]))_e
\end{aligned}$$

In a well-formed system, there is a location state for every capability that occurs in the system. Accordingly, the translation of capabilities relies on the active substitutions introduced by the translation of location states, as follows:

$$[\![l\,.\,\mathbf{Idu}]\!] = \mathsf{idu}(l) \quad [\![l\,.\,\mathbf{Idc}\,(p\,)]\!] = \mathsf{idc}(p\,,\, v_l\,,\, w_l) \quad [\![l\,.\,\mathbf{Rd}\,(p\ V)]\!] = \mathsf{rd}(p\,,\, s_l\,,\, [\![V]\!]\,,\, w_l)$$

The compilation of each location state $l\,.\,C$ introduces name c_l and variables s_l, v_l, w_l, l whose visibility from the environment depend on the exported capability recorded in C. Thus, our translation finally introduces the following top-level restrictions: for every location, if no capability have been exported, all these names and variables are restricted; if C has tag **Idu**, the identifier l is unrestricted. for locations owned by principals in $\mathcal{A}$; if C has tag **Idc**, the variables w_l and v_l are also unrestricted; if C has tag **Rd**, only the channel c_l is restricted.

Example of transitions in the target language. Let us consider how our translation operates on the following transition, which represents player a_1 receiving the result of the game from server e_0 (with $H = h(e_0 + h(s))$).

$$l\,.\,\mathbf{Idu}\,(e_0\ H) \mid a_1[c_1?(x).P_1] \xrightarrow{c_1?l\,.\,\mathbf{Rd}\,(e_0\ s\ \mathbf{11})} l\,.\,\mathbf{Rd}\,(e_0\ s\ \mathbf{11}) \mid a_1[P_1\{^{l\,.\,\mathbf{Rd}\,(e_0\ \mathbf{11})}/_x\}]$$

The translated system $\{\, H \,/\, l \,\} \mid [\![a_1[c_1?(x).P_1]]\!]$ simulates the source transition by an input with label $c_1\,?\,(\,\mathsf{rd}(e_0\,,\, s\,,\, \mathbf{11}\,,\, \mathsf{sign}(\mathsf{h}(s) + \mathsf{h}(s + \mathbf{11})\,,\, \mathsf{sk}(m_{e_0})))\,)$, followed by a series of reductions through the code of parse, including dynamic checks on is_rd and check_idc. In 6 silent steps (including 3 steps for recursive processing of value 11), this yields the process

$$\begin{aligned}
&\{\, H \,/\, l \,\} \mid [\![a_1[P_1]]\!] \{^{\mathsf{rd}(e_0\,,\, s\,,\, \mathbf{11}\,,\, \mathsf{sign}(\mathsf{h}(s) + \mathsf{h}(s+\mathbf{11})\,,\, \mathsf{sk}(m_{e_0})))}/_x\} \\
&\quad \mid \mathsf{repl}\ \mathit{log}!\langle \mathsf{get_idc}(x) \rangle \mid \nu\, r\,.\, (\mathsf{repl}\ r?(_).c_1?(x).\mathsf{parse}\ x\ [\![P]\!]_a) \mid R \mid E.
\end{aligned}$$

After applying structural equivalence with active substitutions and eliminating the dead loop on channel r, we obtain a system

$$\nu\, s_l\,.\,\nu\, v_l\,.\,\nu\, w_l\,.\,(\{\, s \,/\, s_l \,\} \mid \varphi(\mathsf{h}(s_l), \mathsf{h}(s_l + \mathbf{11}))_{e_0} \mid [\![a_1[P_1]]\!] \{^{\mathsf{rd}(e_0\,,\, s_l\,,\, \mathbf{11}\,,\, w_l)}/_x\}) \mid R \mid E$$

that matches the translation of the resulting source system above.

6 Correctness Results

The first proposition states that the behavior of every source system can be simulated by its translation. That is, for any labeled trace of all source systems, there is a labeled trace of the process resulting from its translation. This shows the correctness (or functional adequacy) of our translation. We let $\xrightarrow{\phi}$ (resp. $\xrightarrow{\psi}$) range over series of transitions in the labeled semantics of the source (resp. target) language.

Theorem 1 (Functional adequacy). *Let A be a well-formed source system. For all series of transitions $A \xrightarrow{\phi}{}^{*} A'$, there exist transitions $[\![A]\!] \xrightarrow{\psi}{}^{*} [\![A']\!]$.*

The proof of the theorem is by induction on a series of source transitions between systems in normal forms. For each source transition, we exhibit target transitions that commute with the translation.

The "upwards" direction is more challenging: the trace produced by the translation of a source process A can be related to a trace produced by A *unless* its translation emits the name of a cheating principal on the special channel bad. This property uniformly guarantees the security of the translation of all systems with respect to the source semantics, provided that a proof that a principal cheated is a reasonable exceptional outcome for the other principals.

We let $S \longrightarrow_D^* S'$ denote that a target system S goes to S' with a (possibly empty) series of silent deterministic transitions, and let $S \Downarrow M$ abbreviate $S \longrightarrow_D^* \xrightarrow{bad!M} S'$ for some S'; we then say that M is blamed.

Theorem 2 (Security). *For all transitions $[\![A]\!] \xrightarrow{\psi}{}^{*} S$ starting from a well-formed source system A, we have*

1. *either there are source transitions $A \xrightarrow{\phi}{}^{*} A'$ leading to a well-formed source system A' such that $S \longrightarrow_D^* [\![A']\!]$; or $S \Downarrow e$ for some $e \notin \mathcal{A}$;*
2. *if $S \Downarrow M$, then $M \notin \mathcal{A}$.*

The proof is by induction on the series of transitions in the target language that do not trigger a blame. The first part of the theorem states that either the source semantics is respected, or the implementation at least provides the honest participants with the name of one dishonest principal to blame. Said otherwise, its statement excludes the possibility of cheating without eventual detection. The second part of the theorem expresses that honest participants are never blamed (even in the case some dishonest participants cheat), a necessary property for any optimistic implementation.

The form of our theorem differs from security properties for other programming abstractions (e.g. [7,2]), where any run or labeled trace of the cryptographic implementation of a source program is related to a run or labeled trace of the program on the source level. Reflecting a more flexible approach to security, it enables bad runs as long as malicious principals are reliably detected and blamed.

We illustrate how the Resolution protocol and the verifications made by the translation of receive suffice to detect write-after-commit attacks. Consider the online game example and suppose that $a_1, a_2 \in \mathcal{A}$ and $e_0 \notin \mathcal{A}$, that is, the server implementation is malicious. In particular, the server implementation may commit location l twice, to convince a_1 that he is the winner with his bid 11 and a_2 that he is the winner with his bid 8. The system composed by the translation of the two clients $[\![A_1 \mid A_2]\!]$ generates a trace

$$[\![A_1 \mid A_2]\!] \rightarrow \cdots \rightarrow [\![A']\!] \xrightarrow{c_1 ?(\mathsf{rd}(e_0\,,s\,,\mathbf{11}\,,w))} \xrightarrow{c_2 ?(\mathsf{rd}(e_0\,,s\,,8\,,w'))} S$$

where the seals w and w' sign commitments of l to 11 and 8, respectively.

For the first input transition, there exists a matching source transition, with a resulting source system A'' that includes the location state $l\,.\,\mathbf{Rd}\,(e_0\;s\;\mathbf{11})$. Moreover, the translation of A'' emits the corresponding idc on log.

For the second input transition, however, there is no matching source transition. This would require a capability transition from $\mathbf{Rd}\,(e_0\;s\;\mathbf{11})$ to $\mathbf{Rd}\,(e_0\;s\;8)$, which is excluded by our definition of the $\preceq$ preorder. Instead, the resulting system sends a second **Idc** on log. As soon as the Resolution process reads both commitments, it detects that they are inconsistent, and blames e_0 on bad.

7 Prototype Implementation

We have implemented committable cells as a library for OCaml [9]. We have also coded a series of examples, including simple online games and sealed-bid auctions.

The library provides abstract datatypes and access functions that closely follow those of our source language. Its implementation relies on standard cryptographic libraries and on a public-key (X.509) infrastructure for processing capabilities; it uses pseudo-random number generation for creating fresh secret seeds. Programs that use our library may communicate with one another using OCaml marshalling and network socket interfaces—cryptographic validation of received capabilities then occurs during unmarshalling.

The main difference between the implementation and its formal semantics is the handling of resolution. We refine the idealized resolution mechanism of Section 4 as follows: instead of relying on a central resolution process, our implementation keeps track of all principals and cells involved in a run of the system, and eventually implements the exchange and local resolution for all shared commitments.

8 Conclusions and Future Work

We presented a simple language for specifying systems based on optimistic commitments, and we compiled this language into a realistic concurrent framework modeled in the applied pi calculus. We established two security properties relating the labeled traces of a source semantics with commitment primitives to those of their implementation, with a target semantics that uses only ordinary communications and cryptographic functions. We only consider authenticity for now, but we believe it would also be possible to guarantee some properties of formal secrecy.

Although committable cells provide a reasonably useful (and formally challenging) block for building protocols, we focused on one particular usage of secure logs, rather than proposing a comprehensive language design for optimistic protocols. Our formal approach could be extended to other, more involved datatypes—as long as we can represent their live cycles using a preorder on exported capabilities, as detailed in Section 5.

It would be interesting, for instance, to design compilers for such datatypes with incremental commitment properties.

More generally, audit logs constitute an important tool for designing protocols and applications. Although their efficient implementation has been thoroughly studied, we believe ours is the first work to address their reliable, principled usage from a programming-language viewpoint.

References

1. Abadi, M., Fournet, C.: Mobile values, new names, and secure communication. In: 28th ACM Symposium on Principles of Programming Languages (POPL 2001) (2001)
2. Abadi, M., Fournet, C., Gonthier, G.: Secure Implementation of Channel Abstractions. Information and Computation 174(1), 37–83 (2002)
3. Castellà-Roca, J., Domingo-Ferrer, J., Riera, A., Borrell, J.: Practical Mental Poker Without a TTP Based on Homomorphic Encryption. In: Johansson, T., Maitra, S. (eds.) INDOCRYPT 2003. LNCS, vol. 2904, pp. 280–294. Springer, Heidelberg (2003)
4. Cederquist, J.G., Corin, R., Dekker, M.A.C., Etalle, S., den Hartog, J.I., Lenzini, G.: Audit-based compliance control. Int'l Journal of Information Security 6(2), 133–151 (2007)
5. Chaum, D.: Secret-ballot receipts: True voter-verifiable elections. IEEE Security and Privacy 2(1), 38–47 (2004)
6. Chaum, D., Ryan, P.Y.A., Schneider, S.: A practical, voter-verifiable election scheme. Technical Report CS-TR-880 (2004)
7. Corin, R., Denielou, P.-M., Fournet, C., Bhargavan, K., Leifer, J.: Secure implementations for typed session abstractions. In: IEEE Computer Security Foundations Symposium (2007)
8. Corin, R., Galindo, D., Hoepman, J.H.: Securing data accountability in decentralized systems. In: Meersman, R., Tari, Z., Herrero, P. (eds.) OTM 2006 Workshops. LNCS, vol. 4277, pp. 626–635. Springer, Heidelberg (2006)
9. Leroy, X., et al.: Objective caml, `http://caml.inria.fr`
10. Etalle, S., Winsborough, W.H.: A posteriori compliance control. In: 12th ACM Symposium on Access Control Models and Technologies (2007)
11. ISO/IEC. Common criteria for information technology security evaluation (2004), `http://www.commoncriteriaportal.org/public/expert/index.php?menu=3`
12. Jha, S., Katzenbeisser, S., Schallhart, C., Veith, H., Chenney, S.: Enforcing semantic integrity on untrusted clients in networked virtual environments. In: IEEE Symposium on Security and Privacy (2007)
13. Kremer, S., Ryan, M.D.: Analysing the vulnerability of protocols to produce known-pair and chosen-text attacks. In: 2nd Int'l Workshop on Security Issues in Coordination Models, Languages and Systems (SecCo 2004). ENTCS (2005)
14. NIST Special Publications. Generally accepted principles and practices for securing information technology systems (1996)
15. Schneier, B., Kelsey, J.: Secure audit logs to support computer forensics. ACM Transactions on Information and System Security 2(2), 159–176 (1999)
16. Shamir, A., Rivest, R., Adleman, L.: Mental poker. Mathematical Gardener (1981)
17. Waters, B.R., Balfanz, D., Durfee, G., Smetters, D.K.: Building an encrypted and searchable audit log. In: Network and Distributed System Security Symposium (NDSS) (2004)
18. Xu, W., Chadwick, D., Otenko, S.: A PKI Based Secure Audit Web Server. In: IASTED Communications, Network and Information and CNIS (2005)
19. Zheng, L., Chong, S., Myers, A.C., Zdancewic, S.: Using replication and partitioning to build secure distributed systems. In: IEEE Symposium on Security and Privacy (2003)

Author Index

Lecture Notes in Computer Science

Sublibrary 1: Theoretical Computer Science and General Issues

For information about Vols. 1–4618
please contact your bookseller or Springer

Vol. 4962: R. Amadio (Ed.), Foundations of Software Science and Computational Structures. XV, 505 pages. 2008.

Vol. 4960: S. Drossopoulou (Ed.), Programming Languages and Sstems. XIII, 399 pages. 2008.

Vol. 4934: U. Brinkschulte, T. Ungerer, C. Hochberger, R.G. Spallek (Eds.), Architecture of Computing Systems - ARCS 2008. XI, 287 pages. 2008.

Vol. 4927: C. Kaklamanis, M. Skutella (Eds.), Approximation and Online Algorithms. X, 289 pages. 2008.

Vol. 4921: S.-i. Nakano, M.. S. Rahman (Eds.), WALCOM: Algorithms and Computation. XII, 241 pages. 2008.

Vol. 4919: A. Gelbukh (Ed.), Computational Linguistics and Intelligent Text Processing. XVIII, 666 pages. 2008.

Vol. 4917: P. Stenström, M. Dubois, M. Katevenis, R. Gupta, T. Ungerer (Eds.), High Performance Embedded Architectures and Compilers. XIII, 400 pages. 2008.

Vol. 4915: A. King (Ed.), Logic-Based Program Synthesis and Transformation. X, 219 pages. 2008.

Vol. 4912: G. Barthe, C. Fournet (Eds.), Trustworthy Global Computing. XI, 401 pages. 2008.

Vol. 4910: V. Geffert, J. Karhumäki, A. Bertoni, B. Preneel, P. Návrat, M. Bieliková (Eds.), SOFSEM 2008: Theory and Practice of Computer Science. XV, 792 pages. 2008.

Vol. 4905: F. Logozzo, D.A. Peled, L.D. Zuck (Eds.), Verification, Model Checking, and Abstract Interpretation. X, 325 pages. 2008.

Vol. 4904: S. Rao, M. Chatterjee, P. Jayanti, C.S.R. Murthy, S.K. Saha (Eds.), Distributed Computing and Networking. XVIII, 588 pages. 2008.

Vol. 4878: E. Tovar, P. Tsigas, H. Fouchal (Eds.), Principles of Distributed Systems. XIII, 457 pages. 2007.

Vol. 4875: S.-H. Hong, T. Nishizeki, W. Quan (Eds.), Graph Drawing. XIII, 402 pages. 2008.

Vol. 4873: S. Aluru, M. Parashar, R. Badrinath, V.K. Prasanna (Eds.), High Performance Computing - HiPC 2007. XXIV, 663 pages. 2007.

Vol. 4863: A. Bonato, F.R.K. Chung (Eds.), Algorithms and Models for the Web-Graph. X, 217 pages. 2007.

Vol. 4860: G. Eleftherakis, P. Kefalas, G. Păun, G. Rozenberg, A. Salomaa (Eds.), Membrane Computing. IX, 453 pages. 2007.

Vol. 4855: V. Arvind, S. Prasad (Eds.), FSTTCS 2007: Foundations of Software Technology and Theoretical Computer Science. XIV, 558 pages. 2007.

Vol. 4854: L. Bougé, M. Forsell, J.L. Träff, A. Streit, W. Ziegler, M. Alexander, S. Childs (Eds.), Euro-Par 2007 Workshops: Parallel Processing. XVII, 236 pages. 2008.

Vol. 4851: S. Boztaş, H.-F.(F.) Lu (Eds.), Applied Algebra, Algebraic Algorithms and Error-Correcting Codes. XII, 368 pages. 2007.

Vol. 4848: M.H. Garzon, H. Yan (Eds.), DNA Computing. XI, 292 pages. 2008.

Vol. 4847: M. Xu, Y. Zhan, J. Cao, Y. Liu (Eds.), Advanced Parallel Processing Technologies. XIX, 767 pages. 2007.

Vol. 4846: I. Cervesato (Ed.), Advances in Computer Science – ASIAN 2007. XI, 313 pages. 2007.

Vol. 4838: T. Masuzawa, S. Tixeuil (Eds.), Stabilization, Safety, and Security of Distributed Systems. XIII, 409 pages. 2007.

Vol. 4835: T. Tokuyama (Ed.), Algorithms and Computation. XVII, 929 pages. 2007.

Vol. 4800: A. Avron, N. Dershowitz, A. Rabinovich (Eds.), Pillars of Computer Science. XXI, 683 pages. 2008.

Vol. 4783: J. Holub, J. Žďárek (Eds.), Implementation and Application of Automata. XIII, 324 pages. 2007.

Vol. 4782: R. Perrott, B.M. Chapman, J. Subhlok, R.F. de Mello, L.T. Yang (Eds.), High Performance Computing and Communications. XIX, 823 pages. 2007.

Vol. 4771: T. Bartz-Beielstein, M.J. Blesa Aguilera, C. Blum, B. Naujoks, A. Roli, G. Rudolph, M. Sampels (Eds.), Hybrid Metaheuristics. X, 202 pages. 2007.

Vol. 4770: V.G. Ganzha, E.W. Mayr, E.V. Vorozhtsov (Eds.), Computer Algebra in Scientific Computing. XIII, 460 pages. 2007.

Vol. 4769: A. Brandstädt, D. Kratsch, H. Müller (Eds.), Graph-Theoretic Concepts in Computer Science. XIII, 341 pages. 2007.

Vol. 4763: J.-F. Raskin, P.S. Thiagarajan (Eds.), Formal Modeling and Analysis of Timed Systems. X, 369 pages. 2007.

Vol. 4759: J. Labarta, K. Joe, T. Sato (Eds.), High-Performance Computing. XV, 524 pages. 2008.

Vol. 4746: A. Bondavalli, F. Brasileiro, S. Rajsbaum (Eds.), Dependable Computing. XV, 239 pages. 2007.

Vol. 4743: P. Thulasiraman, X. He, T.L. Xu, M.K. Denko, R.K. Thulasiram, L.T. Yang (Eds.), Frontiers of High Performance Computing and Networking ISPA 2007 Workshops. XXIX, 536 pages. 2007.

Vol. 4742: I. Stojmenovic, R.K. Thulasiram, L.T. Yang, W. Jia, M. Guo, R.F. de Mello (Eds.), Parallel and Distributed Processing and Applications. XX, 995 pages. 2007.

Vol. 4739: R. Moreno Díaz, F. Pichler, A. Quesada Arencibia (Eds.), Computer Aided Systems Theory – EUROCAST 2007. XIX, 1233 pages. 2007.

Vol. 4736: S. Winter, M. Duckham, L. Kulik, B. Kuipers (Eds.), Spatial Information Theory. XV, 455 pages. 2007.

Vol. 4732: K. Schneider, J. Brandt (Eds.), Theorem Proving in Higher Order Logics. IX, 401 pages. 2007.

Vol. 4731: A. Pelc (Ed.), Distributed Computing. XVI, 510 pages. 2007.

Vol. 4728: S. Bozapalidis, G. Rahonis (Eds.), Algebraic Informatics. VIII, 291 pages. 2007.

Vol. 4726: N. Ziviani, R. Baeza-Yates (Eds.), String Processing and Information Retrieval. XII, 311 pages. 2007.

Vol. 4719: R. Backhouse, J. Gibbons, R. Hinze, J. Jeuring (Eds.), Datatype-Generic Programming. XI, 369 pages. 2007.

Vol. 4711: C.B. Jones, Z. Liu, J. Woodcock (Eds.), Theoretical Aspects of Computing – ICTAC 2007. XI, 483 pages. 2007.

Vol. 4710: C.W. George, Z. Liu, J. Woodcock (Eds.), Domain Modeling and the Duration Calculus. XI, 237 pages. 2007.

Vol. 4708: L. Kučera, A. Kučera (Eds.), Mathematical Foundations of Computer Science 2007. XVIII, 764 pages. 2007.

Vol. 4707: O. Gervasi, M.L. Gavrilova (Eds.), Computational Science and Its Applications – ICCSA 2007, Part III. XXIV, 1205 pages. 2007.

Vol. 4706: O. Gervasi, M.L. Gavrilova (Eds.), Computational Science and Its Applications – ICCSA 2007, Part II. XXIII, 1129 pages. 2007.

Vol. 4705: O. Gervasi, M.L. Gavrilova (Eds.), Computational Science and Its Applications – ICCSA 2007, Part I. XLIV, 1169 pages. 2007.

Vol. 4703: L. Caires, V.T. Vasconcelos (Eds.), CONCUR 2007 – Concurrency Theory. XIII, 507 pages. 2007.

Vol. 4700: C.B. Jones, Z. Liu, J. Woodcock (Eds.), Formal Methods and Hybrid Real-Time Systems. XVI, 539 pages. 2007.

Vol. 4699: B. Kågström, E. Elmroth, J. Dongarra, J. Waśniewski (Eds.), Applied Parallel Computing. XXIX, 1192 pages. 2007.

Vol. 4698: L. Arge, M. Hoffmann, E. Welzl (Eds.), Algorithms – ESA 2007. XV, 769 pages. 2007.

Vol. 4697: L. Choi, Y. Paek, S. Cho (Eds.), Advances in Computer Systems Architecture. XIII, 400 pages. 2007.

Vol. 4688: K. Li, M. Fei, G.W. Irwin, S. Ma (Eds.), Bio-Inspired Computational Intelligence and Applications. XIX, 805 pages. 2007.

Vol. 4684: L. Kang, Y. Liu, S. Zeng (Eds.), Evolvable Systems: From Biology to Hardware. XIV, 446 pages. 2007.

Vol. 4683: L. Kang, Y. Liu, S. Zeng (Eds.), Advances in Computation and Intelligence. XVII, 663 pages. 2007.

Vol. 4681: D.-S. Huang, L. Heutte, M. Loog (Eds.), Advanced Intelligent Computing Theories and Applications. XXVI, 1379 pages. 2007.

Vol. 4672: K. Li, C. Jesshope, H. Jin, J.-L. Gaudiot (Eds.), Network and Parallel Computing. XVIII, 558 pages. 2007.

Vol. 4671: V.E. Malyshkin (Ed.), Parallel Computing Technologies. XIV, 635 pages. 2007.

Vol. 4669: J.M. de Sá, L.A. Alexandre, W. Duch, D.P. Mandic (Eds.), Artificial Neural Networks – ICANN 2007, Part II. XXXI, 990 pages. 2007.

Vol. 4668: J.M. de Sá, L.A. Alexandre, W. Duch, D.P. Mandic (Eds.), Artificial Neural Networks – ICANN 2007, Part I. XXXI, 978 pages. 2007.

Vol. 4666: M.E. Davies, C.J. James, S.A. Abdallah, M.D. Plumbley (Eds.), Independent Component Analysis and Signal Separation. XIX, 847 pages. 2007.

Vol. 4665: J. Hromkovič, R. Královič, M. Nunkesser, P. Widmayer (Eds.), Stochastic Algorithms: Foundations and Applications. X, 167 pages. 2007.

Vol. 4664: J. Durand-Lose, M. Margenstern (Eds.), Machines, Computations, and Universality. X, 325 pages. 2007.

Vol. 4661: U. Montanari, D. Sannella, R. Bruni (Eds.), Trustworthy Global Computing. X, 339 pages. 2007.

Vol. 4649: V. Diekert, M.V. Volkov, A. Voronkov (Eds.), Computer Science – Theory and Applications. XIII, 420 pages. 2007.

Vol. 4647: R. Martin, M.A. Sabin, J.R. Winkler (Eds.), Mathematics of Surfaces XII. IX, 509 pages. 2007.

Vol. 4646: J. Duparc, T.A. Henzinger (Eds.), Computer Science Logic. XIV, 600 pages. 2007.

Vol. 4644: N. Azémard, L. Svensson (Eds.), Integrated Circuit and System Design. XIV, 583 pages. 2007.

Vol. 4641: A.-M. Kermarrec, L. Bougé, T. Priol (Eds.), Euro-Par 2007 Parallel Processing. XXVII, 974 pages. 2007.

Vol. 4639: E. Csuhaj-Varjú, Z. Ésik (Eds.), Fundamentals of Computation Theory. XIV, 508 pages. 2007.

Vol. 4638: T. Stützle, M. Birattari, H. H. Hoos (Eds.), Engineering Stochastic Local Search Algorithms. X, 223 pages. 2007.

Vol. 4630: H.J. van den Herik, P. Ciancarini, H.H.L.M.(J.) Donkers (Eds.), Computers and Games. XII, 283 pages. 2007.

Vol. 4628: L.N. de Castro, F.J. Von Zuben, H. Knidel (Eds.), Artificial Immune Systems. XII, 438 pages. 2007.

Vol. 4627: M. Charikar, K. Jansen, O. Reingold, J.D.P. Rolim (Eds.), Approximation, Randomization, and Combinatorial Optimization. XII, 626 pages. 2007.

Vol. 4624: T. Mossakowski, U. Montanari, M. Haveraaen (Eds.), Algebra and Coalgebra in Computer Science. XI, 463 pages. 2007.

Vol. 4623: M. Collard (Ed.), Ontologies-Based Databases and Information Systems. X, 153 pages. 2007.

Vol. 4621: D. Wagner, R. Wattenhofer (Eds.), Algorithms for Sensor and Ad Hoc Networks. XIII, 415 pages. 2007.

Vol. 4619: F. Dehne, J.-R. Sack, N. Zeh (Eds.), Algorithms and Data Structures. XVI, 662 pages. 2007.